Response From Readers

WordPerfect: Desktop Publishing in Style is **a gold mine of useful information!**

—Bruce Lorie, Chicago, IL

Congratulations. *WordPerfect: Desktop Publishing in Style* is **the best** out of all the books on the same subject.

—N. T. Tran, Downey, CA

I use WordPerfect for certain projects and I particularly love to hear people say: "You can't do that with WordPerfect—can you?" **Your book has impressed me** enough to order your *Designer Disk.* What are you going to do for an encore?

—Louis Balbi, N. Babylon, NY

At 20° below we are huddled around our new computer and laser printer and thoroughly enjoying your book! So far **your book is the most-used Christmas present this year.** Looking forward to the *Designer Disk* to boost our creativity!

—Susan Johnson, Fairbanks, AK

Daniel Will-Harris is the very best. He holds your attention, teaches, knows PC's and different brands of printers better than anyone I have ever read. Daniel Will-Harris *is* style—this is an AUTHOR.

—Anne Tuminello, Canyon Lake, TX

I have found your book to be the most interesting computer tutorial I have ever read.

—Mark Lesch, CompuServe

WordPerfect: Desktop Publishing in Style is right on the money. You cannot imagine how much your book has meant to us. **Keep up the good work and keep on including the humor.**

—Chuck McKinney, Columbia, SC

Your book was a tremendous help to me in learning about the desktop publishing aspects of WordPerfect. And it was *the* **easiest to read computer book I've encountered to date.**

—Bari Phillips, CompuServe WP Forum

WordPerfect: Desktop Publishing in Style is **literally indispensable** for any WordPerfect user with a LaserJet. Thanks for your efforts; after laboring through the rest of the literature on WP, **witty instruction is a rare pleasure.**

—Dave Hardy, San Francisco, CA

Great book! I wasted $50 on other WordPerfect books before I found yours.

—Leon Zolman, Cambridge, MA

Your book and *Designer Disk* really saved me on a critical project. They are extremely useful and entertaining, and have **proven to be invaluable tools.** I keep them next to me whenever I work in WordPerfect.

—Nancy Cohen, Minnetonka, MN

I'd like to add to the notes of praise for *WordPerfect: Desktop Publishing in Style.* I found it **extremely helpful and entertaining, a rare combination.** In most such books, I'd just as soon do without the humor and get on with the technical stuff, but Daniel Will-Harris carries it off— dare I say? —in style. Thanks again for the advice and congratulations on the book.

—Nigel Chippindale, CompuServe

Thank you so much for your book, which really makes it **a pleasure to explore** the possibilities of this subject. As a typesetter I am particularly grateful for the pleasant way you ease the transition for me from commercial to desktop publishing. **I really appreciate your guidance and all this information.**

—Alice Bernstein, New York, NY

I want to congratulate you for writing one of the first computer books that I have read that has **substance and useful, easy to understand information.** *WordPerfect: Desktop Publishing in Style* has been **a real godsend.**

—O. C. Spencer, Campbell, TX

Love your book! Love your humor! Love your Designer Disk!

—C. G. Williams, Lake Hughes, CA

I found your book to be **very entertaining and an invaluable source of information on desktop publishing.** I really appreciate your reviews of related products; without your book I would never have known about them. Thank you and keep up the good work.

—Patricia Dickinson, Bridgeport, CT

I have just been reading and experimenting with your **wonderful book,** *WordPerfect: Desktop Publishing in Style,* and look forward to receiving your *Designer Disk.*

—M. L. MacDonald, Hampton, VA

Your book is a perfect compliment for WordPerfect. **Without your book I would be lost in trying to do desktop publishing with WordPerfect.** I have used many of the examples and I am pleased with the results. Please send the *Designer Disk* post haste.

—Rufus Roper, Fountain, CO

If your Designer Disk is near as helpful as the book, it will be like gold.

—R. C. Allison, Denver, CO

I am finding your book enormously helpful (and of course, delightful)! Thank you for putting together such a comprehensive and useful piece of work! I'm thoroughly enjoying your approach to teaching what easily might be dull material, if presented in the usual textbook manner. Levity lifts us from expectations of boredom, keeps us looking forward to more, and allows the joy of learning which should accompany any new experience.

—Melody M. Brinkman, Spencerport, NY

I just wanted you to know how much I enjoyed reading your book. **Your sense of humor is great!** It's so refreshing to read a book on WordPerfect that goes beyond the dull word processing level. **You provided wonderful ideas that I have used very successfully.**

—Susan Perry, Tustin, CA

Wow! Your book makes it easy for me to experiment with my layout as I write (I like the instant gratification). Keep up the good work.

—G. Randolph Davis, Dallas, TX

WordPerfect: Desktop Publishing in Style is **fabulous.** If you have a mailing list for future publications, please put me on it!

—L. S. Wagner, Grand Junction, CO

Enjoyed the book!

—Lowell Kind, Anchorage, Alaska

Using your book with my laser printer is amazing. I can now do most of my school work and newsletter with WordPerfect instead of Ventura and it really saves me time. I'm ready to give the *Designer Disk* a try.

—Mark Valsi, Sierra Madre, CA

Your book is absolutely sensational! I loved the way you made everything so simple and you did it humorously. I have a dot-matrix printer and I got very good results, even though I realize it could have been much better on a laser printer.

—Lucile Cheng, San Diego, CA

I have really enjoyed your book and *Designer Disk.* They have been very helpful.

—Juan de Luis Camblor, Madrid, Spain

Please notify me if Daniel Will-Harris writes any more books, on any subject; I'd like to buy them. I like his style very much.

—Peter Maston, Davis, CA

Your book has been a big help in getting over my resistance to learning yet another program. **Thanks for providing such entertaining and stimulating material to learn from.**

Allen Young, San Francisco, CA

I very much enjoyed your book, and now I'm eager to take a look (and use) your *Designer Disk* templates and concepts. **Thanks again for a fine, readable, and most helpful "manual."**

—Ronald Barritt, Wauwatosa, WI

I have been reading your book and I've found it **informative and helpful.** Since I am barely computer literate, I need all the help I can get at a reasonable cost. Thanks for the support.

—Stanley Beacock, London, ON

I have thoroughly enjoyed reading *WordPerfect: Desktop Publishing in Style.* Your book has been **very entertaining and informative,** and I can now produce a passable newsletter, including columns and graphics, even on my dot-matrix printer.

—Jane Bliss, Los Angeles, CA

I have found *WordPerfect: Desktop Publishing in Style* to be **quite useful.**

—Bill Adams, Washington, D.C.

I just love WordPerfect: Desktop Publishing in Style.

—Kay Young, Maryland Heights, MO

I just got a copy of *WordPerfect: Desktop Publishing in Style,* and would like to convey my appreciation. **Daniel Will-Harris really did a great job. The book is tremendously helpful.** Most WP books have enough good ideas to keep me browsing in the bookstore for about 10 minutes, but this one is **full of great examples, suggestions, and tips.**

P.S. I am not his mother, agent, or publisher. I just think an outstanding job deserves recognition.

—David Vandagriff, CompuServe

The book is great! Thanks, much.

—Ron Wolfson, Burnably BC

—J. E. Burke, Appleton, WI

Daniel Will-Harris is a genius with a huge literary talent. **What a superb book. Many thanks for each and every zinger. He has succeeded in making a dry subject more than palatable.**

—Cheryl Ryshpan, Thornhill, ON

I would like you to know how much I enjoyed your book. **It was, hands down, the best, most informative book about any program that I have ever read.** It was especially helpful for one who is a relative novice about WordPerfect. **If I had read this book a year ago, I could have saved a lot of time and money.** Your suggestions about software, graphics, etc., are invaluable. **Thank you for a most enjoyable and useful book.**

—Henry Milne, Rockville, MD

I want to personally thank you for all the great advice in your book, and all the great humor, too!

—Theresa Wiener, Des Plaines, IL

Your book is my bible for WordPerfect.

—Judi Johnson, Eagle Lake, TX

I have learned much from your book. It's well written and fun to read. More computer books should copy your style.

—Russ Heggen, Eugene, OR

An absolutely superb book.

—Douglas Myall, Dorset, England

Your book supplies exactly what the beginning desktop publishing needs—good advice about working with WordPerfect. For me, the book's main value lies in the way it offers concrete and detailed guidance on how to apply WordPerfect to specific problems. I want to **thank you for providing genuinely useful workarounds for some of WP's limitations.**

—Les Gordon, San Diego, CA

I literally thank Daniel Will-Harris for getting me started. I went to my in-laws on Thanksgiving (without my computer, of course) and I just read his book. His suggestions were **so well done and so beautifully illustrated** that when I returned home three days later I could remember what I'd learned. **I couldn't believe I could learn how to use software without sitting down at the computer. In fact, I barely knew anything about WP, so this book also taught me the essentials.**

—Steve Conrad, Manhasset, NY

WordPerfect: Desktop Publishing in Style **certainly wasn't boring.** And it was **quite informative.** I have a lot of respect and admiration for **Daniel Will-Harris; he really knows WordPerfect, and it shows.**

—James Wright Jr., CompuServe

Daniel Will-Harris

WordPerfect Desktop Publishing in Style

Second Edition

the expert's guide to WordPerfect & graphic design

PEACHPIT PRESS
Berkeley, California

Notice of Liability

The information in this book is distributed on an "As Is" basis, without warranty. While every precaution has been taken in the preparation of this book, neither the author nor Peachpit Press, Inc. shall have any liability to any person or entity with respect to any liability, loss or damage caused or alleged to be caused directly or indirectly by the instructions contained in this book or by the computer software and hardware products described herein.

Peachpit Press, Inc.
2414 Sixth Street
Berkeley, CA 94710
510/548-4393

Art Direction by Toni Will-Harris

Portions of this book have appeared in *Compute!*, *Desktop Communications*, *PC World*, *Personal Publishing*, *Computerland*, and *WordPerfect* magazines.

Library of Congress Cataloging-in-Publication Data
Will-Harris, Daniel
WordPerfect: Desktop Publishing in Style
Includes bibliographical references, index
1. Desktop publishing 2. WordPerfect
I. Title
Z286.D47W536 1990 686.2'254436–dc20

9 8 7 6 5
Printed and bound in the United States of America
ISBN: 0-938151-15-0

This book is dedicated to our parents.

Acknowledgments

I want to thank my wife Toni, a respected [illegible]er, editor, and publication consultant in her own right (usually on my left). When we met, she was Editor-in-Chief of our college newspaper, and she still edits everything I write (no matter how hard I try to sneak it past her). She wrote a majority of the design chapter in this book and compiled the reading list, glossary, and index in the Appendix. She also designed most of the example pages and provided art direction for the entire book. While I could have done this book without her, it wouldn't have been any fun (and this time there was hardly any shouting).

I would also like to thank Louise Domenitz at Bitstream, Brent Garlic and all the crew at WordPerfect, those enterprising LaserMaster mavericks (especially Bill Neuenschwander and Mark Gilbert), everyone connected with Corel (and you know who you are), Jeri Peterson and Mike Lough at Hewlett-Packard, Lavon Collins and Alice Peterson at Adobe, Dr. Robert Fenchel and Scott Taylor at SoftCraft, Kimm Neilson, and Mark Evanier. A very special thanks to Karen Linden, Liz Swoope Johnston, Steve (*Roseanne*) Paymer, and Rowby (*FidoDido*) Goren. I would also like to especially thank Ted Nace, without whom there wouldn't be a book.

Contents 

Introduction

The myth and the reality

DTP in the real world

Your favorite word processing program (or the one your boss forces you to use), WordPerfect, is about to take you to the deep, dark regions of desktop publishing. While some people would like you to believe that desktop publishing is as simple as pressing a few buttons, it isn't. The uncharted territory of desktop publishing is fraught with confusing lingo, dangerous pitfalls, and an intimidating detail called *graphic design.*

WordPerfect is a remarkable program. It's the first PC word processor that combines excellent word processing with a wondrous amount of desktop publishing power. Desktop publishing is simply a way to make printed matter more attractive and effective, and WordPerfect does that better than any other PC word processing program.

You may feel at home with WordPerfect's word processing features, but now you'll be confronted with horrifying details such as fonts, points, rules, grids, readouts, gutters, hairlines, kerning, layout, leading, serif, sans serif, sidebars, widows, orphans, and other frightening characters. It's a jungle out there.

But never fear! This book will guide you through it, making sure you don't step in anything messy or fall prey to cannibalistic dealers trying to sell products you don't need. You'll not only discover how to navigate your way around a page like a pro, but you'll also find the best way to present information, and learn the exact codes necessary to create the many examples you'll find on these pages. This book will show you how to make your publications as professional-looking as possible, without having to spend more time and money than is necessary.

If this book seems different from some of the others you may have looked at, that's because it is. It's not a rehash of the instruction manual. (If that's what you're looking for, there are many such books available.) In my thousands of hours spent consulting and training people to use new programs, I've learned that most people are bored and frustrated with dry, technical manuals. I know I was when I started reading computer books, and I haven't forgotten it.

If you're at all like them, you want a book that you can readily comprehend. This book is written in terms you can understand. The fields of desktop publishing, graphic design, and typography all have separate vocabularies that you'll need to learn. You'll pick up the jargon along the way, without being assaulted and confused by it right from the start. You'll find the definitions for all these new terms in the glossary of this book.

I've written this book so you can feel as if a friend has come over to explain desktop publishing with WordPerfect to you. For some, the tone of my explanations may be too casual, but although the tone may be casual, the information is not. I cover techniques that are not contained in the WordPerfect documentation or in other books about the program, and have attempted to present this material in as accurate, detailed, and lively manner as possible.

This book is for three types of people: first, for those of you who have never used any other type of word processing program; second, for everyone who is upgrading from WordPerfect 4.2; and finally, for those of you who are using or moving on up from WordPerfect 5.0. While this book stresses 5.1, much of the material is applicable to 5.0, and there are still plenty of tips specific to 5.0.

The book is structured in this way because some people are not going to upgrade to 5.1. While 5.1 does have many exciting features, it is slower than 5.0 and requires more memory. If you haven't switched to 5.1 and want to stay with 5.0, this is still the book for you.

Don't let the size of this book scare you. You *don't* have to read the whole thing. There's not going to be a quiz at the end. The book is so big because it's really two, two, two books in one. Your getting the best of 5.0 and 5.1 all in one neat package.

The book is broken down into easily digestible chunks and there's something for just about every occasion or eventuality. The only way to get this much information into a less intimidating size would have been to use type so small you'd need a microscope to read it with. (Besides which, just lifting this book could be considered as your minimum daily requirement of exercise.)

I'll cover everything you need to know to use WordPerfect effectively for desktop publishing. I go into exquisite detail about every little feature—*except one:* equations. If you're the type of person who uses equations, then you can probably figure out how to use them yourself. Since I can't cover equations with the same attention to detail that I give the other features I know so much about, I'll leave them to other books.

◆ DTP for the rest of us

How a feature works and how you actually use it in real life are two different things. This book emphasizes not just the features, but the way you will use them in your daily work. Before we get any further, how about a little more straight talk? I know this is dangerous, and everyone has warned me that you should be careful about telling readers the truth, but I must, at least about desktop publishing.

While desktop publishing is truly a revolution in the way printed communications are created, as in any revolution, it's jam-packed with hype. I have one simple rule about DTP: it's not whether you *can* do something with a program, but whether you'd *want* to. Call it the "sequin" effect. Sequins are dazzling, but would you wear them if you had to sew them on yourself?

So you have to be cautious. To this end, I'm going to tell you exactly what you can and *can't* do. I've seen advertisements that show dazzling pages, actually created with a product. But such jimmied, roundabout, time-consuming measures were required to create the finished page, that it's not really honest. Yes, you *can* create a page like that with the program, but would you really *want* to? Do you have the time, patience, and expertise to manage it?

I've tried to avoid such convolutions in this book. However, I've become such a WordPerfect junkie that I too have found myself using and abusing every one of its tricks (and a few of my own), finally extracting a single correct page after about 20 trial-and-error prints. Rather than resorting to that, I've tried to make everything in this book something you'll *want* to do, rather than just something you *can* do. Even if a particular example seems too complicated to you, you can still use it as a source of design ideas.

Even without resorting to trickery, WordPerfect provides a vast array of features, some not even feasible in expensive dedicated desktop publishing programs, including Ventura Publisher and PageMaker. Using a scaleable font printer, WordPerfect can rotate type, and includes special effects such as outline and shadow for fonts. Fonts can be downloaded to LaserJets in advance, so the print time can be quicker than even speedy Ventura. And WordPerfect's ability to print graphics in draft mode is something I've yearned for in a page composition program.

It's easy to install fonts. (You get a whole slew of superb Bitstream soft fonts for a nominal charge.) In addition, WordPerfect uses files from many graphics programs, has excellent typography (justification, hyphenation, leading, etc.), and is still one heck of a word processing program, with features ranging from search and replace to footnotes, tables of contents, indexes, and a document compare feature that's a godsend for writers and editors.

Most of us equate desktop publishing with the final page emerging from the printer, with type and graphics perfectly positioned—no more rubber cement and X-Acto knives (or whatever you used to cut and paste). But it isn't a sin to use the old tools; there are some effects you may not be able to achieve with your current system, such as upside-down type or scanned artwork at an angle.

If you're working with a super-ambitious design and actually need to cut and paste, there's no need to feel guilty—it's OK. Do as much as you can with what you have on-screen, and then do the rest by hand. After all, this is still a free country (last time I checked). Producing a great-looking document is what matters, and using whatever tools are available makes sense.

So come along with me and discover new ways
to make your documents more attractive, effective,
and — who knows — maybe even fun.

1

Getting it all together

System configuration

WordPerfect has made quite a few changes in their program from 5.0 to 5.1. If you're confused over which version you should use, you're not alone. While WordPerfect makes plenty of good software, it's not easy to know which version of their program will do the best job for you. Let's take a look at what's available and see if we can find the one that best suits your needs. If you've already decided, skip to the next page and go right to *Set me up.* But if you'd like to examine the differences, step into my office, please.

◆ WordPerfect 5.0 or 5.1? Which is right for you?

WordPerfect 5.0 and 5.1 are quite different in terms of functions, memory requirements, and performance. WP 5.0 is much faster and requires less memory, but 5.1 has some tremendously important new features, such as tables, spreadsheet import, and equations. WP 5.1 includes a host of minor improvements such as improved hyphenation, justification, and tabs, all of which make desktop publishing easier and more accurate. 5.1 also adds mouse support and drop down menus which make it *much* easier to learn for beginners. I've found that the mouse isn't used much by people who learned WordPerfect the traditional way.

Both programs are excellent. With the exception of the new invoice in Chapter 4, all the full-page examples in this book were originally created using 5.0, so clearly you don't need 5.1 for DTP with WordPerfect. But, if you don't mind the fact that it's slower, 5.1 does actually simplify many steps which were cumbersome or tedious in 5.0.

Which version you need depends on what you want to do and what type of hardware you will be using. WordPerfect 5.1 requires faster hardware and more memory. While theoretically both 5.0 and 5.1 need the same memory, 5.1 actually needs 50-100K more at print time. 5.1 is also *substantially* slower than 5.0, although this isn't as apparent if you're using a computer that's fast enough, such as a fast 286 or a 386. An XT really isn't powerful enough to run 5.1. 5.0, however, runs fast even on an XT, and is much less finicky about memory.

Basically it breaks down to this: If you have a very fast computer, use 5.1. If you don't, but still need to use the excellent table feature and spreadsheet import, or you're a new user who wants WordPerfect to be easier to learn, use 5.1.

If you don't need tables, spreadsheet import, or mouse support, you probably don't need 5.1. I personally prefer 5.0 for plain text editing because it's so much faster, but 5.1 makes complex formatting easier. The choice is yours, and rather than grumbling about it, appreciate the fact that you *do* have a choice.

❖ Set me up

Before you can get the most desktop publishing power out of WordPerfect, you have to make sure your system is set up properly. If it's not, you're going to waste a lot of time feeling sorry for yourself, something society now deems unattractive.

First, a few conventions so that we understand each other. I was confused when I first started reading (and cursing) computer books because I didn't understand the conventions. I'd see directions like "12n," but I didn't know I was supposed to replace the n with something of my own choosing. I just kept entering "12n" and couldn't figure out why things didn't work. My wife, Toni, took this approach one step further the first time she sat down at a computer. When the software provided her with a list (or menu) and a prompt which read "Type Your Choice," she dutifully typed the words "Your Choice" and wondered why nothing happened.

In this book I try to have as few conventions as possible. If you see letters in bold like this: **BOLD**, it means you type these letters on your keyboard (no, type them on your microwave keypad—sheesh, what does he think we are, gerbils?). If you see CONTROL-F1, it means you hold down the **CTRL** key first and while holding it down, tap the key marked **F1**. Do not type the words CONTROL-F1 or press a dash between the Control and the F1 key (if you do, other people will snicker at you, as they did when I did such things lo, those not-so-many years ago). If you see the word [ENTER], it means you press the key marked **ENTER** (or sometimes **RETURN**) on your keyboard. If you understand the concept, read on. If you don't, join me in the department of redundancy department and I'll repeat myself so you won't be confused.

- INSTANT REPLAY: **ALT-F8** means press the **ALT** key and keep holding it, tap the key marked **F8**, then release both keys. **SHIFT-F1** means hold down the **SHIFT** key while pressing the key marked **F1**.

Keystrokes look like this:

SHIFT F10 OFF ITALIC [ENTER]

(By the way, this particular set of keystrokes does nothing. It's just here to show you the differences between an O and a 0, and a 1 vs. an I.)

In the keystroke font, notice that the zeros are tall and thin and the alphabet letter "O" is very round. Also notice that the number one is indicated by a small serif at the top of its stroke and the alphabet letter "I" has no serif.

Most of the keystrokes in this book are for WordPerfect 5.1. In some cases, these are identical to WordPerfect 5.0, but in many cases they are slightly different. If you are using WordPerfect 5.0. you may want to upgrade to 5.1. If you don't want to, you will not be able to blindly type the keystrokes in this book and get perfect results; you will have to pay attention to what's on-screen and use a little brain power. If you've got slightly more than half a brain, this book will be useful for you, even with WordPerfect 5.0. If you have no intention of ever upgrading to 5.1, you might want to contact the publisher of this book and see if you can get a copy of the first edition which was written entirely for WordPerfect 5.0.

❖ *Keyboard*

If you have a keyboard with the function keys along the left hand side, you're going to have an easier time using WordPerfect than if the function keys are along the top. This is because you can press SHIFT, CONTROL, and ALT at the same time with one hand. The function keys along the top require both hands for three-quarters of WordPerfect's commands.

I would like to put a curse on the head of whoever designed the so-called "enhanced" keyboard because it is illogically, unergonomically, and unproductively designed. If you like it, ignore this little outburst; if you don't, think about getting a new keyboard. I'm not joking. Keyboards with the function keys on the left make life with WordPerfect much easier. If you're not used to working with a mouse, you may end up spending a lot of time with the function keys.

```
Setup

     1 - Mouse

     2 - Display

     3 - Environment

     4 - Initial Settings

     5 - Keyboard Layout                    DWH.WPK

     6 - Location of Files




Selection: 0
```

The ever-popular Setup Menu.

◆ Help

It's also reassuring to know that WordPerfect has an excellent built-in help system. If at any time you need help with a particular feature, press **F3**. Unlike earlier versions of WordPerfect, you can press F3 *at any time,* even when you are in the middle of a menu. F3 should always be your first line of defense when you can't figure out something. Your second line of defense should be either a can of Hershey chocolate syrup or a call to WordPerfect's 800 tech support number (found in the manual or through directory assistance).

If you don't know or can't remember where a particular feature is located, press **F3** and then the first letter of the name of the feature (for help with underlining, you would press the letter **u**).

❖ *On your mark . . .*

Depending on your hardware, WordPerfect has certain limitations. So before you go any further, make sure WordPerfect is installed properly.

➺ Go into the WordPerfect SETUP menu by pressing

SHIFT-F1

This will allow you to make sure WordPerfect is set up in the best way possible for your particular computer and monitor.

➺ Make sure that WordPerfect is installed for the type of monitor and graphics card installed in your computer by pressing

D G

WordPerfect *should* automatically know what type you are using unless you have installed something exotic (like a high-resolution or full-page monitor). If you have, find it listed on the menu and select it; otherwise, you will be unable to use the graphic preview function. If WordPerfect can't figure it out, here are a few hints: If your screen is black and white, black and green, or black and amber, chances are you have either a text-only screen or a Hercules-compatible graphics card. The Hercules card is the most popular and reasonably priced monochrome graphics card for PCs and compatibles.

If you have a text-only system, you're not going to be able to experience the thrill of seeing your pages on-screen, just the way they'll print. Nor will you be able to effectively edit graphics on-screen. You will be missing out on two of WordPerfect's most fun-filled (and useful) new features. If you're serious about desktop publishing with WordPerfect, you should consider purchasing a Hercules-compatible monochrome graphics card. These cards will work with almost any monochrome monitor and cost under $200. If you're not serious, just send the cash directly to me in small, unmarked bills.

If you have a color monitor, you will probably be using either CGA, EGA, or VGA. If your text is grainy, you're using CGA. If it's sharp, you're probably using EGA 640x350. EGA is much sharper for both text and graphics. If you're using an IBM PS/2 computer Model 30 or below, you'll probably want to use EGA 640x350. If you've got your nose pressed to a PS/2 Model 50 or above, you'll have VGA graphics and want to select VGA 640x480. If you don't see your particular graphics system listed, call WordPerfect's 800 support number.

➺ When you find the right monitor, press

S

◆ **For 5.1**

5.1 will present you with a second (and shorter) list of monitors. Find the right one and press

S

again. To ensure that WordPerfect displays in the way I'll describe, press

E A Y S Y [ENTER] [ENTER]

To make sure that WordPerfect saves your files automatically and backs them up in case of trouble, press

E B T Y 5 [ENTER]

O Y [ENTER] [ENTER]

While still in setup, I suggest you select a character such as the double chevron,

ALT-174 (on the keypad), to indicate carriage returns. To do this, press

D E H

then hold down the Alt-key and type

174

on the numeric keypad. This *will not* work if you type on the numbers keys along the top of the keyboard. Now press

[ENTER][ENTER].

One last point and then we're ready to setup the printer. Unlike normal word processing which relies on lines and columns to tell you where you are on the page, desktop publishing needs more accurate units of measure. WordPerfect is able to measure in inches, centimeters, points (72 points=1 inch), and old-fashioned lines and columns.

For desktop publishing, you should set your units to either inches or centimeters, whichever is easier for you to understand. Unless you are a real techie-type, or have a strong typesetting background, you would not want to measure everything in points. Press

E U D" S"

You actually *do* press the quote marks here and press

[ENTER] [ENTER] [ENTER]

to leave the setup menu. That wasn't too hard now, was it?

◆ For 5.0

To ensure that WordPerfect displays in the way I'll describe, press

AY SY [ENTER]

To make sure that WordPerfect saves your files automatically, and backs them up in case of trouble, press

B T Y 5 [ENTER]

O Y [ENTER]

While still in setup, I suggest you select a character such as the double chevron, ALT-174 (on the keypad), to indicate carriage returns. To do this, press

DH

Then hold down the Alt-key and on the numeric keypad type

174

This *will not* work if you enter numbers from along the top of the keyboard. Now press

[ENTER]

One last point and then we're ready to set up the printer. Unlike normal word processing which relies on lines and columns to tell you where you are on the page, desktop publishing needs more accurate units of measure. WordPerfect is able to measure in inches, centimeters, points (72 points=1 inch), and old-fashioned lines and columns.

For desktop publishing, you should set your units to either inches or centimeters, whichever is easier for you to understand. Unless you are a real techie-type, or have a strong typesetting background, you would not want to measure everything in points. Press

UD"S"

You actually *do* press the quote marks here, and to leave the setup menu press

[ENTER] [ENTER]

That wasn't too hard now, was it?

❖ *Performance tips for power users*

If you're a whiz at software, but know zilch about hardware, you may not be aware of two words that can make your computer seem like it's running at double speed. No, these words are not "mush, mush!" but "Buffers and Files."

Without delving into pedantic detail, let's just say that DOS isn't all that bright. It has one small bookshelf for a file, and when that shelf gets too full, it has to pile everything on the floor. Later, it wastes a lot of time looking for whatever it needs. (Of course, I don't mean to infer that *you* are not bright if your work place is like this. Mine unfortunately is, but you'd think a computer would be a little more organized than we scatterbrained humans are.)

Anyway, the magic words, "Buffers and Files" will provide you with more working room for the computer. These words don't give you more memory (in fact, they give you a little less), but they do allow DOS to perform more functions in a shorter amount of time. It's like adding bookcases; they take up space, but allow for a more useful and organized room.

(Forgive me if this sounded like a bedtime story, but what the heck? You might try to pass it off on your kids and see if they start cleaning up their rooms. I suggest you add dinosaurs to the story. Kids love them, and you can infer that because dinosaurs weren't organized and didn't clean up their rooms, they lost their allowances and TV privileges, became extinct, and are now powering cars and other internal combustion engines.)

So how do you use these magic words? First let's see if your computer already contains them. Press

CONTROL-F5 T R C:\CONFIG.SYS [ENTER]

If you do not have this file, WordPerfect will say "Error: File Not Found." If you do have this file, it will appear on-screen. This file should begin with the lines:

Buffers=20

Files=20

If it contains the words "buffers and files," with numbers larger than 20, leave it as it is. If the numbers are smaller, or are simply not there, type them (as above) at the top of the file to create the first two lines.

Don't change any other information contained in this file; it may contain information about a mouse, scanner, or other peripherals. Save the file by pressing

CONTROL-F5 T S C:\CONFIG.SYS [ENTER]

These changes will not take effect until you turn the computer off and on again. You can also use **CONTROL-ALT-DELETE** to reset the computer. (Make sure you exit WordPerfect before using CONTROL-ALT-DELETE.)

❖ *Get set . . .*

Now we turn to what might possibly be the single most important piece of hardware. In the trade it's winsomely called an "Output Device," but that always sounds too anatomical to me; and besides, in plain English it's simply known as a printer.

The type of printer you have (or have access to) determines what type of pages you can produce with WordPerfect. WordPerfect can print using anything from a dot-matrix printer (costing under $200) to a Linotronic phototypesetting machine (costing upwards of $50,000). Naturally, the more expensive printer gives you more expensive-looking pages—true typeset quality, in fact.

For the best desktop publishing results, a laser printer is required. That doesn't mean you need a very expensive laser printer, but it does mean that you can expect to shell out at least $1,000, which some people might consider very expensive. If you can't afford a laser printer, I'll cover some ways to beg, borrow, steal, or rent time on someone else's printer. You can also use ink jet printers, such as the HP DeskJet, or even dot-matrix printers using special third-party software.

◆ Printers

Until recently, laser printers fell into two main categories: LaserJet compatibles and PostScript printers. Now they still fall into two categories, but they are LaserJet and "scaleable font" printers. When I refer to "LaserJet" or compatible printers, I'm talking about the Series II or compatibles. These printers use "bitmapped" fonts which you generate in advance in each size you need.

Scaleable font printers can take any single "outline" typeface and print it at any size or any rotation, portrait (tall) or landscape (wide). The advantage of scaleable typefaces is that you don't have to create them in advance for every size you want, they take less disk space on your hard disk, and you can apply more special effects such as outlines and shadows to them.

The original scaleable font printers were PostScript printers which use the PostScript PDL (page description language). Now there are a number of printers which have scaleable fonts even if they don't use the PostScript language. These printers include the LaserJet III and the Canon LBP III printers. Also in this category are add-in boards for your computer which add scaleable fonts (and higher resolution) to your existing printer. The best known in this category is the LaserMaster line of printer controllers such as the LM 1000.

Scaleable font printers, both PostScript and otherwise, come standard with the basic fonts you will need for the examples in this book.

If you want to add more typefaces to any of these scaleable font printers, you can use the Bitstream Fontware installation program. LaserJet III users can use either Fontware or the Hewlett-Packard Type Director.

The LaserJet Series II is the most popular laser printer in the world. But it comes with almost no fonts (just Courier and a tiny line printer font) and no special effects. However, when you buy WordPerfect, you are eligible to receive a copy of a program called Bitstream Fontware for next to nothing. OK, it's something right around $30, but the point is, if all the components in the Fontware package were sold separately it would cost around $500, so it's a real bargain.

The Fontware Kit includes two typefaces, Dutch and Swiss (aka Times Roman and Helvetica), that allow you to create type up to 144 point (2 inches) tall. If you have a LaserJet, call WordPerfect *immediately* (if not sooner) to order your copy of Fontware (1-800-222-9409). You won't be able to effectively desktop publish without it.

While I can recommend either Fontware or Type Director for the LaserJet III, for LaserJet Series II users I recommend Fontware. All the LaserJet examples in this book are designed using the Fontware fonts, so if you use the Type Director fonts they will not work exactly as they do in this book.

There are two-and-a-half reasons why I support Fontware instead of Type Director in this book. 1) Fontware is *the* industry standard for LaserJet and many other printers as well. It's available for more PC software—and more PC printers. Type Director only makes LaserJet and DeskJet and some dot matrix fonts, while Fontware makes fonts for the LaserJet, Deskjet, PostScript, LaserMaster, Canon—all major printers. 2) The quality of Fontware fonts is clearly superior to those from Type Director. 2.5) Bitstream has a larger library of typefaces from which to choose. Compugraphic has been very slow to get new Type Director typefaces to the market. Compugraphic itself has a huge type library, though, so if they get their act together they certainly have the ability to offer as many typefaces as Bitstream.

Whichever type of laser printer you have, the best way to connect it to your computer is with a parallel cable. Parallel cables are faster and infinitely easier to install than serial cables. If you must use a serial cable, be aware that it will take far longer to print, especially if you want to print graphics or use a LaserJet compatible with Fontware fonts for WordPerfect. You may also need a specially configured serial cable.

If you have any type of PostScript printer, install the driver for your printer. If your printer is not listed, but is fully PostScript compatible, install WordPerfect's generic PostScript driver. I use the QMS-PS/800/810 printer driver. The QMS is a PostScript printer, and all PostScript printers share the same commands, but this is a particularly good PostScript printer. If you want to use any Adobe "soft" fonts, you will need to call WordPerfect and order a special printer driver for $10. You will only need the Bitstream Fontware installation kit if you want to use Bitstream Fontware typefaces that are not built-in your printer.

If you have a LaserMaster printer (like the one this book was printed with) the WordPerfect printer driver probably came with your controller board. If not, LaserMaster will send it to you for free.

The LaserJet comes in several models, the oldest and least powerful being the plain LaserJet. This printer uses only cartridge fonts which are no larger than 14-point. The next step up is the LaserJet Plus, which has enough memory to use the Fontware fonts, but only up to 30 point (less than 1/2 inch) tall. The LaserJet II has the same abilities as the LaserJet Plus, but you can add extra memory, enabling you to use larger fonts and produce more complex graphics. The II comes in three models: the II (a long, low printer which kicks out 8 pages per minute); the IID (similar to the II, but with two paper trays); and the IIP (a very small, very cute, inexpensive printer which prints 4 pages per minute). All three use the same type of fonts.

The new LaserJet III has CG Times and Univers (similar to Helvetica and Swiss, though I like it better), so you should follow the directions for a scaleable font printer, not a LaserJet Plus, II, IID, or IIP.

If you have a LaserJet or compatible, here's what you will need to do. If you are using a plain LaserJet, find out what type of font cartridge is on your printer (it will be sticking out the front of the machine), and install WordPerfect for that particular cartridge. If you are using a LaserJet Plus or Series II, find out what cartridges you have and how much memory your printer has.

If your printer has at least 512K of memory (as all LaserJet Plus and Series II printers do), you will want to install Fontware on your hard disk. The Fontware installation program is easy to use if you follow their instructions carefully (some step-by-step instructions appear in Chapter 7 of this book). However, here are a few words of advice.

When you create fonts, select "Portrait and Landscape" to create fonts for both portrait (tall) and landscape (wide) pages. You will need both "orientations" to complete the examples in this book. You can later delete (or copy to diskettes) the landscape fonts (.SFL) if you don't use them regularly. This will save a lot of disk space.

If you are sure you will only print portrait pages (tall), and will not be following the examples in this book, choose "Portrait Only" in the installation. This will save time when creating the fonts, as well as disk space. Remember, though, to use this book you will need both Portrait (tall) and Landscape (wide), so select both.

If you have a LaserJet IIP or IID, or another printer which can "rotate" portrait fonts for landscape printing, you won't need to create landscape fonts for these printers, even if you follow the examples and print in landscape.

Once you select "Make Fonts" you should press F3 to create what Fontware calls "Starter Fonts." This gives you 8, 10, 12, and 14-point in all weights of Swiss and Dutch, as well as 18 and 24-point in bold. The advantage of this selection is that it creates a set of either typeface which will all fit into the memory of a standard 512K LaserJet. I say either because you can either use all the Swiss fonts created or all the Dutch fonts created, but not all of both at the same time.

You should also create Dutch 30-point Bold for use with the second step-by-step example. While this puts you over the 512K limit, you're not going to use *all* the fonts on the same page at the same time. Also, when fonts are marked with a +, as they are automatically (don't worry about what this means yet, I'll explain it in stifling detail later), you can select more fonts than will fit in your printer and WordPerfect will only load them as necessary.

If you have more than 512K, you may also want to install bold fonts in 36, 48, and 72-point.

In the past, this little process could have taken 18 hours, but now with the newest version of Fontware it should take you no longer than an hour on an XT, about 15 to 30 minutes on an AT, and next to nothing on a 386. Now class, I don't want to hear any complaining about this taking a lot of computer time. Remember that these fonts would cost $500 if you had to buy them but you got them practically free with WordPerfect.

❖ GO!

While Fontware is making fonts, sit down and read the rest of this book, starting with this little aside about bugs.

◆ Is it a bug or a feature? Only her programmer knows for sure

No software is perfect, and any program as large (two-and-a-half times bigger than 4.2) and complex as WordPerfect 5.1 is bound to have a few problems. I know, I feel like I've personally experienced the challenge of all of them.

It's next to impossible to make any software bug free because you may fix two bugs but create another one (a bug you don't know you've created until some crabby user tells you about it). Modern software has gotten so big that it's almost unwieldy, both for the programmers and the users, and like a car with too many power features, you can't expect them all to be in working order at the same time. That doesn't make you feel any better when you can't get the thing to work, but you're not the only one who has to go through software Hell just to print a letter.

When WordPerfect 5.0 came out, it had a few bugs, and this caused some confusion among users. The first version, dated 5/5/88 is especially problematic. If you are using 5.0 to work with this book, make sure you have a version dated after 1/3/89. Remember, too, that 5.1 has many new features which aren't found in 5.0, and so you won't be able to create all of the examples here. WordPerfect Corp. puts out an updated version of WordPerfect about every six to eight weeks. They don't change the number, they just change the date.

To find out the date of your software, start the program, then press **F3** (the Help key). The date will appear in the upper right corner of your screen.

The first release of 5.1 is dated 11/06/89. It's a pretty solid program, and I used it to write this book and create the examples.

The most annoying problems I've had with the program have more to do with memory management than with things related to DTP. Although my system has 640K of regular memory, 1 megabyte of EMS, WordPerfect often still tells me it doesn't have enough memory. "Bull," I think, but it insists. This happens when I try to use View Document, edit graphics, print, or perform some other memory-intensive function. If you get that message, save what you're doing, exit the program, and try it again. That way the memory will be cleared and reset. If you get that message frequently, remove any memory resident programs to clear up as much memory as possible, work with only one document at a time, don't print and edit at the same time, use a smaller soft keyboard, and just be careful in general. That may take care of the problem. If it doesn't, try, try again.

Another good way to improve performance is to have only the fonts you use in your printer drivers. The more fonts in the driver, the slower everything will be.

If you experience other problems with your copy of WordPerfect, call WordPerfect (800-321-3349 or 800-541-5096) *immediately.* First they'll try to solve your problem. If they can't, and your problem is a known bug, they will send you an update for free. If not, and you just want the latest version because you think it will solve your problems, WordPerfect is charging about $10 for this.

While it's great that WordPerfect puts out updates so regularly, these updates sometimes subtly change how features work. If you consistently find that an example is not working for you, and you are absolutely, positively sure that you have followed it to the letter and haven't missed a step, or mistyped, and your program is dated after 11/89, this may be the cause.

- Some new users have a tendency to think that they've hit a bug when they've actually just made a mistake. (I know, because I still do it myself.) Of course, sometimes they *have* hit a bug.

But if you're not sure how to use the program, it's hard to tell if it's your fault or the software's. If a feature doesn't seem to work, or your program is not working the way I describe it, the best thing to do is call WordPerfect tech support. If your problem has been reported as a bug, they'll tell you; if not, they'll try to help you get it right.

WordPerfect has instituted a *Software Subscription Service* for those who want to automatically receive all interim releases and software upgrades. If you call 801-222-1400 and give them your credit card number, or send them a $200 deposit, they will see that you receive the latest material as it's released.

If you are a large corporate user with many registered copies, you only need one subscription and you are allowed to make copies. If you have only one copy of WordPerfect, this service may not be for you, as you may receive (and pay for) disks of new printers drivers, graphic drivers, or other things you don't really need.

And now, as they say in the movies: lights, camera, action!

❖ *Wait! There's more*

•◆ Other ways to improve performance

If you find yourself breezing through the information in this book and still want more, you're in luck. Besides my two *Designer Disks* for WordPerfect, which are available by mail order only (use the form in the back of this book), I've recently completed a *Signature Series* of instructional video tapes for your dining and dancing pleasure.

Proceeding on the basis that all computer videos don't have to be a cure for insomnia, I have plunged into the video arena with a tape about WordPerfect's advanced features that is both fun and easy to understand. Here's the deal. The tape is called *WordPerfect: Desktop Publishing Style & Substance*, and it's not simply a rehash of this book. I cover the creation of several new documents and pass along even more valuable tips (how do I keep coming up with them?). If you follow along with the video you will not only learn how to use the program inside and out, but you'll get a headstart on the competition because you'll already have real, useful, re-useable document formats. The video makes a good companion for this book, and I hope you will find it every bit as useful.

Peachpit Press, the publishers of this book, have included an order form in the back for your immediate ordering convenience. They even have an 800 number, and they actually ship tapes within three days of your ordering. Amazing.

My other videos cover Corel Draw and Ventura Publisher. *Corel Draw: Ideas, Information & Inspiration*, goes far beyond the beginning video that's included in every box of Corel Draw. You'll learn about everything from "Cheese Whiz Draw" (edible line art) to a session on special effects that will help you create dazzling designs in less time (it gives new meaning to the "tastes great, less filling" controversy).

Ventura: Desktop Publishing Style & Substance has a similar title as the WordPerfect video, but the similarity ends there. This is a tape for beginners and those intermediate users who would like to be better acquainted with all of Ventura's many features. Sparky, the Wonder Frog is my co-host, which isn't nearly as stupid as it sounds.

The videos are available immediately for $49.95 each, and are all guaranteed to keep you on the edge of your seat (or rolling on the floor).

2

Conquering new frontiers

or What, me worry?

There's no need to worry about all the new features of 5.1 as long as you know what you're getting into. One advantage of using WordPerfect as a desktop publishing program is that you already know its word processing features. In general, desktop publishing consists of two parts: word processing and formatting. In this chapter I'll explain what some of WordPerfect's new desktop publishing features can do and take you on a guided tour of them.

➾ A note to those of you who haven't used previous versions of WordPerfect:

Read this section to get an idea of what the new features are called and what they're used for. In a book like this it's important to know what things are called because it seems like every program calls the very same feature by a different name. Other programs may call it "Line Spacing," but WordPerfect calls it "Line Height" or "Leading." Once you know what something is called, it is easier to look it up or understand what's going on. You can take solace in the fact that drop down menus and mouse support make WordPerfect 5.1 easier to learn than earlier versions. And remember, any time you're confused press F3, the help key. Unlike previous versions, help is available at all times and is actually helpful. F3 should be your first line of defense when you are confused.

➾ A note to users who are upgrading from WordPerfect 4.2:

Hold on to your hat. You're about to go from word processing to "word publishing." Many of you may be frustrated by the transition from 4.2 to 5.1. The underlying concepts of the program are the same, and in many cases the function key commands are identical. But there are enough changes, especially in items like margins and tabs, that even features you knew like the back of your hand are going to seem like strangers. Don't worry, you'll get the hang of it faster than you can say "antidisestablishmentarianism."

➾ A note to users who are moving up from WordPerfect 5.0:

Calm down, it's not going to be as bad as it was from 4.2 to 5.0. Really. Would I lie to you (this early in the book)? While at times you are going to feel that there are more changes in 5.1 than there were in 5.0, they are generally additional features, rather than changes in the way existing features work. While 5.1 is in reality, quite a different program from 5.0, it's a much smoother transition than the transition from 4.2 to 5. The whole program is now more powerful and easier to use.

➾ One more tip for everyone:

The numbers in parentheses which follows the feature name tells you what version introduced this feature. I've done it this way so you can zoom in on the features which are improved (or at the very least, new to you).

◆ Appearance *CONTROL-F8 A* (5.0)

Allows you to select attributes such as underline, italic, small caps, shadow, outline, redline, and strikeout. Whether or not you can use these features depends on what your printer can do.

◆ Baseline for typesetters *SHIFT-F8 O P B* (5.0)

This feature was really added in the last version of 5.0 and has to do with margins. If you have a 1" top margin you probably expect to have 1" of white space at the top of your page, and normally in WordPerfect you do. That's because WordPerfect places the top of the tallest character on the first line 1" from the top of the page.

But typesetters do it differently. (That sounds like a bumper sticker, doesn't it?) If they set a 1" top margin they want the baseline (an invisible line which marks the bottom of all characters except "descenders," such as "g j p q y.") to be at the 1" mark. I recommend this setting for advanced users only. When using this setting it's possible to have a large headline at the top of the page print off the top of the page, so you have to be careful.

◆ **Color** *CONTROL-F8 C* **(5.0)**

With this you can mix and select colors for type (if your printer is capable of printing in more than one color).

◆ **Columns** *ALT-F7 C* **(5.0)**

WordPerfect's column feature works with any font. You can create newspaper style columns, where text "snakes" from the bottom of one column to the top of another, or parallel columns, which allows you to put paragraphs of information side-by-side.

WordPerfect's column feature has been improved so it works with any font.

You can create newspaper style columns, where text "snakes" from the bottom of one column to the top of another. You can also use parallel columns which allows you to put paragraphs of information side-by-side.

5.0 was fussy about what you could or couldn't put into a graphic box, and this was sometimes a limitation. Now there are fewer things you can't put into a graphics box, and columns are one of them.

One advantage of using WordPerfect as a desktop publishing program is that you already know its word processing features. In general, desktop publishing consists of two parts: word processing and formatting.

But there are enough changes so you'll be happy that you have this book.

◆ **Columns in graphics boxes** *ALT-F7 C* **(5.1)**

5.0 was fussy about what you could or couldn't put into a graphic box, and this was sometimes a limitation. Now there are fewer things you can't put into a graphics box, and columns are one of them.

◆ **Dormant hard return** *Automatic* **(5.1)**

This feature may seem minor, but it has the big effect of saving you time. With 5.0, a blank line between paragraphs could fall at a page or column. This could throw off formatting, and it looked especially bad at the tops of columns because they didn't line up horizontally.

Now when a Hard Return (you press the **[ENTER]** key) is the first thing on a page, or a column, WordPerfect turns it into a "Dormant Hard Return." This means the return is still there, it just goes into hibernation. If your text moves so that this return is no longer the first thing on a column or page, the return becomes active again and shows up as a return.

The only drawback is that this can sometimes be confusing. If you're at the top of a page or column and press **[ENTER]**, it may seem as if nothing happened. Then when the text moves, you suddenly have two returns. Even so, this feature is well worth this minor weakness.

◆ **Equations** *ALT-F9 E C E* **(5.1)**

I was a straight "A" student, except for a "C" in high school geometry. While you surely don't care about my educational background, I'm telling you this so you'll understand why there isn't much about equations in this book. I'll cover it, but if you're the type of person who will use this feature, then you're the type of person who would snigger when they saw the meaningless example I'd create. Hey, all that Pi and Sigma stuff is just Greek to me.

◆ **File Compatibility (5.0 & 5.1)**

This isn't a purely DTP feature but it is an important concern. Both 5.0 and 5.1 can read each other's files and can read 4.2 files, but 4.2 can't read either 5.0 or 5.1 unless they are saved in 4.2 format (CONTROL-F5 A P). Not all versions of 5.0 can read 5.1 files, only those dated in 1989. If you try to print 5.1 files in 5.0, WordPerfect will tell you that the file you are printing is a "newer version," each and every time you print. This isn't very important and you can ignore it, but you will have to press Y to tell it to print. The only way to avoid this is to save the file as a 5.0 file in 5.1 by pressing CONTROL-F5 A W.

◆ **Fonts** *CONTROL-F8 F* **(5.0)**

This feature allows you to specifically select different fonts or styles of type and sizes, depending on your printer's capabilities. WordPerfect has extremely good control over fonts of all varieties, and as a registered user of WordPerfect you can purchase $400 worth of Bitstream Fontware fonts for LaserJets (and compatibles) and DeskJets for about $30.

◆ **Graphics** *ALT-F9* **(5.0)**

WordPerfect allows you to mix text with graphics. WordPerfect automatically wraps text around graphics for professional-looking results. The graphics can be from paint-type programs such as PC Paintbrush, draw-type programs such as Corel Draw, Artline, Micrografx Designer, DrawPerfect, Harvard Graphics, spreadsheet graphs from Lotus 1-2-3, and many other programs (a complete list is in WordPerfect's Reference Manual Appendix).

The Graphics feature also enables you to draw lines (often called "rules" in publishing), and boxes, and it sets quotes out in what are called "readouts" or "pull quotes." This feature is also useful for keeping tables of information correctly formatted when text around them moves.

◆ **Graphic Box Contents** *ALT-F9 F C O* **(5.1)**

5.0 added the ability to include graphics in your document, but it had drawbacks. Since graphics were included inside WordPerfect's document files, the files could easily get *huge*. The on-disk feature allows you to place graphics in a document without actually loading the graphic file into your WordPerfect document. This saves disk space and has another important advantage: it keeps you up-to-date. Each time you print (or use View Document), WordPerfect loads the latest version of the graphics file.

Here's an example. You have a file with 14 different charts and graphs in it. The day before your report is due, your spreadsheet figures all change and so do your charts and graphs. In 5.0 you would have had to have gone into each graphics box, one by one, and load each new file. With the graphics on-disk feature, these updated graphs are all automatically loaded each time you use View Document or print the file.

◆ **Hyphenation** *SHIFT-F8 L Y* **(press** *SHIFT-F1 E Y* **to select** ***external*****) (5.1)**

WordPerfect has always had hyphenation, it just wasn't all that great, even in 5.0. The program used to beep at you incessantly and ask you all sorts of annoying questions. 5.1 can now be set so that it will hyphenate when it can and never ask you questions. If you want to be annoyed, you can set it to ask you whenever it isn't sure. 5.1 also has a better hyphenation algorithm and larger hyphenation dictionary so not only does it do a better job but it does it without bugging you.

◆ **Justification** *SHIFT-F8 L J* **(5.1)**

While 5.0's justification (actually alignment) was better than that of any other PC-based word processing program, it did have some quirks. Unlike programs such as Microsoft Word, you couldn't actually "right align" an entire paragraph. Now don't waste time arguing with me; it may have seemed like you could, but what you were really doing was changing the paragraph into separate lines of text, each ending with a hard return. You had to block it, then press ALT-F6 to make the lines align flush right. You also couldn't center an entire paragraph without marking it and pressing SHIFT-F6. The real problem was that if you no longer wanted all those lines centered or flush right, they had a hard return at the end of each line, returns which you had to remove manually. Even worse, if you changed your typeface or type size, the whole thing could quickly become a mess.

The justification feature in 5.1 is far more sophisticated. You can choose among four different settings: *Left*, which is also known as "unjustified," "Flush Left," or "Ragged Right;" *Full*, also known as "Justified;" *Center* (not to be confused with SHIFT-F6 for centering a single line of text); and *Right*, also known as "Right Aligned" or "Ragged Left."

The nice thing about the way 5.1's justification works is that it's flexible. If you had 10 paragraphs set centered (something you'd only do for an invitation or other special application) and then decide you wanted them all full justified, you'd just move the cursor to where you wanted the alignment to change and press **SHIFT-F8 L J F**. No manual reformatting of the text is required. When you change typefaces or type sizes, the text will reformat automatically. No, it isn't as exciting as manned space flight, but then again, you don't fly to the moon for eight hours a day, every day.

◆ **Kerning** *SHIFT-F8 O P K* **(5.0)**

Kerning is a feature that adjusts the spacing between pairs of letters in tiny amounts so that they look their best. Quality fonts, such as those from Bitstream and Adobe, have kerning pairs defined for each typeface, and WordPerfect will automatically use them if you set this to "yes."

◆ **Labels** *SHIFT-F7 P S A S A* **(5.1)**

Almost everyone would like to print labels now and then, and while this is relatively easy on dot matrix printers, it can be complex with laser printers. 5.1 makes the whole thing much easier with the label addition to the Paper Size function. Now instead of trial and error, you measure your labels and tell WordPerfect the width, height, number across, and distance between labels. WordPerfect does the rest, and now your labels can look as good as your letters do.

◆ **Leading** *SHIFT-F8 O P L* **(5.0 & 5.1)**

WordPerfect calls this feature "Line Height," but in publishing it's called Leading (pronounced ledding), and refers to the white space between lines of text. WordPerfect will adjust this automatically (based on the size of type you choose), providing the right amount of space for any size font. You can also set this manually. 5.1 adds a feature specifically called "leading." This feature allows you to decide how much *automatic* leading WordPerfect will add. The default is 2 points. This means that if you are using a 10-point font, WordPerfect will give it 12 points of leading. This new addition is useful because it gives you control over leading without having to do it manually.

◆ **Location of Files** *SHIFT-F1 L* **(5.0 & 5.1)**

5.0 allows you to tell WordPerfect where your important program files are, and 5.1 takes this a step further by allowing you to specify where *your* important document, style, and graphic files are. If you set these locations, WordPerfect will use these as defaults. This feature is especially important to "graphics-on-disk" because WordPerfect will look in this default graphic directory when it retrieves graphics from on-disk.

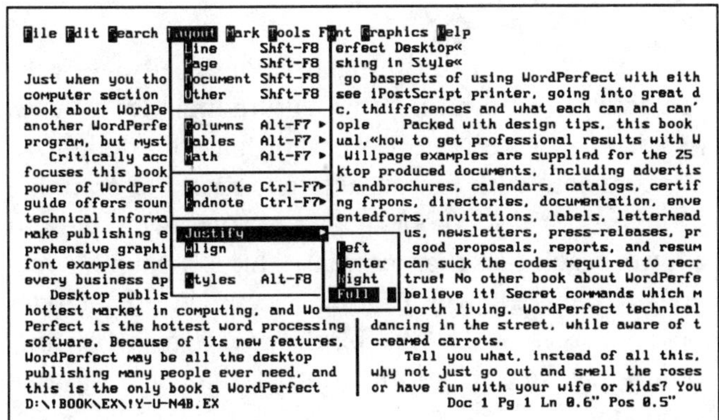

Drop-down menus make learning WordPerfect easier.

◆ **Margins** *SHIFT-F8 L M* **or** *SHIFT-F8 P M* **(5.0)**

If you're used to setting margins such as "10 and 70," get ready for a shock. These same margins would now be 1" and 1". Why? Because now instead of measuring across the page, you have to measure in from the edges of the paper. Margin settings of 1" and 1" mean that your text will begin 1" from the right edge of the paper and end 1" from the left edge of the paper. The same applies to top and bottom margins.

◆ **Mouse support:** *Move Mickey around the screen* **(5.1)**

While mice are essential in graphics-based desktop publishing programs, WordPerfect's mouse is not. Some people like it for editing or using the pull-down menus, but it is really of very little use for desktop publishing. If you like it, use it; if you don't, don't feel bad.

◆ **Outline Styles** *ALT-F8 C T O* **(5.1)**

Outline Styles are a new breed of styles. These are specially designed for creating (no big surprise here) outlines. A single outline style actually contains eight styles, one for each level of an outline. Each of these styles can be either paired or open, and each contains all the features of regular styles. They are applied automatically while in outline mode or manually when an automatic paragraph number is used. The nice thing about these styles is how they automatically change when you change the outline level of the paragraph they are in. If you promoted a second level paragraph to first level, the style would change to first level as well. WordPerfect's outline feature does not allow for "collapsing" the way other outline programs do, but it does allow for moving levels and moving sections (or Families, as WordPerfect calls it).

◆ **Print** *SHIFT-F7* **(5.0)**

WordPerfect's printing function has been so drastically redesigned over time that it might as well be new. In addition to printing, this feature includes a "View Document" mode. This shows you on-screen almost exactly what your document will look like when it's printed, complete with text in different sizes and graphics. The print feature also allows you to print fast "proof" copies of your pages without graphics or with graphics at a lower resolution than normal. This is a valuable feature which saves time when you are checking your pages for accuracy. 5.1 includes the added bonus of speed: if you press **SHIFT-F7 C** after you start printing, WordPerfect will devote all processing time to printing, rather than sharing time with the editing section of the program.

◆ **Print entire Character Set on all printers**

WordPerfect introduced its gigantic character set with 5.0. But it could only print special characters if your printer (or fonts) included them.

- Automatic (use CONTROL-V or CONTROL-2 to access WordPerfect's 5.1's twelve character sets)

5.1 can now print any and all of the entire 1700-character set on any graphics printer, including dot-matrix, ink jet, or laser. This means that even if your printer (or fonts) don't include items such as real opening and closing quote marks, WordPerfect will create them for you as graphics. It also means that you now have access to Kana, Hebrew, Greek, and even fun icons. What's more, you can print the IBM character set, even to a PostScript printer.

◆ **Print Multiple Pages** *SHIFT-F7 M* **(5.1)**

In 5.0, if you wanted to print pages 2-6 and page 19, you had to print from disk, either through List Files or SHIFT-F7 D. Now you can print selected pages from the document currently on-screen. When the program asks "Pages?" you simply type in the page number (or numbers separated by commas) or the range (1-5) you want printed.

◆ **Print multiple pages generated by** *SHIFT-F7 U* **(5.1)**

This feature only sounds esoteric. In reality, it can help speed printing by many times. Many new printers, especially laser printers, have the ability to create multiple copies from the page (or pages) stored in their built-in memory. LaserJets and PostScript printers can make these copies very quickly, about eight pages per minute. In

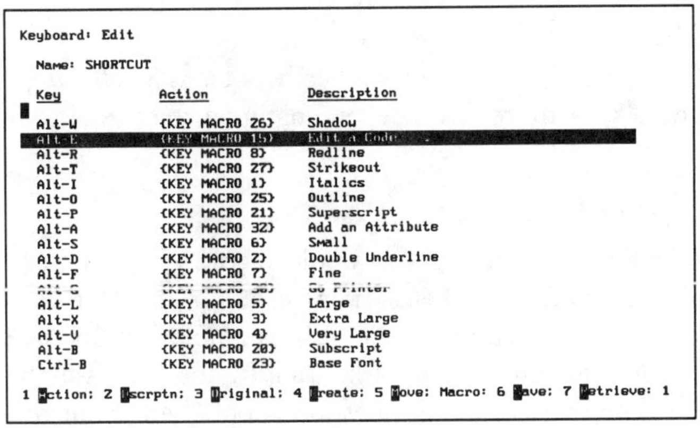

```
Keyboard: Edit

  Name: SHORTCUT

  Key              Action              Description

  Alt-W            {KEY MACRO 26}      Shadow
  Alt-E            {KEY MACRO 15}      Edit a Code
  Alt-R            {KEY MACRO 8}       Redline
  Alt-T            {KEY MACRO 27}      Strikeout
  Alt-I            {KEY MACRO 1}       Italics
  Alt-O            {KEY MACRO 25}      Outline
  Alt-P            {KEY MACRO 21}      Superscript
  Alt-A            {KEY MACRO 32}      Add an Attribute
  Alt-S            {KEY MACRO 6}       Small
  Alt-D            {KEY MACRO 2}       Double Underline
  Alt-F            {KEY MACRO 7}       Fine
  Alt-G            {KEY MACRO [illegible]}  Go Printer
  Alt-L            {KEY MACRO 5}       Large
  Alt-X            {KEY MACRO 3}       Extra Large
  Alt-V            {KEY MACRO 4}       Very Large
  Alt-B            {KEY MACRO 20}      Subscript
  Ctrl-B           {KEY MACRO 23}      Base Font

1 Action: 2 Dscrptn: 3 Original: 4 Create: 5 Move: Macro: 6 Save: 7 Retrieve: 1
```

The "Edit-a-Code" macro is a very important new feature.

the past, WordPerfect ignored this and if you wanted five copies of a complex page which took five minutes to print, WordPerfect sent that page five times. With this new feature, WordPerfect allows the printer to make the copies, so WordPerfect only has to send the page once. This means those same five pages would take a little over 5 minutes instead of 25 minutes.

◆ Shortcut keyboard, Edit macro *SHIFT-F1 K* (5.1)

This is a well-hidden, but very important new feature. Some critics of WordPerfect have complained that it requires too many keystrokes to accomplish something. In some ways they are right. When you're in a hurry, keystrokes such as SHIFT-F8 L J F seem like an awful lot to go through just to change the justification of a paragraph. But 5.1 has added new keyboard definition which many people will overlook, yet it can save them hundreds of keystrokes a day. When you install the program, answer "Y" to installing "Soft Keyboards." These are not keyboards made out of rubber, but files which allow you to redefine what each key on your keyboard does.

The new keyboard is called Shortcut and it contains 32 shortcuts. But one in particular is a minor miracle, and it's called ALT-E, Edit a Code. With this keyboard installed, you can edit virtually any code on-screen just by moving the cursor on top of it (it helps to have Reveal Codes on) and pressing ALT-E. The macro figures out what type of code it is and almost immediately moves you to the menu in the program to edit it. Once you've edited, the macro removes the old code.

If you already use a soft keyboard you can save this to a separate macro file and then retrieve it into your own keyboard file. Whatever you do, *use this macro.* Once you do, you won't complain that I've mentioned this macro four or five times throughout the book. If you want more information about finding and using this macro, look in Chapter 17.

◆ **Size** *CONTROL-F8 S* **(5.0)**

Allows you to choose different sizes of type automatically, such as *Small, Large, Very Large,* or *Extra Large.* These sizes are relative, depending upon the size of your "Initial Base Font" *SHIFT-F8 D F.*

◆ **Size Attribute Ratios.** *SHIFT-F1 I P S* **(5.1)**

I know, I know, this sounds like something you would read in physics class. "What next," you think. A feature called "Isosceles Triangles?" No, this feature is not only simple, it's very important. 5.0 tried to make font sizes simple, but anytime you make something simple, you also run the risk of limiting it, and that was the problem with the size feature. The most common question people had about this was, "Just exactly how large is large?"

Now, if you want to, you can choose exactly how large "large" is, as well as fine, small, very large, and extra large, for that matter. You enter percentages, so if you set Large=150% and your initial base font is 10-point, then your Large font is going to be 15-point. If WordPerfect can't find a 15-point font, it will select the closest size.

If you don't want to bother with this you don't have to, and you get the same sizes you had in 5.0. The only point to remember is that these changes apply to 5.1 overall, not to a particular document. So beware: if you change this setting, your old files will be reformatted automatically on scaleable font printers.

◆ **Sizable Reveal Codes** *SHIFT-F1 D E R* **(5.1)**

Once you start using WordPerfect for desktop publishing, you'll realize how important Reveal Codes (*ALT-F3*) is. I have it turned on *all the time* when working on anything but the most basic formatting. 5.0 improved Reveal Codes by allowing them to be on-screen at all times. And 5.1 makes it even better by allowing you to specify how many lines of the screen Reveal Codes takes. Ten lines is standard, but 15 is not a bad idea. You can make it as large as 20 lines, and this can be helpful when working with heavily-formatted files.

◆ **Spreadsheet import** *CONTROL-F5 S* **(5.1)**

WordPerfect is the second-best-selling piece of software for MS-DOS computers. Lotus 1-2-3 is the first. And yet, even in 5.0 it was a major pain to get them to work together. It was so bad that I had to spend an entire chapter on it, with five pages of really hard stuff just on exporting from 1-2-3 and then importing into WordPerfect. While I lost some good jokes removing most of that chapter, I don't mind, because the new spreadsheet import feature is extremely powerful and extremely easy.

WordPerfect can not only retrieve 1-2-3 and PlanPerfect files, it can turn them into tables. Tables make manipulation easier than tabs, especially because when

WordPerfect brings spreadsheets in as text, it uses "hard" tabs which makes it difficult to change tab types.

As well as importing, WordPerfect can *link* spreadsheet files. This means that when your spreadsheet data changes, so does the information in your WordPerfect file, so your information is never out-of-date. You can set WordPerfect to update every time you load the document or only when requested.

◆ Styles *ALT-F8* (5.0)

Microsoft Word users have been gloating about this feature for years, and with good reason. Style sheets enable you to create what most other programs call "tags." These tags can be applied to your text, speed formatting, and make it much easier to create consistent documents.

Here's an example. Let's say you have a file where all the subject headings in your 100-page document are to be printed in 18-point Times Roman. You (or more likely your boss or client) decide that all the subject headings should be in 14-point Helvetica. Using WordPerfect 4.2, you would have to go through all 100 pages and make the change on each subhead. Using Styles, you change the code for one style, such as the subhead, and every subhead you marked with that style is automatically changed. Because you can share style libraries between more than one file, they too can be updated automatically. Styles can contain any formatting commands, text, and graphics.

◆ Style improvements *ALT-F8* (5.1)

Because Styles was a completely new feature in 5.0, it's not surprising that there have been some improvements and deletions. As well as the new "outline" styles mentioned earlier, the major change to styles is how you delete and rename them.

In 5.0, if you deleted a style from the list of styles, the style codes would remain in your text. If you created a new style with the same name, it would then control the old styles with the same name. Now when you delete a style, you have three choices: Leaving Codes, Including Codes, and Definition only. If you choose to leave the codes, the style codes themselves are deleted, but the formatting codes which were inside remain in the file. If you choose to delete the styles including the codes, then both the style and the codes within them are deleted throughout the entire file. If you delete the style but leave the definition (the way 5.0 did), then the style will disappear from your list of styles, but the style code will remain in your file, complete with all the codes inside it. There is one strange detail about this feature: if you move the cursor past one of these styles in your document, the style name will reappear in the list of styles.

Renaming Styles. In 5.0 you could rename a style, but all the style codes in your document would still have the old name. This means you sometimes had to do a lot of manual work, removing old styles and replacing them with new. But now when you rename a style, WordPerfect gives you the option to either rename all the style codes in your document or not. This is a very valuable addition to the style feature.

The only thing styles can no longer do is contain other styles. "Nesting," as it used to be called, did cause ample user (and program) confusion, so it won't be greatly missed.

◆ Tabs, Relative *SHIFT-F8 L T T R* (5.1)

Yes, I know 5.0 had tabs, but they weren't very good. They wouldn't change automatically and they would completely disappear if you weren't careful when changing your tab settings. Also, if you were using multiple columns and the first line of each paragraph was indented, you had to do math to figure where to set the tabs. This was more of a bother than it sounds.

While the old tabs were always measured from the left side of the paper, the new "Relative" tabs are always measured from the left *margin* (of the page or column). Get the difference? This means that if your page has two columns, you don't have to calculate anything. When you press the tab key in the second column you will automatically be moved the same distance from the left side of the column as when you pressed the tab key in the first column. There's also a new type of tab called a "Hard Tab" which won't automatically change types when your tab settings do. To create a hard tab, press **[HOME][TAB]**. Normal tabs (either Relative, or the old "Absolute") display as **[Tab]** in Reveal Codes, while hard tabs display as **[TAB]**.

◆ Tabs, interactive setting *SHIFT-F8 L T CONTROL -[RIGHT ARROW]* or *CONTROL-[LEFT ARROW]* (5.1)

Another important tab improvement is that they are easier to set. In 5.0 you changed them blindly. You figured out what you thought was right, then pressed F7 a lot, then looked at the results. If you didn't like them you started all over again. In 5.1 your text reformats *as you change the tab settings.* You see how the formatting looks before you ever leave the Tab Set menu. This is a real time-saver and it eliminates the guesswork.

◆ Tables *ALT-F7 T C* (5.1)

This is the most important new feature because it can be used for so many things. You can use it for something as small as putting a box around a paragraph, or as complex as financial tables, or forms, complete with ruling lines, which you can easily fill in over and over again. You can't overestimate how useful this feature really is. And it is genuinely easy to use. You will be seeing a great deal about tables in the rest of the book because they are an easy-to-use, yet powerful feature.

```
«
Classical Accoutrements«
710 N. Bupkiss Pkwy., Helen of Troy, PA 15219, 412-555-1206                «
Invoice«                     | Date«                      | Invoice #«
                             | 12/23/90«                  | 4U-N-E-TH1-N
Bill To:«                                  | Ship To:«
Wilton Veneer«                             | Erica Kane«
MetroSpace Inc.«                           | 17 Agnes Oaks«
2117 Placido Domingo Place«                | Pine Valley, PA 20123«
Newbury, CT 10101«                         | (407) 555-2333«
(201) 555-5555«
F.O.B. Point«  | Customer Order #« | Ship Via«      | Ship Complete«
London UK«     | 555-74-7500«      | Concorde«      | «
Order Date«    | Terms«            | Salesperson«   | Our P.O.«
D:\!BOOK\EX\!INVOI-S.TBL                      Doc 2 Pg 1 Ln 0.75" Pos 1"
```

Tables are the most important and useful of 5.1's new features.

◆ Typographic controls *SHIFT-F8 O P J* (or *W*) (5.0)

Because you are typesetting instead of just printing, features such as Word- and Letterspacing, and Justification limits allow you exceptional control over exactly how the type will appear. If you don't want to deal with all that, WordPerfect's built-in settings attempt to give you the best-looking type possible.

◆ Units of measure *SHIFT-F1 E U* (5.0)

This is an important feature because of *proportionally-spaced fonts.* In the past, you were probably used to *monospaced-fonts,* such as Courier or Elite. With monospaced fonts, every letter takes up the same amount of space horizontally: the letter "i" is exactly the same width as the letter "M." But now you will be using proportionally spaced fonts (the same type of fonts used in typesetting), where each letter is only as wide as it needs to be. Proportionally spaced fonts are easier to read, look better, and allow you to put more information on a page than monospaced fonts.

But proportionally spaced fonts can complicate matters. No longer can you line things up by using the space bar. When using proportional fonts, *tabs* become vital. Tabs are "absolute" measurements, which means that a tab set at 5" will always be at 5", no matter what precedes it. You now *must* use tabs to align columns of numbers or indent paragraphs.

What does this have to do with WordPerfect's new "Units of Measure" feature? Glad you asked. In the past, WordPerfect measured only in lines and spaces, but now it can measure in lines and spaces, inches, centimeters, or points (there are 72 points to an inch). When you use inches or centimeters (whichever is easier for you to understand), WordPerfect will display your exact location on the page.

If you've ever seen those old Italian Hercules movies from Italy, you've learned a valuable lesson about proportional fonts: "Never believe what you see" (on-screen). Sometimes when using tabs, things may not appear to line up on-screen, but they will be in the right place; a quick check in the lower right corner of the screen will show you where you really are.

◆ View Document *SHIFT-F7 V* (5.0)

WordPerfect's View Document feature (formerly known as "Preview"), allows you to see on-screen almost exactly what your page will look like, including graphics. View allows you to perfect your page before you print it. You can see your entire page on-screen at once, in full size, at twice its real size, or even with facing pages. You cannot edit in View mode.

◆ So what?

So now you know what WordPerfect's desktop publishing features are. Big deal. The point is to learn how to use them and even how to abuse them or at least get them to do exactly what you want them to do.

Unlike the WordPerfect *Workbook* (which uses pre-designed forms that make it appear easy, but neglect to show you how to do it yourself), the following chapter will take you through a step-by-step examples from start to finish.

❖ *Preparation*

Desktop publishing entails more than just producing a publication with a computer. Careful preparation will save you time and aggravation in the long run. With WordPerfect, it's easy to try out many diverse styles with a single document. However, users are sometimes so excited with the ease and speed the program offers (after the initial hair-pulling), that they forget about design and content, and concentrate on getting it done fast. This is where a little homework and planning will pay off.

No matter what software/hardware combination you use, the first time you create any publication, it's going to take longer than you think. Some people purchase a program and try to produce their company newsletter with it without spending the time to learn how it works. It takes days longer than it should and they get very frustrated and blame the program.

The importance of planning in advance cannot be over-stressed. Simply reviewing the tutorial or manual is not enough. Sometimes the pressure of deadlines does not allow for experimentation before you actually have to produce a publication. Inevitably, you will waste time learning the program when you are on a deadline producing your first publication.

Try to create a style sheet for your publication before you have to produce a finished product. If possible, take some old word processing files and try to recreate a previous publication to familiarize yourself with WordPerfect's new features. If you follow this advice, you will be thoroughly prepared, confident, and ready to begin desktop publishing.

3

Follow my example

Steps will be taken

Now I'm going to show you, step-by-everloving-step, how to create a desktop published document with WordPerfect. During these examples you'll use almost all of WordPerfect's new features. There are four, count 'em, four long-winded examples in all. Because of the numerous changes between 5.0 and 5.1, two of the examples are specifically for 5.0 and two are exclusively for 5.1. Please do not try the 5.0 examples with 5.1 or the 5.1 examples with 5.0. It will only lead to premature aging on your part. Not only that, I tell the same jokes in both (stop that groaning or I'll report you to Mother Superior). You can find another step-by-step example about calendar creation using tables in Chapter 10, *Table Manners.*

It's important for you to complete these examples because they're going to take you through the basics (and in some cases the complexities) of creating a desktop published page with WordPerfect. Each of the other examples in this book is accompanied by a chart that shows the keystrokes required to recreate the page yourself. The charts will make more sense and be easier to follow if you've completed these examples.

The examples we'll cover in this chapter will provide you with a solid foundation for understanding WordPerfect's new features. The first 5.0 example is fast and simple and the second is more complex. The same goes for the two 5.1 examples in this chapter. The third 5.1 example in Chapter 10 is aimed right between the eyes of the powerful new table feature.

You may not understand all the steps as you are doing them, but just keep following along and it will start to make sense (really, it will. This is also known as the *learn by doing* method).

We're going to be using the Bitstream Dutch fonts in the "starter" set I suggested you make in Chapter 1. You'll need Dutch 10, 12, 14 in normal, bold, and italic, and bold in 18 and 24-point, as well as Swiss 24-point bold. You can make all these by selecting "starter fonts" in the Fontware Installation program. For more information about installing these fonts, see Chapter 7. For the complicated examples, you'll also need to create Dutch Bold 30-point, all of which will fit into 512K *if* you mark Dutch 30 point bold using a + instead of an *. (You may also have to mark other fonts with +s instead of *, depending on your configuration.)

If you are in a hurry and haven't made the fonts, you may attempt the examples. But I warn you, if you substitute fonts, the spacing may not be accurate and your examples will not match the ones in this book.

◆ Font note for scaleable font printer users

If you have a scaleable font printer, such as any PostScript or LaserMaster printer or a LaserJet III, all the fonts you need will be built in. PostScript users will need to substitute Times Roman for Dutch and Helvetica for Swiss. LaserJet III users will use CG Times for Dutch, and Univers for Swiss. If all you have is a daisy wheel printer then you wasted your money on this book, but it's too late to return it because I've already spent the money on a pizza.

WordPerfect does not list each size separately for Scaleable font printers the way it does for LaserJets. To select the size you want, move the cursor to the font you want and press [ENTER]. WordPerfect will then ask for the size you want. Type the number, such as 10 or 12, and press [ENTER] again. PostScript fonts are narrower than LaserJet fonts, so your text will appear shorter than the text in the finished examples. CG Times also has slightly different widths from Dutch, so the amount of text which fits per line or page will differ slightly.

❖ General instructions

Make sure the units of measurement are set to inches, with **SHIFT-F1 E U** (SHIFT-F1 U for 5.0). Otherwise, when I say "type 1.75," you may be entering 1.75 centimeters or 1.75 points or 1.75 WordPerfect units, none of which is even remotely close to 1.75 inches. (If you use a different unit, add " or i to the end of all numbers.)

Before you do any formatting, you'll have to type the text shown in the simple example, including the headlines. Don't do any formatting, just type the text. Using the exact same text will simplify matters, as I sometimes have to tell you where to go (on the page) in accordance with the text in my example.

Make it easy on yourself. After you've typed the simple example text, save the file as "SAMPLE.TXT." When you are ready to work on the examples, retrieve SAMPLE.TXT, then immediately save it under a different name. This will allow you to use the same unformatted text for the complicated example. (If you don't want to type the text for these two examples yourself, and you have $39.95 to spend, it's available by mail order on *Will-Harris Designer Disk* 5, along with most of the other examples in this chapter. We fill orders the same day we receive them and most people get the disk within 10 days of ordering; see the order form on the last page of this book for complete details.)

If it seems as if you have to go through a lot to produce a page that looks so simple, you're right. You must tell WordPerfect what type of font you want, margins, columns, graphics, tabs, tables. That's a lot of information. At first, it's bound to be a slow and perhaps even confusing process, but once you start to understand the features, you can produce pages such as these in anywhere from 5 to 20 minutes, depending on your speed.

Once you've created this format, you can use it over and over again in a fraction of the time it took to create it. You can insert new text or new graphics while retaining the original layout. So think of this as a worthy investment of time rather than as a practice exercise.

Unlike the desktop publishing examples in the WordPerfect *Workbook*, you will be formatting this page yourself. The only completed files are the graphics we'll take from the disks that were included with WordPerfect.

Putting together a page is rarely straightforward, even when you are well-prepared with thumbnail sketches and dummies (Edgar Bergen had a well-prepared dummy, but that's another book). It's a process of give and take; you try something, it doesn't appear quite right, so you change it. With that in mind, this step-by-step example isn't always linear. One change affects another change, creates new problems, and requires more adjustments all around.

Just as in real life, this example won't be perfect the first time through. We'll make a lot of changes until the page looks the way we want.

- I find that it's helpful to work with Reveal Codes turned on when you're creating complicated files. This enables you to see exactly where you are and what you've entered.
- These examples assume that you have a hard disk called C: and a floppy called A:. You should be working on drive C. It doesn't matter what directory you are in.

Just one warning: be patient (and I'll be Nurse). Plan on spending at least a couple of hours working with each example. If you get tired, save the file as it is and then start up again when you're ready, from wherever you left. Mastering these new features will take time and practice, and there's only so much you can comprehend in one sitting. Don't worry if you don't understand everything the first time around. Just do it and let it seep into your unconscious like so much Lady Clairol or Grecian Formula.

- One iron-clad guarantee: experimenting with these examples won't be as bad as having a root canal or passing a kidney stone.

❖ *Simple example for 5.0*

A full page in 10 easy steps. Well, 10 steps more or less (maybe 11).

The first step is to open a new file. Start WordPerfect and say hello to the blank screen. (This may be one of the few times that it won't talk back to you.)

◆ Reveal Codes

First you need to turn Reveal Codes on by pressing

ALT-F3

If you haven't already initialized the printer, do so now. If you have, don't type this next line. If you don't know what I'm talking about, follow this instruction anyway. Press

SHIFT-F7 I

This will ensure that the printer is ready for action. The Bitstream downloadable fonts will be sent to the printer even as you are working on this example. You don't have to stop and wait for them to finish.

Select the printer you are going to use. In this case, we're going to use the printer driver that contains the Bitstream Dutch fonts I asked you to create in Chapter 1. If you haven't created them, I'm disappointed in you, but I'll live. You, on the other hand, aren't going to be able to accomplish much without them. To select the printer, press

SHIFT-F7 S

Mama Rowby's Blue Ribbon Pies

Any way you slice it, we're #1

This last year has been one of great change for Mama Rowby and her family of fine foods. Corporate Raider/Pond Scum Walter Scanlan tried to wrest the company away from the family that has owned and operated it with such great care for lo these past five years, and if it hadn't been for the great spirit of loyalty among management and employees, Mama Rowby's Pies would have become just another corporate conglomerate, instead of the caring, loving, gold mine it is.

Last year pie consumption skyrocketed the world over, partly due to our massive advertising campaign, and the "Miss Cutie Pie" competition, co-hosted by Morgan Fairchilde (desperate to overcome her image as being someone who'll go to the opening of a drawer). Even more important, Mama Rowby is now making mince meat of the competition.

To keep employee morale up during the recent corporate nightmare, Mama decided to institute a "pie-a-day" plan, whereby employees could take home a pie a day. Productivity skyrocketed (as did the bathroom scales of our employees).

This coming year, Mama Rowby is introducing a blitz of new flavors coming out the wazoo. These are revolutionary flavors that will blow the lid off the pie market. Everything from the new "California Cuisine," including "Linguini and Clam Meringue," and "Cactus Ice Cream."

Another hot new line will be retailed under the Cajun Queen moniker, and will include "Blackened Red Cherry," and "Fruit-Slaw Jumbalya." The sleeper of the new trio will be "Dr. Ruth's Good Pies," packaged with illustrated instructions for unorthodox uses. These flavors will be offered in only soft and safe fruits, such as Banana and Cherry.

This fall, Mama will be starring in her own syndicated cooking show where she and her guests (Dr. Ruth is at the top of the list) will help solve world problems and promote "Peace Through Pies." The show is pre-sold in 175 of the largest markets, and will be a perfect platform for increasing customer awareness of "Pie Possibilities," as well introducing new products. Because of Reagan's FCC deregulation (first seen on Saturday morning TV), Mama will sponsor her own show--a first in the syndication market. Dr. Abiner Goren, noted pet psychologist, has said that this unity of information will help to relieve much of the stress that modern television viewers are subjected to, as well as do "Darn good business."

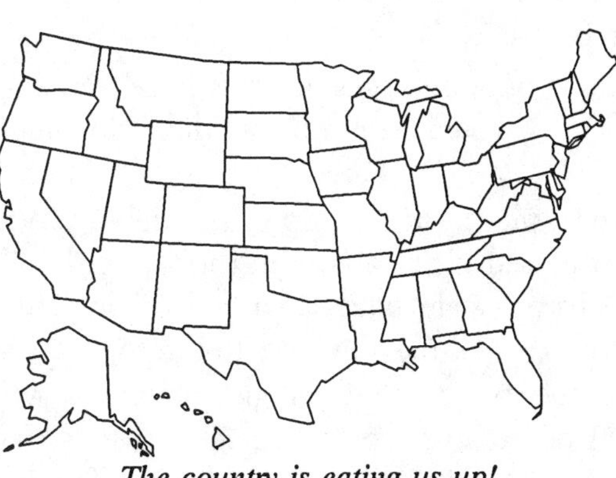

The country is eating us up!

Move the cursor to the name of the printer file you created with the Dutch fonts, then press

S

You should now find yourself at the print menu. The name of the printer you selected should be next to the words "Select Printer." To get back to the editing screen, press

F7

◆ Retrieving a file

Now we're going to retrieve the text file you typed for this example. Press

SHIFT-F10

Type the name of the file you are going to use for text. Press

[ENTER]

You need no justification to turn off justification for this example. Press

SHIFT-F8 L J N F7

You also need to set the initial font for this document. This is the font WordPerfect will use for everything unless we tell it otherwise. We're going to choose Dutch Roman 12-point.

SHIFT-F8 D F

Move the cursor to **Dutch Roman 12pt (ASCII) (Port) (FW)**. This means that the font is Dutch, 12 points tall, the ASCII symbol set, portrait orientation, and made by Fontware. Be careful to choose ROMAN 12pt and not BOLD 12pt or ITALIC 12pt. Press

S F7

◆ Creating a paired style

We're going to create only one style for this page. Since this book is called *Desktop Publishing in Style,* I would be remiss if I didn't include a style, even in a simple example like this.

This is a paired style, placed at the top of the file. I call this type of style a "topper," because (you guessed it) it's always at the top of the file. As you'll see in Chapter 11, *Styles,* this type of style makes it easier to change the document from a simple report such as this to a full-blown newsletter in the least amount of time.

The opening half of the style contains margin commands, while the closing half contains column and tab definitions and a line height setting. I'm going to create the style now. Won't you join me? (Don't give me any lip, just follow along.)

Press

ALT-F8 C N Topper [ENTER] C

The only item on-screen right now is a [Comment] code. Anything you enter before the code will appear in the "Style:On" part of the style, and anything after the code will be in the "Style:Off" half. Let's just place a margin setting in the first half of the style. Press

SHIFT-F8 L M .75 [ENTER] .75 [ENTER] F7

Move the cursor past the [Comment] code. Now it's time to add another return so that there's a blank line between the headline and the two columns. Press

[ENTER]

Now we're going to set up columns. Press

ALT-F7 C D D .3 [ENTER][ENTER] C

◆ Setting tabs

We want the paragraphs to be equally indented on both columns, and so we're going to set tabs. Press

SHIFT-F8 L T [HOME][HOME] [LEFT ARROW] CONTROL-END 1.05 [ENTER] 4.7 [ENTER] F7 F7

Just one more step: set the line height (the white space between the lines of text). Press

SHIFT-F8 L H F .2 [ENTER] F7 F7 F7 F7

◆ Applying a style

Now that we've created the style, we're going to apply it to the file. Brace yourself, excitement like this doesn't happen every day (every other day, maybe).

To use this style, we're going to block the headline and then apply the style. First, make sure the cursor is at the very top of the file. Then, turn on the block by pressing

ALT-F4

Move the cursor from the top of the page to the "T" of "This last year." To apply the style, press

ALT-F8 O

The headline still takes one column, but the body text is now in two columns.

◆ Creating a User-defined box

Are we having fun yet? And you were going to fritter the night away being sociable! Now you get to put in that lovely map of the U.S. of A. instead.

Move the cursor so that it's right after the [Style On:Topper] by pressing

[HOME] [HOME] [UP ARROW]

We're going to create a User-defined box by pressing

ALT-F9 U C

Faster than you can say the immortal Dick Shawn catchphrase, "Suck on a shoe," you've created a User-defined graphics box. We need to make it a page type box and center it at the bottom of the page. Let's do that now, shall we? Press

T A V B H M C

Here's an instant memory tip: just think of "TAV BHMC." (Tav Bhamuc is one of Dickens' all-time favorite characters. You know, the travelling tea salesman in *Oliver with a Twist.* Stop that moaning now, it only took a few seconds of your time and at least *I* enjoyed it. Some jokes you do for yourself—others you should just keep to yourself.)

◆ Retrieving a graphic

Let's retrieve the graphic now. Check that the Fonts/Graphics disk is in Drive A and press

F A:USAMAP.WPG [ENTER]

Voila! You've got a graphic. Now how about a caption? Press

C [BACKSPACE] SHIFT-F6 CONTROL-F8 A I **The country is eating us up!** F7 F7

◆ Placing a horizontal line

Almost finished, cross my heart. Now we're going to place the horizontal line on the page. Press

ALT-F9 L H H C L 2.79 [ENTER] W .1 [ENTER] [ENTER]

Then put some space between the line and the headline by pressing

[ENTER][ENTER]

You should now see two returns after the graphic line and before the headline. If you don't, you obviously missed the boat at some point in our journey (luckily for you, this will not translate into bad karma in your next life, unless you come back as a computer).

My, this desktop publishing sure makes a person hungry. Go get some chocolate chip cookies, then come back. If anyone asks what you're doing, just say "following instructions."

◆ Making a headline extra large

Back so soon? We have only one more little step to do, and we get to do it three whole times. We're going to make the headline extra large, the #1 line large.

Move the cursor to the "M" of Mama Rowby and turn block on by pressing

ALT-F4

Move the cursor to the line that says "Blue Ribbon Pies" and go to the end of the line by pressing

[DOWN ARROW] [END]

We're going to make the headline extra large, or 24-point. Press

CONTROL-F8 S E

The words may not appear any different on-screen, but they will in View Document and on paper. Now move the cursor to the "A" of "Any way you slice it." We're going to block this entire line and enlarge it. Press

ALT-F4 [END] CONTROL-F8 S L

◆ Creating raised caps

We're in the home stretch. We're going to make the "T" of "This" very large so that it becomes a "Raised Cap." Move the cursor over to the "T" of "This last year." Block it by pressing

ALT-F4

And pat it and mark it with a "B" and put it in the oven for . . . no, no, wrong book. Cover the "T" with the block by pressing

[RIGHT ARROW]

To make the "T" into a raised cap, press

CONTROL-F8 S V

◆ Centering a headline

If the headline isn't already centered, do that now. Go to the top of the file by pressing

[HOME] [HOME] [UP ARROW]

Turn block on

ALT-F4

And move the cursor so it covers the entire headline. Tell WordPerfect to center the blocked text. Press

SHIFT-F6 Y

◆ Save your work

It's a good idea to save the file before printing. I've found print time to be sort of like the Bermuda Triangle of word processing (it's the time when the most data-losing accidents can occur). Let's save the file now. Press

F10 [ENTER] Y

◆ View Document

Now, at last, we can take a look-see at this masterpiece with View Document. Press

SHIFT-F7 V

If you can't see the entire page, press **3**; if you can see the page but can't read the text, press **1**. If you're totally confused and thinking of ways to exchange this book for something else like *Larry: the Stooge in the Middle,* don't press your luck. Take it again from the top—it has worked for other people. Who knows, it just might work for you. If it looks something like my example, congratulate yourself. To leave View Document press

F1

◆ To print

Now, print it, quick, before it melts. No, it won't really melt. I'm kidding. (Geez, lighten up, will you?) Make sure that the printer is plugged in and connected to the computer. It's showtime, folks. Press

P

The computer will emit some hard disk noises, and then the lights on the printer should start flashing (just like in an extremely cheap science fiction movie). The page should emerge victoriously from the printer in anywhere from 1 to 5 minutes, depending on the speed of your printer. I don't know about you, but I'm tired. Take the rest of the day off.

❖ *Complicated example for 5.0*

Now that you've been hooked by the first example, let's move on to the hard stuff. As usual, the first step involves retrieving a file. Remember how the *General Instructions* on page 31 told you to save the simple example text file under a different name before you started putting codes into it? This is where that file will come in handy. Start WordPerfect. (Or, start WordStar and really confuse yourself.)

◆ Turn Reveal Codes on

To turn Reveal Codes on, press

ALT-F3

Select the printer you are going to use. In this case, we're going to use the printer driver that contains the Bitstream Dutch fonts. Press

SHIFT-F7 S

Move the cursor to the name of the printer file you created that contains the Dutch fonts and then press

S F7

You should now be at the print menu, and the name of the printer you selected should be next to the words "Select Printer."

To return to the editing screen, press

F7

◆ Retrieving a file

Now let's retrieve a text file. (Can you say "retrieve?" I knew you could.) Press

SHIFT-F10

Type the name of the file you are going to use for text. (If your text contains a table, as this one does, make sure you use tabs, and not spaces, between each column of numbers. If you use spaces, the column will never line up when using a proportional font, such as Dutch.) Press

[ENTER]

◆ Font default

Now you need to set the Initial (default) font for the file. This font will be used for all body text, headers, footers, and captions, unless we specify otherwise. Press

SHIFT-F8 D F

Move the cursor to **Dutch Roman 10 pt** The name of the font will also indicate whether it uses ASCII for Roman-8 symbols, and whether it's portrait or landscape. If you created ASCII symbol fonts, the complete name will be **BSN Dutch Roman 10pt (ASCII Business) (FW, Port)**. The (FW) stands for Fontware (or Fay Wray). Select this font by pressing

[ENTER] F7

◆ Open style

Now we'll create a topper style which contains important global formatting commands. (Doesn't "global" sound important?) I had wanted to create a paired style as in the first example, but WordPerfect kept giving me trouble about margins. Even though I'd set margins after the comment, it wouldn't place them in the style. Whatever the problem was, I came up with a new approach. Create two styles: one for the very top and one containing the horizontal line, the requisite number of returns, and the column definition. Press

ALT-F8 C N TOPPER [ENTER] T O C

◆ Setting margins

Set the margins. We'll use a seven-tenths of an inch margin on the top and bottom, and a half-inch margin on each side. Let's first set the top and bottom margins. Press

SHIFT-F8 P M .7 [ENTER] .7 [ENTER] [ENTER]

Now we're going to set the left and right margins. Press

L M .5 [ENTER] .5 [ENTER] F7

◆ Creating a column style

Now we need to create the column style. Press

ALT-F8 C N Columns [ENTER] T O C

The column style starts with the horizontal line, includes three returns, and has a column definition. Press

ALT-F9 L H [ENTER]

[ENTER] [ENTER] [ENTER]

We also have to set the margins yet again, because otherwise the columns will not be sized correctly.

SHIFT-F8 L M .5 [ENTER] .5 [ENTER] F7

Mama Rowby's Blue Ribbon Pies

Mama takes a big bite out of the pie market

This last year has been one of great change for Mama Rowby and her family of fine foods. Corporate Raider/Pond Scum Walter Scanlan tried to wrest the company away from the family that has owned and operated it with such great care for lo these past five years, and if it hadn't been for the great spirit of loyalty among management and employees, Mama Rowby's Pies would have become just another corporate conglomerate, instead of the caring, loving, gold mine it is.

Last year pie consumption skyrocketed the world over, partly due to our massive advertising campaign, and the "Miss Cutie Pie" competition, cohosted by Morgan Fairchilde (desperate to overcome her image as being someone who'll go to the opening of a drawer). Even more important, Mama Rowby is now making mince meat of the competition.

To keep employee morale up during the recent corporate nightmare, Mama decided to institute a "pie-a-day" plan, whereby employees could take home a pie a day. Productivity skyrocketed (as did the bathroom scales of our employees).

This coming year, Mama Rowby is introducing a blitz of new flavors coming out the wazoo. These are revolutionary flavors that will blow the lid off the pie market. Everything from the new "California Cuisine," including "Linguini and Clam Meringue," and "Cactus Ice Cream."

Another hot new line will be retailed under the Cajun Queen moniker, and will include "Blackened Red Cherry," and "Fruit-Slaw Jumbalya." The sleeper of the new trio will be "Dr. Ruth's Good Pies," packaged with illustrated instructions for unorthodox uses. These flavors will be offered in only soft and safe fruits, such as Banana and Cherry.

This fall, Mama will be starring in her own syndicated cooking show where she and her guests (Dr. Ruth is at the top of the list) will help solve world problems and promote "Peace Through Pies." The show is pre-sold in 175 of the largest markets, and will be a perfect platform for increasing customer awareness of "Pie Possibilities," as well introducing new products. Because of Reagan's FCC deregulation (first seen on Saturday morning TV), Mama will sponsor her own show--a first in the syndication market. Dr. Abiner Goren, noted pet psychologist, has said that this unity of information will help to relieve much of the stress that modern television viewers are subjected to, as well as do "Darn good business."

	WA	AK	TW	MA	NY	CA
Cherry	.50	.55	.83	1.24	1.86	**2.78**
Apple	.70	.77	1.16	1.73	2.60	**3.90**
Coconut	.30	.33	.50	.74	1.67	**1.67**
Pecan	1.10	1.21	1.82	2.72	4.08	**6.13**

Now we create the columns. Press

ALT-F7 D N 3 [ENTER] D .25 [ENTER] [ENTER] C F7 F7

◆ Creating a headline style

For good measure, let's create a headline style, making the text Swiss 24-point bold. Press

C N Headline [ENTER] C CONTROL-F8 F

Move the cursor to "Swiss Bold 24pt" and press

S

Now, turn justification off. It's rarely ever a good idea to justify headlines. Press

SHIFT-F8 L J N F7 F7 F7 F7

So much for creating styles. Now move to the very top of the file by pressing

[HOME] [HOME] [HOME] [UP-ARROW]

And turn on the Topper Style by pressing

ALT-F8

Move the cursor to "Topper" and press

O

◆ Placing a graphics box

Now let's place the first graphic, located in the upper right-hand corner of the page. We're going to use a "User-defined" box because it has no border around it (just like Germany, these days . . .). Press

ALT-F9 U C

We need to tell WordPerfect where to place this box. WordPerfect's default will put graphics along the right margin. In this case, we want them along the left margin. Press

H L

◆ Sizing a box

We will also set the size of the box. The box should only be a half inch high. We'll set the height and WordPerfect will figure out the width when we retrieve the graphic. Press

S H .5 [ENTER]

◆ Retrieving a graphic

Now we're going to retrieve the graphic. Rather than type the name, we're going to use **F5**, the List Files key. Press

F F5 A: [ENTER]

Move the cursor to the file called **AIRPLANE.WPG** and press

R

After the file has been loaded, you'll notice that the size is 1.83" wide by .5" high.

◆ Editing a graphic

WordPerfect allows you to size, stretch, compress, rotate, or invert graphics. To try it, let's go into graphic edit mode by pressing

E

The graphic should appear on-screen. If it doesn't, you may have set up WordPerfect incorrectly for the type of graphics your computer has. Consult the "Getting Started" chapter in the WordPerfect manual or the "Setup" section in the reference manual.

◆ Rotating a graphic

Notice the number between the parentheses in the lower right corner of the screen. This should read 10%. If it doesn't, press the **INS** key until it does. As long as we're here, let's play with the graphic. If you press the **plus** key (next to the cursor or number-pad), you'll see that the graphic rotates 45 degrees (it's doing a nose dive.) To pull the plane up before it goes down in flames, press the **minus** key (next to the cursor or number-pad). The graphic will rotate 45 degrees in the other direction, returning it to where it was.

◆ Enlarging a graphic

Now, let's zoom in on the plane itself. Press

[INS][INS][INS]

until the number in the lower right corner reads "25%." Now let's increase the picture by 125%. Press

[PgUp] [PgUp] [PgUp] [PgUp] [PgUp]

Now we need to move the picture to the right. Press

[RIGHT ARROW]

20 Times. Now we need to move the picture down.
Press

[DOWN ARROW]

20 Times. We have now zoomed in on the plane. We decide that this was a mistake and want to return the picture to its original state. Press

CONTROL-[HOME]

The picture will return to its normal size. Enough fun and games. Press

F7 F7

A box will appear on-screen that displays the approximate dimensions of the graphic we just created.

◆ Replacing a graphic

But wait! We hold an impromptu staff meeting and decide to insert a new graphic file in this same graphics box. Sure, the plane is cute, but maybe just a little too cute. What were we thinking? But at least it won't be difficult to change. Press

ALT-F9 U E 1 [ENTER]

Quick, it's time to replace the current graphic with one called AWARD.WPG. Press

F A:AWARD.WPG [ENTER] Y

Because this graphic is a different size, it is now too small. Let's size it again. We'll instruct WordPerfect to make the new graphic 1" high. Press

S H 1 [ENTER] F7

WordPerfect has automatically calculated how wide the graphic should be and come up with .76".

◆ Enlarging a headline

Now we want to increase the size of our headline. This will be the banner/logo of our publication. Our body text is Dutch and our headlines are Swiss for contrast, but this is not a headline, it's a logo. (It's not a gang, it's a club.) We could use some fancy display or headline typeface (such as Broadway) to match our company logo. But in this case, because I can only be sure that you have either Swiss or Dutch, we'll choose from Swiss and Dutch. The logo will be Dutch.

The reason we're not using "Appearance Extra Large" to enlarge the type in this logo is that when you use a 10-point base font, Extra Large will give you a 24-point font. We want a 30-point font, so we'll have to choose it specifically. If we were using a 12-point base font, Extra Large would give us a 30-point font. Make sure the cursor is on the "M" of the first "Mama" and press

CONTROL-F8 F

Move the cursor to **Dutch Bold 30pt** (ASCII) (Port) (FW), and press

[ENTER]

When you selected this font, WordPerfect automatically adjusted the line spacing so that lines of text wouldn't print over each other. We chose a bold base font, so it will print bold even without using WordPerfect's bold feature. If we used the bold feature, the bold font would print in an even darker shade.

But because of this font change, WordPerfect is now formatting the rest of the file for this large font. We need to change the font. Put the cursor on the "s" of "Pies," then press

[RIGHT ARROW] CONTROL-F8 F

Move the cursor to **Dutch Roman 10pt** and press

[ENTER] F7

◆ Aligning text

Make sure that Reveal Codes is still on. (Some people turn it off so they can see more of their page. They think I won't notice.) Move the cursor so that it's on the "A" of "Any way you slice it." We're going to make this flush right (without having to pay a fortune to a plumber), so press

ALT-F6

and the text jumps to the right margin.

◆ Applying italics

Let's use italics on that "Any way you slice it" line. Turn block on by pressing

ALT-F4

Move the cursor to the end of the line by pressing

[END]

To turn italics on for the block, press

CONTROL-F8 A I

The line is now in italics. Let's re-block it and increase it to Large (or 12-point). Press

ALT-F4 CONTROL-[HOME] CONTROL-[HOME] CONTROL-F8 S L

◆ View Document

Getting curious? Let's use View Document to see how it looks. Press

SHIFT-F7 V

If you've followed instructions carefully, the *headline area* should be *similar to* (but not exactly like—just yet) the printed example in the book.

◆ Enlarging view

You probably can't read any of the type on this full page on-screen view. For a closer look, press

1

You're now seeing the page in 100% view. For a still closer look, press

2

You're now seeing the page in 200% view. This is as close as you can get without getting the pie in your face. Let's return to full page view. Press

3

We still haven't finished this puppy. Let's go back to work. Press

F7

◆ Applying a column style

Now it's time to place three columns in the body text. Move the cursor to the "B" of "Blue Ribbon" and press

[DOWN ARROW]

Turn on the column style by pressing

ALT-F8

Move the cursor to "Columns" and press

O

Extra space will appear under the headline, and the text will be set in three columns.

◆ Applying a headline style

We need to use that headline style on the headline. Block the entire headline ("Mama takes a big bite out of the pie market"), moving the cursor to the "M" and then pressing

ALT-F4

Move the cursor to the space after "Market." To apply the headline style, press

ALT-F8

Move the cursor to "Headline," and press:

O

We want the rest of this column to be blank, so place the cursor on the "T" of "This Last Year" and press

CONTROL-[ENTER]

The remaining text will jump to the second column, leaving the rest of the first column blank. Ahh, white space.

◆ Turning justification on

We didn't want our headline justified, but we would like our text justified. Time to turn on justification. As annoying as hyphenation can be, we'll have to turn it on for an accurate idea of how our text fits on the page.

Justification without hyphenation can result in extremely unattractive type, and you wouldn't want that, would you? I didn't think so. Since both justification and hyphenation are in the same menu, we can turn both of them on simultaneously. Press

SHIFT-F8 L J Y Y A F7

It's always smart to get in the habit of adjusting as many features as you can when you're on a particular menu. This saves a lot of keystrokes. (There'll be a $5 charge for that hint. You'll find my address in the back of the book.)

◆ Hyphenation

Whenever WordPerfect asks you to hyphenate, press **ESC** if you want it to place the hyphen where it recommends, or move the cursor to where you'd like the hyphen and then press **ESC**. WordPerfect sets a hyphenation range, so you may not be able to move the cursor to the precise location you desire. If you don't want the word hyphenated, or can't move the cursor to wherever you want it, press **F1** to tell WordPerfect not to hyphenate that word.

If you get really sick and tired of having WordPerfect pester you about so many words, press **F7** to temporarily turn hyphenation off. Hyphenation will remain off only through the next cursor move or command, and then will turn itself back on.

Let's go back into View Document to see how the page is progressing. Press

SHIFT-F7 V

It's getting there, isn't it? If we didn't have the table at the bottom, we could stop right now. But you paid good money for this book and I'm here to see that you get your money's worth. By the end of this example (and certainly by the end of the book), you'll know more about desktop publishing with WordPerfect than you ever dreamed of (even in your worst nightmare).

◆ Blocking and copying a table

Before we proceed any further, let's take care of that table at the bottom. We've already placed a graphic in a graphics box, but now we're going to put a table in a table box.

Since we want this "graphic" table to span several columns, we're going to create it as a page type graphic. To ensure that it prints on this page, and not the next, we'll place this code at the top of the page, right after the margins.

First we're going to block our table and copy it, then create a table box, and then paste the table into the box. If the phone should ring right now, tell them not to bother you because you're busy pasting a table in a box.

Move the cursor to the beginning of the table. To turn the block on, press

ALT-F4

Move the cursor so that it covers the entire table, and then press

CONTROL-F4 B M

The table will disappear, but it's not gone forever. WordPerfect has put it in a special magic place and will drop it back onto the page as soon as you press return. As a convenient reminder, WordPerfect says, "Move cursor, press **Enter** to retrieve."

Now that the table is safely tucked away, let's hope that it said its prayers and create that table box.

◆ Creating a page-type graphic box

Go to the top of the file, and press

[HOME] [HOME] [HOME] [UP ARROW]

To ensure that the table box is the correct size, we have to check that the cursor is after the two margin codes, so press

[RIGHT ARROW] [RIGHT ARROW]

Before we create the table, we're going to set the options. We'll have a single line above and a thick line below. The table will contain a 10% gray background. Press

ALT-F9 T O B N N S T G 10 [ENTER] [ENTER]

Now we're ready to create the table of "States." Press

ALT-F9 T C

We need to tell WordPerfect what type of box this is, where it will be on the page, and how large it will be. Let's start with what type of box it is. This is a page-type box, so it can span the two columns of text. Press

T A

WordPerfect automatically places this box on the top of the page, flush with the right margin, and makes it 3.25" square. First, let's move it to the bottom of the page by pressing

V B

◆ Placing a box

Next, we'll tell WordPerfect how wide this box is. The box will stretch all the way across the page, from the left margin to the right margin. When you create a page-type box, you can place it on the page based on margins, columns, or exact numerical measurements. We're going to make it flush with both the left and right margins by pressing

H M B

Now, we can finally edit the contents of the box itself. Press

E

Don't worry, our text is still there. The [ENTER] that we pressed when creating the table options didn't count. Now we're going to press

[ENTER]

Zippity do dah, here's our table. (Zippity do dah may be a registered trademark of the Walt Disney Company.)

Make sure there are no extra returns at the top of the table. If there are, your table will be larger than the one in the example.

◆ Changing fonts

Let's make the entire table Swiss 12-point bold. Press

CONTROL-F8 F

Move the cursor to "Swiss 12pt Bold" and press

S

◆ Setting tabs

And now, without further ado, it's tab time! We'll employ one set of tabs for the headings and another for the numbers. First, we need to clear the existing tabs by pressing

SHIFT-F8 L T [HOME] [HOME] [LEFT ARROW] CONTROL-END

Now we're going to set the new tabs. The first one will be a right aligned tab, and we'll tell WordPerfect to set the rest of them 1" apart and right aligned as well. Press

1.88 [ENTER] R 1.88,1 [ENTER] F7 F7

Now move the cursor to the first space of the second line (in this case, right on the "C" of "Cherry"). We're going to set decimal tabs here by first clearing the old ones and then setting the new ones by pressing

SHIFT-F8 L T [HOME] [HOME] [LEFT ARROW] CONTROL-END

1.66 [ENTER] D 1.66,1 [ENTER] F7 F7

◆ Search and replace for tabs

Here's a really neat tip on how to whip tables into shape. Even though we've set these tabs to be right aligned and decimal, WordPerfect uses one type of codes for regular tabs, and another for aligned tabs, and so text may not line up correctly.

What's a mother to do? (It's easier than you think.) Did you know that you could perform a search and replace on just a block? Well, you can. Did you know that you could search for tabs and replace them with Aligns? Well you can (you learn something new every day). First, block the table by pressing

ALT-F4

Move the cursor so that the block covers the entire table. Now it's time to search for tabs and replace them with Align codes. Press

ALT-F2 N [TAB] F2 CONTROL-F6 F2

In a flash (or a flush, depending on the speed of your computer and the length of the table), WordPerfect will replace those nasty old tabs with new-fangled Aligns, and the table will look like a million bucks, even if your numbers don't.

Leave the table box by pressing

F7 F7

I don't know about you, but that trick alone was worth the price of the book.

◆ Moving around in View Document

Golly gee willikers, this page looks mighty unique to me. But then, I'm nearsighted. Let's sneak another peek through the magic mirror of View Document by pressing

SHIFT-F7 V

Go into 100% mode by pressing

1

Did you know that you can move around the View Document screen with any cursor movement keys (including gray [+] or gray [-], the "Screen Down" and "Screen Up" keys)? You can also jump to any page by pressing **CONTROL-HOME**, and then typing in a page number. Will wonders never cease? (Yes, they will, probably around 5 p.m.)

You're spending altogether too much time looking at View Document (stop it or you'll go blind). Press

F7

◆ Measuring a table

Three more steps and we'll call it a day, a week, or a marsupial—whichever you prefer. First, let's put a vertical rule between the headline column and the body text.

Move the cursor to the "M" in "Mama takes . . ." We're going to create a vertical line running from this line down to the table. WordPerfect will automatically start the vertical rule at the current line, but unless we intervene, it will print the line to the bottom of the page, right through the table.

First, let's look at the "States" table to see how tall it is. Press

ALT-F9 T E 1 [ENTER]

We can see that it's 1.4" high. That's all we needed to know. Press

F7

To quickly return to the "M" of "Mama takes," press

CONTROL-[HOME] CONTROL-[HOME]

◆ Creating a vertical rule

Now we're going to create that vertical rule. Press

ALT-F9 L V

We need to tell WordPerfect where to place the rule on the page. We're going to select Between Columns and then tell WordPerfect to place it to the right of column 1. Press

H B 1 [ENTER]

Now we're going to set where the line begins vertically. When we choose Vertical Set, WordPerfect will insert our current location on the page (which should be 2.09"). Press

V S [ENTER]

Next let's tell WordPerfect how long to make the line. WordPerfect has automatically calculated 8.15" as the distance to the bottom of the page. We don't want to print over the table, so we're going to subtract 1.4" (the height of the table) and end up with 6.75. Press

L 6.75 [ENTER] [ENTER]

Viola! the vertical rule is in place. Two more to go. You can see the light at the end of the tunnel, the wind's at your back, and the only obstacle between you and immortality is death. You look Death in the face and say, "The word 'scared' isn't in my vocabulary." Death responds with a snappy "What about the word 'stupid?' " Death has very bad breath, and what's worse, you (and I) cannot keep up this level of witty repartee much longer.

You snap back to reality and experience something akin to psychic whiplash. You ponder the inevitable existential questions, then decide to just finish the example and drown reality in Heavy Belgian Chocolate ice cream (Steve's, of course).

◆ Creating a User-defined box

Move the cursor to the end of the text (in this case, after "business"). Put a blank line after the text. Press

[ENTER]

Now we're going to create another User-defined box, this time with its horizontal position both left and right so that it fills the column. Press

ALT-F9 U C H B

◆ Loading a graphic

It's that time again. Time to load a graphic file. We know the name, so we won't bother using List Files this time. Make sure the Fonts/Graphics disk is in drive A and press

F A:USAMAP.WPG [ENTER] F7

We've already had more than our share of fun playing with graphics, and besides, if you mirror the map of the US, we might be branded as pinko troublemakers.

There. The page is finished at last. Well, a drop cap wouldn't hurt. Then people will be sure you've done the page in Ventura Publisher. They'll think you must be pretty well-off to be able to afford Ventura and, boy, you sure know how to use it. Little will they suspect that you've been using a word processing program all along. Ah, what the hay—if you're game, I'm game. Drop caps can be tricky, but they look fab (some even say gear).

◆ Creating a drop cap

To create a drop cap, we need to set some special options. We don't want to change the User-defined box that contains the captivating map of the US, and so let's make this a Text Box.

Move the cursor to the "T" in "This last year," in the first paragraph of the story. We're going to delete the letter T. Press

[DEL]

First, we have to set the options. We don't want any lines around the box, no border space inside or out, and a background of 0% black (otherwise known as white). If you skip this option, the Drop Cap will not work worth beans. Press

ALT-F9 B O B N N N N

O 0 [ENTER] 0 [ENTER] 0 [ENTER] 0 [ENTER]

I 0 [ENTER] 0 [ENTER] 0 [ENTER] 0 [ENTER]

G 0 [ENTER] [ENTER]

That seems like a lot to suffer through, but just remember how much time and money you'll save, and how you'll get to spend it on trips to the Virgin Islands, genuine diamond jewelry, cheesecake.

◆ Creating a Text Box

Now let's create the Text Box that will contain the drop cap itself. Press

ALT-F9 B C

We'll align it with the left margin by pressing

H L

Now we're going to type the text of the box. First we'll change the font and then we'll type the letter "T." Press

E CONTROL-F8 F

Move the cursor over to **Dutch Roman 30pt** and press

S T F7

◆ Sizing a box

Now for the hard part—sizing the box. Let's use the on-screen measurements to help us. WordPerfect would size the box for us, but it overcompensates and makes the box too large for our purposes.

Put the cursor *on* the letter T. Look at the measurement. Mine says 3.08. Press the **[RIGHT ARROW]** key and check the measurement again. Mine says 3.35. Subtract the first number from the second and you get .27. If you come up with another figure, your math is as bad as mine is.

Back to the drop cap. We've learned that it's .27 wide, and since we know it's 30-point high, we already know how tall it is. Let's get out of here and size this box, complete this example, and do something more interesting (like have some dessert). Press

F7 S B .3 [ENTER]

Before we enter 30pt for the height of the box, I have to add something. Don't worry—it has nothing to do with my family, it has to do with this drop cap.

(By now, you probably feel like you know my family intimately, and I haven't even told about my sister who lived in a teepee or my brother who could argue about the fact that it was daylight outside. I'm only telling you this because it should shed some light on the way I think, and creating a drop cap in WordPerfect is a study in problem solving.)

We could enter 30-point for the height of the box, but we want to make the box to be a bit smaller than that so the text will flow neatly around it. This always calls for some experimentation. I started with 30pt and it was too large.

WordPerfect automatically gives us 12.2 leading with 10-point Bitstream body text. (With 10-point PostScript or other soft fonts, WordPerfect gives you 11-point leading, but Bitstream added extra leading and the improvement is noticeable on the page.) I only know this because I spent hours investigating it. Sometimes I wonder if it's really such a good way to spend one's time.

Since the drop cap will be two lines high, I tried 24-point for the height of the box. It was still a bit too big. I tried 22-point (.3") and it was perfect.

If you make the box too narrow, the letter will print with a hyphen after it. If the box is too short, the letter won't print at all. So we've settled on .3". Press

.3 [ENTER] [ENTER]

Now let's squeeze some juice from the fruits of our labor. Press

SHIFT-F7 V

◆ Printing

A page like this may take some time to display on-screen. On my Victor AT, it takes about 15 seconds. There it is, it looks terrific, and now it's time to print. To leave View Document and go to the Print menu, press

F1

Make sure the printer is plugged in and connected to the computer (rather than the toaster). It's showtime. Press

P

The page should pop out of the printer in anywhere from 1 to 5 minutes, depending on the speed of the computer and printer.

I don't know about you, but it's times like this when I'm proud to be an American: happy to be alive, and overjoyed that someone had the sense to invent computers.

❖ *Simple example for 5.1*

A full page in 10 easy steps. Well, 10 steps more or less (maybe 11).

WARNING: Check and make sure that the .WPG files needed in this example (GLOBE2-M, BALLOONS, TROPHY) are on your hard disk. They will probably be in the C:\WP51 directory (or wherever your program is). *If* you can't find them, run the install program and answer NO to everything *except* Install Graphic Images. This will copy the sample graphics onto your hard disk. Then press SHIFT-F1 L G to tell WP where to look for graphics files.

The first step is to open a new file. Start WordPerfect and say "hello" to the blank screen. (This may be one of the few times that it won't talk back to you.)

◆ Reveal Codes

First you need to turn Reveal Codes on by pressing

ALT-F3

Select the printer you are going to use. In this case, we're going to use the printer driver that contains the Bitstream Dutch fonts I asked you to create in Chapter 1. If you haven't created them, I'm disappointed in you, but I'll live. You, on the other hand, aren't going to be able to accomplish much without them. To select the printer, press

SHIFT-F7 S

Move the cursor to the name of the printer file you created with the Dutch fonts, then press

S

If you haven't already initialized the printer, do so now. If you have, don't type this next line. If you don't know what I'm talking about, follow this instruction anyway. Press

I Y

This will ensure that the printer is ready for action. The Bitstream downloadable fonts will be sent to the printer even as you are working on this example. You don't have to stop and wait for them to finish.

◆ Retrieving a file

Now we're going to retrieve the text file you typed for this example. Press

SHIFT-F10

Type the name of the file you are going to use for text. Press

{type your filename here} [ENTER]

◆ Just off & Initial Font

You need no justification to turn justification off for this example. Press

SHIFT-F8 L J L [ENTER]

You also need to set the initial font for this document. This is the font WordPerfect will use for everything, unless we tell it otherwise. We're going to choose Dutch Roman 12-point. Press

D F

Move the cursor to **BSN Dutch Roman 12pt (ASCII BUSINESS) (FW, Port)**. This means that the font is Dutch, 12 points tall, the ASCII symbol set, portrait orientation, and made by Fontware. Be careful to choose ROMAN 12pt and not BOLD 12pt or ITALIC 12pt.

S F7

◆ Creating a paired style

We're going to create only one style for this page. Since this book is called *Desktop Publishing in Style,* I would be remiss if I didn't include a style, even in a simple example like this.

This is a paired style, placed at the top of the file. I call this type of style a "topper," because (you guessed it) it's always at the top of the file. As you'll see in

Mama Rowby's Blue Ribbon Pies

Any way you slice it, we're #1

This last year has been one of great change for Mama Rowby and her family of fine foods. Corporate Raider/Pond Scum Walter Scanlan tried to wrest the company away from the family that has owned and operated it with such great care for lo these past five years, and if it hadn't been for the great spirit of loyalty among management and employees, Mama Rowby's Pies would have become just another corporate conglomerate, instead of the caring, loving, gold mine it is.

Last year pie consumption skyrocketed the world over, partly due to our massive advertising campaign, and the "Miss Cutie Pie" competition, co-hosted by Morgan Fairchilde (desperate to overcome her image as being someone who'll go to the opening of a drawer). Even more important, Mama Rowby is now making mince meat of the competition.

To keep employee morale up during the recent corporate nightmare, Mama decided to institute a "pie-a-day" plan, whereby employees could take home a pie a day. Productivity skyrocketed (as did the bathroom scales of our employees).

This coming year, Mama Rowby is introducing a blitz of new flavors coming out the wazoo. These are revolutionary flavors that will blow the lid off the pie market. Everything from the new "California Cuisine," including "Linguini and Clam Meringue," and "Cactus Ice Cream."

Another hot new line will be retailed under the Cajun Queen moniker, and will include "Blackened Red Cherry," and "Fruit-Slaw Jumbalya." The sleeper of the new trio will be "Dr. Ruth's Good Pies," packaged with illustrated instructions for unorthodox uses. These flavors will be offered in only soft and safe fruits, such as Banana and Cherry.

This fall, Mama will be starring in her own syndicated cooking show where she and her guests (Dr. Ruth is at the top of the list) will help solve world problems and promote "Peace Through Pies." The show is pre-sold in 175 of the largest markets, and will be a perfect platform for increasing customer awareness of "Pie Possibilities," as well introducing new products. Because of Reagan's FCC deregulation (first seen on Saturday morning TV), Mama will sponsor her own show--a first in the syndication market. Dr. Abiner Goren, noted pet psychologist, has said that this unity of information will help to relieve much of the stress that modern television viewers are subjected to, as well as do "Darn good business."

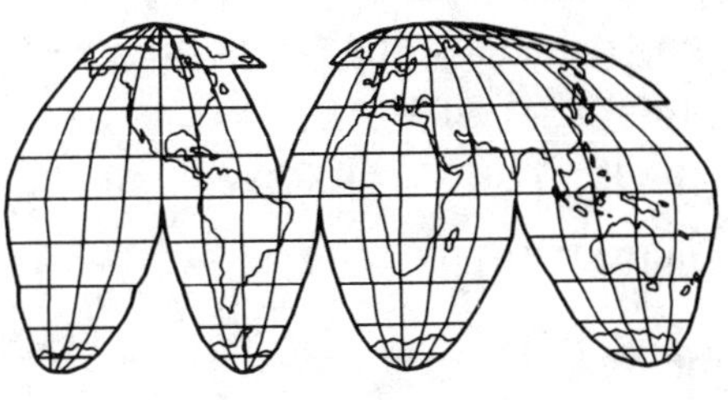

The world is eating us up!

Chapter 11, *Styles,* (or in Chapter 13 if you're filing for bankruptcy) this type of style makes it easier to change the document from a simple report such as this to a full-blown newsletter in the least amount of time.

The opening half of the style contains margin commands, while the closing half contains column and tab definitions and a line height setting. I'm going to create the style now. Won't you join me? (Don't give me any lip, just follow along.) Press

ALT-F8 C N Topper [ENTER] C

The only item on-screen right now is a [Comment] code. Anything you enter before the code will appear in the "Style:On" part of the style, and anything after the code will be in the "Style:Off" half. Let's just place a margin setting in the first half of the style. Press

SHIFT-F8 L M 3/4 [ENTER] 3/4 [ENTER] F7

Notice how 5.1 automatically converts fractions to their decimal equivalents. In this case, 3/4 was converted to .75.

[RIGHT ARROW]

Move the cursor past the [Comment] code. Now it's time to add another return so that there's a blank line between the headline and the two columns. Press

[ENTER]

Now we're going to set up columns. Press

ALT-F7 C D D .3 [ENTER][ENTER] O

◆ Setting Tabs

The normal 1/2 inch tab setting is too big when using columns, so we're going to set them to a quarter of an inch. We need to set them in the closing half, because if we set them in the opening half, WordPerfect would automatically reset them to their default in the closing half, defeating the purpose. This will delete all existing tabs before setting *all* our tabs 1/4" apart.

SHIFT-F8 L T [HOME][HOME] [LEFT ARROW]

CONTROL-END 0 , 1/4 [ENTER] F7

◆ Fixing Line Height

Just one more step: set the line height (the white space between the lines of text). We need to do this or else the big "raised" cap in first line will have too much space under it. Press

L H F 14p [ENTER] F7 F7 F7 F7

We've set the line height to 14-point, then exited the style menu.

◆ Applying a style

Now that we've created the style, we're going to apply it to the file. Brace yourself, excitement like this doesn't happen every day (every other day, maybe).

To use this style, we're going to block the headline, and then apply the style. First, make sure the cursor is at the very top of the file on the "M" of Mama. Then, turn on the block by pressing

ALT-F4

Move the cursor to the "T" of "This last year." To apply the style, press

ALT-F8

Highlight TOPPER, then press

O

The headline still takes one column, but the body text is now in two columns.

◆ Creating a User-defined box

Are we having fun yet? And you were going to fritter the night away being sociable! Now you get to put in that lovely map of the world instead.

Move the cursor so that it's right after the [Style On:Topper] by pressing

[HOME] [HOME] [UP ARROW]

We're going to create a User-defined box by pressing

ALT-F9 U C

Faster than you can say the immortal Dick Shawn catchphrase, "Suck on a shoe," you've created a User-defined graphics box. We need to make it a page-type box and center it at the bottom of the page. Let's do that now, shall we? Press

T A [ENTER] V B H M C

Here's an instant memory tip: just think of "TAV BHMC." (Tav Bhamuc is one of Dickens' all-time favorite characters. You know, the travelling tea salesman in *Oliver with a Twist.* Stop that moaning now, it only took a few seconds of your time and at least *I* enjoyed it. Some jokes you do for yourself—others you should just keep to yourself.)

◆ Retrieving a graphic

Let's retrieve the graphic now. The sample graphics files which come with WordPerfect are probably in your WordPerfect directory, C:\wp51\. If you installed them someplace else, you'll need to type that path. If you can't find them anywhere, run the install program and answer Y to "Install Graphic Images."

F C:\wp51\GLOBE2-M.WPG [ENTER]

Voila! You've got a graphic. Now how about a caption? Press

C [BACKSPACE] SHIFT-F6 CONTROL-F8 A I

The world is eating us up! F7 F7

◆ Placing a horizontal line

Almost finished, cross my heart. Now we're going to place the horizontal line on the page. Press

ALT-F9 L H H C L 2.79 [ENTER] W .1 [ENTER] [ENTER]

Then put some space between the line and the headline by pressing

[ENTER][ENTER]

You should now see two returns after the [HLine] code and before the headline. If you don't, you obviously missed the boat at some point in our journey (luckily for you, this will not translate into bad karma in your next life, unless you come back as a computer).

You can't see graphic lines in normal edit mode, only in View Document. To use View Document, press

SHIFT-F7 V

The line should appear on your screen. To leave View Document, press

F7

My, this desktop publishing sure makes a person hungry. Go get some ice cream, then come back. If anyone asks what you're doing, just say "following instructions."

◆ Making a headline extra large

Back so soon? We have only one more little thing to do and we get to do it three whole times. We're going to make the headline extra large, the #1 line large.

Move the cursor to the "M" of Mama Rowby and turn block on by pressing

ALT-F4

Move the cursor to the line that says "Blue Ribbon Pies" and go to the end of the line by pressing

[DOWN ARROW] [END]

We're going to make the headline extra large, or 24-point. Press

CONTROL-F8 S E

The words may not appear any different on-screen, but they will in View Document and on paper. Now move the cursor to the "A" of "Any way you slice it." We're going to block this entire line and enlarge it. Press

ALT-F4 [END] CONTROL-F8 S L

◆ Centering a headline

If the headline isn't already centered, do that now. Go to the top of the file by pressing

[HOME] [HOME] [UP ARROW]

Turn block on

ALT-F4

Move the cursor so it covers all three lines of the headline. Tell WordPerfect to center the blocked text by pressing

SHIFT-F6 Y

◆ Creating raised caps

We're in the home stretch. We're going to make the "T" of "This" very large so that it becomes a "Raised Cap." Place the cursor on the "T" of "This last year." Block it by pressing

ALT-F4

And pat it and mark it with a "B" and put it in the oven for . . . no, no, wrong book. Cover the "T" with the block by pressing

[RIGHT ARROW]

To make the "T" into a raised cap, press

CONTROL-F8 S V

◆ View Document

Now, at last, we can take a look-see at this masterpiece with View Document. Press

SHIFT-F7 V

If you can't see the entire page, press 3; if you can see the page but can't read the text, press 1. If you're totally confused and thinking of ways to exchange this book for something else like *Larry: The Stooge in the Middle,* don't press your luck.

Take it again from the top—it has worked for other people. Who knows, it just might work for you.

◆ A little short

But before you pat yourself on the back, notice that the second column is a little too short and doesn't reach the end of the page. That looks sort of stupid and is because the graphic in the 5.1 example isn't as large as the one in the 5.0 example. Of course, we could add a few more lines of text . . .

F7

Or, we can get the exciting text to fit. The trick is to fill the space, without having it *look* like we are just filling space. A good way to do that is to increase the line height a tiny bit. Few people will even notice it, but it will make our existing text fill the page.

Because we've set the line height using a style, we can change it quickly by typing

ALT-F8 E C [HOME] [HOME] [DOWN ARROW]

SHIFT-F8 L H F 15p [ENTER] F7 F7 F7 F7

We didn't remove our old line height code, just in case we didn't like the new one. Now go back into View Document

SHIFT-F7 V

Perfecto mundo. And because we've only added 1 extra point (1/72nd of an inch) between each line, your readers won't have the faintest idea they've been had.

◆ To print

If your screen now looks something like my example, congratulate yourself. Print it, quick, before it melts. No, it won't really melt. I'm kidding. (Geez, lighten up, will you?) To leave View Document and go to the Print menu, press

F1

Make sure the printer is plugged in and connected to the computer. It's show-time, folks. Press

P

The computer will emit some hard disk noises, and then the lights on the printer should start flashing. The page should emerge victoriously from the printer in anywhere from 1 to 5 minutes, depending on the speed of your printer.

◆ Save your work

It's time to save your work. But you need to save it with a new name, otherwise you'll overwrite the plain text you'll need in the next example. To do this, press

F10

Type a new file name, anything you want. If you can't think of something, name it "SIMPLE.51" and press

[ENTER]

If WordPerfect asks you to "replace" the file, it means you've typed the name of a file that's already on your hard disk. Try a new name. I don't know about you, but I'm tired. Take the rest of the day off.

❖ *Complicated example for 5.1*

Now that you've been hooked by the first example, let's move on to the hard stuff. As usual, the first step involves retrieving a file. Remember how the *General Instructions* on page 31 told you to save the simple example text file under a different name before you started putting codes into it? This is where that file will come in handy. Start WordPerfect.

◆ Turn Reveal Codes on

To turn Reveal Codes on, press

ALT-F3

Now we're going to make sure the printer is set up correctly.

SHIFT-F7

If the printer driver with the Bitstream Dutch fonts is not selected, move the cursor to the name of the printer file you created that contains the fonts and press S.

You should now be at the Print menu, and the name of the printer you selected should be next to the words "Select Printer." You'll need to initialize the printer by pressing

1Y

◆ Retrieving a file

Now let's retrieve a text file. (Can you say "retrieve?" I knew you could.) Because we want to keep the original, unformatted text file, we're going to use a little trick which comes in handy in many different circumstances. Press

[SPACEBAR]

If you load a file into a completely blank screen, WordPerfect remembers the name of the file so that you can save back to the same file. But if you are loading a file you don't want to accidentally save back to the original name, pressing one single spacebar is enough so that WordPerfect will load the file, yet not keep the filename.

- You'll have to type some new text for this example, such as "Mama takes a big bite of the pie market" and the table at the end. When you type the table, don't try to make it look nice. Just use a single tab between each "column" of numbers, and don't worry if they don't line up on-screen just yet. Also, place *two* [TAB]s in front of the state WA.

To retrieve the text file, press

SHIFT-F10

Type the name of the file you are going to use for text. (If your text contains a table, as this one does, make sure you use tabs, and not spaces, between each column of numbers. Also, make sure you have **two** tabs before the "WA," otherwise the state names won't align with the columns of numbers when we convert it to a real 5.1 table. If you use spaces, you won't be able to automatically turn it into a table. Press

[ENTER]

This spacebar trick also comes in handy if you encounter any strange formatting problems. When you load with a space, WordPerfect is forced to completely reformat the file as it retrieves it, and this can sometimes cure unexplainable formatting weirdnesses. Now, remove that extra line by pressing

[BACKSPACE]

◆ Font default

Now you need to set the Initial Base Font for the file. This font will be used for all body text, headers, footers, and captions unless we specify otherwise. Press

SHIFT-F8 D F

Move the cursor to **BSN Dutch Roman 10 pt**. The name of the font will also indicate which symbol set it uses and whether it's portrait or landscape. If you created ASCII symbol fonts, the complete name will be **BSN Dutch Roman 10pt (ASCII) (FW,PORT)**. The (FW) stands for Fontware. I don't know what the BSN means. Select this font by pressing

[ENTER] F7

Mama Rowby's Blue Ribbon Pies

Any way you slice it, we're #1

Mama Takes a Big Bite out of the Pie Market

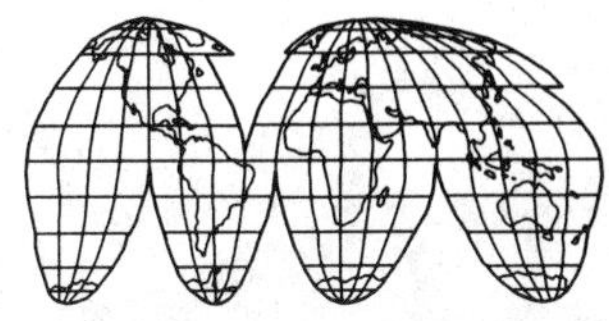

This last year has been one of great change for Mama Rowby and her family of fine foods. Corporate Raider/Pond Scum Walter Scanlan tried to wrest the company away from the family that has owned and operated it with such great care for lo these past five years, and if it hadn't been for the great spirit of loyalty among management and employees, Mama Rowby's Pies would have become just another corporate conglomerate, instead of the caring, loving, gold mine it is.

Last year pie consumption skyrocketed the world over, partly due to our massive advertising campaign, and the "Miss Cutie Pie" competition, co-hosted by Morgan Fairchilde (desperate to overcome her image as being someone who'll go to the opening of a drawer). Even more important, Mama Rowby is now making mince meat of the competition.

To keep employee morale up during the recent corporate nightmare, Mama decided to institute a "pie-a-day" plan, whereby employees could take home a pie a day. Productivity skyrocketed (as did the bathroom scales of our employees).

This coming year, Mama Rowby is introducing a blitz of new flavors coming out the wazoo. These are revolutionary flavors that will blow the lid off the pie market. Everything from the new "California Cuisine," including "Linguini and Clam Meringue," and "Cactus Ice Cream."

Another hot new line will be retailed under the Cajun Queen moniker, and will include "Blackened Red Cherry," and "Fruit-Slaw Jumbalya." The sleeper of the new trio will be "Dr. Ruth's Good Pies," packaged with illustrated instructions for unorthodox uses. These flavors will be offered in only soft and safe fruits, such as Banana and Cherry.

This fall, Mama will be starring in her own syndicated cooking show where she and her guests (Dr. Ruth is at the top of the list) will help solve world problems and promote "Peace Through Pies." The show is pre-sold in 175 of the largest markets, and will be a perfect platform for increasing customer awareness of "Pie Possibilities," as well introducing new products. Because of Reagan's FCC deregulation (first seen on Saturday morning TV), Mama will sponsor her own show--a first in the syndication market. Dr. Abiner Goren, noted pet psychologist, has said that this unity of information will help to relieve much of the stress that modern television viewers are subjected to, as well as do "Darn good business."

	WA	AK	TW	MA	NY	CA
Cherry	.50	.55	.83	1.24	1.86	2.78
Apple	.70	.77	1.16	1.73	2.60	3.90
Coconut	.30	.33	.50	.74	1.67	1.67
Pecan	1.10	1.21	1.82	2.72	4.08	6.13

◆ Open style

Now we'll create a topper style which contains important global formatting commands. (Doesn't "global" sound important?) I had wanted to create a paired style as in the first example, but WordPerfect kept giving me trouble about margins. Even though I'd set margins after the comment, it wouldn't place them in the style. Whatever the problem was, I came up with a new approach. Create two styles: one for the very top, and one containing the horizontal line, the requisite number of returns, and the column definition. Press

ALT-F8 C N Topper [ENTER] T O C

◆ Setting margins

Set the margins. We'll use a seven-tenths of an inch margin on the top and bottom, and a half-inch margin on each side. Let's first set the top and bottom margins. Press

SHIFT-F8 P M .7 [ENTER] .7 [ENTER] [ENTER]

Now we're going to set the left and right margins. Press

L M .5 [ENTER] .5 [ENTER]

◆ Setting tabs

Once again, 1/2" is too big for tabs when using columns. We'll set it to 1/4"

T [HOME] [HOME] [LEFT ARROW] CONTROL-END

0 , 1/4 [ENTER] F7 F7 F7 F7

◆ Creating a column style

Now we need to create the column style. Press

C N Columns [ENTER] T O C

The column style starts with the horizontal line, includes three returns, and has a column definition. Press

ALT-F9 L H [ENTER]

[ENTER] [ENTER] [ENTER]

We also have to set the margins yet again, because otherwise the columns will not be sized correctly.

SHIFT-F8 L M .5 [ENTER] .5 [ENTER] F7

Now we create the columns. Press

ALT-F7 C D N 3 [ENTER] D .25 [ENTER] [ENTER] O F7 F7

◆ Creating a headline style

For good measure, let's create a headline style, making the text Swiss 24-point bold, with justification set to left. Press

C N Headline [ENTER] C CONTROL-F8 F

Move the cursor to "Swiss Bold 24pt" and press

S

Now, set justification to left. It's rarely a good idea to justify headlines. Press

SHIFT-F8 L J L F7 F7 F7 F7

So much for creating styles. Now move to the very top of the file by pressing

[HOME] [HOME] [HOME] [UP-ARROW]

And turn on the Topper Style by pressing

ALT-F8

Move the cursor to "Topper" and press

O

◆ Placing a graphics box

Now let's place the first graphic, located in the upper right corner of the page. We're going to use a User-Defined box because it has no border around it. Press

ALT-F9 U C

We need to tell WordPerfect where to place this box. WordPerfect's default will put graphics along the right margin. In this case, we want them along the left margin. Press

H L

◆ Sizing a box

We will also set the size of the box. The box should only be a half-inch high. We'll set the height and WordPerfect will figure out the width when we retrieve the graphic. Press

S H .5 [ENTER]

◆ Retrieving a graphic

Now we're going to retrieve the graphic. Rather than type the name, we're going to use **F5**, the List Files key. Press

F F5 C:\wp51 [ENTER]

If you don't find any .WPG files in this directory, you may have installed them elsewhere. You can press F1 and repeat this step, replacing C:\wp51 with the directory you installed them to. Or, if you can't find them for love or money, run the install program and answer "Y" to "Install Graphic Images."

If by some stroke of luck you happen to see .WPG files, move the cursor to the file called **BALLOONS.WPG** and press

R

After the file has been loaded, you'll notice that the size is .692" wide by .5" high.

◆ Editing a graphic

WordPerfect allows you to size, stretch, compress, rotate, or invert graphics. To try it, let's go into graphic edit mode by pressing

E

The graphic should appear on-screen. If it doesn't, you may have set up WordPerfect incorrectly for the type of graphics adapter your computer has. (I know it's not correct to end a sentence with the word "has," but this is my book and I make the rules up.) Consult the "Getting Started" chapter in the WordPerfect manual or the "Setup" section in the reference manual.

◆ Rotating a graphic

Notice the number between the parentheses in the lower right corner of the screen. This should read 10%. If it doesn't, press the **INS** key until it does. As long as we're here, let's play with the graphic. If you press the **plus** key (next to the cursor or number-pad), you'll see that the graphic rotates 45 degrees (there must be a strong breeze). To keep control of the balloons before they fly away, press the **minus** key (next to the cursor or number-pad). The graphic will rotate 45 degrees in the other direction, returning it to where it was.

◆ Enlarging a graphic

Now, let's zoom in on one of the balloons. Press

[INS][INS][INS]

until the number in the lower right corner reads "25%." Now let's increase the picture by 125%. Press

[PgUp] [PgUp] [PgUp] [PgUp] [PgUp]

Now we need to move the picture down. Press

[DOWN ARROW] [DOWN ARROW] [DOWN ARROW] [DOWN ARROW]

Now we need to move the picture to the right. Press

[RIGHT ARROW] [RIGHT ARROW] [RIGHT ARROW] [RIGHT ARROW]

And finally, let's zoom in on the star. Press

[PgUp] [PgUp] [PgUp] [PgUp] [PgUp]

We've made it to the lone star state. Either that, or just a deep state of confusion. We decide that this was a mistake and want to return the picture to its original state. Press

CONTROL-[HOME]

Now the picture will return to its normal size. Enough fun and games. Press

F7 F7

A box will appear on-screen that displays the approximate dimensions of the graphic we just created.

◆ Replacing a graphic

But wait! We hold an impromptu staff meeting and decide to insert a new graphic file in this same graphics box. Sure, the balloons are cute, but maybe just a little too cute. What were we thinking? But, at least it won't be difficult to change. Press

ALT-F9 U E 1 [ENTER]

Quick, it's time to replace the current graphic with one called TROPHY.WPG. Press

F C:\WP51\TROPHY.WPG [ENTER] Y F7

Remember, if your graphics are in a different directory, type that directory name instead of C:\WP51.

◆ Enlarging a headline

Now we want to increase the size of our headline. This will be the banner/logo of our publication. Our body text is Dutch and our headlines are Swiss for contrast, but this is not a headline, it's a logo. (It's not a gang, it's a club.) We could use some fancy display or headline typeface (such as Broadway) to match our company logo. But in this case, because I can only be sure that you have either Swiss or Dutch, we'll choose from Swiss and Dutch. The logo will be Dutch.

The reason we're not using "Appearance Extra Large" to enlarge the type in this logo is that when you use a 10-point base font, Extra Large will give you a 24-point font. We want a 30-point font, so we'll have to choose it specifically. (We could go in and change the "Size Attribute Ratio" but I'll leave that type of esoteric nonsense for later in the book.) If we were using a 12-point base font, Extra Large would give us a 30-point font. Let's select a new font. Make sure the cursor is on the "M" of the first "Mama" and press

CONTROL-F8 F

Move the cursor to **Dutch Bold 30pt** (ASCII) (Port) (FW), and press

[ENTER]

When you selected this font, WordPerfect automatically adjusted the line spacing so that lines of text wouldn't print over each other. We chose a bold base font, so it will print bold even without using WordPerfect's bold feature. If we used the bold feature, the bold font would print in an even darker shade.

But because of this font change, WordPerfect is now formatting the rest of the file for this large font. We need to change the font. Put the cursor on the "s" of "Pies," then press

[RIGHT ARROW] CONTROL-F8 F

Move the cursor to **Dutch Roman 10pt** and press

[ENTER]

◆ Aligning text

Make sure that Reveal Codes is still on. (Some people turn it off so they can see more of their page. They think I won't notice.) Move the cursor so that it is on the "A" of "Any way you slice it." We're going to make this flush right, so press

ALT-F6

The text jumps to the right margin.

◆ Applying italics

Let's use italics on that "Any way you slice it" line. Turn block on by pressing

ALT-F4

Move the cursor to the end of the line by pressing

[END]

To turn on italics for the block, press

CONTROL-F8 A I

The line is now in italics. Let's re-block it and increase it to Large (or 12-point). Press

ALT-F4 CONTROL-[HOME] CONTROL-[HOME] CONTROL-F8 S L

◆ View Document

Getting curious? Let's use View Document to see how it looks. Press

SHIFT-F7 V

If you've followed instructions carefully, the *headline area* should be *similar to* (but not exactly like—just yet) the printed example in the book.

◆ Enlarging view

You probably can't read any of the type on this full page on-screen view. For a closer look, press

1

You're now seeing the page in 100% view. For a still closer look, press

2

You're now seeing the page in 200% view. This is as close as you can get without getting the pie in your face. Let's return to full page view. Press

3

We still haven't finished this puppy. Let's go back to work. Press

F7

◆ Save before it's too late

It's a good idea to save your file before printing. That's because I've found print time (including View Document) to be kind of like the Bermuda Triangle of word processing: it's the time when the most data-losing accidents occur. In fact, while I was writing this chapter I went to View Document, and poof, the screen went blank and I couldn't do anything. Luckily, my timed backup is set to every 5 minutes (as yours should be if you followed the directions in Chapter 1), but it's still no fun to try to remember what you did even five minutes ago.

The moral of this story is *save often and repeatedly.* Let's save the file now. Press

F10 {type a new filename here} [ENTER]

◆ Resizing the graphic

It's a good idea to use View Document every now and then because it helps you to spot errors before you get so far along in the formatting that it becomes a pain in the derriere to fix it.

What you *should* have noticed is that the graphic is too small. It should be about the same height as the headline, and it isn't. I know, I know, this is getting tedious, but imagine the pride you'll feel when you're finished. You can frame this page and take it home to your mother (or significant other) and show them what you did all by your little self. Of course, they will probably be completely unimpressed, but this will only prove, once and for all, how little they actually know.

Let's size it again.

ALT-F9 U E 1 [ENTER]

We'll instruct WordPerfect to make the new graphic .75" high and .75" wide. Press

S B .75 [ENTER] .75 [ENTER] F7

Let's check it in View Document again.

SHIFT-F7 V

Hmmm. Still too small. We don't want to make the graphic box any bigger, so we'll need to edit the graphic itself and make it larger. Leave View Document with

F7

Take a deep breath and press

ALT-F9 U E 1 [ENTER]

E [PG UP] [PG UP] [PG UP] [PG UP]

The graphic now fills the box. Leave graphic edit by pressing

F7 F7

◆ If at first you don't succeed

View, View again. Let's use View Document again to see how it looks:

SHIFT-F7 V

The trophy should now be almost exactly the same height as the headline. Good. Let's continue before our eyes glaze over and we go into some type of trance, staring frozen at the screen like a deer in a car's headlights.

F7

◆ Applying a column style

Now it's time to place three columns in the body text. Move the cursor to the "B" of "Blue Ribbon" and press

[DOWN ARROW]

Turn on the column style by pressing

ALT-F8

Move the cursor to "Columns" and press

O

Extra space will appear under the headline, and the text will be set in three columns.

◆ Applying a headline style

We need to use that headline style on the headline. Block the entire headline ("Mama takes a big bite out of the pie market") by moving the cursor to the "M" and then pressing

ALT-F4

Move the cursor to the space after "Market." To apply the headline style, press

ALT-F8

Move the cursor to "Headline," and press

O

We want the rest of this column to be blank, so place the cursor on the "T" of "This Last Year" and press

CONTROL-[ENTER]

The remaining text will jump to the second column, leaving the rest of the first column blank. Ahh, white space.

◆ Hand justification

In this age of computers we sometimes think that machines can do everything. Well, not *just* yet. One important item they can't handle is deciding where to break headlines. Yes, of course, they can figure out how much *can* fit on a line, but they can't yet figure out what *should* be on each line.

Headlines are read very quickly by readers, so it's important to break them in a way that makes sense. The computer wants to break this headline:

Mama Takes a
Big Bite out of
the Pie Market

That's OK, but a really fast reader would see "Mama" and "a," "Big," and "of" and "The" and "Market. "Mama a Big of The Market." This could, and should be better. Better is

Mama Takes
a Big Bite
out of the
Pie Market

This way it instantly makes more sense to the reader. Each line can stand on its own.

Notice that we didn't break the first two lines at

"Mama Rowby's Blue

Ribbon Pies"

If we did, people would be asking us what "Ribbon Pies" were. Think about it.

Since the computer doesn't have enough sense to break this logically, we will. To do it, simply press an **[ENTER]** at the end of each "logical" line. Be careful not to leave a blank space at the start of a line.

◆ Turning hyphenation on

Anytime you justify text you need to hyphenate it as well. 5.1's default for hyphenation is "off," so we'll need to turn it on. Justification without hyphenation can result in extremely unattractive type, and you wouldn't want that, would you? I didn't think so. Position the cursor on the "T" of "This" and press

SHIFT-F8 L Y Y F7

◆ Hyphenation

If WordPerfect asks you to hyphenate, press **ESC** if you want it to place the hyphen where it recommends, or move the cursor to where you'd like the hyphen and then press **ESC**. WordPerfect sets a hyphenation range, so you may not be able to move the cursor to the precise location you desire. If you don't want the word hyphenated, or can't move the cursor to wherever you want it, press **F1** to tell WordPerfect not to hyphenate that word.

If you get really sick and tired of having WordPerfect pester you about so many words, press **F7** to temporarily turn hyphenation off. Hyphenation will remain off only through the next cursor move or command, and then will turn itself back on.

If you never want WordPerfect to ask you about hyphenation again, ever, press SHIFT-F1 E P N F7.

◆ Viewing again

Let's go back into View Document to see how the page is progressing. Press

SHIFT-F7 V

It's getting there, isn't it? If we didn't have the table at the bottom of the page, we could stop right now. But you paid good money for this book and I'm here to see that you get your money's worth. By the end of this example (and certainly by the end of the book), you'll know more about desktop publishing with WordPerfect than you ever dreamed of (even in your worst nightmare). Leave View Document with

F7

◆ Creating a table

Before we proceed any further, let's take care of that table at the bottom. We've already placed a graphic in a graphics box, but now we're going to put a table in a table box, even though it's not really a table just yet. First things first. Get it out of the normal body text and off by itself where we can be alone together.

Since we want this "graphic" table to span several columns, we're going to create it as a page-type graphic. To ensure that it prints on this page and not the next, we'll place this code at the top of the page, right after the margins.

First we're going to block our table and copy it, then create a table box, and then paste the table into the box.

Move the cursor to the beginning of the table. To turn the block on, press

ALT-F4

Move the cursor so that it covers the entire table, and then press

CONTROL-F4 B M

The table will disappear, but it isn't gone forever. WordPerfect has put it in a special magic place and will drop it back onto the page as soon as you press return. As a convenient reminder, WordPerfect says, "Move cursor, press **Enter** to retrieve."

Now that the table is safely tucked away, let's hope that it said its prayers and create that table box.

◆ Creating a page-type graphic box

Go to the top of the file by pressing

[HOME] [HOME] [HOME] [UP ARROW]

To ensure that the table box is the correct size, we have to check that the cursor is after the topper style and its two margin codes, so press

[RIGHT ARROW]

Before we create the table, we're going to set the options. We'll have a single line above and a thick line below. The table will contain a 10% gray background. Press

ALT-F9 T O B N N S T G 10 [ENTER] [ENTER]

Now we're ready to create the table of "States." Press

ALT-F9 T C

We need to tell WordPerfect what type of box this is, where it will be on the page, and how large it will be. Let's start with the type of box. This is a page-type box, so it can span the two columns of text. Press

T A [ENTER]

WordPerfect automatically places this box on the top of the page, flush with the right margin, and makes it 3.25" square. Let's move it to the bottom of the page by pressing

V B

◆ Placing the graphics

Next, let's tell WordPerfect how wide this box is. This box will stretch all the way across the page, from the left margin to the right margin. When you create a page-type box, you can place it on the page based on margins, columns, or exact numerical measurements. We're going to make it flush with both the left and right margins by pressing

H M F

Notice that the size of the graphic has changed. It may look like it's too big, but when you put the table in it will be the right size. Now, we can finally edit the contents of the box itself. Press

E

Don't worry, our text is still there. The [ENTER] that we pressed when creating the table options didn't count. Now we're going to press

[ENTER]

Zippity do dah, here's our table. (Zippity do dah is probably a registered trademark of the Walt Disney Company.)

◆ Changing fonts

Let's make the entire table Swiss 12-point bold. Press

CONTROL-F8 F

Move the cursor to "Swiss 12pt Bold" and press

S

◆ Transmogrifying tabbed text to tables

Make sure there are no extra returns at the top of the table. If there are, your table will be larger than the one in the example. Also make sure that there are TWO tabs before "WA," otherwise the names of the states will not align correctly with the columns of numbers. Do not have a return at the end of the table. When you're ready, press

ALT-F4 [HOME] [HOME] [DOWN ARROW]

You've now blocked the text, and we're going to turn it into a table. Press

ALT-F7 T C T

The table will appear on-screen, but it will probably be formatted all wrong and look terrible. Your data may even seem to have disappeared. Don't worry. Be happy. Everything will work out fine if you can just stand to continue following this example.

◆ Take a break

I know this isn't easy, but then few good things in life are easy. Once you master this you will be the envy of your family and friends, the life of the party, and the world will be your oyster, or, if you're not into seafood, your Rolex Oyster watch, or, if you're not into big, pretentious, expensive watches, your bowl of cherries.

This is a good time to take a short break. First, get out a copy of any Calvin & Hobbes book by Bill Watterson and laugh your head off.

OK, play time's over. Hi-ho, hi-ho, it's off to work we go (another Disney trademark).

◆ Setting the table

The first thing we have to do is make the table full width. To do this, press

O P F [ENTER]

Now we want to block the entire table and set the column widths to 1" (This step is in memory of Frank Lloyd Wright).

ALT-F4 [HOME] [HOME] [DOWN ARROW] F L W .75 [ENTER]

This may have corrected some of the problems with the way the table looks on-screen, then again, it may not. Don't worry, though, your data is still there.

Now let's go back to the top of the table. We'll use the GOTO feature to jump to cell A1

CONTROL-[HOME] A1 [ENTER]

Your table will probably have an extra column in it before the WA column. If it does, you'll need to remove it. To delete the column, put the cursor on it and press

[DEL] C [ENTER]

If you blatantly disregarded my warning to make sure there were no returns at the end of the table, you will find yourself staring at a one or more blank rows at the end of the table. If this happens, move the cursor to the blank row and press **[DEL] R [ENTER]**

◆ Changing the ruling lines

We don't need the ruling lines on the outside of the table, so let's get rid of them. Press

[HOME] [HOME] [UP ARROW]

ALT-F4 [HOME] [HOME] [DOWN ARROW]

L O N

◆ Decimal alignment

The only step left for the table is to give the columns with numbers decimal alignment. Move the cursor to the cell which contains ".50" (Cherry, WA, or cell B2). We'll block all columns but A by pressing

ALT-F4 [HOME] [HOME] [RIGHT ARROW]

Now we'll set the column justification for these blocked columns to decimal by pressing

F L J D

The numbers in the columns should align themselves neatly. If they do, and all the rows are the same height, move on. If the rows aren't the same height, read the next paragraph.

➻ Sore spot

Check your table. *If* one of the rows is taller than the rest, you'll need look for the cell that has a [SRt] code after the numbers and press [DEL]. This sometimes happens when changing decimal alignment.

Say "Adios" to the table by pressing

F7 F7 F7

◆ Moving around in View Document

Golly gee willikers, this page looks mighty unique to me. But then, I'm near-sighted. Let's sneak another peek through the magic mirror of View Document by pressing

SHIFT-F7 V

Go into 100% mode by pressing

1

Did you know that you can move around the View Document screen with any cursor movement keys (including gray [+] or gray [-], the "Screen Down" and "Screen Up" keys)? You can also jump to any page by pressing **CONTROL-HOME**, and then typing in a page number. Will wonders never cease? (Yes, they will, probably around 5 p.m.)

You're spending altogether too much time looking at View Document (stop it or you'll go blind). Press

F7

◆ Measuring a table

Three more steps and we'll call it a day, a week, or a marsupial—whichever you prefer. First, let's put a vertical rule between the headline column and the body text.

Move the cursor to the "M" in "Mama takes . . ." We're going to create a vertical line running from this line down to the table. WordPerfect will automatically start the vertical rule at the current line, but unless we intervene, it will print the line to the bottom of the page, right through the table.

Now we're going to have to do some math. Not anything fancy. Not *new* math, just plain *old* math. Don't let it scare you; if *I* can do it, *you* can do it.

First, let's look at the "States" table to see how tall it is. Press

ALT-F9 T E 1 [ENTER]

We can see that it's 2.13" high. That's all we needed to know. Press

F7

Next, return to the "M" of "Mama takes" by pressing

[DOWN ARROW] [DOWN ARROW] [DOWN ARROW]

◆ Creating a vertical rule

Now we're going to create that vertical rule. Press

ALT-F9 L V

We need to tell WordPerfect where to place the rule on the page. We're going to select Between Columns, and then tell WordPerfect to place it to the right of column 1. Press

H B 1 [ENTER]

Now we're going to set where the line begins vertically. When we choose Vertical Set, WordPerfect will insert our current location on the page (which should be 1.94"). Press

V S [ENTER]

Next, let's tell WordPerfect how long to make the line. WordPerfect has automatically calculated 8.37" as the distance to the bottom of the page. We don't want to print over the table, and so we're going to subtract 2.13" (the height of the table), and end up with 6.24". Press

L 6.24 [ENTER] [ENTER]

Voila! The vertical rule is in place. (It won't show on-screen, but it will appear in View Document and when you print.)

You can see the light at the end of the tunnel, the wind's at your back, and the only obstacle between you and immortality is death. You look Death in the face and say, "The word 'scared' isn't in my vocabulary." Death responds with a snappy "What about the word 'stupid?' " Death has very bad breath, and what's worse, you (and I) cannot keep up this level of witty repartee much longer.

You snap back to reality and experience something akin to psychic whiplash. You ponder the inevitable existential questions, then decide to just finish the example and drown reality in Heavy Belgian Chocolate ice cream (Steve's, of course).

◆ View, View, again

Let's take another look

SHIFT-F7 V

Hmm. Not bad.

F7

but it could use something. Let's put that map of the world in. The only appropriate place would be in the first column. Let's put it near the bottom.

◆ Creating a User-defined box

Move the cursor to the space after the last "t" in "Mama Takes a Big Bite out of the Pie Market." Make sure that you are to the right of the [Style Off: Headline] code. Put a blank line after the text. Press

[ENTER]

Now we're going to create another User-defined box with its horizontal position both left and right, so it fills the column by pressing

ALT-F9 U C H F

◆ Loading a graphic

It's that time again. Time to load a graphic file. We know the name, so we won't bother using List Files this time. Press

F C:\WP51\GLOBE2-M.WPG [ENTER] F7

We've already had more than our share of fun playing with graphics, and besides, if you mirror the map of the world, we might be branded as pinko troublemakers. What we *do* have to do, however, is move it near the bottom of the column. Let's make it start on about the same line as "To keep employee morale up." To do that, press

[LEFT ARROW]

to put the cursor on the graphic box code, and then press

[ENTER]

18 times.

There. The page is finished at last. Well, a drop cap wouldn't hurt. Then people will be sure you've produced the page with Ventura Publisher. They'll think you must be pretty well-off to be able to afford Ventura and, boy, you sure know how to use it. Little will they suspect that you've been using your trusty word processing program all along.

Ah, what the hay—if you're game, I'm game. Drop caps can be tricky, but they look fab (some even say rad, or cooler yet, bitchen).

◆ Creating a drop cap

We're going to create this with a style (and with style). First, create a style by pressing

ALT-F8 C N Drop Cap [ENTER] C

We must use the "advance down" feature to move the drop cap down one line. Press

SHIFT-F8 O A D 12P [ENTER] F7

Now we select Dutch (Times Roman) 24-point Bold

CONTROL-F8 F

Move the cursor to **BSN Dutch Bold 24 Pt** and press

[ENTER]

(Scaleable Font Printer users, move the cursor to Dutch or Times Roman, press [ENTER] 24 [ENTER])

Now we move to the closing half of the style by pressing

[RIGHT ARROW]

Set line height to fixed, otherwise there will be extra space under the first line of the paragraph and it will look tacky.

SHIFT-F8 L H F 12p [ENTER] F7

Remember how we advanced down in the opening half of the style? We now have to advance back up. Remember: Get down. Get funky. Get back up again. So we'll advance up:

SHIFT-F8 O A U 12P [ENTER] F7

Almost done, I promise. Remember, the bell does not excuse you, I do, so stay seated even if the bell rings. And please keep your hands and arms inside the car at all times until we come to a complete stop.

We need to use the margin release to take us backwards one tab stop, and then we tab in. We have to do this because we are actually on top of the tab stop now, and just pressing tab would cause WordPerfect to skip to the next tab. To release the margin to the previous tab stop, press

SHIFT-[TAB]

and then tab in with

[TAB]

And finally, let's save this style with

F7 F7 F7

To apply this style, move the cursor to the first "T" of "This last year" and press

ALT-F4 [RIGHT ARROW] ALT-F8

Move the cursor to "Drop Cap" and press

[ENTER]

Last, and very probably least, place the cursor on the first letter of the first word of the second line. *What?* Put the cursor on the "c" of "change for Mama Rowby." Then press

[TAB]

We have to do this because otherwise the big "T" would run into the second line of text. Now let's squeeze some juice from the fruits of our labor. Press

SHIFT-F7 V

When you're done gawking, press

F7

➻ The best you can possibly be

OK. You're done. Gee, sort of anti-climactic, ain't it? Over so soon. And for the short time we were working on it, it gave us such a sense of purpose in our lives, too.

OK, if we try hard enough we can find something else to complain about. How about that hyphenation! That's not bad. But all you have to do to hyphenate words WordPerfect misses is press **CONTROL–** (that's Control-hyphen). No, there's something bigger, more obvious . . . But what?

Can you imagine what type of world we would live in if everyone would ask that about what they did? If, when people thought they were finished with whatever it was they were doing, they stepped back and asked, *could it be better?* And, if the answer was *Yes,* think of a way to improve it, and then actually *do* it? Of course, everything would take longer to get done, but it would be done right the first time, which, in the end, would save zillions of hours in trying to fix shoddy workmanship after the fact. Let's be the first to refuse to settle for *good enough.* Let's find fault and fix it.

I see it now. It's too short. That seems to be a common problem around here. OK, let's increase the leading again. But can you remember where we set the line height to fixed?

That's right, it's in the drop cap style. Let's go make it 13-point.

ALT-F8

Move the cursor to "Drop Cap" and press

E C

Place the cursor *on* the **[AdvUp:0.167"]** code and press

SHIFT-F8 L H F 13p [ENTER] F7 F7 F7 F7

Now move to the end of the file

[HOME] [HOME] [DOWN ARROW]

Uh-oh. It's too long. Let's change that leading again and make it 12.75 point. It's amazing how much difference in the length of text just a quarter point of leading can make. Press

ALT-F8

Move the cursor to "Drop Cap" and press

E C

Place the cursor *on* the [AdvUp:0.167"] code and press

SHIFT-F8 L H F 12.75p [ENTER] F7 F7 F7 F7

Now we're just one line short. That's perfect, because it gives us room to add an "end piece" to the article. You may have noticed that many magazines place a small graphic at the end of a story, so you know it's really where the piece ends. In this case, let's use the trophy again as if it were a symbol of the *Blue Ribbon Pies.* We'll create a tiny, character-type graphic. Position the cursor following the closing quote on the last line, then press

ALT-F9 U C

We'll select "character" and place it on the "baseline" of the text

T C V A

We'll size it so that it's 12 points high and 12 points wide. That's only a little bit bigger than our text.

S B 12p [ENTER] 12p [ENTER]

And then we'll load the graphic

F C:\WP51\TROPHY.WPG

(Remember, if your graphics are in another directory, use that directory instead of C:\wp51.)

And finally, we'll make the loving-cup a little bigger inside its graphic box.

E [PG UP] [PG UP] [PG UP] F7 F7

Let's take one last look

SHIFT-F7 V

Perfection. At last. At long last. (You may think it took you a long time to complete this example, but try to imagine how long it took me to *write* it...)

◆ Printing

A page like this may take some time to display on-screen. On my Zeos 386 AT, it takes about 15 seconds. There it is, it looks terrific, and now it's time to print. To leave View Document and go to the Print menu, press

F1

Make sure the printer is plugged in and connected to the computer. It's show-time. Press

P

The page should pop out of the printer in anywhere from 1 to 5 minutes, depending on the speed of the computer and printer.

◆ Save the whales

You've done a lot of work, so save your file. Press

F10 {type a filename here} [ENTER]

I don't know about you, but it's times like this when I'm proud to be an American: happy to be alive, overjoyed that someone had the sense to invent computers, and, most of all, delirious that I've finished another chapter.

4

Show & Tell

Examples of applications

This chapter shows you the types of applications you can realistically expect to create using WordPerfect. Each example is accompanied by a brief summary of the specific fonts, software, and hardware used to produce the example, as well as the WordPerfect codes used for that example.

The examples range from the first page of a newsletter to three pages of an annual report. Don't try to make a brunch reservation at *My Old Dutch Pancake House,* or list your house with *HomeFinders*—they are figments of my imagination. The material in these examples is intended primarily for your enjoyment, but it's possible to pick up some useful information along the way, too. Also take a look at Chapter 10, *Table Manners,* for a step-by-step calendar example, and Chapter 18, *1-2-3 Publishing,* for an example (with codes) of a financial report.

❖ *Style sheets on disk*

For novice desktop publishers, predesigned style sheets can be a big help. I have assembled the WordPerfect style files I used to produce the examples in this chapter and they are available on a disk. My *Designer Disk 5* contains many practical tips about the basics of graphic design and shows how to quickly modify a style sheet. Users can load in their own text and graphic files, and instantly tailor any element of the page layout to fit their individual document. These style files work for either WordPerfect 5.0 or 5.1 and include original graphic files (see *Designer Disk* ordering details in the Appendix).

◆ Ready or not

If you do your homework in the graphic design chapter, you'll be ready to play. I say play, not because you're necessarily going to have loads of fun, but because you're going to experiment, and experimentation is the basis of play. (Repeat that line at parties, it never fails.) In the previous chapter we took one page and prepared it a couple of different ways, demonstrating how WordPerfect allows you to be both flexible and consistent. In this chapter, we tackle a slew of examples. Ready or not, here we go.

❖ *Codes dissected*

Don't be intimidated by what looks like a ton-o-codes. When you look the codes for each example, it may seem like there are millions of them and they seem impossible to decipher.

But if you take them code by code, you can put these pages together in less time than you think. And remember, once you've created these pages you can use the design (and all those WordPerfect codes) over and over again with new text and graphics.

I'll admit deciphering this stuff is not unlike reading the Rosetta Stone, but I include a Rosetta Stone/WordPerfect translation chart on the inside back cover of this book that shows each code, what it does, and what keys you have to punch to get it. Refer to this if you want to recreate any of the examples, and it will give you the exact keystrokes you need.

❖ *Flavor of the month*

WordPerfect codes come in two flavors; the first (I'll call chocolate) displays all the information you need to know about them, and the second flavor (vanilla) is cryptic: it shows you the code, but not the variables inside.

- Here's an example of a chocolate code:

[Col Del:3,1",3",3.25",5.25",5.5",7.5"]. This is a column definition code. The first number tells you how many columns, the next numbers tell you the margins of the columns. In this case, the margins of column one are 1" on the left and 3" on the right. Column two's margins are 3.25 on the left and 5.25 on the right. Column three's margins are 5.5" on the left, and 7.5" on the right. Got it?

Remember, most codes display their information in the same order as you've entered it on-screen. Here's an example: [VLine:1.25",2.19",7.81",0.01",100%] This is a vertical line, and the first number if the first menu choice on the screen, Horizontal Position. The second number is the second menu item, Vertical Position. The third number is the third menu item, Length of Line. The fourth is, not surprisingly, the fourth menu item, Width of Line. And last (and who knows, maybe least) is the fifth number and its matching menu item, Gray Shading.

From this one code we can tell that the Horizontal Position is 1.25", the vertical position is 2.19" from the top of the page, the line is 7.81" inches long, .01" inches wide, and is 100% solid black.

- When point sizes are listed in fonts, it means that this specific font was the default font for that file.

◆ A double dip of vanilla, please

- Here's an example of a vanilla code: [Fig Opt]. This code can contain up to 18 different variables, and so the code doesn't show them all. If you want to see what the settings are, you have to put your cursor below the code, and go into the menu where the code was created, in this case, **ALT-F9**.

If you want to recreate these examples, please make sure that your Initial codes (**SHIFT-F1 I I**) in the setup menu don't include any Figure, Table, Text, or User Box options, as this will change your results. I've based the examples in this book on the standard WordPerfect defaults and only mention those variables that I've changed from the default.

Because of the sheer number of variables, it would take a book the size of the *Encyclopedia Britannica* to include them all. When there are vanilla codes, I've included the keystrokes necessary for any important variables in brackets like this <>, and any special explanations in brackets like this {}. If you see anything between in <> brackets, remember that these don't appear on-screen; they aren't the keystrokes to access the command, they are keystrokes you type from within the menu to select the correct variables. If you see anything between {} brackets, please don't type it, just use it as reference to explain what the codes are doing.

I use figures whenever possible because then it's easy for me to search for them. I only use more than one type of box when I need one to have certain attributes, such as lines around or an outside margin and others to have different attributes.

This sounds much more complicated that it really is, but I've tried to make the instructions as clear as possible.

- You'll see a lot of "Advance" codes, often set to .1". I use these to make small adjustments in line height that make a big visual difference. Pressing the return key to add extra white space between a headline and text for instance, usually adds more space than you really wanted. Using the advance code is the best way to make elements fit precisely. It's so good, I've put it in my soft keyboard so that I can press just one key to advance up or down in .1" increments.

And remember, don't press return unless there is a [Hrt] code.

- Here's an example for a mysterious code:

[Fig Opt]<BAAAA> This made sure that the borders around a figure were dashed lines. All the other defaults remain the same. (Please, whatever you do, don't see this code and think you're supposed to make a noise like a sheep.)

Even if you don't want to follow these babies code for code (and I don't blame you a bit if you don't), you can still use them as design examples, and get a good idea of what WordPerfect is capable of when you put your mind and fingers to it.

- **LaserJet examples**

  - All opening and closing quotes are made with double accent marks such as ' and '. Dashes use **ALT-196.**

- **Scaleable font examples**

  - opening quotes use **CONTROL-V 4,32**, closing quotes are **CONTROL-V 4,31**, and dashes are **CONTROL-V 4,34**.

If an example is shown for a scaleable font printer, such as PostScript, it doesn't mean you can't reproduce it on a LaserJet II. The only exception to this involves the LaserJet II's inability to rotate type, thereby prohibiting the printing of portrait and landscape fonts on the same page. Rotated type, outlines, shadows, and gray type are all available on the LaserJet III. All other effects, including outlines, shadows, and gray type could be produced on a LaserJet, using Font Effects from SoftCraft. The scaleable font printer examples will be first.

All of these examples can be created using either 5.0 or 5.1. Any of the examples which rely on tables can also be constructed using parallel columns. While 5.1 can use all of 5.0's codes, it doesn't work the other way around. Unless tables are involved, the codes shown are for 5.0 because they will also work for 5.1.

❖ *Newsletter — Astral Travel*

Experience Level: Advanced

- **Fonts** Bitstream Bodoni 14pt, for PostScript
- **Graphics** MGI Publisher's PicturePak-CGM, Sales/Marketing
- **Printer** QMS-PS 810

Notes: When using a PostScript printer, graphics are opaque. WordPerfect prints in the order they are placed on the page. So in this case, the gray type was on the page after the passport graphic, and so it printed over the graphic. If I had placed gray type after the "TRAVEL" headline, it would have printed gray over the black type.

```
[VLine:1.1“,Full Page,9",1w",100%][VLine:Right Margin,Full Page,9",1w,100%][L/R
Mar:1.25",1“][T/B Mar:1",0.75"]
[Fig Opt]<BNNNN>
[Figure:1;SA0209.CGM;]<TA V2 HMC S .75 E 3 10>
[Txt Opt]<BNNOO I 0 0.05 0>
[Text Box:1;;]<TA VT HMC SW 1.75>[HRt]
[HRt]  {Press [HRt} 8 more times}
[AdvToLn:3.86"][Cntr][Ln Height:0.23"]
[Font:Bodoni Book (WP PostScript) (FW) 125 pt]
 [Color:90%,90%,90%]ASTRAL[Color:Black][C/A/Flrt][HRt]
[Cntr][C/A/Flrt][Cntr][Ln Height:Auto][AdvToLn:3.62"]
[Font:Bodoni Book (WP PostScript) (FW) 125 pt]TRAVEL
[Font:Bodoni Book (WP PostScript) (FW) 14 pt]
[AdvUp:0.5"][C/A/Flrt][HRt]
[Col Def:3,1.25",3.79",3.99",4.79",4.99",7.5"][Col On]
[Tab Set:0",0.5",1“,1.5",5.24"]
[Figure:2;;]<TA V5.21 HC2B SH 4>
[Figure:3;SA0195.CGM;]<TA V5.21 HC2C SW.4>
[Figure:4;SA0194.CGM;]<TA V7.78 HC2C SW.6>
[VLine:Column 1,5.21“,5.04",1w,100%]
[VLine:Column 2,5.21“,5.04",1w,100%]
```

by Swami Macdonaldo

ASTRAL TRAVEL

Love to travel but hate to leave home? That's where **Astral** Travel comes in: to give you the vacation of your dreams (or perhaps literally, in your dreams). Unlock your imagination with the exclusive **Time**Travel network—even the past and future are within your reach.

Let Mark Twain take you steamboating on the Mississippi. Thrill to the Bermuda Triangle at midnight. Help Cleopatra invent the practical joke, and play it on Marc Anthony. Ride a dolphin to Atlantis, a Blue whale to the coast of Mexico, or just take Shamu for a ride around the tank. See the Leaning Tower of Pisa before it leaned. Watch the Divine Sara perform. See how your grandchildren will turn out. Anything's possible!

London
City of Dreams

Paris
City of Light

Ain't no mountain high enough, ain't no valley low enough, nothing is ever out of the question, nothing is ever out of your reach. The only limit is your own imagination. Ask Shirley McClaine, she'll tell you: there's nothing like it. **Astral**Travel operates 24 hours a day, for everything from a daydream to a full night's dream. But rest assured, you'll never have a nightmare.

AstralTravel will make sure you'll see the world like you've never seen it before.

They're out-of-this world!

❖ *Invitation — Sleepwalker's Ball*

Experience Level: ***Intermediate***

- **Fonts:** Palatino, Adobe, 14 pt
- **Printer:** QMS-PS 810

Notes: Most invitations are not a full page like this, so you might want to have the printer reduce the page. Reducing the page by 50% will increase the resolution to 600 dpi, the resolution of some commercial typesetting machines. This invitation is designed to be folded in half right above the line "DayDreamer Alliance." If you have enough money in your budget, you could print the "Z's" and the large "T" in a second color. You might also consider using Galliard Italic, an excellent choice for formal invitations. The gray "ZZZZZ's" at top of page are inside the first figure box, which also provides the double line around the page.

```
[Just On][Comment][Hyph On][L/R Mar:1",1"]
[Fig Opt]<BDDDD>[Figure:1;;]<TA VF WN>
[L/R Mar:1.5",1.5"][Font:Palatino Italic 14 pt]
[AdvToLn:5.5"][Cntr]The DayDreamers Alliance[C/A/Flrt][HRt]
[Cntr]Presents[C/A/Flrt][HRt]
[HRt]
[Font:Palatino Italic 30 pt][BOLD][Cntr]A Sleepwalking Ball[C/A/Flrt][bold][HRt]
[Font:Palatino Italic 14.4 pt][AdvDn:0.1"][Cntr]February 30, 1989,
8 p.m.[C/A/Flrt][HRt]
[HRt]
[Font:Palatino Italic 30 pt][BOLD][Cntr]A Sleepwalking Ball[C/A/Flrt][bold][HRt]
[Font:Palatino Italic 14 pt][AdvDn:0.1"]
[Cntr]February 30, 1989, 8 p.m.[C/A/Flrt][HRt]
[HRt]
[HRt]
[Ln Height:0.25"][Usr Opt]<O 0000 I 0000 G0>
[Usr Box:2;;]<TP HL SB 1.3 2 E [Flsh Rt]
[Font:Palatino 157 pt]T[C/A/Flrt]>o sleep, perchance to dream...
{Here are the codes for the gray Z's:}
[L/R Mar:1",1"][Ln Height:1"][AdvDn:0.7"][HRt]
[Color:99%,99%,99%][Font:Palatino Bold Italic 300 pt]z[AdvDn:0.4"][Color:98%,98%,98%]
[Font:Palatino Bold Italic 200 pt]z[AdvDn:0.4"]
[Font:Palatino Bold Italic 150 pt]z[AdvDn:0.4"]
[Font:Palatino Bold Italic 100 pt][Color:96%,96%,96%]z
[AdvDn:0.4"][Font:Palatino Bold Italic 80 pt]
[Color:94%,94%,94%][AdvDn:0.2"]z[AdvDn:0.4"]
[Font:Palatino Bold Italic 60 pt]
[Color:90%,90%,90%][AdvDn:0.2"]z[Color:Black]
```

Z Z Z Z Z Z

The DayDreamers Alliance
Presents

A Sleepwalking Ball

February 30, 1989, 8 p.m.

To sleep, perchance to dream... a somnambulist's heaven. Come wearing your favorite bedtime ensemble and be lulled by the sounds of Sam and his All-girl Sandman Band. Enjoy a buffet, scientifically formulated to provide sweet dreams. See you there—and don't let the bed bugs bite!

R.S.V.P Essential
Produced by REM Associates

Contact: Rip
212-555-2121

❖ *Book — Babies in Space*

Experience Level: ***Easier than it looks.***

- **Fonts:** ITC Avant Garde, Adobe, 9 pt
- **Graphics:** Baby, Dynamic Graphics, Four Seasons, edited with PC Paintbrush Plus; Astronaut, Publisher's PicturePak-CGM, Sales/Marketing
- **Printer:** QMS-PS 810

Notes: Once again, here's a page that looks hard, but isn't. It's all done with parallel columns. Type a sidehead, press CONTROL-ENTER, then type your text. When you want another sidehead, press CONTROL-ENTER, and repeat the process until you get good and tired of it. The graphic figure box is in the narrow left column, and the CONTROL-ENTER is directly after it. If you want to use Fontware ITC Avant Garde from Bitstream, remember, while the package includes four weights, it lacks an italic (or in this case, Oblique. Don't ask me, I just write about it.) If you wanted italics, you'd have to use a program like SoftCraft's Fontware Installation program to "oblique" the characters.

```
[W/O Off][HZone:10%,10%][Hyph On][T/B Mar:0.75",1"]
[L/R Mar:0.75",0.75"][Fig Opt]<BNNNN>
[Figure:1;BABY.PCC;]<TA V .8 HMR SH 1.5>
[T/B Mar:1.75",0.75"][HRt]
[Font:ITC Avant Garde Gothic Demi 30 pt][Color:80%,80%,80%]
Chapter 1[Color:Black][HRt]Babies In Space
[Font:ITC Avant Garde Gothic Book 14 pt]
[Flsh Rt]NASA's Toddlers[C/A/Flrt][HRt]
[HRt]
[Tab Set:0", every 0.5"][Ln Height:0.18"]
[Font:ITC Avant Garde Gothic Book 9 pt]
[Col Def:2,0.75",2.75",3.25",7.75"]<TP>[Col On]
[Style On:sidehead]A chilling tale of[SRt]
infants out of[HRt]
control: dirty[SRt]
diapers and[SRt]
weightlessness.[HRt]
Ick, Pooey.[HRt]
[Style Off:sidehead][HRt]
[HRt]
[Figure:2;SA0235.CGM;]<TP HB>[HPg]
Dirty Work. That's what NASA called their five year project...
```

Paired Style for Sidehead

```
[Ln Height:0. 22"][Font:ITC Avant Garde Gothic Book 14 pt] [Comment]
```

Chapter 1
Babies In Space

NASA's Toddlers

A chilling tale of infants out of control: dirty diapers and weightlessness. Ick, Pooey.

Dirty Work. That's what NASA called their five year project, *Infanta*. A mission designed to see how babies would fare in deep space. Dr. Albert Gonquin, head of the Juvenile division of NASA, could take it no longer; he leaked the story to the press, and the rest is history. What would drive a bunch of normally sane guys gaga enough to think they could raise a bunch of space cadets from seedlings?

It started in 1987. The space program was in shambles, and the country had begun to forget the dream of space for the sport of TV Evangelist scandals. NASA's budget was being trimmed to a quarter of Tammy Fay Baker's mascara allowance, and heads were going to roll.

It was while he was staring at his pink slip that Al got the idea. He was absentmindedly humming the Don McClean refrain "and babies float by, just counting their toes," and there it was, as clear as a super nova. "I figured we needed a gimmick that would get more publicity than the three billion dollars NASA spent hiring Bill Blass to design haute couture space suits."

"The whole idea kind of started as a joke. We'd say that someone had left a baby in the unmanned rocket launcher, and it was accidentally sent into orbit. I told a pal, and pretty soon the whole theory spread out of control, until the head of NASA approached me, asking how much my 'baby' would cost."

The scam, I mean plan, was to specially train a group of infants for the rigors of space travel. They could fly to the farthest reaches of the galaxy and still be alive to tell about it when they got back to Earth. None of this "suspended animation" hooey—this was practical, and the country would be hooked for years. Just imagine, the sight of those little babes bobbing around the high-tech cabin. You can't buy publicity like that (and I know, I've tried).

Less than nine months after the initial joke, an entire new top-secret division was working on the intricacies of the plan. Robots had to be constructed with electronic breasts. Specially absorbent disposable diapers were a high priority. The PR division was working more feverishly than any part of NASA. Polls were conducted: "Do you think babies should be brought up in space?" and other cleverly veiled questions were being asked to tourists at DisneyWorld by people in dwarf costumes. Disney already had the TV rights to this ultra event.

Gentlemen, we have achieved poopoo

Zero Hour, 6 AM. Six toddlers (three Adams, three Eves), were packed into foil-covered bassinets, hurtling towards the future at light speed. Jane Pauley stopped chatting with the author of a diet book

❖ Catalog — Babs Ryan Originals

Experience Level ***Intermediate/5.1 codes only***

- **Fonts:** Garamond Antiqua , Compugraphic 12 pt
- **Graphics:** Dynamic Graphics, Desktop Art Artfolio, edited with PC Paintbrush Plus
- **Printer:** LaserJet III

Babs Ryan Originals
A Little Night Music
Straws in The Wind
A Breath of French Air

Notes: This is an example of "Table as page," where the entire page design is created using a table. This makes the page design easy, but it *only* works if you don't have text which needs to flow from one cell (or what looks like a column) to another. (See small illustration at right.) The same design can be reproduced in 5.0 using parallel columns, but it's much more difficult to control.

This design requires pictures that are all approximately the same width; they can vary in height, however. The subheads use Garamond bold which is then bolded, creating extra-bold subheads. If you use the bold attribute on fonts that are already bold, WordPerfect prints the characters several times, shifting slightly each time, and this creates extra-bold type. The art at the bottom of the page was edited heavily in PC Paintbrush so that it would match the style and shape of the two other graphics. The text also has a lot of "hand justification." This means I've pressed return (and in this case, also an indent), so that the lines would end the way that looked best rather than the way WordPerfect broke them. Hand justification can make a big difference in the appearance of a page, but can be used only when type is set flush left (ragged right).

Some especially wide letters of hanging caps, such as H, M, or W require a separate style to indent the paragraph a little bit more, otherwise the paragraph will run into the cap. The table is full width, the first column is 2.58", the second is 2.12" and the third is 1.55". All lines are set to none, except those visible.

[L/R Mar:1.25",1"][T/B Mar:0.3",0.3"]
[Tab Set:Rel: +0.3",+1.03"][Tbl Def:I;3,2.58",2.12",1.55"]
[Row][Cell][Font:Garmond KrsvHlb (DT) (TD) 30pt]
[Wrd/Ltr Spacing:80% of Optimal,Optimal]
Babs Ryan Originals[Wrd/Ltr Spacing:Optimal,Optimal]
[Row][Cell][Font:Garmond KrsvHlb (DT) (TD) 14pt][Flsh Rgt]Fashion for the Well
[-]Heeled Broad[Wrd/Ltr Spacing:Optimal,Optimal]
[Font:Garmond Krsv (DT) (TD)11.5pt][Ln Height:0.181"]
[Row][Cell][Style On:subhead]A Little Night Music[Style Off:subhead]
[Row][Cell][Fig Opt]<O 0 0 0 0>[Fig Box:1;ERTE.PCC;]H F S H 2[Cell]
[Style On:hanging cap]E[Style Off:hanging cap]asy does ityou don't[SRt]

Paired Style for Subhead

[AdvDn:0.1"][Wrd/Ltr Spacing:Optimal,150% of Optimal]
[Font:Garmond Hlb (DT) (TD) 14pt][SM CAP][Bold][Comment][AdvDn:0.05"]

Babs Ryan Originals

Fashion for the Well-Heeled Broad

A Little Night Music

Easy does it—you don't want to be placed under Fashion arrest. This design is sure to keep you out of the clutches of the Style Patrol.

Colors	*Price:*
Wine	$429.95
Burgundy	$329.95
Claret	$239.95
Maroon	$199.95
Puce	$129.95
Rust	$109.95

Straws in The Wind

The latest hats are breezy and romantic. We've got two of the most enchanting patterns this side of the Rockies—non-flammable too!

Colors	*Price:*
Cream	$155.50
Eggshell	$135.99
Beige	$122.16
Tan	$114.44
Ostrich	$109.95
Sand	$107.97

A Breath of French Air

He'll fall head-over-heels when he sees your tresses wrapped up in this little satin chapeaux—ooh la la.

Colors	*Price:*
Peach	$122.50
Turquoise	$155.99
Puce	$122.16
Baby Puke	$144.44

Paired Style for Hanging Cap
[HRt]
[AdvDn:0.167"][Font:Garmond Hlb (DT) (TD) 34pt][Comment][Mar Rel][Indent]
Paired Style for Hanging Wide
[Tab Set:Rel: +0.4",+1.07"][HRt]
[AdvDn:0.167"][Font:Garmond Hlb (DT) (TD) 34pt][Comment][Mar Rel][Indent]

❖ *Flyer — Cooking School*

Experience Level: ***Easy***

- **Fonts:** Palatino 12pt, Zapf Dingbats - Adobe PostScript
- **Graphics:** MGI Publisher's PicturePak-CGM, Sales/Marketing
- **Printer:** QMS-PS 810

Notes: This design is really ridiculously easy. It's just three columns, with a thick black line at the top of each. I've created a style that selects the dingbat font, and this makes it easier to globally change size or placement on the line. It's easy to go overboard with dingbats because they're fun, but keep them under control so they add zest, but don't clutter the page.

Because this is a three-fold flyer, the backside of this flyer could be portrait, segmented into three blocks the same size as each of the folds. One segment would contain the mailing and return address, and the other two would available for more sales pitch material, maps, etc.

This same page could easily be done on a LaserJet.

[Ln Height:0.19"][Par Num Def][Paper Sz/Typ:11" x 8.5",Standard]
[L/R Mar:0.5",0.5"][T/B Mar:0.7",0.5"]
[Col Def:3,0.5",3.63",3.93",7.06",7.36",10.5"]<D .3>
[Col On][HLine:Left & Right,3.13",0.2",100%]
[VLine:Column 1,Full Page,7.3",1w,100%]
[VLine:Column 2,Full Page,7.3",1w",100%][HRt]
[HRt]
[VRY LARGE][ITALC][AdvDn:0.1"]I Even Burn Water[vry large] [italc][HRt]
[Fig Opt]<BNNNN PBI>{The caption contains an [AdvUp:2.5"] code to move the text to the middle of the graphic rather than below it}
Paired Style for Dingbats:
[Font:ITC Zapf Dingbats 16 pt][Comment]
Paired Style for Headlines:
[BOLD][Ln Height:0.5"][EXT LARGE][Comment]
Paired style for subhead:
[Ln Height:0.22"][LARGE][Comment]
Paired style for schedule:
[Font:Palatino 10 pt][Comment]

"I Even Burn Water"

Cooking Classes for the Hopelessly Inept

"After being banished from Home Ec, I didn't think I would ever learn how to cook—But CFC taught even me!"

And we can teach you, too. Klutz after klutz has been cured, using our patented CRC *Klutz-Control-System*.

Our staff of highly trained professional "Cooking Counsellors" will not only teach you how to cook, but how to enjoy it! It's almost like being a Stepford Wife! Or if your a man, a Stepford Husband! (Girls can't resist men who cook.)

Classes include:

- Boiling Water 101
- Parboiling Just About Anything!
- Tips For Buttering Toast
- Miracle "Whip It Good"
- Blow Torch Browning
- Microwave Madness!

"My husband was going to leave me for this teenager who worked at KFC. You taught me the true meaning of shake and bake, and saved my marriage!"

Watch your life improve dramatically as you explore the basics of food preparation. You'll learn how to be a cheap date, or a good homemaker.

If you're in a hurry, we offer a special classes for the overworked Executive: *Defrosting Debriefings!*

✲ SCHEDULE OF CLASSES ✲

Course	*Begins*	*Fee*
❶ Defrost 101	May 23, 2 4-hour classes	$90.00
❷ Boiling Water	October 19, 12, 2-hour classes	$285.00
❸ Klutz Control	October 29, 9, 6-hour classes	$1,250.00

Cooking for Klutzes
123 Microwave Dr.
Amana, PA

☎ 800-555-BURN

❖ *Form — Runsheet*

Experience Level: ***Easy to make, easy to use/5.1 codes first***

- **Fonts:** Bitstream Swiss Condensed 12 pt. (body), Swiss Compressed 16 pt titles
- **Printer:** LaserMaster LX6 & LaserJet III

Notes: We used this runsheet while putting together this book. It consists of one large table and there's really nothing else mysterious about it. Of course, you may have no idea what a runsheet is. If you put together any type of publication, from a newsletter to a newspaper, you need to keep track of what's assigned for each issue. I can't overemphasize how important it is to use a form like this one (if not this one itself). It will make the difference between knowing what you're doing and a desktop publishing nightmare. You'll have enough contingencies to contend with, so at least you should try to organize what you can about your publication.

The table is 9 columns by as many rows as you want. The first two rows are marked as headers, so they are repeated on every page. All the cells in these two rows are locked so they can't be changed—not really for security but so the cursor won't stop on them. It's easy to add additional rows in Table Edit by pressing the Insert key, then specifying how many rows you want to add. I've used a large top margin so the page could be bound on top, but you can make it smaller if you want.

[Hyph Off][Brdr Opt]<O .01>[Paper Sz/Typ:11" x 8.5",Standard]
[T/B Mar:1",0.5"][L/R Mar:0.6",0.6"]
[Tbl Def:I;9,0.8",2.78",0.608",1.22",0.507",2.38",0.6",0.348",0.5"]

(This means 9 columns, with the row widths being: Author=0.8; Title=2.78; Page#=0.608; Art=1.22; K=0.507; Head=2.38; Prog=0.6; In= 0.348; Out=0.5)

The top line is extra thick and the outside borders of the table are single lines, as are the lines between rows 1, 2, and 3. The rest of the lines are dotted so that they separate the space without being overly distracting. The bottom line is dotted because this form continues for pages and pages, so WordPerfect doesn't consider it the outside line of the table.

Because a form like this is basically utilitarian, if you're in a rush, you can print it without the graphic lines by pressing SHIFT-F7 G N. Of course, the form *looks* better with the lines, but it also takes *a very long time* to print. This is because the dotted lines must be printed as graphics rather than faster "line commands" in the printer's control language. With dotted lines, the LaserMaster takes about three minutes, while a LaserJet III takes over 15 minutes. With single lines, this will print in about three minutes on LaserJet printers. Without lines this will print quickly on any printer.

The up/down/star dingbats are a form of visual shorthand you create with paired styles. Rather than having to write "great," "good," or "uh-oh," you can simply apply one of these styles. These are optional but fun. Interestingly, WordPerfect can access the entire set of dingbats, something Ventura Publisher can't do. 5.1 users don't need a dingbat style, as WordPerfect will automatically select the dingbat font (if it is available in your printer driver) when you use any character in set 12.

RunSheet **Project: Will-Harris Harbinger** **Page 1**

Author	Title	Pg#	Art	K	Head	Prog	IN	OUT
DWH	Minnie Mouse	4	Broken ❤	16	Minnie's Night of Hell	✏	▲	
TWH	Mickey Mouse	12	Photo	24	Mickey's Torment	✪		▲
SR	Lucille Ball	16	Dumps	12	The only person to loathe Lucy	✍	▲	
ME	Calvin & Hobbes	back	strips	18	"The funniest cartoon in the history of the world?"	✌		▲
KLL	Vance The Pig	3	Trotters	4	My Romance with Vance	✉		
TN	The Great Coffee Houses of the World	22	Java-Logo	6	"Hey, The Donald, why so tense?"	✆		
PO	Women: Hair Horror-Stories	42	Woman in hat	9	"I was a victim of Cindi Lauper's hairdresser!"	✂	▲	

Swiss Condensed is used for the body text because it is narrow, so more text can be placed in the form. While similar, this is not the same font as Helvetica Narrow which is built into PostScript (and other) printers. Helvetica Narrow is an electronically squished version of Helvetica, and isn't really designed to be that narrow. Consequently, it doesn't look very good. Swiss Condensed (or Helvetica Condensed from Adobe) are both designed to be narrow, so they are more attractive and legible.

❖ 5.0 Version of the Runsheet

Experience Level: ***Advanced to make, easy to use***

The page looks almost identical to the 5.1 version, only instead of using tables (which 5.0 doesn't have), it uses many codes placed in the header so they will repeat on every page. This page can also be produced easily on a LaserJet, provided you create landscape fonts with Fontware first.

Notes: This form is a lot of fun because the form prints at the same time your information does. The secret is in the Advance codes. The styles for the form are placed into the header, so they automatically print on every page. The end of Topper3 contains [AdvToLn:0.9"] which moves WordPerfect back to the top of your page. When you watch the page draw in View Document, you see WordPerfect draw the entire form, then move back up to the top of the page and put in your information.

Topper3 looks like a billion codes, but in actuality, you only have to create one line, delete it, and then paste it back 13 times. The settings are the same for all 26 boxes. These figures boxes create the ballot boxes along the right side of the page, and if you don't want them, then all you need is the horizontal lines.

IMPORTANT: Once you save this as a style sheet you can use it over and over, but you must do it correctly. Topper1 is the first code in the file. Topper 2 and Topper 3 are both placed in a header that prints on every page. Once you do that, you can type all the information you want. The titles will not display on-screen, but they will print.

This is the complete file:
[Open Style:Topper1][Header A:2]

HEADER
[Open Style:topper2][Open Style:topper3]

Open Style for TOPPER1
[Paper Sz/Typ:11" x 8.5",Standard][T/B Mar:0.5",0.3"][L/R Mar:0.5",0.5"]
[Font:ITC Avant Garde Gothic Book 14 pt][Ln Height:0.5"]
[TabSet:1.5",3",3.75",6.5",7",8.5"][Wrd/Ltr Spacing:Normal,Normal]

Open Style for TOPPER2 (In Header)
[Font:ITC Avant Garde Gothic Book 14 pt]
[Paper Sz/Typ:11" x 8.5",Standard][T/B Mar:0.5",0.4"]

[L/R Mar:0.5",0.5"][HLine:Left & Right,10",0.1“,100%][HRt]
[AdvDn:0.1“][LARGE][BOLD]Run[bold]Sheet[large][Tab][Tab][Tab][Tab]
[AdvToPos:3.75"]Project: BAM![Flsh Rt]Page ^B[C/A/Flrt][HRt]
[HLine:Left & Right,10",0",100%][HRt]
[Ln Height:0.25"][AdvDn:0.1“][TabSet:1.5",3",3.75",6.5",7",8.5"]
[VLine:1.4",1.07",6.93",0",100%][VLine:2.9",1.07",6.93",0",100%]
[VLine:3.65",1.07",6.93",0",100%][VLine:6.4",1.07",6.93",0",100%]
[VLine:6.9",1.07",6.93",0",100%][VLine:8.4",1.07",6.93",0",100%]
[BOLD]Author[Tab]Title[Tab]Size[Tab]Head/Info[Tab]P#[Tab]Artwork
[Tab]Format/Status[bold][HRt]

Open Style for TOPPER3 (In header)
[AdvToLn:1.32"][HLine:Left & Right,10",0",100%][HRt]
{This is where the repeat begins}
[Flsh Rt][SMALL][Figure:1;;]<TC VB SB 14p 14p> IN [Figure:2;;]<TC VB SB 14p 14p>
OUT[small][C/A/Flrt][HRt]
[HLine:Left & Right,10",0",100%][HRt]
{Enter the above, then cut from [Flsh Rt] to the [HRt] after the [HLine] and paste it 13 times. This will give you figure numbers up to 26. After you paste them all in, enter the following:}
[AdvToLn:0.9"]{If you forget this Advance code, the whole thing won't work}
Paired Style for Up Triangle Dingbat
[Font:ITC Zapf Dingbats 14 pt][129n:12,115][Comment]
Paired Style for Down Triangle Dingbat
[Font:ITC Zapf Dingbats 14 pt][129n:12,116][Comment]
Paired Style for Star Dingbat
[Font:ITC Zapf Dingbats 14 pt][129n:12,74][Comment]

❖ Poster — Lincoln

Experience Level ***Couldn't be easier***

- **Fonts:** New Century Schoolbook, Adobe 18 pt
- **Graphics:** DG Desktop Art, edited with PC Paintbrush Plus
- **Printer:** QMS-PS 810

Notes: This looks tricky, but it isn't. When using a PostScript printer, the shadow type is opaque, which means that it prints white on top of any kind of graphic. The 18 point rotated text along the edge of the page is in a text box, and rotated using ALT-F9 2.

```
[Figure:1;ABE.PCC;]<<TA VF WN>
[Text Box:1;;]<TA VF HMR SB 1 9 WN E ALT-F9 2>
[W/O Off][HRt] [L/R Mar:1.2",1.2"][HRt]
[Font:New Century Schoolbook Bold 72 pt]
[SHADW]Happy[HRt] Birthday[shadw][HRt]
```

Happy Birthday

A Fourth of July Celebration at the Lincoln Memorial

❖ *Storyboard — ASPCA*

Experience Level: ***Easy***

- **Fonts:** Helvetica Narrow, Adobe PostScript, 12 pt
- **Graphics:** Add your own with a scanner, draw them in PC Paintbrush, or paste them in manually.
- **Printer:** QMS-PS 810

Notes: This is a presentation storyboard. You'd be out of your mind to use this to develop a storyboard, but it makes a very sharp presentation once you've already polished the storyboard the old-fashioned way (pencil and paper).

This design uses one paired style, called SHOT. This includes an automatic paragraph number, and automatic flush right for the shot.

Because these are parallel columns, make sure you don't accidentally delete at [HPg] codes between columns when you are editing. If you do, press **CONTROL-[ENTER]** to put in a new Hard Page code, and start the next column.

If you are going to use the two column introduction at the top of the page, type all your text and see how many lines it is. Divide that number in half, and place a Hard Page at the end of the half-way point. In this case it was six lines long, so I put a Hard Page code in after three lines.

To create more pages of boxes: Block a single box, then press CONTROL-F4 BC and copy it as many times as you want (that way you don't have to set the size over and over again).

If you aren't going to print graphics on the page, you can easily do this page on a LaserJet, but at the time this book was done, WordPerfect did not support landscape graphics for the LaserJet. The codes for this example continue on the next page after the example.

```
[Fig Opt]<C [BOLD]1[bold] O 0000 1 .1 .1 .1 .1>
[Paper Sz/Typ:11" x 8.5",Standard][T/B Mar:1",0.25"]
[L/R Mar:0.5",0.5"][Wrd/Ltr Spacing:200% of Optimal,200% of Optimal][Font:Helvetica
Narrow 16 pt][Ln Height:0.16"]
[HLine:Left &Right,10",1w",20%]
S•T•O•R•Y•B•O•A•R•D[Tab]FOR: A.S.P.C.A.
[Flsh Rt][Wrd/Ltr Spacing:Optimal,Optimal]DATE: 6/2/90[C/A/Flrt]
[Font:Helvetica Narrow 10 pt][HRt]
[Col Def:2,0.5",5.4",5.6",10.5"]{For intro text}[HRt]
[Col On]We see two teenage girls in poodle skirts fussing with their hair... {For Storyboard
itself}
[Col Def:4,0.5",2.85",3.05",5.4",5.6",7.95",8.15",10.5"]<TP D .2>
[Tab Set:0.9",3.45",6",9",9.55"][Col On]
[Figure:1;;[Box Num]<TP HB SH 1.76>
[Style On:SHOT] ... ][BOLD]EMMA:[bold] Hey,
Karen, what's that on your[SRt]
```

S•T•O•R•Y•B•O•A•R•D FOR: A.S.P.C.A.

DATE: 6/2/90

We see two teenage girls in poodle skirts fussing with their hair. We see only the back of KAREN's head, and EMMA is watching her try out a new fad. Her face belies a feeling of repulsion.

As they speak, we see the shadow of a giant creature looming outside the window, and hear subtle crunching noises of a mutant Gerbil, seeking revenge on Madison Avenue for promoting this new fad.

1 *TWO SHOT*

EMMA: Hey, Karen, what's that on your hair?
KAREN: It's dreamy, isn't it?

2 *CU - EMMA*

EMMA: I'll say, I've never seen anything quite like it!
ANNOUNCER: It's new.

3 *CU - BACK OF KAREN'S HEAD*

KAREN: Isn't Johnny gonna flip?
EMMA: I'll say!

4 *CU - KAREN'S LIPS*

ANNOUNCER: It's cool.
KAREN: He just loves this kind of thing.

5 *MCU - KAREN TURNS TO WINDOW*

EMMA: All guys do!
ANNOUNCER: It's what you've been waiting for.

6 *TWO SHOT - BOTH TURN TO WINDOW*

KAREN: Don't cha just love it?
EMMA: I'll say...

7 *WIDER REVEAL- KAREN TURNS*

After a pause
EMMA: But, what is it?
KAREN: Beats me...

8 *SLOW FADE*

ANNOUNCER: It's a Gerbil
EMMA: They don't use real poodles in these skirts, do they?
The shadow blocks all light from the window, as we ***FADE***

hair?[HRt]
[BOLD]KAREN: [bold]It's dreamy, isn't it?[HPg]
Paired Style for SHOTS
[BOLD][Par Num:Auto][bold][FlshRt][SMALL][ITALC]
[Comment]
[AdvDn:0.1"][small][italc][C/A/Flrt]

❖ *Sign — Time Management*

Experience Level: ***Really Easy***

- **Fonts:** ITC Avant Garde, Adobe PostScript, 14pt
- **Printer:** QMS-PS 810

Notes: Try it. You'll like it.

[Just Lim:60,120][Paper Sz/Typ:11" x 8.5",Standard][Just On]
[Txt Opt]<BTTTT>[Text Box:1;;]<TA VF WN>{Box around page}
[HRt]
[HRt]
[HRt]
[HRt]
[HLine:Center,2.88",0.2",20%][HRt]
[HRt]
[Font:ITC Avant Garde Gothic Demi 30 pt]
[Cntr][OUTLN]The Fallacy of[outln][C/A/Flrt][HRt]
[Font:ITC Avant Garde Gothic Demi 36 pt][Cntr]Time Management[C/A/Flrt][HRt]
[L/R Mar:2.25",2.25"][Font:ITC Avant Garde Gothic Book 14 pt]
[Ln Height:0.22"][Hyph On][AdvDn:0.1"]While the organization of...

The Fallacy of Time Management

While the organization of material is important, when it is left until the last minute, nothing can be organized because there is not enough time. Organization requires time, and saving time requires organization.

If there is not enough time to organize, there will seldom be logic. Without logic and organization, there can be no judgement. If there is no judgement, then nothing is accomplished. If nothing is accomplished, then there is no reason for organization, and without organization why manage time?

So take a nap.

❖ Overhead projection — GoCo

Experience Level: ***Easy***

- **Fonts:** Univers Bold
- **Graphics:** Gem Artline, printed to disk in HPGL format
- **Printer:** LaserJet III

Notes: The gray type is 30,30,30, and the third line is black. The finger is character 5,21 (press CONTROL-V first). Replace "GoCo DTP" and the graphic with your own company name and logo, and use them at the top of all slides for increased name recognition.

You can also put a box around the page, your company name, and the line under it all in a header so they will automatically repeat on every page. Just make sure to turn wrap to NO on the graphics box. (Come on, beat them over the head with your company name.)

```
[Tab Set:3.5",4"][Paper Sz/Typ:11" x 8.5",Standard]
[T/B Mar:1.25",1"][Figure:1;;]<TA VF WN>{Box around the page}
[T/B Mar:1.75",1.25"][L/R Mar:1.75",1.75"]
[Font:Univers Bold 44 pt][Usr Opt][Flsh Rt][OUTLN]GoCo DTP
[Usr Box:1;ZULU.HPL;][outln][HRt]
[HLine:Left & Right,7.5",0.05",100%][HRt]
[HRt]
[Ln Height:0.5"][ITALC]Choose any two[HRt]
[FINE](all three not available as a package)[fine][italc][HRt]
[HRt]
[Color:30%,30%,30%]
[Tab][Tab][Tab] [■:5,21]Cheap[HRt]
[HRt]<use [Color:Black] before black text>
```

Paired Style for Dingbats

5.0: If you want to use dingbats you must change to the dingbat typeface first. Use the following paired style:

```
[Tab][Font:ITC Zapf Dingbats 36 pt][Comment][Indent]
```

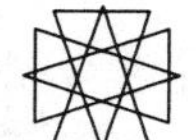

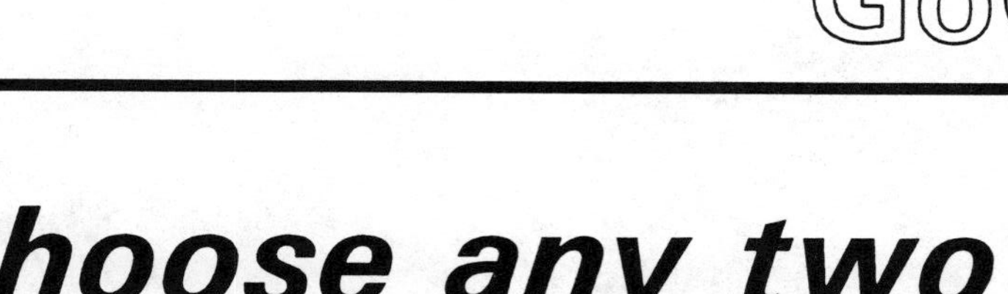

Choose any two

(all three not available as a package)

 **Cheap**

 **Fast**

 **Good**

❖ Outline — WordPerfect 5 DTP in Style

Experience Level: ***Intermediate***

- **Fonts:** Palatino 12pt - Adobe PostScript
- **Graphics:** SpinFont from SoftCraft, with Bitstream Zapf Calligraphic (Palatino)
- **Printer:** QMS-PS 810

Notes: The double outline effect was created by selecting a bold base font, then using both outline and bold attributes. Because the font is already bold, WordPerfect prints the characters several times, shifting to the right each time, in tiny increments.

```
[Tab Set:2", every 0.4"][T/B Mar:1“,0.75"][L/R Mar:1.5",1”][Just Off]
[Fig Opt]<BNNNN>[Font:Palatino 12 pt][Usr Opt]<BSSSS>
[Usr Box:1;;]<TA VF WN>{Box around the page}
[Figure:1;DPIS2.TIF;]<TA VT SW 1.5>
[L/R Mar:2",1.75"][T/B Mar:1“,1”]
[HRt]
[HRt]
[HRt]
[HRt]
[HRt]
[HRt]
[HRt]
[Ln Height:0.55"][Font:Palatino Bold Italic 40 pt]
[Cntr][BOLD][OUTLN]with[outln][bold] WordPerfect
[Font:Palatino 12 pt][Ln Height:0.2"][C/A/Flrt][HRt]
```

Paired Style for Outline Numbers:

```
[Cndl EOP:6][HRt]
[HLine:Left & Right,4.75",0.05",10%][HRt]
[AdvDn:0.1“][VRY LARGE][BOLD][Par Num:Auto][Indent]
[Comment]
```

Paired Style for Chapter Titles:

```
[VRY LARGE][BOLD][SM CAP][Comment]
```

Each numbered line:

```
[Tab][Par Num:Auto][Indent]
```

Desktop Publishing *in Style*

with WordPerfect

Introduction: This is the book that's going to blow the lid off the word processing/desktop publishing industry—and isn't that just what we've all been waiting for? Desktop publishing puts the power and responsibility of designing pages and formatting documents into the hands of the people. This book will show them how to make these publications as professional as possible, without having to spend more time and money than doing it the old fashioned way.

---

1. GETTING IT TOGETHER

1. System Configuration
2. What kind of printer?
3. Make LJ fonts.
4. PostScript vs. LaserJet.

---

2. STEPS WILL BE TAKEN

1. Follow my example
    - a. Concept/Market.
    - b. Writing.
    - c. Designing.
        - I. Selecting font.
        - II. Choosing graphics.
    - d. Assembling with WP commands.
        - I. Sharing the styles with other docs.
        - II. Re-using the format.

LaserJet examples

❖ *Promotional piece — Desktop Publishing in Style*

Experience Level: ***Intermediate (easier than it looks)***

- **Fonts:** Bitstream Korinna, 12 pt
- **Graphics:** MGI Publisher's PicturePak-CGM, Finance/Administration
- **Printer:** Hewlett-Packard LaserJet II

Notes: The graphic of the pen is line art, so WordPerfect was able to rotate and mirror the image so it faced into the page on each corner. Bitstream's Korinna is a wonderful font, so sharp it looks typeset right out of the printer; decorative and suitable for this type of promotional material.

```
[W/O Off][L/R Mar:1“,0.75"][Hyph On][T/B Mar:0.75",0.75"] [HZone:10%,10%][Font:ITC Korinna Regular 11pt (Port) (FW)]
[Usr Box:1;FI0172.CGM;]<TA VT HML SW 1>
[Usr Box:2;FI0172.CGM;]<TA VB HML SW 1 E R 0Y>
[Usr Box:3;FI0172.CGM;]<TA VT HMR SW 1 E R 180 N>
[Usr Box:4;FI0172.CGM;]<TA VB HMR SW 1 E R 180 Y>
[Font:ITC Korinna Kursiv Regular 11pt (Port) (FW)]
 [AdvDn:0.1“][AdvDn:0.1”]
[Font:ITC Korinna Kursiv Ex Bold 18pt (Port) (FW)]
[Cntr]Daniel Will[-]Harris[C/A/Flrt][HRt]
[Font:ITC Korinna Regular 36pt (ASCII) (Port) (FW)]
[Cntr][Ln Height:0.5"]WordPerfect Desktop[C/A/Flrt][HRt]
[Cntr]Publishing in Style[C/A/Flrt][HRt]
[AdvDn:0.1“][Just On][Tab Set:1.25",4.75"]
[Col Def:2,1“,4.25",4.5",7.75"][Col On]
[Txt Opt]<BNNTO I .1 .1 .1 .1>
[Text Box:1;;]<TA VC HC1-2C>
[Ln Height:0.18"][Font:ITC Korinna Regular 11pt (Port)(FW)]
[VLine:Column 1,2.35",1.65",0.01“,155D00%]{Top vertical line}
[VLine:Column 1,7.03",3.21“,0.01”,F2M155D00%]{Bottom vertical line}
[VRY LARGE]J[vry large]ust when you thought...
```

Daniel Will-Harris

WordPerfect Desktop Publishing in Style

Just when you thought it was safe you go back into the computer section of a bookstore, you see it—yet another book about WordPerfect. But wait a sec, this isn't just another book for people who have the program, but (mysteriously) not the manual.

This practical and amusing guide offers sound advice on everything from important technical information such as undocumented features that make publishing easier and more efficient, to a comprehensive graphic design guide with font examples and page layouts for many business applications.

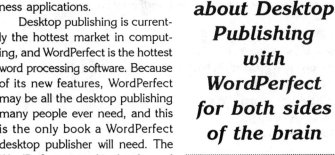

The only book about Desktop Publishing with WordPerfect for both sides of the brain

Desktop publishing is currently the hottest market in computing, and WordPerfect is the hottest word processing software. Because of its new features, WordPerfect may be all the desktop publishing many people ever need, and this is the only book a WordPerfect desktop publisher will need. The WordPerfect manual is sketchy, and actually fails to mention many advanced DTP features. It contains no in-depth examples of how to use the DTP commands, or even clues about many features.

If it can be done with WordPerfect, Daniel Will-Harris will show you how. This book stresses honest, practical desktop publishing—not art director hype.Beginners will learn all they need to know about both WordPerfect and graphic design. Advanced users learn tricks not covered in the manual, or any other books, including hidden commands and highly complex page formatting.

Third party programs that expand WordPerfect's scope are extensively covered, including graphics software, font installation programs, and fonts.

Capsule reviews of monitors and printers are also included. The book specifically covers all aspects of using WordPerfect with either a LaserJet or PostScript printer, going into great detail about what each can and can't do.

Packed with design tips, this book graphically shows how to get professional results with WordPerfect. Full page examples are supplied for the 25 most commonly produced documents, including advertisements, books, brochures, calendars, catalogs, charts, directories, documentation, flyers, forms, invitations, invoices, letterheads, magazines, menus, newsletters, presentations, proposals, reports, and resumes, with all the codes required to recreate them.

No other book about WordPerfect will:

- Reveal secret commands which not even WordPerfect technical support personnel are aware of. (Author beta-tested WP5.)
- Show you full page examples (not teensy-weensy sketches), and all the codes necessary to recreate them yourself.
- Contain specific information for every command from bullets to word spacing.
- Present technical information in an entertaining and amusing way.
- Give detailed information about graphics software for enhancing WordPerfect pages.
- Explain simple tricks to get around major LaserJet deficiencies.
- Be written by an author with as much hands-on WordPerfect experience. The author is a regular contributor to many computer publications and writes a monthly column for a major desktop publishing magazine.

❖ *Magazine — Trends in Type*

Experience Level: ***Easy***

- **Fonts:** Bitstream Zapf Humanist (Optima headlines), Zapf Elliptical (Melior) 12pt
- **Printer:** Hewlett-Packard LaserJet II

Notes: This page design is simple and looks good with almost any typeface. I used this as the test page each time I created fonts with Fontware, and everything looked good in this format. Melior looks especially serious, if not a little dry.

As you can see, sometimes WordPerfect's letter spacing leaves something to be desired, especially in the narrow columns next to the readout. Still, I'd rather have extra letterspacing than huge rivers of white between words, because it gives the page an overall even tone, whereas rivers make the page look blotchy.

```
[Wrd/Ltr Spacing:Optimal,105% of Optimal]{WordPerfect was setting Melior too tight, so
that the letters were almost on top of each other. this code tells WordPerfect to put 5% more
space between the letters}
[Just Lim:60,120][Hyph On][W/O Off][Tab Set:1.25",4.62"]
[Usr Opt]<I .25 .25 .1 .1>[Usr Box:1;;]<TA V 5.9 HC1-2C SW3>
[Font:Zapf Humanist Roman 14pt (Port) (FW)][Cntr]TRENDS IN TYPE[AdvDn:0.1"]
[HLine:Center,1.53",0.03",100%][C/A/Flrt][HRt]
[AdvDn:0.1"][Font:Zapf Humanist Bold 30pt (Port) (FW)]
[Cntr]Putting your best face forward[C/A/Flrt][HRt]
[Font:Zapf Humanist Bold 12pt (ASCII) (Port) (FW)][HRt]
[HRt]
[BOLD]By Daniel Will[-]Harris, Dt.P.[AdvDn:0.1"][bold][HRt]
[AdvUp:0.1"][Col Def:2,1",4.12",4.37",7.5"]<d .25>[Col On]
[Just On][Fig Opt]<BNNNN O 0000 I0000>
[Figure:1;;]<TP HL: SB .25 .35>{Drop Cap}
[Ln Height:0.18"]ypestyles, like clothing styles, go in...
```

Putting your best face forward

By Daniel Will-Harris, Dt.P.

Typestyles, like clothing styles, go in and out of fashion. There's such a variety of printed matter that, like any other kind of fashion, there's always room for the pendulum to swing between the trendy and the outre. This is the kind of thing art directors get paid to think about, but for the typical desktop publisher, font fashions may be a revelation. As Bill Blass says about clothing, certain typestyles "just look right now."

Except for the terminally trendy, desktop published documents should go out of their way *not* to look like desktop publishing. Typefaces can be modern without being extreme, stylish, but not overdesigned or faddish.

For the past few months, the trend for popular type has been leaning towards extremes. The two hottest typefaces now are very sans serif and very serif. In the sans serif corner, Futura Extra Black (and the entire Futura family) are #1 among the avant garde (the people, not the typeface). The type is overwhelming, yet elementary, heavy yet plain, and impossible to miss. As Buster Poindexter says, it's hot, hot, hot.

Of course the trendiest magazines have started using Futura Extra Black. But unfortunately, some of them teamed it with Univers, a combination that Allan Haley, noted authority on type and a VP at ITC, says you should "avoid like the plague."

At the serif end of the spectrum, the type de jour is Galliard. It's simple yet baroque, classic yet flashy, readable yet verging on caricature, especially in the italics. It's today's replacement for Palatino. It's not quite as readable or efficient as Palatino, but it's so "late Eighties." New trends are defined by their radical extremes, and in the future I won't be surprised if the move away from classical faces continues, with even more extravagant faces becoming the norm.

Post-modern neoclassical is becoming dated, and Russian Expressionism looks like the next big thing. If you don't want to have to redesign your publications every year (as some imprudent publishers do), you should think about using more suitable font combinations. Consider a makeover that's more classic, and you won't have to redesign it every 12 months. The combination of Baskerville for body copy and Franklin Gothic for headlines, raised caps, and captions is a well-balanced choice, and one which will retain its clean, distinctive look for a long time.

> When you get hooked on type, you get hooked in the gills, or possibly the Gill Sans. You won't see words in quite the same way again.

This year nostalgia is out, except for maybe Fifties nostalgia. A popular theory holds that whatever people remember from their childhood becomes

❖ *Advertisement — Hollywood Screenwriters*

Experience Level: ***Easy/5.1 codes first***

- **Fonts:** Bitstream Bernhard Modern, 14pt
- **Graphics:** Arts & Letters
- **Printer:** Hewlett-Packard LaserJet II

Notes: Here's an example of using tables as decorative borders. The "film strips" on the left and right are actually tables inside user boxes. The horizontal lines are just graphic lines, placed in styles with advance codes to keep them from running into the text.

The typeface is Bernhard Modern, which exudes glamor and art deco elegance. It's a real "period-piece" but it isn't "dated." This typeface is often used in advertisements and flyers for an upscale look because it is noticeably different than normal body text faces such as Times, Baskerville, and Garamond. It's best used at 14-point and above, although I have seen magazines use it at 12-point for long blocks of text.

You can print this page on any old LaserJet, even if you don't have much memory. Simply print it at draft resolution. Since there are no curves, you'll see no difference between draft and high-quality graphics printing.

Because tables can't normally be side-by-side, these tables are contained within User Boxes: one flush left, the other flush right. Here's the table definitions for the film strips:

```
[Tbl Def:1;3,0.3",0.4",0.3"]
```

Here are the codes for the page:

```
[L/R Mar:0.7",0.5"][T/B Mar:0.75",0.5"]
[HLine:Left,Baseline,7.2",0.1",100%]<top line>
[HLine:Left,10",7.2",0.1",100%]<bottom line>
[Usr Opt]<O .1 0 0 0>[Usr Box:1;;]<TP VT HML SB 1.1 9>
[Usr Box:2;;]<TP VT HMR SB 1.1 9>[HRt][HRt]
[Just:Center][EXT LARGE][BOLD]"Tinsel! Glamour![HRt]
Excitement!"[ext large][bold][HRt]
If you can type with at least three fingers, you can have a[SRt]
lucrative career as a Hollywood Screenwriter! [HRt]
(That's what producers think)[HRt]
[Open Style:thick line][HRt][HRt]
In just three easy lessons, [ITALC]Big [/]Bucks Screenwriting School[italc][HRt]
will teach you the secrets of [HRt]
[Just:Left][HRt]
[Tab][Tab][■:4,2] Power Breakfasts[HRt]
```

Paired Style for "Thick Line"

```
[AdvDn:0.1"][HLine:1.5",Baseline,5.5",0.1",100%][AdvDn:0.1"]
```

"Tinsel! Glamour! Excitement!"

If you can type with at least three fingers, you can have
a lucrative career as a Hollywood Screenwriter!
(That's what producers think)

In just three easy lessons, *Big Bucks Screenwriting School* will teach you the secrets of

- Power Breakfasts
- *Taking* a Meeting
- Using a Car Phone
- Schmoozing at Parties
- Smooth-talking Temperamental Stars

If you successfully complete this course (and thousands have), you can reminisce about the Strike of '88 with the rest of your fellow writers, and remember how David Letterman called the producers "Money Grubbing Scum!"

Have lunch at famous restaurants, meet movie stars, wear Armani as you shop on Rodeo Drive, watch helplessly as know-nothings hack your script to pieces . . . enjoy all the perks big-time writers enjoy.

Don't Delay! Call Today!

☎ 800-BIG-BUCKS ☎

★ *Big Bucks Screenwriters School, Hollywood, Cal* ★

A member of the Big Schmucks School Association

❖ Directory — Astral Travel Agents

Experience Level: ***Easy***

- **Fonts:** Swiss. Galliard, Bitstream
- **Graphics:** Scanned from a Dover Pictorial Archive book with a Hewlett-Packard ScanJet and GEM Scan software
- **Printer:** Hewlett-Packard LaserJet II

Notes: Once you set it up, this design is automatic. Each listing is surrounded with a listing style that contains the line above and a block protect code to insure that listings are broken between columns or pages. This makes them easier to read, and adds extra white space so the page doesn't become confusing. While it's unusual to make the names flush right, it sets them apart from the rest of the text, without taking up much space. While the body text is Swiss/Helvetica, you might want to use Swiss/Helvetica Condensed for the headings. Without the big headline, you could easily do a page like this with just a font cartridge. If you don't use graphics, make sure to leave even more extra white space.

```
[Open Style:Topper;]
[VLine:Column 2,Full Page,10",0.01",100%]
[Footer A:2;[Font:ITC Galliard Italic 11pt (ASCII) (Port) [HRt]
[Fig Opt]<BNNNN>[Figure:1;STARGIRL.IMG;]<TP HB> [HRt][HRt]
[Style On:headline][Flsh Rt]American{one space} [C/A/Flrt][HRt]
[Flsh Rt]Association{one space}  [C/A/Flrt][HRt]
[Flsh Rt]of Astral{one space}  [C/A/Flrt][HRt]
[Flsh Rt]Travel Agents{one space}  [C/A/Flrt][HRt]...[HPg]
[Style On:ENTRY;[HRt]
[Block Pro:On][HLine:Left & Right,2.2",0.01",100%][HRt]
[HRt][Style On:name]Ellen Aires[Style Off:name][C/A/Flrt][HRt]
1-800-555-8768[HRt]
[ITALC]Specialty:[italc] A hard hitting approach[SRt]
to the Zen of software. Takes[SRt]
travellers on a wild adventure[SRt]
[ITALC]Travel Tip:[italc] Always bring enough[SRt]
leading.[HRt]
[BOLD][bold][Style Off:!][HRt]
[Style On:!][Style On:name]Carol T. Download[Style Off:name][C/A/Flrt][HRt]
Paired Style for each Entry
[HRt]
[Block Pro:On][HLine:Left & Right,6.5",0.01",100%][HRt]
[HRt]
[Comment][Block Pro:Off]
Paired Style for Name:
[LARGE][BOLD][Flsh Rt] [Comment]
```

American Association of Astral Travel Agents

AAATA, "Triple A Service with some T&A to spare." Also incorporating the Universal Society of Astral Paranormals (USAP)

Ellen Aires

1-800-555-8768
Specialty: A hard hitting approach to the Zen of software. Takes travellers on a wild adventure through a CRT, dodging electron beams and leaving footprints on the sands of Times Roman.
Channels: Gutenberg, Zapf.
Travel Tip: Always bring enough leading.

Carol T. Download

800-555-4328
Specialty: Running with the "in" crowd.
Channels: Janes, including Jane Austin, Jane Meadows, Jane Jetson.
Travel Tip: When in doubt, guess.
Motto: Don't ask me.

Thomas Filum

800-111-1111
Specialty: Impressionistic Relativity. Leads tours through Paris, circa 1900.
Channels: Serat, Monet, Van Gogh.
Travel Tip: Plimsoles and Bandaids.
Motto: Give me a foot and I'll walk a mile.
Rates: Works too cheap.

Robert E. Lee

800-555-2347
Specialty: Darwinian treks.
Channels: Ben Franklin, Anton Mesmer.
Motto: You can't direct it if you don't respect it.

Bruce Lekec

800-555-7147
Specialty: Excursions into hand-held calculators. Claims 2+2 do not equal 4 (especially on Parisian hotel bills figured with Pascal). Averages a C++
Travel Tip: Always sleep in crepe-soled shoes are as they are non-conductive.
Motto: It's not a bug, it's a feature.
Rates: 2+2 in the fourth dimension.

Sue Marie Harrysun

(Sue) SUE-SUDIO
Specialty: Whisks participants back and forth over the international date line until they get younger.
Channels: Grace Kaeko Kelly Fugitami, Sara Bernhardt.
Motto: Me Habla Japanese

Isaiah Sheven Louis

800-555-5555
Specialty: Astrologer/stock broker, Tao Jones Stock Exchange. Renaissance man, shameless self-promoter.
Channels: Anything for an audience.
Travel Tip: Don't leave home without me.
Motto: Say it with *cash.*

Fred Noodnick

c/o Rosali & Alana's Fungi Factory.
Specialty: Playwrights of the late 20th century. Also dabbles in the healing powers of swing music and the dead languages of China.
Channels: Walt Whitman, Paul Whiteman, Chairman Mao.
Motto: Don't follow a fad, be one.
Rates: The current market price of a leather sofa.

John Tomorrow

800-555-2121
Specialty: All inclusive holidays into harmonic scales; A Flat minor a must.
Channels: Fats Waller.
Travel Tip: It don't mean a thang if it ain't got that swang.
Motto: Be hip, or be gone, real gone.

Sven Wrath

800-555-6792
Specialty: Spys and Smiley faces. Takes side trips into the pseudo-Jungian imagery of undercover ABC affiliates.
Channels: Noah Webster, Hearst.
Travel Tip: It's only worth doing if it can't be done.
Motto: I'd rather be sailing.

Open Style for Topper
[Open Style:3 col w/rul;[T/B Mar:0.5",0.5"][L/R Mar:0.75",0.75"]
[Col Def:3,0.75",2.95",3.15",5.35",5.55",7.75"]<D .3>
[Col On][VLine:Column 1,Full Page,10",0.01",100%]
[VLine:Column 2,Full Page,10",0.01",100%]
Open Style for Vertical intercolumn rules on following pages
[VLine:Column 1,Full Page,9.65",0.01",100%][VLine:Column 2,Full Page,9.65",0.01",100%]
Footer:
[Font:ITC Galliard Italic 11pt (Port) (FW)]Membership Roster Page ^B[Flsh Rt]December 1990[C/A/Flrt]

❖ *Flyer — Estate Finders*

Experience Level: ***Complex***

- **Fonts:** Bitstream Galliard, 11 pt
- **Graphics:** Both scanned from 1920's periodicals using Hewlett-Packard ScanJet and GEM Scan software
- **Printer:** Hewlett-Packard LaserJet II

Notes: Notice how different this example looks from the "HomeFinders" example that follows, even though the layout is almost identical (but flopped). While it should have been straightforward to create three columns, the first two narrow and the last wide, for some reason this page was a pain. The text kept wanting to run around the graphic, one letter at a time. The "HomeFinders" example was much easier to do.

[Hyph On][T/B Mar:0.9",1"][Footer A:2; ...]
[Fig Opt]<BNNNN>[Figure:1;MANSION.IMG;]<TP HR SH 1 WN>
[Font:ITC Galliard Italic 14pt (ASCII) (Port) (FW)]Investment Information[HRt][AdvToLn:1.2"]
[Font:ITC Galliard Italic 36pt (ASCII) (Port) (FW)]{Yes, spaces}
EstateFinders [HRt]
[Font:ITC Galliard Italic 14pt (ASCII) (Port) (FW)][AdvUp:0.1"]
[Flsh Rt]"A Person's Home is their Castle"{Yes, more spaces}[C/A/Flrt]
[HRt]
[AdvUp:0.1"][HLine:Left & Right,6.5",0.01",100%][AdvToLn:1.93"]
[Just On][Font:ITC Galliard Roman 11pt (ASCII) (Port) (FW)]
[Fig Opt]<BNNNN O .1 .1 .01 .1>
[Figure:2;FLYCHAIR.IMG;]<TA V 1.93 H M L SW 3>
[Hyph Off][AdvDn:0.1"][Font:ITC Galliard Bold 14pt (Port) (FW)] ...]
[Col Def:3,1",2.25",2.5",3.8",4.05",7.5"][Col On]
[Ln Height:0.18"][Style On:subhead][Just Off]Schools[HRt]
Paired Style for Subhead (as in "Schools/Neighbors")
[Ln Height:Auto][Font:ITC Galliard Italic 18pt (Port) (FW)]
[Just Off] [Comment]

Investment Information

EstateFinders

"A Person's Home is their Castle"

Post Modern luxury: Geo-classical splendor on 12,000 acres, with 19 bedrooms, 47 bathrooms, 25 fireplaces, tennis court, pool/lagoon

Schools:
Yale University is only 20 minutes away by Lear Jet. No public schools are located within the city limits, although personal tutors are plentiful, cheap and exceptionally well-dressed

Neighbors of Note:
Ron & Nancy
Malcom Forbes
Bob Hope
Abiner & Puppy
Donny Trump
Ivana DuPont
Merv Griffini

Price:
If you have to ask . . .

You deserve it. Just imagine 12,000 carefully manicured acres with all the amenities. Based on the original drawings for Versailles, this magnificent estate is fully furnished—you won't have to do a thing. Everything that can be made out of marble has been, from the floors to the many sunken bathtubs, replete with anatomically correct marble statuary.

Envision unparalleled luxury with no expense spared—including a staff of nine young, blonde, Swedish au pair girls with 5 years still left on their indentured servitude.

This stunning property includes bulletproof windows, and a fully stocked bomb-type shelter, fortified to resist uzis and small armored tanks. The entire neighborhood has been walled and surrounded by moats. Ex-jewel thieves have been hired to design the security systems, then mysteriously disappeared, assuring the highest possible safety. A private police force of 44 is on guard 24 hours a day, and requires a low monthly maintenance fee of just $120,000.

Play tennis on the tournament-grade clay courts, or bowl in Howard Hughes own alley, brought in it's entirety from Las Vegas, and complete with those famous Kleenex dispensers.

And what a pool! Because it's almost a mile wide, you can swim, fish, yacht, cavort with dolphins, or simply relax, as the private hydro-electric plant provides all the energy, with enough left over to sell back to the power company.

The guest house consists of an authentic Scottish castle, imported stone-by-stone and set in it's own island in the middle of the pool. Or if you prefer a tropical flavor, there's always the Polynesian Village, stocked with happy natives who don't even know they're not still in Polynesia. Your own little bit of the islands, without ever leaving home.

Even Aaron Spelling would be jealous!

1 Park Place, El Mirage, California, 90342 • 213•555•8768

Paired Style for Raised Cap
[Font:ITC Galliard Italic 36pt (ASCII) (Port) (FW)] [Comment]
Footer:
[HLine:Left & Right,6.5",0.01",100%][AdvDn:0.1"][HRt]
[Cntr][Font:ITC Galliard Italic 11pt (ASCII) (Port) (FW)]1 Park Place, El Mirage, California, 90342 (213) 555[-]8768[C/A/Flrt][HRt]

❖ *Flyer — Home Finders*

Experience Level: ***Intermediate***

- **Fonts:** Bitstream Serifa, 12 pt, Bitstream Slate Extra Bold
- **Graphics:** Top & Footer: Created in PC Paintbrush; house scanned
- **Printer:** Hewlett-Packard LaserJet II

Notes: Once this format is setup, it's easy to change the text and graphic and use it over and over again. The trickiest thing on the page is the subhead "Vital Statistics," centered over the second two columns. The only way to do this is to make it part of the caption and then center it. WordPerfect was being finicky, and didn't want to let me insert a lot of codes in the caption, but it would let me do this.

[Hyph On][L/R Mar:1.25",0.75"][T/B Mar:0.75",0.75"]
[Footer A:2; ...][Figure:1;HOUSE.PCC;]<TA VT HML SH 1>
[Fig Opt]<O 0 0 .5 0>[Figure:2;BUNGALO.WPG;]<TA V2 HMR SH2>
[HRt]
[AdvUp:0.05"][HRt]
[Font:Slate Extra Bold 36pt (Port) (FW)]HomeFinders
[Flsh Rt][Font:Serifa Roman 11pt (Port) (FW)][BOLD]HomeWork Sheet[bold][C/A/Flrt][HRt]
[AdvUp:0.1"][Font:Serifa Roman 11pt (Port) (FW)]"We don't find houses, we find [BOLD]Homes[bold]"[HRt]
[HLine:Left & Right,5.44",0.01",100%][HRt]
[HRt]
[HRt]
[HRt]
[HRt]
[Just On][Col Def:3,1.25",4.37",4.62",6.1",6.35",7.75"][Col On]
[Style On:drop cap]T[Style Off:drop cap][Style On:firstpar]he Great American Dream of[SRt]
owning your own home is still[SRt]
possible for first[-]time buyers. [HRt]
[Style Off:firstpar][Ln Height:0.16"]
Footer:
[HLine:Left & Right,6.5",0.01",100%][AdvDn:0.1"][HRt]
[Figure:1;HOUSE.PCC;]<TP HR SH .33>
[Flsh Rt]321 Main Street, Alta Mira, Ca 90342
(213) 555[-]1342[C/A/Flrt][HRt]

HomeFinders

HomeWork Sheet

"We don't find houses, we find **Homes**"

The Great American Dream of owning your own home is still possible for first-time buyers.

We at **Home**Finders are dedicated to finding homes that you can afford, no matter what the cost. If we can't find you a home, we guarantee that one of our trained professionals will make you realize that you really didn't want a house after all.

Of course, because we look for low-priced homes, most of them are fixer-uppers (which means they aren't fit for man nor beast). But never mind about that—you want a house, you'll get a house. You want plumbing bills, you'll get plumbing bills (and every other kind of bill, too).

This house is much too nice for the likes of you. Still, drool over this: 2 bedrooms and a half bath. Close to shopping, the kitchen window faces the K-Mart loading dock!

This Week's Hot Home!

This little Spanish bungalow would make the perfect home for a growing family. The second floor is merely a false front to impress the neighbors. But there's plenty of room for expansion, should you want to add a real second story!

The house was built in 1942, just as building supplies were being rationed. But the developer was smart, and you'd never even know that the plumbing was made out of the hoses from his 1932 Model T. Custom-built doesn't even begin to describe this little enchilada.

Talk about local color! The tile roof was made of local mud and seepage from the famed LaBrea Tar Pits, some of which are located in your own backyard (and after big rains, your master bedroom). With a little loving care, elbow-grease, and a lot of cash, this could be the house of your dreams (or nightmares).

PRICE: **$197,500**

Vital Statistics

Bedrooms 2
Bathrooms . . . 1/2
Fireplace . . . . . NO
Garage . . . . . . NO
Pool . . . . NO
A/C . . . . NO
Central Heat . . NO
Carpet . . . . . . NO
Appliances . . . HA!
Ghosts: Does the word "Amityville" ring a bell?

SCHOOLS

Nursery:
Norman Bates Sunshine School (Accredited)

Elementary:
Benedict Arnold Lower School

High School:
Lizzie Borden Memorial Correctional Center

Alta Mira was incorporated in 1911, and has since become famous for it's frozen yogurt stands; 72 of them at last count.

This property is located not far from the Monda Vista Mile of Cars, with the largest assortment of used cars in the West.

The major employer is Asphalt Associated, and 55% of the locals are involved in tar collection.

Caption:
[AdvDn:0.1"][ITALC]This house is much too nice for the likes of...
[Font:Serifa Bold 11pt (ASCII) (Port) (FW)][Cntr]Vital Statistics[C/A/Flrt]
Paired Style for Raised Cap
[Font:Slate Extra Bold 36pt (ASCII) (Port)(FW)] [Comment]
Paired Style for Firstpar (First Paragraph)
[LARGE][Ln Height:0.22"] [Comment]
Paired Style for Subhead
[HLine:Left & Right,3.12",0.01",100%][HRt]
[Ln Height:Auto][Font:Serifa Bold 18pt (ASCII) (Port) (FW)][BOLD] [Comment]

❖ *Proposal — Making It Count*

Experience Level: ***Intermediate***

- **Fonts:** Bitstream Zapf Humanist (Optima) 12pt
- **Graphics:** MGI Publisher's PicturePak-CGM, Finance/Administration
- **Printer:** Hewlett-Packard LaserJet II

Notes: You might want to use the single coin graphics as bullets. Each level of bullets could be a smaller denomination of coin.

[W/O Off][Hyph On][T/B Mar:1",0.75"][L/R Mar:1.25",0.7"]
[Fig Opt]<BNNNN>[Figure:1;FI0146.CGM;]<TA VB HMR SB .3 .3>{Coin at bottom}
[Font:Zapf Humanist Roman 14pt (ASCII) (Port) (FW)]
[Wrd/Ltr Spacing:Optimal,200% of Optimal][ITALC]
Cash in the Real World[italc]
[Wrd/Ltr Spacing:Optimal,Optimal][AdvUp:0.1"][HRt]
[HLine:Left & Right,6.55",0.1",100%][Tab Set:3.33",5.7"][HRt]
[HRt]
[Font:Zapf Humanist Bold 30pt (ASCII) (Port) (FW)][Flsh Rt]
Making it Count[C/A/Flrt]
[HRt]
[Font:Zapf Humanist Roman 14pt (ASCII) (Port) (FW)]
[Col Def:3,1.25",2.75",3",5.3",5.5",7.8"][Col On][HRt]
[HRt]
[HRt]
[HRt]
[Figure:2;FI0143.CGM;]<HB>[AdvUp:0.2"][Figure:3;COINS.WPG;]<HB>
[HPg][Ln Height:0.19"][Usr Opt]<G100>
[Usr Box:1;;]<TC VB SB .1 .1>{This is the square bullet}
[Font:Zapf Humanist Bold 18pt (ASCII) (Port) (FW)]
Time, Money[HRt]and Com-puters[Ln Height:0.22"][HRt]
[Font:Zapf Humanist Italic 14pt (ASCII) (Port) (FW)](or how to use one[HRt]

Making it Count

Time, Money and Computers

(or how to use one to save the other two)

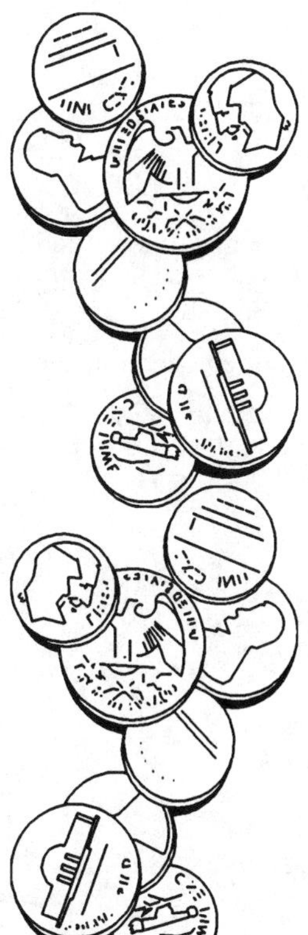

"Time is Money." One of the great cliches of all time. Another popular and pervasive myth, is that if you throw enough money into computers, you somehow create extra time from the ether; sit down in front of a machine and you will instantly work harder and produce more.

The hype that surrounds computers makes you think if you have enough money you can buy time. This fiction is somehow comforting. The truth is that computers *aren't* inherently efficient and productive.

They *are* inherently frustrating, maddening, and difficult. They require much thought and concentration, something not in vogue this year. They also require effort, also unpopular.

And the results? The results are that you work just as hard, but in different ways. At first it's far harder to do something on a computer than to do it by hand. You try to tell the machine to do something, but it doesn't understand what you mean, so you have to learn its language as well as your own.

But after enough trial and error, after enough tension and stress, computers start to pay off. They do what you want. If you leave it at that, you will save time from there on in, until the machine breaks, which it inevitably will.

But if you get hooked, if you get reeled in—that's it. You'll spend hours, days, weeks, months, years, learning new things, experimenting, discovering. And it's wonderful. You have fun in ways you never knew existed.

However, if you're not careful, it can hit you. The desire to learn how to do things you have no intention of ever using, just to learn them. You've never been near a spreadsheet, but you find yourself in a store buying a spreadsheet program, learning what statistical formulas are, even though you don't believe statistics.

And then you're lost. You spend all your time in the quest to master software, to know its ins-and-outs, and you forget that you originally got the computer so you'd never have to retype anything ever again.

Therein lies the danger. Not with the fun. But with forgetting what you originally obtained a computer to do. With forgetting everything but the computer.

Then slowly, almost imperceptibly, the unthinkable happens. Before you know it, you've become:

A SLAVE TO TECHNOLOGY.

[Ln Height:0.19"][Font:Zapf Humanist Roman 12pt (ASCII) (Port) (FW)][Just On][AdvDn:0.2"]
[VLine:Column 1,3.13",7.21",.0155Dc,100%]"Time is Money...

❖ *Cover pages — Butterfly*

Experience Level: ***Easy***

- **Fonts:** Bitstream Galliard, 14 pt
- **Graphics:** Dynamic Graphics Desktop Art, Four Seasons, edited with PC Paintbrush Plus
- **Printer:** Hewlett-Packard LaserJet II

Notes: This graphic is bitmapped at only 75 dpi. Because the resolution is so low, there's no sense to print the page with graphics quality set to high. If it's going to be jagged, you might as well make the most of it. Actually, this should have been either smoother, or more jagged. If the picture of the butterfly had been line-art, I could have scaled it to any size without a loss of quality.

[Fig Opt]<BOOOO>{Oooh, Scary} [Figure:1;BUTTERFL.PCC;]<TA VF WN>{This is the box around the page}[HRt]
[HRt]
[HRt]
[Cntr][Font:ITC Galliard Bold 14pt (ASCII) (Port) (FW)]
[Wrd/Ltr Spacing:Optimal,150% of Optimal]
This year we'll[C/A/Flrt][HRt]
[HRt]
[Cntr][BOLD][Font:ITC Galliard Italic 36pt (ASCII) (Port) (FW)]Sting Like A Bee[C/A/Flrt][bold][HRt]
[Font:ITC Galliard Bold Italic 18pt (ASCII) (Port) (FW)][HRt]
[Wrd/Ltr Spacing:Optimal,Optimal][Cntr]BFD International[C/A/Flrt][HRt]
[Font:ITC Galliard Italic 18pt (ASCII) (Port) (FW)]
[Cntr]Annual Report[C/A/Flrt]
[HRt]
[Cntr]1989[C/A/Flrt][HRt]
[HRt] {*Press [HRt five more times)*
[Tab Set:3",5.5"][AdvDn:0.1"][Font:ITC Galliard Bold 14pt (Port) (FW)]
[Tab]CEO's Statement[Align]3[C/A/Flrt][HRt]
[Tab]Big Bucks[Align]5[C/A/Flrt][HRt]
[Tab]Takeover Attempts[Align]7[C/A/Flrt][HRt]
[Tab]Five Year Plan[Align]9[C/A/Flrt][SPg]

This year we'll

Sting Like A Bee

BFD International

Annual Report

1989

❖ Report/Newsletter — BFD International

Experience Level: ***Intermediate***

- **Fonts:** Bitstream Futura Light, Condensed, & Extra Black, 11 pt
- **Graphics:** Harvard Graphics
- **Printer:** Hewlett-Packard LaserJet II

Notes: Even without the chart, these pages are sharp. Business-like without being dull, stylish without being overly-trendy. They have a subtle insouciance, not unlike a spicy little Diverstrimeiner. Anyway it's a good example of how pages can be interesting even without graphics, and how something as simple as a header can bring continuity, style, and increased corporate (or personal) awareness to a document. Don't try to figure the graph out, it means nothing (no, it means less than nothing as it's really the wrong kind of graph to use). But what the hay, it's impressive.

```
[T/B Mar:1",0.25"][W/O Off][HRt][HLine:Left,2.04",0.05",100%][HRt]
[HRt]
[Font:Futura Extra Black 72pt (ASCII) (Port) (FW)]BFD[HRt]
[AdvUp:0.3"][Font:Futura Light 11pt (ASCII) (Port) (FW)]
[BOLD][Wrd/Ltr Spacing:Optimal,220% of Optimal]International
[Wrd/Ltr Spacing:Optimal,Optimal][bold][HRt]
[HLine:Left & Right,6.5",0.05",20%][HLine:Left,2.04",0.05",100%][HRt]
[HRt]
[Flsh Rt][Font:Futura Condensed Medium 18pt (Port) (FW)]
[Wrd/Ltr Spacing:150% of Optimal,150% of Optimal]5 Year Plan[C/A/Flrt][Wrd/Ltr
Spacing:Optimal,Optimal]
[Font:Futura Condensed Medium 14pt (ASCII) (Port) (FW)][HRt]
[HRt]{23, don't count 'em, 23 returns in all}
[Flsh Rt][Font:Futura Extra Black 72pt (Port) (FW)]'89[C/A/Flrt][HRt]
[AdvUp:0.2"][HLine:Right,1.71",0.05",100%][HPg]
```

5 Year Plan

❖ PAGE 2

[Font:Futura Light 12pt (ASCII) (Port) (FW)][T/B Mar:1“,1”]
[Hyph On][Header A:2;]{See below for complete header}[Just On]
[Col Def:2,1.5",3.9",4.15",7.5"][Col On][Tab Set:1.75",4.63"]
[Fig Opt]<BNNEO>
[Figure:1;US-THEM.CGM;]<TA VB HC2B>{graph}
[Style On:heading][BOLD]Take The Money & Run[bold][HRt]
[Style Off:heading][HRt]

Take The Money & Run

By B. Friedreich Dunn, CEO

Let's face it, greed is hip. Ron & Nancy have made conspicuous consumption the Eighties replacement for Jimmy and Rosalyn's unpopular social consciousness and civic responsibility.

And why not? It works. Who wants to think about the homeless when they can think about remodelling their home? Who cares about the needy when they need a new VCR?

All those poor, sick people are downers; sitting around on the street, making things so dirty you don't even want to take the Mercedes out anymore.

So we at BFD have the alternative. Cocooning is the hot buzz word at the moment, and who better than us to capitalize on it, and wring every last cent possible from this burgeoning market.

This year we've created two wholly-owned subsidiaries: *BFD-TV* and *Serf-City*. The first is dedicated to the new breed of Americans who can entertain themselves at home. They bring back the American ideal of self-sufficiency.

BFD-TV is a combined cable channel, and video tape delivery service. The customer doesn't even have to decide what they want to watch. First, our computerized *Personality-Probe* runs a battery of psychological tests on the customer. Not only does the customer not have to make the difficult decision as to what they want to watch, our system even knows when they want to watch.

The cable arm of *BFD-TV* provides an eclectic mix of programming, consisting of whatever we could get the cheapest. Of course, we are heralding this programming mix as "MacroTV" a clinically-designed system that stimulates, educates, and decorates.

Serf-City is an entirely new concept in personal services. While we live in a "service economy," it seems that good service is hard to find.

For about the same amount as you'd pay monthly on a Range Rover, Serf-City provides a 24-hour hotline. Anything a client wants (within legal limits), we'll get for them.

In our test market, Serf-City was deemed "Indispensable" by 75 percent of the users within the first month. Everything from groceries to plastic surgeons—all the necessities of life are brought to your door within 30 minutes (or you pay nothing). You can't buy time, but you can buy convenience: someone to go to the dry

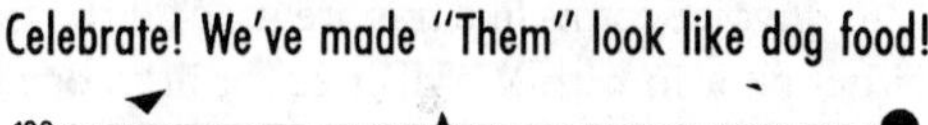

Celebrate! We've made "Them" look like dog food!

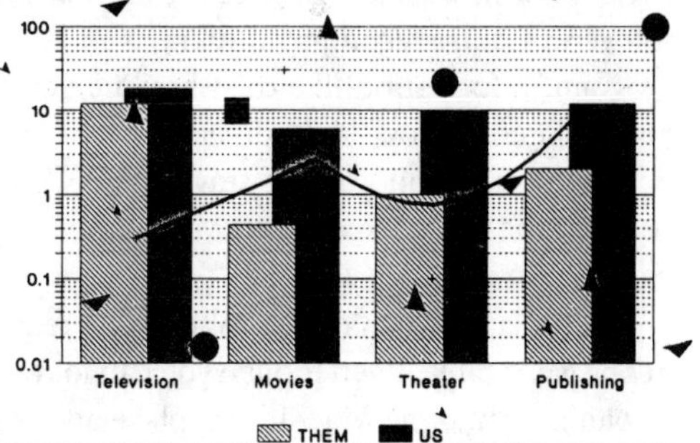

❖ PAGE 3

Everything was automatic, except for the readout, which is text in a graphics figure box. The ruling lines were set with the Figure Options on page 2.

HEADER: {This contains the company logo which automatically prints on each page}
[L/R Mar:0.75",1"][HLine:Left,0.85",0.03",100%][HRt]
[AdvDn:0.15"][Font:Futura Extra Black 30pt (ASCII) (Port) (FW)]BFD[HRt]
[AdvUp:0.15"][Font:Futura Light 11pt (ASCII) (Port) (FW)]International
[Flsh Rt][Font:Futura Condensed Medium 14pt (Port) (FW)] Page ^ B[C/A/Flrt][HRt]
[HLine:Left,0.85",0.03",100%][HLine:Left & Right,6.75",0.03",20%][HRt]
[VLine:1.25",2.19",7.81",0.01",100%]

Paired Style for Heading
[HLine:Left,1.88",0.03",100%][AdvDn:0.M1"][HRt]
[Font:Futura Condensed Medium 18pt (ASCII) (Port) (FW)] [Comment]

❖ Invoice — Classical Accoutrements *Illustration appears on page 139*

Experience Level: ***Easy/5.1 codes only***

- Fonts: Bitstream Swiss Condensed) 10 pt, Bitstream ITC Galliard
- **Graphics:** Publisher's PicturePak-CGM, Sales/Marketing
- **Printer:** LaserMaster LX6 - Hewlett-Packard LaserJet III

Invoice forms like this are used all the time, and this one looks very professional. You can either fill it in with WordPerfect or just copy this and fill it in by hand, or using your database software. I don't recommend filling it in WordPerfect because WordPerfect is not a database program. Information like this should be stored in a database where it can be accessed and manipulated. If you don't already have a database, I recommend either Nutshell (from Iris Software) or, if you want to stay in the WordPerfect family, DataPerfect. You can use merge codes in the table, export from your database, and then do a merge to have WordPerfect print your info in this lovely format.

This is made up of *four* tables. The reason it isn't one giant table is that it can't be done in one giant table. Even though you can join several columns to make them look wider in parts, a column cannot be wider in one place and narrower in another. This means that even though you could join and split the table so that it would have five rows in the middle, you couldn't make these rows even, as they are here. They'd have to be the same width as the rows elsewhere in the table.

cleaner, someone to massage your feet, someone to read bed-time stories to you, whatever.

Serf-City has the potential to change the way people live, and certainly change the way we live (as it requires minimal overhead, yet has maximum profit potential).

Last year it was "excellence," this year it's profits. Wait until you see what we've got up our collective sleeves for the next five years. Huge unjustified profits.

Last, but certainly not least, this year we will launch a new line of personal accessories. The cornerstone to this entire product line is called ''Orb.'' Developed by a noted Dutch psychiatrist (in cooperation with Jackie Collins), *Orb* is the ultimate personal codicil.

Fundamentally, the product is as simple as baby food for adults. The product helps adults to re-live their childhood, but it's also great for commuters, because it doesn't spill. What's more, it's better for your teeth than sucking your thumb.

Orb doubles as a flask or canteen. It can be used be used to sprinkle vinegar on salads. Unbreakable and dishwasher safe, *Orb* helps improve the reflexes and instills a feeling of relaxation and security. Deluxe models are packaged with a small blue blanket.

So much for our plans. As always, or overriding goal, our main ambition, the thing that guides us through those brutal union-bashing sessions is *Money*. People talk about it like it's a dirty word. You're not supposed to admit you like it, you're not supposed to admit you want it, and whatever you do, don't admit that you like making it.

Balderdash. You can like it, you can want it, and you can enjoy making it. But if you're smart, the thing you'll enjoy most is making the most of it.

Something for Nothing, was our motto this year. ''Value for Money'' is passe, but according to our market research, that's what *everyone* wanted. We at BFD were ready to give it to them.

Unfortunately, our demographics sucked the big one, and while the supply was there, the demand wasn't. What went wrong? That's what we asked ourselves all spring. The answer came in the form of my 12 year old daughter. ''Dad, have you lost your marbles? Everyone wants it, but everyone also knows you can't get it. Who'd be taken in by such hype?'' Who indeed? We were. Seeing how Melissa saw right through our $250,000 PR firm's supposed findings, we thought we'd promote her to VP of Marketing. After all, she was exactly the market we were going for: pre-teens, teens, and other minimal IQ individuals.

Melissa's first edict was that we had to hire someone ''neato'' to be our spokesman. Barry Manilow was ruled out immediately with

❖ *Invoice — Classical Accoutrements continued*

To make the four tables *look* like one single table, make sure you don't have any [HRt] codes between the [Tbl Off] code of one table and the [Tbl Def:] of the next table.

The first table includes the word "invoice," the date, and invoice number. Here's the definition code:

[Tbl Def:I;3,2.25",2.25",2.25"]

The second table includes the Bill to and Ship to titles and space for data (the space for data is a single cell for each Bill to and Ship to and will expand and contract in height depending on the data you place in it. This is far easier to enter than having a separate table cell for each row of the name and address. Here is the table def for #2:

[Tbl Def:II;2,3.38",3.38"]

The third table includes from F.O.B to Blanket Order Number:

[Tbl Def:III;5,1.35",1.35",1.35",1.35",1.35"]

The fourth table goes from ITEM# to the Notes cell. The notes cell is a single cell, made by joining all the cells in the last row of the table. Here's table #4:

[Tbl Def:IV;7,0.868",2.16",0.691",0.691",0.691",0.778",0.87"]

In all cases the heading cells are locked for two reasons. First, whoever is entering the information can't accidentally change the normal standing title, and second, you can then press the tab key to jump through the table without landing on any of the heading cells.

The table headings are all bolded through the table, not by F6. To do this, block the cells, then press F C A A B. If your titles are a different typeface or size from the text which you fill-in, I recommend that you create styles for the titles in your table. It's easier that way.

The Table Math feature has been used here to automatically calculate results. The cells in the last column use the same formula copied from row C using the Math coPy formula command. The formula in row C is (C4*F4)*.9 which multiples order times unit price and then multiplies that times .9 to give a 10% discount. The "subtotal" cell's formula is a very simple "+" which tells WordPerfect to add the numbers directly above the cell.

If you place a single $ in the cells which require calculation, WordPerfect will place the calculated figure after the dollar sign.

I've included the 0.00s to show you what happens if you have formulas in cells, but nothing to calculate. Instead of just putting nothing in the cell, WordPerfect puts 0.00.

If you're wondering why the **Notes:** section isn't in the area to the left of the subtotal, it's because of the way WordPerfect handles cells. If you have short notes, you can place them there, but notes as long as this one would have vertically stretched the Subtotal, Tax, and Grand Total cells so that they were twice as tall.

Sometimes when you are filling in these tables, WordPerfect will not move down to the next table when you press a [DOWN ARROW] key. It insists that you use a [RIGHT ARROW] key. I hope they change this, but nobody asks me. Also, don't try to search for text in locked cells (WordPerfect can't).

The LaserMaster controller card (used here in conjunction with a LaserJet III printer), not only provides higher-resolution text, but finer "gray" screens as well. Notice how the shaded areas of the table have a screen so fine you can hardly see the dots.

Classical Accoutrements

710 N. Bupkiss Pkwy., Helen of Troy, PA 15219, 412-555-1206

INVOICE	Date	Invoice #
	12/23/90	4U-N-E-TH1-NG

Bill To:	Ship To:
Wilton Veneer MetroSpace Inc. 2117 Placido Domingo Place Newbury, CT 10101 (201) 555-5555	Erica Kane 17 Agnes Oaks Pine Valley, PA 20123 (407) 555-2333

F.O.B. Point	Customer Order #	Ship Via	Ship Complete	Type
London UK	555-74-7500	Concorde		RUSH!
Order Date	**Terms**	**Salesperson**	**Our P.O.**	**Blanket Order #**
10/29/90	Not so good	Rick Karvasales	N3334218	Pendleton

Item # Serial #	Description	Quantity Order	Back	Shipped	Unit Price	Extended Price
					Discount 10%	
1235PRCA	Obaloogoo Originals	2		2	$755.22	1,359.40
01019	Warhol Xeroxes	4	2	2	8,400.69	30,242.48
						0.00
						0.00
						0.00
						0.00
						0.00
						0.00
						0.00
					Subtotal	**$31,601.88**
					Tax	**$2,054.12**
					Grand Total	**$33,656.00**

Notes: Please inform Miss Kane that even though Mr. Warhol has been dead several years now, he left behind a stack of original signatures and made explicit notes in his will that these be used on new pieces after his death.

Andy's plan is as follows: the purchaser places the Warhol signature on the Xerox machine (preferably color) and then places their face (preferably profile) onto the glass of the Xerox machine. Miss Kane has purchased the right to repeat this procedure up to four times, at which time the signature (signed on special light sensitive paper) will fade.

As per the will, these will be considered signed originals because they are his original idea, and will be treated as such on the resale market.

❖ Catalog — Robot-a-Rama

Experience Level: ***Easy***

- **Fonts:** Bitstream Amerigo, 12pt
- **Graphics:** Left: MGI Publisher's PicturePak-CGM, Finance/Administration; middle & right: Metro ImageBase
- **Printer:** Hewlett-Packard LaserJet II

Notes: This is an extremely easy page to do, and it's good for catalogs or listings that have long descriptions. While the captions don't all look like they're the same length, I've added an extra return on the second one so WordPerfect considers it the same length. If you don't do that, the columns underneath won't all start on the same line.

[Hyph On][T/B Mar:1",0.75"][L/R Mar:1.25",1"]
[Footer A:2;[HLine:Left & Right,6.25",0.01",100%]
[Just Off][Font:Bitstrm Amerigo Bold 48pt (Port) (FW)]
[Wrd/Ltr Spacing:Optimal,160% of Optimal]
[Cntr]Robot[-]a[-]Rama
[Font:Bitstrm Amerigo Roman 11pt (ASCII) (Port) (FW)]
[Wrd/Ltr Spacing:Optimal,Optimal][C/A/Flrt][HRt]
[HRt][AdvUp:0.2"]
[Col Def:3,1.25",3.16",3.41",5.33",5.58",7.5"]<TN D .25>
[Col On][VLine:Column1,2.04",8.02",0.01",F2M100%]
[VLine:Column 2,2.04",8.02",0.01",100%]
[Figure:1;FI0249.CGM;]<TP HB SH 1.97>
{Caption has [AdvDn:0.1"]}
[Ln Height:0.16"][Style On:Raised Cap]B[Style Off:Raised Cap]ig News!
Paired Style for Raised Cap
[Font:Bitstrm Amerigo Bold 24pt (ASCII) (Port) (FW)] [Comment]
Open Style for Paragraph Indents
[AdvRgt:0.5"]

Robot-a-Rama

The Original, the Classic, the One and Only FiFi, as French as an android gets.

Big News! Robo-Fax announcess three new models, guaranteed to knock the socks off Robo-cops.

That's right—not one, not two, but three new house-keeping automatons to choose from.

Fifi is our original model, now **priced to sell, sell, sell.** She cooks, cleans, and tickles humans with her simulated ostrich feather duster.

FiFi may be getting a little long in the transistor, but she's a proven design, kind of like the Dodge Dart of the Android set.

FiFi was the **winner of the 1997 Antarctica World's Fair** Household Robotics competition. Rumor has it that she was modeled after Catherine Denuve, and that's why her head constantly tilts to one side.

She may be a little on the homely side, but you weren't going to take her out dancing... were you?

LaWanda, a hot little number (actually serial # 5117).

Ultra feminine. Now here's an android to take dancing! There'll be a hot time in the old town tonight when you bring home LaWanda to La-Bamba.

LaWanda is specially engineered to withstand extensive shimmying and shaking without breaking.

PlayDroid magazine called LaWanda **"A hot little number in lycra and stainless steel."**

She's a combination drill-sergeant/belly-dancer, and is pre-programmed to kill intruders.

While LaWanda is a little lax on the dustballs, she'll keep you hopping. A few of our beta testers have stated that it's hard to keep up with her, but we didn't hear any complaints.

Andrew Roid, the latest thing in male models. Anatomically correct.

You know a good man's hard to find, but who needs a man when they can have our latest robotic model. He kills scary insets, does household repairs, and doesn't complain about your hair or your cooking. *What more you could want?*

Reliability? You may never have met a male before who was reliable, but Andy's been programmed to run for years without routine maintenance. We guarantee you won't even have to raise his hood for the first 12 months or 12,000 miles.

Power? You got it. Able to leap tall buildings, move heavy refrigerators, even act as a nautilus machine/expert trainer.

Handling? Your wish is his command—it's easy to wrap him around your little finger.

Price? Less than you think for. All with a full 90 minute warranty.

❖ Documentation — Pie Throwing

Experience Level: ***Easy***

- **Fonts:** Bitstream Hammersmith (Gill Sans) 12 pt
- **Graphics:** Scanned from Dynamic Graphics paper clip-art using a Hewlett-Packard ScanJet and GEM Scan software
- **Printer:** Hewlett-Packard LaserJet II

Notes: This page uses parallel columns and is genuinely easy to create. Instead of graphics, you could use keystrokes (with SoftCraft's wonderful KeyCap font) or make the first column wider and use this area for screen dumps. While I've used Hammersmith (Gill Sans) for headlines and subheads in this book, it is an extremely popular typeface for body copy as well, especially in England and Europe. It's a sans serif font with a lot of character, modern without being cold.

[Fig Opt]<BNNNN>[Just On][T/B Mar:1",0.75"]
[L/R Mar:1.25",0.75"][L/R Mar:0.75",1.25"]
[Footer B:4;[Open Style:footer]
[Par Num Def][Just Lim:60,110][Style On:Headline]Pie throwing for fun & profit[Style Off:Headline][HRt]
[HRt]
[Ln Height:0.19"][Col Def:2,0.75",1.75",2",7.25"][Col On][Style On:sidehead]
[LARGE]R[large]eady[HRt]
[HRt]
[Figure:1;BAKERR.PCC;]<TP HB>[HRt]
[HRt]
[HRt]
[Style Off:sidehead][HPg]
Paired Style for Headline
[Font:Hammersmith Roman 36pt (ASCII) (Port) (FW)] [Comment]
Paired style for Headline
[Font:Hammersmith Roman 36pt (ASCII) (Port) (FW)][BOLD]. [Comment]
Paired style for Sideheads
[HLine:Left,1",0.01",100%][HRt][JustOff]
[Wrd/Ltr Spacing:150% of Optimal,150% ofOptimal]
[Font:Hammersmith Italic 18pt (ASCII) (Port)(FW)] [Comment]
Paired style for Readout
[Ln Height:Auto][AdvDn:0.1"]
[Font:Hammersmith Roman 14pt (ASCII) (Port) (FW)]
[Comment]
[AdvDn:0.1"][Ln Height:0.19"]
[Font:Hammersmith Roman 11pt (ASCII) (Port) (FW)]

4. Pie throwing for fun & profit

Ready

Pie throwing is a classic piece of schtik, invented by Cleopatra as a way to pass the time when Marc Anthony was away. It became a favorite of Greek playwrights, and its first known inclusion in dramatic form was in Aristophanes' "The Birds." Pie throwing in film and television reached its apex with Laurel & Hardy, and later, Soupy Sales.

First, you must obtain a pie. The cream variety is preferable to the fruit variety, for several of the reasons listed below.

- It is lighter, and more easily maneuverable.
- It makes a stronger visual impression.
- It is easier to clean up.
- It doesn't stain clothing.
- Cream is more fun to lick off of one's face.

Throwing a pie is a lot like throwing a tantrum, only requiring choreography and a keener aim.

Aim...

When choosing a subject to be the recipient of a pie in the face, you are looking for someone who won't object too much.

1. The subject will be the object of much speculation about his/her level of sportsmanship, so try to choose someone who doesn't have a proven track record of getting even.
2. This person should not be a direct superior with the power to hire and fire (unless, of course, this is no longer a problem, and is in fact, the catalyst for the episode. In that case, go for it—what have you got to lose?).

WARNING: Choose your subjects carefully. Not all personality types react positively to pie attacks. Never, under any circumstances, throw a pie at the President, or President elect. Secret Service agents will wrestle you to the ground, and besides getting a lot of unwanted media attention, your FBI file will expand by leaps and bounds. The Vice President however, is fair game.

Fire!

PIE VELOCITY AND TRAJECTORY

Peanut Butter has a velocity of 120% and a -25° angle correction is advised. Mud pies have a velocity of 77% and a +16° angle correction is needed. Key Lime pie, always a big favorite with the menfolk, has a velocity of 82% and requires a +13° angle correction. Be sure to adjust the trajectory, depending on what kind of pie you are using. If using a cream pie, not as much velocity will be necessary as if using a fruit pie.

Different pies will create different stains, and require different methods for removal of those stains. The easiest stain to remove is created by the Lemon Chiffon pie, and is easily removed with lemon dishwashing liquid. Banana Cream pie stains can be removed with white wine, and Blueberry pie stains are impossible to remove.

Open style for Footer
[HLine:Left & Right,6.5",0.05",100%][HRt]
[AdvDn:0.1"][Font:Hammersmith Roman 11pt (ASCII) (Port) (FW)]Pie Throwing Manual[Flsh Rt] ^ B

❖ *Menu — Dutch Pancake House*

Experience Level: ***Easy***

- **Fonts:** Weaver Graphics BG (Benguiat) 14pt, Weaver Dingbats (both Benguiat and Dingbats are now also available from Bitstream)
- **Graphics:** Corner border: Arts & Letters; Pancake: Metro Image Base
- **Printer:** Hewlett-Packard LaserJet II

Notes: Type the entire menu, then center it at once by blocking it, then pressing SHIFT-F6. Benguiat is a beautiful typeface, perfect for short pieces of text such as this. Don't use it to set the type for an entire book or magazine, though.

[L/R Mar:1.25",1"][Fig Opt]<BNNNN>
[Figure:1;CORNER4.CGM;]<TA VT HML SW 1.5 WN>
[Figure:2;CORNER4.CGM;]<TA VT HMR SW 1.5 WN>
[Figure:3;CORNER4.CGM;]<TA VB HML SW 1.5 WN>
[Figure:4;CORNER4.CGM;]<TA VB HMR SW 1.5 WN>
[Figure:5;PANCAKE.WPG;]<HC SW 2>[HRt]
[HRt] {*Press [HRt eight more times*}
[BOLD][Font:Benguiat 30pt (SF) (LF)][Cntr]M[Style On:dingbat] u
[Style Off:dingbat] E [Style On:dingbat]u[Style Off:dingbat] N
[Style On:dingbat]u[Style Off:dingbat] U[C/A/Flrt][bold][HRt]
[Font:Benguiat 14pt (SF) (LF)]
KES[C/A/Flrt][large][bold][Wrd/Ltr Spacing:Optimal,Optimal][HRt]
[AdvDn:0.1"][Cntr]Ham & Cheese $4.75[C/A/Flrt][HRt]

Paired Style for dingbat (diamonds)
[Font:Zapf Dingbats 14pt (SF) (LF)][AdvUp:0.06"]
[Comment]
[AdvDn:0.06"]
{The advance moves the dingbats up so they print in the middle of the line, rather than on the baseline.}

M ◆ E ◆ N ◆ U

SAVORY PANCAKES

Ham & Cheese $4.75
Gouda or Edam, your choice

Smoked Sausage $4.50
With that farm-fresh flavor

SWEET PANCAKES

Apple $3.75
Warm, cinnamon-spiced apples

Blueberry $3.75
Fresh blueberries, direct from Maine

Raspberry $3.75
Ripe, luscious red berries

Met slagroom (whipped cream) add $1.50

My Old Dutch Pancake House

We reserve the right to serve refuse to anyone.

❖ Brochure — Travel

Experience Level: ***Challenging/Painful***

- **Fonts:** Weaver Friz Quadrata 12pt (SoftCraft LaserFonts Manager installed the fonts, and created the outline and shadow versions of this font)
- **Graphics:** MGI Publisher's PicturePak-CGM, Sales/Marketing
- **Printer:** Hewlett-Packard LaserJet II

Notes: This is a very complicated, very busy layout. It took a long time to figure out and perfect. I almost didn't use it in this book because it was verging on "sequin," but if you like this kind of look, here's proof that you can get it. If you were going to use this over and over, it would be worth the investment, as you'd only need to insert new text and graphics. If you wanted to use photos, you could scan them (use TIF format for photos) or just leave spaces and have the printer insert the halftones.

The "Astral Travel" logo uses the Option Printer Word Spacing function to an extreme, with a different amount of space between each letter, starting at 200% and working it's way down to 100% by the end of "Travel." Very over the top. I haven't included the specs for all the pictures because this book is too long as it is. All are figures with no lines around. Mt. Rushmore and the cruise ship have wrap turned off.

```
[W/O Off][T/B Mar:0.5",0.5"][T/B Mar:1",0.25"][L/R Mar:1",0.5"]
[Fig Opt]<BNNNN>[Figure:1;SA0199.CGM;]<TP HR SH .95>
[HRt]
[Font:Friz Quadrata 30pt (SC)][OUTLN]
[Wrd/Ltr Spacing:Optimal,200% of Optimal]Astral
[Wrd/Ltr Spacing:Optimal,150% of Optimal][outln][SHADW]T
[Wrd/Ltr Spacing:Optimal,140% of Optimal]r
[Wrd/Ltr Spacing:Optimal,130% of Optimal]a
[Wrd/Ltr Spacing:Optimal,120% of Optimal]v
[Wrd/Ltr Spacing:Optimal,110% of Optimal]e
[Wrd/Ltr Spacing:Optimal,Optimal]l[shadw]
[Wrd/Ltr Spacing:Optimal,Optimal]Agents[HRt]
[Font:Friz Quadrata 14pt (SC)]SUMMER BULLETIN[HRt]
[Font:Friz Quadrata 11pt (SC)]Vol. 1. No. 33
"Literally, the Vacation of Your Dreams"
{Spaces, yes spaces to move date to the right}August 8, 1988
[Font:Friz Quadrata 11pt (SC)][HRt]
[HLine:Left & Right,7",0.01",100%][HRt]
[HRt] {Press another [HRt]
[Col Def:4,1",2.5",2.7",5.3",5.4",5.9",6.1",8"]<TP>[Col On]
[Style On:Sidehead]Straighten[HRt]up and Fly[SRt] {Continued...}
```

Astral Travel Agents

SUMMER BULLETIN

Vol. 1. No. 33 "Literally, the Vacation of Your Dreams" August 8, 1988

Straighten up and Fly Right

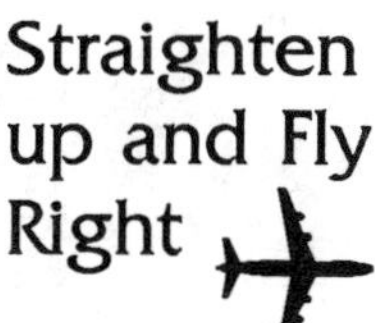

Airports. Reservations. Certain Restrictions may apply. Customs. Long flights with crying babies. Lost luggage. These are a few of the things that make travel, something that ought to be a pleasure, a pain.

That's where we at **Astral**Travel come in: to give you the vacation of your dreams (or perhaps literally, in your dreams).

We supply everything you'll need, from maps of the area, to lists of the best places to eat. There's never an accommodation problem because you never stay overnight!

Astral-Travel: Your passport to a world of potential

Astral travel is fast and easy. And don't worry about safety—time tested by Yogi's over the last three thousand years, at last you'll get exactly what you want—without ever leaving home.

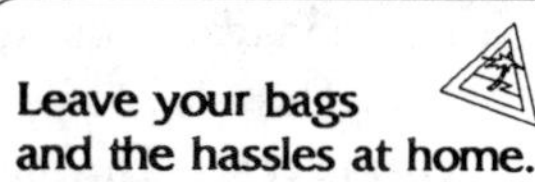

Leave your bags
and the hassles at home.

North by Northwest

There's more than one way to see the sights. How about from the inside of Teddy Roosevelt's nose? Or from an orbit of 25,000 miles above the Earth?

Travel back to ancient Rome and learn the true meaning of "Lorem ipsum dolor sit."

AstralTravel will make sure you'll see the world like you've never seen it before.

Whether it's by stream of consciousness or steam train, Astral-Travel's the only way to fly!

You're the top with Astral-Travel!

Fully guided **Astral**Tours start at only $50 per hour once you've completed our $450 weekend training seminar (includes a vegetarian lunch for both days, and a **AT** beach towel for meditation).

In as little as six hours, Frequent Flyers can start to earn bonus trips to all those out-of-this-world places.

Sea the USA!

Let Mark Twain take you steamboating on the Mississippi. Thrill to the Bermuda Triangle at midnight. See Davy Jones in his locker. Ain't no mountain high enough, Ain't no valley low enough, nothing is ever **out of the question,** nothing is ever **out of your reach.** The only limit is your own imagination. Ask Shirley McClaine, she'll tell you, there's nothing like it.

Around the World in 80 ways

Ride a dolphin to Atlantis, a Blue whale to the coast of Mexico, or just take Shamu for a ride around the tank. **Astral**Travel is open 24 hours a day, for everything from a daydream to a full night's dream. But rest assured, you'll never have a nightmare.

AstralTravel is a fully bonded member of the AAA, the Astral Agent's Association

Paired Style for Sideheads
[Font:Friz Quadrata 18pt (SC)][Comment]
Open Style for Captions
[Font:Friz Quadrata 9pt (SC)][Comment]

❖ Price List — KidStuff

Experience Level: ***Easier than it looks. Intermediate***

- **Fonts:** Bitstream Cooper Light 11pt, Bitsream Cooper Black
- **Printer:** Hewlett-Packard LaserJet II

Notes: While this page was created with parallel columns, it could also be created using tables. Parallel columns were used here because price lists are often more than a single page long and text of this type is easier to handle in columns than in tables.

This is a good example of how you can take advantage of 5.1's ability to print its entire character set. The smilely faces are character 5,8 (press CONTROL-V first). They act as bullets and they're also fun. WP's character set includes many interesting and attention-getting characters which make excellent bullets. (If you're into "cute," the LaserJet III's happy face is "way cute.")

If you print to a LaserJet and WordPerfect is printing these characters very small instead of the size you wanted, it could be because WordPerfect knows that the LaserJet has this character and would rather use it than make it itself. If this happens to you, go into printer edit (SHIFT-F7 S E C) and remove any fonts which say (PC-8). The PC character set has all the little characters you can see on-screen and by removing them, WordPerfect is forced to print these characters as graphics.

The giant exclamation point on the right consists of a WordPerfect graphics box with a 100% background and a 36-point 5,8 character. The bullets are 18-point 5,8's. The KIDstuff logo combines 30-point Cooper Black for the "KID" with 36-point Cooper Light for the "stuff".

5.0: if you need very large bullets, you can use periods from very large fonts. A 30-point Cooper Black period is quite large. With Fontware 3 you could create a custom character set which contained only the period character at 72 or 144 point for really giant bullets that didn't take much disk space or printer memory.

[T/B Mar:1",0.75"][L/R Mar:1",0.75"]
[Fig Opt]<G100>Figure:1;;]<TA VT HMR SB .2 7.5 WN>
[Fig Opt]<G0>[Figure:2;;]<TA V8.4 HMR SB .2 .3 WN>
[L/R Mar:1.25",1.25"]
[Footer A:2; ...]<LH [ENTER] [ENTER]>
[Font:Bitstream Cooper Black 30pt (ASCII) (Port) (FW)]
[Flsh Rt]KID[Font:Bitstream Cooper Light 36pt (Port)(FW)]
stuff[Font:Bitstream Cooper Light Italic 18pt (Port)(FW)][C/A/Flrt][HRt]
[Flsh Rt]What's New![C/A/Flrt]
[Open Style:line][AdvUp:0.1"]
[Font:Bitstream Cooper Light 11pt (ASCII) (Port) (FW)]

KIDstuff
What's New!

☻ **Barbi's Alfred Hitchcock Theatre**

Enter Barbi's world of terror and the unknown. This horrific set includes Norman Bates and Brian DePalma dolls!

Quantity	Price
1	$33.50
5	$33.00
10	23.50
25	$23.00

☻ **Sticky Wickets**

A fun way for kids to clean up their room. Sticky Wickets attract dustballs but are safe for pets!

Quantity	Price
1-10	$3.99
11-25	$2.99
REFILLS:	
10 per pack	$1.50

☻ **Little Baby Peabrain**

A perfectly charming but perfectly stupid little doll. Perfect for those pretend custody battles, and make believe surrogate parenthood!

Quantity	Price
1-10	$19.99
11-25	$17.99
26-100	$15.95

☻ **CLOSE OUT!**

Big sellers from past seasons we can't give away anymore. Yours for a song, even in Quantity 1!

SpaceSlime	$ .99
Nefarious Nutballs	$ .49
Dinky Little Dora	$1.25
Electro-Shock Experiment Kit	$4.99
Michael Jackson Makeup	$2.55
Ed Meese "Blinded Justice Kit"	$4.99
Piranha Pals	$1.99
Mary Hart Leg Waxing Set	$3.55

☻

KIDstuff
(415)-555-1122

"Where great toys are *child's play!*"
Prices good through March 1990

[Tab Set:1.48",7.25"][Col Def:3,1.25",3.08",3.33",5.16",5.41255D",7.25"]
<TP D .25>[Col On][Style On:Name]
Paired Style for Name
[Ln Height:0.27"]
[Font:Bitstream Cooper Black 30pt (Port)(FW)]
[AdvUp:0.06"].[AdvDn:0.06"]
[Font:Bitstream Cooper Bold 18pt(ASCII) (Port) (FW)]
[Indent][Comment]
Open Style for Line (horizontal rules between products)
[HRt]
[HLine:Left & Right,6",0.01",100%][HRt]
[HRt]
[AdvDn:0.1"][AdvUp:0.1"]

❖ Resume — F. Scott Fitzgerald

Experience Level: ***Intermediate***

- Fonts: Pacific Data Products "Z" Font Cartridge, Tms Rmn 12pt
- Printer: Hewlett-Packard LaserJet

Notes: Here's an example of how good a page can look with only relatively small font cartridge fonts and no graphics or artwork. The gray bar over the years is a WordPerfect User-defined box with wrap off, and the dotted lines are .1" tall graphics boxes inside a style.

[T/B Mar:1.5",1.5"][L/R Mar:1.25",1"][Font:Tms Rmn 14pt Bold (Z)]
[Wrd/Ltr Spacing:200% of Optimal,200% of Optimal]
F. Scott Fitzgerald[Font:Tms Rmn 12pt (Z)]
[Wrd/Ltr Spacing:Optimal,Optimal][HRt]
[AdvDn:0.1"][HLine:Left,3.5",0.01",100%][HRt]
[Font:Helv 12pt (Z)][AdvDn:0.1"]RESUME
[Font:Tms Rmn 12pt (Z)][HRt]
[Flsh Rt][ITALC]481 Laurel Avenue[C/A/Flrt][HRt]
[Flsh Rt]St. Paul, Minnesota[C/A/Flrt][HRt]
[Flsh Rt](330) 555[-]0924[C/A/Flrt][italc][HRt]
[Open Style:Horizontal[HRt]
[Col Def:2,1.5",3",3.25",7.25"][Col On]
[Style On:Subhead]Experience[Style Off:Subhead][HRt]
[HRt]
[Usr Opt]<G10>[Usr Box:1;;]<TA V3.25 HML SB.6 4.57 WN>
[AdvDn:0.1"][LARGE]1930[HRt] 1937[large][HPg]
Open Style Horizontal (for long solid lines:)
[AdvDn:0.1"][HLine:Left &Right,6.25",0.01",100%]
[AdvDn:0.1"][HRt][HRt]

F. Scott Fitzgerald

RESUME

481 Laurel Avenue
St. Paul, Minnesota
(330) 555-0924

Experience

1930 1937	Organized and conducted year-round social events for regular members of Hearst's International. Also arranged holiday programs and other fund raising drives for the beautiful and the damned.
1926 1929	Booked travel arrangements for yachting tours, museum days, seasonal picnics, and special "Rented is the Night" theater parties for Charles Scribner's Sons.
1922 1925	Extensively toured Europe, visited Babylon again. Researched and provided source material for quarterly newsletter listing new resorts and villas this side of paradise.
1917 1920	Entered military service. Member of the Army horse guards; aide-de-camp to Commanding General Monte Montgomery. Honorable discharge, 1920.

Education

Graduated Princeton University, 1917.

References

Jay Gatsby, East Egg, Long Island.
Dorothy Parker, Algonquin Hotel.

Paired Style for Subheads:
[Font:Helv 14pt Bold (Z)][Comment]
Paired Style for dotted lines
[Usr Opt]<BNNNO O0000.2>[Usr Box:1;;]<TP HR SB4.25 .1> [Comment]

❖ *Calendar — Bunny Run Preschool*

Experience Level: ***Easier than it looks/5.1 codes first***

- **Fonts:** Bitstream Futura Light, Condensed, Extra Bold, 11 pt
- **Graphics:** Dynamic Graphics Desktop Art, Education; edited with PC Paintbrush Plus
- **Printer:** Hewlett-Packard LaserJet II

Here's another calendar designed using a table. E-Z. What makes it look so dramatic is the use of Bitstream's Futura Light package. This one package contains all the fonts in this calendar: the attention-grabbing Futura Extra Black for the date numbers; the light and modern Futura Light for the body; and the space-saving Futura Condensed Medium for the days of the week and the information in the bottom row. The data numbers are automatic within the style. This is proof-positive what a difference a typeface can make.

The table begins with the days of the week, and the definition is:
[Tbl Def:I;7,1.13",1.13",1.13",1.13",2MI.13",1.13",1F255D.13"]

Here are the codes:
[Par Num Def:]<L>[T/B Mar:0.5",0.5"][L/R Mar:0.3",0.3"]
[Fig Opt]<BNNN>[Fig Box:1;SCHOOL.TIF;]<TP HL SH 1.4>
[Flsh Rgt][Font:Futura Extra Black 30pt]Bunny Run Pre[-]School [HRt]
[Font:Futura Condensed Medium 14pt][Flsh Rgt]for Troubled Teens [HRt][HRt]
[Flsh Rgt] S E P T E M B E R 1 9 9 9 [HRt][HRt]
[L/R Mar:0.3",0.3"][Font:Futura Light 11pt]
[Tbl Def:I;7,1.13",1.13",1.13",1.13",2MI.13",1.13",1F255D.13"]
[Row][Cell][Style On:Day of Week]
Monday[Cell]Tuesday[Cell]Wednesday[Cell]
Thursday[Cell]Friday[Cell]Saturday[Cell]Sunday[Style Off:Day of Week]
[Row][Cell][Ln Height:0.167"][Style On:#][Style Off:#][HRt]
School[SRt]
Begins[SRt]
Psychologist[SRt]
on call[Cell][Style On:#][Style Off:#][HRt]
Nursery[SRt]
School[SRt]
dropouts on parade
[Style On:#][Style Off:#][HRt]
Wet Nurse[SRt]

Bunny Run Pre-School

for Troubled Teens

SEPTEMBER 1999

Monday	Tuesday	Wednesday	Thursday	Friday	Saturday	Sunday
1 School Begins— Psychologist on call	**2** Nursery School dropouts on Parade	**3** Wet Nurse Round-up. Rabies Shots for all	**4** De-Weaning Training	**5** Basketball Practice-Prayer Meeting	**6** Fun with Inner Tubes! Keg Parties were never like this before!	**7**
8 Let's all Wear A Wig Day!	**9** The 1 Minute Scuba Diver Visits (if he's still alive)	**10** RTD Bus Dodging! Don't forget your helmet!	**11** Cat Cleaning day! Bring a cat to our Tabby-mat!	**12**	**13** *"Saturday the 14th Strikes Back"* screens in Room 13	**14** Help the folks at Home: enforced chores, 3 credits
15 Kelp Massage for all 4th graders— wear swim trunks and goggles	**16** Out-Run a Shark at lunch! Win a Month's supply of ear-wax!	**17**	**18** Annette Funicello bares all!	**19** Rehearsals for 1st grade production of "Long Day's Journey into PooPoo"	**20** Trip to the Museum of Scouring Powder (bring Lunch and a clean sponge)	**21**
22 Rummage through Mommie's purse. Most embarrassing secret wins a prize!	**23** Milk Monitor Elections today! Payola suggested	**24** Rummage through Daddy's underwear drawer. More prizes!	**25** Betting pool on Principal's trial closes at 5pm, PST	**27** Verdict in on Principal. Will he be convicted of embezzlement or return triumphant?	**28** *Gouda and Gherkin* day. The Famous Pop Duo performs at lunch	**30** Sweat-Sock extravaganza. Wear nothing but your best dress sweat socks!
31 Hey, what's going on here? This month only has 30 days	**Info:**	**Our Motto: Bunny Run, Where the Turf meets the Smurfs**	**Did you change your underwear today?**	**Have you hugged your cleaning woman today?**	**Mucilage Eaters Club meets Tuesdays at 3. Paste Power!**	

Paired Style for Day of Week
[Font:Futura Condensed Medium 14pt (ASCII) (Port) (FW)] [Comment]
Paired Style for # (big date number)
[Font:Futura Extra Black 30pt (Port)(FW)][Par Num:Auto][Comment]

5.0 *Notes:* You can achieve identical results using parallel columns (and the same styles). It isn't difficult, but you do have to be more careful with parallel columns than with a table. Place a CONTROL-ENTER at the end of each day to take you to the next day. The only detail to remember is that no day can be longer than six lines. If you didn't use such big numbers or used smaller body text, you could have more lines per day.

```
[Par Num Def:]<L>[T/B Mar:0.5",0.5"][L/R Mar:0.3",0.3"][FigOpt]<BNNNN>
[Figure:1;PAGE05ED.PCX;]<TP VL SH 1.4>
[Font:Futura Extra Black 30pt (ASCII) (Port) (FW)]
[Flsh Rt]Bunny Run Pre[-]School [C/A/Flrt][HRt]
[Font:Futura Condensed Medium 14pt (ASCII) (Port) (FW)]
[Flsh Rt]for Troubled Teens   [C/A/Flrt][HRt]
[HRt]
[Flsh Rt] S E P T E M B E R   1 9 9 9  [C/A/Flrt][HRt]
[HRt]
[L/R Mar:0.3",0.3"][Font:Futura Light 11pt (ASCII) (Port) (FW)]
[Col Def:7,0.3",1.21",1.46",2.37",2.62",3.54",3.79",4.7",
 4.95",5.87",6.12",7.03",7.28",8.2"][Col On]
[Style On:Day of Week]Monday[HPg]
Tuesday[HPg]
Wednesday[HPg]
Thursday[HPg]
Friday[HPg]
Saturday[HPg][Col On]
[VLine:Column 1,2.63",7.86",1w,30%][VLine:Column 2,2.63",7.86",1w,30%]
[VLine:Column 3,2.63",7.86",1w,30%][VLine:Column 4,2.63",7.86",1w,30%]
[VLine:Column 5,2.63",7.86",1w",30%][VLine:Column 6,2.63",7.86",1w,30%]
[Ln Height:0.16"][Style On:#][Style Off:#][HRt]
School[SRt]
Begins—[SRt]
Psychologist[SRt]
on call[HPg]
[Style On:#][Style Off:#][HRt]
Nursery[SRt]
School[SRt]
dropouts on[SRt]
Parade[HPg]
[Style On:#][Style Off:#][HRt]
Wet Nurse[SRt]
```

Daniel Will-Harris

May 23, 1989

[L/R Mar:1",1"][Usr Opt]<G100>[Usr Box:1;;]
<TP VT HML S .1 .1>
[Usr Box:2;;]<TP VB HML S .1 .1>
[T/B Mar:1",0.5"][T/B Mar:1",0.75"][Usr Box:3;;]<TP VB HML S .1 .1>[Usr Opt]<G0>[Usr Box:4;SPLAT!.CGM;]<TP VB HMR S .1 .1>
[T/B Mar:1",0.75"][T/B Mar:1",0.65"]
[Footer A:3;[Cntr] ...]<type your return address>
[Fig Opt]<BNNNN>[Figure:1;DWH.CGM;[AdvDn:0.1"]<Insert your graphic logo. Use caption for your name. I've used Bodoni 14 point bold.>
[Font:Bodoni Bold 14pt (ASCII) (Port) (FW)] ...][Header A:4; ...]<the header contains the four user boxes so they will print on every page>[HRt]
[HRt]
[HRt]
[HRt]
[HRt]
[HRt]
[HLine:Center,2",0.03",100%][HRt]
[HRt]
[HRt]
[Cntr][Date:3 1, 4][C/A/Flrt][Ln Height:0.19"][HRt]
[Comment]<This should contain a note to yourself, telling you where to start typing the body of the letter>[L/R Mar:1.5",1.5"]

<NOTE: The DWH graphic was created in Freelance Plus. The Splat! is from Arts & Letters. The default font is Bitstream Fontware Bodoni 12 point. The page was printed on a Hewlett-Packard LaserJet II>

P.O. Box 1235, Point Reyes, CA 94956

5

Communicating by design

Graphic design basics

You're probably eager to delve into the technical wonders of WordPerfect, but don't get too excited just yet. Contrary to popular belief, you don't start desktop publishing by turning on your computer. You begin long before you sit down at your computer. (This is the point where, if this were a movie, the screen would get all foggy and wavy and you'd know you were in for a flashback, or some other piece of information vital to understanding the plot.)

In order to become an accomplished desktop publisher with WordPerfect, you need to know a few things about graphic design. People expect magazines to have a certain "look," while books have another. The more your publication resembles other similar publications, the better it will be accepted. All the sophisticated hardware and software in the world won't produce a truly effective (much less professional) document, newsletter, or other publication unless you have a working knowledge of design fundamentals.

Remember that your number one concern *communication*. It doesn't matter how flashy your publication looks if it doesn't get your message across. Don't risk readability for design. It's better to have someone say, "I read it," than "Oh, doesn't that look hip, doesn't that look modern, doesn't that look pretty . . ." Remember architect Louis Sullivan's advice: "Form follows function."

However, don't be intimidated by this unfamiliar design territory. If you're not the artistic type, that's OK. You don't have to be able to draw to design a newsletter or flyer. You won't be drawing pictures; you'll going to be putting type and artwork together, constructing an inviting, readable format, and that's something anyone can learn to do.

❖ *Understanding the basics*

The process of composing a page in order to attain a specific appearance is called "layout." Page layout simply refers to the arrangement of type and graphics. The most effective arrangement attracts the reader's attention and makes the page easy to read.

All printed material, no matter how simple or elaborate, must go through a layout process. A specific typestyle is chosen. That type is sized; the headlines are one size, the body text another. For a magazine or newspaper, the decision must be made about where to place an article on the page: at the top, the middle, or the bottom? Column widths must be chosen—how many columns should be on the page? Should all the type be set at the same width? What about graphics? Should photos be one or two columns wide? Should they be boxed with a border? What about captions? Should they be set in bold, or italic, or in a different size than the body copy? All these choices must be addressed, even in the most elementary layout.

If wrestling with these decisions is foreign to you, don't be afraid. Once you understand the basics, the layout process will be easier, but you will have to think in a way that may be new to you. You've probably always focused on the *meaning* of words. Now you'll have to pay attention to the format of the words. Print is a highly visual medium, and you must notice how words "look."

What some books about desktop publishing, and many advertisements (especially Apple's), conveniently forget is that the whole idea behind desktop publishing is to produce documents which *don't* look desktop published. If you already know what you want beyond a shadow of a doubt, you can go directly to the step-by-step examples. If there are any shadows lurking in the corners of your mind, illuminate them here.

◆ Decisions, decisions

Your first step is to decide what type of publication you are going to create. Even if your publication is already designed and you just want to produce it using WordPerfect, invest some time ensuring that your design is as fine as it can be. This entails more than simply deciding what typefaces you'll use or how many columns you want. You can't arrive at design decisions until you first answer some eternal questions.

Who is this publication intended for? Who will be reading it? Are they within your organization or outside of it? Have they ever heard of you before? Are they already interested in your organization, or do they have to be sold?

What do you want them to know? What's the single most important point you want them to remember or learn after reading your publication? Do you want to excite them? Warn them? Sell them? Calm them? The appearance of your publication contributes to all of this.

What do your readers expect? People see so many publications that they have certain expectations. Most news magazines have a certain look, and newsletters have a basic format. You don't have to be a slave to tradition, but you should realize that if your design doesn't bear some resemblance to similar publications you'll have to work harder to get your message across.

How much time/money do you have at your disposal? Your budget dictates the limits on your hardware, graphics software, fonts, electronic clip art, number of pages, printing and mailing costs, and most importantly, *time.*

How much material do you have? Do you have tons of text and no graphics, or pictures and no text? Do you have 20 pages of material to fill an eight-page issue? Do you have one page of material for an eight-page issue? Answer each of these questions, then find other publications similar to yours and study them for type, graphics, and layout. Are they easy to read? Are they attractive, or do they look like junk mail? Do you want to read them, or do you have to force yourself to read them? Compare what they did with what you want to do. Learn from their mistakes. If you weren't able to answer these questions, you didn't fail; you just need to learn some new ways of looking at all this.

All the great masters learned to paint by copying paintings they admired. Only after careful study did they attempt to paint on their own. See how your text and graphics fit into someone else's format. Don't be afraid to let yourself be influenced by others who have gone before you. *Plagiarism is the sincerest form of flattery.* Actually, I don't believe in plagiarism (nepotism, or any other inconvenient "ism"), but being *influenced* by some other publication is fair and honest.

If you must use a design almost verbatim, give credit to the original designer or publication. Then you can join the likes of film director Brian DePalma, who claims that his Alfred Hitchcock-like films are an "homage" to the master. He doesn't pretend he invented the genre—he gives credit where it's due, and still manages to bask in the limelight, and/or cash the checks.

Of course, as composer Andrew Lloyd Webber well knows, critics may complain that your work is derivative and may even accuse you of plagiarism; still, most people respond to something familiar with a sense of "Oh, what a catchy tune."

❖ *Fashion vs. style*

You may not have noticed, but graphic design has ever-changing fashions, much the way clothing does. And like clothing, as soon as a fashion comes into widespread use, a new one is cooked up to make the old one obsolete, forcing people to spend even more money. But, there's a difference between fashion and style. Fashion comes and goes, but style never changes. There are classic clothes, and there is classic graphic design.

The art directors at Apple (or Apple's ad agency) are responsible for years of cutesy, cartoony pages which have become equated with "desktop publishing." Their commercials were filled with serious looking executives oohing and aahing over silly-looking pages: giant type, giant graphics, and graphs which resembled animals.

It was all *very* cute and *very* impractical. Trout-shaped graphs are fine and good if you work in a seafood restaurant with a large, full-time art department, but for the most part they trade clarity for cuteness. And, worst of all, they are terribly hard to take seriously.

Now *I* don't equate "serious" with "important," but a lot of people do, and you aren't producing your pages for me, you're producing them for *them.* But does it mean you can't have fun, and it doesn't mean you can't introduce wit, but it does mean that the material should come first, the cute, second. Flash is certainly a legitimate way to attract attention, but once you have someone's attention, you don't want them to concentrate on the flash, rather than on the substance.

Just as there's classic fashion, there's also classic design: pages that illuminate the text with a judicious mix of graphics and white space. They don't overpower the text, they add to it. The design of the page leads the reader's eye to the most important points, without calling attention to itself.

Jan White's *Editing by Design* is one of the bibles of classic design; it stresses design as a way to add to the text, not compete with it. (In fact, I was going to mention it in my introduction, but I wanted you to buy this book first. It does get the full treatment in the recommended reading list in the Appendix, though.)

Classic design doesn't come out and scream anything, but nudges, prods, and subtly guides the reader. Subtle doesn't mean wimpy—it means quietly, without making a spectacle of itself. And as with anything else, it's far more difficult to be subtle than to indulge in over-kill (one of my favorite pastimes).

If your publication is a flash in the pan, something which needs to say "now," just remember that it won't be long before people will look at it and it say "then." Check out some old magazines (especially the ads), and see how quickly they became dated. Classic pages don't show their age — they're useful for years and repeat your message, day after day, year after year.

◆ What's a person to do?

So how can you decide what to do? As my wife Toni loves to tell me, "Put yourself in the other person's shoes." What do *you* want to see? What would persuade *you?* What would inform *you?*

While not everyone in the world shares your personal taste, it's a reasonable starting point. If you find something attractive, chances are other people will, too.

But remember, the best page design results from having a reason for every component. That sounds awfully clinical and fairly obvious, but it's important to bear in mind. Many in the traditional publishing arena were scared to death of desktop publishing because they thought the layman would use hundreds of different typestyles on a single page. While that hasn't happened a lot, there has been a notable proliferation of brain-dead pages.

Some people go wild when designing pages for the first time; they try to use too many different elements for no reason other than that they're available. When a novice designer is asked why there's a big picture above a story when the two clearly are not related, he's likely to say, "I don't know, I hadn't thought about it, it looked good there," or give some equally flimsy response.

Every professionally-designed page you've seen in your life was designed for a reason: to grab your attention, to convey a specific message, to distract you from something else. And it's important to sit down and think about what really attracted you to that page in the first place.

◆ Subliminal messages

Now for the psychological slant: *why* do you like what you do? We often fail to notice just what specifically catches our eye. Mental associations are very powerful persuaders. IBM has an established corporate image which runs through every piece of printed material they produce. If you've ever studied their print advertisements, you'll notice that they always use the same typestyle, and usually the same ad layout: a big picture on top with copy running along the bottom.

You also may have seen, but not realized, that smaller companies often copied this format, right down to the typeface. At first you may look at their ad because you think it's from IBM. But even after you realize that it's not (and not everyone will), you still link their company or product with IBM.

While it's illegal to use IBM's logo (or even their name without proper trademark disclaimers), there has yet to be any type of "look and feel" case for printed pages, unless an actual name or logo was involved. If you want your magazine to look like *Time* magazine, go right ahead. Measure it, study it, use the same typefaces. You're not going to create any image of your own, but people immediately will identify the look of the page with something they've seen before, something respected.

❖ *Does anyone need so many typefaces?*

There were, at last count, more typefaces than I could count. There are literally thousands of typefaces for the English language alone. While only a fraction of these are currently available for desktop-publishing, hundreds of old favorites and new typefaces materialize for desktop publishers each year. Commercial typesetting equipment manufacturers and font companies, such as Compugraphic and Bitstream, promise that it won't be long before the entire library of fonts used by commercial typesetters is available for desktop publishing. (Gee, doesn't that sound like something you'd hear at a World's Fair? Me, I'm still waiting for the picture phones AT&T promised me in 1964. Whatever happened to AT&T?)

A colleague and friend, Allan Ayars, insists that the world could survive with only Times Roman and Helvetica. While he understands that variety is the spice of life, he still sighs in despair when he sees a new, but uninspired typeface. "The world needs a new typeface like it needs a new brand of toothpaste," he tells me. He refers to these useless, spineless imitations as *Upchuck #3*, as if to say it's a new variation on the ever-popular *Upchuck #1*.

Sometimes, when the face is uninspired, derivative, or just plain ugly, I agree. Still, those simple 26 letters can take on countless imaginative, distinctive forms. And even the minor differences between two typefaces can have a marked impact on a publication's appearance.

◆ Two of a kind, or behind the times

Even with the hundreds of typefaces available, several dominate the scene. Times Roman and Helvetica are used for a large percentage of all printed materials. You could get by with just these two if you had to, because they typify the two basic styles of type, serif and sans serif.

A serif is the little doo-jiggy that sticks out at the ends of letters. Okay, okay, you've paid good money for this book and you deserve a better explanation than that. Allen Haley, a noted authority on type, and vice president of ITC (no relation to AT&T), put it this way: "A line crossing the main strokes of a character. It may take on many varieties." Satisfied? Sans serif type doesn't have any extensions at the ends of the letters. Here's a visual example.

Times Roman SERIF Helvetica SANS SERIF

Many studies indicate that serif type, such as Times Roman, is much easier to read than sans serif type, such as Helvetica. The serifs are supposed to lead the eye from letter to letter. Other studies show that we read not letter by letter, but word by word, and the shape of words in serif type is more quickly recognizable. While no study is conclusive (do 8 out of 10 dentists really prefer sugarless gum for their patients who chew gum? Has anyone really asked this question of all dentists, or did they ask just 10 dentists?) you can perform a taste-test of your own. Print a page in Dutch (Times Roman), or Swiss (Helvetica), and compare the two. Depending on how wide the columns are, how long the lines of type are, and how much leading there is between the lines of type, one should be easier to read than the other — it's up to you.

What you'll find is what the latest studies have found: if you grew up reading serif typefaces (as most Americans have), then you'll find serif typefaces easier to read. If you grew up reading sans serif typefaces (as many Europeans have), then you will find sans serif faces easier to read. (See the two full-page examples at the end of this chapter, which illustrate these two typefaces, as well as how to avoid some design mistakes.)

Sans serif type appears to be more modern because it *is* more modern. Sans serif typefaces gained popularity early in the 20th century. Some are more readable than others. Personally, the only sans serif types I can stand to read for any length of time are Gill Sans and Optima. Optima is technically sans serif, but it has a tapered design similar to a serif. Optima is not only one of the most readable sans serifs, it's also one of the most attractive.

For a newsletter, choosing a single type, such as Times Roman for the body copy and a contrasting type, such as Helvetica, for headlines and subheadings is an effective combination. In general, serif fonts like Times Roman are easier to read when set in long columns of text than a sans serif font such as Helvetica is. If you're not sure about which two fonts work well together, don't mix them at all — use one font for both your body text and your headings.

◆ Font follows function

More important than these awe-inspiring technical considerations is how the appearance of fonts dominates, influences, and guides the style of a publication, whether it be a letter, a magazine, or a book.

Typefaces are more than just letters and numbers. They're powerful symbols, with strong connotations. Their ability to stimulate your memory is often as powerful as their capacity to transmit ideas through language.

The next time you leaf through a magazine, consider how you recognize certain advertisements simply by the typeface used. You don't have to stop and read the letters that form the company or product name; you instantly recognize the product or company just by the shape of the words.

In my first book, *Desktop Publishing With Style,* I said (and I quote—I mean who better to steal from than myself?): "Choosing a typeface is like choosing a mate: it says a lot about what you like or dislike, and communicates it to the rest of the world. While divorcing yourself from a typeface is less painful than from a human being, once people get used to associating you or your business with that typeface, it can cause more than a little confusion when you change to something new. People might stop and think, 'What else have they changed? Are they under new management?'" (I couldn't have said it any better myself—though many have tried, including a writer friend of mine while proofing this paragraph: "A face is literally a *face*—the face your publication shows to the world.")

❖ Role playing

Desktop publishers should be aware that the typeface they choose makes a statement about what they want to convey. You must be positive that the typeface matches the message you want to get across. If you're not sure about what looks best, it's perfectly acceptable to study other publications and see what they use.

I've played one of those "first-thing-that-comes-to-mind" games with some common typefaces. In general, if a font is suitable for body copy, it works well in smaller sizes. Fonts that function as headlines are also known as display faces, and are attractive in large sizes. Type can be as decorative as any kind of illustration, and can communicate emotions as well as words. Here are some examples.

Times Roman — **Solid,** *practical,* ***unpretentious***

Effective for body copy and headlines. Newspapers, books, magazines, just about anything. Everyone uses it, and with good reason. It doesn't have a very distinct image, but it's efficient and easy-to-read. If you use Times Roman, also known as Dutch, for body text, these typefaces work well for headlines: Amerigo, Avant Garde Gothic, Benguiat, Bookman, Cooper Light, Friz Quadrata, Futura, Gill Sans, Helvetica, Optima, Souvenir, and Univers.

Helvetica — **Serious,** *modern,* ***impersonal***

Suitable for signs, headlines, etc. I would hate to read a novel or even a magazine set in Helvetica, but reports or business publications have a "serious" appearance when set in Helvetica. Also known as Swiss, it works well with: Benguiat, Bodoni, Bookman, Century Schoolbook, Cooper Light, Friz Quadrata, Garamond, Goudy Old Style, Korinna, Melior, and Palatino.

Helvetica Narrow — **Dense,** *compact,* ***condensed***

May sometimes be hard to read. Good for single column headlines, subheads, price lists, and catalogs. Helvetica Narrow is not really designed to be narrow, it is electronically narrowed, and this can make it harder to read). Not for body copy unless you're really sadistic (although Helvetica or Swiss *Condensed*, fonts specifically designed to be narrow, are OK). As a headline font it works well with the same fonts as regular Helvetica.

ITC Avant Garde — **Modern,** *geometric,* ***worldly***

Avant Garde is perfect for advertisements, signs, headlines. This font takes much more space than Times Roman, and although graphic and striking, it's difficult to read when set in long stretches of text, as for a book. As a headline font it works well with body text set in Benguiat, Bookman, Century Schoolbook, Cooper Light, Goudy Old Style, Korinna, Melior, Palatino, and Souvenir.

ITC Bookman – **Offbeat,** *friendly,* ***casual***

(A little shy, but with a terrible temper lurking underneath.) Bookman is acceptable for body copy, but it's better for headlines because it's more interesting in larger sizes. Brochures, advertisements, short blocks of text (but not too small). Bookman works well with these faces: Avant Garde Gothic, Cooper Light, Friz Quadrata, Futura, Gill Sans, Helvetica, Kabel, and Souvenir.

New Century Schoolbook — **Studious,** *unassuming*

Century is appropriate for both headlines and body copy. Books, newsletters, semi-informal publications. Schoolbook works well with Amerigo, Avant Garde Gothic, Cooper Light, Friz Quadrata, Futura, Gill Sans, Helvetica, Kabel, Optima, and Souvenir.

Palatino — **Formal,** *elegant,* ***classical***

Suitable for body copy and headlines. Books, magazines, reports, advertisements, brochures, menus. Use the italics for very elegant invitations. A more formal alterative to Zapf Chancery, it is also known as Zapf Calligraphic. Palatino works well with Amerigo, Avant Garde Gothic, Friz Quadrata, Futura, Gill Sans, Helvetica, Kabel, and Optima.

Courier – **Old fashioned,** *official*

Useful as body copy and headings for reports, legal documents, office correspondence, memos. This is what you use if you're going for that "typewritten" look. Some people feel that letters printed in Courier have a more personal appearance. I think they are the antithesis of desktop publishing: clumsy and old-fashioned.

ITC Zapf Chancery — Calligraphic, flowing, handmade

Ideal for invitations and announcements, it's also suitable for advertisements, business cards, logos, etc. Most effective in sizes above 14-point, and in short doses.

Zapf Dingbats ❁ ❂ ❃ ❄ ❅ ❆ ❇ ❈ ❉ ❊ ❋ ● ❍ ■ ❏ ❐ ❑ ❒ ▲ ▼ ◆ ❖ ◗

Fun, silly, novel. An entire "alphabet" of symbols, not text. Eye-catching accents such as arrows, stars, fun bullets. Many possible applications, but use judiciously—a little goes a long way.

This selection of typefaces does not include every typeface available, but these are some of the most popular (and not coincidentally, included in most PostScript printers). For many applications, you won't really *need* fonts other than these, but you may *want* them.

❖ *Making the right choice*

Standard typefaces such as Times Roman and Bookman have been employed effectively for years as "body copy" (the main text part of a document). These typefaces are easy to read and do not strain the reader's eye when used for books or newspapers. More flamboyant, attention-grabbing "display" typestyles, such as Cooper Black and Futura Black are used for headlines, advertisements, or brochures.

Futura Black
ABCDEFGHIJKLMNOPQRSTUVWXYZ
abcdefghijklmnopqrstuvwxyz 1234567890&!$

Cooper Black
ABCDEFGHIJKLMNOPQRSTUVWXYZ
abcdefghijklmnopqrstuvwxyz 1234567890&!$

If you are aiming for a modern, slick, up-to-the-minute look for a publication, you may want to choose from among the sans serif typefaces such as Helvetica, Futura, and Avant Garde for headings. If you want an elegant, polished appearance for your pages, you'll probably choose a serif typeface such as Galliard, Korinna, or Palatino. These dignified faces are also appropriate for formal invitations and announcements.

If you are producing a newsletter about schools, you might take a look at New Century Schoolbook, because that's the typeface used in so many "See Jane Run" books. I'm not fond of New Century Schoolbook (I guess it reminds me of grade school), but it's a free country and you can choose whatever typeface you (or your boss, wife, or client) like. The text of this book is set in Bitstream Goudy Old Style, and the headings are Bitstream Hammersmith (a.k.a. Gill Sans).

A serious financial newsletter calls for a dependable, trustworthy font, such as Times Roman or Century Schoolbook. It would lose credibility if it were set in a decorative, lush font, such as Korinna or Benguiat. And it would look foolish if it were set entirely in Tiffany.

Benguiat
ABCDEFGHIJKLMNOPQRSTUVWXYZ
abcdefghijklmnopqrstuvwxyz 1234567890&$

Korinna
ABCDEFGHIJKLMNOPQRSTUVWXYZ
abcdefghijklmnopqrstuvwxyz 1234567890&!$

Tiffany
ABCDEFGHIJKLMNOPQRSTUVWXYZ
abcdefghijklmnopqrstuvwxyz 1234567890&!$

These three art nouveau-flavored fonts were designed by Ed Benguiat for the International Typeface Corporation. Korinna was actually designed in 1904, but

Benguiat is responsible for adding the first true italic design for Korinna, and developing the typeface into a family suitable for typesetting. Tiffany is a combination of two typefaces designed about 80 years ago: Ronaldson and Caxton. Benguiat blended them and created a typeface with long, graceful serifs and strong weight contrast between the thin and thick strokes. These typefaces are useful for short blocks of text copy, advertising, and display type.

Just be sure that the typeface you select is appropriate for the publication or printed material you're creating. And remember that other people's connotations will influence their subconscious reaction to your publication. Take another look at Chapter 4, *Show & Tell*, for more examples of typefaces and how they can be used in various publications.

❖ *Measuring up or get to the point*

Once you've determined which typeface is most appropriate for your document, you'll need to know some specifics about applying the type to the page.

You may be used to measuring print in *pitch*. A 10-pitch typeface is generally larger than a 12-pitch typeface, because 10-pitch signifies that you can print 10 characters in an inch. Pitch is a horizontal measurement used for monospaced fonts, but proportionally-spaced fonts, the kind you'll be using for desktop publishing, are measured in points, a vertical measurement.

- Points are a vertical measurement (72 points= 1 inch).
- A 10-point font is roughly 10 points high, from the tip of the descenders (found in letters such as g, j, p, q, y) to the top of the ascenders (found in letters such as b, d, f, h, l). A 12-point font is about 20% larger than a 10-point font.
- Text set in any size below 10-point is fine print; 10 and 11-point are standard sizes for body copy; 18 to 30-point is standard for headlines; and any size larger than 30 is used for very important headlines (such as those on the cover of the *National Enquirer*).

Not all 10-point fonts are the same size, however. Font size is actually determined by the designer of the font. That's why 10-point Helvetica is larger than 10-point Times Roman. (Try this bit of trivia at your next cocktail party; your friends will be impressed and bored at the same time—maybe they'll even leave.)

While points are a vertical measurement, in traditional publishing the width of a line of text is measured in "picas." WordPerfect offers you the option of measuring in inches, centimeters, or points, and it's advisable to use the unit of measurement with which you're most familiar.

There are six picas to an inch, and twelve points to a pica (which makes as little sense to have twelve inches to a foot). This makes a pica one-sixth of an inch, and a point one-seventy-second of an inch. A standard column width is about twelve picas, or two inches.

◆ Between the lines or beside the point

The amount of white space between the lines of type is called leading, and it should always be at least one point larger than the size of the type. If you're using 11-point type, a leading of 12 or 13 results in maximum readability. This is written as 11/12 and referred to as "eleven over twelve."

Leading also makes an enormous difference in how a page looks. Pages seem gray and hard to read when not enough leading is used. Too much white space between lines of text can also be confusing, because it's difficult to follow a sentence from line to line. (Notice how easily you're following these sentences?)

◆ Sizing up the situation or what's my line length?

When you are calculating the width of columns, there are several details to consider: page size, type size, and the size and number of photos or other artwork that you will be using. Columns should be neither too narrow nor too wide. For a newsletter, it's best to divide the page into two, three, or even four columns if you're using 10-point type on a standard letter-size page.

A single column wider than 42 picas (about seven inches) is not easy to read. Readers "forget" which line they're on with a very wide column, and may get lost starting a new line of text (that's why there are so many people in analysis). Using a single column can be very effective and attract attention if the column is only about 24 picas wide, has a wide expanse of white space on either side of it, and has a generous amount of leading between the lines, such as 11 over 14 or 15.

Columns with lines shorter than about 10 picas (an inch and a half) also may confuse the reader. The fewer times your eye is forced to pause, the faster you can read a line. Narrow columns can break up a sentence's structure until it no longer makes sense, and the same sentence must be read over and over to comprehend it. For an 8 1/2-by-11 inch page, the optimum line length for normal body copy (10 to 12-point type) is between 12 and 36 picas. (See the two full-page examples at the end of this chapter, which illustrate these principles.)

◆ Alignments

➾ There are four basic alignments for text.

Justified type is aligned on both the left and right sides, forming even, solid blocks of text. This book is set with justified text, as are these lines of text.

With **flush left** type, also known as "ragged right," the left margin lines up flush, or straight, but the right margin is ragged, with each line of type a slightly different length.

Flush right type lines up flush on the right side of a column of type. This is not as common as flush left or justified, but it is still used for headlines, readouts, etc.

Centered type is at an equal distance from both margin or column edges. Centered text usually is not set in paragraph form or used for anything with columns (such as a newsletter), although individual lines of type may be centered. Headlines are often centered, as are announcements and invitations.

◆ Set it your way

Both justified and ragged-right have places in publications. While most newspapers, books, and magazines are justified, an increasing number of publications are setting text ragged right. The ragged margins provide a page with a more informal (or less pretentious) appearance. The major drawback with unjustified columns of type is that extremely uneven line lengths may be created—very long lines can be followed by very short ones. These shapes are hard for the reader's eye to follow, and result in an undesirable visual impact. You can always hyphenate ragged right columns to improve unbalanced lines, but if the columns are too narrow, it won't help much.

If you like the look of vertical rules (lines) between columns on a page, then you may prefer ragged margins where the rules can act as a kind of justification. Justified type combined with rules can be a bit much unless there's plenty of white space, but once again, this is not etched in stone.

Justified type is suitable for every type of publishing. The uneven spacing between words that can occur with justified type may be particularly evident in short lines, but for the most part, justification adds a neat, orderly appearance to a page. When it's used properly, justification adds crispness, geometry, and a sense of pleasing formality to a page. The choice is yours.

◆ Deep in the heart of texes

If you justify type, it's an absolute necessity to hyphenate as well. Otherwise, paragraphs will have big, ugly, gaping spaces running through them; these gaps are called "rivers." Hyphenation allows words to be divided, and by splitting syllables across lines, there are fewer oversize gaps in the lines. Letterspacing (adjusting the amount of space between each letter within a word) is another way to avoid those ugly and embarrassing gaps. (See the "bad" example at the end of this chapter.)

An additional ingredient for cooking up appealing type involves adjusting the space between individual pairs of letters. This is called kerning, and is most noticeable with larger type sizes. But remember, everything is relative. Kerning is more vital on a phototypesetting machine than it is on a laser printer. If you plan to send the finished product through a Linotronic or other typesetter, kerning can improve the output.

❖ Gridlock

One of the main concepts in graphic design is the "grid." While this may be useful, the concept is bandied about like it's the holy grail, the be-all and end-all. "Use the grid," some design gurus claim, and everything will fall into place automatically.

Designers have grappled with this concept for years. I have seen examples of five-column grids, but the pages look like three columns. It didn't make any sense. One day I was working with a corporation headquartered in Denmark, and while they didn't speak English very well (their slogan was: "Personal Planning, making your life come true, faster"), their "Corporate Identity" book spoke to me. Their entire corporate identity was based on a 45-millimeter square. Every component of their design system was based on this square, this *grid*; it was a *unit* around which everything revolved.

This is a three-column grid. Don't be intimidated by it. It is nothing but a geometrical pattern that divides the page into shapes that are supposed to make page layout easier. However, your material may not fit into a grid format; don't feel bad. Use your imagination, and arrange your material to communicate effectively without being tied to some arbitrary grid.

Squares and rectangles are convenient shapes for interpreting a grid, and in some cases, you can use circles and triangles. The great architect Frank Lloyd Wright used a grid for all his buildings. It creates a certain rhythm and order.

In essence, a grid is a unit of measure (which can be anything you decide on) that you use as the basis for your design. If your grid is a one-inch square, then your page will be designed with one-inch blocks, or quarter increments of one inch such as 1/4, 1/2, 3/4, 1 1/2, 2, etc. (or, for you decimal fans, .25, .5, .75, 1, 1.25, 1.5, 1.75, 2).

You might design a page with one-inch margins, three two-inch columns (twice the grid size), 1/4-inch gutters between columns (one quarter the grid size), 12-point body copy type (since there are 72 points per inch, 12-point is an even 1/6th of 72-point), 36-point headlines (1/2 of 72-point), etc. The grid acts as a tool which allows all the elements to work together harmoniously.

That's the good news. The bad news is that the grid doesn't always function as it should. Just because you work in increments of a grid doesn't guarantee that your page always will have the correct appearance, and more importantly, doesn't mean that the information you have will fit onto that page. The grid is a tool, not a rule. Strict adherence to the grid can fast lead to visual boredom. Use it to help you make decisions, but don't become a slave to it.

❖ *Creating a style*

Review some of your favorite publications, and note how, while each page is different, there are obvious similarities in style — a header or footer that ties material together, a certain way of boxing readouts, a different typeface (usually italics) for captions than for regular text. These design elements provide a publication with its own unique, easily recognizable style.

"Readout" is a typesetting or newspaper term for text which is set in a bigger size and positioned within an article to highlight an intriguing phrase or emphasize a particular point. It offers you another opportunity to grab the reader's attention and keep it on the page. Readouts are often used to create visual interest when you lack photos or other artwork, and can be thought of as yet another graphic element. They are also handy when you simply need to fill up a page when the text runs short. Magazines refer to this technique as a "callout" or "pull quote." As long as you use them effectively, you can call them whatever you like. Chapter 12, *Graphics*, has many examples of readouts. Here is just one, taken from Dorothy Parker.

Brevity is the
soul of lingerie

Developing a standard page structure helps you organize your words and pictures so they are consistent throughout your publication. While different page layouts within a single publication can add variety, it's easy to overdo it so that the reader is no longer sure what he's reading.

The message you're trying to convey is the most vital element. Your page design should lead the reader's eye to the most important items first. Headlines should not only illuminate the subject, but should be placed so that they sit directly above the article itself; otherwise, the reader won't be able to match the article with the headline, will become confused, and eventually will find something better to do. Variety and contrast are instrumental in creating a pleasant texture on a page, and that can be achieved by using several different graphic techniques. A large capital letter, either raised or dropped, at the beginning of a paragraph attracts attention and serve as an invitation to begin reading.

◆ Tools of the trade

Gray columns of type in long rows are more appealing to readers if you break them up with subheads or set the first few words of a paragraph in boldface. Using different sizes and variations of a single typeface for headlines adds contrast while retaining a sense of consistency and interest. All these elements provide visual clues to amplify the meaning of the words. Some of these design choices have a subliminal effect, and many readers remain largely unaware that they are being manipulated by graphic design. Would-be desktop publishers should notice and apply these techniques to their own publications.

While WordPerfect allows you to have many different typefaces, borders, boxes, graphics, and screens on a single page, using too many of them simultaneously is a sure-fire way to make a page unintelligible. In effective graphic design, every element is on the page for a reason. If you can't come up with a reason why that 2-point border is going to help the reader notice or understand the material inside it, lose it; otherwise, it is just a distraction.

There are many options you must deal with when designing any publication. What size paper will your printed piece use, and what about the margins? Most laser printers require some sort of margin—approximately half an inch all around, because of their paper transport mechanisms—and are unable to print all the way to the edges of the paper. Printing presses also require a margin—usually about a quarter inch—but in either case, the paper can be trimmed after printing so that the final page has no margin.

◆ Less is more

If you are just beginning, try to keep page composition simple and clean. Avoid mixing too many different typefaces and using unnecessary rules (lines), which only serve to muddle the reader. Rules are meant to separate, and they are not merely ornamental. Do not use them to divide material incorrectly. It is seldom advisable to put a full-ruled line under a headline; this separates the title from its related material and defeats the purpose of the headline. This may seem obvious, but it's a mistake novices often make.

Beginners think that by adding lines, boxes, and flashy fonts, their publication will seem professional. Unfortunately, that achieves the opposite result. If you want a ruled line to separate the elements on a page, place the line below the end of one article and above the headline of the other. A *kicker*, however, does look good with a thin ruling line under it. Kickers are a few words, usually aligned flush left, that appear just above a headline to amplify and attract attention to that headline.

"Simple" doesn't mean it has to be Spartan, but you should try to keep the design subtle. Whether you're creating a newsletter, invitation, or advertisement, the purpose is to communicate your message. If readers spend too much time oohing and aahing over the lines, typefaces, graphics, and boxes, they are not spending their time reading. And what's the point of trying to make your publication attractive if it's also hard to read?

❖ Design tips and hints

Page composition can be very complex when you're juggling several unrelated items on the same page. The reader must be able to follow a section of text easily from its beginning to its end. To accomplish this, there are a few practices you should avoid. (Take a look at the "bad" example near the end of this chapter to see what a page that ignores these tips looks like.)

- Don't mix typefaces of body text within a document or publication. Don't set one article in Times Roman and the other in Helvetica (if you do, please remove this book from your bookshelf).
- Don't mix sizes of body text. Body text should always be the same point size.
- Don't mix too many different typefaces in one publication.
- Don't use too many "swash" or special effects typefaces, such as drop caps or raised initial caps. Also do not use outline and shadow fonts to excess.
- Don't set lengthy blocks of text in italic, bold, or all capital letters.
- Don't begin an article without a headline.
- Don't have more white space below a headline than above it.
- Don't use a flamboyant typeface for a serious document.

- Don't place smaller headlines above larger ones. The most important material and the biggest headline should be at the top of a page.
- Don't use the same font, size, and style (such as Helvetica 24-point bold) for every headline. Headline weights and styles should be varied, such as Helvetica 30-point bold for an article at the top of a page, and 24-point italic for one further down the page.
- Don't place two articles directly side by side, so that their headlines "bump." The headlines run together, and are confusing and hard to read (this is also referred to as "tombstoning").
- Don't place advertisements in the middle of the page (floating among articles as if they were illustrations).
- Don't box text without too little white space around it (so that the border is too close to the type).

❖ Headlines

Headlines are usually set in upper- and lowercase letters, since this is easier to read than headlines set in all caps. Headlines in all caps serve a purpose at times, but not on a regular basis. Readers recognize words not only by how they are spelled, but by the shapes they form. Words in all caps form rectangular blocks and are harder to recognize as specific words, which slows a fast reader and discourages a slow one.

The purpose of a headline, or large display type, is to attract the readers' attention, convey a quick message, and persuade them to read the text that follows. Headlines are read more often than the material underneath them—that's where the power to influence comes in. An effective headline should compel a reader to read on.

Headlines can be placed above text, either flush left, flush right, or centered, depending on your design. Headlines should extend across the full width of the column they are in, because a short headline leaves a white space that resembles an unintentional hole. All material requires some sort of identification, including articles that are continued from one page to another. A simple "continued from page 3" in 8-point type is not an acceptable substitute for a headline. When readers turn to that inside page looking for the continuation of the "Dolphins Speak to Researcher" article, they need help to find it. It may just be one or two words from the original headline, such as "Dolphins Speak," or even just "Dolphins," if the story now fits in one column.

Here is an example of how a poorly designed newsletter can be transformed by following the design principles and prepublication planning (spell checking, editing) outlined in this book.

❖ Before—The bad example

This is an example of what not to do with the first page of a newsletter: it has too much material crammed onto the page, and it is in all the wrong proportions. Beginning at the top, the name of the newsletter, "Numismatics Remuneration," tries to be arty by capitalizing the "T," and centering "Numismatics" between the two capital letters. This arbitrary capitalization only succeeds in making readers wonder "Why is the "T" capitalized?" Also, the motto and date line are too large and bold, giving the headlines too much competition and making the top of the page too busy.

The rest of the page is divided into three columns, with white space trapped between the first and second columns, which adds nothing to the overall design. In the first column, blurbs referring to material on the inside pages are overpowered by enormous numbers inside gray screens, and there is no consistency of spacing. Some of the blurbs are directly under the boxes, but the blurb for page 6 is sitting atop the number 8.

The headlines in the first and second columns are the same size, the same typeface (Helvetica), and since they are positioned next to each other, difficult to read. These are "bumping heads." The kicker over the middle headline is too near the nameplate of the newsletter, and should be closer to the top of the headline. There is not enough white space under the headline, so some of the descenders run into the first line of the article. The article flows, newspaper style, into the next column; however, it's also too close to the nameplate, and an article should not appear in a column next to its headline. The headline should be one line, extending across both columns under the nameplate, instead of two lines in the middle column. The headline for the article in the third column is too large, and the byline has too much space underneath it.

All of the body copy is set block style, with no indentation at the beginning of a paragraph. This is not recommended for newsletters. As you can see, it is extremely difficult to tell where the paragraphs begin. Also, the body text is Helvetica, the same font used for many of the headlines and for the nameplate. This overuse of the same typeface gives the page a monotonous, dull appearance.

Photos and artwork should enliven and enrich the material around them, but because of the size and poor positioning of this illustration, it doesn't enhance the page at all. Probably the worst feature of this design is how the narrow boxed text is squeezed into the lower right corner of the page, causing the bottom of the third

NUMISMATICS

RemuneraTion

A journal of know-nothing design and money-grubing slime December 6, 1989

Inside This Issue

Kicker over head

This Headline should be bigger

What is desktop publishing? It means different things to different people. To some it simply means setting type with a computer, on any of a variety of printers. To others it means creating the entire finished page on computer: writing the text, laying out the page, merging in the graphics, and finally printing a finished page on a laser printer or digital typesetter.

According to the ABC program "Business Week," by 1991, desktop publishing will be a three billion dollar industry.

Who will Benefit from Desktop Publishing? You will. Yes, you. The one flipping through the pages looking for the funny drawings. You may already be a publisher. Yes, you!

Publishing doesn't mean just books and magazines. If you're part of an office, school, any kind of organization or club, you're probably already creating a newsletter or flyer of events. If you work in any business, such as a real estate office or travel agency, you need to send out promotional flyers about your hottest listings, or bargain travel packages.

In the past, you've either had to type everything up and stick it on a page, or send it out to a typesetter and have a graphic artist paste up for you, which, before I arrived, cost about $1,000 per issue to produce. After I arrived, the costs dropped to almost nothing (although I must admit the Oreo budget rose dramatically).

The first major expense is typesetting. On a twenty-four page newsletter, if you sent typed pages to a typesetter, you should expect to pay about $500. If you prepared the copy on computer and sent it to the typesetter via modem (over the phone lines), that cost would be lowered to about $300 because the copy would the copy would not have to be retyped by the typesetter.

(These typesetting charges included corrections, inevitable, because some

cont'd p. 4

Headline is Too Big

By Author's name

Either way, an unpretentious little newsletter can quickly become so tedious and time consuming that you'd like to trick someone else into doing it for you.

So, if you're already a publisher, desktop publishing may be for you. It can even be fun, depending on how easily you are entertained.

Where was I?

On the following pages you will find examples of what you can do if you are: a small business, quick-print shop, ad agency, school, theater, fund raiser, restaurant, real estate office, fake estate office, travel agency, mail order catalog, writer, or an unpublished writer

A Word From Our Sponsors

Now you have to measure the type and make a dummy. A dummy is a simple mock-up of a page showing the basic format and where each story, picture, or piece of artwork is going to be placed on the page.

con'd p. 5

column to be too narrow. This is a good example of bad typography—see the river of white space running through this column? Also, notice how the bottoms of the columns are not aligned horizontally, resulting in an uneven page that lacks definition.

❖ *After - The good example*

This design fits practically the same amount of material on the page, but does so in a balanced, inviting way. The nameplate, set in Times Roman, uses two solid black squares to define the corners; the centered motto and dateline are a good size and surrounded by ample white space.

The large one-line headline extending over two columns is aligned flush left, as is the kicker, "From the President." There is an appropriate amount of white space above and below the headline. The author's byline is aligned flush right because of the raised capital letter of the first paragraph. If the big initial letter had been dropped into the paragraph instead of raised, the byline could have been centered above the paragraph.

The font for the body text is Times Roman, and the paragraphs are indented and easy to follow. The body copy is set ragged right to achieve an informal and friendly feeling. A thin rule appears in the gutters between the columns, helping to define the unjustified text. The "News Briefs" headline is the proper size, with the right amount of spacing above and below it. Notice the white space in the far right column next to the "News" headline.

The illustration of the "President" comes from *DeskTop Art,* electronic clip art on disk by Dynamic Graphics, touched up with PC Paintbrush. It's in correct proportion to the other elements on the page, and draws the reader's eye to the pull quote beneath it. Notice the ample leading between the lines of the pull quote. This example effectively demonstrates how type can be used as a graphic element to attract the reader's attention.

The "Inside" listings under the pull quote also are large enough to be highly visible, but not overwhelming. Note the even, consistent spacing between the listings, and between all the elements on the page. A box containing calendar information anchors the lower left corner, and balances the strong visual interest created by the "Inside" listings. And all three columns align evenly at the bottom.

The contrast between the bold sans serif headlines and the casual, free-flowing body text creates an interesting texture on the page, combining many diverse elements without becoming cluttered or crowded.

Numismatics REMUNERATION

Good design for fun and profit *May 1989*

From the President

Publishing Profits Up

By P. Tanner

What is desktop publishing? It means different things to different people. To some it simply means setting type with a computer, on any of a variety of printers. To others it means creating the entire finished page on a computer.

Writing the text, laying out the page, merging in the graphics, and finally printing a finished page on a laser printer or digital typesetter. According to the ABC program "Business Week," by 1991, desktop publishing will be a three billion dollar industry.

Who will benefit from Desktop Publishing? You will. Yes, you. The one flipping through the pages looking for the funny pictures. You may already be a publisher. Yes, you!

Publishing doesn't mean just books and magazines. If you're part of an office, school, any kind of organization or club, you're probably already creating a newsletter or flyer of events.

If you work in any business, such as a real estate office or travel agency, you need to send out promotional flyers about your hottest listings, or bargain travel packages. In the past, you've either had to type everything up and stick it on a page, or send it out to a typesetter and have a graphic artist paste up for you. Either way, an unpretentious little newsletter can quickly become so tedious and time consuming that you'd like to trick someone else into doing it for you. Doesn't that sound nice?

Continued on page 3

May Events

President's Birthday	5
Design Competiton	19
Tree Planting	23
Wall Street Tour	29

News Briefs

So, if you're already publishing something, desktop publishing may be for you. Here's more news for desktop publishers--it can even be fun, depending on how easily you are entertained and amused.

On the following pages you will find examples of what you can do if you are: a small business, quick-print shop, ad agency, school, theater, fund raiser, restaurant, real estate office, fake estate office, travel agency, mail order catalog, writer, unpublished writer looking for a way to do it yourself, home business, teacher, student, or any generally self-employed type.

Do you want to cut costs? Consider the production expenses.

President Tanner

"Who will benefit from desktop publishing? You will. Yes, you - the one flipping through these pages looking for the funny pictures."

Inside

❖ *Tips for handling newsletter design problems*

If an article does not fill an allotted space, there are several things you can do to correct the problem. Don't just use larger type or change the leading—the article will stand out, but for the wrong reason, and that's not how to draw attention to an article. It is usually possible to change the layout, making it more horizontal, or to eliminate the problem by moving artwork around. More often than not are several ways a layout can be rearranged to make it better. Don't be afraid to experiment.

- If it conforms to the design of the page, add a few subheads to the article. Each one takes up a line, so if the article is an inch short, adding three or four subheads fills the blank space, while providing readers with additional information that help them through the article.
- If the story already contains subheads, or if you don't want to use them, find a passage that will grab the reader's attention and use it as a readout. This can be a few words or an entire paragraph—whatever you need to make the article fill the space.
- If the page composition will accommodate it, you can set the entire article two or three picas narrower and box the article with a 1-point rule (or thicker if you so desire). This is one way to add emphasis to an article.

❖ *Steps to success*

Before starting to format your publication, you should take certain steps. Write your material, always remaining aware of your audience. If you already have the text, edit it, bearing the same considerations in mind. Write the headlines—more difficult than it might seem, but it's easier and quicker to modify existing text than it is to create something from scratch when you're trying to format. Place subheads in long articles while word processing (you can always remove them if the article runs too long, and it's more efficient than writing them while trying to design the page). Write all the captions, and run the spell checker, too. Verify that names, addresses, phone numbers, and prices are correct. These are steps over which you have some control, and it's not the fault of desktop publishing if delays caused by spelling and grammatical errors delay the layout and production.

At first, it's tempting at first to head right for the computer and ignore design completely. But try some paper-and-pencil sketches first. They don't have to be beautiful, but they should give you some idea of what goes where. Sketches help you determine how many columns to use, and what size the photos and illustrations should be (if you have any).

Does your company or group already have a recognizable style? Look at your letterhead and other printed material to see if there are elements in your previous publications that relate to this one. Only when you have completed all these steps should you begin working with the composition of the pages.

❖ *Training by design*

Many tools are available for novice desktop publishers. The latest twist in desktop publishing training involves lessons on videotape. Video instruction allows users to observe demonstrations of various techniques, duplicate the designs themselves, compare their work to the tape, and then review the steps again.

◆ Dynamic Graphics

➻ Dynamic Graphics, 6000 N. Forest Park Dr., Peoria, IL 61656.
800-255-8800

A publisher of electronic clip art, Dynamic Graphics, offers a *Step-By-Step Video Series* that includes a tape detailing design strategies and typesetting principles. The VHS tape is entitled “Desktop Design: Basic Electronic Graphic Techniques,” runs 30 minutes, and costs $49.95. It shows the desktop publishing procedures necessary to create three graphics projects, plus an overview of hardware and software.

Dynamic Graphics also offers a series of two- or three-day “Visual Communication Workshops” that cover the basics of graphic design, newsletter design, and design for desktop publishing. Workshops cost between $225 and $725, and locations include Anaheim, Atlanta, Boston, Chicago, Denver, Orlando, and Washington D.C. They also offer a useful catalog of related graphics and design products; Give them a call and request one.

You also might also want to consult local community colleges, universities, and computer training schools for information regarding desktop publishing and design classes.

◆ Style sheets on disk

Many useful utility programs have sprung up around desktop publishing programs. For novice desktop publishers, predesigned style sheets can be a big help. They contain many practical tips about the basics of graphic design, and teach the user how to quickly modify a style sheet. Users load their own text and graphic files, and can instantly tailor any element of the page layout to fit their individual document. See Chapter 20, *Software*, and the Appendix for specific products.

❖ *Dive in*

Now you are ready. WordPerfect’s desktop publishing capabilities are fun, no doubt about it. The only problem is that they can be so much fun that it’s easy to neglect “trivial” details, like composing understandable and well-organized text.

Experimentation is crucial, but you should master the basics of good graphic design before trying anything too complicated. Graphic design is one field where the phrase "if a little is good, more would be better," does *not* apply. Try adding elements one at a time, rather than all at once on the same page. You can't go wrong if you plan in advance and keep it simple.

So be good, eat your vegetables, do your homework, and for dessert you'll get to play with WordPerfect's desktop publishing features, make friends, influence people, and be the life of the party.

◆ What's this? A new book about fonts?

Since I enjoy dispensing advice so much, I've written yet another book, and this seems like a good time to mention it. If you enjoyed learning about the typefaces in this chapter, you should really like my new book. It's called *TypeStyle: How to Choose & Use Fonts,* and it's jam-packed with over 50 new, full-page examples of how to put fonts to work for you. It's also published by Peachpit Press, and is available in bookstores, or directly from the publisher. Ordering details can be found in the Appendix of this book. (When am I ever going to find the time to finish my novel?)

6

Measure for measure

or Give 'em an inch

In the wacky world of desktop publishing, WordPerfect takes you one step away from the typewriter and one step closer to the typesetter. While this is wonderful, it means you are no longer just sitting there typing—you are now sitting there typesetting. And as every good typesetter knows, precision is important.

Luckily, WordPerfect is pretty smart when it comes to distances. You can measure in *inches* (who's foot was the original foot?) or *centimeters.* As much as Americans would like to ignore centimeters, they are far more logical and easy to use than inches. There are 10 millimeters in a centimeter, 100 centimeters in a meter, 10 centimeters in a decimeter. ("Cent" means 100 as in "century" and "dec" means 10 as in "decade"; think of them as pennies and dollars.) You can also use *points* (there are 72 points in an inch, 12 points in a *pica*, and six picas in an inch). Are centimeters starting to look more attractive? WordPerfect also allows you to use the "WordPerfect 4.2" measurement system, based on spaces and lines. This is relatively useless for desktop publishing because it ignores different sizes of type. Even if you are upgrading from 4.2, I recommend that you use either inches or centimeters because 4.2 units can be quite confusing when you combine them with the different way 5.1 works from 4.2. WordPerfect's smallest form of measurement is the "W" unit, which is 1/1200th of an inch.

Remember, however, that just because you can enter a measurement into WordPerfect doesn't mean your printer can recreate it. If you try to create a line 1W wide, and your printer's resolution is 300 dpi, then the thinnest line it can create is 1/300th of an inch wide, not 1/1200th of an inch wide.

❖ Where are you, really?

Because of WordPerfect's measurement system, you can see exactly where you are on a page without having to enter View Document mode. At the bottom right-hand corner of the screen, WordPerfect displays cursor location information. Depending on what measurement format you specified as the default (Shift-F1 E U), WordPerfect will display your location in inches, centimeters, or points.

The **Ln** marker shows you how far down the page the cursor is (the top of the current line), and the **Pos** marker shows you how far across the page it is. These measurements include the header and footer spacing and offer a very accurate position reading. They are also invaluable when you want to calculate distances for advanced formatting.

◆ Get to the point

Luckily, WordPerfect allows you to use any of the forms of measurement at any time. Americans will probably find it easiest to set WordPerfect's default to inches, while Europeans will probably use centimeters as the default. As you will see, you can still enter line height in points or enter any other measurement in any format.

If you enter a number without indicating the units, WordPerfect will use whatever units you selected in Setup as the current default. If the default is inches,

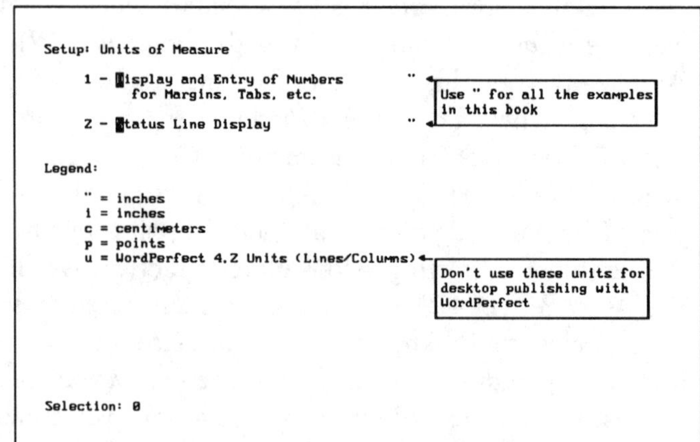

Units of measure.

and you enter 11 [ENTER] for line height, you're going to end up with 11 inches between each line (and wonder why you ever got into desktop publishing).

But if you enter 11P [ENTER] in the Line Height field, WordPerfect will know you mean points and translate it into default measurement units, in this case .15". If you change the default, WordPerfect translates all the measurements in the document to the new default, and displays them in the format you've chosen. Remember: " or **I** is for inches. **P** or **p** is for points. **C** or **c** is for centimeters. **W** or **w** is for 1/1200th of an inch. Don't use **U** or **u**.

REALLY NEAT TRICK: WordPerfect 5.1 is now smart enough to convert fractions for you. If you enter a measurement as 3/4", WordPerfect will automatically convert that to .75". This may not sound like much, but in 5.0 you had to do the math yourself. I don't know of any other program which actually allows you to enter measurements in fractions, so consider yourself lucky. But don't throw away your calculator just yet, as you may want it later on in the book for advanced formatting.

This means you can use whatever format you're most comfortable with. However, WordPerfect *insists* you use points when selecting a font, and you should always use points for measuring line heights.

While points might seem foreign to you right now, they are essential because type is always measured in points. Body type is normally from 9 to 12-point. Subheads range from 12 to 18-point. Headlines generally run from 18 to 48-point, with 72-point and above reserved for declarations of war or advertisements for really good sales.

❖ *Turning leading into gold*

In typesetting, leading (line height) is all-important. It's called leading because in the olden days, typesetters inserted thin strips of lead between the lines of type. Proper leading keeps the descenders (the parts of letters that stick *down* below the base of most characters, such the tail of a "y") and ascenders (the parts of letters that stick *up* above the top of most other letters, such as the top of the "t") from running into each other.

Because type is measured in points, it is customary (and logical) to measure the space between lines (leading) in points. The general rule in deciding on line spacing is to add *at least* 1 point to the size of the type. (For example, 10-point should have at least 11-point leading, and would be referred to as 10/11 or "10 on 11 ".) Two points of leading is also acceptable (that is WordPerfect's default). This means that if you're using 10-point type WordPerfect will give you 12-point leading (10/12).

If I had my choice, I'd choose one and a half points leading. To get 1½ points leading, press SHIFT-F8 O P L –.5p [ENTER] [ENTER] F7. The difference is quite noticeable.

These are good rules of thumb, but they're not gospel. Using less leading is rarely effective, while more leading can be used to fill otherwise blank pages. You can add as much as three or even four points leading, depending on the typestyle and specific application you are working with. However, with type sizes under 12 points, four points additional leading will appear to be double spacing, and that's generally not appropriate for typeset pages.

- It's never a good idea to skimp on leading just to pack in more text. Here's an example of not enough leading:

- When you don't have enough leading, the letters can run into each other and the reader has difficulty distinguishing the letters on each line. The eye becomes confused and forgets which line it was reading. It's also ugly.

- While double- and triple-spacing can be used for draft copies of text, it's not suitable for general typesetting. Here's an example of too much leading:

- When there is too much leading, lines of text are so far apart that they almost don't seem to form paragraphs, and this can make them difficult to read.

- Line height changes placed anywhere in the line affect the entire line they are on—immediately. If you put a line height change at the *end* of a line, WordPerfect uses that line spacing for the entire line, even the part of the line before the code.

This means that if you make the line height greater, WordPerfect adds extra space above the line, as well as below it.

◆ Automatic line height

Because this is WordPerfect's default mode, you don't need to do anything special in order for WordPerfect to automatically set leading for you. If you've turned the feature off, to turn on automatic line height, press

SHIFT-F8 L H A F7

◆ Leading

Here are some examples of the difference a little leading can make. The first number is the size of the type, the second is the amount of leading. WordPerfect's automatic leading corresponds to the 10/12 example. While there is nothing terribly wrong with it, it's a little on the tight side.

- 10/10

  Oh I wanna be a cowboy, but I've never seen a cow. I'd like to punch them doggies, but I don't know how. I've never been in a saddle while following cattle, or had a home on the range . . .

- 10/11

  Still I'd gladly exchange all my three-piece suits for a ten-gallon hat and a nice pair of boots. Oh I wanna be a cowboy, but I don't know how.

- 10/12

  C-O-W-B-O-Y. That's for me, though I don't know why. But a C-O-W-A-R-D, a coward's all I'll ever be. Oh I wanna be an outlaw, but my in-laws say "no."

- 10/13

  They think it's just a phase that I'll soon outgrow. But some mysterious force tells me "go steal a horse" and of course something's got to give.

- 10/14

  Because when you live on the 11th floor, it's hard to get a horse through your elevator door. Oh I wanna be an outlaw, but I don't have the brains.

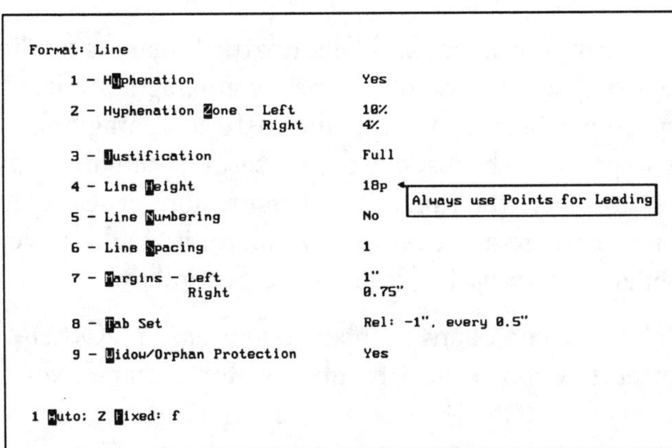
```
Format: Line

     1 - Hyphenation                              Yes

     2 - Hyphenation Zone - Left                  10%
                            Right                 4%

     3 - Justification                            Full

     4 - Line Height                              18p
                                                        Always use Points for Leading
     5 - Line Numbering                           No

     6 - Line Spacing                             1

     7 - Margins - Left                           1"
                   Right                          0.75"

     8 - Tab Set                                  Rel: -1", every 0.5"

     9 - Widow/Orphan Protection                  Yes


1 Auto: 2 Fixed: f
```

Always set line height in points and make it at least one point greater than the point size of the font.

Leading can make a huge difference in a publication. Not enough leading makes lines of text difficult to read and "gray." Too much makes it hard to read and lacks contrast. Some art directors use an abundance of leading to achieve an avant-garde, arty look, but leading that is less than the typesize is never acceptable, unless the look you're going for is "ugly."

◆ Leading feature

WordPerfect's leading feature works with automatic line height only. Fixed line height will completely override any leading settings. Leading allows you to specify how much automatic leading WordPerfect uses. The nice thing about it is that, unlike manual line height, which doesn't change when you change type sizes, leading simply tells the Automatic Line Height feature how much extra space to add between lines, regardless of type size. Leading still remains "automatic"; it's just that you have more control over it. Don't let the fact that this feature is buried deep in the "Other Print Functions" menu deter you from using it.

While WordPerfect's default leading of 2 points is a good average, it might be too much, or too little, depending on the typeface you use.

If you want to use WordPerfect's default of 2 points, leave Leading set to 0. I admit this is a little confusing (at least it was for me, I spent about an hour trying to figure it out), but this number stands for how much more or less than 2 points of leading you want. If you leave it at 0, you get 2 points. If you set it to 1p, you get 3 points. If you set it to -1p, you get 1 point. Ah, the vagaries of "new math." The way to remember this feature is to remember that 2+2 always equals 4 (except when it's -2, in which case it equals 0).

All right now, stop procrastinating. You have to dive right in and try it for yourself. Otherwise life will pass you by and you will be nothing but a shell of your former self, all because you refused to try WordPerfect's Leading feature. Have I worn you down yet? If so, press

SHIFT-F8 O P L

Notice that there are two settings, Primary and Secondary. Primary is for "interline" spacing, which means the spaces between the lines of a paragraph. Secondary is for "interparagraph" spacing, which means the lines between paragraphs. If you want the space between paragraphs to be just like the spaces between lines (and you usually do), set both these numbers the same. If you want more or less space between paragraphs (and while I can see a reason to have more, it would be very unusual to have less), enter different settings for Primary and Secondary.

➥ Make sure to type a "p" at the end of any number you enter here. Otherwise you may inadvertently enter a huge number. If, for example, you typed just plain **1 [ENTER]** and your default measurement was inches, you would be adding 1 inch (72 points) of extra leading between each line. (Mistakes like this often cause premature aging. Avoid it.) Just use a "p" after the number. Remember, we're talking leading, and leading is always measured in points. To leave Leading, press

F7

◆ Fixed line spacing

To set "fixed" line spacing, press

SHIFT-F8 L H F

and then enter a number followed by a **P** for points. Remember that the number should be 1 or 2 points larger than the size of the type. If you use 10-point type, enter either **11p** or **12p** and press **[ENTER]** twice. To leave Leading, press

F7

The only problem with setting leading manually in WordPerfect is that the leading will be wrong if you change the size of the body text. The easiest way to avoid this is to create an open style containing the type you want to use for body text, and the corresponding line height. Then, by changing the style, all the leading will change as well. For more information, see Chapter 11, *Styles.* Unless you really need fixed line height for something in particular (like drop or raised caps), you should consider using the Leading feature (SHIFT-F8 O P L) instead because it will adjust automatically, no matter what size font you use.

◆ Manual leading

Setting leading manually is essential in some circumstances. While mixing typesizes on a line should be done with caution, there are times when it's appropriate (such as in a "raised cap," a single large character at the start of a paragraph). When creating an outline, using larger type for the numbers causes them to stand out. However, when using automatic line height, WordPerfect will put more space above and below a line which has as little as a single character in larger type. In certain situations this can make leading uneven and unattractive. See Chapter 8, *Alignment,* for more information about raised and drop caps.

❖ *When rulers collide*

You may have thought that 1/100th of an inch is too small a measurement to bother with, but that was before you got into desktop publishing. Most laser printers have a resolution of 300 dots per inch (considered rough by typesetting standard, but high enough so that few people notice the difference between lasersetting and typesetting). That means a single laser dot is only 1/300th of an inch wide, and yet it's big enough for you to see. If you don't believe me, look very, very carefully at some type produced by a laser printer. You can see little tiny jagged edges to the characters, and some of these are as small as one single laser dot.

❖ *Formerly secret system "W"*

WordPerfect 5.0 had a secret measurement system called the "W." In the first edition of this book I stumbled upon this undocumented feature one dark and stormy night (it was actually just a hot and sticky night) and now it's such common knowledge that it's even listed on the menu. "W" isn't the fashion tabloid, it's the smallest unit of measure within WordPerfect.

If you enter W for units of measure, there are 1200 units per inch (about four times the resolution of current laser printers). When I first discovered this, I theorized that WP was prepared to see 1200 dpi laser printers soon. (Since this book was printed on a LaserMaster 1000 dpi printer, can 1200 dpi be far away?)

This means you can enter *any* measurement in W's. If you create lines that are 1W wide, they will print as hairlines, a single dot wide, even on 1200 dpi typesetting machines. (Actually, they will be so narrow that they will probably be invisible.)

I don't recommend using this unit of measure for everything (it's too alien), but it's nice to know it's there when you want extremely thin lines or really infinitesimal control.

❖ *Margins*

If you're used to setting left and right margins such as 10 and 70, get ready for a shock. These same margins now will be 1" and 1". Why? Because now instead of measuring across the page from left to right, you have to measure in from the edges of the paper. Margin settings of 1" and 1" mean that your text will begin 1" from the left edge of the paper, and end 1" from the right edge of the paper.

The same applies to top and bottom margins. It really makes sense once you get used to it. Let's try it together by setting left and right margins at three-quarters of an inch. Press

SHIFT-F8 L M 3/4 [ENTER] 3/4 [ENTER] F7

Now let's create top and bottom margins of a half-inch. Press

SHIFT-F8 P M 1/2 [ENTER] 1/2 [ENTER] F7

5.0: You must enter numbers as decimals. In the above example, you'd enter .75 instead of 3/4, and .5 instead of 1/2.

5.1: Notice that once you've entered the fraction, WordPerfect automatically converts it to decimal format. Of course, you can enter it in decimal format yourself, if you like. If you don't like, enter the number as a fraction, as we've just done (and don't give me any lip).

Here's a way to set left/right and top/bottom margins and save a few keystrokes in the process. We'll set left/right to a half-inch and top bottom to three-quarters of an inch.

SHIFT-F8 L M 1/2 [ENTER] 1/2 [ENTER][ENTER] P M 3/4 [ENTER] 3/4 [ENTER] F7

Notice how you can combine your formatting foray into one trip for both types of margins.

WordPerfect's default margins are 1" all around the page. When you are using laser printers, WordPerfect automatically sets a minimum margin of about .25". I say "about" because this limit varies from printer to printer. If you try to set anything smaller, it will automatically return to .25" (or the smallest limit). To be specific, on a LaserJet the smallest allowable margins are .25" on top, .2" on the bottom and the left, and .31" on the right.

Before you complain about this fascist measurement system, remember that WordPerfect's doing this for your own good. Because of the mechanics of paper handling, laser printers can rarely print any closer to the edge of the paper than a quarter of an inch.

And besides, it's very rare that you'd want to set margins less than .4" anyway. Otherwise the print is so close to the edge of the page that readers can't hold the page without putting their fingers over the print, and with some printing methods, this means getting ink on their delicate little fingers. If you want an illustration to "bleed" off the edge of the page, consider trimming the paper.

❖ *WYSMBWYG*

One of the big buzz-words in desktop publishing is WYSIWYG, or wizzywig. This stands for "What you see is what you get," meaning that what you see on-screen is an accurate representation of what you get on the page.

WordPerfect is only near-WYSIWYG in View Document mode, but it's accurate in the ways that really count. It's not totally WYSIWYG because it doesn't display the exact fonts you're using, just generic serif or sans-serif fonts. This isn't terribly important because you only use the View Document mode to be sure that everything is in the right place. Words, and even individual letters, are where they will be on the page.

But when you write and edit in text mode, WordPerfect could best be described as "What You See Might Be What You Get." Text screens have monospaced fonts (like typewriters), but desktop publishing uses proportionally spaced fonts. If the fonts on-screen aren't the same width as those in the printer, you're going to see only the vaguest approximation of the page when in text mode. (You'll see what words are on which lines; lines on-screen will begin and end with the same words on paper.)

Some graphics cards, such as the Hercules RAM-font, can display italics and different sizes of type on-screen, but even these are only approximations of the finished product.

❖ *Run off the screen with the rich & famous*

Some people (me included) find it *very* annoying when their text is so long it runs off the right side of the screen, and yet this happens frequently when your base font is 12-point or less. When using 10-point Times (or Dutch), you can get almost 100 characters on a line, while most monitors display only 80 characters on a line.

So what can you do? You've got a couple of choices. First, you have to remember that it's not good to have such long lines of type because they're too hard to read. If you bothered to read Chapter 5, you know that for best readability, a line of type shouldn't be more than about 60 characters long. So your first choice is to change the margins, making them larger on both sides, which shortens the lines of text.

Another way to reduce line length is to use more than one column of text on a page. Most people don't like doing their actual writing in column mode because it adds a level of complexity to the screen, but try it, you might like it. (I don't.)

You might also consider using a monospaced base font, such as Courier, when you write. I am obliged to inform you that my wife has what she calls "anti-Courier bias," which, simply stated, means that she hates to read anything printed in Courier. She also says that it's nearly impossible to proofread pages set in Courier, whereas mistakes literally jump right off the page when printed in a proportionally spaced font such as Times Roman. I agree with her. Courier is a thing of the past, and while some states demand that legal documents be printed in Courier, there is no law (that I know of) which states you ever have to use Courier again, for as long as you live.

Another idea (and one which is more popular around my house) is to create a style which gives you "temporary" wide margins, or a temporary larger typeface, say 14 or 16-points, so that fewer characters fit on each line. You just have to remember to remove the style before you go to print.

Your other choice is to pester the good folks at WordPerfect, and get them to include a feature like Microsoft Word has, where you can turn off "accurate" on-screen formatting and just see your text. The text still prints correctly, you just don't see real line endings on-screen. When you're just writing, you shouldn't care.

Another solution to the problem for Hercules, CGA, EGA, and VGA users is a program called ScreenExtender. This program permits your current monitor to show up to 100 columns (100 letters wide) and up to 60 lines (depending on your monitor). This allows you to see so much on-screen that your text will probably never run off the screen (see the Appendix for more info about where to get this program).

❖ Tab happy

You probably think you know what the tab key does. It adds a few spaces, usually five, and moves everything over, right? Wrong, hamster breath. The tab key actually inserts a tab code, and this code moves to an exact horizontal location on a line, determined by where you set the tab.

Tabs are *essential* when using WordPerfect as a desktop publishing program, so we're going to spend some time with them. If there's one thing you need to get into your fuzzy little head this very instant, it's that you will never again line things up using the spacebar the way you might have on a typewriter, or even WordPerfect 4.2. Never. Not ever. Not even for your own amusement with another consenting adult. Here's why.

◆ Tabs 'R us

Because WordPerfect isn't completely WYSIWYG (What you see is what you get) in text mode, things may appear to line up neatly on-screen, yet print looking messy and unkempt.

The biggest on-screen deception comes when you use the spacebar. As I've said repeatedly (and will continue to repeat), you simply cannot align text by using the spacebar as you would with a typewriter. Here's an example.

A) This line appears on-screen to be indented the same amount as

B) This line

While they are only 1/100 of an inch off, that can really stand out. The problem becomes increasingly worse as you work with more text. Take a look at the following example.

Presidents and their Dwarf/Reindeer/Substance Equivalents

PRESIDENT	DWARF	REINDEER	SUBSTANCE
Abe Lincoln	Doc	Rudolph	Copper
Dick Nixon	Grumpy	Blitzen	Polyester
Jimmy Carter	Happy	Comet	Legume
Ronnie Reagan	Sleepy	Prancer	Teflon
George Bush	Dopey	Dasher	Silly Putty

Those lines appear to line up on-screen, but they obviously don't print that way. This is because each letter of a proportionally spaced font (such as Dutch/Times,

Swiss/Helvetica) uses a different amount of space horizontally, so each word ends in a different place. Bold and italic fonts usually take up different amounts of space than do medium/roman ones. Even the width of a space varies depending on the typeface and size you use.

Here's the same example using tabs:

Presidents and their Dwarf/Reindeer/Substance Equivalents

PRESIDENT	*DWARF*	*REINDEER*	*SUBSTANCE*
Abe Lincoln	Doc	Rudolph	Copper
Dick Nixon	Grumpy	Blitzen	Polyester
Jimmy Carter	Happy	Comet	Legume
Ronnie Reagan	Sleepy	Prancer	Teflon
George Bush	Dopey	Dasher	Silly Putty

When you use tabs, text lines up on-screen and on paper. In this example, tabs were set every 1.2" so that there is only one tab between each column. At first I set them 1" apart, but when I checked in View Document, I noticed that Sleepy was too close to Ronnie, so I went back into tab setting and moved them interactively until they looked right. Then I went back into View Document, just to make sure.

➾ Tip: Lining up the lines

The horizontal ruling lines for the above chart are not WordPerfect graphics lines, but simply underlined tabs. WordPerfect's horizontal ruling lines do not print far enough down on a line and overprint the bottom of characters. The horizontal lines above are easy to create because you simply press **F8** at the start of each line, and the underline continues under the text and tabs. To make sure WordPerfect underlines tabs, type **SHIFT-F8 O U Y Y F7**. Vertical rules between columns are not quite so easy, but we'll get to that in Chapter 14, *Rules*.

This same table could also be created using the table feature. For more information about tables, see Chapter 10, *Table Manners*.

◆ Musical tabs

Don't forget that all tabs move when you change the tab line. Because of this, you should always set tabs immediately preceding an important table. If you want to keep the current settings, go to the beginning of the table and type

SHIFT-F8 L T F7 F7

This will insert a code containing the current tab settings and keep them from being changed accidentally if you later specify new tab setting somewhere before the table.

If you change tables frequently and have more than one table with the same format, you might consider creating a style that contains nothing more than a tab setting. Then, when you change the style, all the tables will change consistently. For more information, see Chapter 11, *Styles.*

◆ Tab history

The tabs in 5.0 were a feature only a mother could love. They were a sore spot with me for two reasons. First, if you wanted to change them from normal to aligned, or dot leader, or centered, or right aligned, you had to search and replace them. That was a bother, but it wasn't as bad as what happened if you changed the tab settings. In 5.0, tab codes would actually be deleted from your file. One wrong tab setting and boom, your formatting was ruined.

The other problem with 5.0's tabs reared its ugly head when you set text in columns. If you had three columns and wanted the first line of each paragraph indented a quarter of an inch, you had to spend time calculating where to set each tab, based on its column's left margin. Because 5.0 allowed you to work with proportionally-spaced typefaces, you couldn't start paragraphs with spaces, you had to use tabs for control and for the ability to quickly change the amount of indent throughout your file. But in some cases, 5.0 made this all seem unnecessarily hard.

Now 5.1 comes to the rescue with a tab feature which everyone can love. It's even considerate enough to permit you to continue using tabs the old-fashioned way, if you don't like the newfangled way.

◆ Theory of tab relativity

The tabs in 5.1 come in two flavors: chocolate and vanilla . . . no, wait, I was thinking about Ben & Jerry there for a moment. 5.1's tabs can either be "Absolute" (the old way) or "Relative" (the new improved way, which is now the default). An Absolute tab set at .5" will always be .5" from the left side of the paper (unless the cursor is to the right of the .5" mark, in which case it completely ignores you). A Relative tab set at .5" will always be .5" from the *current left margin.* This means that if your page has two columns, you don't have to calculate anything. When you press the tab key in the second column, you will automatically move .5" in from the left margin of the current column.

I recommend that you use Relative tabs for everything, and here's why: they are less hassle. Absolute tabs are an absolute pain in the brain. Don't let the word "Relative" scare you, they aren't at all like the relatives you meet at family reunions. They are accommodating and easy to get along with, and they don't eat the best part of the turkey before you can. When you change margins you don't have to reset all the tabs if they are Relative, as you do with Absolute tabs.

In fact, I firmly believe that the only reason WordPerfect left Absolute tabs in the program is for old fuddy duddies . . . or anyone with plenty of old WordPerfect files which *only* have Absolute tabs. But when you create new files with 5.1, stick with Relative tabs.

One more thing. When you load a file into 5.1 which was originally created with 5.0, the tab settings will all be Absolute, because that's the only type available in 5.0. I recommend you convert them to Relative tabs. To do this, place the cursor to the *right* of the tab setting code and press

SHIFT-F8 L T T R F7 F7

This will keep the tab settings the same, but it will convert them to Relative tabs.

◆ Hard tab time

There's actually one more type of tab, the "Hard" tab. If you want to create a tab which *doesn't* automatically change types (left, right, center, dot leader) when you change the tab line, press **HOME-TAB**. Instead of a **[Tab]**, this creates a **[TAB]**, which will not change types automatically. The amount the tab indents a line will still change with the tab line, however. Hard tabs should only be used when you have formatting that you're deathly afraid might change accidentally.

❖ *On your mark, get set Tabs, go*

Just one more point before we start. Because 5.1 shows your text reformatting as you change tabs, let's get some text on-screen with tabs in it. I don't care what it is, just one paragraph which starts with a tab will be sufficient. Then move your cursor *above* this paragraph so the tab line you're going to create will affect it.

I can tell by your moist palms that you are itching to get out there and set some tabs, so let's go. Press

SHIFT-F8 L T

Notice, if you will, that you now have six, count 'em, six, options, **T L C R D . (dot leader)**. You can forever remember these options by remembering "Type Left Center Right Decimal." But since there's no particular reason why you'd need to know them by heart, don't waste your time.

The **L** stands for a left (or normal) tab. **C** is for a centered tab, which centers the text at the point of the tab. **R** is a right tab, and this aligns the text from the right. **D** is a decimal tab, which aligns text (and numbers) on the decimal point. (Because Americans and Europeans use different decimal characters, you can choose the character you use by pressing **SHIFT-F8 O D**.) The **.** (period) allows you to make any of these four types of tabs into dot leader tabs.

The **T** stands for "Type." You have a choice between Relative and Absolute. You can tell which type of tab line you're on by its appearance. A Relative tab line looks like this:

```
L...L...L...L...L...L...L...L...L...L...L...L...L...L...L...

|    ^    |    ^    |    ^    |    ^    |    ^    |    ^    |    ^    |
^

0"        +1"       +2"       +3"       +4"       +5"       +6"       +7"
```

While an Absolute tab line looks like this:

```
L...L...L...L...L...L...L...L...L...L...L...L...L...L...L...

|    ^    |    ^    |    ^    |    ^    |    ^    |    ^    |    ^    |
^

1"        2"        3"        4"        5"        6"        7"        8"
```

QUIZ: Which type did I recommend you use? (A hint: I described this just four paragraphs back and if you can't remember, you need to check yourself into a hospital to find out just exactly what is causing this short-term memory loss.)

ANSWER: That's right, Relative. (If you cheated and read the answer before you really thought about it, you do not deserve to be quite so proud of yourself.)

Because Relative is WordPerfect's default, you don't have to do anything if that's the type of tab you want. I'm assuming that's the type of tab you want, so we won't press T. (You may try this on your own time at some later date when you have so little to do that it might actually seem interesting.)

There are two ways to set tabs: You can either move your cursor to the place on the line where you want the tab, then press either L, C, R, D, or "." or you can type in a number, then press enter.

But first, let's get rid of all those annoying standard tabs. To do this, type **[HOME] [HOME] [LEFT-ARROW] CONTROL-[END].** This will remove all tabs currently set. Did you notice how the text on-screen changed when you did this? This is a new feature, so appreciate it, you ingrate.

Now move the cursor to the ^ mark between 0" and +1 and press **L**. You have now set a tab in WordPerfect. I imagine this moment is something akin to the very first time you flew a Boeing 747 Jumbo Jet solo, so I will understand if you want to take the rest of the afternoon off.

If you are still here, let's continue. Did you notice how your text reformatted on-screen when you created a tab? I know, it doesn't seem very exciting just yet, but when you use it in real life it will be, if not exciting, then at the very least, practical.

To get an idea how the new interactive feature works, make sure the cursor is on top of the L tab you just created and press **.** (the period). Bingo. If everything has worked according to plan, the "L" will display in reverse and your text will have changed to show a few dots leading up to your tab. This is called a "dot leader," and while it's not an appropriate way to start a paragraph, it has 1001 uses, such as tables of contents, theater programs, and price lists to name but three.

Let's set another tab. Move the cursor to the +1" setting and press R. You've created a right tab, which means that the text will align at the tab and stick out to the left.

◆ Officer, cancel that tab

Let's say you don't like the way your tab change has turned out. You want to go back to the way things were (don't we all). It's easy. Press

F1 F1 F1

This will take you back to the main editing screen with your old tabs intact.

◆ Interactivity

For my next trick, I'd like to show you how to move tabs—interactively. Before we begin, set your base font to Dutch (or Times Roman) 12-point by pressing

CONTROL-F8 F

Move the cursor to Dutch 12 and press **F7 F7**. (If you are using a PostScript or LaserMaster printer, move the cursor to Dutch, then press **[ENTER]** and type **12 [ENTER]**.) Type the following text, with a tab between each item. Don't worry if things don't line up, don't even worry if it looks like a hopeless mess. Whatever you do, press only one tab between each item. I swear they will line up when we are finished. Feel free to change any dwarf, reindeer, or substance if you come up with something you feel is more appropriate (or amusing).

PRESIDENT/DWARF/REINDEER/SUBSTANCE
Abe Lincoln Doc Rudolph Copper
Dick Nixon Grumpy Blitzen Polyester
Jimmy Carter Happy Comet Legume
Ronnie Reagan Sleepy Prancer Teflon
George Bush Dopey Dasher Silly Putty

OK, now it's time to clean up this mess. Move the cursor to the top of the list and press

SHIFT-F8 L T

Move the cursor to the tab at the ^ mark (between 0" and +1") and press the **[DEL]** key. This will remove the tab. Not much will happen on-screen, but be patient. Move the cursor to the 1" mark and press the **[DEL]** key again. Aha, now something's happened. The Dwarf column is now lined up neatly. They may be two short of a full load, but at least they're neat.

Delete the tab at the 2" mark and, shazam, now *all* the columns are aligned neatly. Sure, they're neat, but they aren't even. My, aren't we fussy today. OK, let's make them even.

Move the cursor to the tab set at 1.5", and press **CONTROL-[LEFT ARROW]**. The Dwarf column should move 1 space to the left. Now let's try the same thing with the Reindeer column. Move the cursor to the tab at the 2.5" mark and press **CONTROL-[LEFT ARROW]**. The Reindeer column should move one space to the left. Uh-oh, that's messed up the Substance column. OK, move the cursor to the 3" mark and press **[DEL]** to delete that tab. Now Substance is lined up again.

Now, just for fun, let's make one of those tabs dot leaders. Move the cursor so it is on top of the second "L" and press **.** (the period). The L will reverse so it is white on black, and you will see dots between the first two columns. Ugh, that doesn't look very good; let's change it back. Make sure your cursor is on the "L" and press **.** again. The "L" will return to normal, and the dots between the columns will disappear.

◆ Another way

Like almost everything else in WordPerfect, there's more than one way to set a tab. In this example we've deleted them, or moved them interactively with [CONTROL-ARROW], but there are two other ways. One way is to move the cursor to the place on the line where you want a tab, and then press L, R, C, or D. The other is a more accurate, though less intuitive, way—you can set tabs by entering measurements.

To place a tab based on measurement, all you do is type the measurement. If you want to set a tab at 4 1/4", you type **"4 1/4"** and press **[ENTER]**. If you want to set a tab at a measurement less than 1", you must first type a 0, like this: **0.4"**, setting a tab at .4". If you don't type the 0 first, WordPerfect will create a dot leader tab wherever the cursor is because the first thing it sees you press is the period key. Remember, WordPerfect uses whatever measurement you set as default in setup, but you can enter measurements in any unit, if you follow the number with an " mark for inches, **p** for points, **c** for centimeters, or **w** for WordPerfect's 1/1200th of an inch units. If you so much as even try to use **u**'s, you'll get a splitting headache.

◆ Equally spaced tabs

If you want to set a whole slew of tabs, separated from each other by an even amount of space, type **[HOME] [HOME] [LEFT-ARROW] CONTROL-[END]** to clear all the current tabs, then type **–1** (the very beginning of a Relative tab line if your left margin is set to 1"), a comma, and whatever increment you want the evenly set tabs to occur, such as **–1,.25"**. This will automatically set tabs every quarter of an inch until the end of the line (or at least until the 13" inch mark). The default is a left tab, but if you manually set the first tab to any other type (such as R, C, or D), and then type **–1,.25** the tabs will automatically be the same type as the first tab you set.

❖ *Moving anywhere with precision*

➻ If you want utmost control over the printed page, WordPerfect's *Advance* command is vital. Read on.

When you begin working with desktop publishing, you start to think in terms of fractional inches — tiny increments.

Sometimes you want to move precisely a tenth of an inch down, but a return is too big. Or you want to move exactly a tenth of an inch to the right, but a space is too small and two spaces are too big.

This is when WordPerfect's little-known **Advance** feature comes to the rescue. Advance allows you to move precisely up and down, left or right, or even a specific distance from the top of a page.

In this case, advance doesn't have to mean advanced. While it's terribly precise, it's not terribly difficult.

◆ Advance to go

To use Advance, press

SHIFT-F8 O A

You are now presented with 6 options: **U**p **D**own **L**ine **L**eft **R**ight **P**osition.

When you select one of these options, you won't see any change on the editing screen. If you have reveal codes on, you'll see the code and the measurement status line at the bottom, which reflects the change. The difference will be apparent when you View Document. All text following the code is affected, so if you choose Down 1", everything will be moved down one inch, starting at the code.

```
Format: Other

     1 - Advance  <------------------------------+
                                                 |
     2 - Conditional End of Page                 |
                                                 |
     3 - Decimal/Align Character     .           |
         Thousands' Separator        ,           |
                                                 |
     4 - Language                    US          |
                                                 |
     5 - Overstrike                              |
                                                 |
     6 - Printer Functions                       |
                                                 |
     7 - Underline - Spaces          Yes         |
                     Tabs            Yes         |
                                                 |
     8 - Border Options                          |
                                                 |
          Use "Advance" when you need absolute precision

Advance: 1 Up; 2 Down; 3 Line; 4 Left; 5 Right; 6 Position: 0
```

Advance command.

Up: Moves the text up from its current position. If you are on line 4.48" and advance up .1", the line will print at 4.38". If you edit the text and the line moves to 7.12", it will then print up .1" from that, or 7.02".

Down: Same as up, only down.

Line: While up and down are Relative, based on the location of the code, Line is Absolute. If you're on line 4.48" and select Line 5.58", the line will print at 5.58". If you edit the text and the line moves to 7.12", it will still print at 5.58" because of the advance code.

Left: Same as in up and down, only to the left.

Right: Same as in up and down, only to the right.

Position: Same as in line, absolute from the margins of the page, only horizontally.

I use the advance command frequently because it allows me to move text with great precision and to line up everything perfectly.

◆ Tip: Locking things in place

You'll often run into a situation where the body text is in the correct location, but headline or graphics above them are not.

Once I have material exactly where I want it, I lock it there with the advance command. I press

SHIFT-F8 O A I [ENTER] F7

This places the exact, current horizontal measurement in an advance code, and ensures that the text (or graphics) isn't going to move from this spot.

I can then move the cursor higher on the page and, once again, use the advance command to subtly move headlines up or down, change leading, add or close up space. No matter what I do, I'm sure that the advance command will keep the rest of my page (or pages) perfectly in place.

Advance can also be used to place evenly spaced horizontal lines on a page to create forms, although it's now probably easier to do this with the table feature.

◆ Tip: Safety first

➻ I also save before any major alterations so that in case of an error, all I have to do is clear the screen and retrieve my file.

◆ Old math

I had my 4.0 average destroyed by a C in math class. When the teacher started discussing real vs. imaginary numbers, I figured I might as well make up my own numbers; the teacher didn't agree. So when I say I hate "new" math, I mean it.

Old math, however, doesn't bother me, especially with a $4 calculator in my hand. (I can remember when those things cost and weighed more than a computer—and I'm barely thirtysomething.) The point of all this is that "old" math is often useful in desktop publishing. After using WordPerfect for a while, I realized that I could make my life easier if I stopped guessing at measurements and started using the WordPerfect ruler line instead. Don't bother trying to hold a ruler up to the screen because it won't work. But the numbers in the lower right corner of the WordPerfect screen tell you all you need to know.

Say, for example, you have a page with a table smack dab in the middle of it. You want to create a vertical line between the columns of text above and below the table. To do this, you'd have to know how tall the table is in inches (or whatever units of measurement you are using).

Here's an easy method. Move the cursor to the line below the last line of the table, and write down the number that appears after **Ln** in the lower right of the screen. Now move to the first line of the table, write down the number after **Ln,** and subtract it from the first number. You now know the height of the table. Simple, huh?

If you have the *WordPerfect Library* program (sold separately, just like batteries for kids' toys), you can also use the handy-dandy on-screen calculator which comes with it.

7

About faces

The technical side of fonts

You have IBM to thank for Courier. They designed it for their typewriters and it's probably what you've always used. Pica and Elite are popular, too, and are examples of fonts. Times Roman, Helvetica, Avant Garde, Bookman, New Century Schoolbook, Palatino, and Zapf Chancery are examples of typefaces you'll be using for desktop publishing. These fonts are built into PostScript laser printers, such as the QMS PS 810 or the Apple LaserWriter. They're also available from Bitstream for use with the WordPerfect Fontware system.

The fonts built into scaleable font printers, including LaserJet III, PostScript, LaserMaster, and Canon LBP III printers can be printed in every size from 1 to 1000 point (almost 14 inches high), in 1/10th of a point increments. PostScript and LaserMaster printers can go as high as 1199 point. These fonts can also be printed as outlines, with shadows, or in shades of gray instead of just black. You can also print fonts at any angle (see Chapter 12, *Graphics*), although WordPerfect supports only 90-, 180-, and 270-degree rotations.

All of these printers can also use downloadable fonts. The Fontware Installation Kit can install Bitstream fonts for PostScript, LaserJet III, and Canon LBP III printers, as well as the LaserJet and other laser and DeskJet printers. Type Director can install fonts for LaserJets and DeskJets. While the installation instructions in this chapter are focused towards Fontware, the basics of font installation from inside WordPerfect are identical, no matter what type of fonts you use. Unfortunately for PostScript users, WordPerfect does not yet support all of the fonts available from Adobe (the makers of PostScript). In fact, the PostScript driver shipping with WordPerfect cannot work with any downloadable fonts. WordPerfect updates their printer drivers regularly, so call them for the latest information about which Adobe fonts are supported. But wait, there's more.

LaserJet printers use two types of fonts: cartridge and downloadable (also called *soft*). Soft fonts are most useful in desktop publishing because you copy them from the computer's hard disk to the printer's memory. Cartridge fonts are limited to sizes of up to 30-point, while soft fonts can realistically be as large as 72-point (they can be larger, but then they start to get unwieldy).

The largest size you can use depends on how much memory the LaserJet has. The standard LaserJet II has 512K and can print fonts of up to 30 point. Adding more memory will theoretically allow the printer to print fonts of up to 690 point. Realistically, however, a 72-point font takes up anywhere from 300 to 1000K of disk space and printer memory (depending on the font and symbol set chosen). Larger fonts take megabytes of disk space and take several minutes to download from the computer to the printer. A complete set of bitmapped fonts for a single typeface family can easily take up two megabytes of disk space.

LaserMaster controllers (which were used to print this book) are special expansion cards which fit inside your computer and work with LaserJet printers (or 400 dpi Canon engines) to give them many of the powers of PostScript, but at much higher speed and resolution. A page that might take five minutes to print on a PostScript printer may take only 20 seconds using a LaserMaster-controlled printer. This speed is important when you have deadlines to meet. Also, the LX6 and LM 1000 models can print with such high resolution that they rival typesetting machines costing five to ten times more. While LaserMaster controllers have the power of PostScript, they are not PostScript compatible.

❖ *Waddya print?*

The type of printer you use will determine what fonts you can use. A PostScript printer has all the fonts mentioned at the beginning of this chapter—built-in. This is what they look like:

ITC Avant Garde	ITC Bookman
Helvetica	Helvetica Narrow
ITC Zapf Chancery	Times Roman
New Century Schoolbook	Palatino

If you use a LaserJet, you can print using either Courier or a tiny print called Line Printer. That's it. Of course, if you have a LaserJet Plus or Series II, you can also get Times Roman (Dutch) and Helvetica (Swiss) with WordPerfect's Fontware Installation Kit.

But now it gets confusing. Times Roman is a typestyle, Times Roman Medium is a typeface. Times Roman Medium, Bold, Italic, and Bold Italic are also typefaces, and the four of them together are a typeface family (not unlike the Partridge Family).

Times Roman **Bold** is a totally different font than Times Roman Medium. Times Roman *Italic* is even more different, and Times Roman ***Bold Italic*** is yet another font. So for each typestyle, there are generally four fonts: a medium, bold, italic, and bold italic. And it doesn't stop there; the LaserJet requires separate soft fonts for portrait (vertical) and landscape (horizontal) pages.

LaserJet: *POP QUIZ!* How many fonts does a LaserJet need to print 10-point Dutch medium, 10-point Dutch bold, 10-point Dutch Italic, and 10-point Dutch bold-italic? If you answered four, you can count. The LaserJet requires four separate font files to print the regular variations on 10-point Dutch. Each of these files must be created by Fontware and reside on a hard disk. The four will take up about 20K each for a total of about 80K.

◆ Memory for faces

A note about printer memory. Most new laser printers come with at least 512K of memory. That's enough to do most tasks, but not enough to do a full page of 300 dpi (dots-per-inch) graphics, or to combine a lot of soft fonts and graphics. New PostScript printers have at least 2 or 3 megabytes of memory, and this is enough to print a full page of 300 dpi graphics, along with text. The following section applies mostly to LaserJet and compatible printers.

Everything takes memory: soft fonts, graphics, and even an area of the printer that handles formatting commands. You can't use 350K of soft fonts and expect to have much room for graphics.

If the LaserJet II flashes "20" or "21," this is an indication that the page is too complex to be printed with the available memory. What do you do about it? If you need to print a full page of graphics and only have 512K of memory, you have a couple of choices. You can print the pages using Medium or Draft quality. Medium resolution is 150 dots per inch. While this is only half as good as the laser printer's best output, it also requires only half the memory. With 512K you can print an entire page of graphics, but only at 150 dpi resolution. At this resolution the graphics will have noticeably jagged edges. Type will always print at 300 dpi.

If you really need high-resolution graphics, try using fewer of them on each page, or make them smaller. The bigger they are, the more memory they take.

Remember the "creative use of white space" graphic design rule: don't cram so much on the page and you'll use up less memory.

You can also consider using fewer typefaces (remember that every typeface, even bold and italic, takes up memory). Often simply reducing the number of type sizes you have can help. If you have only one line in 14 point, make it 10, 12, or some other size already in use on the page. If that font has been marked with an * (so that the font is downloaded when the printer is initialized), you need to remove it by pressing **SHIFT F7 S E C** and removing the * next to the font name. If the font is marked with a +, it is only downloaded if it is used on the page.

As of this writing, memory upgrades are getting cheaper. HP sells their own upgrade for the LaserJet; it costs less than $500 for an additional megabyte of memory, enough to print a full page of graphics. Other companies are selling similar upgrades for less. If an upgrade is not feasible you should consider a program like PrintCache that compresses the graphics so they take up less space. PrintCache is reviewed in Chapter 20, *Software.*

One more tip: memory isn't everything. Occasionally you will receive an error message on a LaserJet that has nothing to do with memory. If "21" appears on the LaserJet, the formatting of the page is simply too complex for the printer to follow. It's not the fonts, but the formatting itself: the rules, sometimes the graphics, and the justification and letterspacing. When WordPerfect justifies text, it sends not only text but intricate and memory-consuming codes to the printer that tell it exactly where each letter needs to be placed. If you are confronted with the dreaded "21," place fewer elements on a page, and use smaller graphics, lower resolution graphics, or maybe even ragged text. LJIII owners can also use the "Page Protect" feature.

◆ PS

The fonts built into PostScript printers supply some of the typefaces used most commonly in typesetting. They provide you with an abundance of typographic choices, but PostScript printers also cost at least twice (and sometimes three times) as much as a LaserJet or compatible printer.

◆ Additional fonts

Don't be disappointed if your laser printer fonts aren't quite as sharp and perfect as those you see in the Bitstream promotional material included with WordPerfect. They're the same fonts, but Bitstream prints their material on Linotronic typesetters with a resolution of 2450 dpi, as opposed to a 300 dpi laser printer. Their fonts are specially designed for the resolution of the printer, so they do look excellent on all printers. For a complete list of currently available Fontware fonts, call Bitstream at 800-552-3688.

See Chapter 20, *Software,* for programs that allow WordPerfect access to fonts other than Bitstream's.

•◆ Cartridge

LaserJet: How much is that cartridge in the window? Pretty dear. Font cartridges cost anywhere from $150 to $700, and generally contain fonts no larger than 30 point.

So who needs cartridges when they're more expensive than soft fonts? Owners of the original LaserJet that can't use soft fonts depend on them for attractive type. People who share printers or use them on networks will find that downloading fonts takes years, or at least it seems that way. Networks and most printer sharing boxes work at slow speeds and make downloading tedious and inefficient.

If the printer has enough memory, you'll be able to use Fontware for all fonts, large and small. But using font cartridges allows you to access more than the limit of 32 soft fonts and, more importantly, to save precious memory for graphics and headline type. Cartridge fonts require no printer memory.

LaserJet III: This printer can use both bitmapped and outline cartridges. The *bitmapped* cartridges work exactly as they do on previous versions of the LaserJet (but are mostly unnecessary). Most "Super" cartridges don't work with the III. The *outline* cartridges act like any other scaleable outline, such as the CG Times and Univers, which are built-in. Downloadable scaleable fonts are created using either Type Director or a special conversion program available from Bitstream for use with their Fontware typefaces.

In past years, the most popular font cartridge the B Cartridge, which contains TmsRmn (Times Roman) in 8-point medium and 10-point medium, bold, and italic, and Helv (Helvetica) in 14.4 point bold, portrait only. This is an early design, and type is not of the best quality.

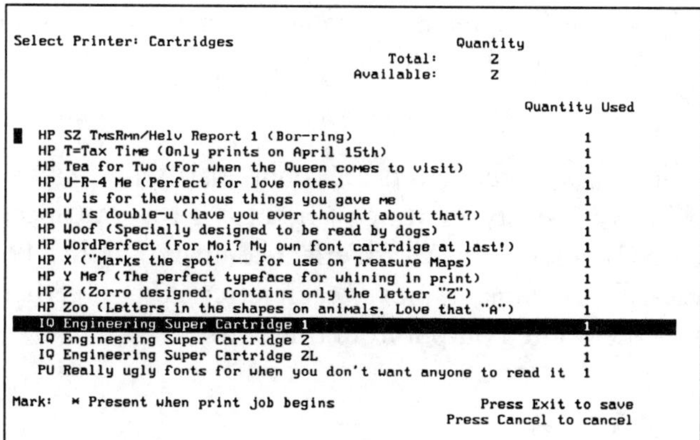

The LaserJet II and III can use two cartridges at a time. The original LaserJet can use one at a time. WordPerfect supports all Hewlett-Packard font cartridges. (SHIFT-F7 S E C F)

HP's new *WordPerfect Cartridge* is specifically designed for use with WordPerfect. It includes Compugraphic Times in 6, 8, 10, 12, 14, 18 bold, and 24 bold, with italics through 14 point. It also includes Univers (a sans serif font similar to Helvetica, but more attractive and elegant) in 14, 18, and 24 point. While 24-point isn't exactly big, it's almost twice as big and useful as the Z Cartridge's 14-point limit. While the Univers type isn't bold, WordPerfect can simulate a bold italic by overprinting each character twice, and although this is not as desirable as a real bold italic, it's more than acceptable.

◆ DTP in a cartridge

For $50 more than the WordPerfect cartridge, UDP's *DTP* cartridge offers a much larger range of weights in either Times Roman-esque or Helvetica-esque fonts than any other cartridge. It is the only cartridge to offer italics all the way up to 30 point, giving you plenty of extra design flexibility. Italics really do look different from the roman members of their family, so the ability to use 30 point italic is exceptional. The cartridge contains 8-point medium, 10-, 12-, and 14-point medium, bold, and italic, and 18-, 24- and 30-point bold, and bold italic. UDP can also boast the highest quality type. (Not for use with the III.)

◆ Super Cartridge

IQ Engineering has introduced a cartridge called the *Super Cartridge,* which just about says it all. This $699 cartridge has *both* a Times Roman-alike and a Helv-alike in 6, 8, 10, 11, 12, and 14 point medium, bold, and italic; 18 point comes in medium and bold, and 24 and 30 point come in bold only. The addition of 11 point is a good one, as 11 point is the size for body text I recommend most often. IQ's cartridge is the only one I know of with 11-point fonts, and the type quality is top quality, equal to UDP's. The cartridge also includes three display faces: Broadway, Cooper Black, and Ribbon (Coronet) in 14, 18, 24, and 30 point, making this the most powerful font cartridge available. They can be reached at IQ Engineering, Box 60955, Sunnyvale, CA 94086; 408-733-1161. See Chapter 21, *Hardware,* for more detailed reviews of font cartridges. (Not for use with the III.)

◆ Tip: Font cartridge spacing

The B Cartridge has very "loose" type; the letters are so far apart that they are difficult to read and don't produce the best typesetting. When using this cartridge, the spacing can be vastly improved by adding this WordPerfect command SHIFT-F8 O P W [ENTER] P90 [ENTER]. This command moves each letter closer together by 10 percent, clearly enhancing the printed output from this outdated cartridge.

```
Select Printer: Soft Fonts                        Quantity      * Fonts
                                        Total:    550 K           32
                                    Available:    165 K           15

FW HP LaserJet Series II                              Quantity Used

   (FW, Port) BSN Dutch Italic 08pt (ASCII Business)          9 K
*  (FW, Port) BSN Dutch Italic 10pt (ASCII Business)         12 K
*  (FW, Port) BSN Dutch Italic 12pt (ASCII Pleasure)         16 K
*  (FW, Port) BSN Dutch Italic 14pt (ASCII No Questions)     20 K
   (FW, Port) BSN Dutch Roman 08pt (ASCII Business)           9 K
*  (FW, Port) BSN Dutch Roman 10pt (ASCII Business)          12 K
*  (FW, Port) BSN Dutch Roman 12pt (ASCII Business)          15 K
*  (FW, Port) BSN Dutch Roman 14pt (ASCII Business)          19 K
   (FW, Port) BSN Swiss Bold 08pt (ASCII Business)            9 K
   (FW, Port) BSN Swiss Bold 10pt (ASCII Business)           12 K
*  (FW, Port) BSN Swiss Bold 12pt (ASCII Business)           15 K
   (FW, Port) BSN Swiss Bold 14pt (ASCII Business)           19 K
   (FW, Port) BSN Swiss Bold 18pt (ASCII Business)           29 K
*  (FW, Port) BSN Swiss Bold 24pt (ASCII Business)           48 K
   (FW, Port) BSN Swiss Bold Italic 08pt (ASCII Business)    10 K
   (FW, Port) BSN Swiss Bold Italic 10pt (ASCII Business)    12 K

Mark:  * Present when print job begins           Press Exit to save
       + Can be loaded/unloaded during job      Press Cancel to cancel
```

Once you've created fonts with Fontware, you need to tell WordPerfect which ones to use. (SHIFT-F7 S E C F).

◆ What's Fontware?

The original LaserJet only used cartridges, but the LaserJet II can use both cartridge and soft fonts.

While the LaserJet II doesn't have the built-in versatility of a PostScript printer, it's low priced and still quite powerful. The Fontware system (available for at a nominal charge to WordPerfect users) allows for useful soft fonts in many sizes (the more memory in the printer, the larger the fonts it can print), but few special effects.

Because there are about four times as many LaserJets as there are PostScript printers, most WordPerfect users will be using Fontware.

Fontware is a software package that takes outlines of fonts and produces bitmapped soft fonts. When a font is bitmapped, it means that each dot of the each character of a font (300 per inch, 90,000 per square inch) is written in a specially formatted file. The printer uses this file to print fonts and requires one bitmapped file for each font it prints.

Fontware can create fonts from 3 point (extremely tiny and hard to read) to 144 point (about two inches tall) for LaserJet II's and compatibles.

While Swiss and Dutch are included with WordPerfect, Bitstream has a huge library of Fontware that WordPerfect can also access. See Chapter 4, *Show & Tell* for examples of most of the typefaces currently available (Futura, Galliard, Korinna, etc.).

❖ *Fontware — Creating soft font files*

Fontware is an extremely self-explanatory piece of software, and yet many people find it confusing. Part of the problem used to be that Bitstream's older documentation was not the most complete. If you read their documentation carefully and follow it completely, Fontware *will* be easy to use. Fontware makes fonts, that's all. There aren't the huge number of commands WordPerfect has, so don't feel threatened by it. *You vill use it. You vill like it.*

Before you install Fontware, however, you must install the .ALL files for either the LaserJet family of printers or a PostScript printer. To do this, you will need to exit WordPerfect and run the INSTALL program, which is located in the same directory as the WordPerfect program (probably C:\WP51).

You must also have DOS version 3.1 or later. I mention this because if you are using an XT or compatible or an older AT, you might have DOS 2.11, or something like that. If you do, *Fontware will not run on your system.* I know this from experience with my Toshiba T3100. If your DOS version is 3.1 or higher, no problem. Upgrading your DOS can be as easy as going out and buying a new copy of DOS, or, in the case of a Toshiba, as tedious as having new BIOS chips installed in your computer. If you don't want to spend the money or take the time to upgrade, you might try installing the program on someone else's computer. Once the fonts have been generated and the .ALL file updated, you can use it on any computer that runs WordPerfect 5.1.

Installing the Fontware program can be treacherously tricky. That's right, if you have difficulty typing the word "Fontware," then I suggest you run screaming from the room with the horrible anticipation of what installing Fontware will be like. If, however, you can type the word "Fontware," you can install it just that easily. Put in disk #1 and type

Fontware [ENTER]

Follow the on-screen prompts to create fonts. Remember, creating large numbers of fonts can take a large amounts of time, so try to do it on your lunch hours (why limit it to just one?) or overnight.

➾ Portrait/landscape

The program will ask you numerous questions about the type of printer you are using and where you want the program copied. The only questions you might need help with are when the program asks if you want Portrait, Landscape, or both. If you only print portrait pages (tall, i.e., 8 1/2 x 11), you can choose "Portrait Only" in the installation. This will save you time and disk space. However, some of the examples in this book are landscape pages, and if you don't create those fonts now you won't be able to reproduce the examples. So, if you need both Portrait and Landscape (wide, i.e., 11 x 8 1/2) select both. After you've worked on the examples in this book you can copy all the files ending in .SFL to diskettes and free up the space on the hard disk. If you have a scaleable font printer, LaserJet III, IID, or IIP, you only need to create Portrait fonts because these printers are smart enough to "rotate" portrait fonts onto a landscape page.

➾ Symbol Sets

LaserJet users have five choices for font sets, while PostScript users have one. If you have a LaserJet, you can choose between ASCII (95 characters—the basic letters, numbers, and punctuation); ASCII Business (110 characters—the normal ASCII set with 15 useful typographic characters such as bullets, trademark symbols, and real opening and closing quote marks); ASCII Technical (187 characters—the ASCII set, plus math and Greek characters not otherwise accessible from Fontware); HP Roman 8 (190 characters—ASCII plus accented characters); IBM PC (254 characters—ASCII, accented characters, plus the entire PC character set of the symbols you can see on a normal text screen).

If you're not going to use foreign characters, don't use the Roman 8 character set. It takes twice as long to create, about twice as much disk space, and twice as long to download.

I recommend the ASCII Business set for everyone except those needing an extensive set of foreign characters. The business character set is a good all-around set that contains the most often used symbols and yet doesn't take up too much disk space or printer memory.

If you use a PostScript printer and don't need to share the PostScript fonts you're creating with any other software, choose WP PostScript. If you are going to share these fonts with any other program, choose the normal PostScript character set.

Fontware will automatically install all the free fonts that come with the program. This includes four weights of both Swiss (Helvetica) and Dutch (Times Roman), and a single weight of Bitstream Charter, a new typeface design from Bitstream. This little taste of Charter is meant to drive you into a buying frenzy wherein you run out and buy the entire Charter typeface package. Those folks at Bitstream are clever marketers as well as brilliant programmers, and I see no reason why you should even try to resist at least one of their excellent typefaces, the best available for the LaserJet and compatibles.

These fonts are special Fontware Outlines. These are the outlines that will be used to create the individual downloadable fonts your printer will use, and they cannot be used *directly* with any printer. These are the outlines for the fonts you use with a LaserJet or compatible printer, PostScript printer, DeskJet (with 128K or 256K additional memory cartridge), or the Canon LBP-8III (Laser Beam Printer) which can scale fonts as Postscript does. Fontware typefaces are also used by LaserMaster controllers, but these are converted using LaserMaster's own software.

Once you've selected "Make Fonts," press F3 to create what Fontware calls "Starter Fonts." This creates 8, 10, 12, and 14-point fonts in all weights of Swiss and Dutch, as well as 18 and 24 in bold. The advantage of this selection is that it creates a set of either typeface that will fit into the memory of a standard, 512K LaserJet. I say either because you can either use all the Swiss fonts created or all the Dutch fonts created, but not all of both at the same time.

If you have more than 512K, may also want to install bold fonts in 36, 48, and 72 point.

Fontware will check to make sure you have enough disk space and tell you approximately how long it will take to build the fonts. If you don't have enough disk space, either copy files to floppies and delete them from the hard disk or reduce the number of fonts or sizes you are trying to produce.

Once you've created the LaserJet fonts, use the following directions for installing *downloadable* fonts.

❖ *Installing fonts (Telling WordPerfect how to use them)*

PostScript: If you use a PostScript printer, especially a "plus" version with the 35 built-in fonts, you may never need to actually install a font. You will simply install the Apple LaserWriter driver and have instant access to all the fonts built into the printer. A list longer than the screen will appear, displaying all the fonts available in the LaserWriter Plus and most other PostScript printers.

- IMPORTANT NOTE: The standard PostScript driver supplied with WordPerfect does not support *any* soft fonts. While you can use Bitstream Fontware to install Bitstream typefaces, if you want to use Adobe soft fonts, you will have to call WordPerfect at 801-225-5000 and ask for the printer diskette that includes soft font support for PostScript printers. There is a $10 handling fee, and WordPerfect does not support all the fonts in the Adobe library. So before you dash out and buy a font, make sure that it's supported.

Let's get right to it. Press

SHIFT-F7 S

- Error, error, everybody to get from street

If WordPerfect asks you "Directory for printer files?" then you have done something horribly wrong, and Ted Koppel will probably do a show about you, right before you're sentenced to hard labor. No, all it means is that WordPerfect can't find the .ALL file. You can remedy this by finding the .ALL file, and either moving it to your WordPerfect directory, or using Setup (Shift-F1 L) to tell WordPerfect where to find it. Once you've accomplished that, press

E D

◆ DO NOT SKIP THIS STEP—Yes, this means you!

In the past two years I've learned that this was the single biggest mistake people made when dealing with soft fonts. You must now tell WordPerfect *where* the soft fonts you just created are located. Unfortunately, if you don't complete this step, you don't print with downloadable fonts.

All you do is type in the full path name where the fonts are located. If you allow Fontware to use its default and want to tell WordPerfect where the fonts are (. . . I'll wait patiently, where the fonts are, where the fonts are, someone waits for me) that path is

C:\FONTS [ENTER]

If you intervened and changed the name of the directory when you installed Fontware, it's your responsibility to remember that directory name and type it in here. If you don't type in a full path name here, WordPerfect will categorically refuse to download any fonts because it won't have the faintest idea where to find them. You should only have to enter this path once, and WordPerfect will remember it, even if you create more fonts.

◆ And now back to our regularly scheduled programming

To select which fonts are used in the driver, press

C

WordPerfect will offer you the choice of Built-in, Cartridges, and "Soft Fonts." You can move the cursor to any of these three and press [ENTER] to select the fonts in each section. In this example, we're especially worried about soft fonts, so move the cursor to

Soft Fonts

◆ How much memory?

Verify that WordPerfect has the correct settings for the amount of memory you have available. If you want to change the amount of memory available for soft fonts, press Q and enter the amount of memory you want for soft fonts.

PS: Most PostScript printers have at least 1.5 megabytes of memory, often 2 or 3 megabytes. Still, not all that memory is available for soft fonts. WordPerfect's default setting is 300K, which is large enough for about two complete families of soft fonts. If you have 2 megabytes of memory or more, you can safely use up to 500K of memory for soft fonts and still have enough room to print a full page of graphics.

LJII, IIP, or IID: The LaserJet II comes standard with 512K of memory, about 350K of which is available for soft fonts. If more memory has been added to the printer, make sure to change this setting accordingly, or WordPerfect will not allow you to select more than 350K of fonts.

LJ III: The standard LaserJet III comes with a megabyte of memory, about 700K of which can be used for fonts. Remember, though, the more memory you fill with fonts the less room you'll have for graphics. If you've added extra memory (you can add up to 4 megabytes more) make sure to press **Q** and change the quantity available.

◆ Selecting fonts

Now we're going to tell WordPerfect which soft fonts we want to use. Press

S

➾ Soft Fonts and Font Groups

WordPerfect now displays a list of "Font Groups." The first one will say:

- FW HP LaserJet Series II

Or it will at least start with the letters **FW** (which stands for Fontware). If you're using Type Director they'll begin with **TD.** This is the group which will contain all the fonts you make using the Fontware installation kit. It should be the first group on the list, and your cursor should already be on it. Press

[ENTER]

The following font groups will also be displayed: "HP AC TmsRmn/Helv US," "HP AD TmsRmn/Helv R8," "HP AE TmsRmn/Helv US," "HP AF TmsRmn/Helv R8," "HP AG Helv Headlines PC-8." These fonts won't print unless you have copied them to your hard disk. Don't mark fonts in any of these font groups unless those fonts are resident on your hard disk. Just because you mark a font doesn't mean it will print.

*Mark fonts with an asterisk * if you want to download them only once a day when you Initialize the printer (SHIFT-F7 I Y). Mark fonts with a + (plus sign) if you want them downloaded each time you print.*

```
Select Printer: Soft Fonts                          Quantity      * Fonts
                                            Total:   550 K           32
                                        Available:   165 K           15

FW HP LaserJet Series II                                    Quantity Used

█  (FW, Port) BSN Dutch Italic 08pt (ASCII Business)                9 K
*  (FW, Port) BSN Dutch Italic 10pt (ASCII Business)               12 K
*  (FW, Port) BSN Dutch Italic 12pt (ASCII Business)               16 K
*  (FW, Port) BSN Dutch Italic 14pt (ASCII Business)               20 K
   (FW, Port) BSN Dutch Roman 08pt (ASCII Business)                 9 K
*  (FW, Port) BSN Dutch Roman 10pt (ASCII Business)                12 K
*  (FW, Port) BSN Dutch Roman 12pt (ASCII Business)                15 K
*  (FW, Port) BSN Dutch Roman 14pt (ASCII Business)                19 K
   (FW, Port) BSN Swiss Bold 08pt (ASCII Business)                  9 K
   (FW, Port) BSN Swiss Bold 10pt (ASCII Business)                 12 K
*  (FW, Port) BSN Swiss Bold 12pt (ASCII Business)                 15 K
   (FW, Port) BSN Swiss Bold 14pt (ASCII Business)                 19 K
   (FW, Port) BSN Swiss Bold 18pt (ASCII Business)                 29 K
*  (FW, Port) BSN Swiss Bold 24pt (ASCII Business)                 48 K
   (FW, P                                                          10 K
   (FW, ┌ Fonts marked with an * download only with SHIFT-F7 I Y  12 K

Mark:  * Present when print job begins      + downloads when needed  ave
       + Can be loaded/unloaded during job                           cel
```

I recommend you purchase Bitstream Fontware typefaces, instead of the bit-mapped font sets packaged by Hewlett-Packard. HP won't be happy with me for saying this, but Fontware typefaces are a better value because you can generate any sizes you need, rather than being stuck with the normal 8, 10, 12, 14, 18, 24 route. There may be times when you actually need 13 point, or 22 point, and you can get them with Fontware. Also, you should seriously consider using 11 point for your body text instead of 10 point. It's only a little bigger, but it's much easier to read and prints sharper on 300 dpi laser printers. Fontware typefaces can also be used with many software programs besides WordPerfect, including Ventura, Windows and Corel Draw.

➾ Marking the fonts for downloading

WordPerfect will now display a list of all the fonts you've installed using the Fontware installation kit. Each font name will be preceded by either (FW, Port) or (FW, Land). This is the *orientation* and tells whether the font is for portrait (tall) or landscape (wide) pages.

If (FW, Land) appears after the font, it means that this is a landscape version of the font. Remember that unlike scaleable font printers, the LaserJet II cannot print portrait and landscape fonts on the same page and will eject the paper before printing the font with a different orientation. This means that you can't use these fonts to "rotate" text inside a graphics box.

The font name will start with BSN. (Since I'm not sure what this stands for, I can only assume it means "Bitstream Soft Nuggets" and was some type of misguided attempt to capitalize on the popularity of McDonalds.) Next comes the name of the typeface itself, such as Dutch or Swiss. Then comes the weight of the font (Roman, Bold, Italic, Bold-Italic), then the character set, and finally the size of the font in K. Then comes a baby in a baby carriage.

Move the cursor to each font you want to use. If you want WordPerfect to download the font each time it is used in a print job, (which may take several minutes using a parallel cable, longer with serial), press + next to the font name. If you share the printer with others and everyone uses different fonts, selecting the font with + will ensure that the fonts you need will be downloaded every time you print (it also ensures that you will be waiting around a while, especially if you use many or large fonts). I normally download about 800K of fonts, and it can take a good five minutes.

If you're as impatient (or busy) as I am, you would have to be put in a straitjacket if you had to wait five minutes every time you wanted to print something, so I suggest you mark the fonts with an

*

If you are the only one using the printer, or if everyone uses the same fonts, mark the font with an *.

Fonts marked with an * are only downloaded when you choose the initialize command: **SHIFT-F7 I Y.**

5.0 Users: You don't need to type the Y. Why? Because we like you.

➻ A word from the impatient

Marking the fonts with an * saves time because they don't have to be reloaded each time you print something; they will stay in the printer memory until you either initialize the printer again or turn it off. When you initialize the printer, all fonts that were previously downloaded are erased.

However, if you forget to use the initialize command, the printer will either substitute another font that is close, or print the page using Courier. Either way, the page will have a different appearance than what you intended.

➻ Equal time for the unorganized

If you're the type of person who never wants to have to remember to download their fonts in advance, who's laid-back enough to not mind a little extra time (from a few seconds to a few minutes) each time they print (the more or bigger the fonts, the more time), then mark them with a +. There's really nothing wrong with it, and what it takes in time it makes up in convenience. This has not been a paid political announcement.

◆ And meanwhile, back at our example

If you accidentally choose the wrong font, simply press the * or + again on that font to cancel it. You can install any or all of the fonts listed provided you have enough memory. If you mark the fonts with an *, WordPerfect deducts the size of each selected font from the amount of available memory (this keeps you from trying to load more fonts than you have memory for). If you mark the fonts with a +, you can mark as many as you'd like, because they aren't all going to be downloaded at once. This isn't as idyllic as it sounds, because it's then possible to use more fonts on a page than will fit into memory.

Once the fonts you have chosen fill the amount of memory you selected, WordPerfect will no longer allow you to mark new fonts without unmarking a previously marked font. When you are finished, press

F7

The next time you go to Base Font (Control-F8 F), WordPerfect will list the new fonts that you added.

◆ A little +, a little *, with the emphasis on the latter

One way to make the most of printer memory is to mark your fonts with both + and *. Permit me to explain. Use an * to mark your most commonly used fonts. These fonts will be downloaded only when you initialize the printer with **SHIFT-F7 I Y**. You do this to save time, so they don't have to be downloaded each and every time you print. Use the + for specialty fonts you don't use as often but still want access to. They will *always* appear on your list of available fonts but will *not* be downloaded when you initialize the printer, and will *only* be sent to the printer if they are included on the page. This method allows you to have access to *all* your fonts and yet conserves printer memory and only downloads special fonts when you use them.

This technique is an especially good way to deal with landscape fonts if you print in portrait orientation primarily. Use an * to mark the portrait fonts and a + to mark the landscape fonts. That way the printer will normally be all ready for portrait printing, but if you want to print landscape the fonts will be available, and download at print time.

◆ When adding a new .PRS file

The first time you create fonts in Fontware, all the fonts you have created will be marked with +'s in your .PRS file. But here's where it can get confusing: If you create more fonts, they aren't automatically marked in your existing PRS files. If you want to use these new fonts with your old .PRS files, you'll need to go in and choose "Cartridges & Fonts" and then select the fonts you've just created.

But if you create a *new* printer driver, all the Fontware fonts you've generated, including the new ones, *will* be marked in this new .PRS file.

Because the fonts are marked with +s, it means that if they are used on a page, they will be downloaded each time you print a page that uses the font. While this is convenient, it also takes a lot of time, each and every time you print. Because of this, I recommend you mark them with an * instead so that you only have to download them once per day.

To remove the + marks, place the cursor on each font and press **+**. Don't forget to remark them with an * or they won't display in the list of fonts.

◆ Where's the fonts?

•◆ **LASERJET II, IID, IIP, or Plus:** If you choose Base Font and all you see is Courier and Line Printer, chances are you haven't told WordPerfect which font cartridges and soft fonts you have. To do this, press

SHIFT-F7 S

Move the cursor to the printer you've installed fonts for. Then press

E C

Move the cursor to "Soft Fonts" and press

[ENTER]

Move the cursor the to font group you want (probably FW HP) and press

[ENTER]

Mark the fonts you want with either an * or a + and then press

F7 F7 F7 F7 S F7

The fonts should now appear when you press Control-F8 F.

◆ Life outside of Fontware

While Fontware is my favorite, there are other font systems. Type Director is OK for use with the LaserJet III, but I don't recommend it for the II. Glyphix, Atech, and MoreFonts all offer low cost systems that allow the LaserJet II and compatibles to scale fonts "on-the-fly." Atech and MoreFonts also support the DeskJet and dot-matrix printers. If you want to use bitmapped typefaces from other vendors, SoftCraft offers a program that will install any bitmapped typeface (even ones you design yourself).

For more information about these programs, see Chapter 20, *Software.*

◆ Cartridges

If you have font cartridges, press **SHIFT-F7 S E C** and move the cursor to "Cartridges" and press [ENTER]. (SEC stands Select, Edit, Cartridges, and Fonts.)

You will see a list of the available HP font cartridges. Older cartridges are listed by letters from A to Z, while HP's newer cartridges are named. Personally, I'm waiting for the "Groucho" font cartridge, but that's another book. You can tell what letter your older font cartridge is by removing it (press the on-line key on the printer first), finding the number at the top of it (92286Z, or whatever letter the cartridge is). If you have a newer cartridge, you can read the name while the cartridge is still in the printer. What will they think of next? Use the cursor to move to the letter of the font cartridge and press

*

Repeat this for any additional cartridge you have available and press

F7

WordPerfect will add the fonts contained in the cartridge to its list of available Base Fonts.

◆ LaserMaster

The standard LaserMaster .ALL file that comes with WordPerfect only contains the standard 35, but the .ALL shipped from LaserMaster contains the information necessary to use the entire Bitstream Fontware typeface library.

Even though this wealth of fonts is listed on your menu, you must, of course, have purchased the fonts before you can use them (isn't that *always* the way?). WordPerfect will automatically select the 35 standard PostScript compatible fonts. If you want to add any other Bitstream fonts, press

SHIFT-F7 S E C

Move the cursor to "Soft Fonts," then press S. Because the LaserMaster board itself takes care of downloading, you should only mark fonts with an *. You do not have to tell WordPerfect the path the fonts are located, the LaserMaster software handles that.

The LaserMaster can download an entire font in about 2 seconds, compared with about 2 minutes for a PostScript printer, so printing is very fast, no matter how many downloadable fonts you use. Also, you'll notice that you can mark every single solitary font with an * at the same time. The way the LaserMaster works, you aren't limited to the number of fonts you can use at once, as you are with LaserJet or PostScript printers. I've never run out of memory using the LaserMaster, no matter how many fonts I've crammed on a page.

◆ Saving precious hard disk space

If you don't plan on generating any more Fontware fonts, you can copy your .ALL file to a floppy for later use. Note: If you're like me, you're having a good day when you can find 400K free on the hard disk. WordPerfect's main printer files are very large, several hundred K each, and WordPerfect does not require that they be on the hard disk in order to print. I keep mine on backup floppies and only use them when I'm adding fonts or changing my printer configuration.

❖ *Downloading (aka Initializing)*

This is so simple it's almost funny. If you marked the downloadable font with a +, WordPerfect automatically downloads the file each time you print anything from a page to an entire file. If you marked the font with an *, Press

SHIFT-F7 I Y

(No Y is necessary for 5.0 users.) If you marked them with a + they will be downloaded automatically each time they're needed. That's it.

Downloading fonts can take anywhere from a few seconds to a few minutes, depending on how many fonts you're downloading, their size, how fast the computer is, and what type of printer cable connects the printer to the computer. Parallel cables are many times faster than serial.

All soft fonts remain in the printer only as long as the power is on. Turn off the power and, zap, they disappear and must be reloaded with the Initialize command before you can print with them. If you forget to initialize, most printers substitute Courier; the text will be there, but it will often be unreadable.

Now there is one catch (oh, you just knew there would be, didn't you?), but it's relatively minor. The fonts you want to download must reside in a single directory (any one you'd like). Copy them from the floppy you copied them to after you generated them or use the directory that Fontware creates called C:\FONTS (or any other name that you specify during installation).

To check that WordPerfect knows which directory contains the WordPerfect soft fonts, press

SHIFT-F7 S E D

Enter the directory where the soft fonts are located, then press

F7 F7 F7 F7

WordPerfect will not be able to download your fonts unless you have entered the directory here. I know I've said this before, but I'm repeating it because this is such a common mistake, and such an easy one to avoid.

◆ Automatic Initializing

If you want to make your fonts with an * for speed, and yet are too forgetful to trust yourself to press SHIFT-F7 I Y once a day, you can create a macro which will cause WordPerfect to automatically initialize the printer every time you run the WP program. My friend (and technical proofreader extraordinare) Liz Swoope Johnson came up with it, and told me (in no uncertain terms) how useful it can be, so I'll pass it on to you.

First, create the macro by pressing

CONTROL-F10

Give the macro a name. Let's call it "download."

DOWNLOAD [ENTER] [ENTER]

Type the "initialize printer command"

SHIFT-F7 I Y

(5.0 users, don't type the Y—yes, I know I've said it a hundred times and you remember it, but I have to include it just in case you are following the directions during a bout of temporary amnesia, a phenomenon which is occurring at an ever-increasing rate.)

End the macro by pressing

CONTROL-F10

When you start WordPerfect, instead of the normal WP, you need to type

WP /M=download

Of course, if you're the type who forgets to download you're probably also the type who will forget to include the /M business. In that case, create a batch file in your root directory called WP.BAT.

If you don't know what a batch file is, ask the person who set up your computer. They may already have created a batch file to start your WordPerfect program and you don't want to mess it up.

If you set up your computer yourself and know you don't already start WordPerfect with a batch file, clear your WordPerfect screen and type the following line:

WP /M=download

Save it as an ASCII text file to a file called WP.BAT by typing

CONTROL-F5 T S C:\WP.BAT [ENTER]

Once you've done this, the next time you start your program with WP, you'll really get WP /M=download, and your fonts will be downloaded without you having to think about it.

◆ Tip: Lots-o-fonts

If you are going to use many typeface families and you want to mark them with an * (so you will only have to download them once a day), you may want to copy your printer definition file (.PRS) and give it a different name, such as PALATINO.PRS, and have one file .PRS file for each major group of fonts. Otherwise, WP will download all the fonts when you initialize, and your printer may not have enough memory to handle them all at once.

◆ Tip: Not lots-o-disk space

If you are always low on disk space, you can download fonts from floppies. Yes, it's true, take it from a hard disk-space miser like me. However, all fonts to be downloaded must fit on a single floppy disk; otherwise, WordPerfect will have a temper tantrum and confront you with two choices. You can cancel the initialization (or print job), or you can start over (which isn't much help if the fonts aren't there). If you have 1.2-megabyte floppies, or the new 1.44-megabyte baby floppies you should be able to cram quite a few fonts onto a single floppy. If you have 360K floppies, you can only store smaller sizes.

Actually, the very best way to save disk space when using LaserJet fonts is to break down a buy a program called *FontSpace.* This program (reviewed in Chapter 20) compresses your fonts so that they take only about a quarter of the space they take now, with no loss in print quality or performance.

◆ Downloading horrors

One annoying problem with soft fonts rears its ugly head when several people using different fonts share the same printer. One person loads his/her fonts, print away merrily, and then leaves the printer filled with those fonts. The next unsuspecting person starts printing and—"Gadzooks!," is he/she going nuts, or is there a gremlin in the printer?

There are several ways to alleviate this problem. If you have enough printer memory, you can simply load all the fonts anyone will ever need. Printer memory, however, doesn't come cheap, so the next alternative is for everyone sharing the printer to always use the same set of fonts. If you think "Corporate Image," then this practice makes sense anyway. You don't want someone using Helvetica on promotional literature, when your stationery and business cards are printed with Times Roman.

You can also avoid this by marking the font files in the printer driver with a + instead of an *. Fonts marked with a + are sent to the printer every time you print. The down side of this method is that it can take a lot of extra time whenever you print.

Another way around this problem is by using common courtesy, a custom that is becoming far too uncommon. If most people who use the printer use a standard set of fonts, a copy of their printer driver (it will end in .PRS) should be handy. When you print, select the printer driver and initialize the printer. When you've finished printing with your fonts, clear the screen and select their printer driver. Press **SHIFT-F7 I Y** to re-initialize the printer. Their fonts will be sent to the printer, and they might even drop all their plans for tarring and feathering you.

◆ A little +, a little *, with the emphasis on the latter

One way to make the most of the printer memory you have is to both + and * marks for your fonts. Permit me to explain: Use an * to mark your most commonly used fonts. These fonts will be downloaded only when you initialize the printer with **SHIFT-F7 I Y**. You do this to save time, so they don't have to be downloaded each and every time you print. Use the + for specialty fonts you don't use as often but still want access to. They will *always* appear on your list of available fonts but will *not* be downloaded when you initialize the printer, and will *only* be sent to the printer if they are included on the page. This method allows you to have access to *all* your fonts, and yet conserves printer memory and only downloads special fonts when you use them.

This technique is an especially good way to deal with landscape fonts if you print in primarily in portrait orientation. Use an * to mark the portrait fonts and a + to mark the landscape fonts. That way your printer will normally be all ready for portrait printing, but if you want to print landscape the fonts will be available, and download at print time.

❖ *What's an Initial font?*

Every WordPerfect file contains an "Initial" font. Unless you insert codes to change it, the Initial font will be the default font that is used for everything from the text to headers, footers, captions, footnotes, you name it. This font does not appear in the file (even if you press ALT-F3 for Reveal Codes). Initial fonts are also always downloaded, whether you use them or not. The only way to see or change it is to press

SHIFT-F8 D F

WordPerfect then presents you with a list of fonts available on the printer. Highlight the font you want and then press **[ENTER] F7**.

◆ Where'd it come from?

If you don't set it specifically, WordPerfect will examine the printer driver to see which font you've set as the initial font. To change this, press

SHIFT-F8 S E F

(5.0 users press SHIFT-F8 S E I)

```
Document: Initial Font

  BSN Dutch Bold 10pt (ASCII Business) (FW, Port)
  BSN Dutch Bold 12pt (ASCII Business) (FW, Port)
  BSN Dutch Bold 14pt (ASCII Business) (FW, Port)
  BSN Dutch Bold 18pt (ASCII Business) (FW, Port)
  BSN Dutch Bold 24pt (ASCII Business) (FW, Port)
  BSN Dutch Bold Italic 10pt (ASCII Business) (FW, Port)
  BSN Dutch Bold Italic 12pt (ASCII Business) (FW, Port)
  BSN Dutch Bold Italic 14pt (ASCII Business) (FW, Port)
  BSN Dutch Italic 10pt (ASCII Business) (FW, Port)
  BSN Dutch Italic 12pt (ASCII Business) (FW, Port)
  BSN Dutch Italic 14pt (ASCII Business) (FW, Port)
  BSN Dutch Roman 10pt (ASCII Business) (FW, Port)
  BSN Dutch Roman 12pt (ASCII Business) (FW, Port)
  BSN Dutch Roman 14pt (ASCII Business) (FW, Port)
  BSN Swiss Bold 12pt (ASCII Business) (FW, Port)
  BSN Swiss Bold 24pt (ASCII Business) (FW, Port)
* Courier 10cpi
  Courier 10cpi Bold
  Line Draw 10cpi (Full)
  Line Printer 16.67cpi
  Line Umpire 16.66cpi

1 Select: N Name search: 1
```

The Initial Font is the default font for a document. Unless another font is specified, this font will be used for text, headers, footers, captions and everything under the sun.

Move the cursor to the font you want and press **[ENTER] F7 F7 F7**. This will automatically be entered as the Initial font for every new file created using that printer driver.

◆ That's a base font

Because WordPerfect can support so many fonts, how you choose them is important. And as with other WordPerfect features, there are several approaches you can use.

The first and most basic is Base Font. Base Font means that all of WordPerfect's other attributes, such as size and appearance, are "based" on this font you've selected. It becomes the default, the standard font. When you enter a Base Font code, it affects all text following it until WordPerfect sees another Base Font code. If you want to switch from one typeface to another, you will always need to use Base Font by pressing

CONTROL-F8 F

A list of the fonts available for your printer will appear, sorted by the name of the font. Most printers will display a single entry for each size and weight of font. The letters following the typeface contain information about the cartridge or soft font vendor they are from.

This list is sensitive to your page orientation. If you are working on a landscape page, you will see only the fonts available in landscape mode on your system.

Base Font uses the same name-search feature as List Files. You can either scroll down the list with the cursor keys or press **N** for **N**ame Search. Then type the first letter of the font you want and WordPerfect will jump to the first font it finds beginning with that letter. Each additional letter you type will narrow the search until you are finally at the font you want.

Base Font is also useful when you want to specify an exact font (such as Times Roman 12 italic), rather than use WordPerfect's appearance attributes.

Because Base Font shows you a list of all the fonts available on your printer, it's also an effective way to determine that the font you're requesting is available. The Base Font list also contains important information regarding what font cartridge or soft fonts WordPerfect expects to be installed in the printer.

➻ Scaleable: PostScript, LaserJet III, Canon LBP III, LaserMaster

Scaleable font drivers work differently from the LaserJet driver in that they list only font names, not font name/size combinations. Once you move the cursor to a font and press [ENTER] to select it, WordPerfect asks what size font you want. You may specify any size from 1 point (which would be unreadable) to 1199 point (where one letter will not even fit on a page).

While WordPerfect can select fonts in one-tenth of a point increments, not all scaleable printers can create fonts in that fine of an increment. The LaserJet III, for example, can scale fonts in 1/4 point increments. WordPerfect will round to the nearest quarter point in when using the LaserJet III, so choosing 11.2 point type will give you 11.25 point.

In actuality, anything less than a half a point makes very little difference. Fractional point increments are rarely necessary, much less noticeable, but they can be useful if the material has to fit with absolute precision (or if people constantly check up on you and you want to drive them nuts trying to measure the type).

◆ Tip: Getting drafted

I normally set my initial font to Courier 12 point (or 10 cpi if that's how your printer displays its standard Courier) for a number of reasons. The biggest reason is that since Courier is monospaced, each line of text will fit on-screen, rather than extending off the right side of the screen.

Courier is also an efficient base font because it keeps you from formatting when you should be writing. One of the great temptations (the vice, not the singing group) of desktop publishing is that you tend to waste time experimenting with formatting rather than writing and editing.

Courier is easily scanned, which means that all Optical Character Recognition (OCR) software can read it. Why is that important? Call me paranoid (you won't be the first), but I hate losing data. I make backups every day (sometimes several times a day) and also print my work daily. Should some heinous mishap occur that prevents me from using my original or my backup, I can still use a scanner and OCR software to read my printed pages and enter everything back into the computer without having to retype it.

Remember, however, Courier is not the best font for *reading* drafts. Courier's advantage is that text printed in it doesn't have that air of finality; it looks like a draft, so it's mentally "easier" to change. The disadvantage is that pages printed in Courier really are harder to read than those printed in proportionally spaced body text fonts. Proofreaders will tell you it's far easier to find errors on a typeset page than on a typewritten one, and Courier is a typewriter font. Keep that in mind and choose your weapon/font accordingly.

If you routinely switch back and forth between Courier (for easier on-screen viewing) and a proportional font for printing, think about creating two macros, one to use Courier as the Initial Base Font, and the other to use your favored proportional font as the Initial Base Font for printing. See Chapter 17 for more information about macros.

When you are ready to start formatting, press

SHIFT-F8 D F

Now select the proportionally spaced font you want to be the default for headers, footers, captions, footnotes, endnotes, etc. Once you've set an Initial Font, you can still override it (in the text, headers, footers, anywhere) by inserting a new Base Font with

CONTROL-F8 F

Or simply by changing the default Base Font again with SHIFT-F8 D F, or by using styles.

◆ Changing fonts with Styles

Styles are often the best way to change fonts because they make *changing* font changes easier. There's no way to search and replace from on3e font to another, but Styles give you this power—so it's a good idea to use them whenever possible.

❖ *Larger than life*

Another way to change fonts is to change size or appearance attributes, rather than changing the base font. Size is obvious, in that you can make fonts bigger or smaller. But rather than use discrete (no, not disc*reet* as in careful or cautious, but disc*rete* as in distinct or independent) font sizes, WordPerfect allows you to choose fonts that are Fine, Small, Large, Very Large, and Extra Large. These sizes are relative, and depend on the size of the base font. (Speaking of relatives, the members of my family aren't "fat"—we're just larger than life.)

Choosing fonts also depends on what you have available in the printer. If you're using a LaserJet with a WP cartridge or the Fontware starter set and a 10-point base font, Fine will be 6 point, Small will be 8 point, Large will be 12 point, Very Large will be 14 point, and Extra large will be 18 point.

If you're using a scaleable font printer, such as PostScript, LaserMaster, LaserJet III (or have a wide variety of sizes available from Fontware and are using a 10 point base font), Fine is 6 point, Small is 8 point, Large is 12 point, Very Large is 15 point, and Extra Large is 20 point.

The advantage of using size attributes over base font changes is that size attributes are relative. If you change the size of the base font from 10 to 12 point, all the other sizes change accordingly. Another advantage is that if you decide to change the body copy typeface, the size changes will still apply to whatever font you choose. On the other hand, if you had entered the sizes individually, you would have to go back and change them all manually (unless you used a style sheet, as covered in Chapter 11, *Styles*). These size change attributes are also easier to use if point sizes confuse you.

Size is applied in the same way as underline and bold. You can either enter the size code as you type the text or block the text you want to change the size of and then press

CONTROL-F8 S

Then press the letter of the size you want (such as L for Large)

Fine 60%

Small 80%

Large 120%

Very Large 150%

Extra Large 200%

◆ Size attribute ratios

I know, I know, this sounds like something you would read in a physics class. "What next," you think, a feature called 'Isosceles Triangles?' "No, this feature is not only simple, it's very important.

I've answered more questions about fonts, downloading, sizes, etc. than anything else in WordPerfect. I know how confusing they can be. So did the designers of 5.0, and they did the right thing in trying to relieve users of the pressure of choosing font sizes. They tried to make it simple. But anytime you make something simple, you also run the risk of limiting it, and that was the problem with this feature. If you didn't know what a point size was, you didn't care what "fine, small, large, very large, and extra large," meant. But if you did know the difference between 18 and 24 point (a point is 1/72nd of an inch and is the standard unit of measure when dealing with type), you probably found it exasperating. "Just exactly what size type am I going to get?"

In 5.1, you can choose exactly how big "large" is (and fine, small, very large, and extra large, for that matter). If you don't want to bother, you don't have to, and you get the same sizes as in 5.0.

To access this feature, press

SHIFT-F1 I P S

You can then enter any percentage you want. These percentages are based on the size of the base font. If your base font is 10 point and you set extra large to be 360%, then extra large will print 36 point. If you are sadistic (and want to confuse your friends and coworkers), you can even make Extra Large smaller than Fine. The only point to remember is that these changes apply to all documents created after you change the percentages, not to a single document. So beware that if you change this setting, your old files will be reformatted automatically.

- Here are my recommendations if you use a 10 point base font (body text). This applies to both the Fontware starter set and to the HP WordPerfect font cartridge:

Fine = 60% (6 point)
Small = 80% (8 point)
Large = 140% (14 point)
Very Large = 180% (18 point)
Extra Large = 240% (24 point)
Super/Subscript = 60% (6 point)

- If you have more fonts to choose from, and your base font is 11 point (the size I recommend for body text), specify the following:

Fine = 55% (6 point)
Small = 73% (8 point)
Large = 127% (14 point)
Very Large = 164% (18 point)
Extra Large = 273% (30 point)
Super/Subscript = 55% (6 point)

- If you are using a LaserJet or compatible, you will need to make fonts in all the sizes listed, otherwise WordPerfect will not choose a font as large as you expected, and instead will substitute the closest size.

◆ Techno-nugget: "The mysterious PTR program"

For those not afraid to delve into their printer files with WordPerfect's PTR program, here's a way to see exactly what font WordPerfect will give you for each size or to tell WordPerfect exactly which font *you* want it to use for each size. You can customize WordPerfect's "automatic font changes," so that the program will select a different typeface when you bold or italics. If you're really fussy, you can also tell WordPerfect not to show you italic and bold fonts as Base Fonts, but to use them only when you select the appropriate appearance attribute. This is useful when you have many fonts and don't want to have to search down the screen for the right one or when you accidentally make the choice of turning all the text into italic or bold.

Before attempting this, ask yourself this question: "Do I feel lucky?" These instructions are meant for advanced or adventurous users. If you are the type of person who tends to make a mess of complex technical things, do this at your own risk. You can make changes using this program that will make WordPerfect print strangely (or not at all). If this happens, you can reinstall the printer from scratch. Modifying your printer driver is purely optional—you can live a long and happy life without the PTR program. So one more time, ask yourself, "Do I really want to get into all this?" If your answer is "no, not the longest day I live, I'm sorry I even read this far," jump to the next subheading. If the answer is "yes," exit to DOS and type

PTR [ENTER]

(If you have a good imagination, you will hear wispy strains of the *Twilight Zone* theme song emanating from a location not far from your computer. If you don't, you'll hear disk drive noises.) If you haven't copied this program to the hard disk, run the install program and answer Y to "PTR program."

PTR uses the same major function keys as WordPerfect, so to retrieve an .ALL (single printer) file or an .ALL (many printers) file press

SHIFT-F10

Enter the name of the file or press **F5** for List Files. One or more printer names will be listed on-screen. Move the cursor to the one you want and press

[ENTER] [ENTER]

```
File: C:\WP5\BODONI.PRS
                    Printer: HP LaserJet Series II
             Font: (FW) Bodoni Book 11pt (ASCII) (Port)
                     Automatic Font Changes For
                 (FW) Bodoni Book 11pt (ASCII) (Port)

 Feature            | Font Name
 Extra Large Print  | (FW) Bodoni Bold 48pt (ASCII) (Port)
 Very Large Print   | (FW) Bodoni Book 18pt (ASCII) (Port)
 Large Print        | (FW) Bodoni Book 14pt (ASCII) (Port)
 Small Print        | (FW) Bodoni Book Italic 11pt (ASCII) (Port)
 Fine Print         | (FW) Bodoni Book Italic 11pt (ASCII) (Port)
 Superscript        | (FW) Bodoni Book Italic 11pt (ASCII) (Port)
 Subscript          | (FW) Bodoni Book Italic 11pt (ASCII) (Port)
 Outline            |
 Italics            | (FW) Bodoni Book Italic 11pt (ASCII) (Port)
 Shadow             |
 Redline            |
 Double Underline   |
 Bold               |

Enter Select Automatic Font Change:
Switch Cross Reference List:
```

WordPerfect's PTR program allows you to change WordPerfect's defaults for automatic font control, but should only be used by the young and the restless, or the brave.

Move the cursor to “Fonts” and press **[ENTER]**. A list of all the fonts in that printer driver will appear. Move the cursor to the font you are interested in and press

[ENTER]

Move the cursor to “Automatic Font Changes” and press

[ENTER]

This will show you the font WordPerfect will use when you select an attribute or size. If you want a printed copy of this, press **SHIFT-PrtSc** (if you are using a LaserJet the page will not eject automatically, and you will have to press the printer’s on-line button, then the form feed button, then the on-line button again).

You can change these AFC selections by moving to the attribute or size you want to specify a font for and pressing **[ENTER]**. You will now be presented with yet another list of fonts. First unmark the font WordPerfect has chosen by pressing the **[BACKSPACE]** key, then move to the font you want WordPerfect to use for this attribute and press *

To leave the font control for that single font, press

F7

Repeat this for each font you want to view or change.

If you want to remove a font from the list of base fonts, but still use it when you want bold, italic, or bold-italic attributes, move down to “Miscellaneous Font Features” and press

[ENTER]

Move down to “Use Font Only For Automatic Font Changes” and press

*

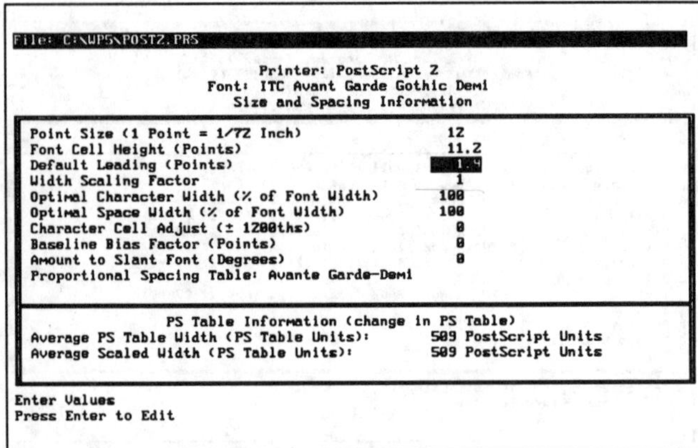

WordPerfect’s PTR program allows you to change the default leading for each font. (But don’t try it unless you are technically inclined.)

Remember, once you do this, the font will *not* appear on the list of base fonts, and you will only be able to access it by specifying appearance attributes such as bold or italic.

If you want to do this for all your bold and italic fonts, you will have to repeat this process for each font individually. (Of course, if you accidentally delete something, you can bring it back immediately by using WordPerfect's Cancel command, the F1 key, to undelete.)

To leave the PTR program, press **F7** several times until the program asks you "Save File?" If you are secure in the changes you made, press **Y** to save the file. If you are not, press **N**.

◆ All appearances

•◆ WordPerfect has nine standard appearance attributes, illustrated at left.

These are the attributes of a PostScript printer: Bold Underline, Double underline, Italic, Outline, Shadow, Small Cap, Redline, and ~~Strikeout.~~ Notice how bold and italic affect underlines. Appearances can be combined in any and all combinations, depending on what the printer will support and what fonts are available.

The true bold version of most fonts is more than just a double strike — it's a completely different design. While a true bold font looks better, if you don't have one or lack the memory for one, WordPerfect will make one for you by double striking the character and shifting it slightly. This pseudo-bolding looks okay, but not as authentic as a real bold version of a font. Sometimes it won't even be discernable. If you're using a light font (i.e., Futura Light), WordPerfect's bolding will show; but if you're using a font that is already fairly heavy, you won't notice the difference.

Bold
Italic
Bold Italic
Normal
Outline
Redline
Shadow
SMALL CAP
~~Strikeout~~

PostScript printers have special effects built in.

◆ LaserJet italics

What happens when you have 30-point Times Roman available, and you choose an italic attribute but don't have an italic font in that size? You will get italic in the size closest to your current font. If the closest size you have is 24-point, you get 24-point italic.

What if you don't have Times Roman 30-point italic but do have a 30-point Helvetica italic font? Usually WordPerfect won't even consider using the 30-point Helvetica italic, because your base font is Times Roman. It will insist on the next size of Times Roman it can find.

If no italic version of the base font exists, as in Bitstream's version of Avant Garde, WordPerfect will *underline* the text, as this is the traditional way to signify italics when none are available. SHIFT-F7 V comes in handy because it helps you to know what you're going to get before you print.

If you use any of these appearance attributes frequently, you may want to create a macro to speed formatting and eliminate keystrokes or change the underline key to italics using the soft keyboard feature. You may also want to use style sheets. See Chapter 11, *Styles,* and Chapter 17, *Macros,* for more tips on speed formatting and changing appearances.

Appearance attributes are applied in the same way as underline and bold: you can either enter the codes as you go or block the text you want to change the appearance of and press

CONTROL F8 A

Then press the letter or number of the attribute you want.

Bold

Italic

Bold Italic

Normal

Outline

Redline

Shadow

SMALL CAP

~~Strikeout~~

Special effects on a LaserJet aren't so special, but PostScript-like effects can be made with Font Effects and LaserFonts, both from SoftCraft.

◆ Tip: Turn it off already

When applying an appearance attribute such as italic, the WordPerfect manual tells you to repeat the process used to turn it on. In the case of italics, this means pressing

CONTROL F8 A I

This turns the appearance on and off. But there's a short cut for turning the attribute off that requires only one keystroke rather than four. Instead of typing **CONTROL F8 A I**, press the **[RIGHT ARROW]** key once.

When you turn italics (or any appearance) on, WordPerfect inserts a matched pair of codes, one to start and one to stop the attribute. This prevents you from accidentally having bold, italic, or underlining on for an entire page (like I always used to have with WordStar).

Pressing the right arrow will move the cursor outside the stop code for italics (or any appearance), thereby turning it off. If you're a skeptic, turn Reveal Codes on with **ALT F3** and see how it operates for yourself.

◆ Tip: Underlines mean *italics*

Always replace underlines with italics when using a proportional font. (The underline is a typesetters code; before desktop publishing, few typewriters had italic fonts.) *Never* underline headlines or subheads. Why? Because it looks tacky. Remember, in most cases, ruling lines should go *above* headlines or subheads, otherwise they visually separate the headline or subhead from the text.

LaserJet III
Effects
Normal
Bold
Italic
Outline
Shadow
SMALL CAP
Redline
Normal
Bold
Italic
Outline
Shadow
SMALL CAP
Redline

The LaserJet III's special effects are really special. But because the Shadow effect is so flashy, it should be used sparingly.

◆ Tip: Underlines *are* italics

Here's an easy way to change attributes globally (throughout the entire document) using styles. Most draft copies are printed in monospaced fonts, such as Courier, and use underlines to signify italics. Since the LaserJet doesn't come with an italic version of Courier, text marked as italic will print with an underline. When you select a proportional font, the italics will print as italic. But if you use a PostScript printer, or an other laser printer that includes an italic version of Courier, use the style trick.

◆ Tip: Underlines *become* italics

If you want to create a style that allows you to instantly change underlines to italics (and back), see Chapter 11, *Styles*.

◆ Color me puce

While there are currently few (affordable) color printers with high resolution, functional color laser printers are on the market, and WordPerfect is ready for them. WordPerfect not only offers you a selection of 11 standard colors, but it allows you to mix your own.

Unlike underline, bold, italic, and other attributes, the codes for color don't have a beginning and end. You can't block text and then select a color for it. Color codes are like base font codes; you select a color and it takes effect until you select another color.

To select a color, press

CONTROL-F8 C

Then press the letter or number of the color you want.

You mix colors by telling WordPerfect what percentage of each primary color you want. Black type is 0% red, 0% blue and 0% yellow, while white is 100% of each.

If you have a black and white printer, what good is the color setting? Plenty, if you have a scaleable font printer, not much if you have a LaserJet, although you can use the color setting to prepare separations for offset printing, as detailed in Chapter 15, *Printing.* For special effects on a LaserJet, see the section on font effects in Chapter 20. If you have a scaleable font printer, read the "Scaleable font extras" later on in this chapter.

◆ Blue feeling gray over you

If you have a scaleable font printer, the colors menu opens up a Pandora's box in shades of gray. Gray type can be attractive and effective when used for emphasis or to lighten the impact of very large type.

While it seems logical that selecting "Other" and choosing 10% would result in 10% gray type, it's just the opposite: 10% gives you 90% gray (almost black). Think of it as mixing light, instead of mixing colors. If you have 90% light, then you only have 10% dark, which means you will have light gray characters.

If you select 90% for **all three** of the colors, you will get light gray characters. WordPerfect allows you to enter numbers in 1 percent increments and, while subtle, each percentage makes a difference. If you are printing the final pages on a Linotronic typesetter, the 1 percent increments will be more pronounced.

Remember to enter the gray screen you want in **all three** of the color categories or you won't wind up with the exact shade you requested. Refer to the chart on the next page.

❖ *Normalcy*

The one function I haven't covered from the Font function key is #3, Normal. While it's fairly self-explanatory, it doesn't insert any code of its own. Selecting

CONTROL F8 N

tells WordPerfect to turn off any attributes you've selected from the Appearance or Size menus (not color or base font) and returns everything to the current Base Font. Normal allows you to turn off all attributes in a single command and saves you

99 99 99
95 95 95
90 90 90
80 80 80
70 70 70
60 60 60
50 50 50
40 40 40
30 30 30
20 20 20
10 10 10
BLACK

OUTLINE
50 50 50
SHADOW
50 50 50
BOLD
50 50 50

While you may not have a color laser printer yet, if you have a PostScript printer you can use WordPerfect's color feature to create gray type.

If you select 90% for **all three** *of the colors, you will get light gray characters. WordPerfect allows you to enter numbers in 1 percent increments and, while subtle, each percentage makes a difference, as you can see.*

Remember to enter the gray screen you want in **all three** *of the color categories, or you won't wind up with the exact shade you requested.*

the bother of having to turn them off individually. Normal does not affect color or any changes to the base font.

The command is also very effective when creating styles, as only opening appearance and size codes are entered automatically.

◆ Put on a happy space

One WordPerfect feature you may never need (but it's nice to know its there) is word- and letterspacing control. The name of this feature is a bit misleading for people who know something about type. The letterspacing control is actually tracking. Rather than controlling the amount of space between letters for justification, it controls the amount of space between letters at all times. The wordspacing command controls the space between words.

You would normally use the letterspacing command if your font appears to have too much space between each letter. When letters aren't close enough to each other, it's hard to differentiate between the spaces between letters and the spaces between words. The LaserJet B cartridge has a real problem in this department. Sometimes you just want to add more or less space between each letter (to strengthen the impact of a headline, for example). Press

SHIFT-F8 O P W [ENTER] P

Then enter a number less than 100% to make the letters print closer together or a number greater than 100% to make them print farther apart. In general, setting the number at less than 90% will make each letter touch the next and make text hard to read. A setting of more than 110% will create a noticeable gap between each letter and, while this is fine for headlines, subheads, kickers, or other larger type, it's dreadful for body text.

If the space between each word seems too large or too small, you can alter it as well. Press

SHIFT-F8 O P W P

Then enter a number larger than 100% to make the spaces larger or a number less than 100% to make them smaller.

If you want to return spacing to normal, press

SHIFT-F8 O P W O O F7

While you did that you may have noticed that there are several functions I didn't mention. Normal returns letterspacing to the spacing the printer (or font) manufacturer set as normal. Optimal sets spacing that WordPerfect thinks is best. Unless you have problems with this setting, I recommend that you use Optimal. The last option is Set Pitch. This should be used only for monospaced fonts.

Whether it's for special effect or just to improve the appearance of type, you may use WordPerfect's letterspacing (or tracking) frequently.

❖ *Jerome Kern, a man and his music*

Oops, sorry, wrong Kern. Kerning is a process that moves specific pairs of letter closer together in order to create a more attractive, easier to read word.

Here's an example:

AWARE (unkerned)

AWARE (kerned)

Notice how there's less space between the letters of the second word. While kerning is more obvious with headlines and other large type, it can make a subtle improvement in smaller sizes. To turn kerning on press

SHIFT-F8 O P K Y F7

To turn it off, press

SHIFT-F8 O P K N F7

I've yet to have any occasion to turn kerning off. In fact, I entered it in my initial codes through the setup menu, so that the kerning on code is placed in all of my files as I create them. To do this, type

SHIFT-F1 I C SHIFT-F8 O P K Y F7

❖ *Making do with less*

What, you don't have a scaleable font printer? You don't have 1.5 megabytes of LaserJet memory? Money *doesn't* grow on trees? Gee, then you can't possibly produce anything that looks attractive and professional, right?

Wrong. While scaleable font printers or large quantities of LaserJet memory offer you power with a lot of options, you can easily do without them if you just use a little imagination.

Some noted designers avoid large type, believing that smaller sizes force the reader to pay attention. (Just as many designers think that you can't grab a reader's attention without using large type, but quoting them would only negate the intention of this section, so I'll simply pretend they don't exist.)

If you have a plain LaserJet with font cartridges or even a LaserJet II with only 512K, your options are limited. The largest font in a cartridge is 16 point (normally only large enough for a subhead, not a headline), while a 512K LaserJet II is limited to about 30 point (adequate, but not really big enough for a commanding headline).

While size is a quick way to garner attention, it's not the only way. You can spruce up pages with small type by simply using ruling lines and white space. Ruling lines take up memory, however, and if your laser printer doesn't have much, you'll have to use it sparingly. But white space takes up no memory, just imagination.

Rule This: Heavy ruling lines above headlines attract the readers eye and make the type seem larger and more commanding. When designing documents with related material, such as newsletters and newspapers, remember to use ruling lines above but not below headlines. This is because lines are a form of separation and a line under a headline breaks the connection between the headline and the material beneath it. In WordPerfect, .01" will give you a thin line, while .1" gives you a thick one. Also, make sure there's enough space under the line and above the headline.

Spaced Out: White space is, if not free, at least reasonable. If the largest type you have is 14 point (as it is with the HP Z cartridge), one way to make it appear larger is to simply put a space between each letter. Make sure to add a couple of spaces between each word and to be consistent with the amount of space you've added. The more complicated WordPerfect procedure is to press

SHIFT-F8 O P W [ENTER] P

Then enter any number above 100 (the normal letter spacing). Entering 200 gives each letter twice as much space as it would normally have, and you can enter any number up to 250. This also automatically makes the space between words larger. Be sure to set this back to 100 after the headline (or any expanded text) so that the regular body text is spaced correctly.

Of course, the ultimate bit of trickery involves both ruling lines and white space. A thick black rule over widely spaced text is going to take up the most space and grab the greatest attention when using small type sizes.

Lest you think that all this work leads only to artificially filled pages, the results, you will be pleased to know, are extremely attractive. Even designers who feel that large type is de rigueur often find it useful/hip to use small type and some of the tricks I've just mentioned. See the resume example in Chapter 4, *Show & Tell.*

❖ *It's all symbolic*

ASCII (pronounced ask-key) no questions and I'll tell you no lies—or so it seems. But even though ASCII is an internationally standardized system for assigning decimal equivalents to letters, numbers, and common punctuation, once you get past ASCII 126 (~) it's Cole Porter time—anything goes.

Many people are used to working with typewriters that lack even such common symbols as {} [] <> ^ | ~‘ and \, and they don’t miss real quotes, dashes, and bullets. Still, when you are ready for serious desktop publishing, these differences are important.

Now, none of this has to be a problem if you have a scaleable font printer (they have the correct characters built-in), or you generate your Fontware fonts using the ASCII Business character set, or if you use the Desktop Symbol set in Type Director.

But if you generate or purchase fonts for the LaserJet that have only the ASCII, then you will not have these characters and WordPerfect will have to create them graphically, which can be slow and won’t look as good as if they’re really in the set. Got it? (For old-fashioned entertainment, the type your grandparents used to have, read this entire paragraph in one breath.)

The moral of this very lengthy and somewhat pathetic discourse is if you use a LaserJet and want real opening and closing quote marks, make sure to use the correct symbol set when you create your fonts with Fontware. This said (about once too often), let us continue with our discussion of quote marks. (Please, let me apologize for all this attention to characters which most people probably don’t even notice. You see, when you start working with desktop publishing in depth, occasionally something becomes important to you, something that the rest of the world finds trivial and inconsequential. Real opening and closing quote marks are just such a detail, and I can’t seem to help myself when it comes to them. My wife suggests I get “professional help.”)

OK, you want those blasted quote marks. How the heck do you get them in WordPerfect when they aren’t on the keyboard? Well, it’s not that easy. Press

CONTROL-V 4,32 [ENTER]

for an opening quote mark, and for a closing quote mark press

CONTROL-V 4,31 [ENTER]

Of course, you can create a macro to simplify this process, or a complex macro to turn all the regular quote marks into opening and closing quote marks automatically.

◆ Incredibly simple quote mark TRICK

Now, after all that, here’s the easy (if not the most accurate) way to create real opening and closing quote marks. Robert Fenchel, Ph.D., of SoftCraft told me about this trick and I could have kicked myself for not thinking of it earlier. Of course, I don’t have a Ph.D., just a Dt.P.

All you do is use the grave accent ‘ (the backwards apostrophe located under the ~ on most keyboards) twice before a word, and the normal apostrophe twice after a word. Here's an example: "Simple." The quotes will appear widely spaced on-screen, but in most typefaces will print perfectly (although a little more widely spaced than the "real" thing. In View Document, the opening quotes will have the correct appearance, but the closing quotes will look straight. Don't worry about it; the spacing will still be accurate. Wasn't that easy?

If you often use special characters, it's going to be faster to find a font that has them than to wait for WordPerfect to print them as graphics.

◆ PostScript/LaserMaster/Fontware Business Set/Type Director Desktop Symbol Set

The simplest way to produce real opening and closing quote marks is by using the same crafty maneuver I just described for LaserJet printers.

If you want the real McCoy, WordPerfect's *compose* feature can insert real typographic quote marks into your publications. To get an opening quote mark, type

CONTROL-V 4,32 [ENTER]

To get a closing quote mark, type

CONTROL-V 4,31 [ENTER]

Because the PC doesn't have real opening and closing quote marks in its character set, you will see a small square box on-screen where the quote mark will print. You can see the real character in View Document.

Macro: If you are going to use these frequently, it's advisable to create a macro. And you will probably want to use an ALT-key macro, as it requires fewer keystrokes. To create a macro that inserts an opening quote mark when you press **ALT-O**, type

CONTROL F10 ALT-O OPEN QUOTE [ENTER] CONTROL-V 4,32 CONTROL F10

Once you've created this macro, you will only need to press **ALT-O** for WordPerfect to insert an opening quote mark. For a closing quote macro, type

CONTROL F10 ALT-C CLOSE QUOTE [ENTER] CONTROL-V 4,31 CONTROL F10

Remember that WordPerfect can now print characters that are missing from your printer or fonts. If you need real opening and closing quote marks, WordPerfect will create them and print them as graphics. The only problem with this is that it makes printing slower, and WordPerfect's opening/closing quote marks only come in a Helvetica-like font, so they aren't exactly going to look elegant with any other typeface.

Here's the way WordPerfect works. If it can find a specified character in any font in your printer driver, it will use it. This means that if you're printing on a LaserJet

```
Here's how regular "quote" marks look on-screen«
«
Here's how the trick LaserJet ''quotes'' appear on-screen«
«
Here's how real compose ■quotes■ look on-screen

                                      Doc 1 Pg 1 Ln 1.67" Pos 3.4"
Here's how regular "quote" marks look on[-]screen[HRt]
[HRt]
Here's how the trick LaserJet ''quotes'' appear on[-]screen[HRt]
[HRt]
Here's how real compose [■:4,32]quotes■ look on[-]screen




Press Reveal Codes to restore screen
```

Since real typographic quotes aren't in the IBM character set, you have to kludge them. This is how they appear on-screen. (You'll get used to it.)

in Courier and you ask for an opening quote mark, WordPerfect knows that Dutch 10 point has it, so it uses it, rather than printing the mark as graphics.

If your printer driver only has Dutch and Courier and you ask for quote marks in Courier, you can bet you're going to get Dutch quote marks. But if you've got both Swiss and Dutch, you'll probably get Swiss. The only way to know for sure is to use the PTR program, look at the font and check out its substitute fonts. This is an awfully long way to go for something so trivial; if you're really concerned, you should just generate a font with the character you need using Fontware.

❖ *Genuinely important note for LaserJet users*

Here's something you're not going to read in the documentation or any place else for that matter. "So what," you think, "I'm not going to hear Barbara Bush sing *Feelings* anyplace either, but what do I care?" Remember, I said important.

Before you start drooling over how WordPerfect can print any of its 1700 characters on any printer, LaserJet users *may* have to do something special. I say *may*, because sometimes you do, sometimes you don't. Try it first and if it works, don't make these changes. If it *doesn't* work—make these changes.

If you use a LaserJet (or compatible) and you want to use any of the IBM-PC character set in any size other than 12 point (10 pitch), you *may* have to deselect any internal fonts that use the PC-8 character set. This is because when WordPerfect can't find a character in a font, let's say a ¢, it then checks to see if any other available font has this character. If it does, it uses it. Now, the PC-8 character set contains *all* the little characters you can see on-screen, including smiley faces, hearts, stars, and more serious symbols, such as paragraph markers ¶, Sigma, little triangles for pointing, all types of elements you might want to use.

While that's nice for people who *don't* have WordPerfect, for people who do, it means that if you want a 30-point smiley face or paragraph marker, you're not going to get one. Now, this does *not* apply to foreign characters because WordPerfect will happily either take existing accent marks or print them graphically to create most foreign characters, even if these characters are available in another typeface. Besides, if you're going to use foreign characters often, you should really use the Roman-8 character set.

You're not going to get them, unless . . . now, you don't *have* to do this, but I recommend it. What we're going to do is go in and remove the built-in fonts. That way, when WordPerfect looks to see if there are any PC-8 characters in any of your fonts, it won't find them, and it will then create the character in the size you want, by printing it as a graphic.

Ready? Oh. OK, fine, use the sandbox first, I'll still be here. Back now? Fine, let's proceed. Press

SHIFT-F7 S

Move the cursor to the LaserJet printer driver. You may have renamed it, but if you haven't, it'll say "HP LaserJet II." When the cursor is on top of it, press

E C

Now, if you a get a message saying it can't find your printer files, you will have to find your .ALL file and make sure WordPerfect knows where it is. Otherwise, if all is well, you will see: Built-In, Cartridges, Soft Fonts. We're interested in the built-in fonts, and your cursor should already be there, so press

[ENTER]

You're presented with a short list that includes Courier, Line Draw, and Line Printer. They are all marked with an * because they're always ready. But we don't want no stinkin' built-ins, so we're going to unmark them all. Press

[DEL] [DEL] [DEL] [DEL] [DEL] [DEL] [DEL] [DEL]

That's eight times (in case you're reading this on a bus and it's bouncing around and it's hard to count) or as many times as you need to remove all those built-in fonts. Now, to save your driver press

F7 F7 F7 F7 F7 (or just a whole bunch of times)

You can now print any character at any size. What you can't do, however, is print in Courier. If you want to print in Courier for any reason, you will need to create a new printer driver. In case you need them, here are the keystrokes without a lot of explanation.

SHIFT-F7 S A {move to the printer you want} [ENTER]

If it asks if you want to replace a file, answer no, or you will be doing just that. Give it a new name, and then press [ENTER] again. To exit the info screen press

F7

I recommend you press

N

Then type some new name, such as "Courier" so you know what the printer driver really is. Press

[ENTER] F7 F7 F7

❖ *Print it, print it good*

One of the wonders of 5.1 is that if you have a graphics printer (such as a laser, ink-jet, or dot-matrix printer), then you can print every single, solitary character in the gigantic WordPerfect character set. You may never need to print in Japanese or Hebrew, but you can if you want to.

There are two ways to see all the characters WordPerfect supports. One way is to look in the back of the manual in the appendix. I'd give you a page number, but they change with each version of the program. And if you don't happen to have your manual handy (I know you *do* have one, it's just too heavy, or inconvenient to get to), then you can print them all out. Here's how:

When you installed your graphics drivers . . . whoa, pardner, you *did* install your graphics drivers, didn't you? You can tell if you did because there will be a file called **WP.DRS** that will take up about 475K worth of disk space in your WordPerfect program directory (probably C:\wp51) and another called **WPSMALL.DRS**, which is about 50K. The WP.DRS file contains all of WordPerfect's 1700 characters for both screen and printer, along with various screen fonts. The WPSMALL.DRS file does not contain the entire character set, only a few screen fonts, and is for use with computers where you can't spare 500K, such as laptops.

If you discover you haven't installed them, do that now, and don't come back until it's all done.

Look in your WordPerfect directory and find a file called CHARMAP.TST. This file contains *all* of WordPerfect's characters. Print this entire file right now by pressing

SHIFT-F7 F

Now here comes the complicated part. The "graphics quality" of the file is set to *Do not print*, so when you printed the file as-is, what you got was three pages, most of them empty. This is because chances are your printer doesn't have most of these characters, so the characters you're seeing are the characters in your printer or font.

To actually print all of the characters, you must press

SHIFT-F7 G H F

This will set graphics to print in high-quality mode and print the entire file.

Be warned, however, printing this file can take a long, long time. On some printers it can take so long that you might as well go out and get an oil change. Why? Because WordPerfect has to print most of these characters as graphics, and that can be very, very slow.

Once you've printed this file, keep it somewhere handy—like underneath your keyboard (we're going to be using it in just a sec). That way, when you want to access a special character, all you have to do is pick up your keyboard, look for the character, see what number it is, then enter it with **CONTROL-V**, the number of the character set, a comma, then the number of the character.

◆ Retain your compose-ure

Because there are far more characters than there are keys on the keyboard, WordPerfect had to come up with a way to enter them. They call this the **Compose** feature, and you can either use **CONTROL-V** or **CONTROL-2** (that's the two above the letters, not on the keypad) for composite characters. It allows you to create characters that are not on the keyboard (foreign characters such as ñ), by using ones that are. You can also enter characters that have no keyboard equivalent at all, such as æ.

CONTROL-V works at the main editing screen and gives you a prompt that says "Key = " while CONTROL-2 works anywhere, but doesn't give you a prompt. Once you've pressed this, you enter the two characters that you want to merge into one. To create a ç, press

Control-V c ,

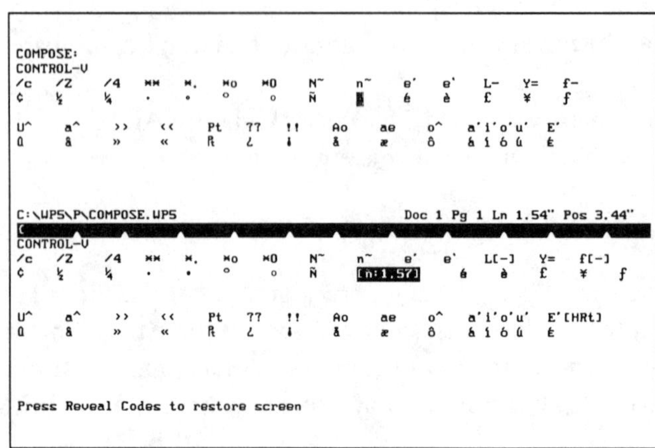

Compose is not a command for budding musicians. No, no, no. It's a way to access characters that aren't otherwise accessible from the keyboard.

WordPerfect will combine the two characters into one cedilla. This is the easiest method if a keyboard equivalent is available for the each of the two characters you want to combine. Many of these characters will show on-screen. If they don't, WordPerfect will display either the first character you entered or a small black square. If you turn Reveal Codes on (ALT-F3) and place the cursor on the character, WordPerfect will show the numerical representation for the character. Ü, for example, displays in Reveal Codes as [Ü:1,70].

You can use Compose to access 1/2 and 1/4 characters as well. **CONTROL-V /2** gives you a 1/2 character, **CONTROL-V /4** gives you a 1/4 character. If your printer or font doesn't have these characters, WordPerfect will print them as graphics, which may or may not look good with the rest of your type.

If the two parts of the character are not available on the keyboard (such as a mathematical character), you must refer to a section of the WordPerfect manual's appendix entitled "WordPerfect Characters." Find the character you need among the 12 different WordPerfect character sets and press **CONTROL-V**. Type the number of the character set, a comma, the number of the character, and press **[ENTER]**. A sigma will be entered as **CONTROL-V 8,36 [ENTER]**. (Because the sigma is also included in the PC character set, it can be entered as ALT-228 or entered using the equation feature).

Now take the three pages you just printed out (look under your keyboard) and let's look at them together. You can print any one of these characters using the Compose feature. Let's enter the frowning face, which is near the top of page 2. We can see it's in character map 5, and then we look over to see what number it is. The first row starts at zero, and the frowning face is 26 characters in, so its number is 5,26.

Before we enter this, we're going to do some finger calisthenics. Most people don't think about it, but typing is very hard work, and to avoid injury, you want to be warmed up. Hold up your right hand at arms length. Do the Vulcan greeting (pinkie and ring finger to the right, middle, index and thumb to the left). Out, in, out, in, out, in. Very good. Now repeat the entire exercise with your left hand. Whew. Now that we've burned up all those calories, it's time for a brownie break.

◆ Chart alert! IBM Character Set and Useful WP Characters

The next two pages show charts of the IBM Character Set, with all the special symbols it includes, and a selection of useful characters from the WP Character Set. All of the IBM symbols will appear on-screen in text mode, whether they can be used with your printer or not.

If you're using a standard LaserJet, HP sells a font cartridge that contains the "line-draw" character set. This includes the entire IBM on-screen character set, and the foreign characters. This would be a good thing to consider because the original

❖ LaserJet ASCII/ALT-Key symbols

Code	1	2	3	4	5	6	7	8	9	10	11	12	13	14	15	16	17	18	19	20	21	22	23	24	25	26	27	28	29
Symbol	☺	☻	♥	♦	♣	♠	•	◘	○	◙	♂	♀	♪	♫	☼	►	◄	↕	‼	¶	§	▬	↨	↑	↓	→	←	∟	↔

Code	30	31	32	33	34	35	36	37	38	39	40	41	42	43	44	45	46	47	48	49	50	51	52	53	54	55	56	57	58	59
Symbol	▲	▼		!	"	#	$	%	&	'	(	)	*	+	,	-	.	/	0	1	2	3	4	5	6	7	8	9	:	;

Code	60	61	62	63	64	65	66	67	68	69	70	71	72	73	74	75	76	77	78	79	80	81	82	83	84	85	86	87	88	89
Symbol	<	=	>	?	@	A	B	C	D	E	F	G	H	I	J	K	L	M	N	O	P	Q	R	S	T	U	V	W	X	Y

Code	90	91	92	93	94	95	96	97	98	99	100	101	102	103	104	105	106	107	108	109	110	111	112	113	114	115	116	117	118	119
Symbol	Z	[	\	]	^	_	`	a	b	c	d	e	f	g	h	i	j	k	l	m	n	o	p	q	r	s	t	u	v	w

Code	120	121	122	123	124	125	126	127	128	129	130	131	132	133	134	135	136	137	138	139	140	141	142	143	144	145	146	147	148	149
Symbol	x	y	z	{			}	~		♀	ü	é	â	ä	à	å	ç	ê	ë	è	ï	î	ì	Ä	Å	É	æ	Æ	ô	ö	ò

Code	150	151	152	153	154	155	156	157	158	159	160	161	162	163	164	165	166	167	168	169	170	171	172	173	174	175	176	177	178	179
Symbol	û	ù		Ö	Ü	¢	£	¥	₧	ƒ	á	í	ó	ú	ñ	Ñ	ª	º	¿	⌐	¬	½	¼	¡	«	»	░	▒	▓	│

Code	180	181	182	183	184	185	186	187	188	189	190	191	192	193	194	195	196	197	198	199	200	201	202	203	204	205	206	207	208	209
Symbol	┤	╡	╢	╖	╕	╣	║	╗	╝	╜	╛	┐	└	┴	┬	├	─	┼	╞	╟	╚	╔	╩	╦	╠	═	╬	╧	╨	╤

Code	210	211	212	213	214	215	216	217	218	219	220	221	222	223	224	225	226	227	228	229	230	231	232	233	234	235	236	237	238	239
Symbol	╥	╙	╘	╒	╓	╫	╪	┘	┌	█	▄	▌	▐	▀	α	β	Γ	π	Σ	σ	µ	τ	Φ		Ω	δ	∞	φ	ε	∩

Code	240	241	242	243	244	245	246	247	248	249	250	251	252	253	254
Symbol	≡	±	≥	≤	⌠	⌡	÷	≈	°	•	·	√	η	²	■

☞ Useful WP Characters ☜

- • 4,0ALT-7 or **
- ○ 4,1 or ALT-9 or *O
- ■ 4,2 or ALT-254
- ● 4,3 or ALT-249 or *.
- ¶ 4,5, ALT-20, or P|
- ¿ 4,8 or ??
- « 4,9 or <<
- » 4,10 or >>
- £ 4,11 or L-
- ¥ 4,12 or Y=
- ¢ 4,19 or c/
- ® 4,22 or ro
- © 4,23 or co
- “ 4,32
- ” 4,31
- – 4,33 or n-
- — 4,34 or - -
- ○ 4,37
- □ 3,38
- ™ 4,41 or TM
- ℠ 4,42 or SM
- ℞ 4,43 or Rx
- ● 4,44
- ° 4,45 or *o
- ■ 4,46
- ▪ 4,47
- □ 4,48
- ▫ 4,49
- ½ 4,17 or /2
- ¼ 4,18 or /4
- ⅓ 4,64
- ⅔ 4,65
- ⅛ 4,66
- ⅜ 4,67
- ⅝ 4,68
- ⅞ 4,69
- Ⓜ 4,70
- ℗ 4,71
- Ⓤ 4,72
- ℅ 4,73
- ‰ 4,75

- № 4,76
- ♥ 5,0 or ALT-3
- ♦ 5,1 or ALT-4
- ♣ 5,2 or ALT-5
- ♠ 5,3 or ALT-6
- ♂ 5,4 or ALT-11
- ♀ 5,5 or ALT-12
- ☼ 5,6 or ALT-15
- ☺ 5,7 or ALT-1
- ☻ 5,8 or ALT-2
- ♪ 5,9 or ALT-13
- ♫ 5,10 or ALT-14
- ⌂ 5,12 or ALT-127
- √ 5,14 or ALT-251
- ◘ 5,18 or ALT-8
- ◙ 5,19 or ALT-10
- ← 5,20
- ☞ 5,21
- ☜ 5,22
- ✓ 5,23
- □ 5,24
- ⊠ 5,25
- ☹ 5,26
- ♯ 5,27
- ♭ 5,28
- ♮ 5,29
- ☎ 5,30
- ⌚ 5,31
- ⌛ 5,32

Remember: Press CONTROL-V or CONTROL-2 FIRST

- → 6,21 or ALT-26
- ← 6,22 or ALT-27
- ↑ 6,23 or ALT-24
- ↓ 6,24 or ALT-25
- ↔ 6,25 or ALT-29
- ↕ 6,26 or ALT-18
- ► 6,27 or ALT-16
- ◄ 6,28 or ALT-17
- ▲ 6,29 or ALT-30
- ▼ 6,30 or ALT-31
- · 6,31 or ALT-249
- · 6,32 or ALT-250
- ∘ 6,33
- • 6,34
- ⇒ 6,56
- ⇐ 6,57
- ⇑ 6,58
- ⇓ 6,59
- ⇔ 6,60
- ⇕ 6,61
- ↗ 6,62
- ↘ 6,63
- ↖ 6,64
- ↙ 6,65
- □ 6,93
- ■ 6,94
- ◊ 6,95
- ♦ 6,96
- ★ 6,112
- ◁ 6,170
- ▷ 6,171
- △ 6,172
- ▽ 6,173
- ★ 6,184
- ℱ 6,212
- ℂ 6,213
- 𝕀 6,214
- ℕ 6,215
- ℝ 6,216

LaserJet (not the LaserJet II) does not have enough memory for graphics, so WordPerfect will not be able to create these characters for you.

Back to work now, if your train of thought hasn't been completely derailed. If you're suffering from short-term amnesia (as I often enjoy doing), we were entering the frowning face, from Character map 5, character 26. To do that, press

CONTROL-V 5,26 [ENTER]

Now just a goll-dern minute. I don't see a little frowning face on your screen, I see it on your face because all you got was a little square on the screen. Don't take it so seriously, you did it right. There's no little frowning face in the IBM PC character set, so you can only see it in View Document mode. The same holds true for the over 1700 characters which aren't in the PC set.

Let's see if we've done it right. Press

SHIFT-F7 V

If it's too small to see on your screen, press **1** or **2** until you've zoomed in on it. (Remember, you can use cursor keys to move around View Document when you zoom in.)

Using this method you can enter *any* WordPerfect character into your document. Let's try another, the SM symbol. No, it doesn't mean what your dirty little mind thinks, it stands for "Service Mark," like the trademark, but for services. It's in character map 4, on the second line. So what's its number? That's right, it's 4,42. If you didn't get that, here's how you do it for the next time. The character is on the second line, and the second line starts at 30. It's over 12 spaces to the right, so 30 + 12 = 42. To enter the character, press

CONTROL-V 4,42 [ENTER]

Another way to make sure you've entered the right character without using View Document is to go into Reveal Codes with

ALT-F3

Then move the cursor on top of the square box and see what it says. If you've done it correctly, the Reveal Codes should read **[■]:4,4**

If the symbol you want is in the IBM-PC character set, you can hold down the [ALT] key, and then type the PC character-set number *on the numeric/cursor keypad*. This will not work if you use the number keys above the letters on the keyboard. This character set is not WordPerfect's, so WordPerfect will translate it into the appropriate character. An example of this is è. This character is 1,47 in the WordPerfect character set, but you can also enter it as ALT-138. If the character *is* in the PC character set, it will display on-screen.

◆ The more, the merrier

Throughout all this I've only concentrated on a few frequently used characters such as quotes and dashes. But there are really hundreds of characters that you, in your particular line of work, might need.

Bitstream Fontware's character set includes 560 characters, and using the Custom Character Set, you can tailor your fonts to your particular needs. If you always need fractions, or ligature, or even a face with its tongue sticking out, you can get them all.

◆ What a bunch of bullets

A quick way to make some bullets in various sizes.

Small bullet:

CONTROL-V * .

(That was "asterisk period")

Medium bullet

CONTROL-V * *

Small hollow bullet

CONTROL-V * o (asterisk, lower case letter "oh")

Large hollow bullet

CONTROL-V * O (asterisk, upper case letter "oh")

◆ Scaleable extras

Scaleable font printers endow you with a wide range of great options and effects. WordPerfect is capable of making fonts print as outlines (unfilled), and shadows can be applied to any font except for Courier. Unlike all other scaleable fonts, Courier is a "stroke" font rather than an "outline," so special effects will not work.

While outline is self-explanatory, the shadow effect has the additional bonus of being opaque; it will print solid white with a black outline, even when you place it on top of a graphic. (See the Abe Lincoln example in Chapter 4.)

But along with the obvious outlines and shadows, WordPerfect offers two additional undocumented extras. The first is gray type, which is controlled by pressing

CONTROL F8 C

For more information about gray type, refer to the section about color earlier in this chapter. The second extra is reverse type, or white type on a black background. While studies have shown (oh, another study, enough already) that white type is at least 18 percent harder to read than black type, there are times when it is effective, especially with larger sizes.

While "White" is an obvious choice in the color menu, you're probably wondering how to produce a black background. The answer? Graphics boxes. While I delve into excruciating detail about this in Chapter 12, *Graphics,* I know the suspense is killing you scaleable-font junkies out there, so here goes.

You should decide what type of graphics box you want to use. It can be a Figure, Table, Text, or User-defined box; it makes no difference (as you will find out if you can hack your way through Chapter 12). In this example, we'll use a figure.

Press

ALT-F9 F O

to set the Figure Options.

Press

G 100 [ENTER][ENTER]

Congratulations, you've just set the background of the box to black.

Now create a graphic Figure with

ALT-F9 F C

Make the box any size you want. If you want the background of the entire page to be black, create a page type box. Press

F

for . . . you guessed it, full. Now to edit the text inside the box. Press

E

Set the type color to white with

CONTROL-F8 C W [ENTER]

Then type and format the text. Text inside a graphics box must not exceed one page. When you are finished, press

F7 F7

You will be returned to the editing screen. If Reveal Codes is on, you will see the marker for the graphic; if it's off, you will see nothing.

If you preview the page with **SHIFT-F7 V,** you will get a great view of a black box. You won't see any type, however, because WordPerfect's View Document doesn't display white type on a black background. I guess they didn't think anyone would figure out how to use it. I guess they didn't know me . . .

You can examine the text only by printing the page. It will print perfectly, with white type on a black background. If you want white type on a gray background, repeat the above steps, but set the Figure Options to a number lower than 100. The background setting works logically, with 100% being solid black and 0 being white. White type requires a background of at least 20% gray in order to be readable, and even that is not quite enough. On lower percentages of gray, the type may appear ragged because it is surrounded with dots placed far apart from each other. When printed on a typesetting machine, the grays will be much smoother and the type easier to read.

◆ LaserMaster note

One thing to remember about the LaserMaster is that it *never* runs out of memory so there are no limits to what you can do.

As well as all the normal special effects, the LaserMaster can do a few more, such as interesting pattern fills. If you choose a color, instead of getting gray fills you get patterns. When you print at 300 or 400 dpi the patterns are large. When you print at high–res (800 or 1000dpi) the patterns are *tiny* so they end up looking like gray fills. If you want a very interesting shadow effect, try using both outline and shadow. It will give you black characters with an outlined shadow, and it's a nice effect.

If you want gray text that's about 50% gray, you can get it by using the Redline feature. Unlike PostScript's gray which is composed of little dots, WordPerfect produces a horizontal stripped affair, which is actually quite interesting.

❖ *Dingbats in style*

Dingbats are not only fun, they're a useful set of characters that can add zing to your pages. This book is full of them (OK, I heard someone in the back of the class say "this book is full of it," and I won't continue until that person makes himself or herself known . . . oh, never mind, it was my pet sheep, Selsdon, practicing his ventriloquism again). The four diamonds ❖, single diamonds ♦, and pen nibs ✎ that appear on these pages as subheads and bullets are all Zapf Dingbats.

If your printer supports Dingbats (PostScript and LaserMaster printers do) they will be located in character set 12 and you will have seen them when you printed out the CHARMAP.TST file. In previous versions you had to change typeface, as well as use Control-V to enter the character, but no more. In 5.1, if you ask for something from character set 12, and you're using one of these printers, you will automatically get Dingbats. This makes life much easier.

LaserJet users: If you aren't satisfied with the characters in the WordPerfect set, and want real, live dingbats, you can buy them from Bitstream. When you are using these fonts, however, you may have to manually switch to the dingbat font, then go through the Control-V rigmarole. If you do, a good way to make this easier is to use a paired Style. The paired style will consist of nothing more than just a [Font:Dingbat 14pt] (or whatever size you want) code. Don't put anything in after the [Comment] code. When you want Dingbats, turn this style on, then use Control-V to choose the character. If you use this feature often you can create a macro which will insert this style faster and easier. See Chapter 17 for more information about macros.

➺ The chart on the next page shows where the Zapf Dingbat set has been mapped in the WordPerfect user-defined character set.

❖ *Big type without really trying*

What if you want REAL BIG TYPE but you don't have enough printer memory or disk space, or, in the case of the DeskJet or dot-matrix printers, the ability to have REAL BIG FONTS.

Well, hold on to your hat. For being so patient and loyal and for reading all the way to the end of this chapter, I'm going to give you a tip that will change your life, or at least change your page.

You can, on any printer, print type up to 1199 points (over 16 inches) tall. That's right. You, yes, you, sitting there forlornly with your lowly printer, can now print gigantic type, or even just 36, 48, or 72-point headlines or drop caps.

How? Well, if I weren't so nice I would say something like "send a check or money order for $29.95 to Box 1235, Point Reyes, CA 94956," but I'm not going to make you pay $29.95. Not even $24.95. For you, and only you, it's on the house. You've already popped for this book, and you're going to get your money's worth.

The secret is to use *equations.*

Even if you don't know a Σ from a π you can still use the equation feature to create giant headlines on any graphics printer: dot-matrix, ink-jet, or LaserJet.

Code	Char	Code	Char	Code	Char	Code	Char	Code	Char
12,33	✁	12,74	✪	12,115	▲	12,190	❾	12,231	➧
12,34	✂	12,75	✫	12,116	▼	12,191	❿	12,232	➨
12,35	✃	12,76	✬	12,117	◆	12,192	➀	12,233	➩
12,36	✄	12,77	✭	12,118	❖	12,193	➁	12,234	➪
12,37	☎	12,78	✮	12,119	◗	12,194	➂	12,235	➫
12,38	✆	12,79	✯	12,120	❘	12,195	➃	12,236	➬
12,39	✇	12,80	✰	12,121	❙	12,196	➄	12,237	➭
12,40	✈	12,81	✱	12,122	❚	12,197	➅	12,238	➮
12,41	✉	12,82	✲	12,123	❛	12,198	➆	12,239	➯
12,42	☛	12,83	✳	12,124	❜	12,199	➇	12,241	➱
12,43	☞	12,84	✴	12,125	❝	12,200	➈	12,242	➲
12,44	✌	12,85	✵	12,126	❞	12,201	➉	12,243	➳
12,45	✍	12,86	✶	12,161	❡	12,202	➊	12,244	➴
12,46	✎	12,87	✷	12,162	❢	12,203	➋	12,245	➵
12,47	✏	12,88	✸	12,163	❣	12,204	➌	12,246	➶
12,48	✐	12,89	✹	12,164	❤	12,205	➍	12,247	➷
12,49	✑	12,90	✺	12,165	❥	12,206	➎	12,248	➸
12,50	✒	12,91	✻	12,166	❦	12,207	➏	12,249	➹
12,51	✓	12,92	✼	12,167	❧	12,208	➐	12,250	➺
12,52	✔	12,93	✽	12,168	♣	12,209	➑	12,251	➻
12,53	✕	12,94	✾	12,169	♦	12,210	➒	12,252	➼
12,54	✖	12,95	✿	12,170	♥	12,211	➓	12,253	➽
12,55	✗	12,96	❀	12,171	♠	12,212	➔	12,254	➾
12,56	✘	12,97	❁	12,172	①	12,213	→		
12,57	✙	12,98	❂	12,173	②	12,214	↔		
12,58	✚	12,99	❃	12,174	③	12,215	↕		
12,59	✛	12,100	❄	12,175	④	12,216	➘		
12,60	✜	12,101	❅	12,176	⑤	12,217	➙		
12,61	✝	12,102	❆	12,177	⑥	12,218	➚		
12,62	✞	12,103	❇	12,178	⑦	12,219	➛		
12,63	✟	12,104	❈	12,179	⑧	12,220	➜		
12,64	✠	12,105	❉	12,180	⑨	12,221	➝		
12,65	✡	12,106	❊	12,181	⑩	12,222	➞		
12,66	✢	12,107	❋	12,182	❶	12,223	➟		
12,67	✣	12,108	●	12,183	❷	12,224	➠		
12,68	✤	12,109	❍	12,184	❸	12,225	➡		
12,69	✥	12,110	■	12,185	❹	12,226	➢		
12,70	✦	12,111	❏	12,186	❺	12,227	➣		
12,71	✧	12,112	❐	12,187	❻	12,228	➤		
12,72	★	12,113	❑	12,188	❼	12,229	➥		
12,73	✩	12,114	❒	12,189	❽	12,230	➦		

Opening Quotes, any font:
4,32 “
Closing Quotes, any font:
4,31 ”

En Dash:
4,33 –
Em Dash:
4,34 —

4,22 ®
4,23 ©
4,41 ™
4,7 ¡
4,8 ¿

You heard me right. Now that 5.1 can print any character on any graphics printer, it means *any* character, including the normal letters of the alphabet. Of course, there are some tricks to this, but they're worth it. First, some rules.

1. WordPerfect can print only Times Roman (Dutch), Helvetica (Swiss), or Courier, and it decides which to use based on the *Initial* Base Font of your document, *not* the current Base font. If you're using any proportionally spaced font, Times Italics is the default, even if your Base Font is sans serif. If you select nonitalics you will get Times if your Initial Base Font is serif, and Helvetica only when your Initial Base Font is a sans serif typeface. All italics are Times.

2. You have to use either ' or ~ characters instead of spaces. A ~ is four times as wide as **a** '.

3. Because we're not using the equation editor as God intended, certain words have to be treated specially. The words Acute, Bar, Check, Circle, Dot, Grave, Hat, Bold, From, Left, Matrix, Over, Phantom, Right, Stack, Sub, To, and Underline all must be preceded by a backslash (\), otherwise WordPerfect will assume they are commands. Here's an example: "Get \Over Here!"

4. If you want multiline headlines, you're going to have to work for it.

5. I can tell the anticipation is making you nervous, so let's try it together. Hold onto my hand, I don't want to lose you once we enter the scary depths of the equation editor. I've heard tales that if you don't have a Ph.D. you can get stuck in there forever or at least for long enough so that when Indiana Jones finds you all that's left is your skeleton. Oooh. Scary. Press

ALT-F9 E C E

Gee, Toto, this doesn't look like Kansas. This doesn't even look like Rhonda Aldrich's old nose, which was also from Kansas (the new nose is from a plastic surgeon in Beverly Hills, but don't tell her you heard it from me).

You are now in the forbidden zone — the equation editor. Actually, it's not anything to fear, it's just a little alien. Pretend you're Richard Dryfuss, and you will have nothing to fear (except possibly type casting).

You want type, well, type

Big~Deal

Remember, you have to use ~'s for spaces. Let's see how it looks, to switch to the display window, press

SHIFT-F3

There it is, plain as the nose on your (or Rhonda's) face. But wait, it's in italics. How come? Well, *all* type in the equation editor comes out as italics, unless you put

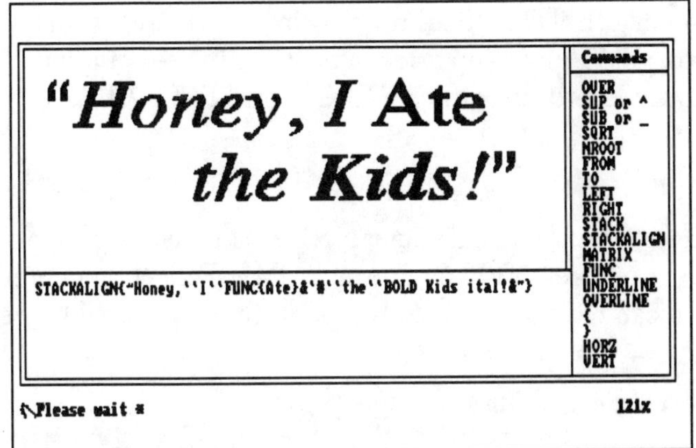

Once you master "equation headlines" you can create headlines as complicated as this.

the word FUNC in front of it, and surround it in { } brackets. Let's try it. We're now in View, and we have to switch to edit, so press

SHIFT-F3

Edit your text so that it reads

FUNC{Big"Deal}

We've used two ' ' marks instead of one ~ because ~ characters tend to be just a little too big, while ' 's are *just* the right size. Call it the *Goldilocks Syndrome.* Now, to see the results, press

SHIFT-F3

Very nice. But don't get cocky just yet, there's more to do (isn't there always). If we left now, this would print at the same size as your initial base font. That's not what we want at all. We want BIG. First, we have to switch back to the edit window by pressing

SHIFT-F3

Now we can set the size of the font by pressing

SHIFT-F1 G S 72 [ENTER]

Very good. What you've done is to tell WordPerfect to print the equation as a graphic (instead of trying to use a printer font) and to print it at 72 point. You can set sizes independently for every equation in your document. Now, let's leave the equation editor and go into View Document so we can see what this really looks like.

F7 F7 F7 SHIFT-F7 V

Oooh. Jumpin' Jehovosafat! Big type that says Big Deal.

You get the idea. Here are a few more tips.

- **Two lines of text:** Pressing [ENTER] does nothing in equations. It starts a new line in the editing half, but it won't start a new line in the equation itself. To do that, you need to use either STACK or STACKALIGN. Here's an example:

STACK {Big # Deal}

The # signifies where the line break should occur. Notice that anything "stacked" has to be placed within { } brackets. When you stack, WordPerfect will automatically center the lines. You can have as many #s as you want, so you could type something like

STACK {Big # Deal # for # a # Few # Bucks}

and get six lines of text.

If you wanted nonitalic text, stacked, you'd type

FUNC {STACK {Big # Deal}}

Notice that it ends with two }}'s. This is because the first { is enclosing the "func" text, and the second is for the stack. If you make a mistake, WordPerfect will say "Incorrect Format" and will place the cursor on the problem.

- **Two Lines, flush left:** Now it starts to get sticky. The only way to have two lines not centered is by using the STACKALIGN command. To produce left aligned text you would type

STACKALIGN {' & Big # ' & Deal}

In this case, you're using the period as the alignment character.

- **Two lines, flush right:** Once again, you have to use STACKALIGN.

STACKALIGN {Big & ' # Deal & '}

- **Combinations:** You can combine all this stuff any way you want:

STACKALIGN{"Honey,"I"FUNC{Ate} & ' # "the"BOLD kids ital !" & '}

Of course, this tip only works for 5.1 users, but if I performed any more miracles with 5.0 I would have to be declared a saint and I don't want my image to be placed on medallions, like St. Christopher, only to have (hundreds of years later) some fickle Pope decide that I am not really a saint anymore. I just couldn't stand the disappointment.

8

What's my alignment?

Paragraph technicalities

Before we explore paragraph alignment, justification, hyphenation, letterspacing, word spacing, and other universal themes, I'm going to try once more to show you how crazy it is to format while you write. Printing out drafts that look typeset is seductive, but dangerous. First, you can easily spend more time formatting than writing; but your written message is the one you are trying to get across, not the formatting.

Second, pages printed in just plain Courier look like just plain drafts. Ephemeral. Inconsequential. Easy to change. Pages printed in Times Roman or Helvetica or even our old friend Upchuck #3, have a final, untouchable appearance.

There is an exception to this rule. If you are creating a document with the same format you've worked with before, and you know you're going to be using a headline, byline, subhead, whatever, it's okay to enter those codes. Just don't spend a lot of time checking back and forth between Edit and View Document mode. Don't worry about page breaks or line endings. Just worry about the text.

In Chapter 11, *Styles*, I'll cover ways to transform a standard Courier draft form into a completely formatted final form in as little as three keystrokes.

❖ *Alignment*

WordPerfect gives you a choice between the four basic forms of paragraph alignment: *Left*, which is also known as unjustified or ragged right. *Full*, also known as justified whereby both the left and right edges of the text line up, as they do in this book. *Center*, not to be confused with SHIFT-F6 for centering a single line of text, and *Right*, also known as right aligned or ragged left. (5.0 can only center by using SHIFT-F6.)

You can turn justification on and off at will ("fire at will" was never a favorite expression of mine) and use them within styles.

Full justification: Many people consider ragged right easier to read, but fully justified type can fit more copy onto a page and still retain its readability. Justification is tricky because it requires careful hyphenation; you must also pay attention to letter and word spacing (covered later in this chapter) and to lines that are too short. Justified type looks more formal, appears more . . . typeset. Good justification is beautiful; bad justification is ugly and hard to read. Bad justification is easy; good justification is harder.

To use full justification, press

SHIFT-F8 L J F F7

Left justification: Ragged type is easier to set and very much in style with many applications (*excluding* books and most magazines). As you can see from this paragraph, it's less formal, takes up more space, and is less intimidating because it requires less attention to hyphenation and letter and word spacing.

For left-justified text, press

SHIFT-F8 L J L F7

Center justification: Centering is good only for short blocks of text. You'd never want to set the text of a book, magazine, or newsletter entirely centered because it would be very hard to read and just plain look stupid, as this paragraph does. Centering is good for invitations, very short advertisements or brochures (and I mean very short, just a few lines).

To turn on center justification, press

SHIFT-F8 L J C F7

Right justification: This is another special form of justification which has limited uses.

If you set a long block of text this way you would probably just end up confusing your readers or making them think you had gone completely, totally, and irrevocably insane. However, right justification has its place. I can't say I've ever right justified more than a single line, but who knows, it's nice to know it's there if you need it.

To get it, press

SHIFT-F8 L J R F7

➔ Put it first

Although you can change alignment anywhere within a line, unless the alignment change is the first item on the line, WordPerfect will automatically follow it with a **[DSRt]** code. This code is called a "deletable soft return" because it will be deleted if the justification code is deleted or moved. A [DSRt] acts just like a return in that it splits a line in two. This means you can't have part of the paragraph fully justified and another part left justified, but then, I can't think of any reason why you'd want to.

The moral of this whole thing is simple: *Always place justification codes at the beginning of a line—never the middle or end.*

➔ Justifying after the fact

Suppose you've got a few lines of text you want centered. How ya gonna do it? Well, of course, you could PS/2 it, if you were so inclined, but in this particular case, the best plan of action is to block the text, and then press

SHIFT-F6

WordPerfect will ask if you want to [Just:Center]? and if you do, you will press Y.

If you're familiar with 4.2 or 5.0, you may expect WordPerfect to place a center code at the beginning of each line, and a [C/A/Flrt] and a [HRt] at the end of each line. But 5.1 doesn't have to do that. What it does is place a [Just:Center] at the beginning of the blocked text and a [Just:whatever you had before you blocked it] at the end.

For those of you who are easily confused, I don't mean to say that WordPerfect really has a code called [Just:whatever you had before you blocked it], I mean that whatever the alignment was before you blocked the text, that's what WordPerfect will return it to at the end of the block.

This same thing takes effect with flush right. If you have a few lines you want flushed (or righted), then block it and press

ALT-F6

There's only one little drawback to this system. If you later change the alignment *above* this block of text, the old [Just:whatever] code does not automatically change, it just sits there with the old alignment. This doesn't have to be a problem as long as you remember that the code is there.

Another way around this problem is to use a paired style for centering blocks of text. Since the closing end of a paired style always returns text to whatever it was before the style took effect, it *will* automatically adjust to whatever the current alignment is, even if you change it.

Centering and the single line

There are many times when you only want to center a single line, not a whole block of text. To do this, before you type the line of text, press

SHIFT-F6

Or if you've already typed the line, move the cursor to the beginning of the line and then press **SHIFT-F6.**

This inserts a **[Center]** code. This code does not change justification except for the line it's on. If the line doesn't end with a hard return, this code can cause text to print over text which precedes it on the line, causing confusion and a good old-fashioned mess.

◆ TIP: Period space space

Never ever use a double space after a period when setting justified type. Yes, I know what you learned in school, but that was for typing, and this is the glamorous world of typesetting. Because justification adds extra space between words, a space could be added after the period, resulting in three spaces that produce a huge gap. Ask any typesetter, and they'll tell you single spaces belong after punctuation.

◆ One lump or two?

Another age-old question. In this particular case, it's one return or two. The answer is simple—it depends on what you're doing.

Naturally, one return between paragraphs is going to take less space on the page than two. But two returns have their advantages. They introduce more white space to the page (hello page, this is white space, nice to meet you), and they help to make pages less gray and text-heavy.

Single returns are best for books and magazines. I can't recall ever reading a novel that used blank spaces between paragraphs. I have, however, seen large format books done this way and have even produced one this way myself. Correspondence can go either way, indented or block form. I like block form myself, but it's a personal decision.

The only word of advice I have is this: if you only have one return between paragraphs, and don't use any extra secondary leading (SHIFT-F8 O P L) then you *must*, you absolutely must have some type of indent (or occasionally outdent) for all paragraphs. Otherwise, readers can't tell where one paragraph ends and another begins. If you don't have any type of indent and no blank line between paragraphs, it's much harder to read. The whole reason we use paragraphs are to put ideas and information into digestible little clumps. Think of them like "Info-McNuggets." If you have gigantic long paragraphs, no one except the truly intrepid will read them. Short paragraphs are not only easier to read, they help you to organize your material so it's easier to write and easier to read.

If you use two returns between paragraphs or have extra leading between them, then do *not* use any type of indent. Using both is redundant. An indent is to show the reader where a new paragraph begins, but if you have a blank line between paragraphs, then either they can figure it out or they're going to be too dense to read the words anyway.

◆ What hard returns do in the dead of winter

Once again we have a feature with a name that sounds like something out of a science class. Let me set the record straight: this feature has nothing to do with sleeping like a bear through the winter because learning WordPerfect is boring. It has all to do with getting rid of those blank lines at the top of a page or column and is a feature that only programs like WordPerfect and Ventura Publisher can boast.

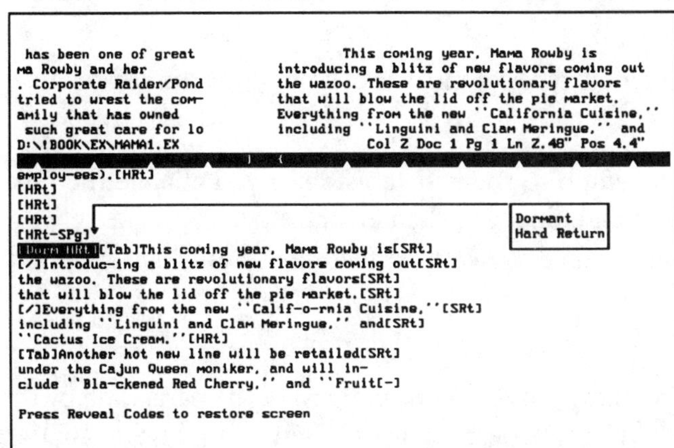

The first [HRt] on a page (or column) becomes Dormant … whether you like it or not.

When you have a page with more than one column, it becomes very noticeable when the columns don't line up at the top. With 5.0 it was all to easy to make this mistake. In fact, you had to go out of your way and visually check the column tops to keep this from happening. The problem was that if you made any editing changes, you could easily end up with another blank line on top. Even worse, if the paragraph moved so it was no longer at the top of the column, you could have two paragraphs without any space between them.

WordPerfect's Dormant Hard Return feature works like this. If WordPerfect sees a hard return as the first item on a page, it changes it into a Dormant Hard Return. The hard return is still there, it just doesn't show up unless it moves so that it is no longer at the top of the page. Glamorous? No. Useful: yes.

Don't be confused by this feature, however. It really is a feature, not a bug, and a useful one at that. But if you normally have a blank line between paragraphs and a page break takes place between paragraphs, on-screen it will appear as if there is no return there. If you meddle and add another return and later make any editing changes that move the location of the page break, you'll end up with *two* returns, and wonder where they came from. Dormant means invisible, it doesn't mean dead.

◆ Indents ahoy!

What's the difference between a tab and an indent? About a dollar fifty (yuk, yuk, just kidding). A tab indents a single line, while an indent (F4) indents an entire paragraph. Indents are indispensable for outlines.

- Using indents allows you to create perfect outlines without hitting returns at the end of each line. You can't justify outlines without using indents. Don't miss the exciting intro to 5.1's new outline feature in Chapter 11, *Styles*.
- For some hints on creating outlines that show on-screen but don't print, see Chapter 17, *Macros*.

There are actually two different types of indents. The first is good old reliable

F4

This indents an entire paragraph to the first tab stop. If you change the tabs, the entire paragraph will reform and indent to the new tab stop.

The second type of indent is called (in Wordperfectese) a Left/Right indent. If you press

SHIFT F4

WordPerfect will indent both the left and right margins of the paragraph by the amount of the first tab on the left. If that doesn't make any sense, try this explanation on for size: if margins are set at 1" from left and 1" from right and tabs are set every .5", pressing **SHIFT F4** will indent both the left and right margins by .5". If you change tab stops so that you have only one and it's set at 1.5", both the left and right margins of the paragraph will be indented by 1.5." Here's how it looks:

> This is a Left/Right indent because both sides of the paragraph have been indented by the amount of the first tab stop. This is useful for quotes and, if you're so inclined, screenplays.

➾ Watch out

As I write this book, WordPerfect 5.1 is still in its first version. One of the peculiarities of this version is that you must *never* place a justification code after an indent. If you do, WordPerfect will keep adding [DSRt]'s every single time the cursor passes these codes. The result will be that every time you move past the codes, the document will become one line longer, and the text will move further and further downwards. I don't know if this is a feature or whether it'll be removed in later versions, but be aware of it. Aren't computers fun?

◆ Playing hangman

They're called hanging indents because the first line of the paragraph seems to protrude or hang out from the body of the paragraph. Hanging paragraphs are useful for numbered lists, outlines, and, in rare cases, regular paragraphs of body text.

There are two ways to create hanging indents with WordPerfect. The first is the simplest, but works only when you have a numbered or lettered paragraph, as in an outline.

I. Type the number or letter of the paragraph (or use WordPerfect's automatic numbering with SHIFT-F5 P [ENTER]). Press **F4** for indent. The cursor will move as if you pressed the tab key; however, the entire paragraph, not just the first line, will be indented.

The second procedure is more complicated, but is still the only way to achieve a hanging indent in a normal paragraph.

This hanging indent was created by first pressing **F4** to insert a WordPerfect indent and then pressing **SHIFT-TAB** to create a margin release. Unlike the margin release on a typewriter (which totally releases the margin), WordPerfect's margin release code moves backwards by one tab stop.

A) Margin release can also be used on numbered or lettered outlines (where you want the first line to jut out from the body of the paragraph). A hanging first line makes it easier to see where each point begins. Thrill to more exciting outline ideas using outline styles. Where? In Chapter 11, *Styles*, of course.

◆ It's only marginal

An important detail to remember about margins is *where* you set them. Because all WordPerfect codes affect everything that *follows*, you have to put the margin codes at either the very beginning of a file (use **HOME HOME HOME [UP ARROW]** to get to the very top) or preceding the part of the file that you want to change (including graphics). This is both good and bad. It's good because it allows you to place graphics, headers/footers, etc., outside the normal working area of the page; it's bad because it can be confusing.

Margins are absolute: everything will print within the margins, nothing will print outside of them. If you set a top margin of one inch and a bottom margin of one inch, the headers and footers will print at least one inch from the top and bottom, and the text will print even farther from the edge of the paper. You can however, change margins anywhere on a page. If you place a new top and bottom margin code halfway down the page, WordPerfect will be able to change the bottom margin but not the top (it's already finished with that part of the page). Left and right margins take effect immediately.

Here's another example: let's say you've set left and right margins of one inch and want the same margins for headers and footers. You must place the margin code *before* the header or footer code.

You'll only put headers/footers and graphics outside the normal margins of the page when you're going for a special effect. Let's say you wanted a margin of one inch from the left and right sides of the text but only a half inch for the headers or footers. If you place a Left/Right margin code of .5" and then the header or footer followed by another margin code of 1", the headers or footers will have a wider margin than the text.

This isn't as obvious as it seems. It's all too easy to move to what you think is the top of the file using **HOME HOME [UP ARROW]**; you will not be at the top, however, but at the top after the codes. If you change the margins there, whatever codes are above the margin (headers, footer, graphics) will not be affected by these new settings.

For desktop publishing, margins are measured *in* from the edge of the paper. If you're used to working with old WordPerfect or a typewriter, this will take some getting used to. You might be tempted to set margins in familiar old WordPerfect units, namely lines and columns. These units are basically "decimal" inches, ten to the inch. But beware; while you can enter the left margin at 10u (the u tells WordPerfect that you're using the old WordPerfect units), you can't enter it at 70u (because this measurement measures *in* from the right side of the page). If you did enter the margin at 70u, you would end up with a printed area only half an inch wide, with 1 inch of white space on the left and 7 inches of white space on the right.

Most laser printers cannot print closer than a quarter of an inch (.25) from the edge of the paper because they have handling mechanisms that must be able to grasp the paper. Since printing can be very light at the extremities of the page, I never set margins less than .3" inches from the edge of the paper.

- One warning about setting margins. If you place a Left/Right margin code anywhere but at the beginning of a line, WordPerfect will automatically place a [HRt] (hard return) *before* the margin change. This is not really a problem it's just kind of annoying. These hard returns don't automatically disappear the way the [DSRt]'s do with justification changes; they have to be removed manually if you remove the margin change. And you *cannot*, repeat, cannot delete them unless you delete the margin change first.

- Attn: Reformed typesetters

If you have a 1" top margin, you probably expect to have 1" of white space at the top of the page, and normally in WordPerfect you do. That's because WordPerfect places the top of the biggest character on the first line 1" from the top of the page.

But typesetters do it differently. (That sounds like a bumper sticker doesn't it?) If they set a 1" top margin, they want the baseline (an invisible line that marks the bottom of all characters except those with descenders, such as g, j, p, q, y) to be at the 1" mark. I only recommend this setting for advanced users because it is possible, when you have a large headline at the top of the page, for the headline to print off the top of the page. To turn this feature on, press

SHIFT-F8 O P B Y

◆ How long, oh Lord, how long?

The question of how long a line should be has been asked repeatedly throughout the ages. According to typography and design expert Jan White, a centuries-old formula for line length is one-and-a-half alphabets, or approximately 39 characters long. Obviously, this will vary depending on the size and width of type. You can go longer or shorter, but very long lines are confusing while very short lines are choppy. Of course, in the very book where he states this, he uses 65 - 75 characters per 5 inch line.

Another formula uses 9 - 10 words per line with serif type and only 7 - 9 words per line with sans serif type. Longer lines often require more leading (line height in WordPerfect lingo), as do heavier typefaces.

It all comes down to what the publication is going to be used for. Books and newsletters can have longer lines because readers are expected to read them thoroughly at arm's length. Advertising copy should have shorter lines in that you don't expect to have the reader's undivided attention. You have to make your point quickly, and short lines do just that. However, you need to be aware of how each line ends so that each line is understandable by itself.

The most important point is never to have lines that are too long or too short. A line should have at least three words on it, and really only be *that* short if you're wrapping around something. Five to nine words is better.

❖ *Hyphenate this*

Can I be frank? I used to hate WordPerfect's hyphenation. It used to beep incessantly, and ask me to hyphenate all sorts of words. As Bones on *Star Trek* might say, "Dammit, I'm not a dictionary, Jim." The program would also attempt to hyphenate words like "the" and in general make a nuisance of itself.

The hyphenation in 5.1 is completely new. The program can hyphenate two different ways: first, by using internal hyphenation rules, and second, by using the external spelling dictionary which has new hyphenation information built-in. The rules feature can hyphenate any word based on rules of the English language. The dictionary version can only hyphenate words in its dictionary. The rule version can, in rare instances, make mistakes. The dictionary version can't. The dictionary version also takes up more memory. I suggest you try both and decide which works best for you. To set this feature, press

SHIFT-F1 E Y

Then choose either **E** for external, or **I** for internal.

F7

The other new feature of hyphenation is that *you* control whether the program will ask for hyphenation help. In 5.0 the program would ask you how to hyphenate words it couldn't figure out (it used to drive me nuts; I want to write, not hyphenate). With 5.1, you can set the help level three ways: *never* will, not surprisingly, never ask you how to hyphenate a word. That's what I use. (I'll be completely honest, occasionally even set at *never* WordPerfect sometimes can't stand staying silent and will break through to ask me how to hyphenate some unhyphenateable word such as "new." It doesn't happen often, but you know what they say, *never* say never.) *When Required* will ask you only if WordPerfect can't figure it out for itself. *Always* will always ask you. The only people who will set it to "always" are those who trust computers even less than they trust car salespeople or the truly masochistic. To set hyphenation help, press

SHIFT-F1 E P

Then press **N** for Never, **W** for when required, or **A** for always.

F7

➻ Turning on

To control whether hyphenation is on or off, you press

SHIFT-F8 L Y

Then press either **Y** for "Yes, turn it on, stupid" or **N** for "Don't even think about turning it on."

To get back to document edit, press

F7

➻ 5, 6, 7, 8, who do we all hyphenate?

If you are going to set justification to Full, you'd sure as heck better hyphenate. Your typesetting won't look good otherwise. Hyphenation is essential in producing attractive, justified text. Hyphenation causes justified lines to appear more even, so large gaps aren't apparent between words and letters (these gaps are called "rivers"). Hyphenation also makes text both easier and harder to read. Easier, because the words and characters are set more consistently, and more difficult, because readers are sometimes thrown by hyphenated words, especially when at the end of a page.

But when you're just plugging along, writing your draft, don't turn hyphenation on—you don't need it. Hyphenation is for the reader, not the writer. It was invented so lines could be hyphenated and so more words could be placed on a page. I don't care about hyphens while I'm writing and neither should you since every little edit will change hyphenation.

◆ Short takes

You can only hyphenate words of more than one syllable. This isn't a WordPerfect rule but a rule of English. Words like "the," "mess," "gross," and "quite," can't be hyphenated because they are monosyllabic. If WordPerfect ever pops up monosyllabic words for hyphenation, press the **F1** key to cancel hyphenation on the word.

Hyphenation can also be dangerous and/or libelous. Witness this famous example: "Throughout his long career he was known as the-rapist to the stars . . ." Uh oh.

Hyphenation requires that you pay attention. When you print the next-to-final copy, take a moment to sit down and check the hyphenation. Is there enough of it or are there gaps in the text? Is there too much of it? Are they in the right place?

One of the more fussy canons about hyphenation is: "Don't have more than two lines in a row hyphenated." It won't stand out like a sore thumb if three lines in a row are hyphenated, but the text will be harder to read. WordPerfect cannot prevent this automatically, so it's one more item you'll want to watch out for.

➺ When WordPerfect asks

When WordPerfect asks you to help it hyphenate, you are faced with four choices:

1) Press the **ESC** key to hyphenate where WordPerfect suggests.

2) Use the left and right cursor keys to mark where you want the hyphen to go.

3) Press **F1** to Cancel that particular hyphen. This causes WordPerfect to insert a [/] command that means "don't hyphenate this word if you care for your life."

4) Press **F7** to have WordPerfect temporarily forget about hyphenation and stop its insistent beeping at you. The temporary aspect is important. WordPerfect typically hyphenates as you move through a file; if you were to go to the bottom of the file, WordPerfect would try to hyphenate the entire file. Pressing **F7** forces WordPerfect to stop hyphenating, at least for the next function. It also works in View Document. But once the function is complete, hyphenation rears its ugly little head again.

◆ Hand tuning

Once you print a publication, you'll notice that certain lines may contain space between the words. Often you can supplement WordPerfect's hyphenation with your own to alleviate these problem lines. If the last word on the previous or problem line or the first word on the next line appear as if they could be hyphenated, move the cursor to where you want the hyphen to be and press CONTROL – (you hold down the control key, then press the hyphen key). This will insert a "soft" hyphen that only appears when used at the end of a line. WordPerfect only reformats the line when you move the cursor back up, above, and back down again, so move the cursor to the problem line and then press the [DOWN ARROW].

If there is room to add the newly hyphenated word, WordPerfect will break the word. But if there isn't enough room, WordPerfect will ignore the soft hyphen you've inserted. Sometimes it looks as if there should be enough room, but WordPerfect is calculating in very small increments; if it determines that there isn't enough room, it won't use your hyphen.

If there are certain words you don't under any circumstances want hyphenated, you can place a [/] before the first character of the word. To do this, place the cursor on the first letter of the word and press

[HOME] /

Unless you are in Reveal Codes, you won't see anything happen. If you *are* in Reveal Codes, you'll see the [/] code appear. As long as that code appears in front of a word, WordPerfect will not hyphenate it.

◆ Tuning out

There are times when you'll want to remove all traces of WordPerfect's hyphenation and start from scratch. I do this when I drastically change the format of a publication (from two to three columns) or make changes in type size. This requires WordPerfect to rehyphenate everything, and then I can make sure I approve of what it's done. To remove all traces of old hyphenation, use search and replace. Search (ALT-F2) for **CONTROL –** and replace it with nothing (not even a space). This will remove all old soft hyphens. Next, move back to the top of the file ([HOME] [HOME] [UP ARROW] ALT-F2). Search for **[SHIFT]-F8 L /**, and replace it with nothing. This will eliminate all the cancel hyphenation codes.

◆ Regular hyphens

When you press the – key (underneath the underline character), you insert what WordPerfect calls a hard hyphen. This is the normal hyphen that you'll use for most words. It will print anywhere; in the middle or at the end of a line. WordPerfect will also use this hyphen to break words that are located at the end of a line. If you want to search for a hard hyphen, you press **F2** and then the - key. You'll notice that WordPerfect will display [-] for any regular hyphen.

◆ Nonbreaking (or hard) hyphens

If you want to use a hyphen in a word or group of words but don't want WordPerfect to use the hyphen to break the words at the end of the line, you should enter a "hyphen character." You do this by pressing **HOME –**. To search for a hard hyphen, you press **F2 [HOME] –**.

◆ Hyphenation zone

Changing the hyphenation zone allows you to specify when you want WordPerfect to hyphenate a word. The default is 10% on the left, 4% on the right. If more hyphenation is desired, make these numbers smaller. If you want less hyphenation, make these numbers larger.

➾ The incredible invisible soft return

There's actually one more way to break words at the end of the line, and it's called an Invisible Soft Return. This is used when you want to break a word but don't want to use a hyphen, for example, when you have an em dash (Wonda—Cleana) or slashes between words (sick/sicker/sickest). Normally WordPerfect won't place a hyphen at an em dash or hyphen, so you can end up with a very short line. To enter one of these creatures, press

[HOME] [ENTER]

This code will remain invisible until WordPerfect needs to use it.

WordPerfect will sometimes insert a Deletable Soft Return if you are working with very short lines or very big headlines that can't be hyphenated. In these cases, WordPerfect *must* break up the word in some way, but since it can't hyphenate and it can't move it to the next line because it won't fit there either, it inserts a [DSRt]. This code acts like a normal return when WordPerfect needs it and disappears when WordPerfect doesn't. WordPerfect also inserts this code if you place a justification change in the middle of a line of text. You can't delete these codes manually; you must correct whatever situation is causing them to appear. There is, as far as I know, no way to enter this code manually, nor would you ever want to anyway.

If you have a headline that won't fit—make it smaller. If you have a word that won't fit on a line, either a word is too long or your line is too short. Either way, something's got to give; otherwise you're going to have a word broken up in the middle, without a hyphen, and people will write you nasty letters or make insulting phone calls.

◆ Dash it all!

There's a big difference between a hyphen and a dash, as you may have guessed from the previous passage. While you may routinely use two hyphens instead of a dash, the real typographic character you want is called an "em dash." It's called this because it's the same width as the letter "m." There's another, shorter dash called an "en dash" character, (you're way ahead of me here), because it's the same width as the letter "n."

En dash: Use the compose feature to create an **en** dash. Type

CONTROL-V n-

(optional) [ENTER] HOME [ENTER].

The **HOME [ENTER]** at the end inserts an "invisible soft return," which, if necessary, causes WordPerfect to break the line rather than hyphenate.

Em dash: To create an **em** dash, you will also use the Compose feature by typing

CONTROL-2 m–

(optional) HOME [ENTER].

As with the en dash, the **HOME [ENTER]** at the end will insert an invisible soft return.

➾ Dastardly dashes

While all PostScript and LaserMaster fonts include em and en dashes, not all LaserJet fonts do. ASCII fonts don't. Fontware's ASCII Business fonts do, as do Roman-8 fonts. If you don't have them, WordPerfect will look for a font in your driver that does (even if it's not the right size) or will print the dash as graphics.

◆ Ridiculously complex simulation pour la LaserJet

If you are using 9-, 10-, or 11-point type, the easiest way to simulate a hyphen is to press **ALT-196** (on the keypad) twice. This dash belongs to the IBM line drawing set and works just fine, while two in a row align perfectly so that there's no blank space between them.

Complicated LaserJet: If you are using larger type, and want or need to simulate an en or em dash with type hyphens, type **HOME – –**. WordPerfect will keep the two dashes together at the end of a line. If you are using ASCII symbol fonts, you won't have a real em dash. Still, you can create a close facsimile. Type **HOME– HOME– HOME– HOME–** and then press the **[LEFT ARROW]** key so that the cursor is on the second hyphen. If you are using 10-point type, enter **SHIFT-F8 O A L .01 [ENTER] F7**. Put the cursor on the third hyphen and repeat this procedure. Now put it on the fourth hyphen and do it again (you probably haven't had this much fun since high school). You won't see any difference on-screen (it will just look like you've got four hyphens in a row). But you will see what appears to be a real em dash in View Document and when you print.

If spaces are still visible between the hyphens, make the .01 number larger. This command tells WordPerfect to move to the left 1/100th of an inch before it prints the next hyphen. Sometimes that's enough, sometimes it isn't. Making the number .02 should work for any 10 point font, but the dash will be shorter.

If you want to repeat this trick with larger headline fonts, you'll have to experiment with the correct number to use. A large font can use .1" or more to eliminate the space between the hyphens. If you type a hyphen at the left margin, you can check the ruler line at the bottom of the screen to see just how long your hyphen is. (This is starting to sound like a Mr. America contest: "Just how long *is* your hyphen?") If the number is bigger than the length of the hyphen, the second hyphen will simply print over the first (or even to the left of it).

Since you obviously don't want to press almost 40 keystrokes every time you want a dash, you can turn the whole dreary procedure into a macro simply by recording your keystrokes. Press **CONTROL-F10** to start the macro. When WordPerfect says Define Macro, type a name; go for something clever like **DASH [ENTER]**. When Macro Definition appears, type a description of the macro. Let's try making a dash out of four hyphens **[ENTER]**. Now you get to experience the thrills and chills of the entire spine-tingling process, starting with **HOME– HOME– HOME– HOME–** and **SHIFT-F8 O A L .01 [ENTER] F7** between each of the hyphens.

When you are finished, press **CONTROL-F10** again. The next time you want a dash, press **ALT-F10 [ENTER]**. WordPerfect will play back your keystrokes and create another dash.

If none of that makes any sense, try it for yourself or see Chapter 17, *Macros* (my fingers are getting tired).

❖ *Limiting yourself*

I told you that justification was more complicated than you imagined. And probably more boring. But before you doze off, this next section will unravel the mystery behind justification limits.

These limits control the amount of space that WordPerfect can add between words when it justifies. You can instruct WordPerfect to add large amounts of space between each word (which looks terrible) or split the extra space between words *and* letters.

With WordPerfect's default, spaces between words can be compressed down to 60% and enlarged to 400% of their normal size. The 60% figure is acceptable, but would you really want the equivalent of *four* spaces between words? I don't think so — it looks unprofessional.

You should aim for a decent mix of space between words and letters. I use a setting of 60% for compression and 150% (a space and a half) for expansion. To enter that setting, type

SHIFT-F8 O P J 60 [ENTER] 150 [ENTER] F7

If you want to use that as the default, type

SHIFT-F1 I C SHIFT-F8 O P J 60 [ENTER] 150 [ENTER] F7 F7 F7

Warning: Some people *hate* letterspacing; they claim it makes text difficult to read and ugly. Personally, I like letterspacing, and I find type with gaping spaces between words hard to read and ugly (so there). Most publications utilize a mix of space between words and space between letters, as I've suggested.

◆ Widows and orphans: A Dickensian touch

Widows and orphans, a staple of 19th century literature. And now these two pathetic characters hit you right where you live, or at least where you desktop publish.

Orphans are desolate little words or lines all by themselves at the bottom of a page or column. Their mothers are widows, lonely lines all by themselves at the top of a page.

But weep no more, WordPerfect now has a feature that prevents single lines from being stranded all by their lonesome. This feature is not a default; to turn it on you need to type

SHIFT-F8 L W Y F7

If you want to use it as a permanent default that will be applied to all new files you create, type

SHIFT-F1 I C SHIFT-F8 L W Y F7 F7 F7

When W/O is turned on, WordPerfect will pause briefly at any page break where a widow or orphan might be occurring. If you have a four-line paragraph, WordPerfect may break it after the second line (so that one page ends with two lines and another begins with two lines). If you have a three-line paragraph, WordPerfect will not be able to break it correctly; it will simply move the entire paragraph to the next page.

Be aware, however, that pages and columns won't end on exactly the same line. WordPerfect has no magic method of spacing (also called vertical justification or feathering) a column so that it ends up equal in length to another column. This is more of an inconvenience than a gaffe; it's perfectly acceptable for columns to end unevenly, and this can actually be an artistic virtue if they end unevenly enough.

While this feature is useful, it's not foolproof. As a matter of fact, it's extremely easy to fool, so be sage enough to keep an eye out for it. While the W/O feature always functions correctly when splitting a paragraph, it doesn't work the way you might expect with single line paragraphs, such as subheads; it completely ignores them, forcing them to become orphans. (Maybe WordPerfect should open an adoption agency).

In essence, the only sure way to avoid widows and orphans is to watch out for them yourself.

◆ Raising initial caps from the dead

Or at least from the lifeless. Raised Initial Caps allow you to easily add visual interest to a page without the use of graphics. You've seen them used hundreds of times in magazines and newspapers; they're the big letter at the start of a paragraph.

Most initial caps are Drop Caps set into the body of the paragraph and can be difficult (but never fear, not impossible) to create with WordPerfect. Raised Caps are easy and provide as much visual interest. Their only drawback is that they take up more space.

Raised caps normally use the same typeface as the body copy or headline. It can also be effective to use a contrasting typeface for drop caps. If you're using Times

Roman for the body copy, try Helvetica (or better yet, something more interesting like Avant Garde) for the raised cap.

➾ Here's how to do it:

1. Set line spacing to fixed with **SHIFT-F8 L H F** and a number that is a point or two larger than the body text (otherwise WordPerfect would leave extra space above *and* below the line for the ascenders and descenders of the large letter), then press **F7**.

2. Press [ENTER] once or twice, depending on how large the first letter is. If the normal type is 10-point on 11-point leading and you want to use a 36-point raised cap, you need at least two blank lines before the paragraph with the raised cap. If you are using the Extra Large size, the amount of space you'll need will depend on whether you've changed the Size Attribute Ratio in Setup; but leave at least one blank line before the paragraph.

3. The easiest way to create the big cap is to block the first letter with **ALT-F4**, then press **CONTROL-F8 S E** for an extra large raised cap. If you have a 10-point base font and haven't changed the ratio, Extra Large will give you type approximately 25 points tall or the nearest size available on the printer. (For the LaserJet, this will probably be 24 point.)

If you want to set a specific font size, put the cursor on the second letter of the paragraph (right after the raised cap). Type **CONTROL-F8 F [ENTER]** (if you have a PostScript printer you'll need **2 [ENTER]**'s). This inserts a code with the current font size. Now place the cursor on the first letter. Type **CONTROL-F8 F**, move the cursor to the font you want, press return (for scaleable printers, press [ENTER] once, type the point size you want, then press [ENTER] again).

4. Print as usual and enjoy the delicious aroma of freshly brewed coffee . . . oh, wrong hype, sorry.

◆ Drop that cap, puppy . . . spit it out

Drop Initial Caps are the opposite of raised initial caps. Instead of sticking out above the paragraph, they are set into the paragraph. While drop caps can be especially attractive, they can also be tricky.

In the previous edition of this book I used a method that placed the letter in a graphics box. This worked well, but was tedious and required much trial and effort so that everything would fit properly. But now after a year and a half, I've finally come up with a better way—the type of thing that comes to you in your sleep. (Why I can't have brilliant ideas like this about feeding the hungry or saving the ozone layer I don't know, but as I always say, don't look a brilliant idea in the mouth. Perhaps it has something to do with the fact that I know more about WordPerfect than about world hunger or the stratosphere. Or maybe it's because life is just unfair.

Who knows? Fools give you reasons. Wise men/women? You got it—they never try.) Now, where was I? Oh yes, drop caps.

This method uses paired styles. This means that you can always see all your text, including the dropped cap, and there's very little trial and error. I'm jumping the gun here getting into styles, but I'll do it anyway because this is fun and besides I'm just that type of person.

This example uses 10 point Dutch or Times Roman. You will also need 24 point Times or Dutch Bold. Since these fonts are created in the Fontware Starter set, you should already have them. Here goes:

1. Before you start, it's a good idea to go into Reveal Codes mode (and remember to set your base font to 10 point Dutch). That way you can see the codes you've entered and get a better idea what on earth is going on.

2. Set tabs. You will want to have tabs set at .27", .33", .40", and .5". This is because certain characters, such as "W," are too wide to be used with .27, and .33 is too wide for most other characters. You can't set them any closer together than this.

SHIFT-F8 L T 0.27 [ENTER] 0.33 [ENTER] 0.4 [ENTER] F7 F7

If in View Document (or through printing) you discover that the drop cap runs into the text next to it, press the [TAB] key to insert another tab directly after the closing half of the style (before the second character).

3. Set line height to fixed. You *must* do this, otherwise WordPerfect will try to protect you from yourself and put extra space above and below the line with the drop cap and this will look awful. While this procedure may seem exceedingly tedious, in actuality it's just monotonous. This may seem like a lot of work, but remember, you're creating a style, so once you've created it you never have to enter all this stuff again.

SHIFT-F8 L H F 12p [ENTER] F7

```
                                         «
Drop Cap using Style                 Mama Rowby's«
                                  Blue Ribbon Pies«
                           Any way you slice it, we're #1«

T      his last year has been one of great        the wazoo. These are revolut
       change for Mama Rowby and her              that will blow the lid off t
family of fine foods. Corporate Raider/Pond       Everything from the new ``Ca
Scum Walter Scanlan tried to wrest the com-       including ``Linguini and Cla
pany away from the family that has owned          ``Cactus Ice Cream.''«
and operated it with such great care for lo               Another hot new line
these past five years, and if it hadn't been for  under the Cajun Queen monike
the great spirit of loyalty among management      clude ``Blackened Red Cherry
and employees, Mama Rowby's Pies would            Slaw Jumbalya.'' The sleeper
have become just another corporate conglom-       will be ``Dr. Ruth's Good Pi
erate, instead of the caring, loving, gold mine   with illustrated instruction
it is.«                                           uses. These flavors will be
       Last year pie consumption skyrocketed      and safe fruits, such as Ban
the world over, partly due to our massive                 This fall, Mama will
advertising campaign, and the ``Miss Cutie        own syndicated cooking show
Pie'' competition, co-hosted by Morgan Fair-      her guests (Dr. Ruth is at t
childe (desperate to overcome her image as        will help solve world proble
being someone who'll go to the opening of a       ``Peace Through Pies.'' The
drawer). Even more important, Mama Rowby          in 175 of the largest market
D:\!BOOK\EX\MAMA1.EX                 Col 1 Doc 1 Pg 1 Ln 2.68" Pos 0.75"
```

This is how drop caps look on-screen when you use this fabulously exciting new style. The indent on the second line is from a tab you must insert manually.

4. Now we create the paired drop cap style.

ALT-F8 C N drop cap [ENTER]

This creates a paired style, and names it "drop cap."

C SHIFT-F8 O A D 12P [ENTER]

This goes into edit mode, then advances down 12p.

F7 CONTROL-F8 F

Move the cursor to Dutch 24 point bold. (PostScript/LaserMaster users will move the cursor to Times Roman or Dutch Bold, press [ENTER], type 24, and press [ENTER] again.)

[ENTER] [RIGHT] SHIFT-F8 O A U 12P [ENTER] F7

This moves the cursor past the [COMMENT] code to the closing half of the style and advances back up to the first line.

SHIFT-[TAB] [TAB]

This creates a margin release, and then tabs to the first tab stop. A margin release is needed because sometimes the drop cap is too close to the first tab, so WordPerfect jumps to the next tab. That can make the space between the drop cap and the next letter much too large. The margin release backs up on the line so that you are assured the next tab code will go to the first tab. The tab then moves to the tab stop.

F7 F7 F7

Incessant pressing will always get you out of whatever you've gotten yourself into.

5. Now, to actually use the style, press

ALT-F8

Move the cursor to the style called "drop cap," and press

[ENTER]

Type the first letter of the paragraph, the one that is going to become the drop cap. In this case, let's try an H. To move the cursor outside of the style codes press

H [RIGHT ARROW]

Then type at least three lines of text.

6. Here's the only manual step of this whole shenanigan. Move the cursor to the beginning of the second line of the paragraph and press

[TAB]

This will indent the second line so that it matches the indent of the first line.

7. WARNING: If you edit the text, the tab can move and mess up the effect. If you edit this text, remember to move the tab to the first space on the second line. *Always* check out the results using View Document before you print.

SHIFT-F7 V

This will give you a very accurate idea of how the drop cap is going to print.

Exceptions: If the second letter of the paragraph appears too close to the drop cap, put the cursor on it and press [TAB] again. This will move the text 6/100ths of an inch to the right (the next tab stop), which should be far enough even for a "W." You will also need to add another tab to the second line of the paragraph.

Not all typefaces are the same width, so when using other typefaces you may have to set the tabs larger or smaller, depending on the typeface and size.

➻ Dropping in a bit later

Of course, drop caps can also be applied after the text is typed. You will still need to make sure to set the line height to fixed and set the tabs, then you block the first letter of the paragraph with ALT-F4, press ALT-F8, move the cursor to "drop cap" and press [ENTER]

➻ Elevensies

Here are the codes for drop caps with 11-point body text and a 30-point drop cap. You will first need to set tabs at .33" and .4".

SHIFT-F8 F

move the cursor to Dutch 11 point

S [ENTER]

L T 0.33 [ENTER] 0.4 [ENTER] F7

H F 13p [ENTER] F7

ALT-F8 C N drop cap [ENTER]

C SHIFT-F8 O A D 13P [ENTER]

F7 CONTROL-F8 F

Move the cursor to Dutch 30 point bold. (PostScript/LaserMaster users will move the cursor to Times Roman or Dutch Bold, press [ENTER], type 30, and press [ENTER] again.)

[ENTER] [RIGHT] SHIFT-F8 O A U 13P [ENTER] F7

SHIFT-[TAB] [TAB]

F7 F7 F7

Using the style works the same way as it does at 10 point. Don't forget to put a tab (or two if necessary) at the start of the second line of text.

You can use this trick with any typeface or size you want, but you will have to make adjustments.

◆ Block party

Search and replace can be a valuable tool for quickly changing paragraph formatting. While styles can be a more efficient way of changing complex formatting, there are times when you haven't planned ahead and created a style. This is when search and replace comes in handy.

WordPerfect doesn't permit you to use all codes for replacing, but it does allow you to use returns, tabs, indents, center, flush right, and column on/off as replacement text.

If you sometimes format paragraphs with the first line indented and sometimes format them in the block style with a line of space in-between, here's an example of how quick and useful replacing formatting codes can be.

The two styles may be cousins, but they're still worlds apart (not unlike the Patty Duke Show . . . *"While Cathy adores the minuet, the ballet Russe, and Crepe Suzette, Patty loves to rock and roll, a hot dog makes her lose control, what a wild duet! But they're cousins . . ."* My, the natives *are* getting restless, aren't they? Settle down, class. Back to work).

To change from block to indent or from indent to block is a simple matter of search and replace. While this system is easy, it depends on the kindness of strangers . . . or at least on your consistency. It will only work on paragraphs indented with tabs; paragraphs indented with spaces are a no-no, and if you are caught using them I will be forced to turn you in to the "space patrol." Likewise, this will not work in a consistent fashion if at times you use one blank line between blocked paragraphs and at other times use two. You know, "Garbage in, garbage out."

INDENT TO BLOCK: Let's say your file is in indent format with a tab indenting the first line of each paragraph. To turn this little baby into block format, press

ALT-F2 N [ENTER][TAB] F2 [ENTER][ENTER] F2

That tells WordPerfect to perform a search and replace to find all returns followed by tabs (the indent of the first line) and to replace them with two returns. Depending on the length of the file, this can take seconds or minutes.

BLOCK TO INDENT: Now we're going to do the opposite, that is, take a file in block format and turn it into indent format. Press

ALT-F2 N [ENTER][ENTER] F2 [ENTER][TAB] F2

Normally search (or search and replace) searches forward in a file. If you want to search backward, just press the [UP ARROW] key while the **Srch:** prompt is displayed. You'll see the little arrow in front of it point backwards, which means the operation will take place from the cursor to the top of the file, instead of the other way around.

Also, if you only want to perform a search and replace on a particular part of a file, you can block it first with ALT-F4. Then search and replace will only occur in the blocked portion of the file.

Uh badee, badee, badee, that's all folks!

9

Columns as I see 'em

or, Columns and their many uses

WordPerfect has always had excellent control over columns and now it's even better. But before you use columns, try to answer this seemingly simple question: why use columns?

- Because they're there
- Because it's hip
- Because they make a personal statement
- Because they are low calorie
- All of the above
- None of the above

Give up? The answer is none of the above. Turn the page for the real reasons.

- Most importantly, columns can make type easier to read by keeping the line from getting too long.
- Columns give you the ability to put several different stories on a page and have them look like several different stories.
- Columns allow you to get more type on a page. It's true—a two-column format can contain more words than a one-column format.
- All of the above.

You won't need columns all the time, and like everything else in design and typography, you should only use them when they are appropriate.

◆ How many is enough?

The next logical question is "How many columns do I need?" The answer is not unlike Abe Lincoln's response to the question, "How long should a man's legs be? Long enough to reach the ground." You need as many as will do the job.

Since almost all laser printers are limited to 8 1/2-by-11 inch paper, you generally won't use more than three columns, lest they get too narrow and become difficult to read and follow. Even most large tabloid-size newspapers use five or six columns at most.

Newsletters and magazines are fine in either two or three columns. Three columns offer you more design flexibility but are also more complicated to work with. The only time you'll use anywhere near WordPerfect's limit of 24 columns is when you are using parallel columns to create complex tables of information, and even then using a WordPerfect table is often going to be easier and more convenient.

5.0 users: this is one area where the keystrokes have changed slightly, but don't let it throw you. Just read the screen instead of following along blindly. You'll have one less keystroke to define a column, and you'll press C instead of O to turn columns on, and C instead of F to turn them off.

◆ In the gutter

When you create columns in WordPerfect, the default places a half inch space between them. While that doesn't seem like much, it's about two times more than you would normally choose. Columns generally have .2" to .3" between them. This area is known as the gutter.

Don't think that just because WordPerfect automatically wants gutters to be a half inch that it somehow knows better than you do. It doesn't. Whenever you create columns, make sure you set the "Distance between columns" at around .2".

◆ It takes two

There are two different types of columns in WordPerfect: Newspaper and Parallel. Newspaper columns "snake" text from the bottom of one column to the top of the next. Parallel columns are designed for several paragraphs of text that must remain side by side. Parallel offers an additional option called "block protect;" this ensures that the text is not split by page breaks. Because WordPerfect permits you to turn columns off and on at any time and set uneven column widths, you have tremendous possibilities at your beck and call.

❖ *All the news*

First we're going to set up two newspaper-type columns. To set up a column, press

ALT-F7 C D

WordPerfect then gives you four choices: **T**ype, **N**umber, **D**istance between columns, and **M**argins. Newspaper column is the default, so you don't have to change it. Two columns is also the default, so you don't have to change that either.

◆ Setting distance between columns

However, you do have to change the distance between the two columns. Press

D .25" [ENTER]

Once you've set the distance, WordPerfect automatically calculates the margins so as to create columns of equal widths. If you want one column to be wider than the other, press **M** and change the margin measurements that WordPerfect is displaying. These margin settings are initially within the margins you've set for the

```
Chapter 9«
Columnation that's the name of
the game«
«
WordPerfect has always had
excellent control over columns,
and now it's even better. But
before you use columns, try to
answer this seemingly simple
question: why use columns?«
«
A)   Because they're there«
B)   Because it's hip«
C)   Because they make a
personal statement«
D)   Because they are low
calorie«
E)   All of the above«
F)   None of the above«
«
Give up? The answer is F, none
of the above. Now, here are the
real reasons: «
«

question ''How long should a
man's legs be? Long enough to
reach the ground.'' You need as
many as will do the job.«
  Since almost all laser
printers are limited to 8 1/2"
by 11" paper, you generally
won't use more than three
columns, lest they get too
narrow and become difficult to
read and follow. Even large
tabloid size newspapers use
five or six columns at most.«
  Newsletters and magazines are
fine in either two or three
columns. Three columns offer
you more design flexibility,
but are also more complicated
to work with.«
  The only time you'll use
anywhere near WordPerfect's
limit of 24 columns is when you
are using parallel columns to
create complex tables of
C:\WP5\P\WP9.TW                 Doc 2 Pg 1 Ln 1" Pos 1"
```

When you create columns, WordPerfect shows the columns side-by-side, even in text mode.

document using **SHIFT-F8 L M**, but you can set these numbers outside the main margins if you so desire.

WordPerfect displays the left and right margins for each column. You enter a measurement and then press return. When you are in the left column, the up and down cursor can be used to move between the measurements for the left side of all columns. But to set measurements for the right column, you must first press **[ENTER]**. When in the right column, you can use the up and down cursor to set the right margin for all columns.

If you set the wrong number, don't worry. If you press **F7 M** WordPerfect returns you to the top of the measurements, and you can enter them again. The measurements are only set when you press **[ENTER]** for the last time and are returned to the one-line columns/tables/math menu at the bottom of the screen.

◆ Turn it on, stupid

While the column margins are now set, they don't take effect until you press

O

for Column On. Once you do, the text will begin to format on-screen.

At first the text will have an odd appearance; one column may overlap with another and there won't seem to be any space between them. The quickest way to format all the text is to press **HOME HOME [DOWN ARROW]**. This moves you to the bottom of the WordPerfect file and forces WordPerfect to format the text and display it correctly on-screen.

In addition to formatting the text, WordPerfect is also calculating the "display pitch,"(the amount of space required between columns on-screen). You can set the display pitch manually by pressing

SHIFT-F8 D D

```
time, and like everything else
in design and typography, you
should only use them when they
are appropriate.«
«
How Many is Enough?«
The next logical question is
''how many columns do I need?''
The  answer is not unlike Abe
Lincoln's response to the
------------------------------------------------------------------------
                                 question ''How long should a
                                 man's legs be? Long enough to
                                 reach the ground.'' You need as
                                 many as will do the job.«
                                   Since almost all laser
                                 printers are limited to 8 1/2"
                                 by 11" paper, you generally
                                 won't use more than three
                                 columns, lest they get too
                                 narrow and become difficult to
                                 read and follow. Even large
                                 tabloid size newspapers use
                                 five or six columns at most.«
C:\WP5\P\WP9.TW                           Col 2 Doc 2 Pg 1 Ln 3.5" Pos 4.37"
```

Sometimes it can be difficult to write and edit with columns side by side. You can force columns to appear sequentially, rather than side-by-side, using Setup. (SHIFT-F1 D S N).

While it's best to leave the setting on automatic, you can set it to manual when WordPerfect has too much or too little space between columns. This feature only affects how text looks on-screen, not on paper.

The standard display pitch setting is .1" (10 characters per inch), and this gives a fairly realistic view of the page. If you use a larger number (such as .02"), the space between columns (or the length of tabs) will appear smaller. If you make the number smaller, the space between columns and the length of tabs will appear larger. No code is inserted in the file when you change the display pitch, but it is saved with the file you are editing.

If you don't want columns to appear side-by-side while you are editing, press

SHIFT-F1 D E S N F7

and columns will appear offset. They still will print side-by-side, however.

◆ Getting around

While it's convenient to have columns displayed side-by-side on-screen, moving around can be very confusing. If you are pressing the **[DOWN ARROW]** key and reach the end of a column, you won't move to the top of the next column but to the next page. And you can't get from the left column to the right one simply by pressing the **[RIGHT ARROW]**.

To move between columns, you must use what WordPerfect calls the GOTO key: **CONTROL-HOME** (most often the 7 on the number pad, although some keyboards have a separate HOME key).

GOTO [RIGHT ARROW] moves to the next column on the right.

GOTO [LEFT ARROW] moves to the next column on the left.

GOTO HOME [RIGHT ARROW] moves to the *last* column.

GOTO HOME [LEFT ARROW] moves to the *first* column.

GOTO [UP ARROW] goes to the top of a column.

GOTO [DOWN ARROW] goes to the bottom of a column.

If you are at the bottom of one column and press the **[RIGHT ARROW]** or **CONTROL [RIGHT ARROW]** key, you will move to the next word at the top of the next column.

If you are at the top of one column and press the **[LEFT ARROW]** or **CONTROL [LEFT ARROW]** key, you will move to the previous word at the bottom of the previous column.

All this moving around can be very bothersome, so I don't suggest you write in column mode unless you need to fit material into a very specific area.

5.0 users: Advance Right (SHIFT-F8 O A R) can be used instead of tabs to indent the first line of a paragraph.

```
     The second and more advanced method is to use Advance Right.
Advance is an absolute fixed value, no matter what column it
appears in. The advantage of this method is that you can set the
tab for other items, change the column layout, and still retain
an exact, uniform indent. The disadvantage is that it requires
more effort than pressing the tab key. And it doesn't change
automatically when you change the tabs.«
To set an indent of .3" with Advance, you'd type «
SHIFT-F8 O A R .3" [ENTER] F7«
Since this is a lot to go through whenever you begin a new
paragraph, you'll want to create a macro if you plan to use this
C:\WP5\P\WP9.TW                                Doc 2 Pg 4 Ln 7.5" Pos 1"
more effort than pressing the tab key. And it doesn't change[SRt]
automatically when you change the tabs.[HRt]
[AdvRgt:0.3"]To set an indent of .3" with Advance, you'd type [HRt]
[BOLD]SHIFT[-]F8 O A R .3" [ENTER] F7[bold][HRt]
Since this is a lot to go through whenever you begin a new[SRt]
paragraph, you'll want to create a macro if you plan to use this[SRt]
system. See Chapter ???, Macros.[HRt]
[Tab]As you've hopefully learned by now, you should never ever,[SRt]
under the penalty of seeming really stupid, indent anything using[SRt]
spaces. [HRt]

Press Reveal Codes to restore screen
```

◆ Indenting tricks or making advances

As you've hopefully learned by now, you should never ever, under the penalty of seeming really stupid, indent anything using spaces. (Although I'll let you in on a secret. I "indented" this paragraph using spaces, just to be a troublemaker—April fool.)

With 5.0 it was a major pain to set tabs correctly for columns. Now with relative tabs there's no trick at all. But remember, when you use columns you should also use relative tabs. If you use absolute tabs for some reason, it's going to be a pain in the largest muscle of your body.

Here's the important part to remember—if you originally created a document in 5.0, when you bring it into 5.1, the tabs are going to be set as Absolute, exactly the type you don't want to use with columns. So if you're bringing in a text file from 5.1, make sure to edit the tabs, changing them to relative.

◆ Parallel columns

Parallel columns are an excellent way to make tables when one or more of the entries is longer than a single line. Yes, I know, in many cases the glamorous new table feature is a better way. But in certain cases, such as when all the information is already typed in a normal format and turning it into a table is tedious, or for those of you with slower computers, parallel columns are more practical. Remember, though, if all the entries are only one line long, tabs will work just as well.

The key to using parallel columns is understanding that a Hard Page [Hpg] (created by pressing CONTROL-ENTER) code doesn't start a new page but a new column. When placed in the last column, it turns columns off, adds a blank line, and then turns them back on.

To define parallel columns, press

ALT-F7 C D T P F7 O

You can now set the number of columns, gutter width, and margins, as in newspaper columns.

◆ Table with block protect

The only difference between ordinary parallel columns and those with block protect is that the information in protected columns won't be split by page breaks. If necessary, WordPerfect will move the entire set of columns to a new page. When you press **CONTROL-ENTER** at the last column, the block protect is turned off, then turned back on with the next set of columns.

To create a table with block protect, type

ALT-F7 C D T B

You can now set the gutter and margin as you did with newspaper type columns.

Remember just a few paragraphs ago I said that parallel columns were good for creating tables when the material was already entered in normal form? Well, do you remember? I said that because if you use the table feature, you'd have to create a table, then individually block and move text paragraph by paragraph into the table. This means pressing ALT-F4 (mark the text) CONTROL-F4 B M (move to the cell in the table you want) [ENTER]. With Parallel columns, once you've defined the columns, all you have to do is move to where you want a new column to be and press CONTROL-ENTER to insert a column break. Which looks faster to you? I thought so.

That's not to say that the table feature isn't the greatest thing since sliced paper napkins—it is. Once text is in a table, it's easier to control and gives you more options. But sometimes tables are overkill. They can be very slow if you need to do much editing within them, and parallel columns are very flexible.

In this example, we'll create a five-column table—join me, won't you? (That wasn't really a question—you'd better join me or else.)

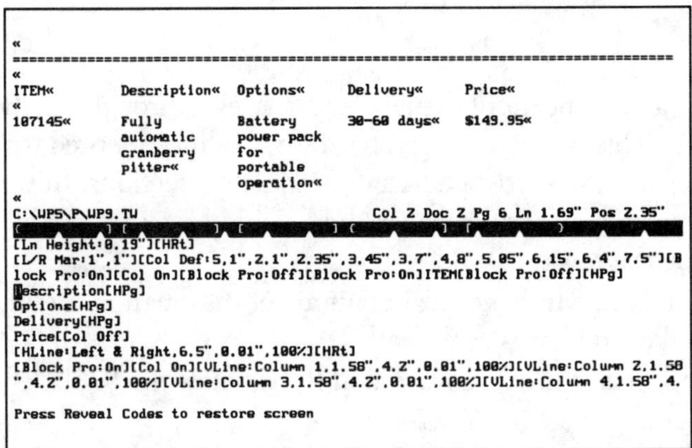

This is how the codes for parallel columns appear. Notice how the text appears side-by-side on the top half of the screen, but not in the lower Reveal Codes (ALT-F3) half.

◆ Set margins

To ensure we're working with the same margins (not unlike playing with a full deck), set the margins to 1" left, 1" right, by pressing

SHIFT-F8 L M 1 [ENTER] 1 [ENTER] F7

◆ Set base font

Set the base font to Times Roman (or Dutch) 10 point.

SHIFT-F8 D F

◆ Create a block protected table

To create a block protected table, press

ALT-F7 C D T B N5 [ENTER] D .25" [ENTER]

We're going to use the margins that WordPerfect set for us. Press **O** to turn columns on.

Now type the table illustrated on the opposite page (soon to be seen on the Home Shopping Network).

Press **CONTROL-ENTER** to end each column.

Isn't that fun? Isn't that easy? Isn't that going to make your life easier and so much more productive? Isn't the world a wonderful place? Quick, slap me.

❖ *Faux table lines for 5.0*

◆ Horizontal rules

If you want a ruling line between each full set of columns, wait until you've pressed **CONTROL-ENTER** at the last column so that WordPerfect turns the columns off and then on again. Then press

[UP ARROW] [ENTER] ALT-F9 L H [ENTER] [DOWN ARROW].

◆ Vertical rules

In the table we created above, horizontal rules lead the eye through all the elements of a single item. The table is easier to read because it is line-oriented; the horizontal rows are the focus, and the vertical columns are just subsections. In this case, vertical rules would only be confusing because they would break up the elements of an item, interrupting the rows.

But in column-oriented tables, where vertical columns of information are important, vertical rules can make a table easier to read.

To create vertical rules between the columns, you must be below the [Col Def:] and [Col On] codes. To select a vertical line press

ITEM	Description	Options	Delivery	Price
107145	Fully automatic cranberry pitter	Battery power pack for portable operation	30-60 days	$149.95
5394875B (beige) 10234723 (red)	Hand carved bust of Marie Osmond, made of genuine imitation plastic. Every tooth a masterpiece.	Genuine Faux marble base. (Faux marble, that's the richest kind)	45 minutes, less on weekends	$1.29
555 (English) 777 (French) 999 (Esperanto)	Hardbound copy of the best selling *Generic Quick Weight Loss Diet,* 2nd Edition	Full Size cutout of Twiggy. Has everything going for it and nothing to lose.	After October 19.	$21.95US

ALT-F9 L V

To instruct WordPerfect to place the line between columns press

H B

Press **1** to put the line to the right of column 1. If the table is full-page, and you want the line to run top to bottom, press return. If you want the top of the line to begin on the line where the cursor is, press **V S [ENTER]**. This inserts the current line location. It also calculates the distance between the cursor and the bottom of the page and inserts this number under "Line Length." If you don't want the line to run to the end of the page, press **L** and type in the length you want for that line.

➻ Repeat this process for each intercolumn line

◆ 5.0 Tip: Making vertical rules float with text

Unlike horizontal rules that float with text, vertical lines are anchored to an exact location on a page. If you set a vertical 4" line to start at 2.25" from the top of the page, it will always start at 2.25" from the top of the page, no matter where the text has moved.

This can be disastrous when you are working with tables and you add or delete text. The parallel "table" will move, but the lines won't. The most basic solution is to put the table on a page by itself. Boring. Or you can wait until the last minute to place the vertical lines when you're sure that all editing is complete and the text is not going to move.

My few remaining brain cells ached as I tried in vain to come up with a way to get vertical rules to move with the text. I even tried using the vertical bar character | but this only produced a broken line and looked crummy.

I gave up. And true to the Zen (and Zulu) cliche, it was then, and only then, that I came up with the answer.

◆ Tip: Superduper tip—so clever it surprised even myself

Are you ready for this? It's no picnic in Holland, but it's not all that tough either. This is how it looks:

Events to look forward to:

Spring	Summer	Fall	Winter
East: Rain West: Clouds Hay Fever, runny nose, itchy eyes	E: Humidity W: Sunstroke Heat frustration, heat rash, insects	E: Leaves W: Sunstroke Weddings Anniversaries	E: Snow W: Sunstroke Colds, flu, family reunions

◆ Here's how the codes look

[Col Def:4,1",2.4",2.7",4.1",4.4",5.8",6.1",7.5"][Col On] [Usr Opt][Usr Box:1;;]Spring[HRt] [HRt]West: Clouds[HRt]East: Rain[HRt]Hay Fever, runny[SRt]nose, itchy eyes[HPg] [Usr Box:2;;]Summer[HRt]

◆ The magic is all in those innocuous little [Usr Box] commands

- Create the table using parallel columns.
- When the table is finished, move the cursor to the last line of the table and write down the number after Ln in the lower right corner of the screen.
- Move to the first line of the table, write down the number after Ln, and subtract it from the first number. You now have the height of the table.
- Go to the first column and line of the table. Type **ALT-F9 U O** to set user-defined box options. Press **B N S N N [ENTER]** to create a box with a ruling line on the right side.
- Press **ALT-F9 U C W N H R S B .1" [ENTER]** and the height of the table. Press **[ENTER] [ENTER]**. You have just created a tall thin box that won't shove text out of the way. All that will appear of this box, however, is the line on the left side; this will print .1" to the right of the right margin.
- Turn on reveal codes with **ALT-F3**, and press **[BACKSPACE]** over the [User Box:] code. Press **F1 R** to undelete it. Move to the next column and press **F1 R**. Repeat the **F1 R** step for each column. This creates a copy of the original box for each column. You will probably not want a ruling line to the right of the last box, so don't bother placing one in the last column.

Impress your friends and neighbors with your handiwork (tell them it was all your idea—what do I care?), and bask in their befuddled indifference. You can move the table wherever your little heart desires, and those lines will move right along with them. (This is great—I only have two more miracles to go.)

Note: This is brilliant but it's not foolproof, as that would be a contradiction in terms; some restrictions will apply (just pretend you're buying an airline ticket). The only item you have to pay attention to is the right margin of each column. Use preview to check that the text doesn't run into the lines. If it does, press a return before the offending word.

❖ *Fast 5.1 tables (Tweety's tip)*

One more bit of unmatched excitement: once you've created a table using parallel columns it's easy to convert it into a real 5.1 table. Do I hear a hint coming on? I do, I do, I do see a 'puttee tip.

When you are working with existing text, it's easier to create a table using parallel columns than with the table feature. So, logically it follows that the best way to create a table out of existing material is to first turn it into parallel columns, then turn them into a table. To learn exactly how to accomplish this prodigious piece of prestidigitation, see the following chapter.

◆ Parallel universes

Now we explore the next major use for parallel columns. A drum roll please. Parallel columns can be used for creating entire multicolumn documents, especially when one column will contain only headlines, sideheads, or pull quotes.

For an example of what this may appear like when in the wrong hands, see the "Babies in Space" example in Chapter 4, *Show & Tell*.

In this example, the first column is used only for pull quotes and artwork. Using newspaper columns would require constant checking to make sure the first column was kept clear and would make it difficult to ensure that pull quotes floated with their respective text.

But using parallel columns actually makes this genuinely easy. The margins here were set at .5" to 2.5" for the first column, and at 3" to 8" for the second column.

The cursor is in the first column when you turn the columns on. You can type an intro or pull quote here, or just press **CONTROL [ENTER]** to end the first column and begin the text column. Because parallel columns will span pages, the wide text column will continue until you press **CONTROL [ENTER]** again to create another sidehead or pull quote.

This format is blissfully simple to use, and the white space of the first column, combined with pull quotes, makes this format easy to read as well.

You could extend this design to a three column format, where the first two columns are used for staggered pull quotes. To create a sense of order (in a somewhat random but not uninteresting design), the first column is always a certain size (in this case 14 point), and the second column is always italics.

The advantage of this system is that it gives you more room to play (why bother with all of this if you aren't going to at least pretend to have fun?). The first column could contain art and the second pull quotes, or the first could be for editorializing, the next for pull quotes; the possibilities are bound only by the amount of time you can play before someone starts bugging you to do some real work.

➻ Uneven and unparalleled

One job WordPerfect can do, which even Word for Windows can't, is uneven columns. Even columns are what WordPerfect sets automatically, each column is the same width. But you can create uneven columns by setting the margins manually.

Sometimes two columns (both the same width) are, let's face it, boring. Uneven columns present a multitude of design possibilities. You can have a narrow first column, one that you use for subheads or graphics only, and then a wide text column. This is what I've done with the "Babies in Space" example. Graphics work well when placed in a narrow column because they tend to have more visual impact than long paragraphs of text. But you usually don't want graphics to overpower the text, so making the column narrower helps to keep a proper balance between their impact and the text.

A little advice about uneven columns: don't make any column too narrow. It's a good idea (but not mandatory) to use the narrower column for something special, not just normal running text. Parallel columns and uneven widths go together like a horse and marriage. Except in special cases, you're not going to want to use uneven widths with newspaper columns. Stick to two different widths.

❖ *Play time—constructing a table*

Okay, I've been talking about having fun, so now we're going to make a valiant attempt at it.

You've been working hard reading this book (even thumbing through the pages while you dawdle in the bookstore has probably been an effort). It's time for a break. You have two choices: you can get out a bath towel, lie down on the floor, and take a nap like you did in kindergarten; or you can play the following game with WordPerfect. The bath towel route will be nostalgic but not much else (floors having become so hard lately), but the WordPerfect game will be enlightening and could possibly develop into this year's hot party item.

Set up two parallel columns. If your retention rate is such that you don't remember how, here's a clue: the codes you need are concealed somewhere in this chapter. (Was that too much of a clue?) Make sure you first define the columns, then turn them on.

This table is going to be full page, and so, let's put a vertical rule down the center (between the two columns). Press

ALT-F9 L V H B I [ENTER]

You can use a regular rule instead of the fancy-schmancy trick because this table is not in danger of moving.

Type the word "HAPPY" on the first line of the first column, then press **CONTROL-RETURN** and type the word "MISERABLE" on the first line of the second column.

Use your new-found knowledge of parallel columns and CONTROL ENTER to produce a list of all the items that make you happy and all the petty annoyances and such that make you miserable. Think of everything (and every*one*) you can, then print the file. Finally, cut or tear the paper down the middle, between the two columns. Throw away the miserable side in a symbolic act of defiance, and tape the HAPPY side at your workplace, or wherever it is you spend the most time.

If your life doesn't change overnight, trade your copy of WordPerfect for a package of Sara Lee frozen brownies. That should make you feel better.

10

Table Manners

or, Right this way your table's waiting

You've read about it in the magazines. You've seen the movie. Now titter to the tingling titillation of tables—today. Thrill as you watch a 1-2-3 spreadsheet appear in WordPerfect. Feel the hitherto unimaginable elation as you are able to create complex tables, right here in your own word processing program. Experience the unbelievable, inconceivable power of knowing that you can also create all types of forms, calendars, and schedules, not to mention very personal cubist interpretations of man's inhumanity to man, all right on your very own screen.

Now that we've dispensed with the hype, let's put it all out on the table. Tables are an extremely powerful, surprisingly easy-to-use feature. They can help you integrate spreadsheet information, but don't just use them for that. Even if you never touch a spreadsheet, you'll use the Table feature to create the forms you always dreamed about, from invoices to monthly calendars, complete with complex equations (for the forms, not the calendars).

Just so you know how much work the Table feature is going to save you, at this point in the 5.0 edition of this book I went on for two pages explaining how to fake out WordPerfect and create attractive horizontal and vertical lines for a table-like effect. The Table feature is going to save you from having to read those two pages and free you up to read the next several pages concerning the powerful Table feature. See how much time you're saving already?

While this chapter covers tables, it doesn't go into great detail about importing spreadsheets. For in-depth coverage of this, see Chapter 18. Remember, though, you'll still need to know how to work with tables in order to import spreadsheets to their best advantage, so don't skip this chapter or you'll be sorry later on and there'll be no one to blame but yourself.

5.0 Users: Parallel columns are an excellent substitute for 5.1's tables. They don't give you automatic lines or gray shading, but they do allow you to format text in almost the same way, and they're much faster than the Table feature. Use the tips near the end of the previous chapter to add lines to parallel column tables.

❖ Basics

Tables are just ordinary text, surrounded by [Tbl Def:] and [Tbl Off] codes. Tables have two modes: Table Edit, and just plain Text Edit. Just plain Text Edit is like editing any other text. You are editing the text inside the table and not the format of the table itself. In Table Edit you are editing the format of the table and cannot edit the text (and never the twain shall meet).

When you are within a table, in either edit mode, you move around by pressing the tab key.

[TAB]

This takes you to the next "cell," which is what the individual blocks of the table are called. You can move to the previous cell by pressing

SHIFT-[TAB]

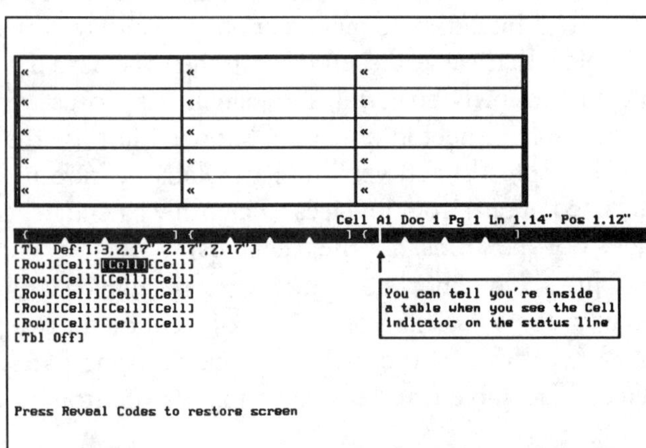

A table in Text Edit mode.

A cell can hold anything—text, graphics boxes, equations, pressed flowers from your prom (as long as they've been scanned), anything. Each cell is a separate entity from the others, although you can join several adjacent cells into one large cell.

Cells will automatically get longer when you add more text. They will get wider only if you specifically widen them in Table Edit mode. Unless you've set tables smaller than the margins, they will automatically expand to fill the current margins. If you make the margins smaller later on, the tables will also shrink to fit. Tables mean never having to say you're sorry.

You can place lines around cells or the entire table. You have a choice of None, Single, Double, Thick, Extra Thick, Dotted, or Dashed. If you select "none," no one need ever even know you're using a table.

Tables can be placed so they align to the right, left, or center of a page, or they can span the entire width of a page.

➻ Yes and no

Tables can be placed in graphics boxes and styles. Tables cannot be placed in columns—unless you first put the table in a graphics box. If you try to create a table when you have columns turned on, WordPerfect will just plain ignore you. No table, no message, no nothing. If you are in columns and insert a style that has a table in it, WordPerfect will automatically turn columns off. It won't insert a [Column Off] code, it will just turn them off. If you remove the style with the table in it, columns will come back on.

All this has been leading up to "how the heck do I put tables in columns . . ."

➻ How the heck do I put tables in columns . . .

The only way to put tables into columns is to first put the table into a graphics box. The box can be in columns, and tables can be in boxes, so you're set. You can

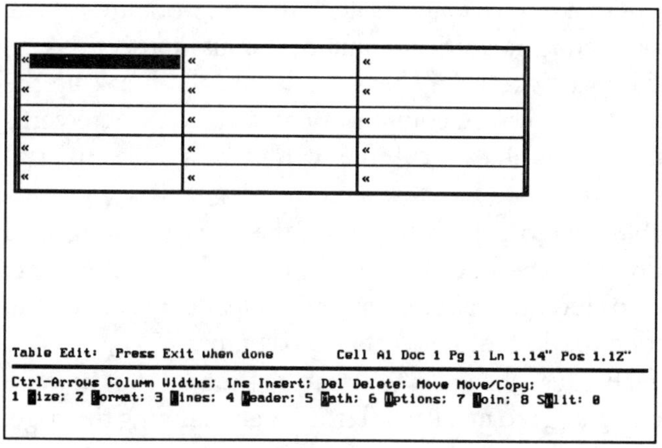

«	«	«
«	«	«
«	«	«
«	«	«
«	«	«

```
Table Edit:  Press Exit when done          Cell A1 Doc 1 Pg 1 Ln 1.14" Pos 1.12"
Ctrl-Arrows Column Widths; Ins Insert; Del Delete; Move Move/Copy;
1 Size; 2 Format; 3 Lines; 4 Header; 5 Math; 6 Options; 7 Join; 8 Split: 0
```

A table in Table Edit mode.

put tables in any type of graphics box, which means you can have a table that spans several text columns. On to the next question.

➾ How the heck do I wrap text around tables?

The answer is: you don't. Unless you place the table in a graphics box, other text will not wrap around a table.

➾ How the heck do I place tables side by side?

You don't. Unless you place them in a graphics box.

➾ Waiting on tables

While tables are great, they aren't exactly what you'd call fast. Not even quick. Certainly not fleet. Yes, the fact of the matter is that unless you have a very fast AT or '386, tables can be slow.

But as so often happens with computers, because tables can be easier to create and set up than other methods such as columns, tables can end up being faster to use. Don't ask me, I just write about this stuff.

The point of this is don't get frustrated when it takes a few seconds to maneuver around your table. The end results are worth it, and, like I said, even though you'll find yourself waiting tables, just think of the tips.

❖ *Lines by design*

One of the things people like most about tables are the ruling lines. But remember, everything on a page should be there for a reason. That includes the lines on a table or form. Just because WordPerfect automatically puts lines around all cells doesn't mean they should always be there. Lines are meant to lead the eye, to structure the page.

Tables can either be *line-oriented*, or *column-oriented.* In a line-oriented table, the horizontal rows are the focus and the vertical columns are just subsections. In this case, vertical rules would only be confusing, because they would break up the elements of an item, interrupting the rows. In column-oriented tables, where vertical columns of information are important, vertical rules can make a table easier to read.

If the columns of your table are more important than the rows, try using solid lines between columns and dotted or no lines between rows. If the rows are very important and you don't want to stop the reader's view, as in a price list, have solid lines between the rows and none (or dotted) between the columns.

Dotted lines are very useful because they help to structure the page, but because they aren't solid they don't cause people to make a full stop when scanning the page.

If you think of lines as if they were punctuation marks, solid lines would be periods and dotted lines would be commas.

Another way to structure a table without using lines is through shading. You can shade every other column or every other row or even just the important rows. When you do this, turn the lines off because having all that shading and all those lines is just going to be overkill.

◆ What's my line: Undocumented tip!

Just as fine, small, large, very large, and extra large are relative, so are single, double, thick, extra thick, dotted, and dashed.

While these settings are unalterable in 5.0, in 5.1 you can get very specific about what each of these settings really means. If you're the type of person who's into control, follow along. (If you're so into control that you don't like taking orders like "follow along," I'll rephrase that: Would you like to try this now? If so, please do. If not, just forget that I even mentioned it.) If you press

SHIFT-F8 O B

Pandora's dialog box of choices appears on-screen. You can control the width and shading of all lines. You have the additional options of controlling the spacing between double lines, the length of the dashes and space between the dashes, and the dot spacing. Control! Power! You can pretend you're Donald Trump as you pare the "Extra Thick" Merv Griffin down to size.

These options are very useful and very important because they give you more precise control over how a page will look. One you set these Border Options a code appears in your file, much like Figure Options. These codes affect all lines from the code to the end of the file.

If you want to change the Border Options on all new files, press **SHIFT-F1 I C** and then press **SHIFT-F8 O B** and choose your settings. Then press **F7** a couple of

```
Format: Border Options

     1 - Single -        Width             0.013"
                         Shading           100%

     2 - Double -        Width             0.013"
                         Shading           100%
                         Spacing Between   0.013"

     3 - Dashed -        Width             0.013"
                         Shading           100%
                         Dash Spacing      0.013"
                         Dash Length       0.053"

     4 - Dotted -        Width             0.013"
                         Shading           100%
                         Dot Spacing       0.013"

     5 - Thick -         Width             0.063"
                         Shading           100%

     6 - Extra Thick -   Width             0.125"
                         Shading           100%

Selection: 0
```

How thick is Thick? As thick as you say it is with SHIFT-F8 O B.

hundred times (it's actually only three times, it just feels like more—I don't know about you, but someone is going to get rich replacing F7 keys . . .) and from now on, each *new* document you create will have these settings as default. This will not change documents you've already created, but you can also go to the top of these files (or Initial Document Codes SHIFT-F8 D C) and place a border option there.

Just remember, you read it here first! Aren't you glad you bought this book? Don't you think you should buy a few extra copies to give away as gifts or pressure your friends into purchasing their own copies?

◆ Mabel, Mabel, if you're able

Let's create our very first table together. To create one, press

ALT-F7 T C

Then tell WordPerfect how many columns and rows you want. Columns are vertical, rows are horizontal. You can have up to 32 columns and some ridiculous number of rows like 32,765. To realize just how big 32,765 is, if you take 32,765 toothpicks and put them end to end—you obviously don't have enough to do and should be donating your time to some worthy cause.

Columns are labeled using letters, while rows use numbers. These labels are invisible, and do not print, but they do display on-screen. When you are in Table Edit, you can use the GOTO feature (CONTROL-[HOME]) to quickly jump to any cell.

In this example, let's create a table with three columns and five rows.

3 [ENTER] 5 [ENTER]

The table should appear on-screen, along with a menu at the bottom that tells you that you are in Table Edit mode. I don't really feel up to explaining Edit mode at the moment (this is how you format the table itself, not the contents), so let's get out of it by pressing

F7

When you are in Table Edit mode you cannot leave the table or move the cursor outside its bounds. Pressing F7 takes you out of Table Edit.

Now I'm going to go off on a tangent for a paragraph. I'm warning you in advance because some reviewers complained that they found it distracting in the first edition of this book when I'd comment on something not specifically related to WordPerfect. Of course, those people had no sense of humor, and I suspect some don't even have souls, but I'll forgive them because I guess I'm more tolerant than they are.

Getting stuck in Table Edit is not unlike the opening of that old TV show, "Outer Limits," where you were told that they had control of your television set. I used to run from the room as soon as that show started because I actually believed that not only did they have control of the TV, but once the show started I would somehow be unable to leave the room and I would be forced to watch really scary stuff and have bad dreams for days. So I'd be stuck there, all alone, watching something terrifying, and I'd hear the refrigerator door slam at the other end of the house, and I'd just know that this time it was some burglar with a big appetite rather than just the fact that my brother was always hungry. I feel better for sharing that with you.

So don't freak out when the cursor won't move outside of a table while you're in Table Edit. *You* are always in control. WordPerfect does not have control of your vertical hold. You can always press F7 or just leave the room for a half hour until the show is over.

◆ Get a move on

OK, so you've got a table on-screen. Kind of decadent, isn't it? You know you are inside the table for two reasons. One, because you have half a brain and can see the cursor sitting inside the little boxes of the table, and two, because in the lower right corner of the screen there's a new addition to the status line, namely, something that says **Cell A1**. This tells you that you are in the first column (A) and row (1). Columns are addressed by letters and rows are addressed by numbers.

This is the type of excitement you just don't get in theaters anymore. I mean, the only excitement in *Les Miserables* was waiting to see if the giant turntable would go crazy and spin so fast that it flung the cast into the audience. For those of you too young to remember, musicals used to have real stories, tunes that weren't ripped off, and lyrics that were witty and clever. Now there are just too many people in overblown costumes, jumping up and down, screaming. Oh, there I go again, off on a tangent. Some day, when I once again write musicals, I'll make sure to go off on tangents where I include WordPerfect keystrokes in the middle of songs. That will even things out.

When inside a table there are many ways to move around. You can use the cursor, but the best way is to press the [TAB] key to move from cell to cell. SHIFT-[TAB] moves you backwards from cell to cell. If you're the type of person who enjoys long strings of meaningless keystrokes, here are some more ways to move around a table:

First Cell Of Table: CONTROL-[HOME] [HOME] [HOME] [UP ARROW]
Last Cell in Table: CONTROL-[HOME] [HOME] [HOME] [DOWN ARROW]
First Cell in Column: CONTROL-[HOME] [HOME] [UP ARROW]

Last Cell in Column: CONTROL-[HOME] [HOME] [DOWN ARROW]
First Cell in Row: CONTROL-[HOME] [HOME] [LEFT ARROW]
Last Cell in Row: CONTROL-[HOME] [HOME] [RIGHT ARROW]
MOUSE: This is one of the few places where using a mouse is easier than using the keyboard. If you have a mouse, you can simply move it and click on any cell to move the cursor there.

◆ A little more, a little less

If you have what's called an "enhanced BIOS," you can also add or delete rows without going into Table Edit. You'll know if you have one or not when you try this—if it works, you do, if it doesn't, you don't. It also won't work if you've redefined these keys using the soft keyboard feature (covered in detail in Chapter 17).
To add a row: CONTROL-[INSERT]
To delete a row: CONTROL-[DEL]

◆ Add-a-tab

To place a tab in a table, you need to press

[HOME]-[TAB]

To place a margin release in a table, press

CONTROL-V SHIFT-[TAB]

❖ *Poof, you're a table*

You know the old joke, "Make me a cup of coffee." "OK. Poof: you're a cup of coffee." Well, the same goes for tables. You can take tables created with tabs or parallel columns, and turn them into real 5.1 tables without all that much ado. In fact, as I said earlier in the parallel column section, it's easier to turn plain text into a table by way of parallel columns than by blocking and moving little chunks into the table itself.

All you do is block the entire table, and then press

ALT-F7 T C

WordPerfect will ask you if the table is made with **T**abs, or **P**arallel columns, and you press either **T** or **P**, depending on what's what.

WordPerfect will sit there for anywhere from a few seconds to a few minutes while it figures out how to turn your mess into a table. Most of the time it will do an excellent job, but just in case, I suggest you save the file first. That way if you don't like the table it's created, you can just clear the screen, retrieve the file, and you haven't lost anything.

❖ Table Edit Depeche Mode

In this mode you are editing the table itself, not its contents. Make sure the cursor is inside a table, and press

ALT-F7

If the cursor isn't currently inside a table, press

ALT-F7 T E

WordPerfect will search backwards to find the last table in the file. If it doesn't find one, it will then search forward for the next one.

It is here that you control the **S**ize of the entire table; **F**ormat and width of columns, row height, and individual cells; **L**ines around the entire table and between cells; **H**eader, the rows of the table, which are repeated if the table is broken by page breaks; **M**ath, the ability to perform calculations on any number entered into a cell; **O**ptions, which include space between cells, alignment of the table, and the percentage of gray background; **J**oin, which allows you to combine several cells into one; and S**p**lit, which does just the opposite, permitting you to take a single cell and break it up into several. You can also insert a row or rows, a column or columns, or delete either or both. You can size columns with the cursor keys and move columns or rows.

When you select either Format or Lines from this menu, the first line menu will display the current settings. This is the only place these settings will display on-screen, and it's all too easy to overlook them and then think you have to go to View Document mode to see what they are.

◆ Press GOTO, collect $200

There's an important addition to the cursor commands I showed you earlier when you are in Table Edit mode. You can press the GOTO key (CONTROL-[HOME]) and then type in the cell address, as you would in a spreadsheet. **A1** is always going to be the first cell. The last one will vary, depending on the number of columns and rows in your table.

❖ Just my Size

Size controls the number of columns and rows. You can add or remove rows at any time. If you change the size and add more rows, they will appear at the end of the table. If you add more columns, they will appear on the right of the table. If you delete columns, they'll come off the right of the table. If you delete rows, they'll come off the bottom. If you want to delete or insert specific rows or columns, you'll want to use the insert or delete keys.

WordPerfect will show you how many rows are currently in the table. If you were following directions, you should have five. Let's add another column right now. Press

S R 6 [ENTER]

A new row should appear at the bottom of the table.

If you type a number smaller than the current number of columns or rows, then one will be deleted. Let's remove the one we just added:

S R 5 [ENTER]

❖ *Format*

This controls plenty. Maybe too much. It's broken up into three sections: Cell, Column, and Row Height.

While Cell is listed first, the one you should use first is Column. This is because WordPerfect formats tables by columns, so if you specify a column setting, all the cells in that column will share the same attributes, size, and alignment (WordPerfect calls it justification). This can save time, and keep you from having to press the zillions of keystrokes necessary to format each cell independently. If you do want to specifically format a single cell differently from the rest of the column, you will choose Cell.

◆ Block and roll

Don't forget that you can use Block (ALT-F4) when formatting cells or columns. This way, if you know you want the first three columns all to be 2 inches wide, you first block them (you don't have to block the entire columns, just a single cell in that column), then set the width, and the one setting applies to all columns within the block. The same action applies to all the formatting options. If you block three cells and use Format Cell, you have to enter the keystrokes only once for them to apply to all three blocked cells.

◆ Let me 'fee what's going on

When you press **F**, WordPerfect displays not only the options but the current settings for the column and cell. On the left, you see the current *cell*'s Vertical alignment, horizontal alignment, and attributes. On the right you see the *column's* width, horizontal alignment, and attributes.

◆ Four fast functions

There are four fast functions in Table Edit that require no delving into menus. To make the current column wider, press

CONTROL-[RIGHT ARROW]

When the table fills up the allotted space, making one column wider will force another (to the right) to get narrower. Unless you change a table's positioning between the margins, cells always grow to the right. If the table is aligned to the right, then cells grow to the left. If it's aligned to the center it will alternate, once to the right, once to the left. But no matter how you have it aligned, CONTROL-RIGHT always makes a cell wider.

CONTROL-[LEFT ARROW]

This will make it narrower. There are times when no amount of pressing either of these keys will make any difference. When one column has been specifically formatted very wide and there is no room to take away from other columns, WordPerfect will ignore all requests to make another cell larger. You will then have to make the wide cell narrower so there is room for the others to grow.

[INSERT]

This causes WordPerfect to ask if you want to insert a Column or a Row. If you select Row, it will first ask how many, then once you enter a number or press [ENTER] for 1, it will add a new row above the current row.

If you select Column, it will ask how many, and you can either type in a number or press [ENTER] for 1, and it will add a new column to the left of the current row.

[DEL]

This works much the same way. After you press [DEL], WordPerfect will ask if you want to delete columns or rows. Once you tell it how many or press [ENTER] for 1, WordPerfect will delete the current column or row (and the number of columns to the right or rows below you specified).

CONTROL-F4

This allows you to move columns or rows or a block of text. When you press it, WordPerfect asks if you want to move a Block, Row, Column, or Retrieve a block. This feature works just like the normal Move feature. If you select Row, then the row will disappear and WordPerfect will ask you to move the cursor to where you want to place the row. Once you've moved the cursor you press [ENTER] and the row will appear, in front of whatever cell the cursor was on. It's the same with columns. If you block several cells, WordPerfect only moves the text inside them, not the cells, and then when you press [ENTER] to finish the move, it will first delete anything that was in the cells, then insert the moved text at a different location.

◆ Column

Because Column is the most powerful, we'll cover it first. Using the column format, you can make all the text in the column bold or large or any other attribute. You can also control the formatting for the entire column and set the number of digits WordPerfect will display in calculations.

➾ Width

CONTROL-[RIGHT ARROW] and CONTROL-[LEFT ARROW] size cells interactively, but this option allows you to enter specific widths for columns. Suppose you want column one to be 2.5 inches wide. You move the cursor to column one and press

F L W 2.5 [ENTER]

WordPerfect will make the current column 2.5 inches wide. Remember, though, that if the table already fills up the available horizontal space and you try to make one column wider, another one (to the right) is going to have to get narrower. If your table is set to full, you may experience great difficulty if you try to widen the right-most column or columns. If you want to read more about it, find the heading titled "Right nightmare" later in this chapter, but otherwise don't worry about it just yet; you'll have plenty of time to deal with it later.

➾ Attributes

This command is like the normal Attribute or size command (CONTROL-F8 A or S) except that it applies to all the cells in a column, rather than just a block of text. Selecting Normal will return the column to the normal base font.

➾ Justify

This command controls the alignment for the entire column. While Left, Right, Center, and Full are all familiar from Chapter 8, Decimal Align is new. This is specifically for cells containing numbers.

Decimal Align aligns the text or number on the decimal point. I know that explanation verges on the absurd, so I'll try again. Decimal Align is similar to right align, except that instead of aligning on the end of the line, it aligns on the decimal point in the line. If you try to use this alignment with standard paragraphs of text, your punishment might involve the vertical hold button on your TV.

➾ # of Digits

This governs the number of digits that will appear to the right of a decimal point (up to 15). While setting this doesn't stop you from entering numbers with more digits to the right of the decimal place, if you type more digits than what you specify here, the digits will wrap and everything will go cracker dog. Also, the higher a number you enter here, the farther to the left the decimal will be placed. This means that there's less room for larger numbers, the only kind I really want to be concerned with. This feature also controls how many digits WordPerfect will use for calculations, but this is a book about desktop publishing, not accounting, so all we really care about here is that the numbers *look* nice (and that the book sells in adequate numbers).

◆ Row height

This is our last formatting option. Whew, what a relief. Unfortunately, this option can be really tricky.

➡ Single line Fixed or Auto

If you choose one of these options, WordPerfect will only allow one line of text in the cell. Yes, this is constricting, but it can be very useful for forms where you don't want some idiot to enter Chapter 1 of *Gone with the Wind* when all you really wanted them to enter was "Yes" or "No." As soon as they press return—boom, they're in the next cell whether they like it or not.

Fixed will permit you to set any height for the cell, up to the size of the page. Auto will tell WordPerfect to size the height of the cell automatically.

➡ Multi-line Fixed or Auto

This setting allows you to set the height for the row, even when it contains more than one line of text. Fixed will make the row whatever height you specify. If you set a fixed row height of 5" and only enter two lines of text, the row will still print 5" tall. It won't look that way in the editing screen, though. You'll only see it in View Document or when you print.

➡ Table Limbo

No, this isn't something you do while listening to Harry Belafonte records. It's something that happens when you put more text into a cell than will fit.

If you try to enter more text than will fit (either because you've entered a fixed height or because the cell would be larger than a page) WordPerfect will go a little insane. To the casual (or hysterical) observer, it will appear that WordPerfect has just lopped off the text, never to be seen again. You can even search for it with **F2**, but you will find nothing.

While it seems like the black hole of WordPerfect, it's really just in limbo. The documentation doesn't warn you about this, but I will, thereby saving you endless hours of heartbreak as your prose goes "poof."

Actually, the text *can* be retrieved by either setting the row height to automatic (if the contents of the cell are less than a page) or by deleting the table definition. This can be dangerous or, at the very least, really really confusing.

Using the **Auto** setting is safer. It means that the row will shrink and grow depending on what text it contains. This is the default setting. Auto has its own little idiosyncracies as well, though. Because a cell can't be larger than a single page, if you type (or copy) more into a cell than will fit, that text will also go into Table Limbo.

◆ Cell

Cell controls the formatting of a single cell. This is useful when you need to format one cell differently from the rest of a column. You might use this for the heading of a column where the type would be larger or bold or something different from the rest of the column. Cell has five more options:

- **T**ype tells WordPerfect whether the contents of the cell are numeric or text. If you don't specify, WordPerfect will think of it as a numeric cell. But don't worry about this, as it mostly concerns the Math feature and not formatting.
- **A**ttributes is just like pressing CONTROL-F8; it controls both **S**ize and **A**ppearance not just for some text, but all the text in the cell. **N**ormal turns off all attributes, while **R**eset returns the cell to the same formatting as the rest of the column. You can also press **F6** to bold the entire cell or **F8** to underline it.

Personally, I don't recommend using this method for cells because you have no on-screen indication of what the settings are. You must go into View Document to see what they are; whereas if you use normal text attributes, they will display in Reveal Codes.

- **J**ustify controls the alignment of the cell. This is in lieu of setting it with SHIFT-F8 L J. You can set this to **L**eft, **C**enter, **R**ight, **F**ull, **D**ecimal alignment (perfect for numbers), and Reset, which returns the cell to the same alignment as the rest of the column. These settings always take precedence over the general alignment of the body text.
- **V**ertical alignment controls where the text sits vertically within the cell. Choose from **T**op, **B**ottom, or **C**enter (middle). When you change these you won't see any difference in the normal editing screen. The differences only show in View Document or when you print.
- **L**ock does just that: it locks a cell so it can't be changed. When a cell is locked the cursor will not enter the cell in normal Text Edit mode; it just jumps around it. This is perfect for the headings of forms, which need to be printed but not changed. It also means that you don't have to waste time when filling forms because pressing [TAB] will not land on a locked

cell, you will just jump from one place to fill to another. Once a cell is locked, the only way to change it is to go into Table Edit, move the cursor back into the cell (you can enter locked cell in Table Edit mode), and turn the lock off.

❖ Line up

One of the niftier parts of the Table feature is its ability to print lines around cells. To those of you new to computing this may not sound like much (you are probably the same people who take VCRs for granted), but it's a good trick, and it has a thousand and one uses for desktop publishing. You can use these lines for everything from boxing a single paragraph to creating decorative borders to creating entire forms.

The point to remember is that the lines around each cell are independent from the other cells, yet there is no space between them. This means that if you put "single" lines around on all four sides of a cell and put single lines around an adjacent cell, you're really going to have two single lines, right next to each other, and end up with a thicker line than you expected.

This is confusing because it doesn't actually display on-screen as it prints. When you set lines inside a cell, they are really inside the cell. If you go to the cell above it and ask for no lines on the bottom, well, you're not going to have a line at the bottom of the top cell but you are going to have one on the top of the bottom cell, so it will look like there is a line, even though you've told the top cell not to have one.

Lines come in seven different flavors—None, Single, Double, Thick, Extra Thick, Dotted, or Dashed. If you don't change any line settings, you will always have double lines around the table and single lines between cells.

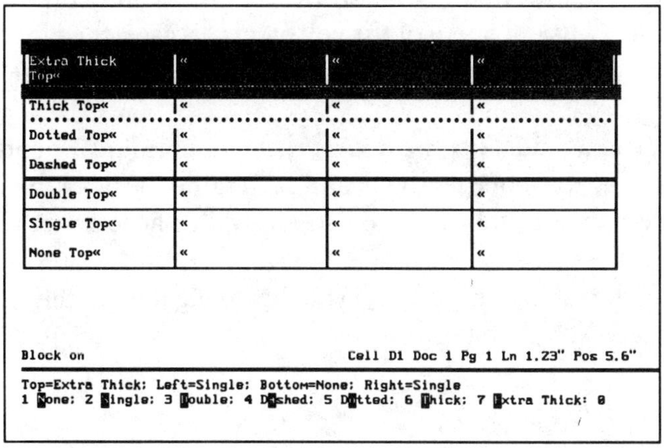

Extra Thick Top«	«	«	«
Thick Top«	«	«	«
Dotted Top«	«	«	«
Dashed Top«	«	«	«
Double Top«	«	«	«
Single Top«	«	«	«
None Top«	«	«	«

Block on Cell D1 Doc 1 Pg 1 Ln 1.23" Pos 5.6"

Top=Extra Thick; Left=Single; Bottom=None; Right=Single
1 None; 2 Single; 3 Double; 4 Dashed; 5 Dotted; 6 Thick; 7 Extra Thick: 0

Here are the seven line styles available with tables. This graphic illustration should not be left where small children might see it.

◆ Inside, outside, all around the cells

Now, for the moment we've all been waiting for. If you haven't done so already, create a table with three columns and five rows and go into edit mode. *If* you haven't done it yet or are hopelessly lost, press the following keys:

ALT-F7 T C 3 [ENTER] 5 [ENTER]

A table should appear on the screen, and you should be in Table Edit mode. If a picture of a raisin appears on your screen, then you are probably watching Saturday morning cartoons and are not really working in WordPerfect.

If your cursor is not in cell A1, press

CONTROL-[HOME] A1 [ENTER]

Your cursor will be in Cell A1, and you can tell that by looking in the lower right corner of the screen. There, sitting casually in front of the word "Doc" as if it doesn't care, is the Cell status.

If you press L for Line right now (don't do it, I was just speaking hypothetically), you would be changing the lines for Cell A1 only. What we want to do is change the lines for the entire table at once. To do this we need to turn block on by pressing

ALT-F4

Then to go to the end of the table, press

[HOME] [HOME] [DOWN ARROW]

If we had blocked only two cells, then the line command would affect only those two cells. But we've gone and blocked the whole table, so what we do next will affect the whole thing. Press

L

Another menu appears with more choices. Don't think of it as another decision, think of it as *control* (you'll like it better that way). You can *control* the lines on the Left, Right, Top, Bottom, Inside, Outside, or All of the cell or, in this case, the block that is the entire table. There's also one more little item called Shade, but we'll get to that in a bit.

Let's try these options, one at a time. First, we decide that a double line around the table looks like something from a science textbook and we'd rather be dead than format our table this way. We're taking this a bit too seriously, but at least we're paying attention.

"Let's make the outside of the table a single line," you say, trying desperately to sound calm as you see the inside. "OK," I reply, "do it."

O S

What we've just done is to make the lines on the Outside into single lines. Already the table looks a little less fifties and a little more nineties. The block turned itself off, however, and we want to block the whole table again. Press

ALT-F4 CONTROL-[HOME] CONTROL-[HOME]

This turned the block back on and marked the same area again. This time we're going to mess with the lines Inside.

L I N

If you've been following along, you'll see all the lines Inside the table disappear. The cells are still there, only the lines have changed. Let's put them back and try some different widths. First we turn the block back on and reblock the same cells. Press

ALT-F4 CONTROL-[HOME] CONTROL-[HOME]

Then we try another line style, such as Dashed.

L I A

Interesting. What about dotted lines?

ALT-F4 CONTROL-[HOME] CONTROL-[HOME] L I O

Elegant, in a sort of Kafkaesque way. But wait, remember how I said that these lines don't really look on-screen the way they print? Well? Hello, hello? Anybody home? Let's see how they'll print by using View Document. We'll first have to leave Table Edit by pressing

F7 SHIFT-F7 V

Hmmm. Very post modern, I'm sure. Let's go back to the table.

F7

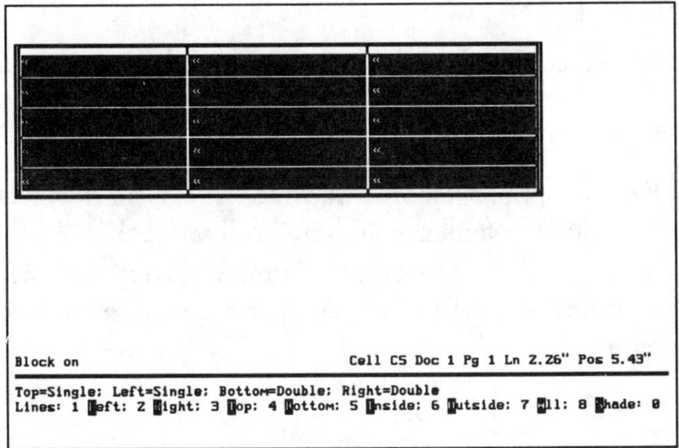

You can block cells and set the line styles for all of them at once. Your grandparents probably never dreamed you'd have so much power.

(Make sure the cursor is inside the table.) Press

ALT-F7

I don't know about you, but I think this is kind of fun. Then again, I don't get out much.

◆ One at a time

We've been working on the whole table, but we can also change the lines on a cell-by-cell basis. If you aren't already there, let's go to Cell A1. Press

CONTROL-[HOME] A1 [ENTER]

Give the Top and Left of this cell thick lines. Press

L T T L L T

Now let's make the bottom into a single line.

L B S

Gee, you pressed the keys, but it didn't seem to change. Well, you've just experienced, first hand, the subtle weirdness of working with tables. You've really given the cell a single line at the bottom, but because the cell below has a dotted line above, that's what you're seeing now. *Both* will print. Let's take a look.

F7 SHIFT-F7 V

See what I mean? (Depending on your monitor, you may *not* see both lines, but they *will* print). Let's get back to the table.

F7 ALT-F7

If we really want just a single line between them, and not a single line with a dotted line stuck right up next to it, we'll move to cell A2 and give the cell no line on top.

CONTROL-[HOME] A2 [ENTER] L T N

Presto chango, the dotted line has turned into a single line, and that's what will print between the cells.

➻ All or nothing

So you get the picture. The only options left are All, which affects all the lines of a cell or block, and None, which turns off all the lines in a cell or block.

None is useful when you want to use the ease of table formatting, but you don't need, or even want ruling lines. When lines are turned off, the printed page gives no hint that you used the Table feature.

◆ Made in the shade

Last, but not least, is the Shade feature. Shade adds a gray background to a cell or cells. Tables and forms often use this to make certain areas stand out or off limits to nonofficial personnel.

Shade really has two parts: you turn it on or off under Lines, and you control the density of the shading under Options. Let's turn it on and off a few times first.

Make sure you're still in Table Edit, and then move the cursor to Cell A1. To turn shading on, press

L S O

You can remember that easily because it's just exactly like USO, only it starts with an L. The only item that changes on-screen is that the Cell address in the lower right of the screen is displayed in reverse video in any cell that has shading turned on.

Shading works just like anything else in tables in that if you turn block on and select a few cells, you can turn shading on or off for more than one cell at a time. Let's try again, this time blocking the first row. Once again, make sure you're in Cell A1.

ALT-F4 [HOME] [HOME] [RIGHT ARROW] L S O

There, you've gone and done it. The entire first row is now shaded. To see how this is going to look when you print, you will leave Table Edit and go into View Document.

F7 SHIFT-F7 V

When you're done looking, go back into Table Edit mode with

F7 ALT-F7

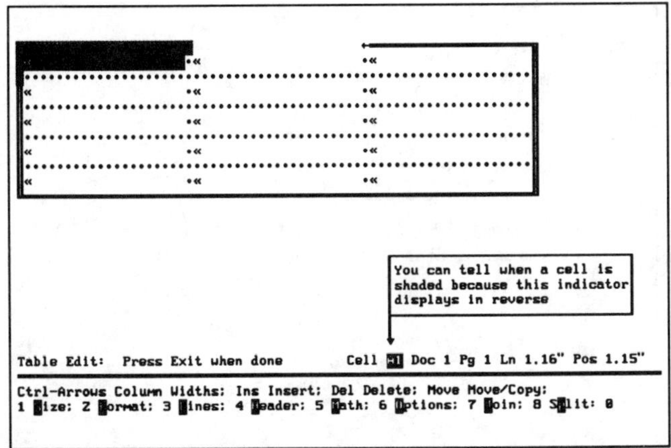

When a cell is shaded the cell indicator on the status line displays in reverse or my name isn't Obie Juan Canobe.

➻ How dark was my shading?

The default setting for a shaded background is 10%. This is really about as dark as you want to go on PostScript printers because anything darker makes it hard to read text. On a LaserJet you can go to about 20% as long as you use bold fonts. Using a LaserMaster at 600 dpi, the grays are very fine, and you can go as high as 30% (although 50% and over all appear as solid black).

You set the percentage on a table-by-table basis, but you can only set one percentage per table. The setting affects the entire table, not just a single cell, so it doesn't matter where in the table you are when you issue the command. To set it to 20% press

O G 20% [ENTER]

Now view the table again.

F7 F7 SHIFT-F7 V

You'll notice that the shading is darker. Shading in View Document is often not very accurate, and on some monitors it is backwards, so that 10% appears almost black, while 90% appears very light. Don't let that throw you; print out various grays on your own printer so you know what they look like.

❖ *Optional equipment*

The options menu allows you to set overall defaults for this table. You can set different options for different tables but not for individual cells.

◆ Spacing

This is a very important function, and luckily the default settings are usually perfect. This tells WordPerfect how much space you want between text and cell

```
Table Options

     1 - Spacing Between Text and Lines
             Left                          0.083"
             Right                         0.083"
             Top                           0.1"
             Bottom                        0"

     2 - Display Negative Results          1
             1 = with minus signs
             2 = with parentheses

     3 - Position of Table                 Left

     4 - Gray Shading (% of black)         10%


Selection: 0
```

Table Options. Need I say more? Yes, and I do on this very page.

borders. These are sort of like mini page margins. I don't recommend that you use settings lower than the defaults because the text can get uncomfortably close to the lines of the table. You can, however, make these numbers larger if you are working with big tables, big text, or just want more space between the text and the lines.

◆ Double negative

This option entitles you to decide how WordPerfect will display negative numbers, either with a minus sign or in parenthesis. When color printers get cheaper I'm sure you'll be able to choose that they just print in red (you'll probably go into the red yourself buying a color printer), but for now these are your choices. Of course, you could always format the text in red using the color command (Control-F8 C).

◆ Assume the position

This tells WordPerfect where to put the table — at the left margin, right margin, centered, a specific distance from the left margin, or the full width of the margin. After a long day at the computer you might think of another option not on the menu, but let's not get into that.

➻ What's Left?

The default is left. But, and this is a big but, WordPerfect always initially formats tables so that they fill the entire margin. So Left really means Full, unless you change the column widths so that the table no longer occupies the full margin area. This also means that unless you change the column widths, Center and Right aren't going to do anything at all. Remember, if you choose Full, and you change margins, the table will "shrink to fit" to the new margins.

❖ *Join up*

Now if tables were just a bunch of rows which always had the same number of columns, it wouldn't be very useful. But you can combine or join two or more cells into one larger cell. Let's get back into Table Edit and try it for ourselves. Press

F7 ALT-F7

Move the cursor to cell A1 by pressing

CONTROL-[HOME] A1 [ENTER]

Now this is a perfectly nice table as it is, but it would be nicer if we could have one big title that went across all three columns. And we can get it if you try hard enough. First, think lovely thoughts, then to turn block on press

ALT-F4

Move the cursor to the end of the first row

[HOME] [HOME] [RIGHT ARROW]

To join these cells in holy matrimony, press

J Y

Now, tell me honestly, isn't that a breeze? And it works on any number of cells, as long as they are right next to each other. Let's try another one. Press

[DOWN ARROW] ALT-F4 [DOWN ARROW] [RIGHT ARROW]

If you've read this correctly (and you'd be surprised at how many people won't) you will have blocked four cells. OK, now join them.

J Y

One mo' time. Press

[DOWN ARROW] [RIGHT ARROW] [RIGHT ARROW] ALT-F4 [DOWN ARROW] J Y

Mondrian would be proud. But let's say your boss (or slave driver or whatever you call them) is an artistic heathen and doesn't appreciate fine art such as this. Let's say that they ask, no, they demand that you put all the cells back to normal—pronto. You have two choices, you can quit, or you can press

P R 2 [ENTER]

Very good! When you put the lines back in they're going to be the default single lines, instead of our customized dotted lines. (I'm trusting that you've followed along correctly and haven't been distracted by something on TV, or completely left the room to order pizza. If you have done any of these other things, then disregard the congratulations.) You probably noticed that WordPerfect already knew how many

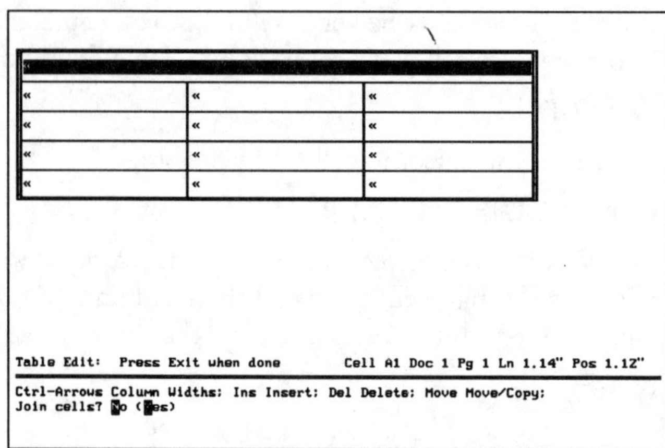

We now join these cells in holy matrimony.

rows you wanted. This is because it read your mind. No, it's actually because it was just assuming that you wanted to return the table to normal. You really could have broken it up into four (or any number of) more rows if you had wanted to.

Now let's split the four cells we joined. Move the cursor to that giganto cell.

[LEFT ARROW] [UP ARROW]

And Split!

P R [ENTER]

Now split the long cells into two normal columns.

P C [ENTER] [DOWN ARROW] P C [ENTER]

Your table is now back to normal (except for the lines), except for the one big cell along the top, which we're going to leave just to rankle to the boss.

Before you go onto the next lesson, clear the screen with

F7 N N

❖ *Putting all this knowledge to good use*

Now the normal uses of tables are obvious. Financial data. Facts, figures. But what about the abnormal, subnormal, aberrant, eccentric, deviant, irregular, peculiar uses for tables. Well, you've come to the right place for those.

◆ Box me up, Scotty

There are many times when you want a single paragraph to have a box around it, as when it contains important information. It used to be hard to do, now it's easy by creating a one-paragraph table.

I'm going to assume your paragraph already exists (so if it doesn't, get those fingers moving). Make sure the paragraph doesn't begin with a tab, otherwise Word-Perfect will create a table with two columns and you'll have to delete the first one.

Go to the top of the paragraph, and turn block on with

ALT-F4

Move the cursor to the end of the paragraph and press

ALT-F7 T C T

Now wait with breathless anticipation while WordPerfect turns your lowly little paragraph into an all-expense paid table, complete with a double line around it. If you want to change the style of the box around the paragraph, read on, I cover that later. OK, I can't keep you in suspense, press

L O

Then choose among the various options. When you're finished, to leave Table Edit mode press

F7

(Some table lines may not appear correctly on-screen, but they will print correctly). If you want to move that paragraph, you won't just be able to use the normal Paragraph Move command because that will only move the text, not the box. You'll have go into Reveal Codes and block the whole thing, including the table [Tbl Def:] code at the beginning and [Tbl Off] at the end.

If you want to move the box from around the paragraph, turn Reveal Codes on and go to the start of the paragraph. Delete the [Tbl Def:] codes and the box will disappear.

◆ Right nightmare

Sizing the right-most columns of a table can become frustrating (to say the least) when the table is set to Full width. This is because no matter how you cajole, plead, or threaten, or how many keys you press or even pound, WordPerfect will absolutely not resize those cells. Why? Is it because WordPerfect is trying to drive you insane? Of course not. It's because it would mean shrinking cells to the left, which it considers a sin or something.

Because of this, if you get in some position where the right-most cells shrink down to next to nothingness (and it's happened to me, that's why I'm mentioning it), here's the only alternative I've found to fix it—throw the computer out the window and do it by hand . . . just joking.

Set your table position to "left" (O P L) and then change the width of *all* the cells to the width of the smallest (block them, then press F L W and enter a number) so that the total table is smaller than the margins. Only now can you start to enlarge, one at a time, the cells that need to be larger. When you're all through, you can then make the table full width again (O P F).

Of course, if your problem was not just a mistake, and you are actually trying to make the columns larger than the amount of space you have, you will need to either make the left and right margins smaller (SHIFT-F8 L M) or get real and revise the width of the cells.

◆ True to forms

Forms. You can't live with them; you can't shoot them. WordPerfect's Workbook presents a complex procedure for creating relatively simple forms, but using the Table feature is a simple way to create complex forms.

Later in this chapter we tackle a calendar, and while you may not think of it as a form, it is. It's a standard format in which you enter changing information. That's a form if Webster ever heard one.

You probably use countless forms without thinking about it—unless you're the person who has to order the forms and keep them in stock, and then you think about it, worry about it, and spend money on it.

Many forms you work with can easily be recreated using WordPerfect's Table feature. You can not only design and print the forms, but fill them in and do complex calculations. Invoices, purchase orders, requisitions, expense accounts, order forms, labels (they're considered a feature now, but I consider them a form), inventory control, packing slips, you name it. Two such forms are shown in Chapter 4, a run-sheet and an invoice, complete with math.

You name it, WordPerfect can do it. Well, pretty much. There is a limit to all this, and it all has to do with the dreaded word "database."

I know many people who have always used WordPerfect as their database. They just put everything into one humongous file, and then they use F2 to find it. While that works in a very simplistic way, it's no substitute for a real database program where you can manipulate information in many ways impossible in a word processing program.

And in the same way, tables are sometimes no substitute for programs specifically designed for creating forms, such as FormBase, Per:Form, FormWorx, and DisplayForm to name a few.

I say this now because I don't want you to think that WordPerfect is always the best solution. It isn't. If you need database power with the information you enter into forms, then you should consider using one of those programs. If you need convenience for designing and printing your own forms, and the ability to enter information (which you don't need to database), then WordPerfect is a good choice.

•◆ Form Tips

Lock up: There's no trick to creating forms, they are just tables. But there are a few things you can do to make filling them easier. First, any cell that isn't going to be filled should be locked. You aren't doing this so much for security as for efficiency. We should all know by now that when you are filling in a table, pressing Tab takes you to the next cell. But not locked cells. The cursor will simply jump over the cell and ignore it completely, and this means there's less time spent tabbing through cells you have no intention of filling in. It also means that headings on the form can't accidentally be changed.

Toe the line: Don't forget that you can specify exactly how thick, how dark, and how dotted you want your lines to be. To do this, press SHIFT-F8 O B.

Template City: Be sure to create form templates. Don't fill in the original form or how are you going to fill it in again? (Not to be confused with "How can I miss you if you won't go away?") The only trick with templates is that when you retrieve a file with WordPerfect, you get the current file name, and it's all too easy to save over the original.

A good way around this is to press the space bar once before retrieving the template. That way WordPerfect will ask if you want to retrieve the file into the current document, and once you do, it will not bring the template's file name along with it. Before you save, remember to delete the space. When you go to save, WordPerfect will insist you enter a new name. Simple. Effective.

Macrotize it: To make it even easier, you can record a macro that will do the same thing. Then all you have to do is type "invoice" or something like that, and the macro will put a space in the file, retrieve your invoice template, and off you go. Recording a macro is easy as pressing CONTROL-F10 to start recording, and CONTROL-F10 to stop recording. For more info about macros, see Chapter 17.

❖ *Tables as full page formats*

All this time we've been thinking about tables as little chunks of words or numbers, nestled among the rest of our text. But tables are also a good way to format entire pages.

I'm not suggesting that you actually write full pages in tables, what I'm suggesting is that you use the formatting power of tables to hold prewritten text. Tables then act like containers into which you pour your text.

Look at the examples in Chapter 4. Both the runsheet and invoice are examples of tables masquerading as full pages. I used a table for the runsheet because it made the ruling lines easier. The invoice was created with a table so the information could be quickly pulled from a spreadsheet. You can use it sort of like a template — first type in a normal document, then block and copy chunks of text into a premade table. Less obvious, but still a full page table, is the Babs Ryan Originals catalog page.

Full-page table pages, where the table really serves as border and ruling lines, are best for a single page, not for continuous text. Trying to use running text in tables is a headache. For continuous text, use parallel columns and styles for ruling lines instead.

The only warning I have is that if you set any of the rows as "fixed height," you can accidentally put more text in a cell than will fit in the fixed height. The only way you will know how much of that text really fits is to use View Document or print the page.

Well, that about wraps it up for these tables (there are some more in Chapter 18, *Spreadsheet Publishing*). I hope you enjoyed your flight and will join us again. To those of you not staying on for the flight to step-by-step calendar creation, please return your seat back and table trays to their upright positions, extinguish any burning items, and make sure your seat belt is fastened securely so you don't get knocked around the cabin during landing.

It's 68 degrees outside at San Francisco International Airport, and if you're really lucky, your luggage will be waiting for you at carousel number 19. From Captain Will-Harris and all the crew here at WP Air, we wish you a very pleasant stay in the city by the bay and remind you to hold tight when you ride them cable cars because those hills are doozies.

❖ Calendar girl

Calendars and schedules are something people use all the time. In fact, they've been in use for about the last 5000 years. However, all those ancient peoples were not able to create them as fast or as slick as you can with WordPerfect. You don't have to hire astronomers, stonecutters, or monks of any kind. In fact, it's so easy it's also scary.

In the next few minutes you're going to create a monthly calendar, or my name isn't Opie Juan Canobe. And once you've created this form you can use it over and over again, even well into the next century. (Hopefully by then computers will be smarter and we'll all just be able to tell them what to do. Of course, the down side is that they'll be able to talk back, precisely the thing so many people dislike about other people, especially spouses and children.) So just creating this one calendar yourself can possibly save you hundreds of millions of dollars on calendars, not to mention putting plenty of people in the calendar business out of business.

If you want to know more about using tables with spreadsheets, see Chapter 18.

◆ Just the table, ma'am

Much of the material here is applicable to all tables, and all forms you create using tables, so don't just press the keys blindly. *Think* about what you're doing so that you can apply it later when I'm not around telling you which keys to press.

If you're not already in Reveal Codes, make sure to turn them on now with ALT-F3.

The actual creation of the table for the calendar uses very few keystrokes. Here they are in their entirety:

ALT-F7 T C 7 [ENTER] 7 [ENTER]

We're going to set the table so that it is full width. Press

O P F [ENTER]

Now we're going to join all the columns in the first row to make room for the month/year title. Press

ALT-F4 [HOME] [HOME] [RIGHT ARROW] J Y F7

That's it. You've created a table with all the cells you need for a calendar.

◆ But wait, there's more...

But while this is the empty form for a calendar, it's not yet a calendar. Sure, you could just type in the month at the top, then the days of the week in the next row, then type in the dates in the other cells. Yes, of course, you *could* do that.

But the whole reason you picked up this book was to learn how to do a really good job of it (well, maybe you just liked the cover), and just plain typing into the table isn't enough.

Not surprisingly, the nicer you want something to look, the more work you have to do. Most computer books I've seen would give you the keystrokes that I just gave you and then show you a picture of a gloriously formatted calendar. Then all you have to do is figure out what they did to make it look like that. I read those books and resented those books for making me figure out what they were too lazy to explain. So this book isn't like that. This book is going to *show* you how to use all the features you need to desktop publish with WordPerfect. It's not just going to tell you what the features do, it's going to give you all the information you need to use them.

You see, it's really all the details—setting margins, fonts, defining automatic numbering, creating an outline style, and inserting the automatic numbers which make the difference between a basic calendar and something which looks professional. They make all the difference and they take most of the work.

◆ Table Edit

Let's start over and work from a blank slate. Press

F7 N N

On your mark, get set, go...

SHIFT-F8 P S

Move the cursor to Standard Wide because you want the page to be landscape (horizontal) rather than vertical. Now we're going to set the page margins. Press

S M .5 [ENTER] .5 [ENTER] [ENTER]

Now it's time to set the line margins. Press

L M .5 [ENTER] .5 [ENTER] F7

May/1990

Monday	Tuesday	Wednesday	Thursday	Friday	Saturday	Sunday
	1	2	3	4	5	6
7	8	9	10	11	12	13
14	15	16	17	18	19	20
21	22	23	24	25	26	27
28	29	30	31			

Now set the Base Font to Dutch 12 point. Press

CONTROL-F8 F

Move your cursor to Dutch 12 point Roman (or Times Roman). (If you have a scaleable font printer you will need to select the font, press Enter, then the size, Enter again, then press F7.) Press

S

◆ Automatic Numbering

Now it's time to define the automatic paragraph numbers which are going to create the date numbers in the calendar. We're doing this because if we just typed the numbers, we'd have to type new numbers for each month. Using automatic numbers, all we have to do is delete the automatic numbers in the blank spaces at the start of the month. The rest of the month will renumber automatically. These automatic numbers are going to use the outline style feature so they will automatically come out large and bold without us having to format each and every one of them. This step is a bit long, but it will save us countless keystrokes later on. First we're going to set the paragraph numbers so they are just Arabic numerals with no punctuation after them. Press

SHIFT-F5 D U 1 F7

Now we're going to define an outline style which will apply itself automatically.

◆ Outline Styles

N C N DATE [ENTER]

We've named the style, now we're going to put in the codes. A style consists of normal text and formatting codes that become one big super code which you can use over and over. If you change the contents of the style, the contents of all the styles you've already placed in your document also change. We're now going to make the automatic number (which is automatically in an outline style) extra large and bold. (Even though you see a Roman number I right now, you've already set the number to appear as an Arabic number 1, and that's the way it will print—looks can be deceiving.) First we have to block the code.

C ALT-F4

Now move the cursor to the right of the **[Par Num:1]** code and make it Extra Large by pressing

[RIGHT ARROW] CONTROL-F8 S E

(You may have to use two [RIGHT ARROW]*'s instead of one.)* The block turns off automatically. But since we want to reblock the same area, we press

ALT-F4 CONTROL-[HOME] CONTROL-[HOME]

Now we're going to make it bold and add a return after it. (If you have a LaserJet and are using the normal starter fonts, you don't even have to specify bold because the only extra large font you have is 24 point bold. In fact, if you include the bold code you'll get extra bold (the bold font with an additional bold by WordPerfect.) But PostScript, LaserMaster, LaserJet III, and other scaleable font printer users should include a bold, or you will just get 24 point medium.)

F6 [END] [ENTER]

We're all finished with styles now, so it's time to leave and select this style. Get ready for a bunch of F7s and get used to them, because you and WordPerfect are going to wear out your F7 key together. Press

F7 F7 L F7 F7

◆ Save it or lose it

Before we create the table, let's save what we've done. It's a good idea to get into the habit of saving often, even though WordPerfect does have a timed backup feature. Let's save now. Press

F10 !CAL.51 [ENTER]

The file will be saved. I started the name with a "!" because that will put the filename at the very top of the list in List Files, making it easier to locate.

◆ Make the table

Now to create the table itself. Press

ALT-F7 T C 7 [ENTER] 7 [ENTER]

We're going to set the table so that it is full width.

O P F [ENTER]

Now we're going to join all the columns in the first row to make room for the month/year title. Press

ALT-F4 [HOME] [HOME] [RIGHT ARROW] J Y

We only have one more step to creating the table itself (many more to finish the whole project). We want all the date cells to be the same height, whether there is text in them or not. Otherwise some weeks would be tall, and some would be short, and it would be a pretty funky looking calendar.

To accomplish this, we're going to set the row heights for these rows to fixed. There are two kinds of fixed row heights, but single-line-fixed only allows for a single line of text entry and we actually should be able to enter up to six lines of text, so we'll set it to multi-line fixed. First, move to cell A3. Cells are numbered so that columns are letters and rows are numbers. The first cell for the days of the month is A3. To move there you can either just move the cursor normally or press

CONTROL-[HOME]

WordPerfect will ask **Go To** at the bottom left of the screen and you respond with

A3 [ENTER]

Now that we're at the right spot, we need to block this row and all the rows which follow so we can format all these rows in one fell swoop (or swell foop, if you're a Peter Sellers fan).

ALT-F4 CONTROL-[HOME] A7 [ENTER]

Now we do the actual formatting. We've will set the height of all the rows we've marked to 1.3 inches high, no matter how little (or much) text is in them. The "much" part is important because even if you type volumes, WordPerfect will only print the text which fits in a cell of this height. In this case, it's about six lines. Press

F R X 1.3" [ENTER]

You won't see any change in the spacing on-screen, but it really *will* print differently. Before we leave, let's go to cell A1 so we'll be in the right place to enter the month name. Press

CONTROL-[HOME] A1 [ENTER]

Now it's time to leave the heady sophistication of Table Edit. This is because you can't enter text in Table Edit mode, and we need to start filling in the table. To exit Table Edit mode, press

F7

◆ Take a look

Now it's time for you to check and make sure your table/calendar resembles mine. The text won't be in yet, of course, but the table itself should be the right shape. To see what it looks like, we'll use View Document. Press

SHIFT-F7 V 3

Well, would you look at that. Amazing. Spectacular. Unbelievable. Unfinished. If your table doesn't look right, if it's not the right width or height, if it doesn't almost fill the page entirely, or if the five rows which will contain the dates aren't all nearly square, you've done something wrong.

Well, maybe it wasn't your fault. You were distracted or hungry or something like that. I don't blame you. Just start over. From scratch. Don't try to figure out where you went wrong, just be very careful to press everything I tell you to press, nothing more, nothing less. This example really does work, and it has for tens of thousands of happy customers. Try, try again.

If it did work, well, aren't you the clever ones. You're bucking for "Teacher's Pet," aren't you. Don't get too cocky, though, you're far from finished.

Let's get out of View Document, and continue with the task at hand. Press

F7

◆ Entering the text

We'll start by centering and selecting Large for the month name. I've chosen May, but you can choose whatever month you'd like. You have enough to worry about in real life, so don't worry about what day the real month starts on just yet. The cursor should be in the first row of the table, the one we created by joining many cells. If it isn't, get it there, and fast.

SHIFT-F6 F6 CONTROL-F8 S E MAY/1990 [DOWN ARROW]

Now we fill in the days of the week. I've started with Monday on the left, because that's the way I think calendars should work. If you want to start with Saturday or Sunday or Lunes, Martes, whatever you want, just do it and don't complain to me about it.

SHIFT-F6 F6 Monday [TAB] SHIFT-F6 F6 Tuesday [TAB] SHIFT-F6 F6 Wednesday [TAB] SHIFT-F6 F6 Thursday [TAB] SHIFT-F6 F6 Friday [TAB] SHIFT-F6 F6 Saturday [TAB] SHIFT-F6 F6 Sunday [TAB]

Now it's time to apply those automatic paragraph numbers we worked on just a few steps back. The cursor should be on the first cell of the third row.

◆ Making a macro

Now we're going to automate the process a little. Otherwise we'd be pressing another 140 keystrokes when, by creating a macro, we could get away with only 35. To create a macro, press

CONTROL-F10

WordPerfect asks for the name of the macro by saying "Macro Define". Press

ALT-D

If WordPerfect responds "**ALTD.WPM already exists, Replace, Edit, Description,**" it means you already have a macro using that name. Press **F1** and try again with a different name. (If you don't plan on saving this macro forever, you can just press [ENTER] when WordPerfect asks for a name. This creates a temporary macro for things you're not going to use forever. If you do this, WordPerfect will *not* ask for a description). If not, enter a description of the macro by pressing

Calendar Date [ENTER]

Now the words **Macro Def** blink in the lower left of your screen, reminding you that every single key you press is being recorded for posterity. We're going to press the keystrokes required to insert the automatic paragraph number. Press

SHIFT-F5 P [ENTER] [TAB]

Now stop recording the macro by pressing

CONTROL-F10

A numeral **1** should appear in bold, and the cursor should be in the second column of the third row. If you get an **I** or anything other than a bold **1**, you haven't created your style correctly and I'm not a bit surprised. Don't feel bad, it happens to everyone. Just try it again.

◆ Running the macro

If your number appeared correctly, press

ALT-D (or alt-whatever-you-called-your-macro)

over and over and over 34 times again until you have filled out all the remaining cells of the calendar. Each time you press, it will replay the macro you recorded. So while you're only pressing one key, WordPerfect is pressing four for you.

Wonder of wonders, your calendar is complete. But *wait*, I can't recall the last time a month had 35 days (I can remember when it felt that way, but that doesn't really count).

Let's save the file again.

F10 [ENTER] Y

◆ Timesaver: Making a template

And now we're going to save it again, only this time under a different name. The reason we're doing this is because the file we just created is now a *template* which we can use over and over again. It can be used for any month or year just by deleting the excess date numbers so that the month begins and ends correctly.

Now you'll see the value of using automatic paragraph numbers instead of just typing the numbers.

IMPORTANT: If we don't change the name now, we're going to lose our template and just save a specific month. If we do that we'll have to add new paragraph numbers next time we retrieve the file. Take my word for it, change the filename now.

Templates are a useful trick (and I wouldn't be surprised if David Copperfield starts using templates in his magic act. I'd pay anything to see him make Gloria Loring and Joanna Kerns disappear, wouldn't you?) because they allow you to set up standard files and use them over and over again. For example, you could create a file which contains your letterhead, margins, memo headings, everything. Then when you want to type a memo, you just retrieve that file, type in it, and save it under a *different* name. You can use templates until the end of time or until you get really sick of them, whichever comes first. Press

F10 [ENTER] Y

◆ Getting the dates right

Look on a *real* calendar (this isn't to say what you've created isn't a real calendar, just that it probably doesn't start and end on the right days) and find out where your specific month starts.

If it starts on Wednesday, move the cursor to the first Monday and place your cursor on top of the bold number 1. Press

[DEL]

(If your are not in Reveal Codes, WordPerfect will ask "**Delete [Outline Lvl 1 Open Style]?** No (Yes)" and you'll press **Y.**)

The number will disappear, and the date of Tuesday, which had been "2" will instantly say "1." Go to Tuesday and delete that number the same way. Wednesday will now say "1." Do the same thing at the end of the month, deleting the dates which don't apply. If your month is February, you are going to be doing the most deleting. But it will still work, even in a leap year! What *will* they think of next?

Let's check out your handiwork in View Document. Press

SHIFT-F7 V

Woo-wee. Get a load of that. Hopefully yours now looks almost identical to mine. Exit from View Document with

F7

Now let's save it as the individual month name, so that we don't overwrite our template file. Press

F10

Type the month name (or an abbreviation) followed by a period, and then the year, such as: MAY.90.

{whatever month you're in} [ENTER]

◆ Advanced revision: Adding graphics

What we've just created is great. And if you're satisfied, stop right now. But if you think it could be better (and what couldn't stand some improvement?), stick around. We're going revise the table and add two graphics.

Before we start—I have a rule about graphics. You only use them for a reason. You don't just stick them on a page because they're nice. The reason we could use one here is because an image which corresponds with the month makes a calendar more effective. You not only look at the date, you think about what events take place that month.

If I had my druthers, I'd probably use some clip art from Metro ImageBase or Publisher's PicturePak, but because I want to make sure you have the same graphic, we'll use one which came with WordPerfect. These graphics were created with DrawPerfect, a graphics program from WordPerfect Corp. While one of the pictures is of a calendar, that would be kind of redundant. If it were June we could use the diploma or if it was the month of my birthday I could use the balloons. But this is an example of WordPerfect, and since WordPerfect's symbol is a butterfly, that's as good a way as any to represent the calendar's creation.

First you're going to have to make sure you've got the graphic on your hard disk. If you said YES to everything during the install, you should find several files ending in ".WPG" in your WordPerfect program directory (probably C:\wp51). If not, exit WordPerfect, put the Install disk in, and say NO to everything except for installing "Graphic Images." This will copy the sample graphics to your WordPerfect directory.

OK, let's get on the rock, and roll. First, move the cursor to the cell which contains the name of the month (A1). Naturally, you are working with Reveal Codes on, knowing that if you had turned them off I'd turn surly, so it's easy for you to put your cursor on the [Center] code which is placed in front of the name of the month.

◆ Advance up

I use the "Advance" command often when desktop publishing because it allows me to precisely place items on a page. But you can also use it to fool the program in order to have more control. In this case, if I just place a graphic in the cell, it's going to have that .1" margin on top, there's going to be space at the top of the graphic itself, and it's going to have to be sized too small to look good.

To get around this, I use the advance command. I advance up .4" inches, then place the graphics boxes. When you use an advance up command, the program literally moves up that far up from where it otherwise would be. So it's like telling someone who's placing something on the page to move it up a little. After we create the graphics boxes we'll be moving down a little for the headline. To create an advance up, press

SHIFT-F8 O A U .2" [ENTER] F7

◆ Creating the graphics box

First, we're going to set some options for a User graphic box. We're doing this because otherwise the box will automatically have an outside margin, and we're really going to be squeezing this in and can't afford that extra space. To set the options, press

ALT-F9 U O O 0 [ENTER] 0 [ENTER] 0 [ENTER] 0 [ENTER] F7

(All those zeros with that one "oh" are confusing, so make sure you pressed "oh," "oh" "Zero" [enter] Zero [enter] Zero [enter] Zero [enter]). Now we're going to create the User graphics box itself.

ALT-F9 U C

Next we set it so it prints at the left of the cell, not the right.

H L

Now we retrieve the graphic itself.

F F5 [ENTER]

List Files here is just like it is when you are retrieving text. If you entered a directory in Setup for Location of Files, WordPerfect will display that "graphics" directory now. If not, look in your WordPerfect program directory, or move to the directory where you put the .WPG files. Move the cursor to BUTTRFLY.WPG and press

R

WordPerfect will load the graphic. Set the height at .6" inches tall. WordPerfect will calculate the width for you.

S H .6" [ENTER]

Edit time! Press

E

We're going to make it smaller and rotate it so it points in towards the name of the month. To make it smaller, look at the lower right of your screen. It should say "(10%)." If it doesn't, press the [INS] key until it does. Once it does, press

[PAGE DOWN] [PAGE DOWN] [PAGE DOWN]

Each time you pressed it, the graphic got 10% smaller. Pressing the gray Plus and Minus key will rotate the graphic. We want it to rotate to the right so it faces *into* the page. To do that, press the Plus key located on the numeric keypad (the "screen down" key in normal editing).

[GRAY PLUS KEY]

And the last bit of tweaking involves moving the graphic down so the top of the wing isn't cut off.

[DOWN ARROW]

And that concludes the editing portion of the program.

F7 F7

◆ Once again, with feeling

We want the exact same graphic on the right side of the calendar, but we want it to face in. Now, we could create the whole thing from scratch again, or we could do the smart thing and just copy the first one. You choose. Good, you chose smart. To make a copy of the graphics box, place the cursor *on* the [Usr Box:1] code, and press

ALT-F4 [RIGHT ARROW] CONTROL-F4 B C [ENTER]

(You may have to press [RIGHT ARROW] twice). You have just copied the graphics box. You didn't for a moment actually believe that this was the end of it, did you? Now we need to place the box on the right side of the cell.

ALT-F9 U E 2 [ENTER] H R

The butterfly is still aiming to the right, but with the box on the right it's now aiming *off* the page. We're going to rotate it to aim into the page. The gray Minus key is on the numeric keypad, and is the "Screen up" key in normal editing.

E [GRAY MINUS KEY] [GRAY MINUS KEY] F7 F7

◆ Advance down (advance funky)

Just one more thing, I promise. Because we advanced up to move the graphics up, we have to advance down or the name of the month will print in the middle of the upper border. We advanced up .4", but we're only going to advance down .2". Why? Because we like you. No, because I said so, that's why. No, that's not it either.

It's because if we don't, the automatic line height feature is going to make this row too tall, and our entire calendar won't fit on the page.

SHIFT-F8 O A D .2" [ENTER] F7

Now comes the moment we've all been waiting for (or dreading, depending on how well you think you've followed directions). Check it out in View Document.

SHIFT-F7 V

How does it look? Good, no? No good? If it looks exactly like the example in this book, print it out and go around your office, or wherever it is you normally go, gloating. If it looks even remotely like the example in the book, print it out. If it doesn't bear the slightest resemblance to the one in the book, but instead looks like the Rosetta Stone, call the British Museum and see if they're interested, then start from the top and try it again.

◆ Print me, print me

To print your masterwork, press

F1 P

It will take anywhere from 30 seconds to five minutes to print the page, depending on the speed of your printer.

I don't know about you, but I'm beat. This intense concentration is a lot harder than people think. Just because you don't sweat like a piglet doesn't mean you haven't worked hard. I think it's time to watch *Murphy Brown*. Then *Designing Women*. So whatever you do, don't call me on a Monday night between 9 and 10 p.m.

◆ One last tip

Paul Friedman, a WordPerfect maven (and one of the sysops of the WordPerfect forum on CompuServe) sent me this great idea.

Tables with lines are standard, but what if you don't want lines? Yes, you can go and remove them from each and every table, but you can also do it automatically! Sound unbelievable? It's absolutely true (despite the "BS" in the keystrokes).

It's *very* easy. Press

SHIFT-F8 O B S 0 [ENTER] [ENTER] F7

What this does is to set the printed width of a single line to 0". While the lines will still appear on the editing screen, they will be invisible in View Document and when you print.

Of course, the table will still have a double line around it, but if you don't want that either, this trick works for double lines, too.

Thanks Paul.

Styles change

Style never does

Flexibility and consistency: the two major reasons for using style sheets. With them you can change the appearance of a document repeatedly in the least amount of time and make sure that the elements remain uniform within that document or a whole slew of documents.

While the idea of style sheets isn't new, the way WordPerfect implements them is. Even if you are familiar with style sheets in Ventura Publisher or Microsoft Word, that will not be of much value since WordPerfect's style sheets are nothing like the others. They're sometimes better, sometimes worse, and perhaps a little easier to comprehend.

WordPerfect's style sheets are really more like formatting macros than the style sheets used in other programs. You create a style by entering all the formatting commands you would usually enter manually into your document. Styles can include any WordPerfect command, including graphics boxes, ruling lines, fonts, line height, colors, leading, indents, and text.

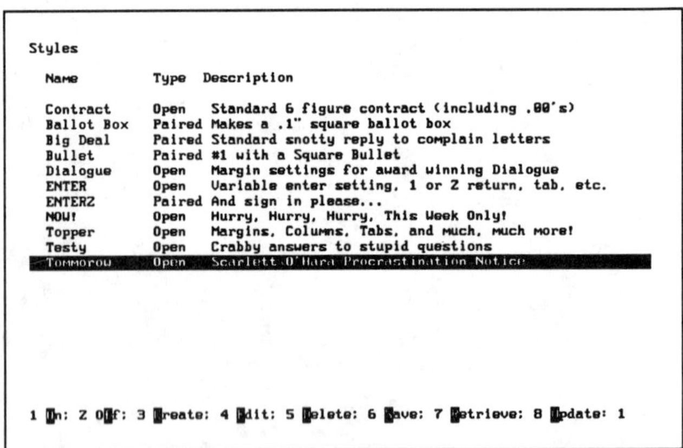

When you press ALT-F8, WordPerfect displays a list of the styles you have created. Not shown on the menu is **N** *for Name Search, a must when using styles with macros.*

There are two types of styles: "paired" (works like bold and underline codes—one at the beginning and one at the end of text to be affected), and "open" (applies to all text following the code). Paired styles can be used on any amount of text, from a single letter to an entire file.

Wait a minute, technically, there's another type of style. In 5.1 there are three types of styles if you include "Outline" styles. I didn't include them because they are really just a special collection of up to eight other styles, either open or paired, and they are used only for outlining, or automatic paragraph numbers.

When you create a style, you first give it a name and then enter all the formatting commands you want. You can also include text and graphics. Then, when you are writing (or better yet, formatting) the text, you select from a list of styles to arrange the text to your liking. When you turn on a style, it inserts a code that contains all the formatting you entered. You can use a style as many times as you like, and each time you use it, it will copy all of those formatting commands to your new document. This means that if you don't remember exactly what font, or line height, or indent you used previously, you can just select a style containing all the correct codes.

But the really "neato-keeno " part comes when you change something. You go into the style, change the codes in the style definition, and voila: every place you've applied that style to the page, the new style codes all change as well, corresponding with the single change you made in the style definition. Change the font in the definition? Zap, it all changes. Change the size? Poof, it's done. No tedious manual search and replace, no fear of missing anything.

You can change the contents of styles to your little heart's content, secure in the knowledge that the text is going to be quickly, easily, consistently, and accurately updated.

◆ But first, a note about disk space

Using Styles takes up disk space. Sometimes an awful lot of it. Some people never notice how much disk space they have, while others are compulsive about it. (If I fit into the second category, it's only because I never have enough.) One of my theories is that no matter how much disk space you have available, you'll fill it. It's always worked for me (or against me).

While WordPerfect 4.2 created very compact files, WordPerfect 5 and 5.1's files are much larger. It's not unusual for files containing identical text to be twice as big in 5.0 or 5.1 as in 4.2. And all this wondrous formatting takes its toll in disk space.

Paired styles take up the most space; they have both opening and closing codes, and each code can contain an abundance of formatting codes. The closing code always returns everything to status quo (as it was before the first code), and this can entail even more formatting.

While I would never advocate being stingy with disk space, you will notice the hard disk filling up much faster than it used to.

One more tip. When you do a repeated editing on a file, it can get bigger and bigger with each save, far out of proportion with the amount of text. One solution is to save the file, clear the screen, and retrieve the file again. When you do this, WordPerfect will delete any unnecessary material as it retrieves the file, and the file size will decrease, sometimes by as much as 50%.

❖ *Just your type*

Recognizing the difference between the two types of styles is important because they are used for different applications.

➾ Paired

Paired styles function like bold or underline commands; an open style code appears before the text you want to style, and a closed style appears after. To apply a style you press **ALT-F8** and move the cursor to the style you want. Then you press **O** to turn the style "on." Two codes are placed in the file: the beginning and ending codes.

Once you turn it on, you can type normally, and press **ALT-F8 F** to turn it off. Or you can simply press the [RIGHT ARROW] key or move the cursor past the "style off" code to turn it off (I find this to be easier and faster).

You can also block text with **ALT-F4**, then apply a style to the marked area by pressing **ALT-F8**, moving the cursor to the style you want, and pressing **O**.

The advantage of paired styles is that, unless you specify otherwise, the ending code returns everything to "normal,"(or at least to the way it was before the Style On code). This means that even if you make many changes (choose a different font, new line height, margins, whatever), they all return to normal after the ending code.

Paired styles can affect anything from a single character to an entire document. They're effective for margin changes, font changes, line spacing, ruling lines, appearance attributes, anything else that will apply to only a portion of text. I use paired styles for headlines, subheads, pull-quotes, even something as simple as italics (which I can instantly change to underlines).

➾ Open

Open styles don't have a beginning and end as do paired styles; you turn them on and they affect all text that follows them. They're good for major formatting changes (margins, fonts, line spacing, headers, footers, bullets, etc.). They also take up less disk space and make editing easier.

Before we get started, let's set our Initial Base Font to Dutch 10 point. Press

SHIFT-F8 D F

Move the cursor to BSN Dutch 10 point Roman and press

[ENTER] F7

❖ *WordPerfect with style*

But enough chit-chat. Let's make a style. Press the Style key

ALT-F8

If you specified a default style library in Setup (Shift-F1 LS), then you will see a list of styles. If not, the screen will display "Styles, Name, Type, Description" but nothing else (except for a menu line at the bottom of the screen).

After you create styles, this blank screen will be filled with a list of styles. You'll see the name, the type (paired, open, or outline), and a description that you can enter. To create a style, press

C

The first step in creating a style is to name it. The name can be up to 11 characters long, and it's best to choose something simple and short (like Dukakis). For this example, press

N

Then type

Subhead [ENTER]

Press

T

This tells WordPerfect the type of style you want; then type

P for paired, or **O** for open (we'll get to outline styles later). For this example press

P

If you want to type a detailed description press

D

You can enter up to 54 characters in length. This procedure can be used to jog your memory when you have so many styles that you don't remember what they do. Humor me and type

A subhead with a ruling line above [ENTER].

It's finally time to instruct WordPerfect about what you want this style to do. Press

C

If you are editing in open style, Reveal Codes will be on but the screen will be otherwise blank. If you are editing in a paired style, Reveal Codes will be on. On the top of the screen you'll see a boxed message which says "Place Style On Codes above, and Style Off Codes below." On the bottom half of the screen, in Reveal Codes, you'll see a [Comment] code. This code will not print, and is there only to contain the "Place Style On Codes..." message and to signify the division between the opening and closing half of the paired style.

```
Styles: Edit

     1 - Name            subhead

     2 - Type            Paired

     3 - Description     Help, I'm being held captive inside a style sheet...

     4 - Codes

     5 - Enter           HRt




Selection: 0
```

When you define a style (ALT-F8 C), you name it, specify whether it's an open or paired style, give it a description, designate what the Enter key will do, and then enter any formatting instructions.

If we were creating an open style, you would enter all the codes, then press **F7.** But we aren't. So don't.

◆ Creating a paired style

Instead we're going to create a paired style for our little example. In paired styles, everything preceding the **[Comment]** mark will be included in the opening code of the style pair and will affect the text inside the code pair; everything following the comment will appear in the closing code. If nothing is placed after the comment, WordPerfect will automatically revert to the codes that were in effect before the opening style code. You can also put any codes you want after the comment; these will affect all text that follows the code, not just the text between the markers.

Now let's create a subhead style that has a horizontal ruling line above. Because we don't want a page or column break between the ruling line and the subhead, we're going to enter a conditional end of page (page break). This will start a new column or page if there isn't enough room for the entire subhead along with several lines of text below it. We're going to set the conditional end of page to six lines. To do this, type

SHIFT-F8 O C 6 F7 F7

To add an extra space above our (we've been through so much together I feel like it's ours to share) subhead, press an additional

[ENTER]

We want to have the ruling line and subhead extend into the left margin. To do this, we're going to change the margins. Press

SHIFT-F8 L M .5 [ENTER] 1 [ENTER] F7

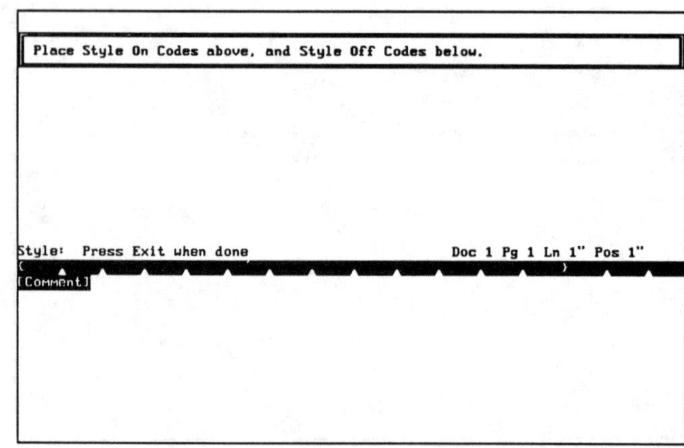

When creating a paired style, any codes placed before the comment appear in the "Style On" code, while comments placed after the comment take effect in the "Style Off" code.

(If you don't have a ruling line and just want a subhead to stick out from the right margin, you could press SHIFT-TAB and insert a [Mar Rel] code, but an actual margin change is necessary for the horizontal line).

◆ Horizontal ruling lines

Now it's horizontal line time. Be a good sport and enter

ALT-F9 L H [ENTER]

This will insert a horizontal ruling line the length of the margin, be it a column or an entire page. Even if you change margins, this line will still run from the left margin to the right margin (a nifty little feature).

◆ Adding white space

We need a little space between the ruling line and the subhead. Add a return and then an advance down.

[ENTER] SHIFT-F8 O A D .1" [ENTER] F7

This enters an advance command that moves us down precisely 1/10th of an inch.

◆ Sizing a font

Because we want our subhead to be a bit larger, we're going to enter a size code using

CONTROL-F8 S L

Notice how only the opening [Large] code appears. There is no need to enter a closing code, because this is a paired style. WordPerfect will automatically switch off all codes entered before the [Comment] mark. Now let's really go for broke and add a [BOLD] code. Press

F6

◆ Selecting a font

If you desire a contrasting typeface for the subhead, you can press **CONTROL-F8 F** and select a font. (If you've just pressed CONTROL-F8, press F1 now to cancel it.)

◆ Letterspacing

We're going to throw all caution to the wind and get downright artistic. Pretend you know what you're doing and follow me right down the garden path. Press

SHIFT-F8 O P W P 200 [ENTER] P 200 [ENTER] F7

You have now unwittingly been a co-conspirator in increasing the space between letters and words by 200%; all the letters and words now have twice as much space between them. This is the type of element people pay big bucks for, but it's yours free, as my personal gift (it was either that or a cubic zirconium ring). If you hate the way the letterspacing looks, you can always come back into this style and delete it, but what the heck—it's good to experiment! (I feel like Auntie Mame.) Now we need to go to the closing half of the style. Press.

[RIGHT ARROW]

Move the cursor to the right of the [Comment] code so we can add codes to the closing half of the style. In this case we want a little additional space below the subhead, so we're going to add yet another advance command. Follow the bouncing ball and press

SHIFT-F8 O A D .1"

[ENTER] F7

Now let's leave style edit

F7 F7

You have now been returned to the list of styles. To turn this style on so we can use it press

O

That wasn't so awful now, was it? Ah, the tales you'll have to tell your wide-eyed grandchildren about working with stone-age computers that everyone thought were so futuristic at the time.

This paired style creates a conditional end of page, a horizontal ruling line above, large type, and additional spacing between each letter. The closing half returns everything to normal, then advances down one-tenth of an inch.

```
Place Style On Codes above, and Style Off Codes below.

Style:  Press Exit when done                    Doc 1 Pg 1 Ln 1" Pos 1"
[Cndl EOP:6][L/R Mar:0.5",1"][LARGE][BOLD][Wrd/Ltr Spacing:200% of Optimal,200%
of Optimal][Comment][AdvDn:0.1"]
```

◆ Reveal codes on

To demonstrate exactly what you've been a party to, I ask only that you press **ALT-F3** and look at the bottom half of the screen.

You'll see two style codes. Move the cursor one position left so it's on top of the [Style On:Subhead] code, and suddenly the code will explode (or at least pop open) and say:

[Style On:subhead;[Cndl EOP:6][HRt]

[L/R Mar:0.5",1"][HLine:Full,Baseline,7",0.013",100%]

[AdvDn:0.1"][LARGE][BOLD]

[Wrd/Ltr Spacing:200% of Optimal,200% of Optimal]

[AdvDn:0.1"]][Style Off:subhead]

See? You receive all the codes you entered into the style whenever you turn that style on. But wait, there's more. Press the **[RIGHT ARROW]** key so the cursor is right on top of the [Style Off:Subhead] code. As in the Style On command, the code will expand to reveal the contents of the style:

[Style Off:Subhead;][AdvDn:.01"][HRt]

[bold][large][L/R Mar:1",1"] [Wrd/Ltr Spacing:Optimal,Optimal]

Paired Styles in 5.0 *may* automatically include a hard return in the closing half if you have changed the margins in the opening half.

If you had changed the font in the opening half of the style, then you'd see another font name in the closing half.

With the cursor on the [Style Off] codes, type some text for the subhead. It may appear highlighted on the screen, depending on how WordPerfect was set up with SHIFT-F1 D C. What you won't see, however, is the additional space between the letters or the horizontal line. These elements will only show up in View Document; let's take a look by pressing

SHIFT-F7 V

Now do you believe me? Good, let's go back to editing. Press

F7

◆ The only certainty is uncertainty: changing a code

Okay, so you didn't go for all that space between the letters. You thought it looked like a mistake. Don't be glum, you're not alone — it's an acquired taste.

So take charge and change it. The real power of style sheets is that they allow you to change your mind, refine the style, without that much manual labor.

Press

ALT-F8

Move the cursor to the subhead style. To edit it, press

E

To reach that pesky little code, press

C

Move the cursor until it is on top of that accursed [Wrd/Ltr Spacing] code and press

DEL

There, all gone. Press

F7 F7 F7

If you were working in the middle of a long document, you might have had to wait a while after pressing the last F7. This is because WordPerfect reviews the entire document from the top, searching and changing the Subhead style whenever it finds it. Let's take another look

SHIFT-F7 V

See the difference?

F7

If the cursor is between two paired styles and you press ALT-F8 to edit the style, the cursor will immediately move to the name of the style you are in.

◆ That's a no-no

Once you've created a style and used it in the text, the one element you shouldn't change is the type of style (paired or open).

While WordPerfect allows you to change the type of a style at any time, these changes are not reflected in the codes you've already applied, and this can make formatting confusing. You might think that when you change a style from paired to open, all the styles in the text change as well. Think again.

If you do need to change from one type to another, you can either remove all the old style codes, or just create a new code altogether.

If you delete a style, you can also have WordPerfect remove all the styles with that name in the document. Or, if you don't want to delete the style, just the styles in a document, you can use search and replace. If they are paired styles, search for Style On; if they are open, search for Open Style. Although you cannot replace them with another style, you can replace them with nothing (an expedient way of kicking them out of the file so you can replace them with new ones). This is why it's important to reflect about what type of styles you will be needing before you start creating and placing them in the text.

❖ *Delete, eradicate, erase, expunge, and obliterate styles*

When you delete a style you have three choices: Leaving Codes, Including Codes, and Definition only.

Leaving Codes: If you choose to leave the codes, the style codes definitions themselves are deleted. The [Style On] and [Style off] codes are deleted, but all the formatting codes which were in the style are inserted in their place. This is a way to "*lock*" the format to insure that it isn't easily changed. And that works both ways; while someone else can't easily change everything globally, neither can you.

Including Codes: If you choose to delete the styles including the codes, then both the style and the codes within them are deleted throughout the entire file. You'd choose this option when you want to strip a file clean of all formatting codes from styles.

Definition Only: If you delete the style but leave the definition (the way 5.0 did), then the style will disappear from your list of styles, but the style code will remain in your file, complete with all the formatting codes inside it. One strange thing about this feature is that even though you delete the style from the list, it can and will reappear automatically.

```
Styles

  Name         Type     Description

  Bibliogrphy  Paired   Bibliography
  Doc Init     Paired   Initialize Document Style
  Document     Outline  Document Style
  eggplant     Paired   Breaded, Deep Fried
  Pleading     Open     Header for numbered pleading paper
  Right Par    Outline  Right-Aligned Paragraph Numbers
  Tech Init    Open     Initialize Technical Style
  Technical    Outline  Technical Document Style

Delete Styles: 1 Leaving Codes: 2 Including Codes: 3 Definition Only: 0
```

There are three ways to delete a style.

This isn't a bug, it's a feature. I call it the "Gas Light" feature, because it's insidiously designed to drive you insane. You delete the style and go about your business and the next time you're back in the style list, there's that style. You were *sure* you deleted it, but maybe not. You delete it again. It reappears again. Pretty soon people find you drooling at your keyboard and putting your car keys in the freezer. Don't let this happen to you.

Remember, if you move the cursor past a "deleted" style where you've only deleted the definition, the style name will reappear in the list of styles as if you hadn't deleted it at all. I don't understand it, it doesn't make sense to me, but that's the way it is. Accept it and get on with your life.

5.0: To delete a style, press the [DEL] key. The style codes will remain in the text and can be edited if you create a new style using the old name.

◆ Please delete me, let me go . . .

Styles can take up a lot of room, and worse, they can get confusing when you have too many, as in a master style list used for a lot of different type of documents. Here's a good trick (for 5.1 only) which allows you to delete only those styles you haven't used in a particular document.

Delete ALL your styles, making sure you choose to delete the Definition only. This will leave the styles in the document. Do not choose "Leaving codes" or "Including codes." Move the cursor to the end of the document. Any styles you've used will reappear on the list.

5.0 users: If you delete all your styles they will be permanently deleted from the list. However, any styles you placed in the document will still be there, full of their original codes. If you want to put them back in the list, block the styles, then select "Copy" (Control-F4). Go into Styles, create a style with the same name, and press ENTER in edit. This will copy the codes from the style in the document into a new style with the same name on the list. As long as the style has the same name, it will control the styles in your document.

◆ Renaming a style

When you rename a style, WordPerfect will ask if you want to rename all the styles by that name throughout the document. If you answer Y, WordPerfect will change all the names. If you answer N, WordPerfect won't. If you elect for WordPerfect *not* to change the names of the styles in the document, what you've basically done is copied the old style with a new name. All the old styles will remain in the document with the old name, and once you move the cursor past one of these styles, it will automatically be added again to your list of styles.

5.0: If you rename a style it will *not* rename the styles in your document.

❖ *Hard facts about the Enter option*

There's one more option you should be aware of at this point. I didn't explain about the "Enter" option because you'll rarely ever want to change it. (Doesn't "The Enter Option," sound like a spy novel title—something about revolving doors?)

To go into styles, press

ALT-F8

Now, move the cursor to a style and press

E

Notice #5 "Enter." This feature only appears on paired styles; it allows you to change how the Enter key works when it's inside a style.

◆ Normal

Press **E** and three choices will appear. If you press **H**, the Return/Enter key will do just that, return or enter. The style will remain on. I find this to be the most practical and efficient method, since the code only turns off when I specifically turn it off. At times I may need to place hard returns in my text, and I wouldn't want them to turn off a style.

◆ Off

If you press **F** the style will turn off the first time you press **[ENTER]** after you have turned the style on. Pressing an *additional* **[ENTER]** will begin a new line.

```
Styles: Edit

     1 - Name              subhead

     2 - Type              Paired

     3 - Description       A subhead with a ruling line above

     4 - Codes

     5 - Enter             HRt






Enter: 1 Hrt: 2 Off: 3 Off/On: 0
```

The often confusing "Enter" option can change the way the ENTER key works when in a Paired Style.

◆ Off/On

The most enigmatic of these choices is O. By pressing the **[ENTER]** key you can turn a code off, then back on. If you can discover a truly effective way to use this feature, write me, because I can't.

Yes, I know what it's supposed to do, and it does, but once you've used it, editing can become quite difficult. Here's an example. Retrieve the style sheet named "LIBRARY.STY." I'm getting ahead of myself here, but it's important to elaborate upon this point.

The file Library.Sty should be in the same directory as your WordPerfect program. If it isn't, use the install program and answer "Y" to install the Style Library.

F7 R LIBRARY.STY [ENTER]

(You may have to type the complete path of your WordPerfect program, such as C:\wp51\library.sty) Once the list of styles is on-screen, press

F7

5.0 users (and *some* 5.1 users if the example above doesn't work): Press ALT-F8, move the cursor to "RightPar" and press O. Skip the next three keystroke commands, then start again at the word *Bingo*.

We're going to demonstrate using an outline style, so we have to define paragraph numbering and turn outlining on. Press

SHIFT-F5 D N

Move the cursor to the style called "Right Par." To seLect this style press

[ENTER]

(This is one of the few places in the program where select isn't "S" so don't let it throw you.)

The Setup menu (SHIFT-F1 L) allows you to specify which style sheet will be the "default." It will automatically be loaded with each new file you create.

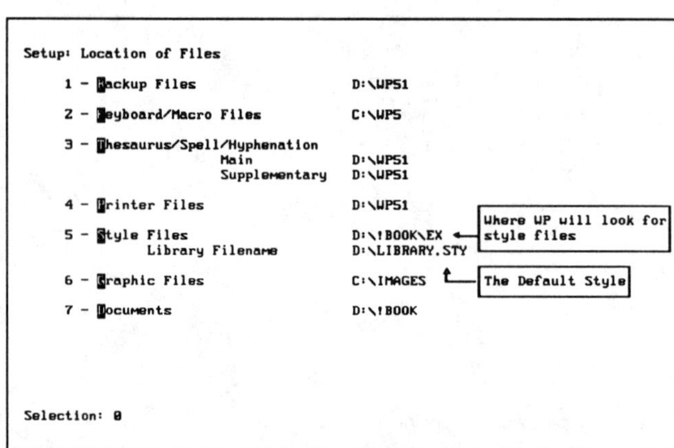

Now we're going get out of the definition, and turn on outlining.

[ENTER] O O

Press return to start automatic outlining. *Bingo*! You'll notice that an automatic paragraph number has been created. When you press a single return, a double return appears on-screen, along with the paragraph number and indented paragraphs. Type a couple of paragraphs here so you have something to work with. C'mon, it's fun (but little do you know what you're getting into.)

Now the mystery and intrigue begins. Why don't you try to combine two of those numbered lines? You can't simply backspace as you normally would to combine two paragraphs. If you do, (and you're not in Reveal Codes) WordPerfect will ask if you want to delete the Style On, and then ask about the Style Off. If you answer **N**, you can't combine the paragraphs. If you answer **Y**, the paragraphs combine, but they lose all their formatting in the bargain: the automatic number, the indent, the whole shebang.

Of course, you could have blocked the second paragraph, deleted it, and then undeleted it back in the first paragraph, but that's tedious (at least for someone with a limited frustration span such as myself).

The biggest drawback is that it just plain gets in the way. It makes editing slower, and in the end, you don't gain very much.

◆ Right out in the open

Now, there's a solution to this mess. If these were open styles, they could still be automatic and there wouldn't be a problem when you tried to join two paragraphs. There's no reason for these to be paired styles, so let's change them.

First, delete all the text in this document, except for the outline definition and the outline on code. Now let's change the style. Press

ALT-F8

Move the cursor to the "Right Par" Style. Press

E T O [DOWN ARROW] T O [DOWN ARROW] T O

Once the styles are changed to Open, you'll see that the "Enter" choice has disappeared entirely. If you press

C

you'll notice that the [Comment] is gone, as are any codes which followed it. (You'll also notice that your entire office has been repainted and has new furniture in it. This is a powerful command.) To get back to the editing screen, press

F7 F7 F7

The styles are now open styles. You'll still get a right aligned paragraph number automatically, but you won't have the hassle. If you want to combine two items on your list, you will have to delete the open style at the beginning of the second item, but this won't affect the numbering of the first item.

The paragraph number will appear, and when you type, the text is indented. The only difference is when you press return, that's all you get—a return. If you need another automatic number and an indent, just press **SHIFT-F5 P [ENTER]**. If that's too much trouble, create a macro (see Chapter 17, Macros). Or, if you turn outlining on with **SHIFT-F5 O O**, then these paragraph numbers will be inserted automatically each time you press **[ENTER]**. Personally, I find this less of a nuisance than having to edit in a special way simply to accommodate my formatting (but hey, that's just me).

5.1 NOTE: If you encounter weirdness (as one of my beta testers did), you'll need to clear everything and start over again. It *will* work.)

5.0 users: To use this new, improved style, press ALT-F8 O.

➾ Here's a hint for bringing back a style you've deleted by accident. Make sure the cursor is in the exact same place it was when you deleted the style, and then press **F1** (the Cancel Key).

❖ *Out and out Outline Styles*

A single outline style (available in 5.1 only) actually contains 8 styles, one for each level of an outline. Each of these styles can be either paired or open, and contain all the features of regular styles. They are applied automatically while in outline mode or manually when you insert an automatic paragraph number.

The nice thing about these styles is they automatically change when you change the outline level of the paragraph they are in. If you promoted a second level paragraph to first level, the style would change to first level as well. WordPerfect's outline feature does not allow for "collapsing," the way other outline programs do, but it does allow for moving levels and moving sections (or Families, as WordPerfect calls it).

Let's quickly create one, and then I'll show you how to use it. Press

ALT-F8 C T T

WordPerfect will now ask for the name of the outline style. Let's call this one...

Pickles [ENTER]

WordPerfect now asks for a "Level Number." Of course, if you're anything like me, you might think it's asking you to choose which level of Hell you want to spend eternity in, but that's not the case. In reality, WordPerfect simply wants to know how many levels deep your outline will go.

For the life of me I couldn't figure out what business it was of WordPerfect's how deep I wanted to go. The reason has nothing to do with WordPerfect being a nosy busybody and all to do with how most outlines are constructed. The last level of most outlines is not the single line of text that the other levels are, but complete paragraphs. If you tell WordPerfect your outline will be three levels deep, the first two levels will be open styles and the last level will be a paired style.

This way, when you are on level 1 or level 2 and press return, WordPerfect inserts a new outline style code, assuming that you are creating the next piece of the outline. When you are on level 3, however (or whatever you say is your last), WordPerfect creates a paired style which allows you to press [ENTER] as much as you want without creating another outline number. Once you turn off the paired style and press [ENTER], another automatic paragraph style will appear.

OK, enough theory. Let's make this a three level outline. Press

3

WordPerfect displays a list of 8 levels of outline styles. Each level is a separate style. Let's begin work on the first level. The cursor will be sitting on Level 1. To edit it, press

C

There will be only one code in the style, [Par Num:1]. This is an automatic paragraph number code. We're going to insert an indent code after it, to indent the text after the number. Press

[RIGHT ARROW] F4 F7

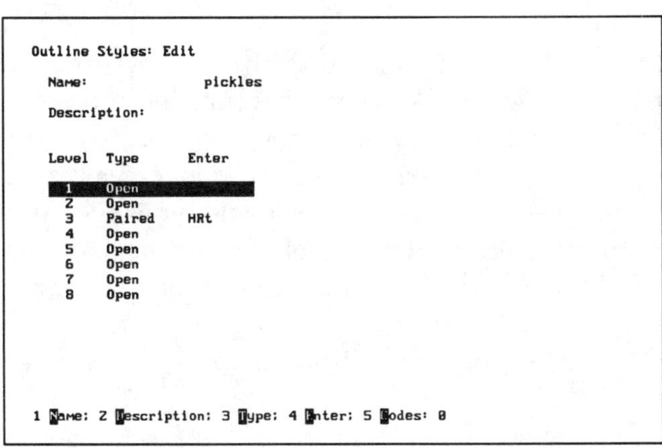

```
Outline Styles: Edit

  Name:                 pickles

  Description:

  Level  Type     Enter

    1    Open
    2    Open
    3    Paired   HRt
    4    Open
    5    Open
    6    Open
    7    Open
    8    Open

1 Name: 2 Description: 3 Type: 4 Enter: 5 Codes: 0
```

The classically beautiful Outline Style Menu.

Move to the next level and give it a tab before the automatic number, and an indent after it.

[DOWN ARROW] C [TAB] [RIGHT ARROW] F4 F7

Very nicely done. Are you sure you haven't done this before in a previous life? Even though there are eight levels, you don't have to bother with all of them, just the ones you need. Let's edit the third level and call it quits. On second thought, let's call it Daphne.

No, all seriousness aside, you can place any code you want into an outline style, just like any other style—except another style. Remember, you can't place a style inside a style and live to tell about it. Now edit the third level. Press

[DOWN ARROW] C F4 F4 F4 F7

Do I hear you saying, "Hey, wait a second. We didn't put anything in the closing half of the paired style. Why didn't we just make it into a open style?" Haven't you been paying attention or did you just flip to this page or what? Remember, just a few paragraphs back I explained that it's a paired style because until you turn it off you can hit return without creating another automatic outline style code. Geez. And you were doing so well for a minute there. Let's start outlining and try to forget that you ever asked such an obvious question. Let's turn it on. Press

F7 O

Huh. Nothing happened. Let's try again. I've got it, press "O" again, but press it REALLY REALLY hard. Yeah, that'll do it...

{really hard} O

Zip. Nada. Zilch. Well. If this doesn't take the cake. What is this world coming to? Oh. I forgot. We can only apply these styles in outlining mode or by inserting an automatic paragraph number. Never mind. Let's leave this now. Press

F7

There's one more ordeal to complete before we can reap the benefits of outline styles. We must bring back the golden fleece. Oh, sorry, I was thinking of the Hercules movies. My favorite part of those movies was when some creature would tell Hercules "never believe what you see," and of course he sees all kinds of really awful stuff and gets scared, but then tries real hard not to believe it and survives because of it. I loved that part. I use that in my daily life. I never believe anything I see. Not the bill for the mortgage, not the MasterCard bill, none of it. They come in the mail and I say, "Honey, I don't believe these bills." And I survive because of it. Someday I hope to be able to afford a golden fleece, but I think Selsdon, my sheep, might get jealous.

Where was I? Does anyone really care anymore? Right, you care, you wanted to learn about outline styles and really couldn't care less about my predilection for bad Italian movies or black sheep. Sorry. Please forgive me. Don't return the book to the publisher or complain to the manager of your bookstore. I promise it won't happen again. (Honey, do you think they believed that?)

OK, our final trial is to define the paragraph number format. If we don't do this, how can we expect WordPerfect to know which style to use? No, software is not yet psychic, let's just humor it. Press

SHIFT-F5 D

Now there are several options here, very few of which we care about. No, that's not true. Geez, I guess maybe I'm just preoccupied with the thought that lightning is going to strike our house again and melt another TV, I don't know.

At this menu we can control a number of options. We can tell WordPerfect what number to start at; what format to use for the numbers themselves; whether we want a number entered automatically when we press [ENTER]; whether we want each new level to be the same as the last one, or go back to the first one; and what we've all been waiting seven paragraphs for, to tell WordPerfect which style to use for outlines.

WordPerfect will automatically default to "outline" numbering format with roman numerals, upper case letters, then numbers. If you want a different type of numbering, press P, L, B, or if you want to come up with your own system (which can use any character in the WP character set (use Control-2 instead of Control-V), press U.

What we're most concerned with at the moment, is pressing

N

```
Paragraph Number Definition

     1 - Starting Paragraph Number                1
           (in legal style)
                                                   Levels
                                 1     2     3     4     5     6     7     8
     2 - Paragraph               1.    a.    i.   (1)   (a)   (i)    1)    a)
     3 - Outline                 I.    A.    1.    a.   (1)   (a)    i)    a)
     4 - Legal (1.1.1)           1    .1    .1    .1    .1    .1    .1    .1
     5 - Bullets                 •     o     -     ■     ⌘     +     •     x
     6 - User-defined

     Current Definition          1.    a.    i.   (1)   (a)   (i)    1)    a)
     Attach Previous Level             No    No    No    No    No    No    No

     7 - Enter Inserts Paragraph Number           Yes

     8 - Automatically Adjust to Current Level    Yes

     9 - Outline Style Name                       pickles


Selection: 0
```

If you want WordPerfect to automatically apply outline styles, you've got to give it a hint as to which style to use.

WordPerfect will display a list of the available outline styles. (You can have as many as you want.) Move the cursor to the one you want (Pickles) and press

L

I know, I know, everywhere else in the program "S" selects, but right now it doesn't. If it bothers you that much you can just press [ENTER] instead. If you want WordPerfect to use an outline style, and just want an automatic paragraph number code, you could move the cursor to - -none- - party pooper. Press

[ENTER] O O

We've just saved the definition, and turned outline mode on. Now, to see what you have wrought, press

[ENTER]

There it is—the automatic paragraph number, and an indent code. Go ahead, indulge yourself, type some text. When you press

[ENTER]

again, you get another number. If you want to move to the next level of the outline, before you type anything, press

[TAB]

Faster than you can say "Is it just me or is this kind of boring?", you are now at level two of the outline. Type another bit of text, then press

[ENTER]

again. Not only did it create a new number, but at the same level as the last one. Type a little more, then press

[ENTER] [TAB]

one mo' time. We're now at level three. If we press [ENTER] now, we don't get a number because we're in that paired style. If we want to get out of this style before sanity sinks slowly into the sunset, we can press

[RIGHT ARROW] {or} ALT-F8 F

Just for fun, press

[ENTER]

again. We're back at level 2. How do we get level 1? Just press

SHIFT-[TAB]

(also known as margin release) and you move backwards to the previous outline level.

Just to remove any remaining mystery from outline styles, let's do one more thing. Make a few more level 1's, and a few more level 2's and 3's under them. Then, turn outline mode off by pressing

SHIFT-F5 O F

If you've done good, it should look something like:

1. What women like about men.
a. They kill bugs.
b. They're amusing.
c. Their brains are so slow it's fun to torment them.

> Brute strength, stupidity, and a sense of humor were all the women who responded to the survey were interested in.

2. What women dislike about men.
a. They don't kill *enough* bugs.
b. They're not as funny as a puppy.
c. Their brains are too slow.

> Women seem to complain that they dislike the exact same things about men they like about them. The real question here is, why do women bother with men? The answer? Ah, but you'll have to buy my next book for that. It's titled *Women Who Are Mean to Men and the Men Who Love Them for It.*

(Don't send me letters about this—my wife collaborated with me on it and it's a joke. If you don't think it's funny, just reverse the roles or make up your own statements.)

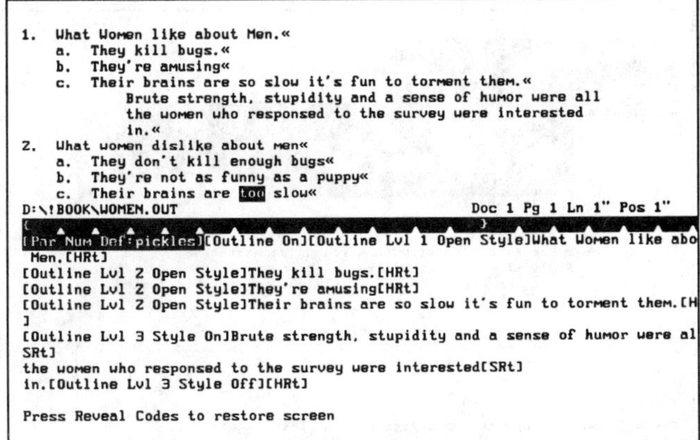

"Look my way, and a thousand violins begin to play" ... oh, wrong caption. Here's how the codes look for the outline above.

Now we didn't go through all of this just for a few outline letters, no sir. We don't need no stinkin' outline letters. What we need is some semblance of outlining. Well, hold onto your sombrero because here it comes. What outlining allows you to do is to treat entire limbs of the outline tree as individual units. Let's say we want to take one of the sub-levels of level II (in this case c., "Their brains are too slow") and make it a sub level of level I. Move the cursor to the first position after the number and press

[TAB]

Zingo. It moves down a level. Keep it there and press

SHIFT-[TAB]

Watch it move up a level. But wait, it gets better. Let's say we wanted to move the entire branch of this family tree. We wanted "What women dislike about men" to come before "What women like about men." OK, fine. Be that way. Move the cursor to anywhere in the line that says "What women dislike about men" and press

SHIFT-F5 O M

The entire branch is now highlighted. To move it up before "What women like about men," press

[UP ARROW]

The whole paragraph will move, and remain highlighted, just in case you want to move it somewhere else. Now we decide this is too negative and that men might take offense, so we want to move it back. No sweat, it's still highlighted, so just press

[DOWN ARROW]

But we're not through yet. (Haven't you learned by now that you're not getting off the hook that easily?) We've changed our minds again (not only a woman's

Outline styles allow you to move an entire branch of an outline tree. And you don't even need a working knowledge of horticulture. (As Dorothy Parker once said: "You can lead a 'ho to culture, but you can't make her think.")

```
1.  What women dislike about men«
    a.  They don't kill enough bugs«
    b.  They're not as funny as a puppy«
    c.  Their brains are too slow«
          Women seem to complain that they dislike the exact
          same things about men that they like about them. The
          real questions here is, why do women bother with men?
          The answer? Ah, but you'll have to buy my next book
          for that. It's titled, Womeon who are mean to men and
          the men who love them for it.«
2.  What Women like about Men.«
    a.  They kill bugs.«
    b.  They're amusing«
    c.  Their brains are so slow it's fun to torment them.«
          Brute strength, stupidity and a sense of humor were all
          the women who responsed to the survey were interested
          in.«

Press Arrows to Move the Partridge Family; Enter when done.
```

prerogative), and we decide that we want "What women dislike" to be part of "What women like" instead of a whole separate branch. OK, no problem-o. Press

[RIGHT ARROW]

Faster than you can say, "I should have had a V-8," the whole branch has moved to the right, one level. The only fly in this otherwise 99.99% pure ointment is that we didn't set up level 4 of the outline, so it just sits there kind of pathetically, no indent, no nothing. We can take care of that, though. First, unhighlight the outline by pressing

[ENTER]

Then move the cursor to "Women seem to complain" and press

SHIFT-F5 O M [LEFT ARROW]

The natural tendency is to press the [RIGHT ARROW] because you want it to move right, but because it's really at level 4 and we want to move it to level 3, we press the [LEFT ARROW]. One final change and then we can go watch something mindless on TV. Let's take this current branch (Women seem to want), make it level 2, and move it up. Press

[LEFT ARROW] [UP ARROW]

Notice that the entire branch moved all the way above item D. One thing you might have noticed is that outline styles are the only types where WordPerfect can automatically change an open style into a paired style, and vice versa. It doesn't change them when you change the definition, however, just when you promote or demote them in the outline itself.

OK, so the excitement is waning (it's not my fault, outlines are not intrinsically exciting). But here's a way to make them so exciting that you might just spontaneously combust.

◆ Hey, big number

One of the hallmarks of the Mac-ish style I normally deplore is giant-sized numbers. I still denounce the Apple ads that lead you to believe serious business people sit around poring over cutesy pictures. However, these outlines with large numbers are lighthearted and quite effective as attention grabbers. The numbers are used in outlines in the same way raised caps would be used in paragraphs.

A few words of warning regarding graphic design since we are treading on Machiavellian territory. These big numbers can easily overshadow the actual content of the outline. They're a good device for diverting attention if you don't want people to read too closely. But if careful and prolonged work with the outline is required, or the subject is formal or serious, these big numbers will probably be obtrusive. Also, this Mac-hination is best for small outlines; on long outlines they become tedious or just plain silly.

Now that you've been warned, go ahead, live the Mac fantasy, but at a fraction of the cost. Intimidate your business acquaintances. Sit on the terrace of your beach house and intone, "We did that in-house, on our computer system, with just a word processing program." Sneer at them smugly when they snivel, whine, and beg to know what type of computer you used. Don't give in too much—just say: "Not a Mac . . . something less expensive and more efficient."

This style automatically numbers the paragraph by using WordPerfect's numbering feature (the #s automatically update when you change the outline, saving you tons-o-time and aggravation), makes the number big and bold, and then indents the body of the outline to the next tab stop.

IMPORTANT: Make sure to set the line height to fixed in your document. If you don't, the big numbers will make the line spacing uneven.

You don't have to limit this formatting to outline styles; you could use it for any type of style. It's just that outline styles will be applied automatically. Make sure to choose a proportional font (not Courier), otherwise the Size Very Large won't do anything (except on PostScript and LaserMaster printers).

Create an open style called BIG NUM by pressing

ALT-F8 C N Big Number [ENTER] T O C

CONTROL-F6 SHIFT-F5 P [ENTER] [LEFT ARROW]

ALT-F4 [END] CONTROL-F8 S V

Pressing CONTROL-F6 commands WordPerfect to temporarily make the next tab a decimal tab and align the number of the decimal. This allows for a neater presentation when the numbers go from 9 to 10, or from 99 to 100.

ALT-F4 CONTROL-[HOME] CONTROL-[HOME] F6

[END] F4

The codes should look like this:

[DEC TAB][BOLD][VRY LARGE][Par

Num:**1**][vry large][bold][-Indent]

You'll have to turn this style on for each numbered paragraph, and if you want anything other than the default roman numerals, you'll have to use define **SHIFT-F5 D** to tell WordPerfect what type of numbers you want.

◆ Outside numbers

You can take this one step further (some might say one step too far). We can "outdent" the number itself. This will cause the numbers to pop out one tab stop to the left. The indent code will cause the rest of the paragraph to align with the normal margins. To do this, you need go back into styles, and, with your cursor at the very tippy top of the file, press

SHIFT-[TAB]

AKA, dba [Mar Rel] or Margin Release to you and I. This will outdent the line to the previous tab stop. [Mar Rel] reminds me of a band I once saw called the *Mar Dels.* They were from Del Mar. If that isn't funny enough, the band leader could play two saxophones at the same time: one right side up, the other upside down. And as if that weren't enough, he also played the piano and sang, all at the same time. That's what I call entertainment value.

For more entertainment value, other outlining tips (and perhaps another music review), see Chapter 8, *Alignment,* and Chapter 17, *Macros.*

❖ *It's not my default*

If you want WordPerfect to automatically load a specific style library whenever you create a new document, you can tell WordPerfect to do so. *Any* group of styles which you have saved to disk can be a library and you can name the file anything you want.

To set a special directory for styles, press

SHIFT-F1 L S

Type the directory you want WordPerfect to save and retrieve style files from.

You can take this all a step further and tell WordPerfect the file you want as your "library." To do that press

[ENTER]

Then type in the complete path name of the file containing the styles that you want to become defaults. The subdirectories must also be included in the full path name. Here's an example: \WP50\STYLES\IZZY.STY. While you can name the default style whatever you want (it doesn't have to be in a directory called STYLES, have the file name IZZY, or end in the letters .STY), the file name alone isn't enough. Use the whole path name so that if you change directories in WordPerfect, the program knows where to look for the file. To finish up, press

F7 F7

Once you do this, WordPerfect will automatically load the style library you've specified into each new file you open.

❖ *Save that thought*

If flexibility and consistency are the two major reasons for using style libraries, it's only natural that these benefits extend beyond one single library.

Any big project should be broken down into individual chunks or chapters. This allows for improved comprehension and is easier and faster for WordPerfect to process. While WordPerfect can theoretically handle documents thousands of pages long, it's most efficient when files are kept well under 100 pages.

If you want format 17 chapters consistently, you don't have to recreate the style for each document. WordPerfect allows you to save a group of styles into a style library and then load it into another document. Even after you've created a style library, you can still load a different library into the file. You can overwrite styles with the same name or load only the styles that don't already exist.

If you're up to this pulse-pounding excitement, follow along with me in this next example.

◆ Saving a style library

Press **ALT-F8** to enter the style menu. Press **S** to save the styles to a separate file. WordPerfect will ask you for a file name. It's advisable to end style library with .STY because it makes them easier to distinguish from files containing text. It's not, however, mandatory, so if you want to end all your style librarys with .POO (for your favorite bear), go right ahead.

If the name you select already exists, WordPerfect asks you to press **Y** (to write over it) or (**N** to choose another name), just as it does when you save a file.

◆ Retrieving a style library

For this example, we'll be using a style library that came with WordPerfect. However, you can also retrieve style libraries you've made yourself, or styles from any WordPerfect file that contains styles.

ALT-F8 R F5 [ENTER]

That's right. You can access good old List Files right here. Move the cursor to the file you want (in this case it's the library.sty file which comes with WordPerfect, and it should be in your WordPerfect program directory). Move the cursor to the file and to retrieve the style file, press

R

If the name of any of the current styles matches the name of a style in the file you are retrieving, WordPerfect will say "Style(s) already exist. Replace? Y/N?" If you answer **Y**, WordPerfect loads the new style, replacing and deleting the old one. If you answer **N**, WordPerfect loads all the styles that don't have the same name, but leaves the ones with the matching names unchanged.

❖ *Tip: Sharesies, sharesies*

If you want to load the style sheet from a particular file, but forgot to save it to its own file, don't worry. You can extract the styles from a file, even if you haven't saved them separately.

Once you press **R** for retrieve (from within the styles menu), you can type the name of the document file (as opposed to a style library) that contains the styles you want and press **[ENTER]**. WordPerfect will only retrieve the styles, not the text within a document. This will also work if you use List Files from the styles menu.

◆ Updating

If you've selected a default style library (SHIFT-F1 L S), WordPerfect provides you with an extra convenience. Let's say you're sharing a style library between several different files, as in the chapters of a book. You've created a style called "subhead" and now want to change all the subheads in all the book files.

You can change the styles from within any of the chapters. Press

ALT-F8 S

Save the style library, using the name of the existing library. WordPerfect will ask if you want to overwrite the file. Answer **Y** for yes. The changes will be saved to the default style library.

When you load another chapter, simply update the styles by pressing

ALT-F8 U

for Update. WordPerfect will copy all the styles from the default file into your current file.

Warning: This will **overwrite** all the styles with the same name in your current file and the default style library. It will do this *without warning*, and will not even have the courtesy of asking you to confirm first. However, it will not delete any new styles you might have added to this chapter.

❖ How high the line for 5.0

This is for 5.0 users only: WordPerfect 5.0's automatic line height does not always give you sufficient leading. That's why I add the Line Height Fixed command to my styles.

If you are using specific point sizes, remember to add 1 point to the leading. All you have to do is include a Fixed Line Height command inside the style: **SHIFT-F8 L H F**. Now enter a number that is 1 point larger than the size of the font, followed by a **P** (so WordPerfect knows that the measurement is in points). If you were using 10-point type, you'd enter **11P**.

If you are using size attributes such as Large, Very Large, and Extra Large, remember that these sizes are based on the size of the body text. Large is 20% bigger, Very Large is 80% bigger, and Extra Large is 250% bigger. Take that into consideration when you are setting the line height.

❖ Graphics secrets

Almost every WordPerfect command can be placed in a style. The most notable exception is graphics files. Graphics boxes can be placed in styles, but not graphics files. However, you can get around this by specifying that the graphic file is "on-disk."

5.0: If you wanted to create a style for a newsletter that contained a logo with an accompanying graphic, you could not place the entire logo into the style. You would need to use a paired style, and place the graphics box between the opening and closing style codes.

5.1: You can place any graphic inside a style as long as it is marked as "on-disk." When a graphic is "on-disk," it is not stored as part of the WordPerfect file, but is kept in its original format in your graphics directory (which you set up by pressing SHIFT-F1 L G). When you go to view or print a page, WordPerfect loads the file from the disk. *If* you have moved or deleted the file, however, WordPerfect will just leave the space blank and will not tell you that the file is missing.

WordPerfect also has a quirk (it's not a bug or a feature) about creating graphics boxes between paired style codes. If you put the cursor between the two style codes and create a graphics box, the box code will appear *following* the closing style code.

A more important problem (possibly a bug, clearly not a feature) is that sometimes the graphics box may not even be created, or may somehow place itself inside the style (as it did when I used the "Subheading" style from the LIBRARY.STY file on the Conversion disk). The graphic completely disappeared the next time I changed a style and they were updated.

All of this could cause you much grief, but in return for your loyal readership, I'm going to tell you how to get around this problem by letting you in on a hard-earned secret.

The first solution is to place any type of text, even a space, between the two codes, and then create the graphics box. That one tiny space will cause the graphics box code to appear between the paired style markers.

If you should forget this trick and find that the graphics box appears outside of the styles, delete the graphics box code, move between the two codes, and press **F1 R.**

◆ Intercolumn rules

WordPerfect will not automatically place vertical lines between columns on all pages. (These lines are not surprisingly called "intercolumn rules.") You can remedy this by putting the intercolumn rules inside an open style that is placed on every page. For more information about using lines in styles, see Chapter 14, *Rules*.

❖ *Table simulation*

Believe it or not, there *are* times when you'd rather use columns than tables, such as in running text that isn't easily encapsulated into a table. Because WordPerfect styles can contain column definition commands, you can reuse column definitions without having to recreate them.

This is especially useful when you create complicated uneven width columns or tables. The advantage of using styles for tables (whether they are created with tabs or columns) is that styles guarantee the tabs, margins, and columns will be consistent even if you change them for the rest of the document. Also, with a paired style, everything (tabs, margins, columns) reverts to normal after the closing code of the style.

To create a "table" style, create a paired style that contains specific column or tab settings. If you want to get fancy, with a horizontal line above and below the table, move the cursor to before the [Comment] code and press

ALT-F9 L H [ENTER]

Then move the cursor after the [Comment] code and press

ALT-F9 L H [ENTER]

❖ Headers, footers, and all that jazz

While I don't recommend putting headers and footers into styles, I do recommend putting styles into headers and footers. This is not unlike taking the girl out of the country and yet being unable to take the country out of the girl.

The only trick to using headers and footers is that they must be among the first codes on a page. This means you can have other codes before them, but if you place any text, and I'm talking anything, even a period, before the header or footer code, it won't take effect until the *next* page.

This is a bummer, because 5.0 wasn't quite so persnickety. In 5.0, footers will print on the page as long as they're anywhere on the page, even near the bottom. But with 5.1, you can't place footers in the middle of the page and expect them to print at the bottom. This actually is a problem because it means that your footers are not going to be as up to date in 5.1 as they can be in 5.0. Ah well, you can't have everything. ("But I *want* everything!" you say, whining ever so slightly. You're a grown-up now, it's about time you learned that you can't always get what you want. Blow your nose and let's get on with the rest of the chapter.)

Serious Warning: (Try to imagine submarine depth-charge alert noises here such as "Wooop Wooop.") If you place a header in a style, WordPerfect will dupe you into thinking that you can edit it from within the text. You will see it, edit it, even View Document with the changes in place. But if you edit any style, WordPerfect will go back through the document and update the codes (including the header that you changed) with the current style codes. The changes you made will be lost and you will be mightily confused, if not downright irate.

If you are using a standard header or footer that you know you won't change, it's fine to include it in the "Topper" style (to be covered momentarily). You can edit the header or footer if you remember to go into the style editor and change it. My problem is that I tend to forget, edit it from the regular text, and then pull out little clumps of hair when my changes disappear. (I don't know about you, but I don't have enough hair or Minoxidil left to afford losing little clumps on a regular basis.)

Now that you've been duly warned, I'll tell you how to use styles inside headers or footers for consistency. Create an Open style that contains all the formatting for a header or footer, but not the header or footer itself.

Here's an example of a footer that has a ruling line above:

```
[Hline:Left & Right,6.5",.05",1][HRt]

[AdvDn:.01"][Font:Helv 8pt][Flsh Rt]Page ^B
```

This code inserts a horizontal ruling line, advances text down an additional .1" (one return isn't enough, two is too much), changes the font, and even sets the page number flush right.

```
Chapter 10«
Style Sheets«
«
Flexibility and consistency: the two major reasons for using
style sheets. With them you can change the style of a document
repeatedly in the least amount of time, and make sure that the
elements remain uniform within that document, or a whole slew of
documents.«
     While the idea of style sheets isn't new, the way
WordPerfect implements it is. Even if you are familiar with style
sheets in Ventura Publisher or Microsoft Word, it will not be of
C:\WP5\P\WP10.TW                              Doc 2 Pg 1 Ln 1" Pos 1"
[Open Style:topper:[Paper Sz/Typ:11" x 8.5",Standard][T/B Mar:0.5",0.3"][L/R Mar
:0.5",0.5"][Font:Stalagtite Roman 36 pt (UKASCII) (Land)][Ln Height:0.5"][Tab Se
t:1.5",3",3.75",6.5",7",8.5"]][Footer A:Z: ... ]Chapter 10[HRt]
Style Sheets[HRt]
[HRt]
Flexibility and consistency: the two major reasons for using[SRt]
style sheets. With them you can change the style of a document[SRt]
repeatedly in the least amount of time, and make sure that the[SRt]
elements remain uniform within that document, or a whole slew of[SRt]
documents.[HRt]

Whack Reveal Codes to restore screen
```

A Topper style is placed at the top of a file, and contains global formatting commands for the entire document.

If the text in headers and footers varies from chapter to chapter, using a style in this manner will guarantee consistent formatting.

When you create a header or footer, simply press **ALT-F8**, move the cursor to the header or footer style and press **O**. The style code will appear.

❖ *Where's Cosmo?*

If you are creating a large project that has been split into many separate WordPerfect files, you can take style sheets one step further by creating what I call "Topper" files. I call them that because they contain all the codes used repeatedly at the top of each file (and because I've always liked Cosmo).

There are disadvantages to placing all these codes into a single style, especially when you use headers and footers. To change a header or footer created in a style, you'd have to first go in and edit the style and then edit the header and footer. If you accidentally edited the footer directly (not in the style editor), the next time you edited any style, WordPerfect would update all the styles. As a result, changes you made directly to the footer (not from within the style editor) would be lost.

Putting headers and footers in a style compromises your ability to share styles between files; if you updated the styles in a file, the header and footer specifics for that particular file or chapter would be lost.

Bearing all this in mind, I like to create a WordPerfect file that contains the styles I want (including header and footer styles), along with formatting, such as headers and footers, margins, even graphics boxes if they are used at the beginning of each chapter.

I also place a comment code at the end of my "Topper" file, consisting of information about what formatting is contained in the file.

◆ Library Card

Consider going into Setup, **SHIFT-F1 L L** and entering the name of the "Topper" file. Then simply press **ALT-F8 U** to update the styles from the "Topper" file to the current file.

❖ *But baby, it's cold outside*

Brrrr. It's the software equivalent of a Dove Bar!

One of the most useful features of style sheets can also be one of the most dangerous. Because a change in a style affects *all* text within that style, it's possible to change a style to suit your current purpose without remembering that those changes will also be made in the rest of the file.

With 5.0 you could simply delete the style from the list and it would remain in the document with all its codes. But 5.1 "fixes" that so you have to be even more clever.

There are three ways to "freeze" the formatting of the file. The first is to delete the styles but leave the codes. While this will ensure that you can't globally mess up something, it also defeats the purpose of styles.

But I found it very important to be able to control who can change styles, so I came up with two better alternatives.

1. Go into styles and save your styles to a file by pressing

ALT-F8 S

Enter any file name you want. This way, if someone changes your styles by accident, you only have to retrieve your correct styles.

2. This is more devious and verges on downright mean. You can completely disable the style key. To do this, look in Chapter 17, *Keys to success,* to find out how to reprogram any key on your keyboard. Once the style key has been disabled, no one can change a style even if they want to — unless they know enough about WordPerfect to change the keyboard layout themselves.

❖ *With six you get egg roll*

No, WordPerfect can't give you the ability to squeal like Doris Day. But can Doris give you the ability to use as many style sheet files as you want? WordPerfect can.

Normally one style sheet is quite sufficient, thank you. But there are times when you might want more than one. WordPerfect files can only use one style sheet at a time, but you can retrieve style sheets as often as your little heart desires.

Remember that when you retrieve a new style sheet, the style codes you've placed in the text still have the same name; only the formatting codes within them change. When you retrieve a new style sheet, only those styles with the same name as the ones in use will have any immediate impact. The others will be added to the list of files but won't function until you turn them on.

Here's a prime example. Suppose you have several standard types of documents: a report, a newsletter, and a standard draft format. Your draft format is Courier, double spaced, 1.5" margins on both sides, 1" margin on the top and bottom. You use this format for printing drafts so that there's plenty of room to write notes. You have a style sheet called DRAFT.STY for this format.

As you write, you know what will be used as a headline or subhead, so you include those styles. The draft style sheet centers, emboldens, and underlines headlines, and emboldens subheads with two extra spaces above each one.

Once you've completed the text corrections, you should format the text into a standard two-column report. Retrieve the REPORT.STY and zap: the text is set ragged right in two columns with hyphenation, the headline is Extra Large, the subheads are large and bold with ruling lines above. The document is complete with footers and ready to go. Total time for formatting: about 15 seconds. Finally, consider adding some snazzy and misleading charts and graphs (this will take 15 minutes on a good day).

You present the report, get a bonus, a raise, a company car, and a vacation in the Bahamas (remember, this is an ideal example—no one said that it had anything to do with reality).

Now it's time to take the revised report (everyone's a critic) and publish it for your customers. You retrieve the NEWSLET.STY sheet and bingo: you've got a three-column justified newsletter. The charts and graphs have re-sized themselves to fit into the new columns automatically. Total time for formatting: oh, say 15 seconds, give or take another half hour to futz around with details.

The moral of this story is that sometimes two (or three) style sheets are better than one. In this case I've included footers in the Topper style because they are standard and won't have to be customized for a series of chapters. While 5.0 allowed for "nested" styles, or styles within styles, 5.1 does not.

Here are the codes for the three style sheets. Remember, the [Comment] code is built-in to the paired style (so don't enter the comment, just the codes after it; comments meant just for you have been inserted between {} brackets and aren't to be typed into the style). Unless you see a [HRt] code, don't press return—the codes are on separate lines for clarity, but they may not appear that way on your screen. For PostScript users: Times Roman is identical to Dutch.

❖ *Draft.sty*

➾ FOOTER *(open): Selects the font, centers the text, and adds the current page number and date.*

CONTROL-F8 F {Move cursor to Courier 10}[ENTER]

SHIFT-F6 DRAFT [-] SHIFT-F5 C

{This is a date code: the current date will be printed automatically on the bottom of each page.}

[-]Page ^B [ENTER]

{The ^B is for a page number}

➾ HEADLINE *(paired): Centers, underlines, and bolds the text.*

SHIFT-F6 F6 F8[Comment] [ENTER]

[ENTER]

[ENTER]

➾ SUBHEAD *(paired): Underlines and bolds the text.*

[ENTER]

[ENTER]

F6 F8 [Comment]

➾ TOPPER *(open): Sets left/right, top/bottom margins, set margins ragged, and sets line spacing to 1.5 and adds footer.*

SHIFT-F8 L M 1.5 [ENTER] 1.5 [ENTER]

S 1.5 [ENTER]

J L [ENTER]

P M 1 [ENTER] 1 [ENTER]

[ENTER][ENTER]

CONTROL-F8 F {*Move cursor to Courier 10*}[ENTER]

❖ Report.sty

➾ FOOTER *(open): Adds a horizontal line, advances the text down, sets the font, and adds the current page number and date flush right.*

ALT-F9 L H [ENTER][ENTER]

SHIFT-F8 O A D .1" [F7][F7]

CONTROL-F8 F {*Move cursor to Dutch 10 point italic*} [ENTER]

ALT-F6 REPORT [-] SHIFT-F5 C [-] Page ^B [ENTER]

➾ HEADLINE *(paired): Centers the text and makes it Extra Large.*

SHIFT-F6 CONTROL-F8 S E [Comment] [ENTER]

➾ SUBHEAD *(paired): Makes the text Large and Bold.*

CONTROL-F8 S L F6 [Comment]

➾ TOPPER *(open): Turns hyphenation on, sets left/right, top/bottom margins, changes the font, and creates a footer.*

SHIFT-F8 L Y Y

M .5 [ENTER] .5 [ENTER]

J L [ENTER]

P M .5 [ENTER] .5 [ENTER][ENTER][ENTER]

CONTROL-F8 F {*Move cursor to Dutch 10 point*} [ENTER]

ALT-F7 C D D .3 [ENTER] [ENTER] O

❖ Newslet.sty

➾ FOOTER *(open): Same as Footer in Report.sty.*

ALT-F9 L H [ENTER][ENTER]

SHIFT-F8 O A D .1" [F7][F7]

CONTROL-F8 F {*Move cursor to Dutch 10 point italic*} [ENTER]

SHIFT-F6 NEWSLETTER NAME [-] Page ^B [ENTER]

- HEADLINE *(paired): Creates a horizontal line, advances text down, and makes it Extra Large.*

ALT-F9 L H [ENTER][ENTER]

SHIFT-F8 O A D .02" [F7][F7] F6

CONTROL-F8 S E [Comment]

- SUBHEAD *(paired): Adds a conditional end of page to keep subhead and ruling line on the same page or column as the text which follows, adds horizontal line, advances text down, and makes text Very Large.*

SHIFT-F8 O C 5 [ENTER] [F7]

[ENTER] ALT-F9 L H [ENTER]

SHIFT-F8 O A D .1" [ENTER] [F7]

CONTROL-F8 S V [Comment]

- TOPPER *(open): Turns hyphenation and justification on, sets font, left/right, top/bottom margins, adds footer, creates three columns.*

SHIFT-F8 L Y Y

J F

M .5 [ENTER] .5 [ENTER][ENTER]

P M .5 [ENTER] .5 [ENTER][ENTER][ENTER]

CONTROL-F8 F {*Move cursor to Dutch 10 point*} [ENTER]

ALT-F7 C D D .3 [ENTER] N 3 [ENTER] [ENTER] O

◆ Tip: "Topper" too

While the Topper styles I've presented so far are all open styles, there are times when you might want to use a paired style for a topper. One such situation is when you have a multi-column page and want the headline to span all the columns (as most headlines do).

In this little scenario, we create the following styles:

- TOPPER *(paired):*

L M .5 [HRt] .5 [HRt][HRt]

P M .5 [HRt] .5 [HRt][HRt][HRt]

[Comment]

ALT-F7 C D D .3 [HRt] N 3 [HRt] [HRt] O

➳ HEADLINE *(paired):*

SHIFT-F7 CONTROL-F8 S E[Comment]

Notice how the Col Def and Col On are *after* the [Comment]; this ensures that they won't go into effect until the Style Off code.

To use these styles, turn the Topper style on, be sure the cursor is highlighting the Style Off code, and turn on the HEADLINE style.

The codes will look like this:

[Style On:Topper][Style On:Headline][Style Off:Headline][Style Off:Topper]

Type the headline between the Style On:Headline and Style Off:Headline codes. The headline will be extra large and centered across the entire page, but all text following the Style Off:Topper code will be in three columns.

◆ **Tip: The name game**

Vanna vanna bo banna, banana fanna fo fanna, me my mo manna, Vanna! Yes, relive those stupid Sixties with this collection of your favorite hits! Hits like, *The Name Game!* (I only put this in so you'd remember how you used to joke around with your friends about what rhymed with "Chuck"). By the way, can you name the artist who recorded this monster hit?

Back to business. I almost always use Topper Styles even if I'm not using columns and other fancy formatting. It's reassuring to know that no matter what style sheet I load, they will all work together because they have a Topper style.

It's advisable to be consistent about what you call your styles, so that you can change style sheets at any time without having to block text and apply styles again.

Okay, so you knew the singer was Shirley Ellis. Now, for the trip to Hawaii, who wrote the song? (Big hint: his name is in the game.)

❖ *Red letterhead day*

Tired of the high cost of stationery? Fed up with running out of letterhead just when you need it most? Fatigued, listless? You've got two choices: Vitametavegamin or styles. A single style can contain an entire letterhead.

One advantage of using a style for a letterhead is that it's instantly available. You turn on the style and voila! Here are two examples of letterheads one of my favorite baddies might have used (sans the suspicious spots).

The first one is for personal use, is rather on the loud side, and takes up a good portion of the page all by itself. The second is for business purposes and is far more tasteful. However, each has its use; sometimes you want to brag, other times you want to stun them with modesty. Because these are both styles, you can choose the one best suited for you right before you print.

(Remember, don't press return unless there's a [HRt] code. Keystrokes are inside <>, and comments are inside {}.

◆ Personal (open):

[L/R Mar:0.4",0.4"][T/B Mar:0.4",0.6"][Figure:1;;]

[L/R Mar:1",1"][T/B Mar:0.3",0.3"][Footer A:1;][HRt]

[Font:Palatino 8 pt] ...][HRt]

[HRt][Font:Palatino 12 pt]

[EXT LARGE][Cntr]C[ext large]ruella

[EXT LARGE]D[ext large]e[EXT LARGE]V[ext large]ille[HRt]

[HLine:Center,Baseline, 3",0.01",100%][HRt]

[HRt]

[Cntr][Date:3 1, 4][HRt]

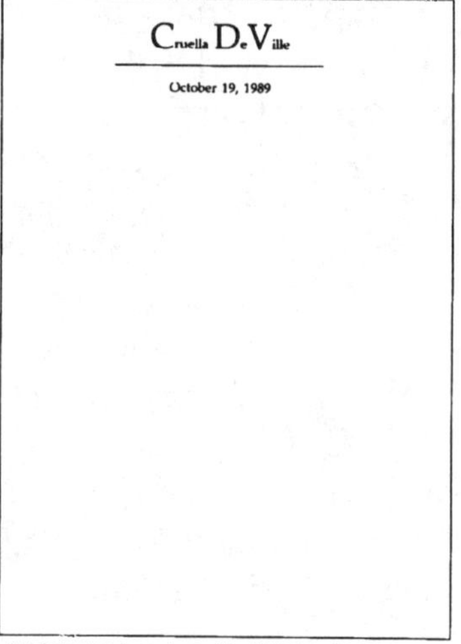

Cruella DeVille

October 19, 1989

999 Dalmation Lane, Spotsville, NY 10011, 212-555-7475

◆ Business (open):

[L/R Mar:0.4",0.4"]

[T/B Mar:0.3",0.5"][Figure:1;;]<TP VF WN>

{I've set a wide margin before the figure because it actually is a full page box with a ruling box around it, and I didn't want it to interfere with the text. Notice how I change the margin next so that the body of the letter is well within the full page box.}

[L/R Mar:1",1"][HRt]

[Font:Palatino 12 pt][EXT LARGE][Cntr]C[ext large]ruella

[EXT LARGE]D[ext large]e[EXT LARGE]V[ext large]ille[HRt]

[HLine:Center,Baseline, 3",0.01",100%][Ln Height:0.12"][HRt]

[Cntr]999 Dalmatian Lane[HRt]

[HLine:Center,Baseline, 3",0.01",100%][HRt]

[Cntr]Spotsville, NY 10011[HRt]

[HLine:Center,3",0.01",100%][HRt]

[Cntr]212[-]555[-]1212[HRt]

[Cntr][Date:3 1,4]

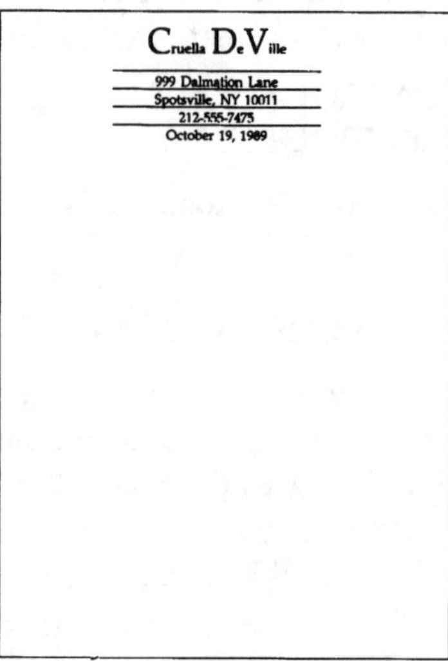
Cruella DeVille
999 Dalmation Lane
Spotsville, NY 10011
212-555-7475
October 19, 1989

If you want to create a letterhead with a graphic logo, remember to make it "on-disk." 5.0 users will need to create a separate letterhead file containing the text and the graphic. I close mine with a comment, so it's easy to delete the letterhead graphics before saving the file, thus conserving disk space. Place the cursor under the comment and just backspace until all traces of the letterhead format have been deleted.

For an example of a letterhead with a graphic, see Chapter 4, *Show & Tell*. (You'll notice I haven't included a sample of my signature on my stationery, lest anyone start signing my checks as well as duplicating my letterhead.)

❖ *Changing your mind, changing your style*

We've seen how styles can affect a paragraph, but they're also useful for text as small as a single character.

◆ Tip: Underlines become italics

Instead of pressing F8, or using **CONTROL-F8 A U** for underlines, create a paired style called UND/ITAL. Type

ALT-F8 C N UND/ITAL [ENTER] C F8 F7 F7 F7

Use this style every time you want an underline. When you are ready to print the final draft, edit this style by typing

ALT-F8

Move to the UND/ITAL style, press

E C [DEL] CONTROL-F8 A I F7 F7 F7

All previously underlined text will now appear in italics.

To hasten this even further, create a macro that will apply this style with a single keystroke. To create the macro, press

CONTROL-F10 ALT-U UND/ITAL [ENTER] ALT-F8 N UND/ITAL [ENTER] O CONTROL-F10

This will automatically summon the UND/ITAL style anytime you press **ALT-U.**

❖ *Searching and replacing styles*

What if you want to replace all the underlines with the UND/ITAL style? No can do. You can't search and replace styles because WordPerfect doesn't permit you to utilize styles as replacement text. But you can achieve identical results with a macro. No, don't start scouring through the macro chapter (you can put down that Brillo pad), I'm including it here.

In this example we're (is this like a nurse saying "Now we're going to have a shot?") going to create a macro that searches for [UND][und] codes and replaces them with the Und/Ital style you just created. (That's if you've been following along like a good reader. If you haven't been paying attention, it doesn't hurt me; it's *you* who will be sorry for it when you can't get into a good college or hold down a good job. Anyway, that's what they always told me when I was caught goofing off.)

This may seem endless, but once you've created this macro you can use it over and over again. Be aware that you must follow the directions exactly—leaving out a single keystroke will mess everything up and could even make the macro destructive. (Kind of like a little Arnold Schwarzenegger running around inside the computer. Don't you love reading stuff like that? Doesn't it make you want to give up and find a job as a mud wrestler or something?) Don't try this unless you've already created a style called "UND/ITAL" that is currently available in the list of styles.

Make sure Reveal Codes is OFF, then type:

CONTROL-F10 UND2STY [ENTER] Turn underlines to UND/ITAL style [ENTER] F2 F8 F2 ALT-F4 F2 F8 F8 [LEFT ARROW] [BACKSPACE] F2 ALT-F8 N UND/ITAL [ENTER] O [LEFT ARROW] [BACKSPACE] Y CONTROL-F10

This will find only a single set of underline codes and replace them with the style. If you want this to automatically find and replace all the underlines with the UND/ITAL style, use the same keystrokes for the macro but add the following before the last CONTROL-F10:

ALT-F10 UND2STY [ENTER]

This will repeat the macro until all the underlines have been found and replaced. In case you didn't notice, this style was a perfect segue to the next tip...

❖ *Tips, tricks & techniques*

When I first started using WordPerfect 5, I created macros that called up styles. Unfortunately, the macros would no longer work when I added or deleted styles because they were relying on cursor movements to select the correct style.

I have my own unique method for learning about software. I press every key on the keyboard, see what it does, and when it does it. I try out every feature in every conceivable way, and while this technique takes time, it works.

This method led to a solution for this macro problem. In the great tradition of American explorers, I stumbled onto a vital feature that WordPerfect's manual fails to mention.

◆ Undocumented boon—styles & macros

Okay, okay, enough breathless anticipation. The feature is none other than our friend "name search," found in almost every list WordPerfect presents. List Files, Base Font, all of these have **N** on the menu. You press it, type the name you are searching for, and WordPerfect jumps to that name.

Style offers this feature as well, although it's not on the menu (possibly because there's no room for it). Still, even if the programmers at WordPerfect didn't think it was important enough to acknowledge, I *know* that it's indispensable when you are devising macros.

Whenever you create a macro that uses a style, use the Name Search feature rather than moving the cursor to the style you want. Then, no matter how many styles you add or delete, the macro will still call up that particular style.

Call me silly, but I feel like I've discovered a planet somewhere. Maybe they'll name it after me. (Probably not.)

◆ Block protect in styles

Block protect is a useful WordPerfect feature that protects a block of text from being interrupted by column or page breaks. While the WordPerfect manual does not mention it in relation to paired styles, you can still use them together to great advantage.

To create a block protect, you turn block on with

ALT-F4

and highlight the text to be protected, then press

SHIFT-F8

To use it in a paired style, the area you've blocked should extend over the [Comment] marker.

When you press **SHIFT-F8**, WordPerfect asks you to confirm. Press **Y.** [Block Pro:On] appears at the beginning of the area and [Block Pro:Off] appears at the end of the area you blocked.

This maintains text between the Style On and Style Off in the same column or on the same page. This is especially helpful if you are including horizontal lines in styles; you don't want the line printing at the bottom of one page or column and the text at the top of another. Block protect keeps the lines with the text.

Of course, you can't block protect more than a page or WordPerfect will be forced to put in a page break anyway.

◆ Conditional end of page

This feature is similar to Block Protect and permits you to keep an absolute number of lines together.

To create a [Cndl EOP], type

SHIFT-F8 O C

and then the number of lines you want to stay together. Example: **SHIFT-F8 O C 10** dictates that the next 10 lines will stay together. If there's not room on this page, a page break will appear and all the lines will be together on the next page or column.

You must place a conditional end of page code on the line before the lines you want to keep together.

❖ *[Just on] in time (5.0 only)*

One of the petty complaints I have about WordPerfect's styles is how it handles justification. When you create a style, WordPerfect considers the default for the document as the default for the style. If you haven't changed Initial Codes using setup **SHIFT-F1 I I**, then the default is justification on.

This means that if you create a style where you turn justification off, WordPerfect will work just fine and will insert a [Just Off] code in the style. But if you want to include a [Just On] code in a style, and press **SHIFT-F8 L J Y,** WordPerfect won't enter any code in the style; it assumes it's already on, so you're not really changing anything.

The fix for this is simple. If the default is Just On and you want to include a Just On code, you should first enter a Just Off code and then another Just Off code, like this: **SHIFT-F8 L J N J Y**. Both codes will be in the style, but only the code that changes the state of justification applies.

◆ Taking it hard

If your chapters always begin a new page, consider creating a style called CHAPTER to include a hard page break at the beginning of the style. If you want the chapters to always start on a right-side page, include a Force Odd code with **SHIFT-F7 P O O**. Then the chapters will automatically start on a new right-hand page with an odd-page number.

❖ *Temporary tunnel vision*

When you start working with proportional fonts, you'll notice that oftentimes your lines are too long to fit on-screen. So your text meanders off the right side of the screen, and it's difficult to get the entire view of your text. Microsoft Word has long had a feature which basically turns off on-screen formatting so that all text fits on-screen, but WordPerfect doesn't.

Just like Mighty Mouse, here come Styles to save the day. I frequently use a style I call "Edit Margins" whose sole purpose in life is to create temporarily narrower margins so that text fits on-screen during editing. Right before print time you delete this style.

Now you could just place a margin change code in your text, but chances are you would forget about it. Because a style can contain text as well as codes, you can place a warning message in this style reminding you to remove it before printing. If you don't remove it, your warning notice will print out, reminding you just exactly why your page formatted so strangely. Follow me:

ALT-F8 C T O N Edit Margin [ENTER]

We're now going to set the margins at 1" left and 3" right. That will keep the text all on-screen, even at 10-point.

C SHIFT-F8 L M 1 [ENTER] 3 [ENTER] [ENTER]

This next line is optional. It sets your current page number to 1000. Since chances are you aren't working with documents that are 1000 pages long, this will be a constant on-screen reminder that you are not in final formatting mode.

P N N 1000 F7 F7

This reminder will appear wherever you place the style

———-REMOVE BEFORE PRINTING——-

and now you'll save the style. Press

F7 F7 F7

I generally place this style at the top of my file. I don't mind the gigantic page number, because it does start at 1000, so when I'm at 1015, I know I'm really at page 15.

Before you print, simply delete this style. Your margins will return to normal.

If you want to spend a little money on a more sophisticated solution to this problem, check out a program called *Screen Extender* (address in Appendix).

➾ Try it with a topper.

If you use topper styles, another way to approach this is to use a style sheet called "edit." The only style in this style file is a topper, and the only code in it (or the only important code, you can have as many others as you like) is the margin change of 1" left, 3" right. When you are ready to print, you retrieve your "final" style and this margin will change.

❖ *Ventura with love*

As wonderful as WordPerfect is for desktop publishing, there will be those among us (even myself at times) who yearn for more power. My choice for this is Ventura Publisher. It's a brilliant program and its design has inspired many WordPerfect features. Did I hear somebody snicker, "What's Ventura got to do with WordPerfect?" Well here's the answer: This book *is* called *WordPerfect: Desktop Publishing In Style,* and Ventura is but one more way to desktop publish with WordPerfect.

If someone has sold you a copy of PageMaker, fear not (well, fear a little: PM is too slow for the likes of me). This trick works almost as well with the "P" word; the concept remains the same, only the codes have been changed to protect the innocent.

One annoying element with Ventura is that its codes can clutter a text file until it becomes unreadable. But WordPerfect's style sheets are a prodigious (don't you love that word?) way of keeping files readable right up until you plug them into the Big V. This is contingent on WordPerfect's ability to include text in a style, and so even Microsoft Word can't do this (ha, ha, ha).

The heroes of this little adventure are two style sheets: the first for easy-to-edit, double-spaced draft printouts, and the second for fully-formatted, code-clogged Ventura-ready files. Both are simple.

The draft style allows headlines, subheads and readouts (or pull-quotes) to stand out from regular text by using additional hard returns, underlines, bold, centers, or indents. The final style removes all extra returns and replaces them with Ventura tag names. Even underlines become real Ventura italics codes. Woo-wee.

◆ **Here's the VPDRAFT.STY:**

➻ BYLINE *(paired):*

[Tab][BOLD][UND][Comment]

➻ HEADLINE *(paired):*

[HRt]

[HRt]

[Cntr][BOLD][UND][Comment][C/A/Flrt][HRt]

[HRt]

➻ READOUT *(paired):*

[Indent][Indent][BOLD][Comment]

{You can use either left indent F4 or Left/Right indent SHIFT-F4}

➻ SUBHEAD *(paired):*

[HRt]

[UND][Comment]

TOPPER *(paired):*

[L/R Mar:1.25",1.25"][Ln Spacing:1.5]

➻ UND/ITAL *(paired):*

[UND][Comment]

◆ **Here's the VPFINAL.STY**

➻ BYLINE *(paired):*

@BYLINE =

[Comment]

➻ HEADLINE

@HEADLINE =

[Comment]

•◆ READOUT

@READOUT =

[Comment]

•◆ SUBHEAD

@SUBHEAD =

[Comment]

•◆ TOPPER

[L/R Mar:1",1"]

UND/ITAL

<MI>

[Comment]

<D>

<MI> stands for Medium Italics, and <D> stands for Default because it returns text to its normal attribute.

While Ventura will read the 5.0 and 5.1 format, you'll want to save the file to WordPerfect's 4.2 format when you use this tip. This locks the formatting and text tags in place so that Ventura doesn't ignore it.

Once you've run the file through Ventura, those codes are going to be there forever and ever . . . unless you use a fancy-schmancy macro. For another Ventura tip, see Chapter 17, *Macros*.

•◆ Ventura 2 users ought to read this:

Ventura was one of the most bug-free programs I know. But it did have one really nasty bug—with WordPerfect 5.0 or 5.1 files. If you had any character over 125 ASCII (such as é), Ventura would place some kind of byte-from-Hell right next

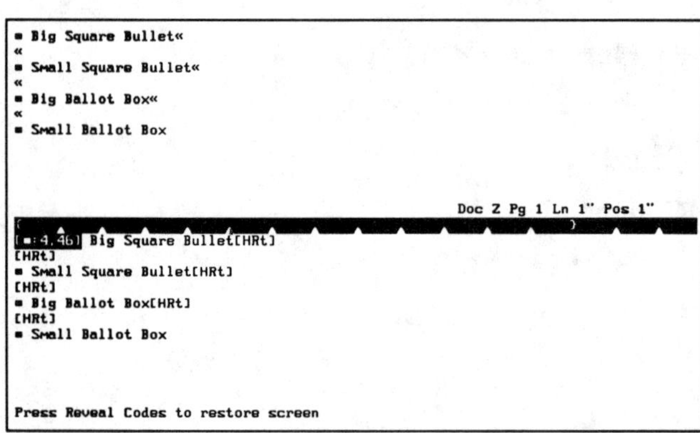

5.1 users: In normal text mode, these three different bullets all look the same. If you want to see the real thing, use View Document.

to it. Once saved in Ventura, you could not load the file again, either in Ventura or WordPerfect.

This has since been fixed, so if you have Ventura 3 it shouldn't be a problem. But if you're using Ventura 2, you will need to call Xerox and get a "patch" for this problem. If you are on CompuServe you can also download the fix on the Xerox Forum.

❖ *Square bullets and ballot boxes*

"What a segue to Graphics," or "Pardon me, Miss, is that the Pottsylvania Choo Choo?" (In case you didn't get it, that was for all our Rocky and Bullwinkle or Moose und Squirrel, fans.)

Square bullets and ballot boxes are de rigueur for anyone who is anyone, or at least for anyone who wants square bullets (so much more Vienna Secession/Josef Hoffman than round bullets) or is preparing a questionnaire.

In 5.1, you can create them simply by pressing

CONTROL-V 4,46

for a big square bullet

CONTROL-V 4,47

for a small square bullet

CONTROL-V 4,48

for a big ballot box

CONTROL-V 4,49

for a small ballot box

```
[Indent]«
{Can be either F4 or SHIFT-F4}[Comment]«
«
SQUARE BULLET (paired):«
[Usr Opt]<<G 100>>[Usr Box:1;;]<<TC SB 12p [ENTER] 12p>«
{Again, vary the size of the box in accordance with the size of
your type. Enter the size in points by following the number with
a P and make the box the exact size of the type.}«
[Indent]«
{Can be either F4 or SHIFT-F4}[Comment]«
«
█     Ballot Box«
█     Square Bullet«
«
↑ They look the same on-screen«
«
At Long Last Answers«
Okay, gold star time. You survived until the end of this chapter.
You now know more about penguins than you ever dreamed of
(what?). So here's the answer to the songwriting question: One of
the names is Lincoln, because the song was written by Lincoln
Chase, Shirley Shirley bo Birley's Beau. If you have a hankering
for more trivia, this time about movies, pick up a copy of Howard
Cohen's book <169>The Official Movie IQ Test<170> published by
C:\WP5\P\WP10.TW                                  Doc 2 Pg 26 Ln 4.39" Pos 4"
```

❑ *Ballot Box*
■ *Square Bullet*

Ballot boxes and square bullets appear as solid blocks on-screen.

◆ **If, then**

If these don't work on your printer, if you need more exact control over sizing, or if you're using 5.0, do the following:

Using a combination of styles and graphics, WordPerfect allows you to produce bullets in any size (and I mean any size): from a hundredth of an inch (since this would bear an uncanny resemblance to a period, why bother) to full page (which would be more akin to a bomb or hand grenade than a bullet).

These two styles are almost identical. The only component that changes is the graphics option. For this example, I've used the User-defined box since it's unlikely that, with three other types of graphics boxes to use, you'll need this for any other purpose.

While you might think these would be open styles, I've created them as paired styles for one simple reason. User-defined boxes normally have no shading or lines around them, but this little ruse changes all that. The square bullet is nothing more than a user box with a 100% background and no lines around it, while the ballot box is nothing but a 0% background and single lines all around it. If I should become delirious and create other graphics as User-defined, they will have the normal user defaults of 0% gray background and no lines around them.

If you are sure you won't lose control in the middle of a work day and start a User-defined frenzy, you can create these open styles. None of the codes will change. And the area after the comment is left blank anyway, so that the style will automatically return the text to how it was before the style.

◆ **Ballot box (paired):**

[Usr Opt]<BSSSS>[Usr Box:1;;]<TC VA SB 12p [ENTER] 12p>

[Comment]

[Indent]

You will need to vary the size of the box depending on the size type you are using. Remember that you can enter the size in points by following the number with a P and by making the box the exact size of the type. If you want a more three dimensional ballot box, use <BSTST> for the options.

The indent can be either F4 or SHIFT-F4.

◆ **Square bullet (paired):**

[Usr Opt]<G 100>[Usr Box:1;;]<TC VA SB 12p [ENTER] 12p>

[Comment]

[Indent]

Again, vary the size of the box in accordance with the size of your type. Enter the size in points by following the number with a P and make the box the exact size of the type. The indent can be either F4 or SHIFT-F4.

◆ At long last, answers

Okay, gold star time. You survived until the end of this chapter. You now know more about penguins than you ever dreamed of (what?). So here's the answer to the songwriting question: One of the names is Lincoln, because the song was written by Lincoln Chase, Shirley Shirley bo birley's beau. If you have a hankering for more trivia, this time about movies, pick up a copy of Howard Cohen's book *The Official Movie IQ Test* published by Putnam. (Come on, there's more to life than WordPerfect and desktop publishing . . . well, just a little.)

12

In graphic detail

Graphics boxes for every occasion

A picture's worth a thousand words, or so the saying goes. Of course it took words to express this cliche. Graphics are the other half of desktop publishing, but to many people graphics are the darker, more mysterious half. Few of us consider ourselves artistic, and the mere mention of the word "graphic" can conjure up images of beatniks in black tunics with bongos and berets. "It's cool man, real graphic."

In true desktop publishing, text without graphics is like Lucy without Ricky, Fred without Ginger (or Ethel), Rocky without Bullwinkle . . . you get the picture (pun intended). Graphics don't have to be intimidating. They may be messy, confusing (especially file formats, which I'll cover later), often slow to print, but not intimidating.

Graphics don't have to be pictures (or charts or graphs or diagrams) either; and in WordPerfect, the graphics features includes both horizontal and vertical lines. (Don't confuse this feature with Line Draw, which uses a font built into printers such as the LaserJet II.) In fact, lines are so important that I've decided to grant them a chapter of their very own. Lucky them.

WordPerfect's graphics can print on any printer capable of graphics, such as laser, ink jet, and dot matrix printers. Most daisy-wheel printers do not have the ability to print graphics.

WordPerfect's graphics feature is the most sophisticated available for any PC-based word processing program. That's not just hype. WordPerfect's graphics feature borrows considerably from some of Ventura Publisher's bag of tricks: WordPerfect automatically wraps text around graphics, attaches captions to pictures that always remain with their assigned graphic, and floats graphics so that they always stay with their associated text. And WordPerfect is the only word processing program I know of that allows you to edit graphics. You can make them larger or smaller, flop (believe it or not, the industry jargon for "flip") them so they are facing in the opposite direction, crop them so you use only a portion of the graphic image, rotate them in 1-degree increments, even invert them so that everything that was black prints as white, and vice versa.

As if that weren't enough, WordPerfect also allows you to use graphics boxes for text. While this may seem like a contradiction in terms, text is often used as a graphic device, specifically in readouts or pull quotes, small chunks of text taken out of context and enlarged on a page as an attention grabber.

❖ One for all and all for five

There are five types of WordPerfect graphics boxes: Figure, Table, Text, User-defined, and Equation. Before you put your hand to your forehead and sigh melodramatically at how complex this must be, here's the good news: all five types of graphics boxes work identically.

Since one of these boxes is solely for equations, I'm doing my best to ignore it. As I told you in the introduction, I don't know nothing about birthin' equations.

So, why on earth are there so many of them? As creative as WordPerfect is, its uses have still been dictated by the needs of academia and big business. Long technical documents, whether for documentation or theses, require "lists of figures" (special appendices that list all the charts, pictures, or other graphic items in the document). WordPerfect offers five different types of graphics boxes so that you can compile five different lists. One list is for figures, another for tables, equations, and while Text and User-Defined are not traditional categories, these too can be used for lists that may be specific to a particular field.

Remember that captions will automatically be included if you are creating lists. Figures are included in list 6, Tables in list 7, Text boxes in list 8, User-Defined in list 9 and Equations in list 10. So there you have it: an explanation for this apparent redundancy.

```
Options: Figure

     1 - Border Style
              Left                          Single
              Right                         Single
              Top                           Single
              Bottom                        Single
     2 - Outside Border Space
              Left                          0.167"
              Right                         0.167"
              Top                           0.167"
              Bottom                        0.167"
     3 - Inside Border Space
              Left                          0"
              Right                         0"
              Top                           0"
              Bottom                        0"
     4 - First Level Numbering Method       Numbers
     5 - Second Level Numbering Method      Off
     6 - Caption Number Style               [BOLD]Figure 1[bold]
     7 - Position of Caption                Below box, Outside borders
     8 - Minimum Offset from Paragraph      0"
     9 - Gray Shading (% of black)          0%

Selection: 0
```

Graphics box options, in this case, Figure Options (ALT-F9 F O) allow you to set the type of border to print around a box, as well as spacing inside and out, caption positioning, and numbering style, and the percentage of gray for the background.

◆ These are the defaults

Each of the five box types have their own defaults for borders, numbering method, position of the caption, and gray shading (whether the box is filled with a gray pattern, and if so, how much).

- **Figure:** Arabic numbers, single line around the box, .167" border of white space outside the box. "Figure 1" as the caption number, with the caption below the box and outside the borders.
- **Table:** Roman numerals, a thick line at the top and bottom, none at the sides, a .167" border of white space both inside and outside the box. "Table I" as the caption number style, with the caption above the box and outside the borders.
- **Text:** Arabic numbers, a thick line at the top and bottom, none at the sides, a .167" border of white space both inside and outside the box. "1" as the caption number style, with the caption below and outside the borders, and a 10% gray shading.
- **User-Defined:** Arabic numbers, no border lines, .167" border of white space outside the box, 0" inside, "1" as the caption number style with the caption below the box and outside the borders.
- **Equation:** Arabic numbers, no border lines, .083" outside and inside borders, (1) as the caption number style, captions on the right side, 0% gray background.

These defaults can be changed at any time using the Options menu described later in this chapter.

◆ Class, suborder, genus, species

The folks at WordPerfect are great with programs, but not so great with words. Once they latch onto a word, they like to employ it for as many functions as possible. That's economical, but confusing. *Styles* refers to both style sheets and the individual styles within them. *Borders* refer to both the lines around boxes and the margins inside and outside them. There are eight *types* of graphics boxes but five of them are one type (based on what you put in the box) and three of them are another type (based on how they are anchored on the page).

Let's call the first *type* "type1" and the second "type2." While "type1" only makes a difference in what lists are generated, all three type2 graphics boxes are worlds apart.

Any graphics box you create must be one of the type2 boxes: a "Page" box, which is attached to a particular position on a page and will not move with text; a "Paragraph" box, which is attached to a particular paragraph and moves with the text; and a "Character" box, which replaces a single character in a paragraph and moves with the very words of that paragraph. Each type of box has its own strengths and weaknesses; each has its own use.

◆ Page

Always prints in the exact position you select on a page. You can place Page boxes by margins or by column. They are the only type2 graphic that can span several columns and have the text from all columns wrap around correctly.

Uses: Full-page graphics; boxes around an entire page; logos/banners/flags; letterheads; "inside this issue" box; pull quotes or graphics to be placed on a particular part of the page or to span several columns. Any text that requires precise placement on a page or that needs to span several columns.

◆ Paragraph

Always stays with the paragraph it is attached to. Will automatically resize box and graphics inside when margins change. Can be placed to the left or right of a paragraph or be set to fit within both margins. Graphic will resize itself automatically if you change margins or columns.

Uses: Illustrations that must be accompanied by their associated text, such as diagrams, charts, and graphs; tables (yes, you can place tables inside graphics boxes) with complex formatting that you don't want to change; pull quotes or readouts that float with text or resize with changing margins or columns.

◆ Character

Replaces a single character and moves with the letters of a paragraph. The only type of graphics box that will print in footnotes or endnotes. Text doesn't wrap around character boxes as in page and paragraph boxes; when the line containing the character box wraps around, the next line begins below the box. If you copy or move any other type of graphic into a footnote or endnote, it automatically becomes a character box.

Uses: Small graphics, bullets, ballot boxes, company logos, special graphics such as "key caps," anything that must move not only with paragraph but letter by letter in paragraph. Also effective for placing graphics in headers and footers.

➾ Tip: Scan a fancy headline alphabet (public domain, please) letter by letter and utilize character boxes for each letter of the headline.

◆ Creating a graphics box

Let's stop talking about it and start doing it. Creating a graphics box is about as tough as opening up a box of cereal. Before you get the hang of it you rip the box top off, but a few boxes later you're keeping that little tab intact and closing the box top again like a pro. WordPerfect's graphics are similar, but 100% salt- and sugarfree (although possibly high in roughage).

ALT-F9 is the graphics key. You will press this to access any graphics command, to create graphics, or to edit them. In this modest little example, we're going to create a paragraph type2 figure box, fill it with a graphic supplied on the Fonts/Graphics disk, edit the graphic, and change the type of graphics box (page, paragraph, character) as well as defaults (figure, table, text, user). We'll also experiment with the options feature.

To create a figure box press

ALT-F9 F C

You are now cheek to jowls with the graphics menu. This menu remains the same no matter which type1 graphics box you choose.

```
Definition: Figure

     1 - Filename                SPLAT.WPG
     2 - Contents                Graphic
     3 - Caption
     4 - Anchor Type             Paragraph
     5 - Vertical Position       0"
     6 - Horizontal Position     Right
     7 - Size                    0.376" wide x 0.244" (high)
     8 - Wrap Text Around Box Yes
     9 - Edit


Selection: 0
```

Figure Definition allows you to choose the size and placement of the graphic box on the page, as well as its contents.

Filename allows you to enter the name of the graphic or the WordPerfect file you want inside the box. If you are going to use a WordPerfect file, remember that graphics boxes cannot be longer than a single page. If you try to make them longer, WordPerfect will warn you, and won't permit you to leave the edit mode until you've shortened the file.

◆ On-Disk, on Prancer, on Donner, on Vixen

Contents (5.1 only). This allows you to specify whether the graphics file will be included inside the WordPerfect file or whether WordPerfect will just load the file from disk whenever it needs it. If you are going to be transferring the files to other disks, choose **G** for "Graphic." This means that WordPerfect will take the entire graphic and store it inside the document file. When you copy the document file to another disk, the graphic will go with it. The only drawback to this is that if you have several graphics or if the graphics are large, your WordPerfect file can become brobdingnagian.

If you want to avoid the attack of the giganto-files, you can select **O** for "On-disk." WordPerfect will *not* include the graphic into its file, but will load the graphic from disk whenever necessary (to edit, view, or print). This can save mucho disk space and has another important advantage—it keeps you up-to-date. Each time you print (or use View Document), WordPerfect loads the latest version of the graphics file even if you've changed the file in your graphics editor or even if you've saved a new graphic over the old one.

Here's an example. You have a file with 14 different charts and graphs in it. The day before your report is due, your spreadsheet figures all change, and so do your charts and graphs. In 5.0 you would have accessed each graphics box and loaded the new file, one by one. With the graphics on-disk feature, these updated graphs are all automatically loaded the very next time you use View Document, or print the file.

There is one important detail to remember about "on-disk," and that is WordPerfect has to know where on your disk to find the graphic. Unfortunately, WordPerfect won't remember a complete path name, just the file name itself, so there are two ways to make sure WordPerfect can find the graphic.

The first is to designate a specific directory for all graphics files you're going to mark as "on-disk." To do this, press SHIFT-F1 L G and enter the complete path name (such as C:\GRAPHICS). No matter what directory holds your text file, WordPerfect will *only* look in the directory you've specified in setup for the graphic.

The second way is to make sure in Setup that the directory for graphics is blank. If you do this, WordPerfect will always look in the *current* directory. That doesn't mean the directory you retrieved your text file from, it means whatever directory you've made default, either through setup (SHIFT-F1 D) or with List Files (F5 =, or F5 [ENTER] O). The drawback to this is that if you change your current directory for any reason and then decide to edit, View Document, or print, WordPerfect won't be able to find the graphic, and will leave the graphics box empty.

No matter which one of these you choose, there's no simple way of automatically copying graphics associated with WordPerfect files. If you're going to use graphics "on-disk" and ever need to copy the file to another disk or computer, you will need to keep a list of all the graphic files you use and copy them individually. (Remember, List Files, F5, allows you to mark several files using the * and then copy, delete, or move them in one pass.)

◆ What type, my love?

Type allows you to choose between paragraph, page, and character type boxes. This is the option I set first. You would base this decision upon how you plan to use the box. Let's start out by creating a paragraph type2 box to move along with the paragraph. Since this is the default for all graphics boxes, we don't have to change it.

◆ Verticalities

Vertical Position tells WordPerfect the distance from the top of the paragraph that you want this graphics box to start. With the 0" default, the top of the box will start at the top of the paragraph. You don't have to change anything if this is what you want. If you want the box to begin in the middle of the paragraph, type V and enter the correct distance from the top of the paragraph you want the box to begin. If you create the graphics box in the middle of the paragraph, WordPerfect will automatically measure the distance from the top of the paragraph and place that number here. For now, leave it at 0".

◆ Horizontal and proud of it

Horizontal position differs depending on the anchor type of the type2 box you are creating. The default is "right" so that the right side of the graphics box is aligned with the right margin. Let's make this box align with the left margin. Press

H L

The other choices are C (for centered), and F (so that the graphics box stretches from one margin to the other), The "F" setting can also resize itself automatically when the margins change. However, you cannot change the width of the box because it is dependant on the margins. (5.0: use B instead of F.)

Editing may change the size of a graphics box automatically as the text inside it gets longer or shorter. However, WordPerfect has a tendency to ignore this, and will not change the size unless you force it to. You can have WordPerfect resize the box automatically (that sounds like a contradiction but it's not) by pressing **H F** again and WordPerfect will resize the box to fit the new text.

◆ Height, width, serial number

Size allows you to change the ________ of a graphics box. Fill in the blank for yourself. If you guessed "size," buy yourself a special treat. If you guessed "potato," there'll be no dessert for you tonight.

You can set either the width, the height, both the width and height, or have WordPerfect Automatically decide how large to make the box. Automatic is really meant for graphics because when a graphic is created in a graphics program (or with a scanner) the art does have a specific size. Automatic is especially good for bit-mapped paint-type and scanned graphics because it keeps them from getting jaggies or gray fills from unwanted "plaid" patterns.

If you set only the width, WordPerfect calculates the correct size for the height so that the graphic is sized proportionally. If you choose the height only, WordPerfect calculates the correct size for the width. If you choose to size both, you can stretch the graphic and distort it. For this example, press

S W 2" [ENTER]

Notice how the width changed to 2".

If you select both, WordPerfect will not change either of them and will place the graphic inside the space you've chosen. The graphic may have large uneven margins but will always be sized proportionally, unless you specifically distort it using the scale command.

◆ That's a wrap!

Wrap Text Around Box allows you to specify whether WordPerfect should wrap text around the box or print text through the box as if it weren't there. You would rarely choose **N** (so that WordPerfect would print the graphic right over the text). You could use this to create a box around the entire page (specifics on this a little later), to print a gray screen, or to print a very light graphic in the background. If you choose to use this with dark graphics, you will not be able to read the text which has been overprinted by the gray screen.

◆ Get a graphic

Edit allows you to edit the contents of the box, be it graphics or text. Since we have nothing in the box right now, let's hold off on this option for just a sec.

For this example, we're going to load one of the graphics that comes with Word-Perfect. These will probably be in the same directory as your WordPerfect program.

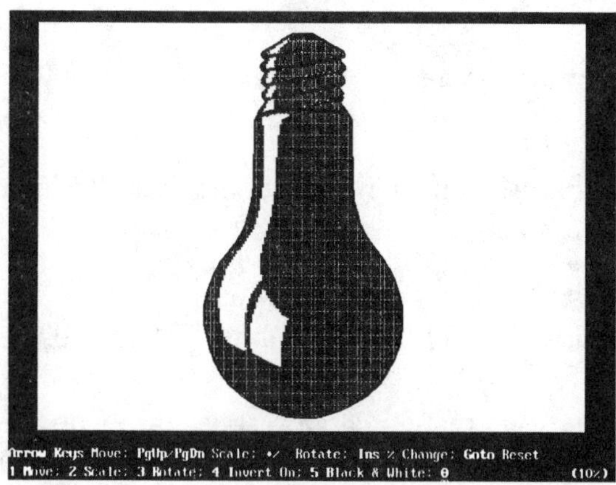

Graphics Edit (ALT-F9 F E E) gives you the power to alter the size and rotation of graphics as well as mirror or invert them. The graphic has not been edited . . . yet.

If they aren't, run the install program and answer "Y" to "Graphic Images." This will copy the example graphics to your WordPerfect directory.

To retrieve a graphic file, type

F

From here you can either type the name of the file you want. I'm going to assume that your graphics files are located in C:\WP51. If they are in any other directory, type the name of *that* directory instead.

BULB.WPG [ENTER]

The file will take a couple of seconds to load, but then you will notice that while the width of the box is still 2" (as we set it), the height of the box is now 1.45".

◆ Let's all play "What was that filename?"

I don't know about you, but I've got a memory like a sieve. I can't remember names, dates, places, or sometimes even which vegetables I like.

Remembering file names is way down on the list of things that I remember. Thankfully, you can use List Files to select files for graphics boxes.

Let's try it. Press

F

Now we're going to select a file. Press

F5 [ENTER]

Voila! Our friend List Files appears, to jog our short term memories. You can do everything you can do in normal List Files, including copying, renaming and deleting files.

F7

◆ Captions-a-plenty

Let's create a caption for our masterpiece. Press

C

The screen says "Figure 1," and if that was sufficient, you could press **F7** right now. But we don't believe in compromise, so press

[BACKSPACE] CONTROL-F8 S V Great Ideas! F7

Unless you specifically change it with CONTROL-F8 F, WordPerfect will use the Initial base font (as set with SHIFT-F8 D F).

If you plan to use captions, I suggest you create a caption style, an open style that includes the font you want and perhaps even an [AdvDn] code (SHIFT-F8 O A D .1") to add a little white space between the line around the graphic and the caption. Remember, a style will not only increase consistency between pages, but will enable you to change caption styles without having to edit each and every one by hand.

The excitement mounts. You're about to edit a graphic. If you have a weak heart, experience motion sickness, or have back problems, throw caution to the wind and follow along anyway.

❖ *Editing expedition*

Press **E** to edit the graphic.

If the monitor and video card you are using has graphics capabilities, you will see the light bulb on-screen in all its line-art glory. If you use a nongraphics screen, such as those on basic IBM PC's, you should seriously consider buying either a Hercules graphics card, or an EGA card and a new monitor. (Or you could always just use your imagination and send that money directly to me.) Although, WordPerfect is incredibly clever in using periods to represent lines, it's only approximate and doesn't work at all for bitmapped graphics.

Now you have a plethora of ways at your disposal to control the unsuspecting light bulb on the screen.

The first row of the menu displays shortcuts for manipulating the graphic. The second line contains menus for more precise movement. Right now you'll see a single thin line around the graphic. This is the default for figures. If you changed to a thick, dashed, or other type of line with Options (explained sooner than you think), these lines would appear on-screen, as you selected them.

You will see (10%) in the lower right hand corner of the screen. This is an important number because it indicates the amount of movement, rotation, or sizing that WordPerfect will employ when you use the short-cut keys. You can change this number by pressing the **[INS]** key. Pressing it once will give you 5%, another press gives you 1%, and another gives you 25%. They are the only automatic increments you can choose from, although you can move in larger increments by using the menus along the bottom. Press the **[INS]** key until 10% is once again displayed at the bottom of the screen.

Now we're going to try out some of the quick keys. (I bet you didn't know a person could have this much fun in front of a computer, did you? What? You're not having fun yet? Just wait.)

◆ Quick move

Press the **[LEFT ARROW]** key a few times and notice how the picture moves to the left. Press the **[RIGHT ARROW]** key and watch the picture move to the right. **[UP ARROW]** moves the picture up, and **[DOWN ARROW]** moves the picture down. Am I moving too fast for you?

The distance the picture moves with each keystroke depends on the percentage displayed in the corner. At 25%, the picture will move 25 times more in a single keystroke then it will at 1%.

Since the picture has moved, press **CONTROL-HOME** (the GOTO key) to reset it to its original position. This can be very helpful should you accidentally mess up the picture.

◆ Quick size

Not let's play with another shortcut: sizing. When you press the **[PgUp]** key, the picture will enlarge by the percent specified in the corner. Pressing **[PgDn]** reduces the size of the picture by the same increment. If the picture is too large, it won't all fit into the box. This is useful if you only want to use a portion of the picture.

If you've set the options so that the box has an internal margin, the edges of the picture may disappear (even though they are still inside the box). When you're

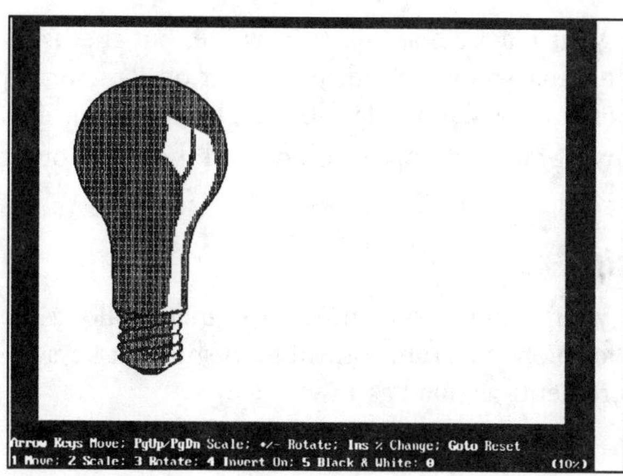

Here's the edited light bulb. It has been rotated and sized. Line art can be sized, rotated, and mirrored; bitmapped graphics can be sized and inverted.

through experimenting, press **CONTROL-HOME** to restore the picture to its original form.

◆ Quick rotate

WordPerfect has the unique ability to rotate all graphics in 1-degree increments. Early versions of the program would only rotate line art formats such as CGM (from Harvard, Freelance, Corel, Arts & Letters, Publisher's PicturePak), Lotus .PIC files, and AutoCAD .DXF files. All versions of 5.1 and versions of 5.0 dated after 4/29/89 can rotate bitmapped graphics, such as PC Paintbrush, TIF, and Halo, to any printer. You can find more information on file formats later in this chapter.

Press the + key on the keypad (not the one over the =), and the graphic will rotate counterclockwise by the percent indicated in the corner. 25%=90 degrees, 10%=45 degrees, 5%=27.5 degrees. (If that's too complicated, just stand on your head.) Pressing the – key on the keypad will cause the graphic to rotate clockwise. When you start to feel nauseous from all this rotation, take a Dramamine or to restore the picture to normal, press

CONTROL-HOME

◆ Quick invert

Pressing **SHIFT-F3** turns everything white to black and everything black to white, presenting you with a negative of the original image.

But (and you should always know it's going to get sticky when you see the word "but"), while you can invert both line art and bitmapped graphics on PostScript and LaserMaster printers, you can't always print inverted line art on LaserJets or compatibles. This is because these printers cannot print white on black. I'd like to be able to tell you for certain whether not this works with the LaserJet III, but while you theoretically can (the LaserJet III can print white on black), at the time I write this book you can't.

When you invert line art, all your black areas will turn white, but the background will not change. This means that you will need to set your options so that the background is 100% black, otherwise you'll print black on black and get nothing.

If you have a color monitor, invert may not appear to do anything at all, but it will have an effect at print time.

❖ *Precision craftsmanship*

If you require precision over your editing, you can use the menus along the bottom of the screen. This allows for more accurate control than shortcut keys because these movements can be increments as small as 1W.

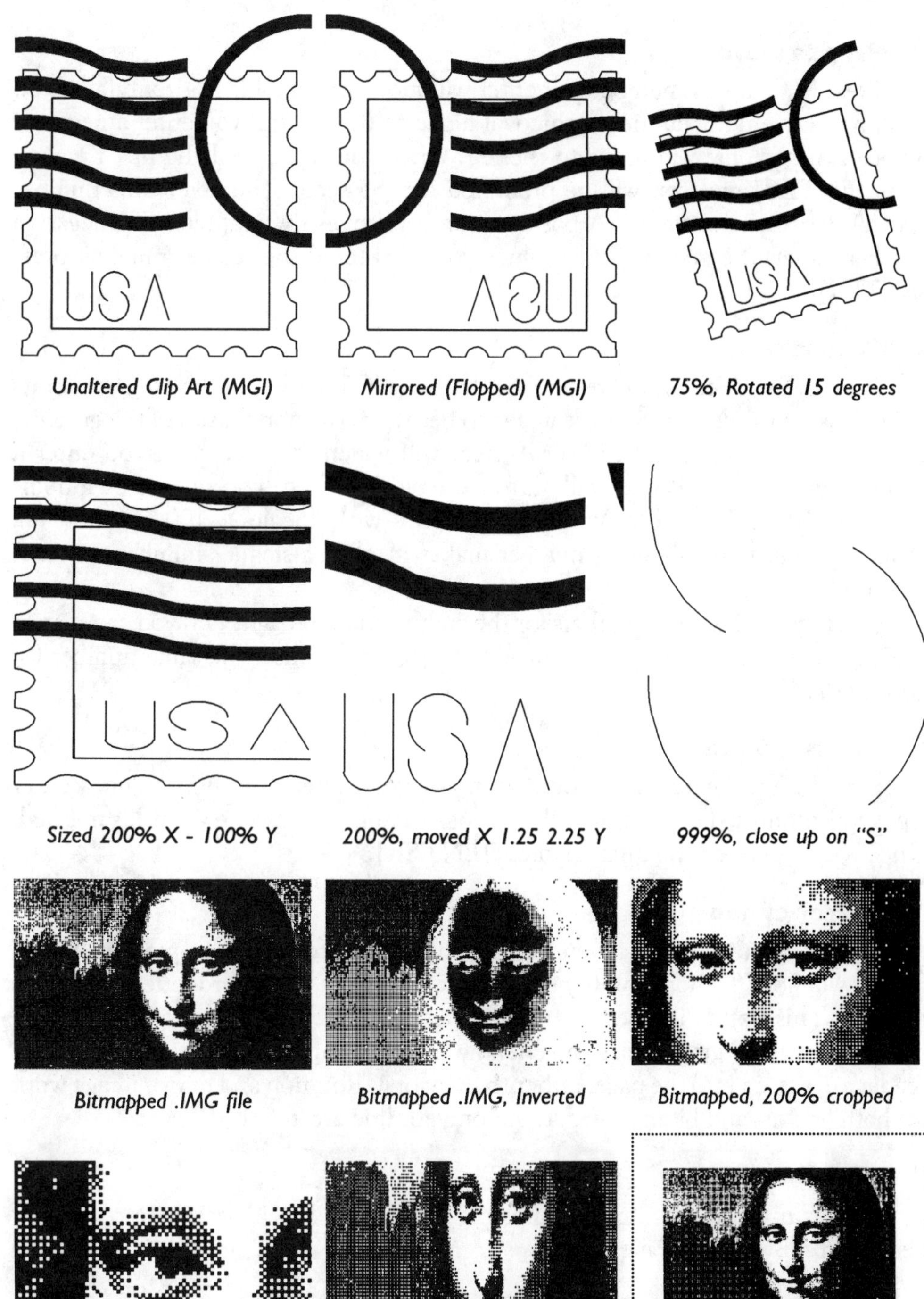

Unaltered Clip Art (MGI)

Mirrored (Flopped) (MGI)

75%, Rotated 15 degrees

Sized 200% X - 100% Y

200%, moved X 1.25 2.25 Y

999%, close up on "S"

Bitmapped .IMG file

Bitmapped .IMG, Inverted

Bitmapped, 200% cropped

Bitmapped, 400% cropped
Moved -2.87 H 1.54 V

Sized non-proportionally
100% X 200% Y

100%, Inside Margin of .2"
(Dotted line shows box size)

◆ **Precise move**

Press **M**. The first number you enter will move the graphic horizontally. If you enter a positive number, the graphic will move to the right; if you enter a negative number, the graphic will move to the left. Once you've entered the first number, press **[ENTER]** and you will be prompted for the second number. This number controls vertical movement. A positive number moves the graphic up, a negative number moves the graphic down. Once you've entered the second number, press **[ENTER]**.

◆ **Precise scale**

Press S. WordPerfect will respond with "Scale X: 100." What the program wants to know is how *wide* you want the image to be. 100 is the normal size of the graphic. If you enter a larger number, WordPerfect will widen the picture; if you enter a smaller number, WordPerfect will narrow the picture. Once you've entered a number, press **[ENTER]**. Now WordPerfect replies with "Scale Y: 100," or how *tall* should the image be. A larger number makes it taller, a smaller number makes it shorter.

By entering different numbers for the width (X) and height (Y), you can distort the image. If you don't want the image to be distorted, enter the same number for both X and Y.

◆ **Precise rotate**

Press **R**. You can enter the rotation in 1-degree increments, but you must enter a positive number. The graphic will only rotate counterclockwise with this method. Once you've entered the number, press **[ENTER]**.

◆ **Mirror or flop**

WordPerfect now asks if you want to mirror the image. If you press **Y**, WordPerfect will flop (flip horizontally) the graphic. If you press **N**, WordPerfect will leave it as it is. This feature is especially useful when you have a graphic that faces off the page. Professional graphic design generally calls for graphics that face inwards; the reader's eye is led into the page, rather than off of it. Rotation and mirror image work for both line art and bitmaps in 5.1, but only for line art in 5.0.

◆ **Invert**

This is no more precise than pressing **SHIFT-F3**, but it's easier to remember because it's listed on the menu.

◆ **Black & white**

While WordPerfect can import color graphics, it can't print them. Ah, well, maybe next version. Of course, you probably don't have a color printer either, so what's the dif? Well, the dif is that WordPerfect maps various colors to various shades of gray. If you press **B**, WordPerfect will not print various shades of gray, just black and white. You're always better off working with black and white graphics in the first place because the results will be more predictable.

◆ **Sharing and caring without swearing**

If you've got a graphic in one file and want to get it into another file, what do you do?

When you're in Edit mode inside any graphics box, you can save a graphic as a .WPG graphic. Press **F10** and give the file a name. The editing changes are not included in the new file.

❖ *Save or abandon?*

To leave editing you press the EXIT key:

F7

If you wanted to restore the picture to its original state, press **CONTROL-HOME F7**. If you want to cancel the changes you just made but keep previous changes, press **F1**.

Normally, if you were pleased with the changes you'd made or the graphic you'd created, you would press **F7** to exit. If you were unhappy with the outcome, you would press **F1**. (But since you never saved the graphics box with F7, *you will lose it if you press F1 now.*)

If you're ever dissatisfied with changes to a graphic, pressing **F1** will cancel the changes and restore the graphic to its previous state.

Now you're back at the figure menu. To save the graphic as a code in the file, again press

F7

To behold your masterwork, live and in-person, press **SHIFT-F7 V**. You should see the light bulb, surrounded by a thin line, with the caption underneath and outside the border. The text in your document (if any) should flow around the graphic. To exit View Document, press **F7**.

❖ *More changes*

You can change any part of a graphics box at any time, its type1, its type2, its location, its size, its caption, even its contents.

Let's say you're in a fickle state of mind and now want the box to print in the lower-left corner of the page. We're going to change the box anchor type to Page; it will now print in the lower left corner of the page, no matter where the paragraph is.

(If the brass upstairs change their tiny, feeble minds, tell them it's impossible and titter behind their backs. Then barge back in a few minutes later, say you just made word processing history and figured out a way. Of course, they'll respond by giving you a large raise, a company car, and a long vacation. C'mon, you'll never know unless you try.)

◆ Changing type: Paragraph/page/character

First, go back into Figure Edit.

ALT-F9 F E 1 [ENTER]

To change this to a page anchor type box, press

T A [ENTER]

That changed the type and told WordPerfect to print the graphic on this page. If you wanted to print the graphic three pages from now, you could have entered "3 [ENTER]" instead of selecting the default of 0.

With WordPerfect's default, this box will print in the upper-right corner. To move it to the bottom of the page, press

V B

To move it to the left-hand corner, press

H M L

◆ Changing size

Now let's make the box exactly 3" high and let WordPerfect calculate how wide it should be. Press

S W 3 [ENTER]

Notice that the graphic is now 2.17" wide.

◆ Changing graphics files

If you want to place a new graphic in this box, type F and the name of the new graphic. WordPerfect will ask "Replace Contents with (your filename here) Y/N?" If you press **Y**, WordPerfect will remove the current file and replace it with the new file you've selected.

◆ **Remove a graphic**

If you want to remove the graphic file from the graphics box, press **F** and then the **[DEL]** key until the name has been erased. Press **[ENTER]**. WordPerfect will ask, "Delete Current Contents of Box?" If you press **Y**, WordPerfect will remove the graphic (but keep the graphics box). If you press **N**, WordPerfect will leave the current graphic in place.

◆ **Change partners and dance**

You get the picture. You can re-edit the picture, change the caption, whatever your little heart or your employer's little mind desires.

◆ **Changing type: Figure/table/text/user**

If you want to transform a figure into a table (and you're not Doug Henning), or any type1 graphic into any other type1, press **ALT-F9** now. A list of the types will appear at the bottom of the screen. Press **U** and you will have changed the graphic into a User-Defined box. Press **ALT-F9 F** to turn the box back into a Figure. To go back to normal text edition, press

F7

❖ *Text in graphics boxes*

While we've experimented with placing graphics in graphics boxes, you can also place text in graphics boxes. To do this, you create a graphics box by pressing

ALT-F9 U C

Then, instead of retrieving a graphics file, to edit you press

E

From here you can either type text or retrieve a WordPerfect or ASCII file using either F5 CONTROL-F5 (for Text In/Out or spreadsheets) or SHIFT-F10.

> **Tip:** WordPerfect can get cranky when the text inside graphics boxes has too much formatting. If WordPerfect tells you "Too much text" even though you have less than a page of text, what it's really telling you is that it isn't in the mood to do whatever it is you're trying to do. Simplify the formatting bit by bit until WordPerfect becomes more congenial.

- **Spreadsheets:** You can either import or link a spreadsheet, both work inside a graphics box.
- **Tables:** Graphics boxes are a great way to place tables in your document. If your table is full width, then it makes little sense to put it into a graphics box, but if it's not, a graphics box allows the body text of a document to flow around the table as if it were a graphic.
- **Columns:** Yup, you can put columns of text inside graphics boxes. One note: when you resize the width of graphics boxes, the column settings do not adjust automatically.
- **Styles:** They work great, both in graphics boxes and in captions.
- **Graphics boxes:** You can't put a graphics box inside a graphics box.

◆ The Rotated Text Times

For text printed at an angle on scaleable font printers: Here's yet another fun (or as chichi New Yorkers say, "important") extra you can tap with a scaleable font printer. While LaserJets alone can't print both portrait and landscape text on a single page, PostScript, LaserMaster, and LaserJet III printers can. Using a graphics box with text instead of a graphic, you can print text rotated by 90, 180, and 270 degrees.

To rotate type, while you are in the Text Editing mode of a graphics box, press

ALT-F9

You won't see any difference until you go into View Document, or print, so this feature does take some trial and error.

◆ Searching for text in all the wrong places

If you place text in graphics boxes, it can sometimes be tedious to remember which box contains which text. It can also take a slew of keystrokes just to get inside a box and work on the text.

To quickly edit text in a graphics box, use Extended Search: **HOME-F2.** This will find the text in the box and immediately put you in edit mode. Once you've finished editing, press **F7 F7** to get out. When using Extended Search, you can use the up and down arrow keys to search forwards or backwards, or go to the top of the file first (by pressing HOME HOME HOME [UP ARROW]) and then press **HOME-F2.** I find this much easier than using **ALT-F9 F E 1 [ENTER] E.**

◆ Back to where you once belonged

There's no place like CONTROL-HOME, *there's no place like* CONTROL-HOME, *there's no place like* CONTROL-HOME.

When you edit a graphic, WordPerfect moves to where the graphics box code is. It could be hundreds of pages away from your current position, and WordPerfect would automatically find it.

While this is helpful, once you edit the box and press **F7** to leave, you are returned not to where you were when you decided to edit the box, but to the position of the graphics box code.

This is not unlike Dorothy's house being dropped into the Land of Oz. But you don't have to find a professor with a balloon to instantly get back home.

Simply press **CONTROL-HOME CONTROL-HOME** and WordPerfect will zip back to where you were before you edited the graphics box. Put that in your $165,000 ruby slippers and smoke it.

❖ *Optional equipment*

There's only one more major function you need to be familiar with in graphics: how to control the options.

(LONG SENTENCE ALERT: This next sentence/paragraph is very, very long. Not as long as E.L. Doctorow's, but getting there. Any readers who get woozy or confused reading really long sentences should avoid it.)

Graphic Options include the type of border around the graphic box, how much blank space is kept between the graphic box and the surrounding regular text, how much blank space is kept between the contents of the box (graphics or text) and the line around the box, the numbering method, the position of the caption, and the background shade of the box. (Try to say that in one breath.)

As long as we still have that figure with the light bulb graphic, why don't you join me in seeing how the options can affect the graphics box. (Afterwards you can take me out to dinner. Just remember, I'm a peanut butter and chocolate man, and I can't stand caviar. Oh, and if you live in Idaho, you don't have to take me out to dinner, just send potatoes.) Where were we?

The Options code must be placed in front of the graphics box code. So you'll need to place the cursor ON the graphic box before creating this next option.

[LEFT ARROW]

In this example, we're going to change whatever we can, just for the sake of change. To select options, press

ALT-F9 F O

You *must* set options separately for each of the four box types; these options will remain in effect until you create a new option code.

◆ Borders

WordPerfect provides you with seven different types of borders: None, Single, Double, dAshed, dOtted, Thick and Extra thick. All that's missing is Original Recipe and eXtra Crispy.

You can set the border independently for each of the four sides of a graphics box. For most graphics, you'll probably want either none or a single line on all four sides. But for special uses such as readouts and pull quotes, you might consider an extra-thick line on the top, a dotted line on the bottom, and none on the left and right sides. For coupons, you'd use dashed lines on all four sides.

Let's lose control and demonstrate our utter lack of good taste by choosing a different type of line for each side. Some call this look "new wave," others call it "funky." Those who still think that it's 1968 call it "cool," and eight to ten-year-olds call it "rad." I don't care what you call it as long as you call me for dinner. Actually, I recommend that you never use more than two different types of lines around a single box (but total disregard for decorum never hurt anyone too severely).

To put a dashed line on the left, a dotted line on the right, a double line on top, and an extra-thick line on the bottom, press

B A O D E

(While I don't think this has a very "hip" appearance, the code sounds like something straight out of Michael Jackson: "Oh yes, I'm BAoDe, I'm BAoDe.) You'll get to examine the results in a minute.

◆ White space

Okay, campers, time to change another default. Let's create a larger margin of white space between the box and the text. WordPerfect, in yet another display of semantic economics, has employed the same word for two more functions. Imagine all those words they're saving. (I only wish I knew what they were saving them for.)

WordPerfect is insisting on calling both the lines and the white space around the box "borders." I'm tired of numbering words, so let's be rebellious and go with something different. The lines around are borders, the white space around is "space" (the final frontier). To increase the space around the box to a quarter of an inch, type

O .25" [ENTER].25" [ENTER].25" [ENTER].25" [ENTER]

Since we have a graphic and not text inside the box, let's leave the inside space the way it is, at 0" all the way around.

◆ Numbering

Now let's play cops and robbers (or Perry Mason) and change the numbering method from numbers to letters, as in "Exhibit-A." Press

F L

We could also have selected any of four options: **O**ff, **N**umbers, **L**etters, or **R**oman numerals (for when you're in Rome). If you press S, you can set the second numbering method in the same way. Since I hardly believe in numbering of any kind, I'll leave this up to you.

You can change the caption numbering style if you press

C

Using the Perry Mason analogy, this is where WordPerfect (or Raymond Burr) would label the graphic "Exhibit A" rather than "Figure A." You can call this word whatever you want (including "Balustrade," if you are into stair accessories).

◆ Caption positioning

As we near the end of this odyssey, it's time to put all decorum aside as we reach another important option. To position the caption, press

P

You can place it either above or below the graphics box, and either inside or outside the borders. We're talking real borders here, not space: if you put the caption inside and you have a printing border, it will appear inside that printed border. Let's place the caption above the box and inside the border. Press

A I

◆ Minimum offset

If you've entered a Vertical offset so that a paragraph box prints a certain distance from the top of the paragraph, WordPerfect tries to keep this measurement unless the paragraph is near the bottom of the page. In this case, WordPerfect will make this offset smaller in order to keep the graphic on the same page as the paragraph. This option allows you to specify how small that offset should be. The default is 0" and so WordPerfect will move the graphic to the top of a paragraph before moving it to the next page.

If you've set 1" as the vertical offset and don't want the graphic closer than 1" from the top, enter 1" here. If you don't care, leave it at 0". If you want to ensure that the offset measurement is never reduced, enter some ridiculously high number here. Remember, this number is not the offset, but the smallest number WordPerfect can reduce the set offset to. It won't make the offset any bigger, but it won't allow it to get smaller.

◆ **Amazing grays**

This is one of the more entertaining options, as it permits you to create a gray background for the box. These backgrounds (below) can cause a graphic (or readout, pull quote, or table) to stand out from the rest of the page. You can choose any percentage of gray from 0% (white) to 100% (black). In this case, let's choose 10%. Type

G 10 [ENTER]

◆ **LaserJet**

A 10% background will be dark enough to be visible without making text hard to read. You shouldn't use a background darker than 20% or text will be difficult to read. While 6% is the lightest you can use, it appears identical to 10% when printed.

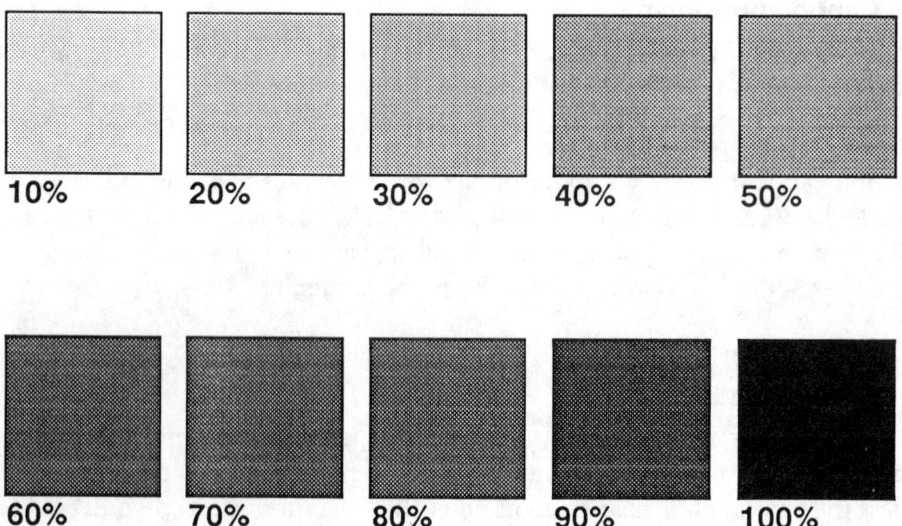

❖ *PostScript news*

PostScript grays are both darker and coarser than the same percentage on a LaserJet. Even 10% can be too dark. 6% is the lightest gray you can use, but it looks so similar to 10% that I couldn't notice any appreciable difference. Remember that even though laser printer dots seem tiny at 300 per inch, they can be quite obtrusive behind text, especially when printed on PostScript laser printers.

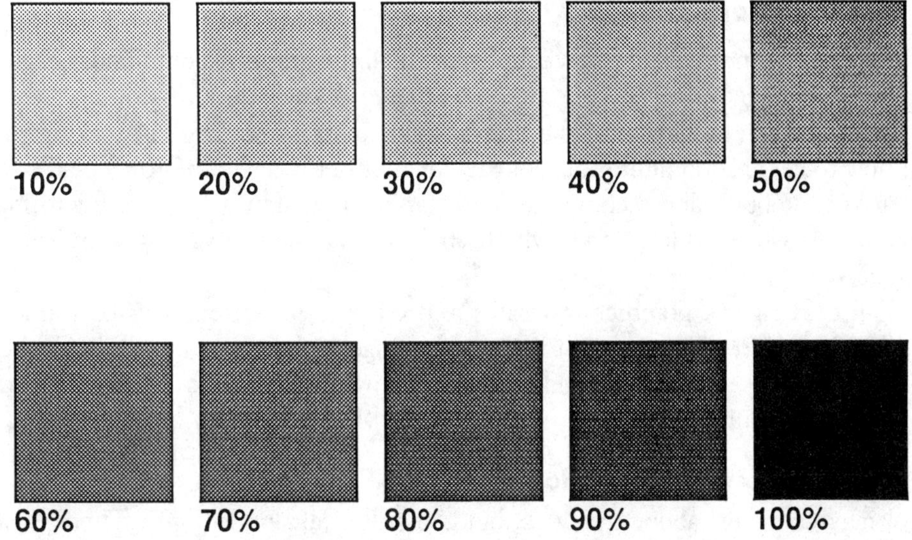

Two more notes for PostScript users: If you choose 100% for the background, set the surrounding borders to None; otherwise, there will be a tiny white line between the border and the background of the box. (This might be an interesting effect when printed on a high-resolution Linotronic typesetter, but on a laser printer it just seems like a mistake.)

For reverse type on PostScript printers (white text on a black background): Set the background to 100%. Enter the text inside the box by pressing **E**. Before typing any text, press **ALT-F8 C W [ENTER]** to make the text white. The white text will not appear in View Document, but it will print correctly. LaserJets can't print white text on a black background. Sorry Charlie—that's another reason why PostScript printers cost three times what a LaserJet does.

If you are going to print the final output on a Linotronic PostScript typesetter, the gray patterns are much finer, resulting in easier-to-read text. But remember, the quality of the offset printing or photo copying must be high-grade or the gray backgrounds will look inferior.

Now that we've all but exhausted the possibilities, to exit the options menu press

F7

Hold onto your hat, it's time to see what this assault on quality design looks like. Go into View Document with **SHIFT-F7 V** and take a gander at your handiwork.

Reverse type: white on black

❖ *Summa cum graphics*

Believe it or not, you are now familiar with all the graphics commands (excluding lines that are covered ad nauseam in a chapter of their own).

From here on in it's gravy. The rest of the chapter is chock full of corking good fun: how to get around limitations, particulars neither your mother or WordPerfect ever told you about, and a complete (and frank) discussion of graphic file formats (which ones work, which don't, which should, and their advantages and disadvantages).

Full coverage of graphics programs and clip art collections can be found in Chapter 20, *Utility Software*, right next to the lingerie department. While all those lonely male execs scramble to find that chapter, why don't you and I cover a little more graphic ground?

◆ **Drop shadows (dark shadows)**

I may complain about the Mac, but I'm still a fair kind of guy. There is one graphic design trick popularized by the Mac that I admire. It's called a "drop shadow." This creates a dark shadow (graphic element, not the soap opera) on one side of a picture, providing it with a three dimensional effect (almost as if it's raised above the page and has a shadow). You can achieve a drop shadow with WordPerfect by using the graphic options that we were just playing with.

Make sure the cursor is located ahead of the figure you want to place the drop shadow on.

Go into graphic options by pressing

ALT-9 F O

(This is assuming your box is a figure box. If the graphics box is a table box, text box, user box, or equation box, you'll need to set the options for those types of boxes. Remember, options are set separately for each type of box.)

Because we read from left to right (at least those of us who are not dyslexic), drop shadows are usually on the right, as if the light were coming from the left. To create a thick drop shadow, we're going to have single lines on the left and the top and thick lines on the right and the bottom. (See the illustration below for a preview of how it will look when printed.) To make the lines, press

B S T S T [ENTER]

Get out of figure options by pressing

F7

If you want to see how this will appear, go into View Document by pressing

(SHIFT F7 V)

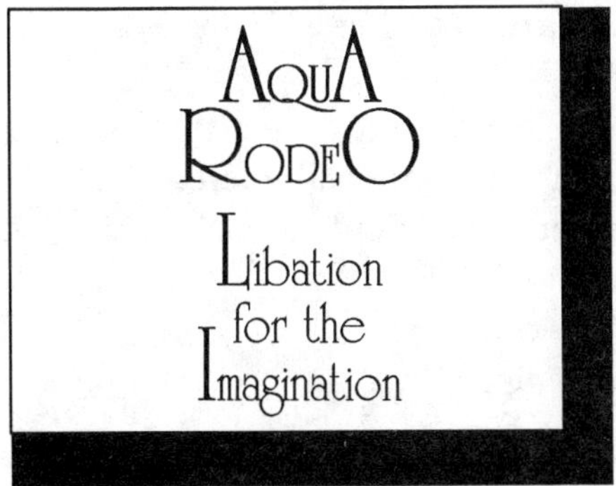

Freze Dried H_2O

At last, relief for the sun-drenched masses.

The 5.0 drop shadow on the left, and the new, improved 5.1 shadow on the right.

If you want an extra thick drop shadow, type

ALT-F9 F O B S E S E [ENTER]

➾ 5.0 users: Your drop shadow will not look quite as flashy as those from 5.1. It won't be a drop shadow, but a "simulated" drop shadow, and it still looks good.

◆ Box around the page and format fixing

Don't worry, this is no relation to ring around the collar. At times, a box printed around a page may be warranted (on title pages, report covers, slide presentations, and signs, to name just a few examples).

To accomplish this formidable task without any formid, simply ignore the advice found in the WordPerfect manual. The manual claims that a full-page graphics box should be used "on a page by itself." Baloney. Salami. Chicken franks.

Take a look at the Abe Lincoln example in Chapter 4, *Show & Tell*, and you'll see one example of how to use full-page graphics with text. The report cover with the butterfly is another. All you have to do is set wrap to NO. But let's stand up to authority together so you can blame me if anything goes wrong.

The first step is to jimmy around with the margins; otherwise the text will run into the box around the page. When you create a full-page box, it sizes itself by how the margins are set. We need to make the margins bigger so the box itself will be bigger.

If you already have Left/Right and Top/Bottom margin codes in the file, move the cursor above them (or to the left).

If you don't, you're going to try a technique I use all the time that I call "*Format Fixing.*" This has nothing to do with what happens at racetracks and is completely legal. What I often do prior to any major changes (like margins) is to enter the current settings as codes. If I'm going to change tabs, I save the tab-line to a code without changing anything, thereby fixing the current settings. (To fix a tab, type SHIFT-F8 L T F7 F7)

To fix any other code, just go to the menu (such as line), select the function, and press return to accept the current value. Some functions will insert a code, but others, such as justify and hyphenation, will insert a code only if you're changing settings. This means you have to change settings and then restore them to the way they were, thereby inserting two codes.

In this case we're going to fix the margins, so type

SHIFT-F8 L M [ENTER][ENTER][ENTER] P M

[ENTER] [ENTER] F7

Now our text won't change even though we're about to set new margins for the box around the page.

These new margins should be at least .25" wider than their previous setting. We're going to make them .5" wider for this example, leaving plenty of breathing room between the box and the text.

If the margins were Left/Right 1" 1" and Top/Bottom .75" .75", make them Left/Right .75" .75" and Top/Bottom .5" .5".

Remember that most laser printers require at least a .25" margin around the page. Any text or graphics positioned closer to the edge will not be printed. For this example, I'll assume you're using the WordPerfect defaults of 1" all around, and so we'll enter the following

SHIFT-F8 L M .5" [ENTER] .5" [ENTER][ENTER] P M .5" [ENTER] .5" [ENTER] F7

Move the cursor to the left of these new margins by pressing

[LEFT ARROW][LEFT ARROW]

Now it's time for our willful act of defiance! We're going to create a full page graphics box and turn wrap off. Type

ALT-F9 F C T A V F W N [ENTER]

Are you ready to experience a thrill that your grandparents would never have dreamed of? Check out how it looks in View Document. Press

SHIFT-F7 V

Pretty niftoid, wouldn't you say? As in any other graphics box, you could use Figure Options to make the line around it single (the default, so we didn't need to change it), double, dashed, dotted, thick, or extra thick.

AN AUTOMATIC BOX AROUND EVERY PAGE (and a chicken in every pot): To print a box on each page, put this graphics box in a header, and set the header to print on every page. You may have to fool around with the margins in order for this to function properly. I had the best luck with at least 1" of margin all around the graphics box and then a 1.25" margin around the page for the text.

Or just create a paired style that contains large margins and a full page figure with wrap turned off. (Use a paired style so that the margins will automatically return to normal after the Style Off code.) Place this in any position on any page that you want surrounded with a box.

◆ Readout all about it

A readout (also known as a pull quote) is one of those wonderful multi-purpose design elements that readers love. They reiterate the highlights or essential points of an article, allow you to editorialize in such a way that people don't even notice you're editorializing (taking words out of context), and add to the readability and style of a page. (The term readout is derived from newspaper jargon, while pull quote comes from magazine jargon. They both have the same meaning.)

With WordPerfect, they aren't even difficult, illegal, or fattening. What more could you want, except for fame, fortune, happiness, and perhaps a vacation or two at Robin Leach's (Mr. *Lifestyles of the Rich & Famous*) expense.

Achieving these minor miracles requires nothing more demanding than creating a graphics box and packing it with text. Who said this desktop publishing stuff was hard?

Because it's such a snap, I've come up with oodles of variations and tips for using graphics boxes as readouts/pull quotes.

◆ Tip: What font glory?

Don't forget about WordPerfect's default font (SHIFT-F8 D F) because this will also be the default for the readout.

But readouts are almost never the same size, and rarely use the same typestyle as the body text. Readouts are most effective when they contrast the type.

It is acceptable to use the same typeface, but with a different weight. Here's an example: If you use Times Roman/Dutch for the body text but also want Times Roman/Dutch for readouts, use the italic or bold italic versions of the font.

It's also proper form to utilize the same font you've used for the headlines, only in a smaller size. With 10 point body text, readouts are generally set with 14-18 point type.

Here are some good fonts to use as readouts with Times/Dutch body text: Times/Dutch italic or bold italic, Helvetica, Helvetica condensed, Avant Garde, Optima, Futura light/oblique/extra bold, Korinna, Serifa/Glypha.

Here are some bad choices for fonts when you are creating readouts with Times/Dutch body text: Palatino/Calligraphic, Century Schoolbook, Galliard, Baskerville.

◆ Tip: What type glory?

Should you work with a paragraph type box or a page type box? Or should you use a graphics box at all? Why not use the header or just lines? (For tips about using lines for readouts, see Chapter 14, *Rules*.)

Using a page type box offers you two advantages: 1) Precise positioning; it's easy to make sure a readout will be at the top or bottom of the page, regardless of where the code is or how the text moves. 2) The ability to create a readout that spans several columns, so that it floats between two columns with text wrapping around all sides. Remember, if you want a page box to print on the top of the current page, the code must also be on top of the page; otherwise, it will print on the next page.

Using a paragraph type box assures that the readout remains close to its associated text. It will automatically resize itself should you change any margins or columns.

If you use any type of graphics box, the options should be set with some sort of "Inside Border Space," generally at least .15". You need plenty of white space between the readout and the body text.

You can also use a header for readouts. If your page design incorporates a large top margin, the header can be used for a headline on the first page with readouts on subsequent pages. Use a style for the basic header information (this will simplify matters on pages without headlines or readouts). For detailed information about utilizing the header for readouts, see Chapter 11, *Styles*, and a section called "Under the Big Top."

◆ Tip: Don't get out of line

Readouts can be completely enclosed in a box with lines all around it, or contain lines on the top and bottom only. I personally think that lack of lines on the sides appears more elegant and prefer readouts with lines above and below only.

If you are working with a graphics box, set options for the type of line you want. It's usually advisable for the lines to be of two different weights (i.e., a thick line on top, with a single line on the bottom; an extra thick line on top, with a dotted line on the bottom).

There are two schools of (design) thought as to whether the heavier line should be on the top or the bottom. Either one is okay, so take your pick. See examples on following pages.

◆ **Tip: Hey, big letter!**

One of desktop publishing's most wonderful features is the freedom of "choice." You don't have to use any lines at all if you don't feel like it. I'm not going to force you. The only ones who might force you are those people you work for, and what do they know?

If lines aren't your scene, you can use lots of extra white space instead, or a raised cap (easy to do, see Chapter 7, *About faces*), or a little black box above and below, or a gray background (no darker than 10%).

The following eight different examples employ the fonts that are built into PostScript printers, but they are also available from Bitstream for use with Fontware. Notice how the different typefaces allow for a wide divergence of appearances. In all the examples, remember to set the line height to fixed when you use raised caps; otherwise, WordPerfect will leave extra space below the first line. The line height in these examples is fixed at .22".

❖ *Readout examples*

The first example doesn't even use a graphics box. The advantage to this is that you can always see the text in normal Edit mode. The disadvantage is that it cannot span columns. The top line is entered with **ALT-F9 L H W .1 [ENTER]**, and the bottom line is **ALT-F9 L H W .01c G 10.**

Although the examples on these pages have been reduced by 18%, I'm going to use the actual point sizes in these explanations. The big S is 36-point Palatino in a paragraph box .6" wide by .4". The options are set for no lines on all sides with an outside border space of 0" all around. The rest of the readout is 14-point Palatino italic. Simple and elegant.

Should you feel the urge to exercise, lie down until the feeling passes.

Robert Benchley

The second example (on the next page, with the two square bullets) is comprised of either one or two graphics boxes. If your readout is going to stay in a normal column, you need only two graphics boxes, one each for the black squares. (5.1 users can also use ALT-254 to create the black squares.) The little squares are User-defined boxes .1" by .1", centered, with options set to **G 100**. The big S is 36-point Palatino italic; the rest is 14-point Palatino italic. Always keep plenty of white space around this type of readout.

■

Should you feel the urge to exercise, lie down until the feeling passes.

■

The third example (with a vertical line on the left side) is a single figure box, with options set for a border of a single line on the left side only and an inside border of .2" all around. The big S is 30-point Times Roman bold, and the rest of the text is 14-point Times Roman italic. This type of readout works well between two columns, so use a page type box.

S*hould you feel the urge to exercise, lie down until the feeling passes.*

The fourth example (dotted line on top, thick line on bottom) is also a single graphics box, with options set to dotted line on top, thick line on bottom, .1" inside border. The big S is Avant Garde 30-point, and the rest of the text is Avant Garde 14-point. It's amazing how effective a change of fonts can be. The "S" in this font is so different (especially in contrast to the very traditional S of the second readout), that the entire readout has a much more modern appearance. If you make this a paragraph box and set the horizontal to "both left and right," it will fit perfectly into a column. If you want this to straddle two columns, use a page type box and have at least .15" of outside border in options.

Should you feel the urge to exercise, lie down until the feeling passes.

The fifth example (at the top of the opposite page) is a single graphics box, with a dotted border all around and a .1" inside border. The big S is 30-point Helvetica bold, and the text is 14-point Helvetica Condensed. I find this attractive, but I wouldn't use more than one of these on a two page spread, lest they appear too busy. (Don't you think Campbell's should start catering to us desktop publishers and come out with a Helvetica Condensed soup? Mmmmm good.)

Should you feel the urge to exercise, lie down until the feeling passes.

The sixth example has a single line on the top and left, and thick lines on the left and bottom. The font is Bookman 30-point bold for the S, and Bookman 14-point light for the text. (Didn't that sound frighteningly like the description of a Miss America Contestant? And while we're on the subject, where else do people wear high heels with bathing suits? And who's responsible for that silly combination?)

Should you feel the urge to exercise, lie down until the feeling passes.

The example below sports double lines above and below, single lines on the left and right. It somehow appears to be academic, if you ask me. The big S is 30-point Times Roman bold, the text is 14-point Times Roman medium.

Should you feel the urge to exercise, lie down until the feeling passes.

The last readout is the most extreme and calls the most attention to itself. It has a classic yet modern look, a bit wacky, but still elegant. Basically, it's just fun. It's also difficult. It can be a pain if the text moves, because the little black boxes may separate from the main gray box. Careful preview in View Document is required prior to printing. It consists of five, count 'em, five, graphics boxes.

The four black squares are each one user-defined box. I created the first two on top and simply copied them for the bottom two. They are .1" by .1", with options set to **G 100**. The readout itself is contained in a figure box, with .25" inside borders on the right and left, .1" inside borders on

Should you feel the urge to exercise, lie down until the feeling passes.

Robert Benchley

the top and bottom, no lines on any side, no outside margin, and gray shading set to 10%. To make the bottom two squares touch the bottom of the box, I had to use Advance Up .3" (SHIFT-F8 O A U .3"). This example is 14-point Palatino bold (it must be bold, otherwise it would be harder to read), with a big S in Extra Large size.

For 5.1: You can also get a similar effect (with less hassle) by putting your single paragraph into a table with only one column and one row. Turn off all lines, turn on the background shading. Use four graphics boxes for the little squares.

❖ *Put the table in the box*

It shouldn't come as any great surprise that you can place tables inside graphics boxes (especially since one of the box types is called table, and because I went on about it ad nauseam just a few chapters back). The question is *why* would you want to do this? The answer is sixfold.

- It's the only way to get tables into columns.
- It's the only way to get side by side tables.
- (5.0) You can set columns, tabs, and engage in any type of complex formatting without worrying about it changing by accident, or by moving it.
- (5.0) To put a box around tables made of tabs.
- (5.0) To put a gray screen behind tables made of tabs.
- (Everybody) Lack of anything better to do.

5.0 users have a dilemma: What if you want horizontal lines in the table—after all, wouldn't tables seem naked without them? You can't place graphics inside of graphics, so what's a mother to do? It all has to do with **SHIFT-F8 O U YY,** so that tabs are underlined continuously. Check out Chapter 6 for some glamorous ways in which you can use the normally mundane underline.

❖ *Text in a box*

There are times when you really want a paragraph to stand out, such as when you have a warning such as the following.

> WARNING: Feeding Miracle Whip to children under the age of eight may permanently warp their taste buds so that they will never be able to differentiate between "sandwich spread" and genuine mayonnaise.

Anything of such vital importance should certainly be boxed with lines all the way around, lest your readers miss it. Remember, however, that when you box text, you must first create an option that contains an Inside border space of at least .15". Otherwise, the text inside the box will run into the line around the box and you will be humiliated, or, if you are Japanese, lose face. It would be a pity too, because it's a cinch to avoid. If you were creating a figure box, you would set the option by pressing

ALT-F9 F O I .15 [ENTER] .15 [ENTER] .15 [ENTER] .15 [ENTER][ENTER]

Then you would create the figure box itself by pressing

ALT F9 F C E

Then type the text that you want to appear inside. If the text is already available in a file, press **SHIFT-F10** to retrieve the file into the graphics box. (Remember, it can't exceed one page, and WordPerfect won't let you leave the graphics box until you shorten it. It reminds me of one of those horrible French plays, like *No Exit*, where the audience is made to feel that there is no escaping the boredom of the play and you get an idea of what Hell must be like.)

This text will not appear in normal editing mode. You will only see it when you are in View Document mode, which leads to my next point.

➾ Table that motion

Of course, if you're using 5.1 you can also "box" a paragraph (or more) by placing it into a table. The advantage to this is that you can always see the text on-screen, it's not hidden away in some horrid little graphics box.

Just create a table with one column and one row. You can make it full width, or centered, or whatever you feel you must have to retain some shred of self-confidence. You can use any type of lines or no lines, just a shaded background.

And remember, you can control the amount of space between the text and the lines (or shading) by going into table edit and pressing **O S** (as in OS/2, Brutus?)

◆ See what you're missing

Text in a box is not visible when you are writing and editing. I find this inconvenient because I can't refer to it. A worst-case scenario has me forgetting it's there and writing it all over from scratch. Since I'm loathe to repeat myself repeat myself, I came up with this solution. When you are finished editing the text inside the graphics box, mark the entire contents by pressing

HOME HOME [UP ARROW] ALT-F4 HOME HOME [DOWN ARROW]

You will now copy this block, so press

CONTROL-F4 B C

WordPerfect will respond by removing the highlighting and saying "Move Cursor; press **ENTER** to retrieve." We're going to move the cursor completely out of the box, so press

F7 F7 [ENTER]

This will create a copy of all text inside the graphics box. Now you can't just leave it there, or it will print *twice* (once here and another time inside the graphics box). So we're going to place this text in a nonprinting comment that will display on-screen, but not print.

Block all the text copied from the box by pressing

ALT-F4

(If that didn't confuse you, this will: The vessel with the pestle has the pellet with the poison, the chalice from the palace has the brew that is true.)

To turn this text into a comment, press

CONTROL-F5 Y

To change the comment into regular text, place the cursor below the comment and type

CONTROL-F5 C T

◆ Box text alternative for 5.0

The one disadvantage of putting a table inside a graphics box is you then have to edit the graphics box in order to edit the text. Here's a procedure to keep the text out in the open and still print a box around it.

Create a User-defined box, set it for horizontal both left and right, and wrap text around to NO. Set the height of the box for at least .1" larger than the height of the paragraph (or paragraphs) you intend to box. Use the LN marker on the bottom of the screen to calculate the height of the paragraph.

Use a Left/Right indent (SHIFT-F4) to indent the text so it won't touch the box around it. You could also use a paired style to achieve this. The text will superimpose itself on the box, fitting neatly inside. If the paragraph gets longer, you will need to edit the user-defined box and lengthen it too.

There is a disadvantage to this method: if the paragraph moves too close to the end of a page, it may print on one page while the box will print another.

13

Do you want me to draw you a picture?

Graphics file formats

With WordPerfect you create text, but not graphics. You'll need to use a paint or draw program or a scanner to create graphics, or purchase pre-drawn clip art. If you can't draw a stick figure that a four-year-old would be proud of, don't worry. Two agreeable solutions are scanners, which act like a copy machine (only they copy to a file in the computer rather than to another piece of paper), and clip art graphics that others have scanned or created directly on computer. Both of these can provide professional pictures even for the non-artistic among us.

So you get into more than just WordPerfect when you get into graphics. Don't fret, you don't have to get in over your head. If all else fails, WordPerfect includes a program that "grabs" what's on the screen and allows you to enter it into a WordPerfect file.

This chapter will cover the many types of graphics files that WordPerfect can use, some it almost can use, and even some it can't. Chapter 18, *1-2-3 Publishing,* and Chapter 20, *Software,* explore graphics programs in detail, and also cover clip art packages.

❖ *Illustrating*

Before we talk tech, just a reminder that you don't have to use graphic pictures at all. Despite their power, you may never use graphics. If basic typesetting is all you desire, if you never want to do full-page layouts, or add graphics of any type, you don't have to use them. No one's keeping score. There won't be a test at the end of the chapter. If you need graphics, use them; if you don't, don't worry about it (although I have a feeling WordPerfect might entice you into using them).

As with everything else in graphic design, use pictures for a reason, not just as mere ornamentation. It's not a good idea to use pictures if they don't *illustrate* something. Remember the old theatrical adage: don't introduce a gun in the first act if it's not going to go off in the third. In this case, don't use a picture of a cow unless it goes off in the third act—no, no, unless the text is addressing cows, dairy products, or Belgian leather sofas.

Using a picture just because you admire it has some built-in pitfalls. People will spend more time studying the picture and trying to figure out what it has to do with the text than reading that text and getting the message. If there is no legitimate reason for the picture, people will use their overactive (or underactive) imaginations to come up with one, which is more than likely not what you had in mind.

◆ Illumination

First, you need to understand the differences between a "paint" program and a "draw" program.

Paint-type graphic (Metro)

Paint programs

A paint program provides you with the same sensation as freehand drawing does. You paint on the screen as if you were sketching on a piece of paper. You use the mouse or cursor to draw lines, circles, and boxes, and then fill them with various patterns.

Everything is part of a single "painting." If you want to change anything, such as the pattern you've used to fill in a circle, you usually have to erase the circle and start over. You are creating a finished painting that is comprised of many little dots; if you try to increase or decrease the size or the picture, the quality deteriorates, and solid grays can become unwanted tartan plaids.

Draw programs

Draw programs employ the same basic idea of drawing on-screen with a mouse, but they treat what you draw in a completely different fashion. In a draw program, whatever you draw is a distinct object. If

Draw-type graphic (MGI)

you draw a circle, and then place a box halfway inside of it, you still have two separate graphic items. You can fill the circle with one pattern and the box with another, and even change the patterns later on. You can control the circle independently from the box, place one on top of the other, and then switch which one is on top. This makes creating (and revising) complex graphics easier than using a paint program.

Drawings do not consist of little dots, as in a paint program, but of shapes—squares, circles, lines, etc. When a drawing is made larger or smaller, it changes sizes perfectly, because the shapes themselves are being resized, not the dots. This is known as "object-oriented" graphics (shapes), as opposed to "bitmap" graphics (dots).

The printed output will also be sharper, no matter what device it is printed on, because, once again, you aren't dealing with dots, but with shapes. A graphic created in a draw program will print at the highest resolution possible: from 300 dpi for laser printers, to 2450 dpi on Linotronic typesetters.

Draw programs are best for creating structured, technical, or geometric-based graphics (such as technical illustrations, floor plans, architectural drawings), and presentation graphics. Since draw programs allow for freehand lines, they can be used for artistic drawing as well, including logos, line art, and visual aids (such as slides, maps, and graphs). The newest draw programs, such as Corel Draw and Micrografx Designer, allow you to mix paint and draw files in a single image.

Even if you aren't an artist, you can still produce cleaner, more attractive graphics with draw programs because they employ precise tools that don't demand painstaking skill to master.

Programs that create draw-type files include AutoCAD, Corel Draw, Artline, Micrografx Designer, Draw and Graph, Harvard Graphics, Lotus Freelance, Lotus 1-2-3, .PIC files, and WordPerfect's own graphics program DrawPerfect and its spreadsheet, PlanPerfect.

◆ Conversion problems

WordPerfect will sometimes refuse to load a graphic, for any number of reasons. For example, you might have the 1/19/90 version of the program which can't read most .TIF files directly, or a version of 5.0 which has taken a dislike to graphics from Publisher's Paintbrush.

When this happens, the very first thing you should try is the GRAPHCNV program. This program will be in your WordPerfect directory if you installed utilities and graphics drivers.

Run the Graphcnv program on the graphic you've had difficulty importing. This program seems less finicky than WordPerfect, and I've had much success using this program to convert graphics into .WPG, which WordPerfect will then use without complaint. For more info about this program, look near the end of this chapter.

◆ Line art alert

While line art graphics will print sharper than bitmapped, WordPerfect finds it harder to print them. It not only takes more time for WordPerfect to display them in View Document and print them to the printer, it seems to take more memory as well.

It's not unusual for WordPerfect to load a CGM or line art WPG file just fine, and then repeatedly tell you "not enough memory to print graphics." This problem is not severe in 5.0, but it can be a real problem in 5.1.

The way to get around it is to 1) have as much computer memory as possible; 2) exit WordPerfect and come back, then print the file immediately without doing anything else before WordPerfect has the chance to gobble up a lot of memory; 3) use bitmap graphics.

Bitmap graphics will print just as sharply as line art, as long as you create them (or in the case of a program like Corel Draw, export them) at the same size you are going to print them.

If you create a bitmapped graphic in exactly the size it will be printed, there is little or no discernable difference in quality between line art and bitmap. This means that if you want to print an image 3" wide, you should make it 3" wide in your graphics program. If you make it 1.5" wide and scale it up, it's going to be jagged. If you make it 4.5" wide and scale it down, it's going to get darker, which is fine if it's just black and white line art, but disastrous if it has too many fine lines.

Programs such as Corel Draw give you the choice between saving artwork as line art or bitmapped. You should save as bitmapped if the graphic is simple black and white and you know the size you're going to print it at. If your graphic has many levels of gray, or if you need to scale the graphic larger or smaller, use line art.

◆ Lucky 13

Have you ever seen a building with a 13th floor? Think about it. The elevator buttons go from 12 to 14. There's an episode of the *Twilight Zone* in there somewhere, but if you write it, I want to share story credit. Also, *Friday the 13th* inspired the ultimate spoof of horror movies, *Saturday the 14th Strikes Back.* (There's nothing

Before. This line art comes from the Pictorial Archive series of copyright-free Dover books, and is a fairly straightforward illustration. But when scanned and edited by my wife Toni in PC Paintbrush, look what happens to those poor unsuspecting geishas.

After. Mere moments later, the geishas have been turned into Mr. Spock and Captain Kirk—complete with pointy ears, raised eyebrows, and Enterprise emblems on their kimonos. Notice their hands now making the familiar Vulcan greeting. Beam me up, Scotty.

really violent or disgusting in this movie—just me. Pop in the video, pop some corn, and watch in awe as I try to upstage the rest of the cast.)

Why the discourse about the lucky number 13? Because WordPerfect can read 13 different graphics file types, that's why. If you've ever tried to read a WordStar file or one from Microsoft Word directly, you're aware that almost every word processing program uses a different file format. This format contains not just the text, but formatting codes for underlines, bold, margins, etc.

Graphics programs file formats have many more differences than do word processing programs and are less standardized, as well. But WordPerfect accepts 13 different formats directly. (Actually 14, if you include Windows Paint, which I don't because I've never seen anything good produced with that program, and besides, I can't think of anything interesting to say about the number 14.) Anyway, we'll all agree that there are enough graphics programs and file formats to choose from.

❖ Unlucky 13

It would be convenient if it were that simple, but it's not. Just because a program claims to make files in a format that WordPerfect accepts, the files still may not function as they should; this is because so-called standard file formats are far from standard.

Here is a list of the file formats WordPerfect accepts, including some comments on the programs that create these files and particular problems inherent in the file format. Hopefully this will help you avoid expensive software mistakes when purchasing graphics software.

◆ Paint formats

PCX

This is the industry standard paint format for MS-DOS computers and is called .PCX format. This format was created by a company called ZSoft for use with their PC Paintbrush line of paint programs. A variation of this format is called .PCC. Both .PCX and .PCC are about as standard as a graphics format gets. This means that while they work most of the time, occasionally they don't. The only problems I've seen are with graphics created in Publisher's Paintbrush, the high-end version of PC Paintbrush. Occasionally these files will import as garbage. If this happens, try re-saving the graphics, or "cutting" them as .PCC files.

Many scanners can also save files in .PCX format, and I have yet to see a scanned image in .PCX format fail to load correctly. PC Paintbrush itself can run a scanner and then edit the scanned images, such as the ones pictured here. Clip art packages are often in .PCX format, and these work fine, too. Popular programs that create .PCX files include PC Paintbrush, Publisher's Paintbrush, Corel Draw (TIF format is more reliable for 5.0), Micrografx Designer (again, TIF is a better choice for 5.0), Artline, HP Drawing/Charting Gallery, and HP Scanning Gallery.

IMG

This is another industry standard, because .IMG (for image) files always work. Popular programs that use this format include Artline, GEM Paint, Halo, Halo DPE, SLed. An excellent 3-D charting and graphing program called Perspective Junior also creates .IMG files. (I'm waiting for 4-D graphics: a program that would "channel" the spirit of Leonardo DaVinci and create charts and graphs without human intervention. I'm not holding my breath, however.)

TIF

Also known as "TIFF," or "Tagged Image File Format." This is the newest bit-mapped format, and while TIF itself has countless variations, there's no guarantee that WordPerfect will accept a TIF file.

TIF files can be compressed and may contain "gray scale" information. WordPerfect reads uncompressed and 8-bit (16-level) gray scale TIF files consistently. However, it occasionally has problems with compressed TIF files. This is unfortunate as these take far less disk space than uncompressed files. My only suggestion is to create a TIF file and try to bring it into WordPerfect. If it works, great; if it doesn't, save it as an uncompressed file, try another format, or try to convert to .WPG using the Graphcnv program.

Sometimes it reads TIF other times it doesn't. The more compressed the files are, the less likely WordPerfect is to read them. WordPerfect will not read 16-bit, 256-level gray scale TIF files. Also, different versions of WordPerfect are better or worse with TIF files. The 6/89 version of 5.0 can read any TIF file you throw at it. The 11/89 version of 5.1 has some TIF trouble, and the 1/19/90 version seems to have some deep-seated hatred of *all* TIF files.

Popular programs that create TIF files include Corel Draw, Micrografx Designer, HP Scanning Gallery, GEM Scan, Perspective Junior, and HP Drawing/Charting Gallery. SnapShot, from Aldus, creates and edits TIF files obtained from video sources.

PIC, DHP

Halo DPE is a popular paint program. It can read and write its own format and .IMG files. Don't confuse this paint-type format with the Lotus 1-2-3 draw-type .PIC format.

MSP

Microsoft Windows Paint is a very limited program included with Microsoft Windows (a "GUI—Graphic User Environment").

MacPaint, PNTG

MacPaint is a popular paint program for the Macintosh computer. Macs use 3 1/2 inch disks, but the disk format differs from MS-DOS 3 1/2 inch disks. Because of this, moving files from one machine to another can require a network, modem, or internal hardware board, such as the "MatchMaker" from Micro Solutions. Some companies sell clip art in this format, namely Software Publishing's "PFS: First Publisher Art Portfolios."

PPIC

PC Paint Plus. Another paint program for the PC. Not as competent or popular as PC Paintbrush.

❖ *Draw formats*

CGM

"Computer Graphic Metafile" is potentially the most useful, and the most troublesome, of the line art formats. CGM files are compact, so they display and print quickly. Many programs are capable of creating CGM files.

Unfortunately, despite its reputation as an industry standard, there are so many versions of this format that it is anything but standard.

The only CGM files WordPerfect will use are straight line art, black and white. A few programs, such as Harvard Graphics, can include gray patterns, but WordPerfect will convert patterns from some CGM files into unadulterated garbage.

And so, although many programs can create CGM files, not all of them can be used with WordPerfect. A single program may create files that you can use, and others that you can't, depending on what you've included in the files. Even Harvard Graphics can produce some CGM files which WordPerfect uses flawlessly, while others may appear all black inside WordPerfect. The cardinal rule to remember is: **ALWAYS CHOOSE PATTERNS, NEVER COLORS.** If a program doesn't offer you a choice, it probably won't work with WordPerfect.

This can be enormously frustrating, so make sure that you can create CGM files with a program, and test them with WordPerfect first. Most graphic editing programs can read a wider variety of CGM files than WordPerfect can; so a program may create a technically perfect CGM file, but WordPerfect still may not read it.

CGM files created by Corel Draw and Arts & Letters usually work perfectly with 5.0 and 5.1.

Some popular programs that create CGM files include Corel Draw, Micrografx Designer, Freelance Plus, Graphwriter, Harvard Graphics, and PlanPerfect. More explicit directions for using Harvard Graphics with WordPerfect are given later in this chapter, and in Chapter 18, *1-2-3 Publishing.*

DXF

"Data eXchange Format" is a format which was standardized by the AutoCAD computer-aided design program. Most CAD software supports this format, but the format itself is limited. Text has a resemblance to stick figures. This was not designed as an artistic format and so lacks useful features.

To use DXF files with WordPerfect, you must first convert them by using the GRAPHCNV program supplied on the Conversion disk. This is the only supported format that WordPerfect can't read directly.

HPGL

Hewlett-Packard Graphics Language was designed for pen plotters. One drawback is that WordPerfect works fine with black and white or stick-figure graphics, but it will not accept HPGL files containing objects filled with patterns. These files are made up of smaller line segments that appear coarse when enlarged and do not size as well as other line art files. For example, to fill a circle with black, this format packs the circle with countless closely spaced lines. If you enlarge the picture, the individual lines become visible and no longer appear solid.

If you are having trouble retrieving CGM, you might consider using HPGL (if your graphics program supports it). With Harvard Graphics, some files are compatible with CGM, while others, notably those with a patterned background, work more effectively in HPGL format.

If a graphic program supports an HP plotter, simply print the file "to disk," rather than to the printer.

EPS

Encapsulated PostScript may sound as if it's inside a cold capsule, but it's easy to swallow *if*, and only if, you have a PostScript printer.

Because PostScript is a language, these files are actually programs that describe an image to the printer. Some people create these program files themselves, but the more sane among us utilize graphics programs to create EPS files.

WordPerfect will only print EPS files if they are "well-behaved"; in other words, they must conform exactly to EPS specifications.

EPS files do not display on-screen unless they include a .TIF file for a screen image. The .TIF file is used for display only, not for printing. If they don't include a .TIF file (and many don't), nothing will be apparent in either Graphics Edit or View Document; the graphic will appear as an empty box.

EPS files can contain dazzling special effects, including rotated types, "fountain" fills which contain a smooth progression of gray tones, and even photographs using gray scale information for high-quality reproduction.

Corel Draw and Micrografx Designer are the best ways to create EPS files on the PC. On the Mac, Adobe Illustrator and Aldus Freehand are the top programs for creating EPS. The EPS format is the same, whether created on a PC or a Mac.

Harvard Graphics and the spreadsheet Quattro (uno, dos, tres) also create EPS files. If the software you are using doesn't create EPS files, you can attempt to print the file to disk using the PostScript printer driver rather than the printer. These files will sometimes function as EPS files.

WPG

Just what the world needs, another graphic file format. This is a new file format devised by WordPerfect Corporation. The WPG format can hold both line art and bitmapped files, so you can't tell whether the file is line art or bitmapped just from the name. DrawPerfect, WordPerfect's graphics program, creates WPG files, as does Corel Draw.

This format is no better or worse than the other formats, it's just different, and if a graphics program can create a "correct" WPG file, it's almost guaranteed that

WordPerfect will accept it. I say almost because, like all graphics formats, *always* does not apply.

.WPG files are also created if you save a graphic from inside WordPerfect. If you load any graphic into a graphics box, then edit it, you can press F10 to save that file to disk. The resulting file will be a .WPG file.

◆ Local color

WordPerfect can display color graphics on-screen if you have a color monitor. What it can't do is print them, even with a color printer. I would be surprised if WordPerfect doesn't add this capability sometime soon, but for the moment you'll have to settle for black-and-white output of your color pictures.

WordPerfect converts colors to different shades of gray and while this is usually accurate, at times the outcome can surprise you. A light color like yellow may print black. If you are using a monochrome monitor (black and white), View Document will give you a good idea of what the printed graphic will look like. But a color monitor will display the graphic in color (unless you press SHIFT-F1 D V G Y), and you will have to print it to see exactly how the colors translate.

◆ Corel drama

Corel Draw is a favorite graphics program (graphics in the sense of pictures, not charts and graphs). It does for pictures what WordPerfect does for text. And it works especially well with WordPerfect because it can save directly into .WPG format.

But as I said earlier, there are times when it's better to save in .PCX or .TIF format. Those are the times when the graphic is complex and WordPerfect balks at displaying or printing it.

Also, certain versions of WordPerfect have idiosyncracies about .TIF and .PCX files. If you're using 5.0, use .TIF files, as 5.0 doesn't like Corel's .PCX files at all. Certain versions of 5.1 (such as 1/19/90) won't accept any .TIF files, while it can use the .PCX files which 5.0 refuses. While .CGM and .WPG files seem to work with all versions, WordPerfect may claim it doesn't have enough memory for them.

As well as being a great graphics program, Corel is a good way for users of nonPostScript printers to tap into the large collection of .EPS clip art which otherwise prints only on PostScript printers. Corel can import .EPS and then export it in .CGM, .WPG, .TIF, or .PCX formats for use with nonPostScript printers.

◆ Ivy league tips

One of the most popular charting and graphing programs for the PC is Harvard Graphics, from Software Publishing. If you don't already use Harvard, you may want to use DrawPerfect instead, because its interface is similar to WordPerfect's.

If you already use HG, here are some tips for creating files that will function effectively with WordPerfect whether you use CGM or HPGL.

- Always select a "Pattern" fill style of instead of color. While color may be attractive on-screen, WordPerfect tends to print out several colors as black, and this can be quite unappealing in charts.
- **CGM Files:** Select patterns from the "Printer Pattern" wheel in Appendix F.
- **HPGL Files:** Select patterns from the "Plotter Pattern" wheel in Appendix F.
- **ONLY USE COLOR 1** (white, which prints as black) to print in black, and **SET BACKGROUND COLOR TO 16** (black, which prints as white) to print in white.

◆ Grab bag

If your graphic program does not create files that WordPerfect can use, there is one last resort, in the form of a program called GRAB.

This is a "screen grab" program that literally grabs whatever is on the screen and creates a copy of it on-disk. WordPerfect can then load the disk file into graphics boxes.

There are limitations, however. First, the program doesn't work with all monitors. The most popular graphics systems, including CGA, EGA, VGA, and Hercules, are supported, but less popular monitors, such as full-page, high-resolution, or video cards in special modes, are not.

The other limitation is that the resolution of a GRAB file is only as high as the screen it was used on. With CGA monitors, that's very low. Hercules, EGA, and VGA are higher, but at approximately 72 dpi, these are still relatively low resolution. These images will appear somewhat jagged when printed full size on a 300 dpi laser printer, such as the LaserJet. The quality will improve if you print them at a smaller size, but these files are not large to begin with, so reducing them may lead to tiny graphics.

◆ Grab for it

Using this program is quite effortless, as there is only one command: GRAB. Located on the Fonts/Graphics disk, the program can either be run from the floppy or copied to the hard disk. The program can be in any directory.

To start the program, type

GRAB [ENTER]

The program will display a message, reminding you that the command to grab is

ALT-SHIFT-F9

It will also tell you that typing

GRAB/H

will enable you to ask for help with the program. Grab takes up a mere 10K of memory, but it may find itself in conflict with other memory resident programs, such as SideKick.

GRAB only operates in graphics mode so don't bother trying to grab a screen full of text. When you are in graphics mode, and want to save a copy of the current screen onto a disk file, press

ALT-SHIFT-F9

If your graphics card is supported, GRAB will emit a two-tone chime. Ding-dong. No, it's not the Avon lady; it's simply proclaiming that it is saving the screen picture onto disk.

If GRAB makes a low buzzing noise that sounds as if you answered incorrectly on a game show, don't bother checking behind Door Number Three because you really have lost. This soothing sound indicates that GRAB doesn't support your graphics card in its current mode. If you try all the modes and GRAB still buzzes, well, it's time for Truth or Consequences, and you're getting the consequences.

If you are a lucky winner, GRAB will save the screen in the "default" directory (usually whatever directory you started the graphics program in). However, the graphics program may have changed directories, and so the file might not be where you think.

To ensure that the file goes where you want it, begin the program with: **GRAB/d=C:\WP51** (or your WP document directory). This forces GRAB to save its files in the WP51 directory. You can specify *any* directory after the "/d=" and GRAB will save its files in that directory.

GRAB calls the first file it saves GRAB.WPG. When you press **ALT-SHIFT-F9** again, it creates a file called GRAB1.WPG. This predictable scenario goes on ad nauseam until you've saved GRAB9999.WPG. If you delete or rename the GRAB files, GRAB will commence renumbering from the beginning. It's often wise to rename these files with something a trifle more descriptive than GRAB894.WPG. Once you've loaded the file into a graphics box, that name will be displayed in Reveal Codes, and you'll know what the graphics box contains, even if you don't have a caption. You can use List Files, **F5** to rename the files.

GRAB has two more options up its sleeve. If you start the program with **GRAB/F=JUNK**, GRAB will name its first file JUNK.WPG, its second, JUNK1.WPG, and so on. Of course, you can use any four letters you want (yes, *any* four letters); this will give your file a more specific name right from the start. You could use a name like **GRAB/F=PIES,** if you were grabbing pie charts from a graphics program, or **GRAB/F=FLEA** if you were grabbing pictures of dogs.

If you use this last option, type

GRAB/R

GRAB will remove itself from memory. You may not be able to remove GRAB from memory until you remove any other memory resident program loaded *after* GRAB.

One sure-fire way to remove GRAB from memory is to turn the computer off, press the reset button (if you have one), or press **CONTROL-ALT-DELETE** simultaneously. Remember to save your work and exit any program (especially WordPerfect) before you use any of these options. Otherwise, you may lose material that was not saved to disk.

❖ *Be a convert*

WordPerfect is accompanied by another program for graphics files. This one is called GRAPHCNV (for graph convert), and converts all the supported formats into .WPG files. If you are using files in any format other than .DXF, this program will not be necessary.

If you are using .DXF files, you must first convert them with this program, as WordPerfect doesn't read them directly.

You can use this program in batch mode by using DOS wildcards instead of complete filenames. If you wanted to convert a whole directory containing .DXF files in one swell foop, you would type

GRAPHCNV *.DXF [ENTER]

WordPerfect will ask if you want to replace all the .WPG files in the current directory. If you answer **N**, the program stops and returns to DOS (maybe it's offended because you didn't agree to its terms). If you answer **Y**, the program is overjoyed and leaps into action. It asks what directory you want the .WPG files to be created in. Press return for the current directory or specify any other directory you want. When you press **[ENTER]**, the program begins converting files with relish (catsup or mustard).

❖ Clip art tips

If you plan to buy clip art (professionally-designed graphics on-disk), you can purchase it in several different file formats. (See Chapter 20, *Software*, for reviews and examples of clip art packages.)

◆ Bitmapped

The most popular file format for clip art is .PCX, with all the advantages and disadvantages of bitmapped files. These files are easy to edit using programs such as PC Paintbrush. Even minor editing can customize clip art so it appears less generic and more specific to your individual needs.

As with all bitmapped files, however, they will print jagged and look as if they were produced on a computer if you enlarge them too much. Also, any gray patterns in the file may turn into plaid patterns. While it might be amusing to argue about what clan these patterns belong to, they are not terribly attractive and distract from the picture itself. But as long as you don't resize them radically they can be indistinguishable from handmade artwork.

One other item to check for when purchasing clip art is resolution. Because laser printers usually print 300 dots per inch, clip art at 300 dpi will print sharper than clip art of lesser resolution.

If you shrink low resolution graphics, they will print as sharply as 300 dpi graphics. A 75 dpi picture printed at one-fourth its original size will look identical to a 300 dpi picture (only smaller).

◆ Line art

There is not nearly as much clip art available in line art format. The advantage of clip art in these formats is that it retains its high quality no matter what size you print it or what printer you print it on. Clip art in line art format will print at full resolution on a typesetter with 2450 dpi resolution.

MGI's PicturePak series is some of the best line art available. If you have 5.0, the clip art included comes from MGI's collections. The clip art in 5.1 was done in-house at WordPerfect using DrawPerfect. Each image in MGI's PicturePaks comes in both .CGM and .PCX formats.

If you have Corel Draw, you can convert .EPS clip art and save it in .CGM, .WPG, .TIF, or .PCX for use with nonPostScript printers.

14

Rules to live by

or What's my line?

Graphic designers call them rules, and there are many rules related to these rules. Rules are important in design because they help organize the page and make it easier to read. WordPerfect has two types of rules: horizontal and vertical. These can be used in a wide variety of ways, as you will find out all too soon.

You can place lines between columns (and learn how to have them print automatically on all pages, not just one). You can place them above headlines and subheads or on separate charts or readouts. Don't confuse these with the Line Draw feature that allows you to draw with the cursor, but does not print with all printers. I'll cover that later in this chapter as well.

Best of all, the lines are blissfully easy to use with WordPerfect. And to prove my point, I shall now attempt to show you everything you need to know about lines, and I won't even have to rely on a translator from the U.N. It's a tall order, and I'll probably spend a half page just hyping what a terrific feat this will be, but I'll bet I can do it. At no time will my fingers leave my hands.

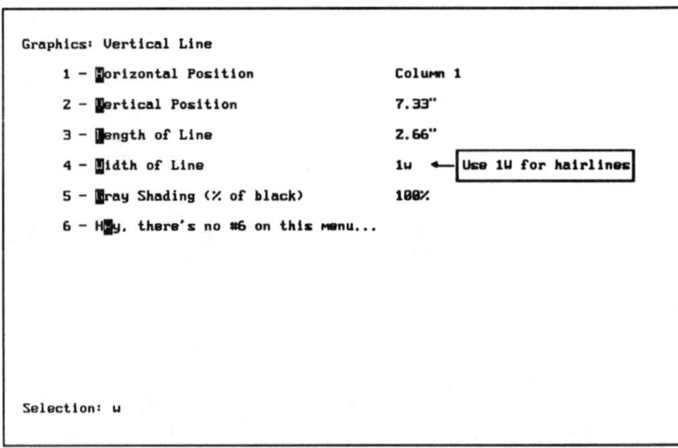

Vertical lines are set to an absolute position on a page. They don't move with text like graphic boxes or horizontal lines. Notice how I've set the width of line with 1w, the thinnest setting possible with WordPerfect.

◆ Creating lines

The main command for creating lines is

ALT-F9 L (V or H)

If you follow this with a **V**, you will create a vertical line; if you follow it with an **H**, you will create a horizontal line.

TA-DA!

That's it. With that information alone, you can create a line in WordPerfect. Of course, you'll have to expand your attention span to cover some of the more involved options (having the line print somewhere other than across the width of the page or down the left margin, for example). To learn how to make vertical rules float with text, see Chapter 9, *Columns.*

◆ Horizontal lines

Let's be alphabetical and start with horizontal lines. Press

ALT-F9 L H

You are now staring at the horizontal line menu, a sight that would have been shocking a mere 100 years ago. Today, of course, it's commonplace, and you'll be seeing a lot of it.

If you press return now, you will be asking for a line that runs from the right margin to the left margin (and changes lengths automatically if you change margins). The line will be .013" (or .03c) wide (5.0 default is .01"), and 100% black.

◆ Line positioning

If you want something other than this default line, you have five choices:

The first is **H** for horizontal position. When you press **H**, you are faced with five options: Left starts the line from the left margin, **R**ight starts the line from the right

```
Graphics: Horizontal Line

     1 - Horizontal Position          Full
     2 - Vertical Position            Baseline
     3 - Length of Line
     4 - Width of Line                0.013"
     5 - Gray Shading (% of black)    100%
     6 - Dance Music (Just kidding)   Strauss

Selection: 0
```

Horizontal lines can be set to start at the left or right margin and can be any length or thickness. When they are set to Full (as seen here), they change length automatically if the margin changes.

margin, Center centers the line, Full (Both for 5.0) is identical to the default (it creates a line that travels from the left margin to the right margin), and Set position allows you to specify the precise distance you want the line to start from the left edge of the paper (not the margin).

For our example, let's center the line. Press

H C

Notice that the length of line is set to 0"; if you were to press return now, you would create a line 0" long (which is a pretty short line). To avoid this embarrassing turn of events, we're going to make the line 3 inches long. To do this, press

L 3 [ENTER]

5.1 users have an additional option here. They can choose that the line prints at the current baseline (the bottom of the letters, excluding descenders such as g, j, p, q, and y) or they can place the line at any vertical point on the page. This is useful if you need to have lines at specific places, such as 3" from the top of the page. When you set a position, the line will not move with the text, as a baseline line does, but will stick to a particular position on a page. If you add or delete enough text, the line may move to the next or previous page. For this example, we're going to leave the line at the baseline.

The next step is to tell WordPerfect how thick a line to create. In most cases, the default of .013" (5.0 default is .01) is just right. It's not too thin or too thick. But we're going to make this a thick line by pressing

W .1 [ENTER]

The last item to decide upon is whether the line will print solid black (the default) or in a shade of gray. Since we seem to be living life in the "lite decade," gray lines are often a lighter alternative to those heavy black lines. Let's make ours a 20% gray line. Press

G 20 [ENTER]

Now let's double check our handiwork. The screen should read:
Horizontal Position = Center
Vertical Position = Baseline
Length of line = 3"
Width of line = .1"
Gray Shading (% of Black) = 20%
If it does, press

[ENTER]

A code will be placed in the text. If you want to see the code, press **ALT-F3** for Reveal Codes. The code will look like this: **[HLine:Center, Baseline,3",0.1",20%]**. This tells you everything you need to know about the line: it is centered, positioned at the baseline, 3" long, .01" wide, and 20% gray. To finish the line, press

[ENTER]

Now press **SHIFT-F7 V** to view this on-screen. C'mon, admit it. Isn't that about the prettiest horizontal line you've ever seen?

◆ Tip: Get down (get back up again)

When using a horizontal ruling line, it's often a good idea to have an Advance Down of .1 (SHIFT-F8 O A D .1 F7) before and after the rule, to keep it from getting too close to the text.

Even if you use a hard return before and after the line, the extra .1" adds white space and keeps the page from looking crowded.

◆ Vertical lines

With horizontal lines under our belt (don't you hate it when those lines dig into your stomach?), let's give our all to creating a vertical line.

But first, a few particulars. Unlike graphics boxes and horizontal lines, vertical lines do not move with text when you edit. They are anchored onto a page in a particular position, either from top to bottom or at a specified distance from the top margin, extending down to a specified length.

Because of this, they can be annoying to work with, especially if you edit text and paragraphs move but lines don't. I'll have a fix for that later on, but it is vital that vertical lines not move with text.

Vertical lines are most often used between columns of text, and so that's what we're going to create. Your first intercolumn rule, oh isn't this exciting? Someday you'll look back on all of this and smile, or hopefully just pay someone to look back and smile for you.

As Peter Pan says 11,234 times a day at Disneyland, "*Come on everybody, here we goooooooo.*" (Pneumatic clicking noises are heard, a shadow of Peter flits across the wall, and the windows of the nursery open themselves magically to allow a flying sailboat to soar over London—and you didn't even have to wait 45 minutes in line, you lucky stiff.)

◆ Intercolumn rules

Because we're going to create an intercolumn rule, we'll first have to create a column. For more information about columns, see Chapter 9. We're going to leave room for a headline, so press

[ENTER]

until the measurement in the right corner is at approximately **Ln 2.00"**.

To create a two column page, press

ALT-F7 C D D .3" [ENTER][ENTER] O

(5.0 users will press **C** instead of **O**). We're now going to create a vertical line that runs from the top of the columns (not the top of the page) to the bottom of the page. Press

ALT-F9 L V

If you were to press return now, you would create a default vertical line .013" (or .03c) wide running from top to bottom of the left margin. But we're not about to settle for that, are we? We're too busy striving for self-enlightenment, self-improvement, and world peace, and we aren't about to accept any crummy defaults.

The first item on the menu (the appetizer so to speak) is **Horizontal**. This is similar to horizontal lines, only different. The difference is that the "Center" choice is replaced with **Between Columns**. Since that's what we want, press

H B 1 [ENTER]

When you press **B**, WordPerfect replies "Place line to right of column." WordPerfect put the line to the right of that column because you pressed 1. If you had more than two columns on a page, you would have to repeat this command for each column (except the last, because a line is not needed at the right margin).

Behind Door #2 lies **Vertical**. **Full Page** is displayed right now because that's the default. The choices are **Full Page**, **Top**, **Center**, **Bottom**, and **Set Position**. These measurements are always set from the margins, not from the edge of the page.

Because we want the line to start at the top of the columns rather than the top, center, or bottom of the page, we're going to press

V S [ENTER]

When you press [ENTER], WordPerfect displays your current vertical location on the page (2" here). If you want, you can type a new number here, and the line will start in that position and then print down the page. A more efficient way to use this feature is to position the cursor on the line of text where you want the vertical line to start printing before you define the line, as you did here. WordPerfect will then calculate the vertical position for you.

Length of line is also filled in correctly so that the line reaches from its current position to the bottom of the page. You could enter a different number here if you wanted the line to stop before the end of the page. But you don't want that, do you?

◆ Line width

It's Width of Line time. In the case of intercolumn rules, thin is best, and so leave it at .013"

Don't try it right now, but if you wanted an even thinner line, you would press

L 1W [ENTER]

➻ Remember, W is WordPerfect's internal measurement system (that I can only dream they named after me). There are 1200 Ws per inch. If you print onto a PostScript typesetter, you'll see a huge difference (called a "hairline"). If you print to a PostScript laser printer, you'll see a considerable difference. If you have a LaserJet, you'll see a less dramatic but still noticeable difference.

We're going to create an even thinner line by using tiny little dots. We'll do this with the Gray Shading (% of Black) command. Press

G 10 [ENTER]

The vertical line is now complete. To finish, press

[ENTER]

If you want to admire your handiwork, press **SHIFT-F7 V**. If you don't see anything (and you may not because it's so thin and light), press **1** or **2** to zoom in. On some monitors you still might not see the line, even at zoom level 2, but it's there.

◆ Your line or mine?

If you have an early version of 5.0, you cannot edit lines. But later versions of 5.0 and all versions of 5.1 allow you to edit lines you've previously created.

If you want to edit a *vertical* line, press

ALT-F9 L E

WordPerfect will search *backwards* and edit the first line it finds. If it can't find one above the cursor, it will search forward and edit the next line.

If you want to edit a *horizontal* line, press

ALT-F9 L O

❖ *The wrap rap*

Text will wrap around graphics boxes, but will not wrap around lines. In other words, the text won't budge if you try to place a horizontal or vertical line to print above or below it. Therefore, you have to exercise a little more caution when working with lines.

While horizontal lines set to "Left & Right" *will* shorten themselves to keep from printing over graphics boxes, a vertical full-page line can only be shortened by using a top and bottom margin change, or by adding headers and footers.

◆ Creating readouts

This means that if you create a page with a readout in the middle of two columns, and then place a full-page vertical line between the columns, it will print right through the middle of the graphics box readout. This can only be averted by setting two vertical rules. One runs from the top of the column to the top of the graphics box readout, and the other runs from the bottom of the graphics box readout to the bottom of the page.

This isn't too difficult if you move to the lines where the readout begins and jot down the LN measurement from the lower right corner of the screen. Then move to the line below where the readout ends, and write down that measurement.

Move to the line on the page where you want the vertical line to begin. Create the first vertical line and press

ALT-F9 L V V S [ENTER]

This will tell WordPerfect to insert the current vertical position. Press

L

Here comes the math, so you might want to get out your $5 pocket calculator. (If you can figure this type of stuff out in your head, you should probably sell your computer and become a card counter in Vegas.) Subtract the measurement at the top of the readout from your current position. This will tell you the length of line you need. Enter this number, then press **[ENTER]**

Now we're going to create the line from the bottom of the readout to the bottom of the page. Move the cursor to where the readout ends. You'll be able to see it on-screen. Press

ALT-F9 L V V S

Enter the measurement of the line where the readout ends. Press

[ENTER]

WordPerfect will calculate the distance to the bottom of the page and enter it in Length of Line.

The intercolumn rule will now stop at the readout box, and continue underneath it, allowing for a thoroughly professional appearance. You are now a horizontal and vertical lines whiz-kid.

◆ Line draw

(Note: If you're using 5.0, you can use Line Draw characters only if you are going to print to a LaserJet. If you're using 5.1, you can use this feature with any graphics printer.)

While horizontal and vertical lines are codes, lines created with "line-draw" are actual characters. The LaserJet II, IID, IIP, and III all contain a line-draw font built-in that matches the line characters available on all MS-DOS computers. The original LaserJet does not have these fonts built-in, but they're available on cartridge.

One drawback with line-draw and desktop publishing is that line-draw characters are monospaced, while DTP type is proportionally spaced. This is why WordPerfect doesn't recommend using line draw with proportionally spaced type. If you want to, go right ahead, but it's really not worth the trouble. It requires writing all the text, then using line-draw, then going back and inserting tabs so that the lines print as they appear on-screen. You should use horizontal and vertical lines instead, or use graphics boxes to create boxes around text. However, if you're careful, you can use this feature to create presentable bar charts.

Not surprisingly, there are a few tricks involved here. Notice how (in the following illustration) I never place text on the same line as a line-draw graphic, except at the end of a line. That's a surefire and simple way to have line-draw work for you.

LINE HEIGHT: Here's another important point to remember. Because these line-draw characters are part of the Courier 10 pitch PC-8 font, you must set line (fixed) height at .16" in order for the line-draw characters to print as they appear on-screen. Additional line spacing will result in horizontal white gaps between each line of characters, while less spacing will cause the line-draw characters to overlap.

Because the line spacing for the entire graph is fixed at .16", it doesn't change even when I add text at the end of a line.

BASE FONT: If you're not using a LaserJet compatible printer, you will need to make sure that the base font is set to "Courier." Otherwise WordPerfect will use proportional spacing for these characters, and they will not print correctly.

◆ Drawing lines

Okay, kids, what time is it? Why, it's play time! To get into Line-Draw mode, press

CONTROL-F3 L

You now have six choices. If you press **1**, you can draw a single line; **2** allows you to draw with a double line; **3** draws an asterisk (and other characters we'll discuss in a minute); **4** allows you to change the character drawn with 3; **5** erases as it moves; and **6** moves without erasing.

Unlike the normal word processing mode, line-draw will automatically create new lines when you press the **[DOWN ARROW]** key. Press

1

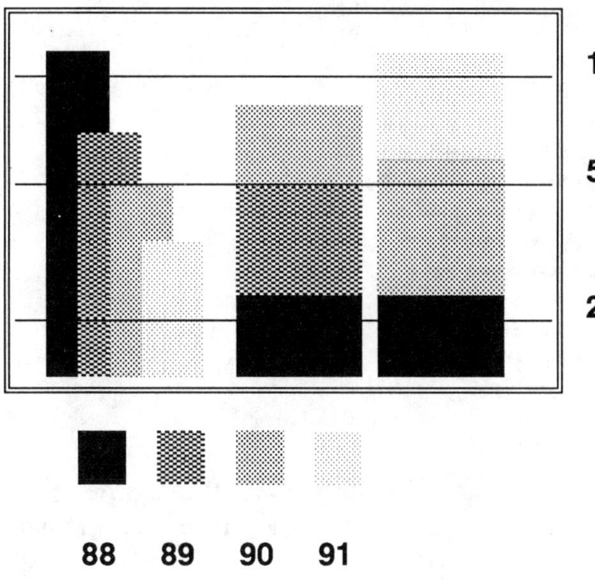

These line-draw characters can be useful for LaserJet users. You can easily create bar charts, such as the one pictured here.

Now move the cursor. You'll see that WordPerfect is drawing a line as you move. And WordPerfect will automatically create corners.

If you study the graph on the previous page, you'll notice that it's derived from characters that aren't shown in either 1, 2, or 3. I selected these characters using option 4. So join me, won't you? Press

4

You'll see nine more options displayed here. Press

4

This will select the thick solid-black box. Now when you move the cursor, WordPerfect draws a thick black line. For the graph on page 325, I used five different types of lines: the #2 double line for the box around, and #4, #3, #2, and #1 within option 4.

◆ Character sets

This is so cute it could make you want to watch a Doris Day movie. Press

4 9 [ALT-3]

Be sure to press the 3 on the keypad, not the 3 under the "#," or F3. A precious little heart will appear, and now, when you move the cursor, WordPerfect will draw a line of hearts. Use the cursor to design a heart like this:

Write a syrupy-sweet message underneath it and send it off to mother. (Who knows? — She might get off your back. On the other hand, she might want to move in with you.)

For a complete list of the IBM-PC character set, see Chapter 7, *Fonts.* You can use any of these characters by pressing

4 9

Then hold down the **[ALT]** key and type the number corresponding to the symbol you want (use the numeric keypad).

The mysterious option 9 allows you to draw with any character included in the 12 character sets. Because only the IBM-PC character set offers you WYSIWYG, those are the only characters I can recommend. However, if you do want to utilize special characters, you can use the Compose feature, **CONTROL-2**. Special characters will appear on-screen as a small square box, but they will display properly in View Document. 5.0 note: remember, the character can't print if it's not available in the printer.

➻ Style tip

For a safer and simpler line-draw, create a "line-draw" paired style. This should contain a font change to the Courier PC-8 font, and a fixed line height of .16" before the [Comment].

Use the Line-Draw feature, then use **ALT-F4** to block the line-draw graphic, and apply the "Line-Draw" style. Now no matter how you change the body text, the line-draw graphics will be in the right font with the correct leading.

➻ Grids

Many graphs include a "grid" to help the viewer relate to the height of bars. The grid on the line-draw chart is yet another in the grand tradition of surreptitious work-arounds. You cannot create horizontal grid marks with line-draw and still have continuous vertical bars.

The secret is in the lowly underline. That's right. All I did was leave line-draw, then underlined the segments of the line-draw graphic where I wanted a horizontal grid. Pretty simple. Pretty nifty. Pretty sneaky.

◆ Idiosyncracies

As wonderful as WordPerfect's line feature is, it still has its idiosyncrasies. In Chapter 6, *Measure,* you (hopefully) read about achieving the thinnest possible line by entering the measurement in centimeters instead of inches. .01c gives you a hair-line, while .01" gives you a line three times thicker.

But there are other little peculiarities as well. For anyone familiar with a page composition program, WordPerfect's inability to print ruling lines on all pages can be frustrating. But rather than simply complain about the situation, I've come up with some ways to get around it. (Well, *someone* has to.)

❖ *Automatic rules*

There are two solutions to the non-automatic intercolumn rule dilemma. The first is an efficient method that will put ruling lines on any page. The second seems rather complicated, but once you've set it up, it provides the entire document with a consistent design.

◆ Totally automatic

If you are using 5.1, you simply enter the same column definition (and column on code) in the header as you have in the text. Then place vertical line codes which are set to "between columns." The vertical rules will then automatically print on each page.

Here's a fast example which will create a two-column definition and an inter-column rule between the two columns:

ALT-F7 C D F7 O

ALT-F9 L V H B 1 [ENTER] F7

Easy enough. But while the columns will continue onto page 2, the ruling lines won't—unless you copy them to the header. Follow me. First, place your cursor *on* the [Col Def:] code, then turn on the block with

ALT-F4

Now move the cursor *past* the [VLine:] code and copy the block with

CONTROL-F4 B C

Now create a header. Press

SHIFT-F8 P H A P

Once inside the header editor (you'll know you're there because it will say "Header A:" (or B, depending which you chose) along the bottom of the screen. To retrieve the block you copied, press

[ENTER]

You've now got a duplicate of your column def and VLine codes, and because these are in the header, the vertical line will print on every page. If you don't want it to print on a particular page, press **SHIFT-F8 P U S**. If you want to stop it from printing on all further pages, press **SHIFT-F8 H A D** to discontinue the header. (Use SHIFT-F8 H B D if you were using header B.)

◆ Rules: Open

Using a single style, you can instruct WordPerfect to place rules between several columns. If you're working with two columns, press

ALT-F8 C N intercolumn rules [ENTER]

T O C

ALT-F9 L V H B 1 [ENTER] F7

If you've followed this instruction correctly, you should see the following code, or at least something similar: **[VLine:Column 1,Full Page,9",.013"100%]**. Now save the whole thing with

F7 F7 F7

Remember to place this style at least once on every page when you want an intercolumn rule to appear. It doesn't hurt if you place it more than once on a page, since the lines will simply print over each other.

If you're working with three columns, you'll need to insert *two* vertical line codes, so the results should look like this: **[VLine:Column 1,Full Page,9", .013"100%] [VLine:Column 2,Full Page,9",.013"100%]**

If you place this on a page where columns are not turned on, the line will print on the right side of the page. If you have only one column, there's no such animal as an intercolumn rule, so WordPerfect will print the rule in the right margin.

Because these rules are set to "full page," they will adjust their length in accordance with the margins on the page, and headers and footers. But remember: these vertical lines will only stop for headers and footers, not for headlines or readouts.

❖ *Under the big top*

One of the advantages of WordPerfect is that all the features seem to mesh together. This next pointer combines styles, headers, and vertical ruling lines to create a pleasing page design, with a large top margin for headlines and pull quotes, and automatic vertical ruling lines on every page. Best of all, thanks to the design of the page, you don't have to ruminate about turning column rules on or off.

This works for both 5.1 and 5.0, although I provide a different header style for 5.1, because it can include column definitions in headers.

In 5.0 this is vaguely reminiscent of a catch-22 because you can't enter column definitions into headers or footers, and you can't place intercolumn rules unless columns are turned on. But my little brain churned away until I conjured up a solution.

You'll need the following styles.

➾ 5.1 TOPPER: PAIRED

[L/R Mar:1",1"] [T/B Mar:1",1"]
[Comment]
[AdvToLn:2"] [Col Def:Newspaper,3,1",3",3.25",5.25",5.5",7.5"] [Col On]
{*Use a distance between columns of .25"*}
[Just:Full] [Hyph On] [VLine:Column 1,2.2",8",0.013",100%]
{*Use the Vertical Set command, and type in the number 2.2"*}
[VLine:Column 2,2.2",8",0.013",100%]
{*Use the Vertical Set command, and type in the number 2.2"*}

➾ 5.1 HEADER: OPEN

[AdvToLn:1.7"] [Col Def:Newspaper,3,1",3",3.25",5.25",5.5",7.5"]
[Col On] [VLine:Column 1,2",2",8",0.01",100%]
{*Use the Vertical Set command, and type in the number 2"*}
[VLine:Column 2,2",2",8",0.01",100%]
{*Use the Vertical Set command, and type in the number 2"*}

➾ **5.1**

The file should look like this:
[Style On:topper] [Font:Dutch 30pt]Headline!{*or whatever headline you want*} [HRt] [Font:Dutch 14pt] [HRt]
[Flsh Rgt]Subhead{*or whatever subhead*} [HRt]
[Flsh Rgt]Subhead2{*another subhead, optional*}[Style Off:topper] [Open Style:header] [HRt]

➾ 5.0 TOPPER: PAIRED

[L/R Mar:1",1"] [T/B Mar:1",1"]
[Comment]
[AdvToLn:2"] [Col Del:3,1",3",3.25",5.25",5.5",7.5"] [Col On]
{*Use a distance between columns of .25"*}
[Just on] [Hyph On]

➾ 5.0 HEADER:OPEN

[AdvToLn:1.7"] [VLine:3.15",2",8",0.01",100%]
{*Use the Horizontal Set command, and type in the number 3.15"*}
{Use the Vertical Set command, and type in the number 2"}
[Vline:5.35",2",8",0.01",100%]
{*Use the Horizontal Set command, and type in the number 5.35"*}
{Use the Vertical Set command, and type in the number 2"}

•➜ 5.0: The first header contains the following:

[Font:Dutch 30pt]Headline{*Whatever headline you want*}
[Font:Dutch 14pt] [HRt]
[Flsh Rt]Subhead[C/A/Flrt]
{*Created when you press [ENTER]*}
[HRt]
[Flsh Rt]Subhead2[C/A/Flrt] [HRt]
[Open Style:header]

The header has .7" worth of space built-in for text at the top of the page. That text can be a headline, or, on later pages, a pull quote. The Header Open style contains an advance command (so it's in exactly the right place, no matter what the leading or how much text you've used) and then rules, set to print between the columns.

•➜ There are a few points you need to remember about headers.

WordPerfect automatically takes the height of headers and footers into account when it is calculating the number of lines available for text. If you are using this method, the headers must always be the same length, hence the [AdvToLn:1.7"] code. If the headers change length, the bottom margin of the page may print off the paper.

In addition, a header can't print on the top of a page unless it's either the first code on the page, or located on a preceding page. If you place a header in the middle of page 1, it will only take effect on page 2.

Also, if you put text in the header, it will repeat on every page until WordPerfect hits another header code. This means that unless you want the headline or pull quote to print on every page, you should place another header code in the text. A header only has to contain the header style, so you don't have to worry about complicated formatting.

If you want neither a header nor a readout in the extra 1" top margin, you can discontinue the header by pressing **SHIFT-F8 P H A D**

◆ Readouts and pull quotes in style

Remember when we discussed using graphics boxes for readouts? I know, you're probably still reeling from the excitement, but you'd better brace yourself. We're now going to accomplish the same task by using paired styles. This method has its advantages and disadvantages.

The main advantage of this system is that the actual text of the readout appears on-screen with the rest of the text. You don't have to go into a graphics box to edit it. The main disadvantage is that you can't put these readouts between two columns because the readouts aren't in graphics boxes and text won't wrap around them. A readout created with this method will be the width of whatever column it's in.

This type of readout is popular and accepted, so don't envision it as just some type of shortcut—it's attractive, and works just as efficiently as graphics box readouts.

This style consists of several elements: ruling lines above and below, space above and below the ruling lines, and a block protect (because readouts should never be interrupted by pages or columns). See Chapter 12, *Graphics*, for some examples of readouts.

◆ Readout: Paired

[Block Pro:On][AdvDn:0.1"][HLine:Full,Baseline,6.5",0.013",10%] [HRt]
[AdvDn:0.1"][VRY LARGE][Comment][AdvDn:0.1"][vry large][Hrt]
[HLine:Left & Right,Baseline,6.5",0.1",100%][AdvDn:0.1"][Block Pro:off]

In this example, I use a dotted line above the readout and a thick line underneath it. You can create the lines at any thickness and at any percentage of gray you want.

◆ Underline setting

In Chapter 9, *Columns*, I showed you how to make horizontal lines in nontable tables (those created with tabs). Because you may not have read that chapter, I'm going to repeat myself (in slightly condensed form) here.

The only rules for using underlines as rules in tables are:

- You must use tabs so that tables line up on the page as they do on-screen.
- You must set underline to print under spaces and tabs. Accomplish this by typing: **SHIFT-F7 O U Y Y F7**
- You cannot use bold and italic type on an underlined line. Each font has its own underline character (isn't that interesting?), and the underline will not look continuous. (The bold or italic underlines will print a bit lower than the regular underline.)

❖ *Forms-a-plenty*

Earlier in the book I showed you how to create forms using tables. That's fine if you've got 5.1, but if you've got 5.0, or a slow computer, you're not going to be able to use tables. There *is* another way, and not the complex rigmarole described in the WordPerfect *Workbook*.

It all hinges on one elementary function: underlined tabs, the very same function you employed for horizontal rules in tables.

Leave one space (yes, a space) after the word and before the horizontal line. This prevents them from running into each other. They still align because all the tabs end in the same place. Don't ask why, it works. If you want several lines of the form to align, you *must use tabs, not spaces, for the underlines.* (I've typed that phrase so many times that my keyboard is wearing out on the letters u-s-e t-a-b-s).

The ballot boxes are a simple graphics box trick. Read all about it in Chapter 11, *Styles.*

◆ Dotted or dashed vertical lines

What, you say WordPerfect doesn't have these? And you're going to let that stop you? Ha! Where there's a Will-Harris, there's a way, or in this case, ways.

You have two choices for dotted vertical lines. The first is easiest. Simply set the width of the vertical line to .01", and the Gray Shading (% of Gray) to 10%. This will give you a very thin gray line. This line may not always display in View Document, but it will print.

The second choice is also the procedure used to create vertical dashed lines. You don't actually create lines at all, you create graphics boxes. We're going to create an *intercolumn vertical dashed line.*

For this example, the dashed line will run down the center of the page, as an intercolumn rule for two columns. Let's quickly set up the columns (normally you would have already done this, and so this step is not mandatory for creating dashes or dotted vertical rules). Press

ALT-F7 C D D .3" [ENTER] [ENTER] O

(5.0 users: use a C instead of an O)

Here are the steps. (We're going to be using a User-defined graphics box, but you could use any of the four types.)

1. Set figure options so that you have a border on only the right side by pressing

ALT-F9 U O B N A N N

2. Create a User-defined box. You can place a page-type box exactly on the page. A paragraph-type box will float with the text. If you want an intercolumn rule, you must use a page-type box, and that's what we'll use for this example. We also want to turn WRAP OFF, so that it won't push text aside. Press

ALT-F9 UC WN TA [ENTER] VF HS 4.25" [ENTER] SB .01" [ENTER] 9.25" [ENTER]

This vertical line code can also be put into a style or a header, allowing you to use it on every page.

What's horizontal, Doc? You can produce horizontal dotted or dashed lines by using these same tips. Dotted lines can just be .01" 10% gray, but dashed lines require a graphics box.

◆ On-screen graphics ruler

Here's a rather esoteric trick that should give you a better idea of the size relationship between on-screen View Document and the real world. If you've ever seen a page composition program, you'll know that they have on-screen rulers to simplify working with pages.

Using this method, the on-screen ruler will appear when you are in View Document, with tick marks every half inch. *Use this for reference purposes only, and remove it before you print the final draft.*

You will want to create this all within a style. You create a style by pressing

ALT-F8 C N Ruler [ENTER] C

For more information, check out Chapter 11, "Styles."

Yes, this looks complex, but you don't have to enter all the codes manually. Create the codes, then block and copy the underlined area below *20 times.*

[T/B Mar:0.3",0.3"][L/R Mar:0.3",.3"]
[VLine:0.3",Full Page,10.5",0.01",100%] [HLine:Left,Baseline,0.2",0.01",100%]
[AdvDn:0.5"] [HLine:Left,Baseline,0.1",0.01",100%] [AdvDn:0.5"]
[Comment][AdvToLn:0"]

The [AdvToLn:0"] code moves WordPerfect back to the top of the page. If you don't use this command, the ruler will appear on a line by itself, and this defeats the whole purpose.

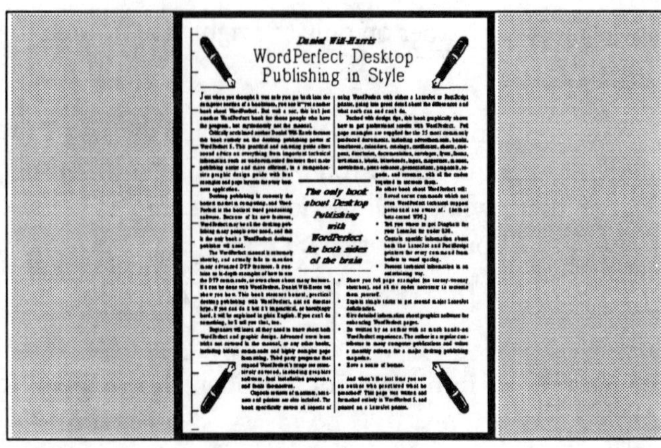

These on-screen rulers help you perfect a page by allowing you to see on-screen distances. You can create these visual aids with a paired style.

15

Printing

Off the screen and onto the page

Some day my prints will come, some day, da dum dum dum . . . Despite what those clever folks at Hewlett-Packard might say, that song was not written about laser printers. While the final print-out is the last step in desktop publishing (unless there are minor revisions, and there always are), it's one of the simplest operations.

I was going to assume that you had chosen the correct printer and then created a file. But a woman wise beyond her years (my wife, Toni) once told me to "never assume anything," and I will follow her advice.

We will cover printer installation and all the options involved with printing. Remember: you have to use **SHIFT-F7 S** in order to select your printer. If you don't, you will be using WordPerfect's standard printer, which has *no* font options. Bo-ring.

❖ *Let's start at the very beginning*

A very good place to start. Lest you think I'm channeling the spirit of Oscar Hammerstein (again), there are some basic steps you must follow before you print (or even write) a document.

This is the print menu, window on a wonderland of desktop publishing. (Gag me with a laser beam, what a sickening caption.) Actually, this menu is the place for printing, viewing, selecting, and editing printers.

```
Print

     1 - Full Document
     2 - Page
     3 - Document on Disk
     4 - Control Printer
     5 - Multiple Pages
     6 - View Document
     7 - Initialize Printer

Options

     S - Select Printer                    Dolores Del Rio
     B - Binding Offset                    0"
     N - Number of Copies                  1
     U - Multiple Copies Generated by      Printer
     G - Graphics Quality                  High
     T - Text Quality                      High


Selection: 0
```

To access any printer command, press SHIFT-F7.

Before you burn up the laser printer, you need to use this command to set up your document for that printer.

◆ Installing a printer

If you still haven't installed a printer, it's now or never. Press

SHIFT-F7 S

- If you *do* see your printer listed, *do not* press A [ENTER] [ENTER] F7; instead, jump to the next little pen bullet which says "printer found." If you don't see your printer listed, follow the steps in the next few paragraphs. Start by pressing

A

A list of printers will appear if you install any of the three WordPerfect ".ALL" files on the hard disk. I'm going to assume that you're using a LaserJet (or compatible). If no printers display, run the WordPerfect install program and install the .ALL file.

Move the cursor down to the specific LaserJet model you are using. (If you're using a compatible and have at least 512K of memory, select the LaserJet Plus. You should only select the Series II if the printer's manual specifically states that it's compatible with the LaserJet II.) Press

[ENTER]

WordPerfect will now suggest a file name for the printer. You can type a new name for the file as long as it ends with .PRS. If you want to use WordPerfect's name, press

[ENTER]

```
Print: Select Printer

  Bodoni-o-do
  Dragon
  Dutch
  Futura
  Galliard
  Gumby/Pokey
  Goudy
  Goudy - Hammersmith 18, 36
  Hammersmith
  Headlines
  HP - Melior
  HP Helv - Boring
  HP LaserJet Series II
  Koosh Ball
  Korinna - FW
  Melior/Optima - FW
  Palatino
  PostScript 2 (Dingbats in User 12)
  PS Beta (Has the great condensed Times/Helv missing in release)
* QMS PS Jet Plus /800 II/810
  Zulu

1 Select; 2 Additional Printers; 3 Edit; 4 Copy; 5 Delete; 6 Help; 7 Update: 1
```

WordPerfect allows you to access countless printers. I use a separate printer for each font family. (SHIFT-F7 S)

WordPerfect will display a screen containing "Helps and Hints" about the printer you've selected. If you want a printout of this, make sure that the printer is turned on and press **SHIFT-[PrtSc]**. If you are using a LaserJet, the page will not eject automatically. You will need to press the on-line key on the printer, then the form feed key, and then the on-line key again.

To leave this screen, press

F7

Don't press the next "E"

➻ Printer Found

Highlight the printer you are going to use and press

E

Everybody together now! WordPerfect now displays another menu (menus, menus everywhere and not a byte to eat). Now you can change the name of the

```
Select Printer: Edit

     Filename                          LX800.PRS

  1 - Name                             Dolores Del Rio

  2 - Port                             LPT1:

  3 - Sheet Feeder                     None

  4 - Cartridges and Fonts

  5 - Initial Base Font                Hammersmith Roman 11pt

  6 - Path for Downloadable            D:\FONTS
        Fonts and Printer
        Command Files




Selection: 0
```

Printer Edit (SHIFT-F7 S E) allows you to set defaults for each printer, including name, port, sheet feeder, forms, fonts, initial font, and the location of downloadable soft fonts.

printer (for your reference only), change the port the printer is attached to, select a sheet feeder, select fonts, choose an initial font, and tell WordPerfect where the downloadable fonts are located.

◆ Any port in a storm

Since you are only installing one printer, leave the name as it is. As I've said many-a-time before, try to use a parallel connection to the printer if at all possible. If you have one parallel port, this will be LPT1; if you have two ports, it could also be LPT2. If you need to change the port, press **P**, and then the number of the port you'll be using.

◆ Sheet-feed me, Seymour, feed me

Unless you have a LaserJet IID, 500+, QMS-PS 820, Mannesman Talley 910, Kyocera F series, Dataproducts LZR-1230, or optional sheet feeder, do not select any other sheet feeder. If you do, you may find a strange letter at the top of every page.

◆ True to form (5.0)

WordPerfect is set up for four forms: Standard, Legal, Envelope, and Letter. If you regularly use some odd-sized form, you can enter its specifications here. Once you do, you can simply select that form and avoid entering all sorts of dimensions whenever you create a file. Don't bother to set up custom forms unless you are going to use them frequently.

5.1: This command has been moved in 5.1. It's no longer in the printer section at all. To access it (this is not a good time, trust me; we're in the middle of something else and I cover forms in Chapter 16, *Labels*), press SHIFT-F7 P S to select, create, or modify printer forms.

◆ Fonts-a-plenty

Time to select your fonts. See Chapter 7, *About faces*, for complete information about installing fonts.

◆ Number I font

After you have selected the fonts for a printer, you can specify the Initial Base Font which WordPerfect will use as the default font. This will become the initial font for any document using this printer unless you specifically change it from the format menu.

◆ A Better mousetrap

If you are using downloadable fonts, Path is the place to inform WordPerfect of their whereabouts. If you don't specify this, WordPerfect will *not* be able to download

```
Select Printer: Soft Fonts                          Quantity     * Fonts
                                          Total:     550 K          32
                                      Available:     165 K          15

FW HP LaserJet Series II                                   Quantity Used

   (FW, Port) BSN Dutch Bold 08pt (ASCII Business)               9 K
 * (FW, Port) BSN Money Bold 10pt (ASCII Business)              12 K
   (FW, Port) BSN Spanky Bold 12pt (ASCII Business)             15 K
   (FW, Port) BSN Alphalpha Bold 14pt (ASCII Business)          18 K
   (FW, Port) BSN Shrimp Cocktail Bold 18pt (ASCII Business)    28 K
   (FW, Port) BSN Wheat Germ Bold 24pt (ASCII Business)         45 K
   (FW, Port) BSN Ingrown Toenail Italic 08pt (ASCII Business)   9 K
 * (FW, Port) BSN Power Bold Italic 10pt (ASCII Business)       12 K
   (FW, Port) BSN Testosterone Bold Italic 12pt (ASCII Business) 16 K
   (FW, Port) BSN BLT Bold Italic 14pt (ASCII Business)         19 K
   (FW, Port) BSN Splat! Italic 08pt (ASCII Business)            9 K
*  (FW, Port) BSN Fiction Italic 10pt (ASCII Business)          12 K
   (FW, Port) BSN Neep Italic 12pt (ASCII Business)             16 K
*  (FW, Port) BSN Fame Italic 250pt (ASCII Business)           519 K
   (FW, Starbord) BSN Lyric Roman 08pt (ASCII Business)          9 K

Mark:  * Present when print job begins             Press Exit to save
       + Can be loaded/unloaded during job       Press Cancel to cancel
```

Select Printer Cartridges and Fonts (SHIFT-F7 S E C F) is how you tell WordPerfect which fonts you want to use with each printer. These particular fonts are only available for those with a warped sense of humor.

your fonts. In fact, it won't even print; it will just beep at you and say that it can't find your fonts.

Once you've filled WordPerfect in on all the particulars, press

F7 S

If you have selected downloadable fonts with an *, press **I** now and WordPerfect will download them. If you marked them with a +, WordPerfect will download them automatically each time you print.

◆ View Document: Take a gander at this

No, don't print. Not just yet. If you do, you'll be missing out on one of WordPerfect's snazziest tricks: View Document. This feature displays the finished page on-screen, almost exactly as it will print.

As if that weren't enough, it's such a snap that even a child could do it (a cat could do it, for that matter, if it stepped on the right keys). Press

V

- Full Page: Before your very eyes, a page will appear in living black and white (or in living color, if you're using a color monitor). You can view the page at four different zoom levels. The default is Full Page. Unless you have a full-page display like the MDS Genius or a high-resolution monitor like the WYSE, you will not be able to read the text.
- Changing pages: At any zoom level, you can press **[PgDn]** or **[PgUp]** to move from page to page. You can also use **[HOME][HOME][UP ARROW]** to move to the first page and **[HOME][HOME][DOWN ARROW]** to move to the end of the file. Don't forget: when you press

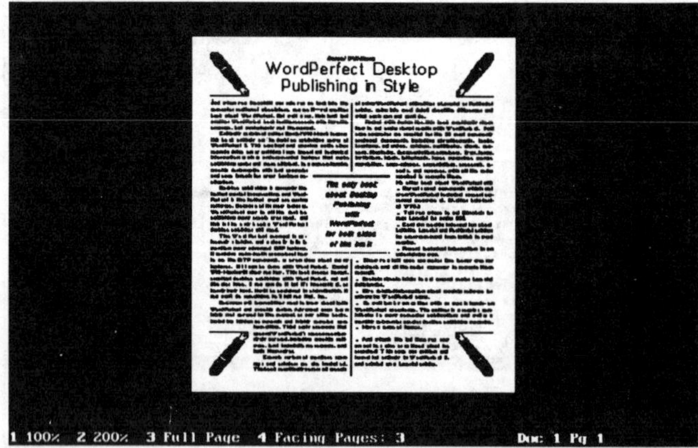

View Document in Full Page view.

CONTROL-HOME, WordPerfect moves to whatever page number you enter.

- Full Size: For a closer look, press 1 for "100%." This is approximately 100% of full size, although it may be slightly smaller or larger depending on the monitor. You will not see the entire page on-screen unless you have a full-page monitor.
- For a better view: You can move around the page by using the cursor keys. The gray + key moves you down one screen at a time, the gray – key moves you up a screen at a time. **[HOME] [RIGHT ARROW]** moves you to the right side of the screen, **[HOME] [LEFT ARROW]** moves you to the left side of the screen.
- Larger than life: Zoom in even closer by pressing 2 for a view that is twice as large as life.

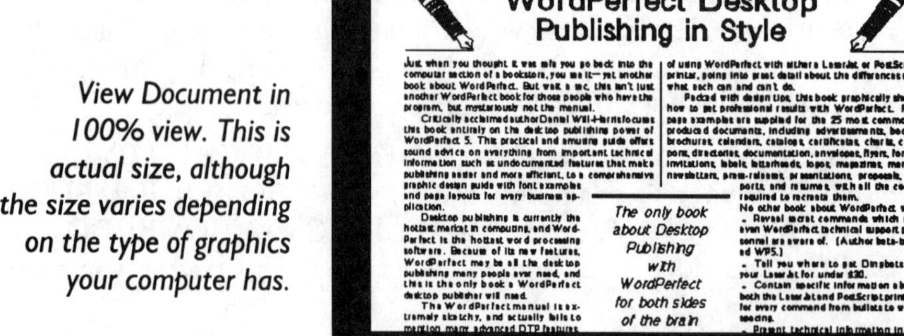

View Document in 100% view. This is actual size, although the size varies depending on the type of graphics your computer has.

View Document in 200% view. This is twice actual size.

- Two, two, two pages in one: Pressing **4** gives you a "facing pages" view so you can look at left and right pages simultaneously. If you are creating a book, magazine, or newsletter (where the pages are printed back to back and "face" each other when open), this will provide you with an accurate representation of how the pages will appear.

WordPerfect has three on-screen fonts: a serif for Dutch/Times fonts and the like, a sans serif for fonts like Swiss/Helvetica, and a typewriter font for Courier-like fonts. These fonts are in a file called WP.DRS, located on the Fonts/Graphics disk. If you are not seeing all three, you may have installed WPSMALL.DRS (on the WordPerfect 2 disk), which only contains the typewriter-like font. If you want to see all three (and it's recommended because it gives you a better idea of the page's appearance), copy WP.DRS to the same directory containing the WordPerfect program.

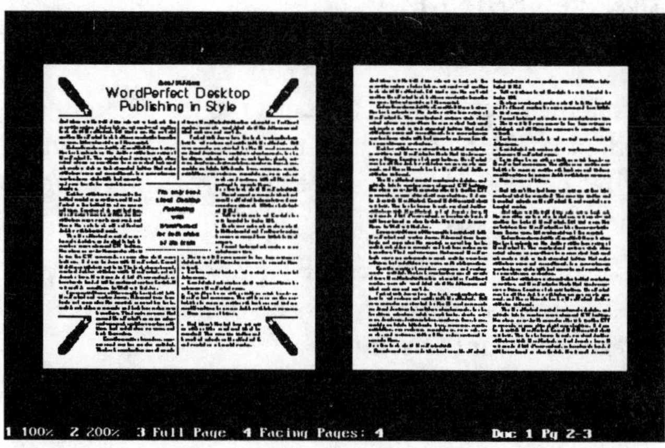

View Document in Facing Pages view. See two pages at once, on-screen. Many people never know this particular brand of excitement.

◆ Initial reaction

If you have selected fonts using an *, you will *must* use the Initialize command **SHIFT-F7 I Y** (no Y for 5.0 users) before attempting to print. This will download any font that you marked with an * in **SHIFT-F7 S E C**.

If you forget to initialize the printer, both the LaserJet and PostScript printers will substitute Courier for any fonts that should have been downloaded. These pages will be unusable, and you will have to initialize before printing again.

Unlike many programs, where you must stop and wait and wait and wait until the fonts are downloaded (which can routinely take five to ten minutes, depending on the number and size of fonts), WordPerfect can download fonts in the background while you continue to write and edit.

You don't have to wait for WordPerfect to finish initializing before you start to print other files. These files will be put in the "print queue" and will print automatically *after* all fonts have been downloaded.

When you press **I**, WordPerfect clears all the fonts that are currently in the printer's memory. Only the fonts downloaded upon initialization will be available.

If you consistently forget to initialize the printer and download the fonts, you might try marking them with a +. WordPerfect will then download the fonts it needs every time you print, and you will get so tired of waiting for them that you will mark them with an * and put them in the printer for baby and me. You might also consider using the automatic initialization macro offered in Chapter 7, *About faces*.

◆ Selecting pages to print

Okay, *now* we can burn up that laser printer with those masterful pages of yours. You've installed a printer, selected it, created a file, and now you want to see it on paper.

Of course, you will need to select the pages to be printed.

- To print the current page: Press **SHIFT-F7 P**
- To print the entire document: Press **SHIFT-F7 F**
- To print a block of text from the screen: move the cursor to the beginning of the block to be printed, press **ALT-F4**, highlight all the text you want to print, and press **SHIFT-F7 Y**. This block can be as short as one character, or as much as several pages long.
- To print selected whole pages from 5.1: Press **SHIFT-F7 M**. WordPerfect will make you wait a bit as it saves a temporary version of the file to disk. It will then ask for the pages you want to print.

Here's an example: If you want to print pages 10 and 14, you would type **10,14**. If you wanted pages 10 through 14 printed, you would type **10-14**. Typing **10-** would print from page 10 through the end of the file. **-10** would print from the beginning to page 10. You can even combine these: **3,7,9,10-14,25-** would print pages 3, 7, 9, 10 through 14, and 25 to the end of the file.

➾ You can also select pages in this way if you are printing from List Files or Document on disk, and this works for 5.0 as well as 5.1.

If you are printing from List Files, or from Document on Disk, once you've selected the file, WordPerfect will ask: "Page(s): (all)." If you press return, WordPerfect will print the entire document; if you need only specific pages printed, type in the correct page numbers.

➾ List Files is convenient in that you can print many files at once. Press **F5**, move to the file you want, and press **P**. WordPerfect will ask you which pages to print. Follow the examples above. You can move to as many different files as you want and press **P**, adding them to the print queue.

You can also mark files with * and then press **P**. WordPerfect will ask if you want to print all the marked files. If you answer **Y**, they will all be added to the print queue. If you answer **N**, WordPerfect will sigh, frustrated about how fickle people are and then ask if you just want to print the file the cursor is currently on.

If you answer **N** again, WordPerfect will get surly, and late at night while you're asleep, it will call another computer with WordPerfect and the two of them will trade potentially embarrassing stories about the people that use them and gossip about which computer is networking with which other computer. It's true, I'm not making it up. They just talk really fast and use such high, squeaky voices that they are out of the range of human hearing. Dogs can hear every last word of it and get a good laugh out of it, believe you me, but we don't have the faintest idea it's going on.

◆ Mysteries of printing from disk

Whenever you print a file from disk, WordPerfect checks to see if the file was formatted with the same printer that is currently being used in Document 1 or Document 2.

If the file was not formatted with this printer, WordPerfect displays this message: "Document not formatted for current printer, Continue? Y/N?" In other words, if you print this file now, it will not be reformatted, but it will be printed with a different printer's format (which may not have the same fonts or abilities).

This shouldn't matter too much if you're working with a draft copy. WordPerfect will try to find substitute fonts (more about this later) and use whatever it thinks is best.

If you want the file to print exactly as you formatted it, you should answer **N** for no. Then you either will need to make the printer used for that file the currently selected printer, or retrieve that file and print it from screen (which will perform the same function automatically).

◆ Checking printer status

How can you tell what WordPerfect is printing, how many copies it's printing, and where it's printing them? With Control Printer, that's how. Press **SHIFT-F7 C** to access the Control Printer menu. This will: tell you what job number is currently printing; tell you the status of the print job (initializing, printing, downloading, etc.); tell you that the printer is not accepting characters; tell you the type of paper and paper tray being used; and confront you with suggestions or out-and-out demands (check cable, make sure printer is turned on), and tell you the current page and copy being printed. This is also where you can control the print queue and cancel print jobs.

If you are typing along, minding your own business, and you hear a beep, it could mean that WordPerfect is trying to tell you something important about the current print job. A beep can either mean an error has occurred or that WordPerfect is patiently waiting for you to put paper in the printer's manual feed before it sends the page. Whatever it is, if you don't fix it, you don't print, so if nothing emerges from the printer and you're wondering why, press SHIFT-F7 C.

◆ Print queue and cancelling printing

"Your call will be answered in the order it was received." I don't know about you, but I don't put much stock in that sort of talk.

But with WordPerfect, you can believe it. Its sophisticated print queue will permit you to print several files in sequence. WordPerfect prints these in order, one after another, without any intervention from you. This is a very convenient way to churn out printed material.

This requires no great effort from you. Every time you tell WordPerfect to print, it adds that job to its list of print jobs. If it's not currently printing anything, then there's no queue, and it just prints the file. But if it is currently printing, WordPerfect adds the latest job to the list and prints it in "the order received."

If you have a long list of print jobs and need something printed quickly, add the print job to the list. Then press **SHIFT-F7 C R**. WordPerfect will ask which job you need to rush. Press the number beside the desired print job. WordPerfect will ask if you want to interrupt the file that is currently printing. If you do want to interrupt, press **R**. WordPerfect will keep track of the last full page it printed and pick up where it left off after the rush job. If you can wait until the job is done, the rush file will move to the second spot on the list, and will print next.

◆ Jane, stop this crazy thing!

What should you do if you are printing and paper begins to fly out of the printer or, even more exciting, jam? Go to Control Printer, go directly to Control Printer, do not pass GO, do not collect $200.

The simplest way to stop printing is to press **C** for cancel. WordPerfect will ask which print job you want to cancel. Type in the number and press **[ENTER]**. If you want to cancel all print jobs, press **C * Y**.

Remember, however, that most laser printers have very large buffers. You can tell WordPerfect to stop, but it may have already sent several pages to print. In this case, you will have to have it out with the printer directly.

If you are using downloadable fonts, do not turn the printer off to clear its memory unless you are prepared to re-initialize the printer. If you are using a LaserJet II, press the **ON-LINE** button (to take the machine off-line). Then press and hold down the **Continue/Reset** for about five seconds until the word "RESET" appears on the LCD. You can then press the **ON-LINE** button again. Any fonts downloaded with * will still be in the printer's memory.

> ➺ Stop it! If you have some sort of tragic printing accident, such as a paper jam, you should just stop the print job, not cancel it. To do this, press **S**.

WordPerfect will stop printing, and a message will advise you to press **G** when you want to resume printing. Fix the jam (ooh, that toner's messy and sometimes even dry-cleaning is a dismal failure) and then press **G**. WordPerfect will ask you to enter the page number where it should resume printing on.

❖ *Quality, not quantity, or memory for faces*

Laser printing can be a slow affair. Laser printers generally print 300 dots per inch. That entails a lot of dots, a lot of information, and a lot of time. When you are proofing pages, you don't need high quality print jobs, you need everything to work as quickly and efficiently as possible.

You may not have much memory at your disposal if you have an older LaserJet, but you still may want to print graphics. And if you have a PostScript printer, you are probably well aware that they are notoriously slow at printing bitmapped graphics. Draft printing works with all laser printers, both LaserJet and PostScript. That's when WordPerfect's Quality options come in handy. Pressing **SHIFT-F7 G** allows you to determine the sharpness of printed graphics.

> ➺ Tartar: If you choose **N** for "Do Not Print," WordPerfect prints the text but none of the graphics, pictures, or lines. This is the most expedient method when you just need to check the text. But it can be difficult to visualize the finished page without any graphics. Do Not Print will also

Want a fast printout of your page? Set WordPerfect's Graphic Quality feature (SHIFT-F7 G) to Medium (150d dpi), Draft (75 dpi), or Do Not Print. When you're ready for a final printout, select High (300 dpi).

```
Print

     1 - Full Document
     2 - Page
     3 - Document on Disk
     4 - Control Printer
     5 - Multiple Pages
     6 - View Document
     7 - Initialize Printer

Options

     S - Select Printer                    Quick-Like-A-Bunny-Beam-Printer
     B - Binding Offset                    0"
     N - Number of Copies                  1
     U - Multiple Copies Generated by      Printer
     G - Graphics Quality                  Draft
     T - Text Quality                      High

Selection: 0
```

suppress graphics from View Document. This can save you time if you're using bitmapped graphics, which often take a while to display on-screen. (If the graphics don't appear in View Document, and you can't figure out why, this is probably the reason.)

- Rare: If you want a rough idea of a page's appearance, select **SHIFT-F7 D** for graphics in Draft mode. Graphics will print at 75 dpi, or a quarter of 300 dpi quality. They take up a quarter of the memory and about a quarter of the time to print. This is very useful for draft copies. (While desktop publishing, it's not unusual to print many draft copies.)
- Medium: Press **SHIFT-F7 G M** to reach the next plateau. This medium resolution is 150 dpi, or half the quality of 300 dpi. If you have a LaserJet Plus or LaserJet II with no additional memory, this will be the highest setting you can use when printing a full page of graphics.
- Well-done: High resolution graphics can be yours by pressing **SHIFT-F7 G H**. These are full 300 dpi babies, sharp and slow.
- Text quality. Although WordPerfect uses these same four settings for text, only two of them work with laser printers: Do Not Print and High. If you set this to Draft or Medium, WordPerfect will still print high quality text, because downloadable and PostScript fonts are always 300 dpi.

❖ *Extras, extras, read all about it*

Three more extras we haven't covered yet are Binding Width, Number of Copies, and Multiple Copies Generated By. Number of copies is basically self-explanatory. If you want three copies of a print job, pages, or a document, press **SHIFT-F7 N** and enter the number three.

What's not so self-explanatory is that WordPerfect will send three entire copies to the printer, in order. Laser printers can create any given number of copies from a single page of data automatically, and this expedites the printing of multiple copies. However, WordPerfect sends the entire page, pages, or document for each copy you print.

That's where Multiple Copies Generated By comes in. Don't look for it in 5.0, it's not there. It's only in 5.1, probably because so many people complained about it. Press **U P** if you want the printer to do the work. This will save you plenty of time, but the copies will not be collated. Press **U W** if you've got all the time in the world or if you want WordPerfect to print one whole copy of the document, then another whole copy, in time-consuming, but collated fashion.

If the pages are to be bound into book or magazine format, the area between left and right pages is referred to as the "binding margin." Because books and magazines rarely lie flat, it's wise to leave extra space in this area so the reader doesn't miss anything.

WordPerfect's binding margin feature adds extra space to the right side of left pages and the left side of right pages. It accomplishes this by shifting the entire left page to the left and the entire right page to the right by the amount you enter here. For example: if you had .5" margins on both sides and entered a binding width of .25", the left page would have a left margin of .25" and a right margin of .75", while the right page would have a left margin of .75" and a right margin of .25".

This is simple enough, but you must remember to enter this number before you print, as this setting is not saved with the file. And, once you set it, this number will be in effect for whatever you print until you reset it or leave the program.

◆ Making a commitment

You can also set any of these options (Binding Offset, Number of Copies, Multiples Generated By, Graphics Quality, Text Quality, as well as Redline Method and Size Attribute Ratios) by pressing **SHIFT-F1 I P**. This will set these options "permanently" (or at least until you set them again). Even if you've set an option here, you can override it at print time by choosing any option on the print menu.

❖ *Change printers and dance*

What should you do if you create a file with, say, Dutch/Times and Swiss/Helvetica fonts, but decide you want to print it with Goudy Old Style and Futura?

Good question, glad you asked. You press **SHIFT-F7 S**, move the cursor to the printer that accommodates those fonts, and press **[ENTER]**. WordPerfect will do its best to match the fonts you've chosen with the new ones it has available. If the same typeface is available, it will use it. If not, it will substitute another font with similar qualities. If you select Palatino but the new printer driver only has Dutch/Times and Swiss/Helvetica, WordPerfect will choose Dutch/Times because it is a serif font. Avant Garde would become Swiss/Helv.

While WordPerfect is fairly proficient at substituting fonts, it's certainly not perfect. In one test, I took a file that had been created using Korinna on a LaserJet and printed it on a QMS PostScript printer. WordPerfect selected Zapf Chancery as a substitute for Korinna. While this might have been a proper choice technically, the serif styles and other attributes resulted in a frankly hilarious appearance. My wife said it looked like a romance novel should look. Well, who cares if it's terribly hard to read? It looks very "gothic."

This is why it's always a good idea to retrieve a file and ascertain what fonts WordPerfect has chosen. You can search for font changes by typing: **F2 CONTROL-F8 F F2**.

If you're not happy with a font substituted by WordPerfect, delete the font code and add the one you want using **CONTROL-F8 F**.

Another good way to handle this is to make all your font changes using styles. That way you only have to change a single style to make countless font changes throughout your file.

◆ Foolproof substitutions

These translations will be almost foolproof if you keep each typeface in a separate printer file. If you created it with Dutch/Times and want to print it with Korinna, simply select the printer containing Korinna fonts by typing **SHIFT-F7 S**. Since WordPerfect has nothing to choose from but Korinna, it can't make a mistake in the translation; all it has to do is match the point sizes.

You might also want to try a printer file with one serif face and one sans serif. WordPerfect is usually good at substituting serif fonts with other serif fonts, *but not always*.

The other advantage of using printer files with very limited font selections is that they will make WordPerfect run faster and take less memory. If you've got 50, 20, or sometimes even 10 different typefaces in your list, WordPerfect can run as if it's in half-set jello. You press CONTROL-F8 F and just sit there, watching your life slip away as WordPerfect brings up the list of available fonts. Keep the selection small and you'll save a lot of time.

If you have hyphenation on, remember to press **HOME HOME [DOWN ARROW]** so that WordPerfect can re-hyphenate the file with the new font.

❖ Going from 5.0 to 5.1

This is really a much bigger problem than you might think. Because WordPerfect 5.1 formats lines and pages of text differently than 5.0, when you load a 5.0 file into 5.1, Jimmy the Greek will spot you 99 to 1 that the formatting will change. Line breaks and page breaks will probably not be in the same places. Graphics may have moved. In some cases, all hell may have broken loose.

If you've got a giant project in 5.0 and it works fine, don't try to bring it into 5.1 at the last minute and expect everything to be right. *It won't be.*

If you have several font changes which aren't in styles, don't expect them to be right either. Check them out. Print out the file and make changes. Font changes in styles are far easier to correct than those just sitting in the document. You can search for font changes with **F2 CONTROL-F8 F.**

Another plug: use styles for font changes. It will make your life easier.

◆ Worst case scenarios

When you save a file in WordPerfect, the name of the printer file (.PRS) you used is included in that file. This tells WordPerfect what printer to use the next time you edit the file.

If WordPerfect can't locate that file, it will automatically reformat the file for the currently selected printer. This is replete with all the potential problems related to WordPerfect font substitution.

If the printer file has vanished (for whatever reason: you deleted it accidentally, someone you despise deleted it for you, your dog ate it), the best course of action is to recreate it. That means reinstalling the printer from the WordPerfect disk. If you used Fontware, you must go into Cartridge and Fonts using **SHIFT-F7 S E C** and mark those fonts for downloading.

If you used Fontware fonts but no longer have the .ALL file, you must have Fontware regenerate all the fonts you want to use. There is no other way to install them in the .ALL file without purchasing a third-party font installation program (such as the one from SoftCraft). If you have Type Director, you can reinstall previously created fonts into your .ALL file.

If you merely renamed the printer file, or possess another file that uses the same fonts, select that printer *before* you load the file. WordPerfect will inform you that it can't find the correct printer but will then use the current printer (containing the same fonts) and life will be just hunky-dory . . . probably.

◆ It can happen to you

WordPerfect has been known, even when the exact same fonts are available, to plead temporary insanity and choose whatever fonts it feels like. Unfortunately, when those aren't the fonts you want or need, the entire document is reformatted. The best course of action in these cases is *don't save the file.* If you do, you'll get stuck with the bizarre font selection. Exit, then retrieve the file again, hopefully with the right printer driver.

Another bit-o-WordPerfect-weirdness can occur with scaleable font printers. If you update your printer driver, even though the exact same fonts are available, WordPerfect will get neurotic on you, and while it will *probably* choose the right typefaces, it will *probably not* choose the right sizes. I don't know why; it doesn't make any sense, but it happens. Your body text was 11-point. You change printer drivers and suddenly WordPerfect wants to print your body text at 9.6-point. It's almost always some really stupid number like that. There's nothing you can do but keep an eye on it, and if it happens, fix it.

◆ High (quality) anxiety and "printing to disk"

You can print absolute, top-o-the-line typeset pages with WordPerfect. While most laser printers are 300 dpi, typesetting machines are generally 600, 1250, or 2450 dpi.

The typesetters that WordPerfect can drive are called "Linotronic," from the famous typesetting company, LinoType. These typesetters use the PostScript language (the same language employed in PostScript laser printers, such as the QMS 800 series or Apple LaserWriter).

These huge machines also cost from $30,000 to $50,000 and require connections to running water, so they're probably not items you can afford or get onto a desktop.

However, you can rent time on these machines at desktop publishing service centers. These ancillary businesses perform a variety of high-end tasks, such as Linotronic typesetting. You give them a PostScript file on disk and about ten bucks

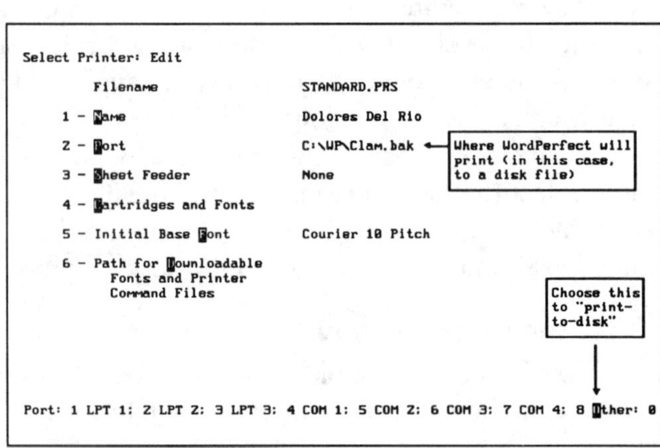

Printing-to-disk is the latest craze. This allows you to print to a file instead of a printer. You can then use this file to print the file on a remote printer.

(per page, usually), and they give you a fully typeset page of the highest quality typesetting.

I once told someone about this type of service and he said, "I don't know if it's worth having to drag my computer across town and hook it up to their big machine." I didn't laugh in his face, I simply told him what I'm going to tell you now.

It's not done with wheelbarrows or mirrors but with a feature called "printing to disk." Instead of having WordPerfect send information from the computer to a printer, it sends it to a file on a disk.

Once you have this file on-disk, you can forget about WordPerfect, and print the file wherever you want. Printing-to-disk differs from saving a file as an ASCII or generic file; those files contain text only. These files contain all the formatting and printer codes that are necessary to print the file with proper formatting and fonts.

We'll assume that you'll be printing the file on a PostScript typesetter, so you'll need to install the printer driver called "Apple LaserWriter" or "QMS PS Jet Plus /800 II/810."

You must select this printer before creating your document. This driver includes many different PostScript fonts that can be selected in sizes from 1 to 1199-point, in 1/10th-of-a-point increments.

Once the PostScript printer is selected, edit the configuration. To do this, press

SHIFT-F7 S

Move the cursor to the PostScript printer and press

E

Now all you have to change is "Port." Press

P O

WordPerfect asks for the "Device or Filename." Since you want to create a file, you will type a file name here.

PS.PRN F7 F7 F7

You are now at the print menu. If you press **P** for a single page, or **F** for the entire document, WordPerfect will create a file on disk containing the exact same material it would otherwise send to a printer.

Each time you print, WP will send the output to the file you have named, overwriting any previous print job. If you have several different files to print, remember to rename the print file after you print so that WordPerfect won't erase the previous print job when it prints again.

When you want to print to a printer again, instead of to a file, press

SHIFT-F7 S E P

Press the number that corresponds to the printer port and then press

F7 F7 F7

WordPerfect will now print to a printer rather than to a disk.

◆ Gimmie proof (5.0 style)

All this inevitably leads to the next question: What if you want to print to a PostScript typesetter, but don't have a PostScript laser printer? How do you "proof" the pages—print them for an approximation of the document's appearance?

Simple, mi amigo, as long as you're using 5.0. First, save the file to disk. Then press

SHIFT-F7 S

Move the cursor to "LaserJet" (or whatever printer you have). Press

S D

This will select the LaserJet printer and then instruct WordPerfect to print a "document on disk."

WordPerfect will respond that "Document not formatted for current printer, Continue? Y/N?" Answer: Y

WordPerfect will then print the file using whatever printer is currently selected for the document you are in. The document will not be reformatted, and all line breaks will be as they were. WordPerfect will substitute the font and, whether it's similar or not, will space all the words and letters correctly.

Proofs such as this often don't look very attractive, but they are precise and help you to know where line and page breaks occur. For most proofs, this is more than adequate.

5.1 Proofing problems

While this works great in 5.0, it doesn't work worth beans in 5.1. This is another case of software being too smart for its own good. WordPerfect won't just print the file with the available printer driver and fonts, it will first look to see if the correct printer driver *is* available. Even though it has just said "Document not formatted for Current Printer," WordPerfect has a secret "third document." This document can't be used for editing, just printing. When you print a file from List Files or from disk, WordPerfect loads the file into this third document. As it does this, it also loads the correct printer driver, if it's available.

This is all well and good if you're a casual user who just wants to make sure that WordPerfect prints the page correctly. But if you're a smart user, and you want to be able to proof the page, you can't.

If you move all the printer drivers to another directory and then try to print again, WordPerfect will reformat the entire document for the available printer. While the page will print, the line and page endings may bear absolutely no resemblance to the file you thought you were proofing.

As I write this, I don't know if this is a bug or a feature. It doesn't actually work wrong, it just works differently, and in doing so it eliminates what was actually an important benefit in 5.0.

Unless something changes between this writing (which is based on the first release version of the software) and future software updates (which can occur as frequently as every six weeks), you cannot design a page for one printer and "proof" it on another.

The only option this leaves you is "View Document." If you're designing a page for a PostScript printer, and all you have is a LaserJet, you're going to have to be content with View Document, as anything you print will be formatted differently than the "PostScript version."

There *is* a solution to this, but it's going to cost you . . .

◆ PS, I can't afford you

There are two more ways to get PostScript printing with the printer you already have. If the printer is a LaserJet II or IIP, you can add a PostScript font cartridge, called "Pacific Page," from Pacific Data Products. This is slow, but it works. If you have a IIP, IID, or III, you can add HP's Adobe PostScript cartridge. This is true Adobe PostScript, and performance is comparable to standard PostScript printers. Either of these cartridges requires at least 2 megabytes of printer memory.

Another way to proof pages is to buy a software-based PostScript interpreter. There are three popular packages on the market which can turn a dot-matrix, DeskJet, or LaserJet into a PostScript printer.

These programs allow you to print *almost* any PostScript file on a nonPostScript printer. GoScript comes with Times and Helvetica, or the Deluxe package comes with the 35 fonts standard in PostScript printers. UltraScript comes with Times, Helvetica, and Lucida, a modern typeface design. Freedom of Press comes with the 35 typefaces and also handles full-color PostScript output to printers such as the PaintJet.

All these programs are capable, and they all suffer from the same problem — performance. GoScript and UltraScript require only 640K of RAM, but with that amount of memory it can easily take 20 minutes to print a page on a DeskJet or LaserJet. Adding at least 512K of EMS to your computer cuts that in half, but it's still a long time to wait for a page. Freedom of Press requires EMS and is slightly faster than the others. These programs will also work significantly faster if your computer has a math co-processor chip such as the 8087, 80287, or 80387.

If you're going to be doing much PostScript proofing, you should either have a PostScript printer or one of these programs along with 2 megabytes of EMS, and, if your budget can stand it, a math co-processor.

◆ Proofing laser output on DeskJet and dot-matrix

The very same trick can be used to proof "laser" pages on DeskJet and dot-matrix printers. Design and format the page for a LaserJet or PostScript printer, and then proof on the printer you have.

While the PostScript printer driver comes standard with the built-in fonts, the LaserJet driver doesn't come standard with any fonts. If you know the fonts that are available on the LaserJet you will be printing to, install a printer driver which can use those fonts. If those fonts are from cartridges, they will be available in the normal .ALL file. If they were produced with Fontware, you will need to do one of two things. Either create them on your machine (even though you can't print with them) just so that they will update your .ALL file, or get a copy of the .PRS file set up for the LaserJet you will be using.

There are two more alternatives for getting "laser-like" output on the printer you use regularly. Both Atech's *Publisher's PowerPak* System and *MoreFonts* scale fonts on-the-fly, much as scaleable font printers do, and can print these fonts to both DeskJet and dot-matrix printers. Atech also sells a product which then allows you to print the exact same file to a Linotronic, without any changes in formatting.

❖ *Living color*

Color laser printers. I give it a year or two until color laser printers become affordable. Right now you could count the number of color laser printers on one hand. The same hand you chew on as you wonder how many convenience stores you'd have to knock over to afford one of your very own. The only color laser printer I am familiar with is the QMS ColorScript 100. If you've got $10,000 burning a hole in your pocket, you can get one fabulous machine.

This PostScript printer has all the standard PostScript typefaces, 8 megabytes of memory, and a 20 megabyte hard disk for downloadable fonts. It uses a thermal transfer process that takes color from waxy sheets and puts it on the page at 300 dpi. The results are truly dazzling.

But while WordPerfect can print text in color (CONTROL-F8 C) and even display graphics in color, version 5.0 cannot print graphics in color.

There is *one* way to print color graphics. If the graphics are in EPS format, created with Corel Draw, Micrografx Designer, Adobe Illustrator, or Aldus

Freehand, then a color PostScript printer will print both color text and color graphics. This is because the color information is part of the graphics file and not something that WordPerfect has to create. If you have a color ink-jet printer such as the PaintJet or PaintJet XL, you can use Freedom of Press to print color text and graphics.

◆ See spot color, see spot color run

Spot color is a term referring to the use of color on a page. This doesn't use full four-tone color, but adds a second color on a page. The page is run through an offset printer once for black and then once again for an additional color. This is not a fancy technique, but it does add areas of color on a page, which can add visual impact.

Using WordPerfect's "Graphics Quality" and "Text Quality" features, you can print out two pages for each single page: one for black text, and another for the graphics (including ruling lines and shaded background) in a second color. Remember, though, color won't magically appear out of your black and white printer; you'll end up with two black and white pages. When you go to your print shop, the printer will substitute a color for one of the black and white pages.

This only requires changing the printer settings. For the text elements press

SHIFT-F7 G N

This will set the graphics to "Do Not Print." The page will include text, but not graphics.

Once you've printed the text portions of the page, press

SHIFT-F7 T N G H

This sets text to "Do Not Print" and only prints the graphics. When you're finished, don't forget to set the print mode for both text and graphics in a single pass. Press

SHIFT-F7 T H G H

When you take your publication to an offset print shop, keep the related pages together. Indicate the text pages are to be in black and the graphics pages in color. Because spot color doesn't always involve high tolerances, you need to watch the alignment of the black and color; it can be a little bit off, one way or the other, so have the printer take extra care.

❖ Tidbits

◆ A few additional morsels to chew on

⊸ FACING PAGES WARNING: This is a rather bizarre and confusing tip. If you want to produce facing pages with a large outside note margin, read on. If you are easily confused, skip it.

At last, a practical use for backwards thinking. In most book and magazine designs, the binding margins dictate that the inside margin be larger than the outside. But in some designs, the outside margin is wider than the inside margin. This design is employed when you want to create a publication with room for the reader to make notes or for certain aesthetic impact.

Usually you can't do this with WordPerfect. What you can do, however, is fool the program as long as you don't use automatic page numbers. On the first page of the document, use this command:

SHIFT-F7 P O E

This command "forced" WordPerfect to create an odd page when you press O and an even page when you press E. The first page is usually an odd page, but this time it's going to be even.

For a design like this, you will need both a wide margin (so that the binding isn't reduced to nothing) and a wide binding margin. Press

SHIFT-F7 L M 1.5 [ENTER] 2 [ENTER] F7

to create left and right margins of 1.5" each. Now change your binding margin to .5" by pressing

SHIFT-F7 B 5 [ENTER]

This will add an additional .5" onto the binding and remove .5" from the other margin. We forced the first page to be an even page, so the wide margin will be on the right, or the outside edge of the page, rather than in the middle at the binding.

Of course, the problem with this system is that the page numbers are going to be incorrect. Page 1 will say "page 2," because WordPerfect still thinks of it as a left-hand page, while you're going to use it as a right-hand page.

But as long as we've come this far, let's take one additional step. Place an added .25" margin at the bottom of each page if you are going to want a footer, or put an additional .25" at the top for a header. Now print out all the pages sans page numbers (but don't let them get out of order).

Next create a file consisting of nothing but a footer (or header). Put the pages you printed back into the printer, and run them through again to print the footer or header. Now page 1 will say "page 1," instead of the page 2 WordPerfect thought it was. I told you it was bizarre, and sometimes the paper crinkles, so use it only as a last resort.

◆ Disk space and temporary files

Each time you print from the screen, WordPerfect creates a file on-disk that contains the information to be printed. This is so WordPerfect will know what to print if you change anything while the file is printing or move to another file.

These files take up disk space. If you are printing a single page, they use the amount of room that the single page takes, and if you are printing an entire file, they take the space of that entire file. WordPerfect deletes these files when the print job is finished so they don't clutter up the hard disk.

The reason I'm bothering with all this is that if you live on the hard disk borderline as I do, these files can sometimes fill the hard disk, albeit temporarily. Does this sound familiar? You finish typing, try to save a file and—whoops, no disk space. Gee, there was a couple hundred K just a few minutes ago. This problem can be especially severe if you are working with floppies. WordPerfect saves print files to whatever directory is current so if you have a hard disk and are working with a floppy, it can save them on the floppy as well.

Of course, there is one way around all this. If you print files from disk, using either List Files (F5) or Document on Disk (SHIFT-F7 D), WordPerfect won't need to create a temporary file. Printing the files from disk, especially if they are large, is the best way to avoid the horrors of a full hard disk.

Also, occasionally you can check the printer for files called **WP{WP}1** (or 2, or 3, or whatever print job it is). If you're all through printing and any of these files remain on your disk, it's because you left WordPerfect abnormally or something else aberrant occurred. Once you leave WordPerfect, you can safely delete any of these files and clear up wasted disk space.

◆ May I? Yes, you might

All printers have limitations, and WordPerfect is very forthright about telling you what it can and can't do with certain printers. For example, in 5.0, PostScript printers don't support the line-draw feature, and earlier versions of 5.0 won't print landscape graphics on LaserJets.

Later versions of 5.0 (and all versions of 5.1) *can* print landscape graphics on a LaserJet, and all versions of 5.1 can print line-draw graphics on PostScript or any other graphics printer.

You can see precisely what the limitations of the printer are by pressing

SHIFT-F7 S

Move the cursor over to the name of the printer you are using (there may only be one) and press

H

A screen chock-full of information about the printer driver will appear, and you can determine which features are supported and which aren't. To exit, press

F1 F1 F1

PostScript

WordPerfect supports all the built-in fonts in PostScript "Plus" printers, but the standard PostScript driver does not support *any* Adobe downloadable fonts. If you need to use Adobe downloadable fonts, call WordPerfect and find out which fonts are supported. Then be prepared to part with 10 bucks for the disk.

◆ Legal-ease

If you use a LaserJet and *occasionally* want to print legal-size pages, you may have found that your LaserJet doesn't like it. You place the legal paper in the manual feed and the LaserJet seems to take it just fine. But then it jams in the middle.

Liz Swoope Johnson, who did a wonderful job of technical editing on this book, told me about the problem—and the solution. The LaserJet wants to have a legal-paper tray any time you print *any* legal-sized pages. If you're going to print lots of legal-sized pages, a special tray makes sense. If not, there's a way around it.

You'll need to define a new Form that tricks the LaserJet into accepting a legal-sized page. Here's how. First you need to select paper size. Press

SHIFT-F8 P S

Highlight LEGAL (not Legal-wide), then press

E L M

This tells the LaserJet to use manual feed. The minute you say you want manual feed, WordPerfect assumes you want it to be prompted to put the paper in the printer. In this case, you don't want to be, (you're big enough to remember all by yourself) so press

R N [ENTER]

You're now back at the list of forms where you'll want to select Legal size. Press

S

To return to the editing screen, press

F7

Now the LaserJet will accept manual-feed legal-size paper just fine with no jamming. This tip is for LaserJets only and won't work on LaserJets using the PacificPage PostScript cartridge. If you want to print legal pages using the PacificPage, you must have a legal-sized paper tray.

❖ Organization tips

◆ A font for all seasons *or* I left my font in San Francisco *or* How to organize fonts and have thin thighs in 20 minutes

When you start amassing a huge assortment of fonts, you realize that you don't want them lumped together in a single printer file. Your printer probably doesn't have enough memory, and you probably don't have enough time or patience to download them all at once. Not only that, but good design sense suggests that you should never (never say never) use too many different typefaces all at one time.

Since I have more typefaces than there are grains of sand on the beaches of Hawaii, I create a separate printer driver for each font family or for certain combinations.

Right now I have 20 different printer drivers on my hard disk. When I select a printer, I have 20 from which to choose, all of which were spawned from a single LaserJet driver. All but one is for the LaserJet. And each one for the LaserJet contains a single typeface, such as Korinna or Futura, or a tasteful combination of the two, such as Dutch and Swiss, or Futura and Bodoni. While my .ALL file contains all my fonts, I only use a selection of them for each printer file.

I create them by going into printer selections with **SHIFT-F7 S**. Then I highlight the file I want to duplicate (in this case, the LaserJet II driver), and press **C**. WordPerfect asks for a name for the new driver and even offers a suggestion. You can use it, or, as I do, enter a new name corresponding to the fonts it will contain. The driver named KORINNA.PRS contains Korinna fonts. It's one less detail to tear your hair out over.

I change the name of each printer (Select Printer/Edit/Name) so I don't have 20 "HP LaserJet Series II" printers with no clue as to which fonts each one supports.

Before I create a document, I select the printer driver containing the fonts I want to use. I press **SHIFT-F7 S**, move the cursor to the printer I want, and press **[ENTER]**.

I then press **I** immediately so that WordPerfect will start downloading any fonts marked with an * while I am writing and editing the file. The fonts are all downloaded by the time I'm ready to print.

The other advantage to this system is that changing fonts becomes fast and accurate. Select a new printer with **SHIFT-F7 S** and all the fonts are changed.

◆ Not lots-o-disk space

If you are always low on disk space, you can download fonts from floppies. Yes, it's true — take it from a hard disk space miser like myself. The trick is that they must all fit on a single floppy disk, otherwise WordPerfect will stamp its feet and give you two choices. You can cancel the initialization (or print job) or you can start over (which isn't much help if the fonts aren't there). If you have 1.2-megabyte floppies or the new 1.44-megabyte baby floppies, you should be able to cram quite a few fonts onto a single floppy. If you have 360K floppies, you will only be able to store smaller sizes.

LaserJet users can also save a ton of hard disk space with a program called *FontSpace*. This program compresses fonts so they take less than half of their original size. Then, a memory-resident program expands them any time WordPerfect downloads them to the printer. A complete review can be found in Chapter 20, *Software*..

◆ Subculture

If you are creating a document with multiple chapters and multiple WordPerfect files, you should be familiar with the Subdocument feature. This feature allows you to create a "master document" that will automatically combine many different files so that page numbering will be automatic throughout the entire document. It can also create tables of contents, indexes, tables of figures, tables, boxes, etc.

The subdocument feature consists of only three commands. The first command, **ALT-F5** S, allows you to insert a file name that WordPerfect will call a "subdocument." The second, **ALT-F5** G E, directs WordPerfect to "expand" the document. WordPerfect looks at each subdocument code and retrieves the file it names until it has one colossal file that contains all the subdocuments. The third and final command, **ALT-F5** G O, instructs WordPerfect to "condense the file," or to write all the files (and any changes you may have made in them) back to their original file names.

There is only one cautionary note regarding this feature. Once you've expanded a file, *do not remove any of the subdoc codes* that appear on-screen like comments. If you do, WordPerfect will not be able to condense the file correctly, and several files may be saved under one file name. Nothing will be lost, but the files will contain more or less text than they originally did.

❖ Printer notes

◆ Wait until dark (or light)

Does the output from the printer appear dark and heavy? Or too light? Most printers have a darkness control, and this can make a world of difference in the way type appears.

With the LaserJet II (or any Canon-based printer), the lightness control is *inside* the top of the printer. Press the big button on the top of the printer and the top will pop up. (If you're cheap, it's a great way to entertain the kids.) If you look straight down into the printer, the Light/Dark control (usually a green wheel) is located in the left front corner. This wheel will probably be set at 5, for medium. A setting of 9 is very light, and 1 is very dark.

Most typesetting fonts look best at 7 or 9, because the lightness makes them appear sharper. On the other hand, jagged edges are more obvious when the type is sharper. Extra toner can be used by setting the printer to 3 or 1. This toner melts around the edges, filling in the jagged edges. However, it also makes the type look heavier, and on typefaces with a small x-height (the height of a lower case "x"), the insides of a letter such as "e" can get filled in.

In general, you should set the printer to 5 (medium) if you are going to use the laser printer pages as originals. Setting the printer to light also offers an additional plus: it saves toner and prolongs the life of the printer cartridge. The only negative is that blacks will not be as dark and solid; this is fine for reproduction but may be inadequate for originals.

"Camera ready" pages (for photocopying or offset printing) should print at a light setting, at 7 or possibly 9. The lighter black should not give you any problem and should reproduce as solid, dark black.

◆ Toner Hell

If you use a LaserJet II, or any other printer based on a Canon engine, you know how wonderfully simple these printers are to maintain. The toner, drum, and most of the moving parts are in a single enclosed cartridge. There's never any toner mess (unless you let the piece of tape that covers the toner stick to you), and it's an efficient and pleasant system.

But if you have a printer based on the Ricoh engine (Ricoh, IBM, TI, Destiny, Acer), then you know the horrors of spreading toner all over the place.

This is just a helpful hint about what to do if you get toner on yourself.

NEVER WASH IT OFF WITH HOT WATER!!!!!

Since toner is designed to melt (that's how a laser printer works; it melts the toner onto the paper, not unlike a Tuna Melt, but not as tasty), it will also melt onto your hands.

Use cold water and soap. If it gets on your clothes, chances are it's there to stay—but wash them in cold water anyway. Desktop publishing may be a lot of things, but it should not be dirty.

◆ Paper chase

Laser printers have special needs, such as special laser paper. These papers may cost a bit more than regular copier paper, but they are generally worth the extra expense to cut down on the paper dust and wear and tear on your expensive laser printer.

We used Nekoosa Laser 1000 to print the original pages of this book, and never had a single paper jam. We have also used Hammermill LaserPlus paper, which has a "wax holdout," so that it can be waxed for paste up. This is a very strong, reliable paper. We've also used James River LaserUltra with good results. Here are the addresses of those paper companies, should you wish to contact them for samples.

- Nekoosa Laser 1000, Nekoosa Paper Inc., 100 Wisconsin River Dr., Port Edwards, WI 54469. (715) 887-5271
- LaserPlus, Hammermill Paper, 1540 E. Lake Road, Erie, PA 16533. 800-242-2148.
- LaserUltra, James River Corp., 356B Sewall St., Ludlow, MA 01056. 800-451-5501, 800-521-5035.

Quickcolor Formats

Colored paper is a quick attention-getter for your documents. Intergraphix offers a new brand of colored paper with a difference. Their preprinted, colorful 70 lb. stock has color printed on just two-thirds of one side, making it perfect for three-fold flyers. The paper can be run through offset presses and copy machines, too. The paper is sold in single color reams of 500 sheets and comes in blue, green, red, gray, and yellow. A rainbow assortment is also available. Call them for more information. Intergraphix, 800-451-2515, or inside Massachusetts, 331-8088.

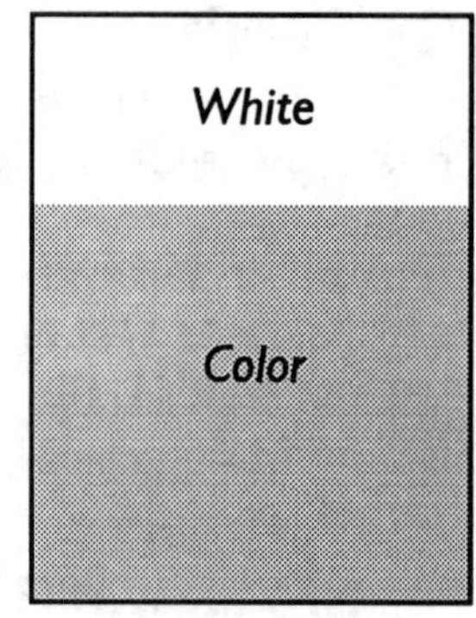

16

Put a label on it

The urge to merge

In the past, trying to create labels with WordPerfect has been equivalent on the suffering index to severe nausea or water weight buildup. But now labels are much easier and only rank with something like postnasal drip. The label feature is a new addition to the Paper Size menu. To use it, you only have to measure the labels you are using and enter the measurements into WordPerfect.

But even if you don't print mailing labels, this feature can work for you. When you create mailing labels, WordPerfect treats each label like its own "mini-page." It prints it, then moves to the next place on the page where the measurements indicate another mini-page is to be printed.

I'm going to give you two examples of labels. The first will be an actual honest to goodness label, and the second one is a great way to print side-by-side pages which can then turn a photocopy machine into a printing press. I'm also going to swoop down and buzz the barest basics of merging. Don't be scared of merging. I used to be. I never merged in WordPerfect until I was doing this version of the book because it just seemed like too much trouble.

I used to have my database "print-to-disk," then read it into WordPerfect, and format it there. That's always an option, although it means having to do some formatting by hand. But if you learn a few basics, you can have WordPerfect do all the work. WP 5.1 simplified merging to the point where I was willing to try it, and hey, it isn't bad at all. It only took me about 15 minutes to learn how to merge, and hopefully I can explain it to you in less time than that.

◆ Printer tip: Going straight

While copier labels work just fine in laser printers, not all printers like to take anything as thick as a sheet of labels. While one LaserJet may like printing labels, another may enjoy eating them. If your printer has an appetite for labels, set the printer so that the labels have the straightest possible paper path.

For the LaserJet II, IID, III (or any other Canon SX printer, including the QMS-PS 810), this means pulling down the face-down paper exit in the back of the printer. Instead of the labels having to make a 90 degree turn, they go straight through the paper path, making it more difficult for the printer to snack on them.

◆ As easy as ALT-F10

The easiest way to create labels is to use the macro cunningly named "Labels," which comes with WordPerfect. As of this writing, the macro will automatically set up WordPerfect for the following labels: Avery 5160/5260, Avery 5161/5261, Avery 5162/5262, Avery 5163, Avery 5164, Avery 5266, Avery 5267, Avery 5196, Avery 5197, Avery 5165, 3M 7730, 3M 7721, 3M 7733, 3M 7712, 3M 7709, 3M 7701, Avery 5293, Avery 5294, Avery 5295.

If you are using any of those products (or think that WordPerfect might have added more), press

ALT-F10 Labels [ENTER]

WordPerfect will display a list of the available formats. You can either press the letter next to the format or move the cursor to the format you want.

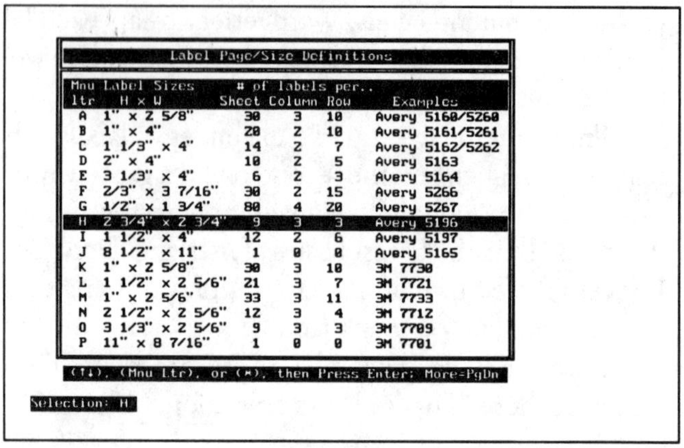

Label Page/Size Definitions

Mnu ltr	Label Sizes H x W	# of labels per.. Sheet	Column	Row	Examples
A	1" x 2 5/8"	30	3	10	Avery 5160/5260
B	1" x 4"	20	2	10	Avery 5161/5261
C	1 1/3" x 4"	14	2	7	Avery 5162/5262
D	2" x 4"	10	2	5	Avery 5163
E	3 1/3" x 4"	6	2	3	Avery 5164
F	2/3" x 3 7/16"	30	2	15	Avery 5266
G	1/2" x 1 3/4"	80	4	20	Avery 5267
H	2 3/4" x 2 3/4"	9	3	3	Avery 5196
I	1 1/2" x 4"	12	2	6	Avery 5197
J	8 1/2" x 11"	1	0	0	Avery 5165
K	1" x 2 5/8"	30	3	10	3M 7730
L	1 1/2" x 2 5/6"	21	3	7	3M 7721
M	1" x 2 5/6"	33	3	11	3M 7733
N	2 1/2" x 2 5/6"	12	3	4	3M 7712
O	3 1/3" x 2 5/6"	9	3	3	3M 7709
P	11" x 8 7/16"	1	0	0	3M 7701

(↑↓), (Mnu Ltr), or (*), then Press Enter; More=PgDn

Selection: H

If you want to print on standard labels, this macro will automatically set WordPerfect to use them.

WordPerfect will ask if you want the labels to be manual feed, and you can make that decision all by yourself. If you're going to be printing many sheets, it's probably a good idea not to select manual feed, unless you enjoy standing around feeding a printer.

◆ Merging a sheet of labels

The first detail to note is that every brand of label on this planet has slightly different measurements, so the measurements I give you here are purely for experimentation.

Most copier/laser printer labels are three-across. They work fine for big mailings, but if you want to print just one or two labels you can end up wasting the sheet. So, you can, at your own risk, use one-across tractor feed labels. I've done this successfully for years (in many different laser printers), because I rarely need more than four or five labels at a time. Label manufacturers warn you that the labels can come off in a laser printer, but I've never had this happen with the Avery 6040 labels that I use. Still, I'm not recommending you do it because I don't want to be sued. I've got a list of people I would *love* to sue (don't we all), but I don't want to be on the receiving end.

So to steer well clear of litigation, this example is for three-across copier labels. If *they* stick you can sue the label makers, not me.

◆ Be prepared

The first step in any type of merging is to have your data file (also called secondary merge file) ready. The data file is the list of names, addresses, whatever type of information is going to be merged. This information is best kept in a database, but you can also type it into WordPerfect directly.

These records are made up of two parts: fields and records. Each record has several fields. Each field stands for something like first name, last name, city, state, zip. Fields must always be in the same order in all records.

In this example, field 1 is the first name, field 2 is the last name, field 3 is the address, field 4 is the city, field 5 is the state, and field 6 is the zip.

If you keep this info in a database, you will need to export the information to a format that WordPerfect can use for merging. If you use DataPerfect or the WordPerfect Library/Office "Notebook" program, the info will automatically be in the correct WordPerfect format.

If you need to export from another program, choose "Comma Delimited ASCII" because WordPerfect can now use this format directly. When WordPerfect asks for your "secondary file" enter the name of this file (or press F5 for list files). WordPerfect will know this is not its normal format and will ask you what the delimiters are for the field and record.

The fields are the individual parts of each record, such as the first name, last name, etc. These will either be separated by a single comma or by commas surrounded with quotes. If they are just commas for "Field," enter nothing for the begin and a comma for end. For "Record" enter nothing for begin, and press CONTROL-M so that "[CR]" appears in end.

If the fields are surrounded by commas with quotes, enter a quote mark (") for begin of field, and a quote comma (",) for the end of field. Enter nothing for begin of record, and press CONTROL-M so that a "[CR]" appears in the end.

If you are typing the data directly in WordPerfect, you will type one field, then press F9. That will enter an {END FIELD} code, and a return. Repeat that for each field, and at the end of the record, press SHIFT-F9 E to {END RECORD}. This will also insert a page break.

◆ On with the codes

OK, I'm going to imagine that you understood all that, and that if you didn't, you looked at the merge section in the WordPerfect reference manual. If you're still confused, try the merge lesson in the WordPerfect Workbook (that's how I learned how to merge). We're not here to talk about merging anyway, we're here to talk about DTP merging, so on with the codes.

Once the secondary file is complete, you have to create a primary file. This is the file that the information from the secondary file will be merged *into*.

◆ Initial codes

In this case, we're doing labels, so we need to set up the labels as the first item in the file. We *could* place these paper/size labels codes right at the top of the file, but if we did it would be repeated for each and every label we merged. It would make merging slow, it would make the files huge, and it would cause problems. So instead we're going to place those codes in the "Initial Codes" of the file. This way, they sit invisibly at the top of the file, and they are not repeated during the merge.

To enter initial codes, press

SHIFT-F8 D C

◆ Tabs

We need to set a relative tab at .25":

SHIFT-F8 L T 0.25 [ENTER] F7 F7

◆ Paper size

You can now enter codes just as you would anywhere in the file. In this case, you're going to place a paper size code here for labels. But before we can place the code in the file, we have to set up the label format. To set paper size, press

SHIFT-F8 P S

A list of existing forms will appear on-screen. These will probably include (I say probably because it varies among printers) an envelope format, legal, legal wide (landscape), standard 8 1/2 x 11 (portrait), and standard wide (landscape). We're going to add a label format, so press

A L

This adds a new format and specifies it as a label format. If we had chosen Other under Paper Type, we could have entered a more descriptive name for these labels, rather than just the default label. This would come in handy when you use more than one type of label stock.

◆ Paper size options

From here we can control the size of the paper; the "type" of the paper (really just what it's called on-screen, you can use "O," other, to give it a descriptive name); the font type (portrait or landscape); whether or not you want WordPerfect to prompt you to load the paper; whether the paper is continuous (in a tray) or manual (hand fed); if printing is double sided (for the IID and other duplex printers); whether the binding edge is on the top or the left; whether or not the form is for labels, and adjustment on the top and side. Adjustment is useful when margins aren't printing where they appear in View Document. This can happen when the paper is loaded into the printer in a different place than WordPerfect expects. You can adjust these numbers rather than changing the margins. You can move up,

```
Format: Edit Paper Definition

     Filename                        STANDARD.PRS

  1 - Paper Size                     8.5" x 11"

  2 - Paper Type                     Labels

  3 - Font Type                      Portrait

  4 - Prompt to Load                 No

  5 - Location                       Continuous

  6 - Double Sided Printing          No

  7 - Binding Edge                   Left

  8 - Labels                         No (Yes)

  9 - Text Adjustment - Top          0"
                        Side         0"

Selection: a
```

If you want to create labels, you need to answer "Y" here.

down, left, or right. They won't look different on-screen, but WordPerfect will position them differently when it prints.

◆ Label options

Even though we've already told it that we want labels, we have to tell it again by pressing

A Y

WordPerfect will come up with defaults for a page of 3-across, 10-deep labels, a standard copier label format. (Standard copier labels are 3 x 11, standard laser labels are 3 x 10.) We're going to stick with this format as is. Press

F7 F7 S F7

We've now set up a label format and inserted the paper/size/label format into the initial codes of the file. To leave Initial Codes, press

F7 F7

◆ Merging with style, or at least Styles

Let's say we want the first line of the label to be in one typeface, and the rest in another. We could just place these codes in the file and WordPerfect would repeat them while merging each label. Or we could do the smart thing and create a style. The reason it's smart is because after we merge, our boss (or ourselves) may decide we hate the fonts we originally chose, or they may look stupid, or any number of things. If we put the codes in manually we either have to replace them all manually or redo our merge file and merge again. If we put them in styles we can change the finished merged file in seconds, over and over and over until we become kind of dizzy or find what we want, whichever comes first. Let's create a style by pressing

ALT-F8 C N Name [ENTER]

The style is going to consist of a font change to Dutch 14-point bold italic, and the WordPerfect code for the right-pointing-finger icon. First, select the font

C CONTROL-F8 F

Move the cursor to Dutch 14-point bold italic and press

S

Now we're going to enter the pointing-finger icon followed by an indent.

CONTROL-V 5,21 [ENTER] F4

A little square block will appear on-screen, and then we're through. Press

F7 F7 F7

◆ Putting in the fields

Now it's actually time to put in the merge fields. We first need to set our Initial Base font to something small, otherwise the text of your labels may wrap and things won't be in the right place. To set the base font, press

SHIFT-F8 D F

Select a small font, such as Dutch 10. Press

S F7

WordPerfect will replace the merge codes you're going to enter with the data in the secondary file. First we're going to apply the style.

ALT-F8

Highlight the NAME style and press

O

Now we'll insert the fields

SHIFT-F9 F

WordPerfect asks for the field name. Unless your fields are named in the secondary file (with SHIFT-F9 M [Field Names]), you will need to enter field numbers instead of names here.

1 [ENTER]

WordPerfect will insert {FIELD}1 ~. Let's insert the rest of the fields.

[SPACEBAR] SHIFT-F9 F 2 [ENTER]

Now it's time to turn off the style and start a new line

[RIGHT ARROW] [ENTER]

[TAB] SHIFT-F9 F 3 [ENTER] [ENTER]

[TAB] SHIFT-F9 F 4 [ENTER] , [SPACEBAR] SHIFT-F9 F 5 [ENTER]
[SPACEBAR] [SPACEBAR] SHIFT-F9 F 6 [ENTER]

Go to the top of the document by pressing

[HOME] [HOME] [HOME] [UP ARROW]

It should all look like this:

[Style On:Name;[Font:BSN Dutch Bold Italic 14pt (ASCII Business) (FW, Port)] [■:5,21] [Indent]] [Mrg:FIELD] 1 ~[Mrg:FIELD]2 ~[Style Off:Name] [HRt]

[Tab] [Mrg:FIELD]3 ~[HRt]

[Tab][Mrg:FIELD]4~, [Mrg:FIELD]5~ [Mrg:FIELD]6~
If it does, save it

F7 Y label.1 [ENTER] N

◆ **Merge mania**

Now it's time to actually merge the two files. To start merging, press

CONTROL-F9 M

WordPerfect asks for the name of the primary file. Type

LABEL.1 [ENTER]

WordPerfect asks for the name of the secondary file. Type the name you gave to your secondary file.

{secondary file name} [ENTER]

WordPerfect will now say * MERGING * in the bottom left corner of the screen. When the message disappears, you will see each label, separated by a hard page break. When you use View Document

F7 SHIFT-F7 V

You'll see the whole page of labels, just the way they'll print.

◆ **Printing**

To print a page of labels, it would seem natural to press SHIFT-F7 P. But don't. While View Document automatically shows you a whole page, if you print the page you'll only get page one of the file, one single label.

Since our format calls for one page to hold 30 labels, we have to tell WordPerfect to print the first 30 pages to get one real page. To print the whole page in this example, press

SHIFT-F7 M 1-30 [ENTER]

When you're all finished, you'll want to clear the screen with

F7 N N

◆ **Merge alert**

As I write this there is a rather annoying bug in Merge. The merge proceeds correctly, but when you're done, the resulting file is huge. In this example I used a data file with 49 records and got 49 labels. The resulting file was 380K. When I then blocked the entire file and copied it to Doc 2, the resulting file was then only 17K, the correct size. I don't know what the other 363K of data was, but whatever it was it was, it was unnecessary.

If you find that your merge files are becoming gigantic, just block the text and copy it to the other document that should help. Of course, if you have hundreds of records, then the file size can easily become hundreds of K; but if your merge isn't big and your file is, try this. If WordPerfect fixes this and you never run into it, so much the better.

❖ *Side by side*

Printing a book used to mean taking pages to a printer, having them shoot stats, make plates, then print the pages on printing presses. While most books are still done this way (this one was), that's not always the most practical way for short-run books, or booklets. If you're not going to print more than a few hundred copies, why not think of the Xerox machine (I know, I should have said photocopy) as your printing press.

If your book is going to be 8 1/2 x 11", there's no problem, Just print the pages and copy them back to back. But many books are smaller than that, and if you just want to be able to fold the photocopied pages in half and staple them in the middle, how can you do that in WordPerfect? Here's a hint: you don't have to print on label stock just because you used a label format.

The answer, my friend, is blowing in the labels, the answer is blowing in the labels. Excuse me, it's late and I'm tired and all this table business has been exhausting. You're probably tired too. Everyone's working too hard these days. Why don't you close your eyes, take three long, slow, deep breaths, and relax.

Don't you feel better? Well, you would have if you had tried it. Are we ready to try side-by-side pages? It all starts with adding a new paper size/type label format.

◆ Faking the "labels"

SHIFT-F8 P S A

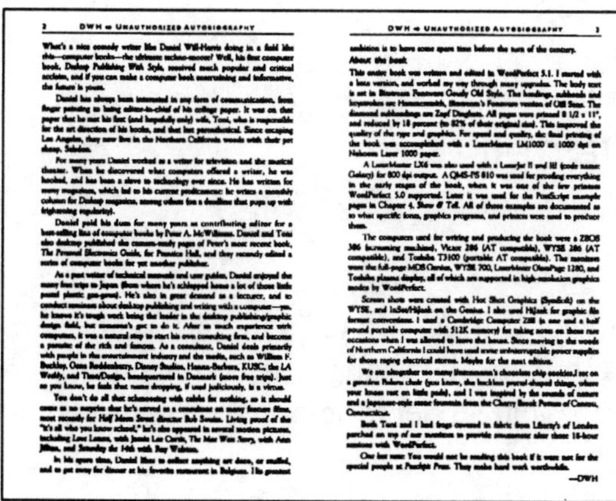

Side-by-side pages are not only possible, they're probable, using the label feature.

We don't have to choose the label type to use a label format, so let's call this one "side by side"

O Side By Side [ENTER]

We now get a menu which tells us that we're using paper that's 8.5" x 11", among other things. Well, this page is going to have to be printed landscape, otherwise we're going to get very silly, tall, and narrow pages, which might be OK for an invitation or something unusual but not for a normal booklet. To choose landscape paper, press

S T

We also have to tell WordPerfect to use landscape fonts, otherwise it isn't quite bright enough to figure this out, even though we've already told it that we're using a landscape page. To do this, press

F L

To set up the label format, press

A Y

Now we're going to set up the labels into two labels, side-by-side.

S 4.5 [ENTER] 8 [ENTER]

N 2 [ENTER] 1 [ENTER]

We're going to set the top left corner at .3" so it's as close to the edge of the paper as it can be and the left margin to .5" so that there's enough margin that your fingers don't touch the type when you hold the page.

C .3 [ENTER] .5 [ENTER]

Now we'll place 1" between the two "labels" so that there's enough binding room in the middle where the page will be folded.

D 1 [ENTER] 0 [ENTER]

And finally, we'll set all the margins to 0"

M 0 [ENTER] 0 [ENTER] 0 [ENTER] 0 [ENTER]

We're finished, so press

[ENTER] to exit.

Whoops, if your printer is like mine, WordPerfect will tell you that you need to have more of a bottom margin and will automatically change the bottom margin to .1" Fine, if it wants to be like that we're not going to let it upset us, we're just going to leave.

Press

[ENTER] S [ENTER]

◆ Headers, footers, and other niceties

As you should know by now, the real trick to DTP is in the details. We've now set up the page format, but no book is complete without page numbers and enchanting headers or footers. So we're going to add them, and then go to sleep for the night.

First, let's set our page numbering. We'll make it so that it's always on the outside of the page.

P N P 4 [ENTER]

That was easy enough. I can see your eyelids are getting heavy from all this reading, so we'll move on quickly before you fall into a deep and sound sleep, from which you'll awake refreshed, with complete and detailed memory of everything you've learned in this chapter. You'll also stop smoking, cut out fats to lower your cholesterol, and learn to enjoy it. (How's that for a far-fetched posthypnotic suggestion.)

Let's make that header.

H A P

First, we'll select a typeface.

CONTROL-F8 F

Move the cursor to Dutch Roman 10 point (or Times Roman, or anything else you want as long as it's a point or two less than the body text), and press

S

We're going to center this baby, so press

SHIFT-F6

We're going to give the words extra spacing between each letter so it won't conflict with the body text. This step is optional, but probably more fun than you've had in ages, so go ahead, press

SHIFT-F8 O P W P 120 [ENTER] P 200 [ENTER] F7

Now, we'll set the whole thing in small caps

CONTROL-F8 A C

Type the header here. I won't even make you think of something, just type

The Elvis Hip Replacement Report [ENTER]

Now for a ruling line below, press

[ENTER] ALT-F9 L H F7 F7 F7

We're done, we're done! At last, this chapter is almost over! Type some text now or better yet retrieve another file and you can bask in the full glow of your accomplishments.

If you want the first page to be a right side page, put in a hard page break now by pressing CONTROL-[ENTER]. If your first page is some type of title page and you don't want a header or page numbers, press SHIFT-F8 P U A F7.

Now, get ready for the thrill of a lifetime as you burst into the hyperspace-like View Document feature.

SHIFT-F7 V

Yes, it's true. Side-by-side pages on a single sheet of paper. If you don't have the faintest idea why I am excited it can only be because you don't appreciate the magnitude of your accomplishment. If nothing else, be gracious enough to pretend that you are slightly amused if not trembling with delight.

Really, this type of thing was impossible with 5.0, and is still impossible with many programs. Please, use it only for the powers of good, and not in some misguided attempt to rule the galaxy.

17

Keys to success

Macros/Soft Keyboard

No, *mac*ros are not a new Chef Boy-ar-dee product comprised of pasta in o-shapes. Nor are they the macaroni equivalent of McNuggets, and whatever you do, don't confuse them with macrame. And soft keyboards are not designed by Claes Oldenburg (the soft sculpture artist), are not squishy, have nothing to do with frozen yogurt, and of course, are not *hard*ware at all.

Macros allow you to accomplish much by doing a little. By pressing two keys you can type your entire address, or change fonts, or search and replace countless variables in a single bound. I've already covered a wide variety of applications in which macros can be used. Review those chapters for information about 1-2-3, converting underlines to italics, converting underlines to styles, dashes, fonts, graphics, indents, lines, paragraph numbering, quotation marks, spreadsheets, or styles.

This chapter will show you how to use two extremely important macros which are cleverly concealed in "soft keyboards," as well as offer some helpful macro tips (to prevent a macro from wreaking havoc with a file). It will also cover some useful but little-known macros included with WordPerfect. In addition, we'll throw in some miscellaneous macros, and fill you in on WordPerfect's "soft keyboard" feature, which allows you to modify the function of any key on the keyboard.

❖ *Two indispensable macros*

These are more than just macros. These are *features.* So, before I regale you with the basics of creating macros, I'm going to show you how to use a couple of the macros which come with WordPerfect. That way, those of you who never ever want to record a macro (or so you think right now) can use these two important critters.

◆ If you read nothing else in this chapter, read this

⊸ Edit any code with only one keystroke (5.1 only)

This is a well-hidden, but very important new feature. Critics of WordPerfect (and users with tired little fingers alike) have complained that too many keystrokes are required to accomplish something. In some ways they are right. When you're in a hurry, keystrokes such as SHIFT-F8 L J F seem like an awful lot to go through just to change the justification of a paragraph. But 5.1 has added a new keyboard definition which most people will overlook, yet it can save them hundreds of keystrokes a day. When you install the program, answer "Y" to installing "Soft Keyboards." These are not keyboards made out of rubber, but files which allow you to redefine what each key on your keyboard does.

The new keyboard is called "Shortcut," and it contains 32 shortcuts. One in particular is a minor miracle: it's ALT-E, for Edit a Code. With this keyboard installed, you can edit virtually any code on-screen just by moving the cursor on top of it (it helps to have Reveal Codes on) and pressing ALT-E. The macro figures out what type of code it is and almost immediately moves you to the menu in the program to edit it. Once you've finished editing, the macro removes the old code.

This even works for replacing bold, italic, or any attribute, or changing one size to another. With "paired" codes such as attributes or size, you place the cursor on the opening code, such as [BOLD] and press ALT-E (or whatever name you decide on). The macro blocks the entire area which uses that size or attribute, then it asks what new size or attribute you want. What a timesaver.

If you already use a soft keyboard, you can save this to a separate macro file and then retrieve it into your own keyboard file. Whatever you do, *use this macro.*

If you just want to use this macro, and don't want to mess with some soft keyboard that will change the functions on your keyboard, follow these steps:

SHIFT-F1 K

Move the cursor to "SHORTCUT" and press

E

Now to edit the keyboard file. Press

[DOWN ARROW]

```
Keyboard: Edit

  Name: SHORTCUT

  Key            Action            Description

  Alt-W          {KEY MACRO 26}    Shadow
  Alt-E          {KEY MACRO 15}    Edit a Code
  Alt-R          {KEY MACRO 8}     Redline
  Alt-T          {KEY MACRO 27}    Strikeout
  Alt-I          {KEY MACRO 1}     Italics
  Alt-O          {KEY MACRO 25}    Outline
  Alt-P          {KEY MACRO 21}    Superscript
  Alt-A          {KEY MACRO 32}    Add an Attribute
  Alt-S          {KEY MACRO 6}     Small
  Alt-D          {KEY MACRO 2}     Double Underline
  Alt-F          {KEY MACRO 7}     Fine
  Alt-G          {KEY MACRO 30}    Go Printer
  Alt-L          {KEY MACRO 5}     Large
  Alt-X          {KEY MACRO 3}     Extra Large
  Alt-V          {KEY MACRO 4}     Very Large
  Alt-B          {KEY MACRO 20}    Subscript
  Ctrl-B         {KEY MACRO 23}    Base Font

1 Action; 2 Dscrptn; 3 Original; 4 Create; 5 Move; Macro: 6 Save; 7 Retrieve: 1
```

The "Edit-a-code" macro. Not just another pretty macro, but an important, time-saving feature. Don't use 5.1 without it.

(Or whatever it takes to move the cursor to ALT-E, Edit-a-Code.) We're now going to save this as a stand-alone macro. Press

S ALTE [ENTER] F7

(If WordPerfect asks you if you want to replace ALTE.WPM, it means that you already have a macro with that name. If you aren't sure, press **N**, and try another ALT name; if that macro is expendable, press **Y**.)

You've just saved this as a stand-alone macro file. Now whenever you press **ALT-E** WordPerfect will edit any code the cursor is sitting on. If the cursor isn't on a code or is just on a letter or number, the macro will do nothing.

Not only will this macro take you to wherever in the program you need to be to edit the code, but once you make the change, it will not only insert the new code, but it will, if necessary, delete the old code.

This macro will not, repeat, will not work in 5.0. If you try it in 5.0, WordPerfect will spew forth a string of letters and numbers and you will need to press F1 or die trying. Oh, this type of excitement wears me out. I have no choice but to lie on the couch and eat ice cream.

◆ Replace any attribute with any other attribute (5.0 & 5.1)

The next indispensable macro which WordPerfect includes is in yet another soft keyboard file. This soft keyboard is called "Macros" and the macro will permit you to search and replace attributes or sizes. While the Edit-a-Code macro only allows you to change one code at a time, this macro permits you to replace *all* underlines with italics, or all bolds with small caps, or all larges with extra larges, or smalls with fines.

Without this macro, you cannot search and replace attributes, and you either have to use styles or replace them (gasp) by hand. This macro is easy and painless, but it can take a while on long files because it's having to search for the start of the attribute, turn the block on, search for the end of the attribute, apply the new attribute, remove the old attribute, and then search again.

5.0 *users:* 5.0 includes a different version from 5.1. The 5.0 version can search and replace attributes or sizes, but not text. It's still tremendously useful. If you can reach the keyboard, follow along, won't you?

SHIFT-F1 K

Move the cursor to "MACROS" and press

E

Move the cursor to ALT-R Replace Size, Attribute, or Text and press

S ALTR [ENTER]

(If WordPerfect asks you if you want to replace ALTR.WPM, it means that you already have a macro with that name. If you aren't sure, press **N**, and try another ALT name or, if that macro is expendable, press **Y**.)

You've just saved this as a stand-alone macro file. Now, whenever you press **ALT-R** WordPerfect will—well, wait a second. It depends on what version of WordPerfect you have.

5.0: If you have 5.0, it will ask if you want to confirm replace, just like regular search and replace. If you want to check each one before WordPerfect does its dirty deed, press **Y**; if you just want it to change everything without bothering you, press **N**. WordPerfect will then say "Type of AFC" and offer you the choice of Size or Attribute. Choose whichever you want, I don't care. Then it will ask "Replace With" and if you changed size, it will present you with sizes; if you replaced attributes, it will display attributes to choose from. When you choose one, WordPerfect will go off on its merry way (just like Mission Pak), and it will replace everything you asked for.

5.1: If you have 5.1, this macro does more, but unfortunately it requires more keystrokes. It will first ask "W/Confirm," just like regular search and replace. If you read the last paragraph you know what to do. If you didn't, thinking you'd spare yourself some time, then I'll repeat myself. Press **Y** if you want WordPerfect to stop and ask each time it wants to replace, or press **N** if you want WordPerfect to replace everything without asking you first.

The macro will now ask "Delete Original Attributes?" It's asking this to confuse us. It wants to get us off balance so it can take over our lives and replace us with clones.

Maybe not. Maybe it's really asking us that because it can either delete the old stuff or leave it there, so that where once there was only **bold**, there is now ***bold italic.***

The macro now asks us just exactly what it is that we want to "convert from." We can replace size, attribute, or text. We can replace any of these with any others of these; make small text into italics, bold into extra large, you name it.

Once you choose the attribute you want to replace, WordPerfect asks you what you want to "convert to." As I said, you can choose size, attribute, or text. This macro also allows you to automatically replace all normal straight quotes into "real" quotes. (But we'll get into all that a little bit later.)

Again, be aware, this macro can be slooooooow. If your file is long, your children could have children before it's finished. Or WordPerfect could be on version 25.1. But it works, and it's automatic.

One word of warning. The text replacement feature is intended for matched sets, like opening and closing quotes. If you have not matched all the sets, then WordPerfect could end up making the "quote" marks look like that.

❖ Basics

Recording macros is a breeze. Just press

CONTROL-F10

WordPerfect will ask for a name by saying "Define Macro." A name can up to eight character, no spaces or **ALT** and any one letter (letters only, no punctuation, numbers, or function keys). WordPerfect will then ask you to type a description of the macro you want to record. You can type a line of text or just press return.

From then on WordPerfect will record whatever you type, and each and every command.

To save the macro, press

CONTROL-F10

There are two ways to run the macro. If you typed ALT and a letter, just press ALT and that letter, and the macro will run. If you typed a name for the macro, press

ALT-F10

Then type the name. Normally, you won't see anything while a macro is running, but while recording a macro you can type **CONTROL-[PgUp] D Y** and WordPerfect will display everything it's doing during the macro. It's a kick to watch WordPerfect working by itself, but remember that macros run much slower with Display On. Don't turn this feature on if you're in a rush or recording a complex macro.

If you want WordPerfect to pause so that you will be able to type, press

CONTROL-[PgUp] P

Now the macro will stop whenever it encounters this pause and will restart when the **[ENTER]** key is pressed.

If you never do any more than this, macros can save you much time and tedium. If you never want to do any more than this, skip to "Undocumented boon again."

◆ Macro editing (for the macro-nically inclined)

If you're in an adventurous mood, you can now edit this macro. To do this, type: **CONTROL-F10** and type the name of a previously recorded macro (or press ALT and a letter). WordPerfect will point out that "BLAHBLAH.WPM" is already defined. (Of course, it will substitute whatever name you entered for Blahblah.) You now have three alternatives: you can **R**eplace the macro (record a new one from scratch), you can **E**dit the macro, or you can change the **D**escription, then edit the macro. (5.0: choose between Replace or Edit.)

To edit the macro, press **E**. 5.1 users are thrown directly into the Macro Edit window. (In 5.0, WordPerfect displays the macro in a window and presents you with two choices. You can **D**escribe the macro or you can change the **A**ction of the macro. Let's try the latter. Press **A**.)

You're now deep in the depths of the macro. You can change whatever you like, and even add new commands or text. You can also mess something up if you're not careful. If you do change something accidentally, press **F1 Y**.

When editing a macro, commands appear in bold, surrounded by curly brackets like this: **{Search}** refers to the F2 key. Text that you typed (including letters such as Y and N in response to prompts from WordPerfect) appears as normal. Spaces appear as little dots.

You can move around the macro using normal cursor keys. Function keys, however, will not perform their usual functions and will place a code in the macro instead.

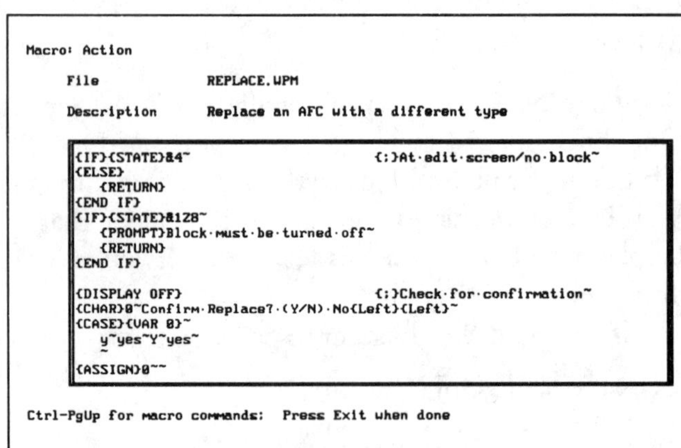

Macro: Action
File REPLACE.WPM
Description Replace an AFC with a different type
{IF}{STATE}&4~ {;}At·edit·screen/no·block~
{ELSE}
{RETURN}
{END IF}
{IF}{STATE}&128~
{PROMPT}Block·must·be·turned·off~
{RETURN}
{END IF}
{DISPLAY OFF} {;}Check·for·confirmation~
{CHAR}0~Confirm·Replace?·(Y/N)·No{Left}{Left}~
{CASE}{VAR 0}~
y~yes~Y~yes~
~
{ASSIGN}0~~
Ctrl-PgUp for macro commands: Press Exit when done

Recording macros is easy, but editing them requires technical understanding.

Inserting cursor movements: You will need to change modes if you want to add a cursor movement code, keystrokes such as ESC, F1, F7, or [ENTER]. Pressing **CONTROL-V** will put you in code mode. Now the next key you press will insert its code into the macro. If you need to insert many codes, pressing **CONTROL-F10** will make every key you press insert its code, and pressing **CONTROL-F10** again will bring things back to normal.

◆ Special macro commands

WordPerfect's macros are actually an entire programming language. Wait, don't run screaming from the room; you don't have to learn how to program them (although you can if you're so inclined). These commands tell WordPerfect whether Reveal Codes is on or off; they can also pause the macro, display messages on the screen, make the computer beep, or wait for a specific amount of time. You name it, a macro can do it (if you can figure out how).

You access these commands by pressing **CONTROL-[PgUp]**. A small window pops up in the top right corner of the macro window. You can either use the cursor to scroll down the list, or press the first letter of the command to jump to that command. To leave this window, select a command and press **[ENTER]**, or press **[ESC]**.

We're going to use a few of these commands to create fail-safe macros later on, but fear not, we're not going to dwell on the subject for long.

Get me out of here: To leave the macro editor and save the macro, press

F7

Or, if you want to leave and abandon any changes you may have made, press

F1 Y

◆ Undocumented boon again

If you read Chapter 11, this is all old hat. But because it's not covered in the manual and is essential for creating macros that call styles, I'm repeating myself (for your benefit).

When you create macros that call styles, don't press ALT-F8 and move the cursor to the style you want. If you do, the macros will no longer work when you add or delete styles because they rely on cursor movements to select the correct style. There will be more, or fewer, styles, and the cursor may move to the wrong one.

WordPerfect includes a feature to solve this problem, but WordPerfect's manual neglects to mention it.

The feature is none other than our friend Name Search, a feature found in almost every list WordPerfect presents. List Files, Base Font, all of these have *N* on the menu. You press it, type the name you are searching for, and WordPerfect jumps to the name that matches what you type. Style offers this feature as well, although it's not on the menu (possibly because there's no room for it).

Still, even if the authors of the manual at WordPerfect didn't think it was important enough to acknowledge, *we* know it's important, don't we? In fact, it's indispensable when you are creating macros.

Whenever you create a macro that uses a style, use the Name Search feature instead of moving the cursor to the style you want. Then, no matter how many styles you add or delete, the macro will still call the style you want.

◆ Big tip #2

Some macros will run differently, depending on whether Reveal Codes is on or off. When you are deleting codes, WordPerfect will ask if it's OK to delete the codes if Reveal Codes is off, but will not ask if it's on.

This can lead to problems if you create macros that search for one code and replace it with another. If you forget to turn Reveal Codes off before running the macro, the search and replace will not function, and you'll have several extra characters in the file. This messes up spelling and garners complaints from sticklers who believe that "the" should be not spelled "they." These same people know that even WordPerfect's wonderful spell check program can't find errors like this (because "they" is a word, too).

There are two solutions to this dilemma, and each involves editing the macro once you've recorded it. It's no great thrill entering complex macro codes in each of your files, and so we're going to use a macro that comes with WordPerfect, hidden deep inside a soft keyboard. (Oh boy, we get to do it all at once. Isn't this going to be fun? Say "yes"; who knows, it might be fun. You'll never know unless you try.)

First we'll get the WordPerfect macro, then record another macro that converts underlines into italics (without the need for a style), and finally combine the two together into a fail-safe macro.

OK, time for some macro merriment. Get out the "Conversion" disk and copy a file called "Macros.wpk" to your WordPerfect directory. If at any time during this procedure you don't understand what I'm doing, play along anyway. No one but you will know that you're hopelessly lost and confused.

Now we're going to edit this keyboard file and save one of the entries as a macro. Press

SHIFT-F1 K

Move the cursor to "Macros" and press

E

(If you don't see Macros listed, you may not have copied the file correctly, or you may have neglected to tell WordPerfect where to look for keyboard and macro files. To tell WordPerfect where to look, press **SHIFT-F1 L K** and type the directory where you want macros and keyboard files to reside.)

You're now presented with a long list of keys on the left and definitions on the right. The cursor should be on "ALT-E," and conveniently, this is what we want. To save this as a macro, press

S

WordPerfect will ask you to "Define Macro," which is its own roundabout way of asking for a file name. Why it doesn't just come out and ask for a file name is not ours to ponder. In that we're going to use this macro to save us from ourselves (for those times when we forget to turn Reveal Codes off), let's call it ALT-S for "Safety." Press

ALT-S [ENTER]

We delve into all this keyboard jazz later in the chapter, but for now, let's get outta here. (A prime tidbit of information: 80% of all Saturday morning cartoon shows contain the line "Let's get outta here!!!" I should know. I wrote for a couple. Other popular lines (in descending order) include, "Let's Go!!!", "(terrified) Whadda we do now!?!", "I've got an idea!!!", "Not again!!!", "Hold it right there!!!", "Yaaaaaoooowwwwwww!!!", "I've heard of ____, but this is ridiculous!!!", and my personal favorite, "And then the world will be mine!!!" Notice how all sentences must end in exclamation marks, preferably three of them. I hope you found this aside entertaining, educational, and at least as informative as the "Cheers and Jeers" section in *TV Guide*.)

Let's get outta here! Press

F1 Y F1 F1

Now you have this macro called ALTS.WPM. All WordPerfect macros end in .WPM, which stands for "WordPerfect Macro" (and not for "Words Per Minute," or "Wealthy Pinhead Movement," as previously and erroneously reported in the *National Intruder*). To run this ALT-key macro all you need to do is press ALT-S.

This macro will turn Reveal Codes off automatically. The next time you record a macro, press **ALT-S** after you've named and described it. That will insure that Reveal Codes will never be a problem in your macros again.

Bear with me as we use this to help us create a macro to turn all underlines into italics. You don't have to follow along if you are just going to use the "replace" macro I told you about earlier. But if you want to learn more about macros, stick around.

◆ Underline to italics macro

Underlines become italics right before your very eyes

If you already have a document with underlines, and you want to typeset these as italics, you can search and replace underline codes and replace them with italic codes. It's easy, but not very straightforward. Don't confuse this with a similar example in Chapter 11, which creates a style that allows you to easily change underlines to italics, or the macro in the same example which enables you to use that style in a single keystroke.

Okay, I admit it. I've got this thing for turning underlines into italics, what can I say? But it's one of those items you may find yourself using on a daily basis. You're right, I did state earlier that "WordPerfect automatically prints italics as underlines." But it does that only when italics are not available (and even then it may get confused and use another font's italics instead of underlining the current font). Are you *happy* now?

The major advantage of all this is that you only have to do it once; one single underline to one single italic. After that, the macro will do it all for you, over and over again, without getting crabby. It will automatically run through an entire file and change all underlines into italics.

Are we ready? Good. Since you now know the basics for creating a macro, I'm going to give you all these keystrokes in one big lump (and if you skip ahead now, you won't be hurting anyone but yourself).

This macro works by searching for an underline, turning block on, searching for the closing underline (which extends the block to cover the entire underlined area), applying italics, and then deleting the underline. The macro then calls itself, searches for the next underline, and keeps calling itself until it can no longer find another underline. Gee, wouldn't this be painfully dull if you had to do it by hand? Remember, as in all macros, don't press the **[ENTER]** key unless you see the word **[ENTER]**. And don't put in any spaces, except where you see a ^. *And make sure Reveal Codes is OFF.* Okay, here goes.

CONTROL-F10 UND2ITAL

[ENTER]turn^underlines^to^italics[ENTER]

CONTROL-[PgUp] D Y ALT-S F2 F8 F2

ALT-F4 F2 F8 F8 [LEFT ARROW][BACKSPACE] F2

CONTROL-F8 A I [BACKSPACE] N [BACKSPACE] Y

ALT-F10 UND2ITAL [ENTER]

CONTROL-F10

Okay, you now have a macro that will turn underlines into italics. Because you pressed ALT-S (a macro we had created to turn Reveal Codes off), you don't have to worry about whether Reveal Codes is on or off.

Now let's run this macro. You should really test it on a file you've already saved, so if for some reason it doesn't work, you won't lose anything important.

First, turn Reveal Codes on to verify that it works. Next, find a file with plenty of underlines, or put some underlines in a file. Now start the macro by pressing

ALT-F10 UND2ITAL [ENTER]

You can now see every step the macro makes, because we turned Display on when we were recording it. Unfortunately, this really slows it down. If you get tired of watching the macro do its thing, rerecord the macro but do not type **CONTROL-[PgUp] D Y**. (This was the command we used to turn Display on.) The default is "Display Off," so unless you press **CONTROL-[PgUp] D Y**, WordPerfect will not show a macro as it is running.

◆ A more technical way to do the same thing

If you are going to use this macro on long files, you might want a quicker (albeit more technical) method to convert underlines into italics. When WordPerfect has to call the other macro, it takes extra time whenever the macro is run. This procedure uses simplified macro programming features to enable it to run faster. Create a macro as usual, then go in to edit it. Add the following commands

{IF}{STATE}&512~

{Reveal Codes}{ELSE}{END IF}

These commands instruct WordPerfect to check if Reveal Codes is on. If it is, WordPerfect will turn it off; if it's off, WordPerfect will leave it off.

◆ True typographic quotation marks

Some people are real sticklers about typographic quote marks. I'm not one of them, although I do feel they add an extra touch that takes laser printing one step closer into the realm of typesetting.

Don't let the apparent complexity of this macro fool you. It took all of two minutes to create, and you can use it over and over and over until you become sick and tired of word processing in general and move to a small island in the South Pacific to paint naked natives.

But who wants to enter CONTROL-V 4,32 [ENTER] by hand whenever they want a quote (on a PostScript printer). And who wants to enter " or " instead of " (when they have a LaserJet). Meanwhile, people read your rough draft in Courier and keep asking, "What are those strange marks?" until you want to throttle them, scream, or force-feed them lots of diuretics.

You've got two choices. If you're using 5.1 you can use the ALT-R "Replace" macro with which I bored you senseless earlier in this chapter, or if you have 5.0 or just like to enter depressingly long macros, you can use the one I came up with all by myself while waiting for a pop tart to pop.

First, let's use the ALT-R macro. Before you run any macro that makes massive changes, it's always a good idea to save your file. That way, if something untoward happens you can just clear the screen and reload your file.

Now, gee, I wonder how we start this thing . . .

ALT-R Y Y

We've told WordPerfect we want to confirm all replacements (to make sure that the quote marks come out right if we've forgotten to match them) and to remove the old quote marks. Now we choose User-defined text. Press

U

WordPerfect will respond: "ON code - Enter the text you wish to use and press Enter" to which we will reply

" [ENTER]

WordPerfect now says "OFF code - Enter the text you wish to use and press Enter" to which we respond

" [ENTER]

WordPerfect asks us what we want to "Convert to." We could press A I to remove the quote marks and make the text between them italic. That's a valid typographic way to replace an abundance of quote marks, but instead, we're going to replace them with " and ". To do this, press

U CONTROL-2 4,32 [ENTER] [ENTER]

CONTROL-2 4,31 [ENTER] [ENTER]

IMPORTANT: You hold down the control key, then press the 2 underneath the @. Pressing the 2 on the keypad won't work.

WordPerfect will work like a little beaver and display messages telling you what's going on. A counter will show you how many changes it's prepared to make, and then, sometime later that same year, WordPerfect will highlight a block of text and ask "Replace? Y/N?" If you press **Y**, WordPerfect will replace the quote marks. If you press **N**, WordPerfect will not replace them and will go on to the next set of quote marks.

If you are absolutely, positively, unequivocally sure that all the quote marks are matched, you can have WordPerfect run this macro without confirmation. But if any of the quote marks are unmatched, some of your text is going to turn out like "this" and you're going to do something rash or break out in one.

◆ Alternative quote mark therapy

This is a relatively simple macro that searches for the first quote mark and turns it into a ", and then replaces the next " with a ". Unlike other macros, this method will not mess up a file if you happen to have a mismatched set of quotes.

The macro works by finding all the quote marks preceded by a space, a tab, indent, double indent, or a hard return. These would be the opening quote marks. Once it has searched and replaced through your file three times, it then converts all other quotes into closing quote marks.

Of course, if you want to use " for inches, you'll have to enter them as some other code in the document (perhaps a ~), then replace them with regular inch marks.

I'm going to present two variations of this macro. The first one is for LaserJet users, and uses ' ' ' ' for double quotes. I found this to be very effective (although a few people thought there was too much space between them).

For PostScript users, the macro will replace " marks with **CONTROL-V 4,32** for authentic opening quotes ", and **CONTROL-V 4,31** for authentic closing quotes." These will not appear as quote marks on-screen, but as little black boxes. It's a bit disconcerting initially to see text with all these bullet-like characters, but you get used to it. If you can't stand to see them on-screen, use the LaserJet method; the printout is almost identical, although authentic quote marks are closer together.

A word of warning. This macro won't find a quote mark directly preceded by a code. This means that if you ever have a bold, italic, underline, or other WordPerfect code before a quote mark, you should search and replace it manually. Of course, underlining or italicizing text in quotes can be redundant, but you need to execute these changes before running this macro.

I've tested this macro on a number of files and they all performed perfectly, but none of my quote marks was preceded by a WordPerfect code. You can't always remember if you've placed a code before a quote mark, but it's the one obstacle that this macro can't overcome. Once you've run this macro, any quote mark that didn't fit into the opening quote mold (preceded by a space, tab, indent, double indent, or hard return) becomes a closing quote, and they can be hard to find.

Always save your file before running a macro like this. Then if there is some problem, you can exit the current file without saving, and retrieve it from disk.

- LASERJET QUOTE MACRO: (Don't press the space bar unless you see ^)

CONTROL-F10 QUOTE [ENTER] Turn ^ " ^ marks ^ into ^ real ^ quotes [ENTER]

[HOME][HOME][UP-ARROW] ALT-F2 N ^" F2 ^"F2

[HOME][HOME][UP-ARROW] ALT-F2 N [TAB]" F2 [TAB]"F2

[HOME][HOME][UP-ARROW] ALT-F2 N [ENTER]" F2 [ENTER]"F2

[HOME][HOME][UP-ARROW] ALT-F2 N F4" F2 F4"F2

[HOME][HOME][UP-ARROW] ALT-F2 N SHIFT-F4" F2 SHIFT-F4"F2

[HOME][HOME][UP-ARROW] ALT-F2 N " F2 "F2

- POSTSCRIPT QUOTE MACRO: (Don't press the space bar unless you see ^)

CONTROL-F10 QUOTE [ENTER]

Turn ^ " ^ marks ^ into ^ real ^ quotes [ENTER]

[HOME][HOME][UP-ARROW] ALT-F2 N ^" F2 ^ CONTROL-V 4,32 [ENTER] F2

[HOME][HOME][UP-ARROW] ALT-F2 N [TAB]" F2 [TAB] CONTROL-V 4,32 [ENTER] F2

[HOME][HOME][UP-ARROW] ALT-F2 N [ENTER]" F2 [ENTER] CONTROL-V 4,32 [ENTER] F2

[HOME][HOME][UP-ARROW] ALT-F2 N F4" F2 F4 CONTROL-V 4,32 [ENTER] F2

[HOME][HOME][UP-ARROW] ALT-F2 N SHIFT-F4" F2 SHIFT-F4 CONTROL-V 4,32 F2

[HOME][HOME][UP-ARROW] ALT-F2 N " F2 CONTROL-V 4,31 [ENTER] F2

❖ *Disabling a feature*

There are certain people who shouldn't use certain features. I'm talking about the people who always manage to mess things up royally. They go into Styles and change the formatting of your entire document, and then even manage to save the style so you can unknowingly mess up all the other documents which use it.

These are the type of people who shouldn't even have access to the style key. And this is where a tip comes in. You can turn off any key on the keyboard. If you decided that the "E" key is dangerous, you could set WordPerfect so that when someone pressed "E," nothing would happen.

Naturally, you can use this to drive other people insane, but since this book isn't called *WordPerfect: Insanity with Style,* or even *Gaslight,* we're not going to dwell on the darker side of the force here.

In this particular example, we're just going to save ourselves from the people who shouldn't use Styles. To do this, go into "keyboard layout" and create a keyboard file (or edit an existing one) and change the action of the style key. Let's create a new keyboard and try it. Press

SHIFT-F1 K C NOSTYLE [ENTER] E

C ALT-F8 Don't Touch! [ENTER]

[DEL] CONTROL-[PgUp]

Move the cursor to {Bell} and press

[ENTER] CONTROL-[PgUp]

Move the cursor to {Prompt} and press

[ENTER] Don't Touch That Key or the Computer Will Explode!~ F7 F7 S F7

Don't forget to type the tilde ~, or the computer really will explode.

Now, when someone presses ALT-F8, they get a scary message and a nerve-wracking beep, but they don't get Styles. If they know enough to change the keyboard back, then they probably also know enough to use the style key safely.

Heh, heh, heh. Won't it be great to do this to someone who has been a real pig around the office? Just think of the hours of fun, tormenting them by suddenly disabling important WordPerfect features. I know, this could probably land you in jail, but they deserve it for all the mean, rotten, nasty things they've done.

❖ *Outlines (for anyone who writes)*

Most of the tips in this book have been meant for people who want to desktop publish. This one is meant for people who want (or have) to write.

As I've learned (the hard way), the real key to writing is organization. It's almost impossible (or at least extremely difficult) to write a long and involved manuscript, be it a novel or a manual, without some type of outline.

I wish that some clever teacher had come up with a way to make outlining fun. I hated it and everyone I knew hated it. The only thing worse was sentence diagramming.

If you already use outlines, you'll appreciate this tip. If you don't, try to get the hang of them, because, like them or not, they're a tremendous help. My outline for this book was 30 pages long. I didn't sit down and write a 30-page outline, but every time I had an idea of any type (an occurrence that merits a celebration, complete with chocolate chip cookies), I would write it down in the outline, in the proper chapter (or at least in what seemed like the proper chapter at the time).

When I actually sat down to write this book (which I did in about 90 days—90 very long days), I reviewed the outline and expanded upon my ideas. I wouldn't have been able to remember them otherwise, and this book would have been a mere pamphlet.

◆ Automatic paragraph numbering and nonprinting comments

Two of WordPerfect's most useful tools for outlining are automatic paragraph numbering, and nonprinting comments. All of these can be enhanced with macros (or at least that's the excuse I'm going to use for addressing them here).

Let's start with automatic paragraph numbering. **SHIFT-F5 P [ENTER]** inserts an automatic paragraph number. If you've defined paragraph numbers to use a style, it inserts an outline style. Now you'll never have to manually renumber lists after you make changes (which you always do).

Once you put one of these little babies into a file, you'll see a number on-screen that resembles any other number. But when you remove one of these numbers, all the rest of them renumber themselves. But wait, there's more. These numbers also change their format, depending on what tab stop (or level) they're on. When you tab one in, or backspace one out, they change format, and the rest of the list renumbers. Chalk another one up for outlines.

WordPerfect gives you four standard numbering methods (Paragraph, Outline, Legal, Bullets), and creates one of your own design called "User-defined."

But that's not good enough for me, and it shouldn't be good enough for you either. We're but a mere step away from 2001. We want more automation! More, more, more! (Enough already.)

In any event, a simple macro will insert a number and indent the text. Now the numbers are "outdented" and the outline is easier to read. Because I use this macro often, I've made it an **ALT-KEY** macro and called it ALT-P (for paragraph number). Here it is. Press

CONTROL-F10 ALT-P automatic paragraph numbering [ENTER]

SHIFT-F5 P [ENTER] F4 CONTROL-F10

If you don't love this macro, you should have your head examined, or you should forget about it and get on with the rest of your life; one or the other.

◆ Fill in the blanks or connect the dots

My next little tip for the writer, would-be writer, or has-been writer involves WordPerfect's nonprinting comments. These appear on the screen but not on the page. In other words, they melt in your mind, not on your keyboard.

Once you've created this divine outline, you're going to use it as a . . . um . . . outline. But not just an ordinary run-o-the-mill outline; a super outline! (How's that for hype?) This outline will appear on-screen, but doesn't print. Each heading of the outline appears in glorious color (if you have a color monitor) or in glorious black and white (if you have a black and white monitor).

This macro turns each entry in an outline into a comment, right before your awestruck little eyes. It's almost too wonderful to believe (unless you've seen Microsoft Word's outliner, which doesn't require this type of maneuvering to be effective. WordPerfect's outlining hopefully will be better the next time around. Who said that?)

Because this macro is fun to watch, we're going to turn Display on. Well, not just because it's fun. This macro can't determine when it reaches the end of the outline, and it keeps trying to turn nothing into a comment. Soon WordPerfect will start beeping at you about every second and will continue to do so until the cows come home. To stop this electronic tantrum, press **F1**.

Are we ready? Press

CONTROL-F10 OUT2COMM Turn outline into comments [ENTER]

ALT-F4 [ENTER] CONTROL-F5 Y [ENTER]

ALT-F10 OUT2COMM [ENTER] CONTROL-F10

Now all you need to do is look at the comment, type anything you can think of on the subject, then press the **[DOWN ARROW]** key so you are under the next comment.

Now you see them, now you don't department: If you get sick of seeing the comments, you can set WordPerfect so they won't appear on-screen but will still be in the file.

5.1: Press **SHIFT-F1 D E C N F7** if you *don't* want to see comments, and **SHIFT-F1 D E C Y F7** when you *do* want to see them.

5.0: Press **SHIFT-F1 D D N F7**. When you want to see them again, type **SHIFT-F1 D D Y F7**.

Better yet, create two macros: one called *No Comment* (the type of macro the Bush administration uses so frequently), and another called *Comment*. *No Comment* tells WordPerfect not to show comments, while *Comment* tells it to go right ahead and show them.

5.1: *NO COMMENT MACRO:*

CONTROL-F10 NOCOMMENT [ENTER] Turn off comments [ENTER]

SHIFT-F1 D E C N F7

5.1: *COMMENT MACRO:*

CONTROL-F10 COMMENT [ENTER] Show comments [ENTER]

SHIFT-F1 D E C Y F7

5.0: *NO COMMENT MACRO:*

CONTROL-F10 NOCOMMENT [ENTER] Turn off comments [ENTER]

SHIFT-F1 D D N F7

5.0: *COMMENT MACRO:*

CONTROL-F10 COMMENT [ENTER] Show comments [ENTER]

SHIFT-F1 D D Y F7

◆ Revision markers *or* the Mrs. Samuel Clemens macro

Comments can also be used as a revision marker. Most documents require a seemingly endless progression of minor changes, and these markers will indicate who changed what and when. You can use this macro anywhere; it doesn't have be on a blank line. WordPerfect will insert this comment in the middle of a sentence, between two letters, anywhere you want.

If you want to be doubly sure about what has changed, use one of these markers at the beginning of the revised text, and another at the end. Then the revised text will be surrounded by revision markers.

The comment looks like this:

↓May 23, 1989 - 2:06pm - (Your Initials Here)↓

While you cannot search for text that is inside a comment, you can search for comments, and in this way move quickly from one revision to another.

Once again, this macro seems complicated, but you'll only need to type it once. WordPerfect won't allow you to use its automatic date feature within a comment, so the macro will have to do all the text, block it, then turn it into a comment.

I call this macro ALT-C (for Comment). I've made it an ALT-macro because I use it frequently. Here's the macro to create the revision marker. **ALT-25** means that you should hold down the ALT-key and press 25 on the keypad. When you see (Your initials here), type your own initials.

CONTROL-F10 ALT-C Revision marker [ENTER]

ALT-25 SHIFT-F5 F CONTROL-END 3 1, 4 - 8:90 [ENTER]

T (Your initials here) ALT-F4 SHIFT-F2 ALT-25 SHIFT-F2

SHIFT-F2 SHIFT-F2 [LEFT ARROW] CONTROL-F5 Y

❖ On-screen calculator

While WordPerfect's math feature is powerful, it isn't always convenient. There is an on-screen calculator that comes with WordPerfect though, and it's great for handling those all-important desktop publishing measurement calculations.

The only drawback to this clever calculator is that it uses whole numbers only, no decimals. An easy way around this is to multiply everything by 100 before you enter it. (Oh no! Now he's asking me to do math to enable the computer to do math. Will this madness never cease? *No, the madness will never cease; get used to it.*)

This is easier than it sounds if you remember elementary school math. All you have to do is move the decimal two places to the right. Here's an example: 1.47 becomes 147, .24 becomes 24, 10.5 becomes 1050. Basically, just leave out the decimal point. That's not so tough, is it?

I find this on-screen calculator much more convenient than having to look all over my desk for my pocket calculator only to find that the batteries are dead. You might too. Of course, this is a very long, complex, and involved macro, but you don't have to type it in. Just save it as a macro from the WordPerfect keyboard file called Macros.WPK on the Conversion disk. Here's how to do it.

Press

SHIFT-F1 K

Move the cursor to "Macros"

E

Move the cursor to CTRL-C

S CALC [ENTER] F1 Y F1 F1

Now, let's try the calculator. Press

ALT-F10 CALC [ENTER]

The calculator should appear on the left side of the screen. Use it as you would a regular calculator. If you want to insert the total into the text, press the **SPACE BAR**. This will also remove the calculator from the screen. Press **C** when you want to clear the totals, and **F1** or **F7** will get you out of it.

◆ Temporary fonts

Another simple to use (but extremely complicated to create) macro enables you to insert a "temporary" font. When you are in block mode, this macro will assign any new font you choose to the block, then return to the base font. When not in block mode, this macro inserts two font codes: the new font you've selected, followed by the base font. This allows you to temporarily switch to a new font and then return to the base font.

An important note: this macro does not involve Styles. Therefore, if you should change base fonts, the "base font" placed in the text by this temporary macro will still be the previous base font. If you plan on making many changes, it's always wise to use Styles, even if the style contains nothing more than a single font change. That way, the Style Off code will always contain the current base font.

As with the Calc macro, you save this macro using the WordPerfect keyboard file called Macros.WPK on the Conversion disk.

SHIFT-F1 K

Move the cursor to "Macros"

E

Move the cursor to CTRL-F8

S ALT-F [ENTER] F1 Y F1 F1

Let's try it out. Press

ALT-F

Notice that a new item has been added to the menu. To use it, press **T**. This will operate like the regular font key, except that instead of just entering one code, this macro will insert two: the font you've just chosen, followed by the current base font.

I don't recommend using this macro in your soft keyboard file as it appears in Macros.WPK, because it will then act as a substitute for the normal CONTROL-F8 key. As a result, you will be unable to search for fonts and will have difficulty selecting fonts within other macros, and just generally complicate your life.

❖ The hard facts about the soft keyboard

WordPerfect's soft keyboard feature is tremendously powerful. It's akin to attaching macros to any key on the keyboard. Well, almost any key. You can't redefine the following by themselves: Shift, Control, ALT, Caps Lock, Num Lock, Scroll Lock, or Sys Req. This Sys Req key is only included on the keyboard if you have an AT. (I still lie awake nights trying to decide if this key has any practical benefit.)

Soft keyboards permit you to customize WordPerfect in any way you like. I grew up with WordStar, so I use the WordStar Control-key cursor movement keys. I also use Control-B for block, Control-W for the thesaurus, and Control-L for search (or look). I use other WordStar commands as well, such as Control-G for delete character, Control-T for delete word, and Control-Y for delete to the end of the line.

I'm not suggesting that you should set up your keyboard in this manner. Still, because these commands are so firmly entrenched in my mind after years of use, and because I'm a touch typist, I find these faster and easier to work with than WordPerfect's usual commands.

I also carry this .WPK file with me for those times when I might be working with another person's WordPerfect. That way I can still use my own commands, even on someone else's computer. All I have to do is copy my keyboard file into their WordPerfect directory, select it using **SHIFT-F1 K**, move the cursor to my keyboard file, and then press S.

I'm going to show you how to create a new keyboard for yourself, and then offer you a couple of keyboard entries I find useful for desktop publishing.

◆ Keyboard definitions

Start by pressing

SHIFT-F1 K C

```
Keyboard: Edit

  Name: !DWH

  Key          Action               Description

  Alt-E        {KEY MACRO 27}       Edit a Code
  Alt-R        {KEY MACRO 18}       Subliminal message to get dates
  Alt-I        {KEY MACRO 11}       Change "Love Boat" script to MurderSheWrote
  Alt-O        {KEY MACRO 24}       Start coffee maker
  Alt-Enter    {KEY MACRO 3}        Clear trashy novel from screen
  Alt-S        {KEY MACRO 25}       SHOW spreadsheet instead
  Alt-F        {KEY MACRO 15}       How to tell Joanna Kerns from Gloria Loring
  Alt-H        {KEY MACRO 21}       Joke Generator
  Alt-L        {Search Left}        search backwards in time
  Alt-;        [■:4,32]             Open Quote
  Alt-'        [■:4,31]             Close Quote
  Alt-X        {KEY MACRO 14}       Stock Calvin & Hobbes Fan Letter
  Alt-N        {KEY MACRO 17}       Secret of the Universe
  Alt-M        {KEY MACRO 12}       Anti-gravity equation
  Num 5        {Block}              Block on, block on harvest moon...
  Ctrl-Num *   {Macro Commands}     Send electro-shock through keyboard
  Ctrl-PgDn    {KEY MACRO 29}       Ouijua Board Simulation

1 Action; 2 Dscrptn; 3 Original; 4 Create; 5 Move; Macro: 6 Save; 7 Retrieve: 1
```

The Soft Keyboard feature allows you to make any key on the keyboard do whatever you want.

WordPerfect will ask for a file name. Why not be terribly unoriginal? Type in your own initials as a file name, and press

[ENTER] E

You will now see a screen which is totally blank except for a menu running along the bottom. You may create a keyboard definition by pressing **C** and then the key you want to redefine. If you have already created macros and want one or more of them to become a new definition for any key, press **R**, the key you want to redefine, and then type the name of the macro. The macro will now be copied into the keyboard file.

First, let's create a definition from scratch. For this example, we're going to modify F6 so that it will insert a code for italics rather than underlines. If you use italics often, this is much more efficient than typing **CONTROL-F8 A I.**

Now we're going to give a short description of what the key will do and then change that function. Follow me by pressing

C F6 Italics [ENTER]

Notice that it says {Underline}. We're going to change that function. Press

[DEL] CONTROL-F8 A I F7 F7 S F7

5.0 users, do the following instead:

C F6 D Italics [ENTER] A

Notice that it says {Underline}. We're going to change that function. Press

[DEL] CONTROL-F8 A I F7 F7

Once you save and select this keyboard, pressing **F6** will give you italics instead of underlines. If you use underlines and italics equally, you might want to put italics onto CONTROL-I. Follow the same procedure as you did using F8, except now when WordPerfect asks which key to define, you press CONTROL-I.

Inserting functions and cursor movements

You will need to change modes if you want to add a cursor movement code, such keystrokes as ESC, F1, F7, or [ENTER]. Pressing **CONTROL-V** will put you in code mode. Now the next key you press will insert its code into the macro. If you need to insert several codes, pressing **CONTROL-F10** will make every key you press insert its code, and pressing **CONTROL-F10** again will bring things back to normal.

Here's another keyboard definition. This one calls the Und/Ital style that you learned how to make in Chapter 11. You could have F8 call this style, but since we've done F8 to death, let's make this ALT-U.

C ALT-U D Underline/Italic Style [ENTER]

A [DEL] ALT-F8 N UND [ENTER] O F7 F7

When you're satisfied with all your keyboard definitions, press

F7

This saves the keyboard file. Check to see if the cursor is in the keyboard name you just created, and press

S

to select that keyboard. You can work with as many keyboard files as you want, and simply switch between them. If you want to return to the original WordPerfect keyboard quickly, press

SHIFT-F1 K O F7

◆ A little something for ex-WordStar aficionados only

Once a word processing junkie, always a word processing junkie. I'm an ex-WordStar addict, but now I get my fix with the hard stuff—WordPerfect. Even so, I'm still addicted to how you can move the cursor in WordStar without taking your hands off the typing area and moving them to the cursor pad.

If you're a touch typist, you will find the WordStar cursor diamond is the absolute greatest way to move the cursor. It's not mnemonic, but it does make sense once you study the arrangement of the keys on the keyboard.

It was invented because at one time not all computers had cursor keys. What a wacky computer world we once lived in (as if we still don't). The only way this tip relates to desktop publishing is that it can make your life easier, and that's what I believe desktop publishing is supposed to do.

Here (in rapid succession so that we don't bore those people who wouldn't touch WordStar with a 10-foot keyboard) is the cursor diamond.

Create or edit the keyboard of your choice. Note: [-] is the WordPerfect Screen Up key, [+] is the WordPerfect Screen Down key.

5.0 users: you'll need to press a **D** after the key you want to redefine, and an **A** after you type the description. To create the diamond, type the following:

C CONTROL-**E** UP [ENTER] [DEL] CONTROL-V [UP ARROW] F7

C CONTROL-**X** DOWN [ENTER] [DEL] CONTROL-V [DOWN ARROW] F7

C CONTROL-**S** LEFT [ENTER] [DEL] CONTROL-V [LEFT ARROW] CONTROL-V F7

C CONTROL-**D** RIGHT [ENTER] [DEL] CONTROL-V [RIGHT ARROW] F7

C CONTROL-**C** DOWN SCREEN [ENTER] [DEL] CONTROL-V [+] F7

C CONTROL-**R** UP SCREEN [ENTER] [DEL] CONTROL-V [-] F7

C CONTROL-**F** WORD RIGHT [ENTER] [DEL] CONTROL-V CONTROL-[RIGHT ARROW] F7

C CONTROL-**A** WORD LEFT [ENTER] [DEL] CONTROL-V CONTROL-[LEFT ARROW] F7

18

1-2-3 Publishing

Uno, dos, tres, WordPerfecto cinco

Lotus 1-2-3 is unequivocally the single most popular piece of PC software in the world. WordPerfect is the most popular word processing software in the world. In the past, they didn't work so well together. In fact, pairing 5.0 and 1-2-3 was like pairing Ethel Merman and Ernest Borgnine, or Sylvester Stallone and Brigitte Nielson: it was so rocky that most people gave up after a brief time.

It was so bad that I had to spend an entire chapter on it, with five pages of really hard stuff just on exporting from 1-2-3 and then importing into WordPerfect. While removing most of that chapter meant that I lost some good jokes, I don't mind (too much), because the new spreadsheet import feature in 5.1 is extremely powerful and extremely easy.

WordPerfect can not only retrieve 1-2-3, PlanPerfect, and Excel files (or any program which can save in .WKS or .WK1 format), it can turn them into tables. Did I hear someone say, "oooooh," or was I just imagining Merv Griffin? Tables make manipulation easier than tabs, especially because when WordPerfect brings spreadsheets in as text, it uses "hard" tabs, which make it difficult to change tab types.

WordPerfect can also *link* to spreadsheet files. This means that when the spreadsheet data changes, so does the information in your WordPerfect document. The advantage to this is that your information is never out-of-date. You can set WordPerfect to update every time you load the file or only when requested. There is one important drawback to all this wonderfulness: Any formatting or number changing you do to linked spreadsheets in your WordPerfect document will be *lost* when you update the link. Additionally, any text you have typed or retrieved between the link codes will also be lost.

While WordPerfect imports 1-2-3 .PIC graphic files, it's not easy to use Excel graphics. Never fear — I'll show you how.

For all those forlorn 5.0 users, this chapter will include the information you need to import and properly format a 1-2-3 file.

For everyone, this chapter will give formatting tips for spreadsheets in tables as well as cover ways to spruce up charts and graphs.

❖ Import or link? Only your hairdresser knows for sure

There are two basic ways to get spreadsheets into WordPerfect. You can *import* them or *link* them. Each of these has its advantages and disadvantages.

❖ Import

I was once obliged to attend a motivational seminar. It turned out that the place had cameras in the bathroom, a fact I somehow sensed, so I turned off the lights when using the facilities. But that's another book. Anyway, at one point we had to tell the person next to us our life's goal. The guy who sat next to me smelled like he had been in an unfortunate cologne accident, and his life's goal was to import fine men's footwear. Not exactly Mother Teresa. My life's goal at the time was to import spreadsheets, but I was way ahead of my time. Neither of us was ready to devote our lives to saving the rain forests, the whales, or even saving face by claiming something enlightened like that as our goal.

While the aspiring shoe importer had to deal with shipping, the falling value of the dollar, and customs, I had to deal with file formats, proportional fonts, and tabs.

Well, I've grown since that time and so as WordPerfect. Today, if given the choice between importing spreadsheets and saving the whales, you can bet that I'd be in scuba gear, playing whale songs underwater and terrorizing Japanese whalers.

But, like you, I've got a living to make, and part of that depends on getting the right numbers in the right places at the right times, and that's what importing spreadsheets is all about.

Once you import a spreadsheet, it's yours to keep. You can format it any way you'd like. It become text, or a table, just as if you'd typed it into the program directly.

If you change the spreadsheet, your document does *not* (and cannot) change with it. That's both an advantage and a disadvantage.

It's good because it means that once you get the figures into WordPerfect, they're there to stay and you can do whatever you want with the spreadsheet itself, such as start making numbers for next month or next year, without affecting the numbers in your WordPerfect document. It's bad because if you make major spreadsheet changes and then want them to appear in WordPerfect in place of the old numbers, you have to manually import the spreadsheet again, then redo any formatting enhancements you've made.

When you import a spreadsheet you have two choices. You can import it as text with each column separated by tabs, or as a table. If you import it as text, WordPerfect will try to figure out where the tabs should be set and place an absolute tab setting at the beginning of the imported spreadsheet. (That makes it sound like caviar: yes, we have rare imported spreadsheets.) WP will also place another absolute tab setting at the end of the spreadsheet so that the tabs revert to the settings in effect above the table.

The problem with importing a spreadsheet as text is that it comes in with [TAB] and [RGT TAB] codes. These are different from normal [Tab] codes because they are *hard* tabs. (Made hard from years of neglect and having to fend for themselves.)

Hard tabs don't change types, even if you change the tab line, so the only way to change them is to search and replace them into normal tabs.

To insert a [TAB] or search for one, press HOME TAB

To insert a [CNTR TAB] or search for one, press [HOME] SHIFT-F6

To insert a [RGT TAB] or search for one, press [HOME] ALT-F6

To insert a [DEC TAB] or to search for one, press CONTROL-F6

I find that a bother, so, while *you* can do it this way if you want, for these examples, and for most of your spreadsheet work, I recommend that you use tables. Tables also make it easier to create ruling lines that add visual impact to tables as well as making them easier to read. That's what we're going to do right now.

Before we begin, you're going to need a spreadsheet file from 1-2-3, Excel, or PlanPerfect. WordPerfect accepts either .WK1 or .WKS files from any program which creates 1-2-3 compatible files, such as Quattro, SuperCalc, VP Planner, or Words & Figures.

I suggest you go into your spreadsheet program and create a spreadsheet which looks like this (remember to format the numbers with fixed decimal places, and put the Rabbit Industries title in column A):

	Rabbit Industries: If It's Fuzzy, It's Rad					
	Jan	Feb	March	April	May	June
Roger	0.50	0.55	0.83	1.24	1.86	2.78
Crusader	0.70	0.77	1.16	1.73	2.60	3.90
Bugs	0.30	0.33	0.50	0.74	1.11	1.67
Ricochet	1.10	1.21	1.82	2.72	4.08	6.13
Peter	0.10	0.11	0.17	0.25	0.37	0.56

That way it will be easier for you to follow along. Once you create the spreadsheet, save it, exit the spreadsheet program, and go back into WordPerfect, your software home away from home.

◆ Font Facts

It's always a good idea to set the font before importing a spreadsheet. Whenever you format either tabs or tables, the font you use will greatly affect where you set your tabs and how wide the table columns will be. You can either set the initial base font with **SHIFT-F8 D F** or insert a base font code by pressing

CONTROL-F8 F

For this example, move the cursor to **Dutch (or Times Roman) 12 point** and press

S

```
Spreadsheet: Import

     1 - Filename              D:\!BOOK\EX\RABBIT3.WK1

     2 - Range                 <Spreadsheet>        A1..G7

     3 - Type                  Table

     4 - Perform Import




Selection: 0
```

When you want to import a spreadsheet, think of this menu as your "customs office."

◆ File at will

To import the spreadsheet, press

CONTROL-F5 S I

From here you have four choices: **Filename**, **Range**, **Type**, and **Perform Import**. Conveniently, they are listed in the order they should be performed. First, tell WordPerfect the name of the file. Press

F

If you know and want to type the entire path and name, go ahead. If you're sick of typing the file name just a little bit wrong and having to type it over and over again, press

F5 [ENTER]

If you've got as many files in your directories as I do, you might find it difficult just to see the .WKS and .WK1 files. If you just want to see them, move the cursor to "Current" and press

[ENTER] [END] [BACKSPACE] wk? [ENTER]

This will cause list files to display *only* files ending in .wks or .wk1. Move the cursor to the file you want to retrieve and press

R

◆ Home on the range

The next step is to choose how much of the spreadsheet you want WordPerfect to import. WordPerfect will read the spreadsheet and permit you to import all of it or just selected ranges. Hopefully, you know enough about spreadsheets to know what a range is and how to name it because I never promised to teach you how to use your spreadsheet. If you don't know what ranges are, then you either don't need

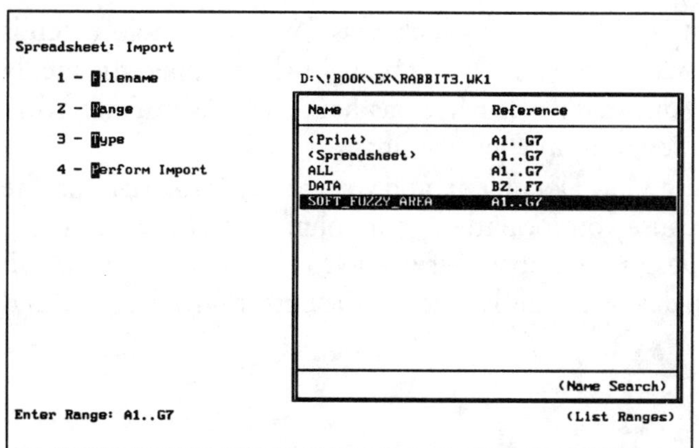

The next best thing to a Range Rover—range import. You can import a particular range of a spreadsheet, or the whole frightening thing.

them or you need to ask a friend in the privacy of your own home or office, or failing that, read the spreadsheet's manual.

WordPerfect always defaults to the entire filled area of the spreadsheet. In this case, you should see something like: <Spreadsheet> A1..G7.

To test this, press

R

WordPerfect will list the cells it's planning on importing. You can either type in a range name or, better yet, press

F5

to display a list of available ranges. If you haven't created any ranges, all you'll see is "<Speadsheet>," which means the whole worksheet. If you have created ranges, you'll see a list which includes the range name and the cells included in that range.

For this example you'll import the entire spreadsheet but remember you can name ranges and import only those ranges.

Move the cursor to <Spreadsheet> and press

[ENTER]

◆ Just my type

This is where we decide if we want the spreadsheet imported as text or as a table. As I said, I find importing to tables easier, formatting-wise. Remember, tables can be turned into regular tabbed text just by removing the [Tbl Def] code, so if you decide you would rather have regular text, it's easy. It's far more efficient to turn a table into text than to turn text into a table, so let's proceed. Press

T A P

◆ Warning

You've probably just noticed a warning which says "Warning, table extends beyond right margin." But don't worry, you haven't brought shame upon the family name, at least not just yet. And that's just what has happened. WordPerfect has created a table which is too wide to fit in your margins.

If you don't believe me, use View Document, and you can see it run right off the page. (If you haven't, it's because you formatted your columns narrower than the default in 1-2-3.) As stewardesses on British Air are so fond of saying, "That will never do." The easiest way to deal with this is to move the cursor into the table and press

ALT-F7 O P F F7

(Note: your display *may* go haywire at this point, but the formatting will be correct; don't worry about it.) This will force WordPerfect to cram the entire table into your margins. If you *haven't* chosen Dutch or Times 12, the only adverse effect this will have is that the first column, the one with the bunny names, may be too short for the names, in which case they will be hyphenated or just broken in the middle.

◆ Finishing touches

For all intents and purposes, the spreadsheet is done. But there are still ways to *improve* it.

➾ A note about fancy formatting of spreadsheets

When you *import* a spreadsheet, nothing in it will change unless you change it, so you can do as much formatting as you want. When you *link* a spreadsheet, doing much formatting is dangerous, because the next time you update the link, your formatting will be lost. Not only that, but any text you have typed or retrieved between the link codes will also be lost.

While the default of double lines around, single lines inside is good enough, you didn't get this book to learn how to be good enough. OK, maybe you did. But I didn't write it to tell you how to be *good enough,* I wrote it to help you do your *best.* Just imagine, if everyone always tried to do their best what a better world this would be. (I got that line from Miss Texas 1989.) And just as every Miss Texas is a good example of before and after, Guy/Rex style, here's a good example of our own personal before and after, WordPerfect style.

Before: This is the standard way WordPerfect imports a spreadsheet into a table. It's OK.

Rabbit Industries: If It's Fuzzy, It's Rad						
	Jan	Feb	March	April	May	June
Roger	0.50	0.55	0.83	1.24	1.86	2.78
Crusader	0.70	0.77	1.16	1.73	2.60	3.90
Bugs	0.30	0.33	0.50	0.74	1.11	1.67
Ricochet	1.10	1.21	1.82	2.72	4.08	6.13
Peter	0.10	0.11	0.17	0.25	0.37	0.56

Rabbit Industries: If It's Fuzzy, It's Rad

	Jan	Feb	March	April	May	June
Roger	0.50	0.55	0.83	1.24	1.86	2.78
Crusader	0.70	0.77	1.16	1.73	2.60	3.90
Bugs	0.30	0.33	0.50	0.74	1.11	1.67
Ricochet	1.10	1.21	1.82	2.72	4.08	6.13
Peter	0.10	0.11	0.17	0.25	0.37	0.56

After: After a little work with fonts, shading, and lines, here's the finished product. The "after" results are not blatantly flashy. What they are is more attractive and, more importantly, more readable. In the "before," everything gets the same attention: the headline, titles, data. Nothing is more important than anything else.

While that's very democratic, that isn't the point of most tables. They're designed to impart some particular slice of information, and with careful use of lines and shading, you can convey that information faster and more accurately, and also control which parts of the information the user thinks is most important.

In the "after" example, the titles are distinctly different from than the data, and the data is cleanly separated with two types of lines, so that the reader's eye is lead more firmly across the data that you think is most important.

Who: on earth is Guy/Rex? I wondered how long it would take you to ask. They're the Siegfried and Roy of the Miss USA set. These two guys act like Professor Henry Higgins in *My Fair Lady* (played in the movie by Rex Harrison, no relation to Guy/Rex) to prepare young women to win the title that prepares them to be the future anchorwomen of America. They've coached all the Miss Texas candidates, and they won the big title five years in a row. You probably never expected to learn this type of life-changing, instantly-useful, hard-hitting information when you picked up the book with the pretty blue marbled paper cover, but life has this way of surprising you. And now we return to our regularly scheduled example . . .

How: If the "headline" came in with a couple of blank columns before or after it, block all columns in the first row join them.

ALT-F4 [HOME] [HOME] [RIGHT ARROW] J Y

◆ Fontastic

Headlines are important, even on tables. In our "after," the headline is extra large and bold, so there can be no doubt as to what the table is about.

There are two ways of applying size changes and attributes to the text in tables. You can either do it in normal text mode, or you can format the cells directly. Both give you the same results on paper.

The advantage of using text mode is that the formatting codes are visible in Reveal Codes. The advantage for formatting directly into the table is that you can use the table as a template, replacing the text without having to worry about formatting codes.

In this example we're going to do a little of both, just so you can try it both ways. Go into Text Mode by pressing

F7

To place the codes in the text, put the cursor at the start of the title, in text mode, and press

SHIFT-F6 ALT-F4 [END] CONTROL-F8 S E

Move the cursor down to the first cell in the next row (A2). Now we're going to format the table itself. We're doing this because it will be faster since we're applying both bold and shading to the same blocks of text. First, go into Table Edit. Press

ALT-F7

Make sure the cursor is in cell A2. To bold the column of month names, press

ALT-F4 [HOME] [HOME] [RIGHT ARROW] F6

Since the same block of text also needs shading, we can remark the block by pressing

ALT-F4 CONTROL-[HOME] CONTROL-[HOME]

And then we can shade the text by pressing

L S O

Now we want to format the column with the rabbit names. In this case, it's easier to format the table than insert normal bold codes, because otherwise you'd have to bold each word individually. If you tried to block the text, you'd have to block the entire row, not just the column. Move the cursor to cell A3 (press [DOWN ARROW]) and press

ALT-F4 CONTROL-[HOME] [HOME] [DOWN ARROW] F6

We also want to shade that part of the table, so reblock by pressing

ALT-F4 CONTROL-[HOME] CONTROL-[HOME]

and add the shading by pressing

L S O

◆ Line Alert!

Working with table lines can be tricky. Remember that each cell has its own lines inside, so even if you give the left side of a cell dotted lines, the right side of the cell to the left will still have the standard straight lines.

In this case, the easiest way to create these new, improved lines is to remove *all* the old lines. Believe me, I've done it both ways, and removing them all takes less time than changing the left and right lines on each column. To remove all the lines, move the cursor to the first cell (**A1**, or, in this case, it's the title "Rabbit Industries,") by pressing

CONTROL-[HOME] A1 [ENTER]

and then remove the lines by pressing

ALT-F4 [HOME] [HOME] [DOWN ARROW]

to mark *all* the cells, and then press

L A N

Faster than you can say "Strum und Drang" all the lines will disappear. This has *not* removed the shading behind the month and rabbit names.

◆ Rules on the horizon

Now it's time to create the horizontal rules. Put the cursor in cell **A1** and press

L T T L B S

This makes the thick line above the table and the single line below the title. Move to cell A3 by pressing

[DOWN ARROW] [DOWN ARROW]

Now create the horizontal rule which runs under the entire row by pressing

ALT-F4 [HOME] [HOME] [RIGHT ARROW] L B S

Move down to the next row with the

[DOWN ARROW]

and then create a horizontal rule for this row by pressing

ALT-F4 [HOME] [HOME] [LEFT ARROW] L B S

You get the picture. Keep moving to each new row, blocking it, and creating a single line below.

If, after having just completed these last two rows, you still can't figure out how to do this on your own, you obviously have just been pressing keys while your brain was out getting a tan. I know you can do it, so I'm not going to give you the keystrokes. Sometimes you have to take control of your own life and forge ahead.

◆ Going dotty

I'm going to assume you were able to figure out how to do those horizontal lines, and that if you weren't, you were resourceful enough to trick someone else into doing for you.

I'm a firm believer in being resourceful, and an equally firm believer in dotted lines. Too many solid lines can be distracting. If the rows are the most important part of the table, then use solid lines for the rows and dotted (or none) between the columns. That way, you're guiding the viewer's eye along the right path.

So in this case, I made the column separators into dotted lines. Move the cursor to cell **B2**, then press

ALT-F4 CONTROL-[HOME] [HOME] [DOWN ARROW] L R O

This marks the entire column, then places a dotted line on the right. Repeat this for each column, except the last, because we don't need a dotted line on the left edge of the table.

When you're finished, to leave Table Edit, press

F7

To use View Document press

SHIFT-F7 V

Now get a load of the most rabid spreadsheet this side of the Rockies. Now *this* looks good. Sure, it took a little time, but it was time well spent. An investment in your future. An investment in America. A glowing tribute to Yankee ingenuity, viewed on a Japanese monitor, and printed on a Japanese printer.

◆ Border options

If you want to get really picky, you can even take control over WordPerfect's dots by using the border option to make them finer and lighter. To do this, move the cursor so that it is on [Tbl Def] code and press

SHIFT-F8 O B O .003 [ENTER] [ENTER] [ENTER] F7

Border options are just like graphics box options: they affect all the borders on all the tables from the [Brdr opt] code to the end of the file, or until another border

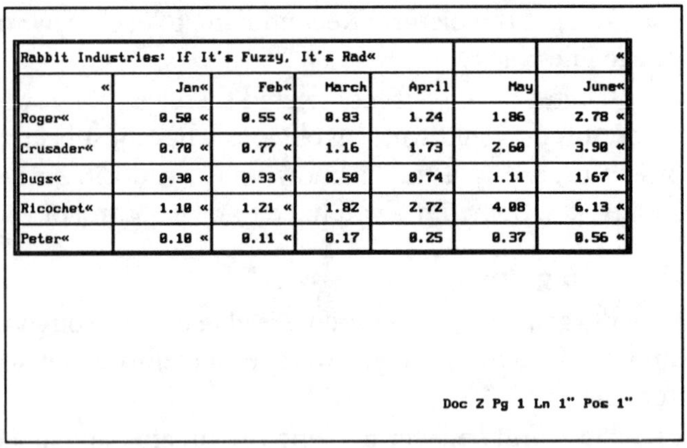

Rabbit Industries: If It's Fuzzy, It's Rad«						«
«	Jan«	Feb«	March	April	May	June«
Roger«	0.50 «	0.55 «	0.83	1.24	1.86	2.78 «
Crusader«	0.70 «	0.77 «	1.16	1.73	2.60	3.90 «
Bugs«	0.30 «	0.33 «	0.50	0.74	1.11	1.67 «
Ricochet«	1.10 «	1.21 «	1.82	2.72	4.08	6.13 «
Peter«	0.10 «	0.11 «	0.17	0.25	0.37	0.56 «

Doc 2 Pg 1 Ln 1" Pos 1"

When you first import a spreadsheet it comes in looking like this.

option code is encountered. These same options would allow you to make any of the other lines thicker, thinner, or grayer.

◆ Gray Bars

You have probably seen the special computer paper for long printouts of numbers. It has alternating stripes of gray and white or green and white. This makes it easier to follow the rows of printed materials.

Well, you can create that effect yourself, without any special forms, and here's how. First, import the spreadsheet into a table. Then go into table edit and make sure the cursor is in cell A1.

Block the first row of the table by pressing

ALT-F4 [HOME] [HOME] [RIGHT ARROW]

and then "shade" the area by pressing

L S O

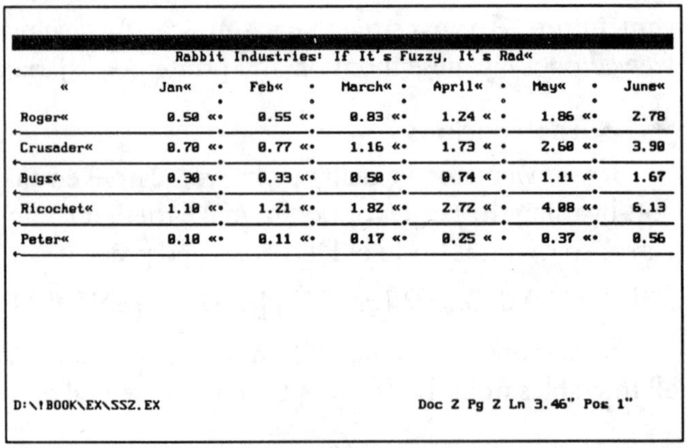

Rabbit Industries: If It's Fuzzy, It's Rad«						
«	Jan«	Feb«	March«	April«	May«	June«
Roger«	0.50 «	0.55 «	0.83 «	1.24 «	1.86 «	2.78
Crusader«	0.70 «	0.77 «	1.16 «	1.73 «	2.60 «	3.90
Bugs«	0.30 «	0.33 «	0.50 «	0.74 «	1.11 «	1.67
Ricochet«	1.10 «	1.21 «	1.82 «	2.72 «	4.08 «	6.13
Peter«	0.10 «	0.11 «	0.17 «	0.25 «	0.37 «	0.56

D:\!BOOK\EX\SS2.EX Doc 2 Pg 2 Ln 3.46" Pos 1"

After a little futzing around it looks like this.

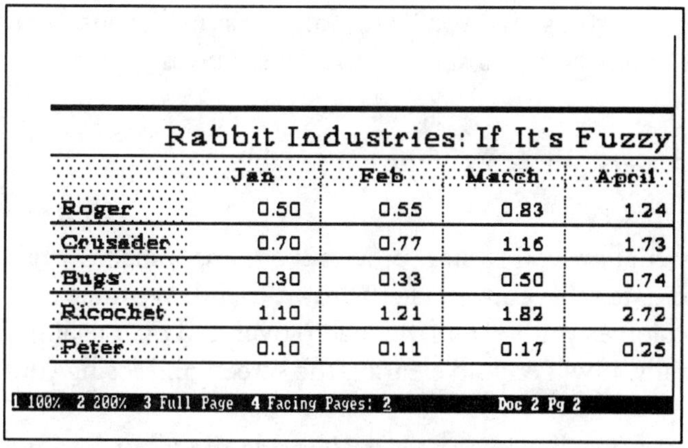

Rabbit Industries: If It's Fuzzy				
	Jan	Feb	March	April
Roger	0.50	0.55	0.83	1.24
Crusader	0.70	0.77	1.16	1.73
Bugs	0.30	0.33	0.50	0.74
Ricochet	1.10	1.21	1.82	2.72
Peter	0.10	0.11	0.17	0.25

1 100% 2 200% 3 Full Page 4 Facing Pages: 2 Doc 2 Pg 2

Here's how the same thing looks in View Document

You've now shaded the first row of the table. Now press

[DOWN ARROW] [DOWN ARROW]

to take you to the third row of the table. Remember, you're going to shade every *other* row, not every row. Because you're now at the far right side of the table (the last column), you could either press [HOME] [HOME] [LEFT ARROW] to get back to the first column, and then repeat the steps above, or, you could save yourself a few keystrokes and press

ALT-F4 [HOME] [HOME] [LEFT ARROW]

to block the row from the right to the left, and then press

L S O

to shade the row. You'd then alternate between the first step, where you block from left to right, and the second step, where you block from right to left.

If you want to make a macro of this, place the cursor in cell **A1** and do the following (I've named it GB for Gray Bar):

CONTROL-F10 GB [ENTER] Gray Bars [ENTER]

ALT-F7 ALT-F4 [HOME] [HOME] [RIGHT ARROW] L S O

[DOWN ARROW] [DOWN ARROW]

ALT-F4 [HOME] [HOME] [LEFT ARROW] L S O

[DOWN ARROW] [DOWN ARROW] F7

This will shade the first and third rows and move the cursor to the fifth row so that you can run it again.

To run the macro, press

ALT-F10 GB [ENTER]

The macro will not display anything, and you'll only know it's run because your cursor will be two lines down from where you started. You'll then press

ALT-F10 GB [ENTER]

again until you've shaded every other row of the entire table.

•◆ Advanced Macro-holics

Because WordPerfect won't allow you to start or stop recording a macro while in a table, this macro has to initiate table edit, shade the rows, then leave table edit. This takes more time and also forces you to start the macro over and over again. If you try to repeat it automatically, it will end up clearing the screen and losing your work.

You can't even edit the macro to have it repeat itself inside the table, because WordPerfect won't allow you to start a macro while editing a table.

Because of this, the best way to use this macro, if you want to use it a lot, is to put it in the soft keyboard. That way you can call it at any time, even when editing a table.

If you choose to put it in a soft keyboard, I suggest you only use the following commands

ALT-F4 [HOME] [HOME] [RIGHT ARROW] L S O

[DOWN ARROW] [DOWN ARROW]

ALT-F4 [HOME] [HOME] [LEFT ARROW] L S O

[DOWN ARROW] [DOWN ARROW]

This way, only the actual blocking and shading are taking place, and you don't have to go in and out of table edit.

❖ *Link*

If this subhead conjured up images of the rolling, verdant hills of a golf course, you are not in the right frame of mind. If you knew, right off the bat, that it had something to do with spreadsheets, you're the type of person I want to be stuck in a life raft with (not that I really want to be stuck in a life raft with anyone, or even alone).

Spreadsheet links are similar to spreadsheet import, except that they can be updated at any time to reflect all changes in the original spreadsheet. You can have as many different links as you want, and you can update them individually.

While this is a very important feature for anyone working with fast-changing data, it is not the best choice if you wanted to do a lot of fancy footwork and make those spreadsheets look like a million bucks, even if the largest number in it was

Link: D:\!BOOK\EX\RABBIT3.WK1 <Spreadsheet>

Rabbit Industries: If It's Fuzzy, It's Rad«						«
«	Jan«	Feb«	March	April	May	June«
Roger«	0.50 «	0.55 «	0.83	1.24	1.86	2.78 «
Crusader«	0.70 «	0.77 «	1.16	1.73	2.60	3.90 «
Bugs«	0.30 «	0.33 «	0.50	0.74	1.11	1.67 «
Ricochet«	1.10 «	1.21 «	1.82	2.72	4.08	6.13 «
Peter«	0.10 «	0.11 «	0.17	0.25	0.37	0.56 «

Link End

Doc 2 Pg 1 Ln 1" Pos 1"

Spreadsheet links have almost nothing to do with golf.

$12,285. That's because each time you update the link, WordPerfect removes all the old text, including all your meticulous formatting, and just inserts its standard old "double line around, single line between" type of table.

I know, I've told you this three times now, but it's only because I don't want you to spend countless hours gussying up a table only to have WordPerfect delete your handiwork in a few milliseconds.

Is there a way around this madness? Yes, sort of, and we'll get to that in a few pages, after I've coached you on the basics on spreadsheet linking.

◆ Link-a-dink-a-doo

OK, are all us yuppies ready? Most of these steps are identical to importing a spreadsheet, but I'll repeat them in case you didn't bother to read the earlier parts of this chapter. To create a spreadsheet link, press

CONTROL-F5 S C

We first tell it the name of the spreadsheet we want to link. Press

F

and enter the complete path name of the file. If you can't remember (or can but just want to be obstinate), you can press F5 and use List Files to locate the spreadsheet.

Once you've entered the name, press [ENTER]. If you're using List Files, press **R** to retrieve the file.

➾ Home on the . . .

You can now select a range by pressing **R**. If you don't select a range, WordPerfect will link the part of the spreadsheet containing information.

➺ Type Table/Text

This is where you specify whether the spreadsheet will be linked as a table or as text. To choose, press **T**, then **A** for Table or **E** for Text. If you don't choose, it will give you a table.

➺ Command performance

Pressing **P** initiates the link. When you press this, the spreadsheet will be linked for the first time.

◆ Editing Links

Once you've created a link, you can edit it or update it. The editing menu controls the exact same items as the link-create menu we just covered. When you press

CONTROL-F5 S E

WordPerfect searches backwards for a spreadsheet link. If it doesn't find one, it then searches forward. If it finds one, it displays a menu which looks uncannily like the spreadsheet create-link menu.

Unless you want to change the file, range, or type, chances are you'll mostly use this to update the link. To update the link, press

P

WordPerfect will bring in the latest version of the spreadsheet file.

◆ Breaking links

Remember that I said (over and over) how formatting a linked spreadsheet is a waste of time? Well, it is, unless you are willing to break the link. Once you break the link, the table or tabbed text acts just as if you had imported the spreadsheet, rather than linked it.

Breaking the link is very, very easy, so I'll give you three guesses. Do you:

1) Take a ball-peen hammer to your screen?

2) Delete the opening link code?

3) Perform a rap version of Neil Sedaka's "Breaking Up is Hard to Do?"

Of course, the answer is 3. This is a very special undocumented feature, and I know this only because WordPerfect sent out audio cassettes called *The 5.1 Rap*. I'm not kidding. An unnamed rapper (or should it be spelled "wrapper"?) extols the virtues of 5.1 in syncopated rhyme. Unfortunately, this tune never hit the charts, but it definitely deserves a spot in the annals of WordPerfect history.

If this step doesn't work for you, you probably don't have the right mixture of soul and rhythm. So in your case, you can also use option 2, which seems to work for everyone, no matter how white bread they are.

Once you break a link, it's broken for good. If you need to link again, create a new link.

◆ Optional Equipment

Links have several options. To see what they are, press

CONTROL-F5 S L

- **Door #1:** Do we want WordPerfect to automatically update this link every time we retrieve this file? The default is no, mostly because it's time consuming, but if you're going to bother to link at all, you're probably doing it to make sure the figures are the most current. If you want to change this to yes, press **R Y**. WordPerfect will not insert any type of code you can see in the file, but it will make note of it.
- **Door #2:** Do we want to show the link codes? The default is Yes, which means that non-printing Link/Link End codes will display on-screen, alerting you to the fact that everything between them is linked data. I suggest you leave it on for two reasons. First, you don't want to accidentally delete one of the link codes. Second, these act as on-screen reminders that you should not spend much time formatting these tables because your formatting will be for naught when the link is updated.

◆ Updating *all* links at once

- **Door #3:** While we've yet to encounter Carol Merrill, this is where the you can, in presidential terms, put your finger on the button. You try not to think about the fact that the entire world as we know it could be disintegrated in only six minutes and then remind yourself that this only updates the links in WordPerfect and has absolutely no effect on the Strategic Defense System.

If you press **U**, *all* the links in the current file will be updated at once. If you have several links, this can take some time. And of course, everything old within the links, including text you've typed there, is lost when the link is updated. Use this option with care.

❖ *Spreadsheet graphics*

Now that we've exhausted the possibilities with spreadsheets themselves, it's time to turn our attention to the pie charts, bar charts, line charts, and whatever charts that spreadsheets can produce.

Since 1-2-3 is the most popular spreadsheet, it's hardly surprising that Lotus .PIC files are among the most popular of this genre. Happily, WordPerfect accepts .PIC files directly into graphics boxes.

But there's more to nice-looking graphics than just loading plain .PIC files. The rest of this chapter is devoted to making them look better.

◆ Graph titles

When using graphs, don't use your graphics program's fonts for titles. The fonts will either be stick figures (1-2-3) or you will be limited in your choice of typefaces (Harvard). WordPerfect allows you to put captions inside rather than outside the graphics box.

This allows you to produce handsome titles in the graphics that match in the rest of the text. The results improve the appearance of both the text and graphs. To do this, set graphics box options as follows:

ALT-F9 F O P A I [ENTER]

The only program this doesn't apply to is DrawPerfect. Because DrawPerfect can export directly to .WPG format, the fonts you see on-screen in DrawPerfect will be the ones you get on-screen and on paper in WordPerfect.

➾ Problem: Crummy graphs

Now you have a top-notch, typeset presentation, and you decide to use a graph created in 1-2-3. It looks like this:

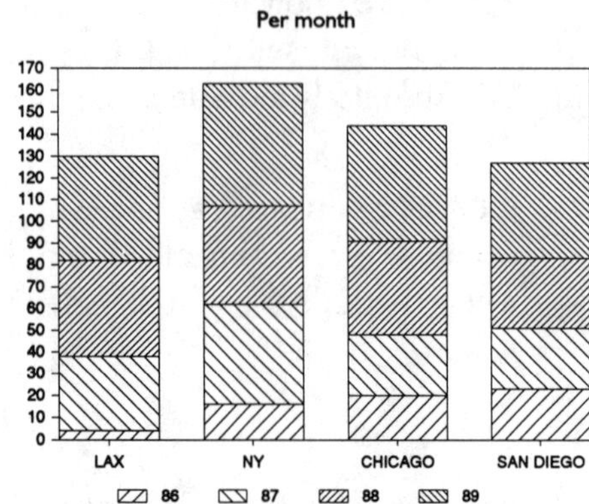

A 1-2-3 graph saved as black & white

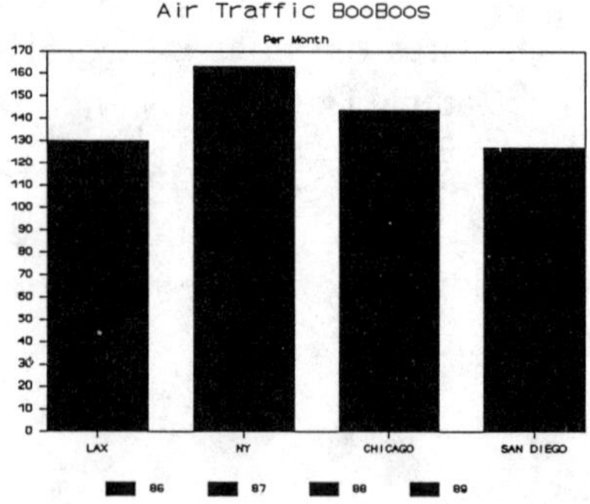

A 1-2-3 graph saved as color

If you've ever seen an emu, then this graph isn't the ugliest thing you've ever seen. Even so, it certainly doesn't live up to the quality of the typesetting that WordPerfect usually produces. It's the chart equivalent of a stick figure. This graph was created and saved in 1-2-3 as a color graph. When saved as black and white, the patterns filling the slices are even uglier and the pie is not very effective.

This graph would be more than satisfactory for casual documents, but is not recommended for important proposals or presentations.

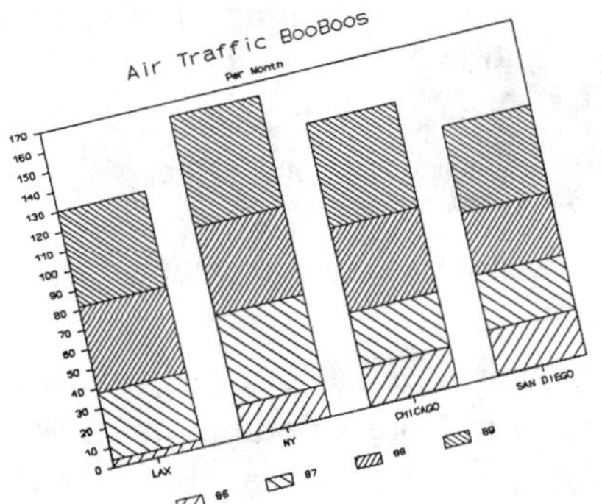

ASKEW: One way to add interest to these otherwise insipid graphs is to employ WordPerfect's rotate feature so that instead of the graphics just sitting on the page like a lox, they are angled.

This technique should not be used recklessly: one might conceive of it as the DTP equivalent of television's Batman (where the camera shot scenes at wild angles). It grabs attention, adds interest and visual energy to the page, but it's far from traditional and even a bit on the whimsical side. It looks as if you just threw the charts down on the page and left them wherever they landed. You either love this or you hate it.

It's important to angle the graphs enough so that the effect looks intentional; otherwise, people may think that you pasted it up by hand and simply did a lousy job. I also recommend that you turn borders off; otherwise, the graph just appears crooked in a straight box.

If you have more than one graph on a page, place each graph at a different angle to accentuate the haphazard look. I have a feeling that this "Dada" look is going to be the new hot trend over the next few years. It happens whenever the real world becomes so surreal that mere parody falls flat.

◆ Excel-lent

If you're among the growing ranks of Excel users, you're sort of out of luck. Currently, there are *only* two ways to get Excel's excellent graphs into WordPerfect. From Excel, the first way is to copy the graph to the clipboard using

Edit, Copy, Picture, OK

This will copy a "metafile" or line art graphic to the Windows clipboard, a temporary electronic storage area. This can then be copied into other Windows-based

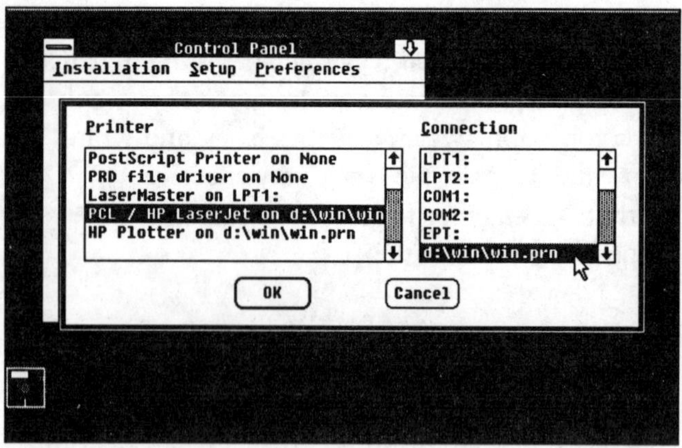

The Windows control panel—your key to the exciting world of trying to get graphics out of Windows and into WordPerfect.

graphics programs, such as Corel Draw, then exported to a format which WordPerfect will accept, such as .WPG.

If you hold down the SHIFT key while pressing OK, a "bitmap" will be copied to the clipboard. These bitmaps can be placed into Corel or edited using Windows Paint or PC Paintbrush for Windows, both of which create files that WordPerfect can import.

If you don't have any other Windows-based graphics program, the only way to get the graphic to WordPerfect is to use "print to disk" using the HP 7470 plotter driver. This creates an HPGL file which WordPerfect can import. While HPGL files are OK, you can't scale them much or the quality deteriorates. You especially can't make them bigger, as areas which were once solid will become striped.

I am now going to attempt, in as little space as possible, to tell you how to "print to disk." First, you'll need to install the Plotter driver. To get this to "print to disk," you need to leave Excel and edit the file called WIN.INI using WordPerfect. Find the section of the file which says

[ports]

; A line with [filename].PRN followed by an equal sign causes

; [filename] to appear in the Control Panel's Connections dialog.

; A printer connected to [filename] directs its output into this file.

LPT1:=

LPT2:=

COM1:=9600,n,8,1

COM2:=9600,n,8,1

EPT:=

and add a line which reads

C:\win.prn=

You can actually type any file name in here, but if that file already exists, it will be overwritten when you go to print and you will not be a happy camper.

➾ MAKE SURE TO SAVE THE FILE AS ASCII by pressing

CONTROL-F5 T S

If you don't do this, Excel will not run and you will spend a lot of money on long distance calls to Microsoft (no nice toll-free numbers like WordPerfect) to find out what's gone wrong.

➾ Repeat

I'll repeat myself: **Do not save the file with F10 or F7. Save it with CONTROL-F5 T S.**

Once you've done this you can install the plotter. To do this, enter Excel and press

ALT-SPACEBAR-U

This starts the "control panel," a program which allows you to install printers and set defaults for the Windows environment which Excel runs in. To install a printer, choose

Installation, Adding a Printer

It will ask you to put various disks in the floppy drive. Follow the on-screen directions.

Once you've done this you need to set up how the printers are connected. In this case, you don't really have a plotter (or even if you do), you just want to send the plotter print information to disk, to a file called **C:\WIN.PRN**. To do this, select

Setup, Connections

You'll see a list of the available printers and the available ports or disk files. **C:\WIN.PRN** should appear on the list. If it doesn't, you've done something wrong in WIN.INI and you'll need to go back and fix it, or leave a 12-year-old alone with your computer for a few minutes. When you return, they will either have fixed it or will be playing some kind of game which you weren't even aware was on the hard disk.

Click on the Plotter

Click on C:\WIN.PRN

Click on OK

Now there's only one step between you and an HPGL file. You still have to tell Windows what printer to use. To do this, select

Setup, Printers

Click on the plotter

Click on OK

Windows will now display all this nauseating information about the plotter. Basically, you just want to choose the model, and choose 7470. That's the first on the list and the simplest. The others *might* work, but then again, they might not, depending on the chart or graph.

Once you've made your selections, click on

OK

and then to close the Control Panel press

ALT-SPACEBAR C

Now, finally, at last, you can print the chart. Open the chart, make sure the chart window is current, and then choose

File, Print

If the gods were smiling on you, Excel will tell you that it's printing the chart to a plotter on C:\WIN.PRN.

Leave Excel, start WordPerfect, create a graphics box, and load this file:

ALT-F9 F C F C:\win.prn

To see the file on-screen, press

E

➾ A few more caveats

Now that you've selected the plotter, Excel will want to print everything, including your spreadsheets, to this nonexistent plotter. So remember, go back into Control Panel and select your normal output device. Before trying to print again, press

Setup, Printer

Do not try to print two charts in the same Excel session. If you do, you will simply write the second chart over the first chart in the C:\WIN.PRN file. If you have a full copy of Windows, you can use the Windows Executive to rename WIN.PRN to some other name, then you can print again, creating a new WIN.PRN file. If you don't have a full copy of Windows, you will need to leave Excel, rename the file, and then go back into Excel before printing another chart.

❖ *Baking a better pie (chart, that is)*

Depending on your budget, you can convert charts into a finished product that can range from attractive to spectacular. I'm going to cover several different ways to turn ordinary 1-2-3 charts into extraordinary graphics for use with WordPerfect.

◆ If you've got the money

If you can afford an expensive graphics program, your best bets are Corel Draw, DRI's Artline, or DrawPerfect, depending on exactly what you need. If you need a program to create charts and graphs primarily, go for DrawPerfect. DrawPerfect specializes in charts and graphs.

If you need something to spruce up your spreadsheet graphs, and want a program which gives you the most power over typestyles and the most control over graphics, choose Corel Draw.

Corel Draw

While Corel cannot create charts or graphs on its own, it does do a bang-up job of importing .PIC files. Rather than just bringing them in as straight graphics, it interprets them and turns stick figure type into one of its 105 standard typefaces. Pretty cool. Corel Draw can export any graphic to WPG format, and these files are can be imported reliably with WordPerfect.

My only warning is that if you save .PIC files as color, Corel will turn those colors into various shades of gray. While these shades print wonderfully from Corel, sometimes when you export to WPG and import them into WordPerfect, WordPerfect does a poor job of differentiating the separate shades, and you end up with bar charts where you can't tell one shade from another. This isn't really a Corel flaw, so remember, take care when bringing any color art into WordPerfect as it is not always predictable in the way it converts colors into shades of gray.

If you do want those various shades of gray, the best bet is to export to PCX. That way the shades of gray won't print too dark. Also, be wary of WordPerfect's "automatic" sizing of these PCX files. It doesn't always work. When I tried it, they always sized the graphic too large, so it looked jagged. Make note of the real size of the graphic while in Corel.

DrawPerfect

This is WordPerfect's sibling graphics program. While DrawPerfect can create freehand graphics, as Corel Draw does, I find that it's really best at Harvard-like charts and graphs. DrawPerfect uses function keys which are similar to WordPerfect, but don't expect to be able to use it instantly, just because you use WordPerfect. DrawPerfect automatically creates .WPG files which work perfectly with Word-

Perfect, and Chapter 19 will explain how to use the two programs together for the best results.

➾ Artline

Artline 2.0 can now import .PIC files. If you've got an XT, Artline is going to be the fastest and most efficient program for you. While WordPerfect will read .GEM files from GEM Draw, it cannot read .GEM files from Artline directly. Artline 2.0 wasn't shipping at the time I wrote this, so I can't tell you exactly how their export feature works. I do know, (or at least *think* I know) that you will choose Export from the file menu and be taken into a conversion program. DRI (the distributors of the program) have stated that the conversions will include PCX, IMG, TIF, CGM and HPGL. Of these, CGM is probably the best choice.

◆ General graphics secret of the universe

The one magic maxim to remember when creating any type of CGM, HPGL, or even WPG graphics is: *SAVE IT IN BLACK AND WHITE OR PATTERNS*, not in color. (They don't call me the master of subtlety for nothing.)

◆ LaserGraphics

If you need the simplest and least expensive way to improve .PIC files, check out a program called LaserGraphics from SoftCraft. This program is part of a package called LaserFonts. The entire package contains a font installation program called LaserFonts Manager; this can install any HP-compatible soft font as well as create outline and shadow versions of any font.

LaserGraphics contains a program called CNVRTPIC that takes a standard 1-2-3 .PIC file and turns it into a .PCX or .TIF file. It will also use any soft fonts (including Fontware fonts) in place of 1-2-3's stick figure type. Since the files it creates are bitmapped, the graphs can contain attractive even tones of gray (rather than the sometimes dizzying patterns of black and white in .PIC files). They also occupy much more disk space and require more time to print. LaserGraphics doesn't add all that much to pie charts; in fact, they don't look much different from standard .PIC files (although the bar charts look extremely different and definitely improved).

Instead of a sickening array of patterns (which can actually make the bars look as if they are bent), LaserGraphics gives you an assortment of simple gray tones that seem elegant without being flashy. Simple, yet baroque. Most importantly, LaserGraphics allows for clear, easy-to-read graphs for those special occasions when you actually want the reader to learn something.

There is only one caveat. Because these are bitmapped graphics, the gray patterns in particular do not scale well. LaserGraphics allows you to specify the exact size of graph you want to produce (from 1" to 10"). It's important to have at least an

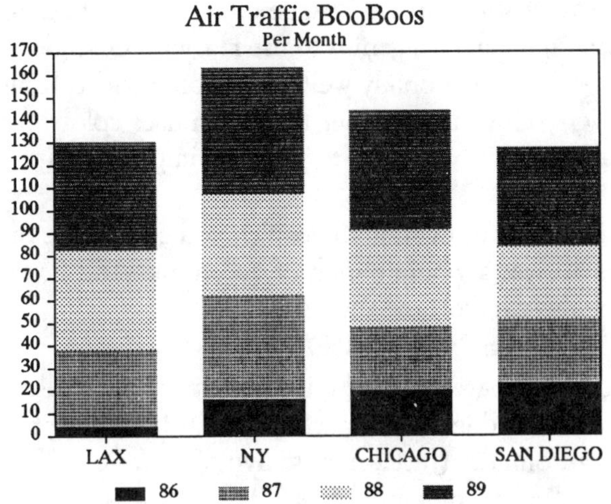

LaserGraphics gives you an assortment of simple gray tones that seem elegant without being flashy. This program allows for clear, easy to read graphs, for those special occasions when you actually want the reader to learn something.

approximate idea of the graph's size before you create it in LaserGraphics. If you know the exact size, so much the better. The final printed graph will be most attractive if it is the same size as the original size of the graphic. If you're using 5.1, use automatic graphic sizing to make sure the gray tones print perfectly.

LaserGraphics is about as difficult to use as typing

GRAPHMW AIR-BAR.PIC OUTPUT:AIRBAR.PCX

Typing that line took me all of five seconds (I'm a fast typist), and the program needed approximately one minute to process the file. LaserGraphics will save files in either .PCX or .TIF format (although the .PCX files usually require only 10% as much disk space as the TIF files). The .PCX files are normally about 30K while the .TIF files are about 250K. When the .TIF files are loaded into a graphics box, they use the same amount of space as the .PCX files; aside from that, they take up much more room and offer no other advantages.

The LaserFonts package, including LaserGraphics, costs $180, a fairly small price to pay for convenient font installation with genuinely easy and much improved graphics. (For the address of SoftCraft, and of all the programs mentioned in this chapter, see the Appendix.)

◆ Harvard Graphics

Come on, admit it, you always wanted an Ivy League education. Whether you went to Harvard or not, you don't have to be a genius to use Harvard Graphics from Software Publishing. Harvard works exceptionally well with WordPerfect. It allows you to change virtually whatever you want (whether the graph uses colors or patterns) and provides you with all the tools you need to properly import a graph into WordPerfect.

If you can create a graph in 1-2-3 (or even if you can't), you can create one in Harvard. All you have to do is answer a whole bunch of questions. And in case it didn't register the first time, the most important answer is:

ALWAYS CHOOSE PATTERNS, NEVER COLORS.

Before proceeding any further, however, you must set up what's called the "VDI" (Virtual Device Interface). Although you have to install this separately from the program, installation is still automatic. (Just a note to avoid confusion: Harvard refers to .CGM files as "Metafiles," as in "metamorphosis.")

The VDI interface uses what's called "Device Drivers"; these are automatically loaded into the computer's memory when it starts up and so take up memory. Depending on the version of DOS, these will take up different amounts of memory. On my 286 computer, the VDI used 50K of memory, a rather large chunk. If you are working on long WordPerfect files, or files with many graphics, removing the VDI when you're not using it will make more memory available for WordPerfect. You can do this by renaming a file called CONFIG.SYS that contains the VDI information.

There are two more important options you need to set, options that I spent far too long trying to decipher. Once you get the hang of them, they're a breeze. But believe you me, after *days* spent agonizing over this kind of crud, you begin to appreciate it. Don't bother searching for this in the manual—it's not there.

- ONLY USE COLOR 1 (white, which prints as black)
- and SET BACKGROUND COLOR TO 16 (black, which prints as white)

When asked if you want to **USE HARVARD GRAPHICS FONTS** when converting to a metafile, always answer **Y**. Otherwise, you will wind up with stick figure letters. The Executive (Swiss/Helvetica) and Square Serif fonts look the best. The Roman is sketchy, as are Script and Gothic.

It takes some doing, but once it's done, WordPerfect and Lotus 1-2-3 can make beautiful music together. The graph and logo on the opposite page were created with Harvard Graphics and printed on a QMS-PS 810.

1-2-3 WordPerfect 5

Everything you always wanted to know about WP and 1-2-3 but had no one to ask...

Winter 1989 - Vol 1. No. 3

WordPerfect and Lotus 1-2-3

By Daniel Will-Harris

What is desktop publishing? It means different things to different people.

If you work in any business, such as a real estate office or travel agency, you can use desktop publishing to send out promotional flyers about your hottest listings, or bargain travel packages.

Consider the production expenses of publishing. Try not to get depressed as you do so, but consider them all the same. Take a newsletter for example, which, using the old method, cost about $1,000 per issue to produce. With desktop publishing, the costs dropped to almost nothing (although the Oreo budget rose dramatically).

The first major expense is typesetting. On an eight page newsletter, if you sent typed pages to a typesetter, you should expect to pay about $300. If you prepared the copy on computer and sent it to the typesetter via modem (over the phone lines), that cost would be lowered to about $80 because the copy would not have to be retyped by the typesetter. (These typesetting charges included corrections, inevitable, because somehow mistakes are easier to see once something has been expensively typeset, and corrections are expensive.)

When you get the copy back you must "proof" it, to make sure the text, fonts, line widths, line spacing, etc. are correct. (A proof is a copy of text used for review and correction.) If you find mistakes, you have to go back to the typesetter.

While I've already added the cost of the typesetters' corrections, I haven't figured your time into it.

I'm not sure what your time is worth, but mine is worth plenty, and I have more to do than just wait for the type to be just right. I'm going to say that the amount of time spent proofing, correcting and working with the typesetter comes to about five hours.

Counting the costs

Your time (or the person you have doing this work) is worth around $15 an hour. If you are making less than this, complain immediately. If you are making more, spill something on this paragraph. Five hours at $15 equals $75. Now you have to measure the type and make a dummy. A dummy is a simple mock-up of a page showing the basic format and where each story, picture, or piece of artwork is going to be placed on the page.

A dummy on paper is very simple and rough, and gives you an approximation of the finished page. Dummying eight pages should take about an hour. Simply cutting out the type alone can take an hour. So, it takes an hour to make a dummy, and an hour to cut out the type. You can then expect to spend about three hours to paste up the type and art work onto the pages.

Harvard comes with a large assortment of clip art and will import .CGM files using its separate "Meta2hg" program. You might also consider purchasing an option package, such as "Business Symbols" (more cute clip art to distract people from the figures in the graphs) and "Designer Galleries" (which allows you to plug your own numbers into a large assortment of pre-designed graphics; or, if your numbers aren't so hot, why not just use theirs?).

Harvard saves graphs in .CGM, HPGL, and .EPS formats. I find that .CGM is by far the most compact (about one-fourth the size of EPS), the fastest to draw on-screen, and the fastest to print. CGM is line art, so you can scale it to any size and it will still print at the highest resolution. If you will be using a PostScript typesetter, .CGM will print quickly (and cost you less) while offering you the sharpest output possible.

Harvard reads and extracts graph information from 1-2-3 .WKS and .WK1 files. Or, if you find some of 1-2-3's commands ridiculous (as I do), retrieve only the data from the 1-2-3 file so that you don't have to retype all those numbers.

Harvard even includes a spell checker so you don't make embarrassing errors in front of those very same people you spent all this time desktop publishing to impress.

Naturally, graphs this attractive are going to require more time to create (not to mention another program to learn). The graph with the butler took me about 30 minutes to create, but since it was the first graph I produced, I didn't think that was

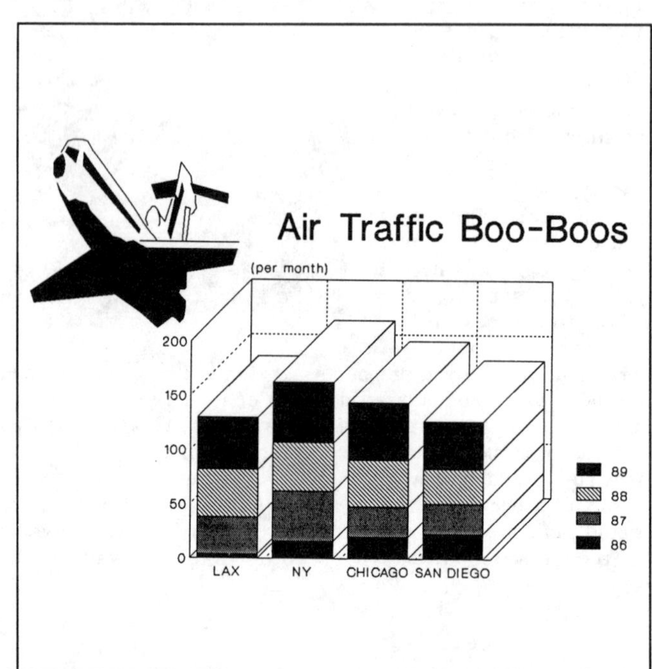

Harvard Graphics creates truly "wow-inspiring" graphics, complete with clip-art and 3D effects. All it takes it a little time, and enough sense to SAVE IN BLACK AND WHITE AND PATTERNS ONLY. I don't think one can repeat something important too many times.

too bad. My next graph took about 20 minutes, and now I can make one in about 10 minutes. (I should make a graph showing how fast I can create a graph.)

Harvard lists at a pricey $395, but we're not the type that pays retail, are we? The street price (through mail order and discount software stores) is approximately $200.

◆ Lotus Freelance

From the people who gave you 1-2-3, here comes Lotus Freelance Plus. This graphics program reads Lotus worksheets and .PIC files, and also creates .CGM and HPGL files that WordPerfect can read. The program even employs the 1-2-3 style of moving bar menus, so 1-2-3 users will feel right at home.

Freelance allows users to dress up charts with fonts, symbols, designs, and, true to its name, freehand graphics. The program combines several functions so you can create various types of charts and graphics. You can combine and modify text, lines, circles, rectangles, slices, polygons, arcs, and arrows, in whichever way you like. The program also includes a number of design tools: fonts, fill patterns, and a symbol library.

Freelance's graphic editing is more powerful than Harvard's: .CGM files can be read into the program directly, enabling you to illustrate and enhance charts with clip art. Freelance is excellent for editing CGM clip art. It imports the file not as a single picture, but in individual pieces, which allows you greater control over line art graphics. This means that you can both use and abuse clip art, forcing it to conform to your exact specifications. The zoom feature enables you to zoom in on even the tiniest detail, and so the editing control of this program is noteworthy.

However, the charts are not nearly as exciting as those made by Harvard. You can't explode pie slices and there are no 3-D effects. It's also disappointing that when creating a .CGM metafile, the built-in Freelance fonts are not exported, leaving you with stick figure type. If you create an HPGL plotter file, the fonts are exported, but the file is larger and doesn't scale as well.

◆ Get some Perspective, Jr.

There's not too much you can depend on in this world, but rest assured that a graph from Perspective Junior will never bore anyone. Confuse them, maybe; distract them, probably; give them a queasy stomach, possibly; impress them, most assuredly. If you are seeking a whole new dimension in graphics, consider the Perspective Jr., a program from Three/D/Graphics that creates genuine 3-D graphs.

Perspective Jr. reads 1-2-3 files directly, so there's no need for retyping. It also creates .IMG and .TIF files, so you can add these little dazzlers right into your WordPerfect document. Since these are bitmapped files, they will not scale as well as

Perspective Junior produces flashy, though sometimes obtuse graphs. They are retreived into WordPerfect as .IMG paint-type files.

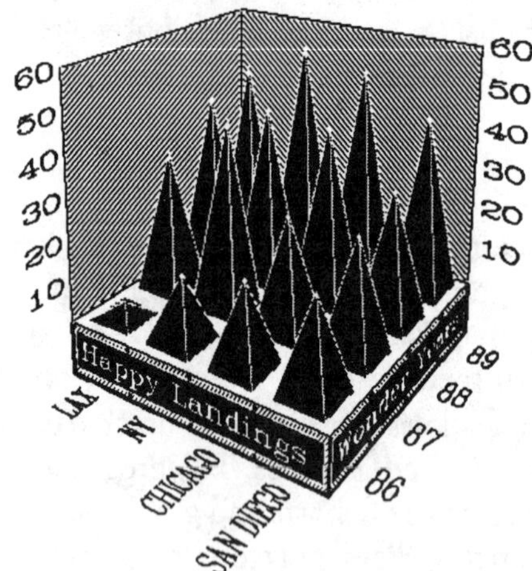

.CGM files, but they look beyond compare. They have depth, they have graph types no one outside a university has ever heard of, but most importantly, they have *sizzle.*

Perspective Jr. includes 180 (count 'em, 180) different fill patterns, some the likes of which you've never seen before. As well as a huge variety of gray tones, there are push pins, fish scales, squares, circles, diamonds, random patterns resembling wood grain, and a few patterns that can only be described as "wallpaper-like" from the 1930's to the 1950's.

To use Perspective Jr., just save the files as "Picture" files by pressing

F3 F2 F5

Perspective Jr. knows what type of picture file to create by the extension (last three letters after the period) that you add. If you use .IMG, Perspective will create a GEM paint file, and .TIF will create a TIFF file.

Perspective Jr. creates image files that are 4.16" wide and 3.15" high, so it's best to use them at their actual size. If you want to make them larger or smaller, use quarter increments (half or three-quarters as big, or one-and-a-half or two times larger). That enables the patterns to scale smoothly.

◆ PC Paintbrush IV

PC Paintbrush is the best paint program for the PC. So what does this have to do with 1-2-3 graphics, you ask? Plenty, I answer. PC Paintbrush Plus contains a feature called "Chart Interpreter" that can read 1-2-3 .PIC files and convert them into ZSoft's .PCX format (which WordPerfect reads directly).

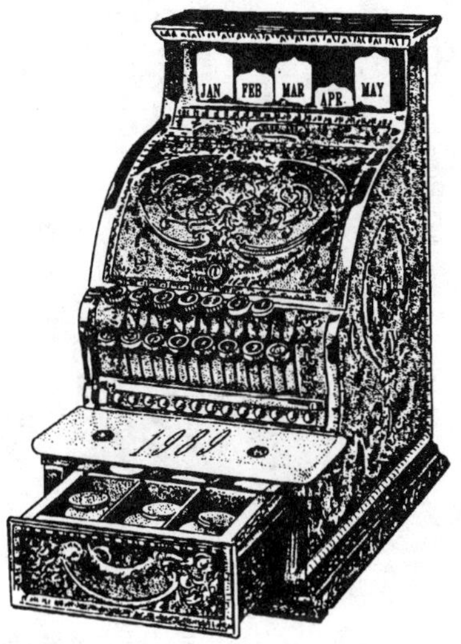

PC Paintbrush permits you to create cute graphs (the kind I decry in this book). But what can I say? It's fun, and there are times when you want cute. What's more, PC Paintbrush is perfect for editing scanned images, and great for customizing clip art, such as this cash register from the Metro Image Base.

Although .PCX files are bitmapped, take up more space, and don't scale as well as .PIC files, they provide you with much more flexibility for editing. Since .PCX is *the* standard bitmapped format for PC's, there's a wide range of clip art available in this format. You can enhance graphs with clip art or scanned images (since the program supports scanners directly), and as LaserFonts, obtain attractive, even gray tones in bar charts.

It's also easy to create those cutesy type of graphs that I have spent so much time decrying. While they aren't suitable for all occasions, they are suitable for framing. They can be especially effective for less formal documents, such as newsletters (where regular charts and graphs may come across as too formal and off-putting. See the example with the cash register graph).

In addition, PC Paintbrush is a truly fun piece of software. It's not unlike an electronic Etch-a-Sketch, but with more control. It's easy to spend hours drawing, or, if you can edit clip art, give the Mona Lisa a moustache. Whatever you find enjoyable. After all, desktop publishing should be fun, even if it is work.

◆ Artsy smartsy

Arts & Letters is another program that gives you the power to enhance 1-2-3 .PIC files. The major advantages here are A&L's high-quality typefaces and large library of clip art. A&L automatically replaces 1-2-3's stick figure type with any of its fonts. Any type in A&L can be outlined, shadowed, compressed, expanded, or rotated to any angle. At times, simply enhancing the text of a graph will greatly improve its appeal.

The graphs themselves are not substantially improved for LaserJet users who must make do with striped graphics similar to standard .PIC files. Trying to use color yields only black and white. PostScript users can obtain a full range of gray tones through EPS files.

A&L saves .CGM files in black and white only. If you have a PostScript printer, A&L converts its files into EPS, and these files can include gray patterns. Otherwise, you'll use the black & white .CGM files created by A&L.

Text manipulation is very good, with 15 high-resolution typefaces. (Unfortunately, only two of these are serif fonts, similar to Times Roman medium and bold.) Another 17 typefaces are optional and cost $25 each. These display faces range from a version of "Broadway" to "Quadrata." These fonts can be rotated to any angle, can be filled with a variety of patterns and gray tones (which only show up with PostScript printers), and can also be outlined or reversed.

Arts & Letters gives you the power to create headlines which are really graphics. These can be sized like any other graphics, and allow you to break the standard LaserJet Plus type size limit of 30 point.

In the past, due to the unstandard nature of CGM, I've noticed that files can sometimes appear different in WP than they do in A&L. In those cases, WordPerfect can cause white fill patterns to become black, and vice versa. As a result, you must reverse everything, and this can be annoying. Still, A&L is a practical program, especially for people who have limited printer memory but want giant headlines and/or special type effects. The clip art and type effects are excellent, and the program is simple to use.

◆ Future graphics

While Harvard and Freelance are fine, they don't hold a candle to what Micrografx's Windows Graph Plus can do. Windows Graph runs, not surprisingly, under Windows, but doesn't seem sluggish like many Windows programs. It's more intuitive than Harvard and Freelance, and supports a wider range of monitors (including full page screens, such as the MDS Genius) and printers.

As I write this, however, the only way to get these remarkable graphics into WordPerfect is by way of EPS files. That's fine for people with PostScript printers, but LaserJet users are out of luck.

Micrografx has announced a new utility called *XPort* to convert their files into the CGM format (which WordPerfect can use). The program will be bi-directional, and will include batch processing to convert groups of files automatically. I've yet to be disappointed by any of Micrografx's software, so I imagine this convert program will work as advertised. If so, Windows Graph will be a sensational graphics partner for WordPerfect.

◆ The low-priced spreads

Some people use word processors for a living, while others use spreadsheets. Individuals who use word processors instantly recognize the differences between WordPerfect and "El Cheapo WP." Individuals who use spreadsheets know the difference between 1-2-3 as compared with the low-priced knock-offs.

But spreadsheet addicts are content to use "El Cheapo WP," and word processing junkies are happy to use one of 1-2-3's lower-priced competitors. They may not have all of 1-2-3's features, but they cost less than half as much (in one case, one-fifth as much), and roughly perform the same function: crunching numbers. (No one ever calls word processing, "Word Crunching," probably because while numbers crunch, words turn to mush if not handled very carefully.)

In the grand old spirit of cheapness (or cheap shots), we present the "Michael Dukakis Balanced Budget Award" to two 1-2-3 clones: VP Planner Plus, and Words and Figures. Both these programs are keystroke-identical to 1-2-3; if you can use 1-2-3, you can use either of these. VP Planner Plus reads 1-2-3 files (either .WKS or .WK1). Words & Figures reads only the older .WKS files. Each of these produces .PIC files that can be imported directly into WordPerfect (or into other graphics programs, such as Harvard and Freelance). 1-2-3 costs $495 (the same as WordPerfect), VP Planner Plus costs $179, and Words & Figures costs $99.

In all cases, 1-2-3's graphs are superior to the other two programs, but in some cases by only slight margins.

Pies: Charts by 1-2-3 and VP Planner Plus are quite similar, with 1-2-3's being denser and rounder. Words & Figures' pie is frankly pathetic: no fill (even though it was saved as black and white) and no exploded slice; what's more, the pie isn't very round and the words aren't in the right location.

Bars: But the WAF bar chart is almost identical to the 1-2-3 chart (although the bars are slightly thinner, and there are fewer tick marks on the left-hand scale). The VP Planner Plus bar chart is the thinnest, and lacks top and side rules. (You might like this; it does allow for a somewhat cleaner look, especially when the entire graphics box is boxed.)

The moral of this story is that if you don't know the difference, don't pay the difference.

❖ *Parting shots for LaserJet users*

Those PostScript people can get pretty uppity, what with their giant fonts, outlines, shadows, rotated text. But once again, ingenuity (and software) can triumph over hardware.

If you have Corel Draw, Arts & Letters, or Harvard Graphics, you can create "headlines" in them which can have all sorts of effects. Outlines, shadows, pattern fills. If you save these as .CGM or .WPG, you can bring them into WordPerfect and rotate them to any angle, or even just print big headlines without having to have big downloadable fonts.

◆ The Harvard Yard

Here's one more way to use that copy of Harvard Graphics (or any other program that saves in acceptable CGM format, such as Corel Draw or Arts & Letters) to add jazzy logos or headlines to your pages (including outlines, shadows, huge sizes, and compressed or expanded text). This method also exceeds the 30-point limit of the LaserJet Plus and standard Series II printers. You can see examples of this in Chapter 4, *Show & Tell.*

This example is for Harvard: Begin with a new empty chart. Don't enter any data, just go immediately to the main menu and press **F7.** Select either the Executive or Square Serif fonts. (The other fonts will work, but won't be as attractive and will not allow you to create outline or shadow effects.)

Next, go to Draw/Annotate. Select **Add Text,** then press **F8** to set Text Options. Here you can select the size of text and also choose among solid, outline, or shadowed. Change whatever you like, but the color should always be **1** for white, which prints black. (If you're skimming this book, you'll have no idea why white would print as black, but that'll teach you a lesson about not reading every chapter in order.)

When you've set the options, press **F8** again to start typing. Remember that this text will be a graphic in WordPerfect; you won't be able to edit it, so get it right here.

Type City!

Harvard Graphics Normal Size

Harvard Graphics 100X 40Y

Type City!

Harvard Graphics 50X 100Y

Harvard Graphics Normal Size

Save the file, then export it to a "metafile." Load this file into a graphics box as a .CGM file. You can now size it, stretch it, compress it, rotate it. This text takes up as much memory as any graphic, but not nearly as much as a large downloadable font; it also offers more versatility. In addition, this is the only method LaserJet users have for printing both portrait and landscape text on the same page.

While this chapter is finished as far as 5.1 users are concerned, the rest of the chapter is devoted to helping 5.0 users lead a normal life without the spreadsheet import feature of 5.1.

❖ *How 5.0 users can beat 5.1 envy*

If you haven't upgraded to 5.1 (for whatever reason, maybe the speed, or lack of it, in 5.1), and yet you still want to import 1-2-3 files, you've got a long road ahead of you, but it can be done. What's a person to do? Problems in transferring data from one program to another are easily avoided if you know what they are. Relax. Have a pickle, turn down the lights, and enjoy this 1-2-3/WordPerfect horror story.

The most obvious task you'll need to do is move numbers from the 1-2-3 file into the WordPerfect file. The most obvious problem you'll encounter is that WordPerfect can't read 1-2-3 "worksheet" files. If you try to do this, you'll wind up with something like this:

^@^@^@^H^@^@^@^C^@^@-^@^B^@^@^@^X.

Gee, that doesn't look anything like next year's sales projections, and unless the folks in your company are extremely nearsighted, they may sense that something is amiss.

So you're pretty distraught, but then this colleague tells you he knows how to do it. No sweat, he'll explain it to you over lunch. Over the salad he says, "Print the 1-2-3 worksheet to disk. It's easy. Hey, pass the crackers, will ya? Oh yeah, then you just press"

/PF [ESC] C:\wp50\123.prn

This instructs 1-2-3 to print the file to disk rather than to the printer, and to send the disk file to a file called 123.prn in the \WP50 directory. "Of course, you could give this file any name you wanted," he tells you, smugly expecting you to pay for his lunch in return for this priceless advice. You just wish he would remove that piece of radish between his teeth.

"Now you need to tell 1-2-3 which part of the spreadsheet to print," he says. "If you want to print it all, type the following:"

R [HOME] . [END] [HOME] [RETURN]

"Gee," you think, naively, "This isn't so bad." "Oh, one more minor detail," he says. "Press"

O M L 0 [ENTER]

M R 240 [ENTER]

M T 0 [ENTER]

M B 0 [ENTER]

O U

Q

This procedure told 1-2-3 that you wanted the file to start at the left margin, print 240 characters wide with top and bottom margins of 0, and to print an unformatted, straight ASCII file.

We're having some fun now. But since your friend is probably getting tired of telling you what to do, he'll probably forget to tell you to press

G Q

Does this means that some guy in an expensive Italian suit is going to appear on-screen and shoot you a withering glance? No, the command has nothing to do with a men's fashion magazine. You merely told 1-2-3 to Go and then Quit from the print menu.

"Lo and behold," your friend tells you, "the spreadsheet is in a form that WordPerfect technically can read." And just think, it only took 46 keystrokes and one lunch.

WordPerfect can technically read this file called C:\wp50\123.PRN, if you use the retrieve command.

There it is, on your screen, just like your friend promised between bites of saltines. But why did that guy make such a fuss about this in his WordPerfect book? Geez, everything is such a production with him.

And then you print the file using Times Roman/Dutch 10-point, and you see this:

```
                Jan            Feb              March             April            May
June
     Roger                    0.50            0.55              0.83              1.24
1.86            2.78
     Crusader                  0.70             0.77             1.16              1.73
2.60           3.90
     Bugs            0.30            0.33            0.50             0.74           1.11
1.67
     Ricochet                   1.10             1.21             1.82              2.72
4.08           6.13
     Peter                    0.10            0.11              0.17              0.25
0.37           0.56
```

Instead of this:

	Jan	Feb	March	April	May	June
Roger	0.50	0.55	0.83	1.24	1.86	2.78
Crusader	0.70	0.77	1.16	1.73	2.60	3.90
Bugs	0.30	0.33	0.50	0.74	1.67	1.67
Ricochet	1.10	1.11	1.82	2.72	4.08	6.13
Peter	0.10	0.11	0.17	0.25	0.37	0.56

Gee, who can we take out to lunch next week? Of course, the mess on the previous page was caused by creating columns with spaces instead of *tabs*.

Fear not! You didn't cough up the price of this book for naught. You're about to learn what you couldn't learn anywhere else (even if you bribed someone with a really nice Italian lunch): how to get that pesky 1-2-3 file to print correctly in WordPerfect while using proportional fonts.

You have a choice of two methods to accomplish this task. The first is free (and so naturally requires more of your time), the second costs about 100 bucks, but is worth it if you use it often.

◆ Do it yourself 1-2-3 conversion

There are a few drawbacks to this method, but what the heck, it's free, so you can't expect everything. Well, you can expect it, but you'll probably be disappointed. It works, and that should be enough for you. If you ask for perfection, people are only going to brand you as an obsessive-compulsive troublemaker or call you an ingrate.

The first method is a two-step, not to be confused with a polka. You must first properly format the 1-2-3 worksheet for conversion, and then you will use a WordPerfect macro for the rest.

Go into 1-2-3 and insert an additional column between each existing column with

/WIC

Repeat this for each column. Type an exclamation marks (!) in each cell of these new columns. If your worksheet is 20 lines long, you can enter 20 !'s quickly by placing the cursor on the first one, then typing:

/C [ENTER] [DOWN ARROW] .

Move to the last line in the column and press

[ENTER]

This will fill the column with !'s. Repeat this for each of the new columns you added. Move to any cells containing spaces in labels, and edit them with

F2

Replace any spaces in words with an _ character, like this: Rabbit_ Industries_Inc. Consult the print-to-disk instructions at the opening of this chapter.

Rabbit_Industries: If_It's_Fuzzy,_It's_Rad

!!Jan!Feb!March! April! May! June

Roger!0.50!0.55!0.83!1.24! 1.86! 2.78

Crusader!0.70!0.77!1 16!1.73! 2.60! 3.90

Bugs!0.30!0.33!0.50!0.74! 1.11!1.67

Ricochet!1.10!1.21!1.82!2.72! 4.08! 6.13

Peter!0.10!0.11017! 0.25!0.37! 0.56

Load the file into WordPerfect and create the following macro (to save you time whenever you convert a file). *The space character is shown in this example as a ^. When you see a ^, press the space bar.* Press

CONTROL-F10 123 [ENTER] convert 123 print file [ENTER]

ALT-F2n^ F2 F2

[HOME][HOME][UP ARROW]

ALT-F2n_ F2^ F2

[HOME][HOME][UP ARROW]

ALT-F2n! F2 [TAB] F2

CONTROL-F10

This macro first removed *all* spaces from the file (because 1-2-3 uses spaces between columns when it prints to disk). Then it replaced all underlines with spaces, and finally it replaced all !'s with tabs.

And voila, faster than you can say "I want my money back," the file is formatted and ready for WordPerfect. Once you've created the macro, you can use it over and over again by pressing

ALT-F10 123 [ENTER]

- **Set those tabs:** Now all you need to do is set **decimal** tabs. If all the columns are the same width, it's a pushover: measure one column on-screen using the measurements in the lower right-hand corner of the screen. Set the tabs to be equally spaced. Remember: **SHIFT-F7 L T [HOME][HOME][LEFT ARROW] CONTROL-END 0,.75** (or whatever increment you want to use) will set equally spaced tabs across the page.

If the columns have different widths, it becomes a bit more involved. Because on-screen appearances can be deceiving, here's a quick way to print out the data so you can measure it on paper.

Set the left and right margins to .25 (the smallest allowed with laser printers). If you are working with a very wide spreadsheet, choose a landscape orientation for this print out so the spreadsheet will not be broken up when it prints. Print the page and find the longest column. Measure it and set tab spacing to be slightly larger than that width, or measure each column individually and make notes for tab settings.

◆ High-class conversion

If you resented having to mess up the spreadsheet with exclamation marks and underlines, then you're going to have to shell out 99 bucks for a program called "Corel Tabin."

This program can take a plain 1-2-3 print file filled with spaces and convert it so that it uses tabs instead. The file can then be immediately loaded into WordPerfect using the Text In/Out feature of List Files.

In addition, if you tell Tabin the point size of the font you're using, it will analyze the file and offer you suggestions about where you should set the tabs. (What a time-saver this can be with big spreadsheets.)

Corel Tabin is the most sophisticated spreadsheet conversion program available because it enables you to change any or all of its options. It does not require strict adherence to formatting rules, as some other spreadsheet converters do. It's also remarkably fast. In my tried and true tests, it never took more than 15 seconds to convert a file.

No other program provides such a high degree of control and customization. Tabin allows you to change its configuration file to specifically tailor any aspect of the program's conversion. If you are using foreign currencies, Tabin allows you to use European punctuation for commas and periods. The French use spaces instead of commas, and Tabin can automatically format in this way as well. You can place the currency marker before or after the numbers, line them up, or remove all but the first and last in a column.

Overall, Tabin is the most powerful and versatile program in its class and an excellent value. (The address for Corel is located in the Appendix, along with the addresses for all the other programs mentioned in this chapter.)

❖ *Advanced formatting for 5.0*

Now that you know the basics, here are some advanced tips for making the spreadsheet look its best.

- **Use a style sheet:** You use larger headings in the text, so why not in the spreadsheet? Create a paired tag called headings, and use the Size Large or Very Large (**CONTROL-F8 S V**) command. Embolden the important points. If you are going to mix type sizes on a line (the titles here are larger than the numbers), you should use fixed line height so that the line spacing will be even.

	Jan	Feb	March	April	May	June
Roger	0.50	0.55	0.83	1.24	1.86	***2.78***
Crusader	0.70	0.77	1.16	1.73	2.60	***3.90***
Bugs	0.30	0.33	0.50	0.74	1.67	***1.67***
Ricochet	1.10	1.21	1.82	2.72	4.08	***6.13***
Peter	0.10	0.11	0.17	0.25	0.37	***0.56***

- **Separator Rows:** Most spreadsheets contain "separator rows," rows of dashes or equal signs to segment the spreadsheet into readable chunks.

But standard dashes and equal signs can appear rather clunky when you start typesetting the spreadsheet:

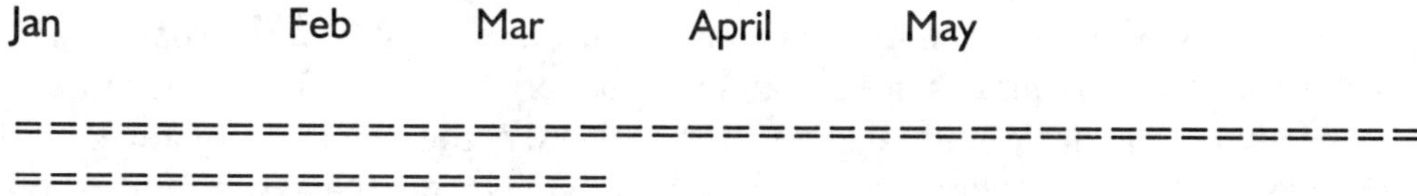

Jan Feb Mar April May

==
===================

In addition, because all of this doesn't line up on-screen, it's difficult to see where these lines really end. In this example, the equal signs stop a few characters after "April," on-screen, while they print as two lines.

The solution to this problem is simple: delete the rows of dashes or equal signs, and replace them with WordPerfect graphic lines. Since most separator rows run from the beginning to the end of a line, create a "left & right" like this:

ALT-F9 L H [ENTER]

If you want to stop the line at the last column, move the cursor to the right of the last word and note the measurement. Subtract the left margin from that number, and you will have the correct length of line you need. Create a left aligned line by pressing

ALT-F9 L H H L

Then press **L** and enter the length you just calculated.

Jan	Feb	Mar	April	May

You won't be able to use graphic lines if you want to place the spreadsheet into a graphics box. In this case, underlines will create a solid line. The larger the type size, the thicker the line.

❖ *Putting it all together*

Now you know the truth about 1-2-3 worksheets and 1-2-3 graphics, and it's time to put them all together. What report could be complete without a financial statement? Here are all the codes for the following example.

◆ Financial Statement Funny Business

Experience Level: ***Intermediate***

- **Fonts:** Bitstream Swiss 12pt, Bitstream Swiss Extra Compressed
- **Graphics:** Harvard Graphics
- **Printer:** Hewlett-Packard LaserJet II

Notes: Tabs work differently with math on. Math doesn't work properly with leader tabs (you can make some *serious and costly* errors this way). Tabs don't automatically change from normal (or math) to leader; they must be removed and replaced (you can use search and replace for this). The pies have wrap turned off, so they can overlap slightly. This allows them to be larger. The dates under the pie charts are captions.

```
[T/B Mar:1“,0.5"][Tab Set:4.75",5"][L/R Mar:1.25",1”]
[Usr Box:1;PIE87-2.CGM;]<TA VB HML SW 2.25 WN>
[Usr Box:2;PIE88-2.CGM;]<TA VB HMC SW 2.25 WN>
[Usr Box:3;PIE89-2.CGM;]<TA VB HMR SW 2.25 WN>
[Font:Swiss Extra Comp Roman 30pt (ASCII) (Port) (FW)]
Funny Business Productions[Flsh Rt]
[Font:Swiss Extra Comp Roman 18pt (ASCII) (Port) (FW)]
1989[-]1990 Financial Statement
[Font:Swiss Roman 12pt (ASCII) (Port) (FW)][C/A/Flrt][HRt]
[AdvUp:0.1“][HLine:Left & Right,6.25",0.1”,100%][HRt]
[HRt]
```

Funny Business Productions

1989-1990 Financial Statement

Assets:

Joke Library	$14,797,119.82
Rumor Mill	69,455.99
Whoopee Cushion Factory	45,211.16
Joy Buzzer Franchise	999,321.09
Collection: Stars' Hangnails	291,778.99
Total Assets	**$16,202,887.05**

In Development:

Agnes of Dog	$320,234.11	Shocker: A girl discovers a mysterious litter of puppies
The Pirate Caterer	12,350,000.00	Rollicking Broadway-bound musical comedy, full of food-services humor.
My Mother the Virgin	4,222,900.01	Sit-Com on fall schedule. Ogilvy & Mather pegs this for sure hitdom.
Unauthorized Autobiography	411,432.11	Autobiography of an amnesiac, won in fierce bidding war.
Total Development	**$17,304,566.23**	

Debts:

Junk Bonds	$4,555,006.01	All Ted Turner's fault.
Junk Food	655,991.08	Those Oreos really add up.
Just Plain Junk	43,621.09	Lots of stuff from K-Tel.
Chinese Junk	14,214.06	For promotional tour.
Total Debts	**($5,268,832.24)**	

Funny Business Bottom Line **$28,238,621.04**

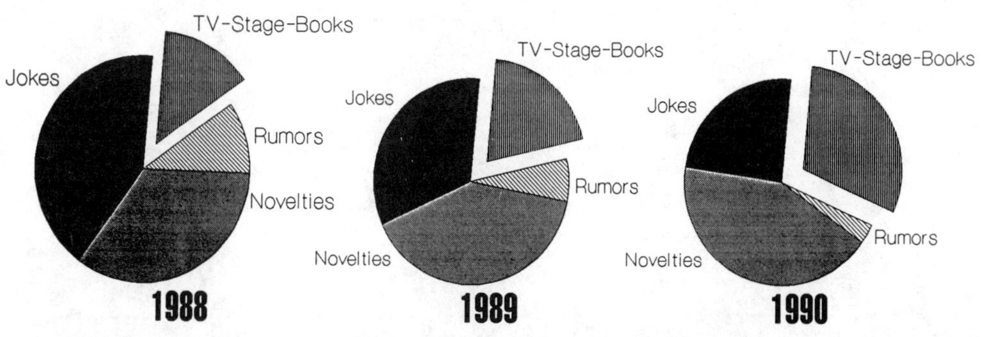

◆ *Paired Style for subheads:*

[Font:Swiss Extra Comp Roman 18pt (ASCII) (Port) (FW)] [Comment]

◆ *Paired Style for Total lines:*

[AdvDn:0.1“][BOLD][Comment][AdvDn:0.1”][HLine:Left & Right,6.5",0.05",20%]

◆ *Paired Style for Grand total:*

[HLine:Left & Right,6.5",0.01“,100%][HRt][AdvDn:0.1”]

[Font:Swiss Extra Comp Roman 18pt (ASCII) (Port)(FW)]

[Comment][AdvDn:0.1“][HLine:Left & Right,6.5",0.05",100%]

And you'll have fun, fun, fun 'til her daddy takes the T-bird away. Goodnight, Chet. Goodnight, David. There's nothing like mixing show biz metaphors (add two parts alliteration and one part onomatopoeia) to help end a complex chapter.

19

Get the Picture?

WordPerfect & DrawPerfect—Together, at last

WordPerfect has a baby brother. Or is it a baby sister? No one's quite sure, so we're not going to embarrass anyone by asking. It's wearing yellow, so that's not a good clue either. All we really do know about it is that it's supposed to do for charts and graphs what WordPerfect does for words; in other words, process them.

DrawPerfect's biggest appeal for WordPerfect users is that it shares a similar command interface. In plain English, this means that some of the same commands are on the same keys. The drop-down menus work in the same way: F1 is cancel, F3 is help (you get the picture).

This chapter won't teach you how to use DrawPerfect in all its glory. There probably will be a whole slew of books about it before you can say "but all I want to know is how to use it *with* WordPerfect," so that's what I'm going to cover here—how to use it *with* WordPerfect.

❖ Shell, the program, not the oil

Have you ever driven past a Shell gas station and noticed that the S was burnt out? This has nothing to do with either WordPerfect or DrawPerfect, it's just one of those things you think about at 3 a.m. as you write about computers.

I've been reminded of this little slice of Americana because the important link between WordPerfect and DrawPerfect is a program called *Shell*.

Shell is also from WordPerfect Corp., and has been sold for many years as menuing, program-switching software. It works great, especially in these big-software days, when programs require so much memory that you can't run much of anything just by "going to DOS" with CONTROL-F1 because there's too little memory left over. Shell allows you to freeze WordPerfect (or any other program which can go-to-DOS) in its tracks and jump into another program. Even if you don't have DrawPerfect, you would probably find Shell useful.

Shell works by taking the program you are running currently out of DOS memory and sending it on a short, all-expense paid trip to either EMS (if you have it) or to a hard disk. With DOS memory free, you again have plenty of room to run another program, without having to first exit from WordPerfect.

EMS is vastly faster, with the whole process taking only about a second. If you use a hard disk, Shell takes between 15 and 30 seconds, depending on the speed of your hard disk.

Shell also allows you to grab text off the screen of any program which is running under it, and then paste it into any other program running under it. Very handy.

I use Shell all the time to jump to my communications program, database, spreadsheet (I don't actually use a spreadsheet, but I feel compelled to keep the charade going), and now, DrawPerfect.

So when you get DrawPerfect, install Shell; otherwise you can't just jump back and forth between WP and DR (they call it DR because DP is used for DataPerfect).

Setup Menu

W	WordPerfect 5	B	WordPerfect 5.1
N	Nutshell	D	VHR MDS
X	Xtree	K	Lync
L	Magellan	Z	BLACK OUT!
M	MCI	E	DOS
S	CompuServe	V	Ventura
G	Guild	T	Desktop
A	Appointment	R	Draw Perfect
C	Calculator	H	Lotus 1-2-3
I	mcI - Norton	U	Sub Menu

1 Edit: 2 Options: 3 Add: 4 Delete: 5 Move: (F7 = Exit, F3 = Help)

Shell comes with DrawPerfect and is your link between DrawPerfect and WordPerfect.

◆ Beam me up, Scotty

Once you've installed DrawPerfect *and* Shell, you're ready to go. You'll press **D** to start DrawPerfect, or **W** to start WordPerfect. If these programs don't run correctly, press **4**, place the cursor on the offending program, and make sure that the Shell knows the correct drive and directory of both WordPerfect and DrawPerfect.

Once you're in either WordPerfect or DrawPerfect, there are several ways to switch from one to the other. At the WordPerfect editing screen, you can press CONTROL-F1 G and then select D from the Shell menu.

Yes, of course you *could* do that. But wouldn't it be easier to just press

CONTROL-ALT-D

Which blasts you into DrawPerfect. You may never have encountered a command where you had to hold down both the CONTROL and the ALT key at the same time (other than CONTROL-ALT-DELETE), but you have now.

When in DrawPerfect, do as the DrawPerfectionists do. To zip from DrawPerfect to WordPerfect, press

CONTROL-ALT-W

◆ Captain Zlog

The first way of jumping back and forth is merely rudimentary, something Scotty might have come up with when all life support systems were down and they had to divert power to the shields. But this next way is how Captain James T. Kirk would do it, if he hadn't been born about 400 years after WordPerfect. (You may never have noticed, but even on the oldest *Star Treks*, the ones made in the Sixties, Kirk and the gang did all their word processing using WordPerfect version 500.1, and my book on that particular version will be out in a few hundred years.) I apologize to anyone who never watched the show and doesn't have the faintest idea who these characters are. (What rock did you crawl out from under?)

If you don't care, jump to the next diamond subhead; but if you do, I'll give you a quick rundown on some of my favorite characters. Captain James T. Kirk is the often bare-chested commander, has only three expressions: determination, anger, and love (always with some doomed alien girl who must die by episode's end). All three expressions look pretty much alike, so it's often hard to tell them apart. He introduced each episode with "Captain's log, Stardate something-or-other," and for the longest time I thought his name was "Captain Zlog."

Then there's Bones, the ship's doctor. His biggest moment always comes when he pronounces Kirk's alien girlfriend D.O.A.: "She's dead, Jim." Next comes Scotty, the easily excitable ship's engineer: "She's gonna blow, Captain!"

And finally, Chekhov (not the Russian playwright). I'm not really sure what he did; steer, I think. Just thank your lucky stars I'm not going into detail about the *Next Generation* characters, such as Lucien Picard, the watchmaker reincarnated as a ship's captain.

◆ Launching pad

The really trekkie way of linking the two programs is to switch right from WordPerfect's graphics edit to DrawPerfect. To do this, let's use the sample file called "BURST-1."

First, let's load it into a graphics box. Press

ALT-F9 F C F F5

Move the cursor to BURST-1.WPG and press

R

If you don't see the file in the current directory, use List Files (which you're already in) to move through the directories until you find the file.

Now go into graphics edit. When you're using DrawPerfect, this term takes on new meaning, as you shall soon see. Press

E

You will see the action-packed graphic on-screen. You'll also notice that suddenly, there's a new addition to the menu along the bottom of the screen. Item #6 now says DrawPerfect.

This is the really neat way to get into DrawPerfect, and it appears just where you need it. Let's say you decide that this graphic is simply *too* exciting for your readers. You're afraid they'll suffer some type of irreparable trauma if they get a load of this shocking, explicit, no-holds-barred graphic.

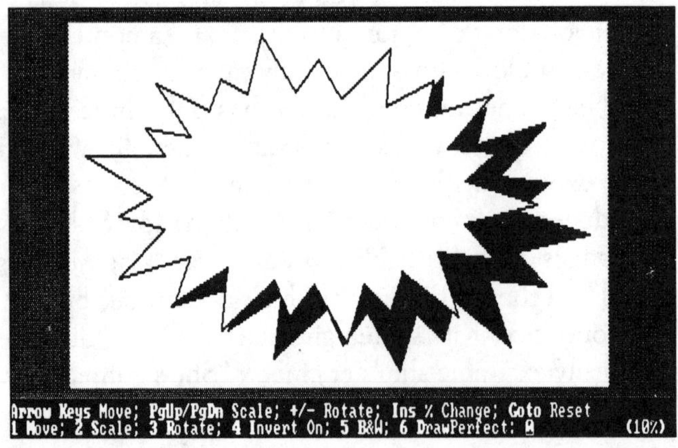

Here's the gaudy "burst" graphic. Notice the new menu item along the bottom of the screen. This allows you to jump to DrawPerfect from Graphics Edit.

So you decide to tone it down a little. Make it a bit more tasteful. Turn it into something that you would not be embarrassed to show your mother or resident DTP expert. Lucky you, you don't have to do anything more than just press

D

Now you're into DrawPerfect to do some *real* editing.

◆ Drawing Conclusions

Before you know it, you will be whisked away to the magic fairyland of DrawPerfect. And there, on-screen, in living-color (if you have a living-color monitor, dead-color if you have a dead-color monitor, or shades of gray if you have a monochrome monitor) will be the burst.

DrawPerfect does not require a mouse. Instead, it just begs for one. You can use the program by moving the cursor around, a slow, tedious and inefficient process, or you can zoom around using any old mouse.

Along the left side of the screen you'll see a bunch of little pictures. In the 1990s, these are called "icons." In the 1890s icons were something you worshipped, and, I guess, with the hordes of Mac fanatics, they still are. Each of these little pictures represents a function of the program.

For this example, we're going to use the fourth icon in the left row. It looks like a dotted rectangle with a solid rectangle in front of it, and it stands for *move*. You can also select *move* from the Edit menu, either with a mouse, or tap and release the ALT key, then pressing E O.

Once you select the icon, you select the object you want to move. In this case, you want to move the burst in the background so that it is closer to the one in the foreground, thereby creating a smaller, less frenetic shadow.

You can select the background burst either by clicking on it with the left button of your mouse, or by moving the cursor there and pressing [ENTER]. If you accidentally select the wrong object, click again until you've selected the correct one.

To move the object, click the right mouse button. A dotted box will appear around the object you've selected, and it will move when you move your mouse. Once you've moved the box where you want the object to be (in this case, move it so that it is closer to the other burst), press either mouse button.

The burst will redraw on the screen, but the other burst probably won't. DrawPerfect does not automatically redraw the entire screen, just the object you're working on, because it's a much faster way to work than redrawing every object.

If you want to redraw the entire screen, select reDraw from the View menu.

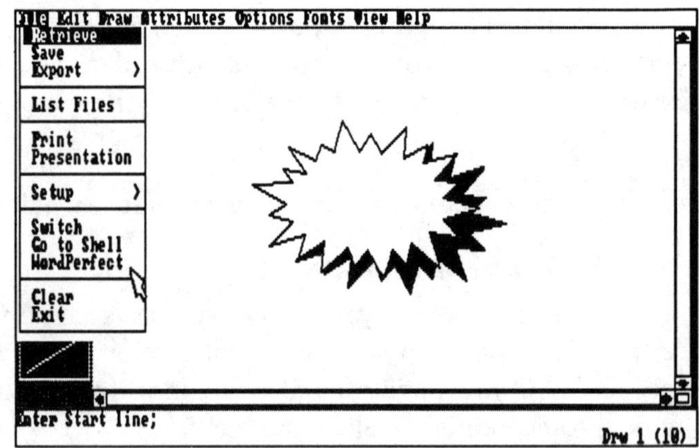

From WordPerfect's Graphics Edit to the real graphic editing power of DrawPerfect. The arrow is pointing to the menu item which will whisk you back to WordPerfect, edited graphic in tow.

◆ Get back, Jack (you can't get down)

You've moved the burst so the two are closer and slightly less garish and you're going to change just one more thing. You're going to make the background burst gray, instead of solid black.

Note to confused readers who see the burst as white on their screen: You know, everything is relative. You call it white, I call it black. In this case it has nothing to do with everyone creating their own reality, and all to do with the fact that on some graphics screens the background will be black, while on others it will be white. If you're using a color screen it will also be either black or white (at least it was on the VGA monitor I used).

Now you're going to switch back to WordPerfect with the edited graphic in tow. To do this, click on (or if you're mouseless: tap the Alt key, then press)

F O

Because you entered DrawPerfect from WordPerfect's graphic edit mode, you are returned to graphic edit. The old, tired, unedited graphic is automatically removed, and the new, improved, edited graphic replaces it.

◆ Getting back when you're not Jack

If you entered DrawPerfect from anyplace other than WordPerfect's graphics edit mode, pressing ALT F O in DrawPerfect will produce slightly different results.

You will be transported to WordPerfect (or back to WordPerfect if that's where you came from). When you arrive you will immediately be asked if you want to Retrieve the graphic from the clipboard, or Leave it in the clipboard.

If you press

R

WordPerfect will create a figure box, insert the graphic, and take you to edit mode.

If you press

L

You will be back in WordPerfect as if nothing had happened. The graphic will be safe and sound in the Shell clipboard.

If you try to retrieve it from a normal editing screen by pressing CONTROL-F1 R, WordPerfect will tell you that the clipboard data is not in the correct format to be inserted in the text portion of the program.

What it won't tell you is that you *can* insert the data into a graphics box. To do this, create a graphics box by pressing

ALT-F9 F C

Now act as if you are going to specify a file. Press

F

But instead of typing a file name or pressing F5, press

CONTROL-F1

WordPerfect will ask "Retrieve contents from clipboard?" and if you answer

Y

WordPerfect will insert the graphic into the box. To see or edit it, press

E

❖ *Table to graph, table to graph, come in, graph*

These two playful siblings have a few more tricks up their collective sleeves. For instance, you can take the data from any WordPerfect table and turn it into a graph. Here's how:

First, create a table. You can import a spreadsheet, or type the data from scratch. I'm going to use that same (by now tedious) rabbit table I've used elsewhere so that neither of us had to retype it from scratch.

Turn block on with

ALT-F4

Block the data that you want graphed. Then press

ALT-SHIFT-G

Now watch in awe as WordPerfect disappears, DrawPerfect appears, and a whole bunch of stuff happens.

Unfortunately, as I write this with the first release of DrawPerfect, dated 2/6/90, this feature doesn't always work. You get into DrawPerfect, a chart is created, and DrawPerfect gets ready to import your data from the Shell clipboard, and then—nothing.

The problem, at least with the version I'm working with, is that this macro (the ALT-SHIFT-G thing is really just a macro, you know), tells DrawPerfect to use *Tabs* as the "delimiter" between columns of data. Well, WordPerfect doesn't put tabs between columns, it puts spaces, so this just plain doesn't work.

This problem probably will be corrected by the time you read this, but if it isn't, just press

I Y A S P

and the graph will be imported properly.

(If the "sample data" feature has been turned off, you'll need to press **CONTROL-F5 Y A S P** instead.)

◆ Text to graphic text

For your final trick of the evening, you shall take normal, everyday text in WordPerfect and turn it into graphic text in DrawPerfect. This graphic text can then be brought back into WordPerfect and used for a headline or any other text which should be especially large, or perhaps compressed or expanded to perfectly fit an area. (Best of all, this one actually works!)

First, block the text you want to turn into graphic text by pressing

ALT-F4

Once you've blocked the text, press

ALT-SHIFT-T

Count to 5, and you should be inside DrawPerfect, staring at a blank screen. (If you had previously gone to Shell from DrawPerfect with a graphic on-screen, that same graphic will appear.)

DrawPerfect will go through some quick gyrations, and then prompt you either to click twice (for the text to fill the whole page) or click the mouse and drag to create a box where the text will flow. Once you do that, the text flows and is at your mercy. Change the typeface, size, or color. (Remember, though, WordPerfect can't print color graphics . . . yet.)

◆ My type isn't your type

I've only experienced a bit of confusion when using the two programs together. When I created text in DrawPerfect using a typeface like Chelmsford Book, it appeared in Helvetica when I brought it into WordPerfect.

If you experience a similar problem, when the typeface you used in DrawPerfect doesn't appear in WordPerfect, it's because you've failed to copy DrawPerfect's WP.DRS file to your WordPerfect directory (replacing your current WP.DRS). This file contains all the typefaces, and unless WordPerfect can get to it, it can only use the basic typefaces it has, Times Roman and Helvetica.

And there you have it — the basics for getting WordPerfect and DrawPerfect to play together without painful sibling rivalry.

20

Coordinating your accessories

Utility software programs

Many useful utility programs have sprung up around WordPerfect. While I would like to fill you in on all of them, I have to draw the line somewhere, so I'm just going to hit the highlights. If something is mentioned in this chapter, you can bet it's software that I've given a workout and probably use regularly. I try not to play favorites and just evaluate the programs based on their features, but it's difficult. Often there are two or three competing programs that basically cover the same ground; they all just do it a little bit differently. In these cases I try to give you an idea of their strengths and weaknesses so you can make an informed decision. Anyway, these programs are frequently updated with new versions, so check them out for yourself before you buy.

For novice desktop publishers, pre-designed style sheets can be a big help. They contain many practical tips about the basics of graphic design and show how to quickly modify a style sheet. Users load in their own text and graphic files, and can instantly tailor any element of the page layout to fit their individual document. Read on.

◆ **Designer Disks**

➺ Will-Harris Designer Disks, Dept. B
PO Box 1235, Point Reyes, CA 94956.
$39.95 Mail order only;
not available in stores

As a tutorial for graphically design-impaired WordPerfect users, *Will-Harris Designer Disks* explain and demystify some of the program's more intricate functions, and illustrate proven design techniques to help users quickly produce attractive, effective documents. Culled from the examples in Chapters 3 and 4 of this book, the style sheets serve as templates for newsletters, manuals, catalogs, directories, and many other applications. Designed for use with both LaserJet compatibles and PostScript printers, *Designer Disk 5*, containing 30 style sheets, is available by mail order only. See the order form in the back of the book.

◆ **FontSpace, the final frontier**

➺ Isogon Corp., 330 Seventh Ave., New York, NY 10001. (212) 967-2424, 800-662-6036. Fontspace $89.95

I've been a fan of the LaserJet since it was introduced. While Mac-a-holics yap incessantly about the LaserWriter, I've always said that bitmapped LaserJet fonts are sharper than scaled PostScript fonts. It's true, but unfortunately it's also true that those sharp fonts take tons of disk space.

I routinely had 4 to 12 megabytes of fonts on my hard disk. Eventually, I resorted backing up typeface families to floppies and restoring them to the hard disk when I needed them.

But now there's an easy, efficient way to save 50-75% of the space used by fonts. It's called FontSpace, and in about 10 minutes your fonts will take less than half the space they did before. FontSpace is a memory-resident program which automatically decompresses fonts *as* they are downloaded to the printer. There is absolutely no loss of font quality. It does this with such speed that you don't notice any performance loss, and it works with *all* programs: Ventura Publisher, WordPerfect, Windows; they (and you) don't even know it's there.

My 12 megabytes of fonts shrank to 4 megabytes. That means the program gave me 8 more megabytes of available hard disk space. The program literally installs itself. You only have to tell it to compress your fonts once. FontSpace searches for your fonts on every drive and directory and then compresses them. Once you've done this initial compression, you need do nothing else. If you use Fontware or other font generation programs, FontSpace automatically compresses these fonts *as they are generated.* Fontspace even compresses fonts automatically as you copy bitmapped fonts from a floppy to your hard disk.

If you have EMS, FontSpace takes a mere 3K of DOS memory, and 18K of EMS. If you don't, it takes 22K of DOS memory. Either way, I've yet to see it conflict with any other memory-resident program. This program is the personification of transparency;, it's even frugal with its own use of disk space, occupying only 65K. If you use a LaserJet and have many fonts, *buy this program.* You'll wish you'd had it years ago.

◆ Fontware

➾ Bitstream Fontware, Athenaeum House, 215 First Street,
Cambridge, MA 02142. 800-522-3668. $129 per package

Bitstream deserves a lot of credit for supplying us WordPerfect aficionados with high-quality fonts for free. In the past, users have had to pay dearly for Bitstream fonts, but now an installation kit and two typefaces are available for about $30 from WordPerfect. Normally I would be suspicious of a company that gives away fonts in order to persuade you to buy more, but buying Fontware is never a mistake.

If Dutch (Times Roman) and Swiss (Helvetica) suit your applications, then there's nothing more to buy. As with all Fontware kits, you can create fonts in sizes from 3 to 144 points for LaserJets and compatibles, as well as PostScript printers.

But once you start using Fontware, how can you resist buying Goudy Old Style, Zapf Humanist, Korinna, Hammersmith (Gill Sans), or Futura (including the ever-popular Extra Black)? And how long will it be before you succumb to the childhood catch phrase "collect 'em all!" (each sold separately, of course). Each package contains either four weights of a single typeface such as Palatino, (medium, italic, bold, and bold italic) or four special fonts packaged to be used as display faces only, such as Headline Package No. 1: Cooper Black, University Roman, Cloister Black, and Broadway.

The most economical way to buy Bitstream fonts is found in their six collections of fonts. Each contains three typeface packages. These packages are only $70 more than single typeface packages. The packages are: Spreadsheets, which includes Zapf Elliptical (Melior), Monospaced 1 (typewriter faces), and Zurich; Books & Manuals includes Baskerville, Goudy Old Style, and Zapf Calligraphic (Palatino); Reports & Proposals includes Activa (Trump Medaeval), Bitstream Amerigo, and Zapf Humanist (Optima); Newsletters contains Bitstream Charter, Headlines 1, and Swiss Light; Flyers includes Futura Light, Headlines 2, and Headline 4; Presentations consists of Slate, Swiss Condensed, and Headlines 5.

Fontware does have a few flaws. You can't use it to install fonts from any other manufacturer. You might wonder why that is a problem, but as good as Fontware is, other vendors have typefaces Bitstream doesn't.

All the typefaces used in this book are from Bitstream (except for the PostScript examples, which use the Adobe typefaces built into the QMS-PS 810). I used them because Bitstream produces the highest-quality type for LaserJets, compatibles, and many scaleable font printers, such as the LaserMaster.

Bitstream's typefaces don't come cheap, but then again, their typefaces are the very best. (For significant discounts on Bitstream fonts, you might try mail order firms such as 800-Software and PC Connection. These companies offer discounts as high as 50%.)

◆ Type Director

➻ Hewlett-Packard, 19319 Pruneridge Ave., Cupertino, CA 95014. 800-752-0900, 800-538-8787.

While I'm a big fan of HP's LaserJet printers (especially the LaserJet III), and recommend them above all other laser printers, I'm not a big fan of HP's Type Director.

There are a couple of reasons for this, but mostly because I'm not a big fan of Compugraphic's typefaces. While CG is one of the largest typesetting equipment manufacturers in the world, I don't think they've done a very good job with their type for PCs. I find the characters uneven and heavier than comparable Bitstream faces. If you look at CG fonts by themselves, they're OK, but if you compare them to Bitstream typefaces, you'll see how much sharper, cleaner, and more professional the Bitstream type looks. CG also offers fewer typefaces than Bitstream.

If you have a LaserJet III, you might want Type Director simply because, as of publication, Type Director is the only software which creates scaleable fonts for the LaserJet III, and that's an awfully good reason to buy it. Bitstream has announced they will release some type of conversion utility for their fonts for use with the LaserJet III, but it may not be available at the time you are reading this.

If you do use Type Director, Garamond Antiqua is their most attractive typeface. It even looks good at 10-point, something which can't be said of CG's version of Times Roman. Garamond Antiqua is the old-fashioned Garamond, as opposed to the new-fashioned ITC Garamond. This older version of Garamond is currently far more "fashionable" than the more modern ITC version, and I like it very much.

If you have a LaserJet II or compatible, which uses bitmapped fonts, I don't recommend Type Director.

❖ *Third-party font installation*

Installing fonts unassisted in WordPerfect can be a nightmare even for the technically inclined, and a near impossibility for almost everyone else. Three third-party programs ride to the rescue to let you install fonts from any manufacturer.

◆ LaserFonts

➻ SoftCraft, 16 N. Carroll St. Suite 500, Madison, WI 53703
(608) 257-3300 Manager, Font Effects $95 each; LaserFonts/
LaserGraphics $180; Word Processor Pack $595; Spin Font $95

The best of the bunch is SoftCraft's LaserFonts Manager. This reasonably-priced program installs any soft fonts for WordPerfect, including the Fontware fonts. If you've already generated the fonts, but for some reason you don't have the modified .ALL file, the LaserFonts Manager can reconstruct it for you. You can also install any Fontware fonts you might have created for other programs.

The program is similar to "WYSIfonts," SoftCraft's font installation program for Ventura and PageMaker. Whether mouse or menu driven, it's both quick and easy, even for the occasional user.

If you have an eccentric font (not listed in the long list of font names), the LaserFonts Manager allows you to enter any pertinent information so that it can be installed correctly and called up by name from within the word processing program.

The installation for WordPerfect is particularly, shall we say, entertaining. WordPerfect has built-in commands for outlined and shadowed characters, so LaserFonts Manager includes a portion of SoftCraft's Font Effects power. It will create shadowed or outlined fonts of *any* bitmapped font automatically, and install them so they will be instantly accessible in WordPerfect.

The LaserFonts Manager fully supports automatic kerning for the finest-looking output with any font, and it lets you install special effects fonts you design yourself, using the full version of Font Effects.

It provides an on-screen preview of font appearance during selection (supporting CGA, EGA, VGA, and Hercules), includes complete support for all symbol sets (including user-defined sets, no small feat with WordPerfect 5), and installs any font in either portrait or landscape orientation, creating landscape fonts when necessary. I dare say the next release will offer "shampoo carpet" and "deep fat fry" features as well.

The LaserFonts Manager also enables you to use SoftCraft's own $15 per disk fonts in a wide variety of styles. These are the least expensive quality fonts I know of, and include hard-to-find fonts such as Hebrew (Serif and Sans Serif), Cyrillic, Phonetic, and even sign language for the hearing impaired.

The Manager also installs Fontware fonts created with SoftCraft's own Fontware installation program. This program has an advantage over the free Bitstream installation program because you can choose your own symbol sets from the 560 character Bitstream character set, and slant fonts, as well as compress or expand them.

The LaserFont Manager can even handle unusual fonts such as Weaver's DB (Dingbats) for LaserJets. These inexpensive fonts use the standard ASCII character set and require two font sets to include the entire Dingbat typeface. Each set costs $29. Even if you have limited memory, these entertaining little symbols can add a lot of fun, spice, and whimsy to publications. With these fonts, WordPerfect LaserJet users will be one up on WordPerfect PostScript users who may not be able to access the Dingbats built into PostScript printers without obtaining the PostScript (Additional) printer driver.

If you also want to improve the appearance of Lotus 1-2-3 .PIC files, a LaserFonts/LaserGraphics package includes several programs to enhance graphs.

For the most comprehensive font control available in word processing programs, you might consider SoftCraft's "Word Processor Pack." This includes the installation program, a Bitstream Fontware typeface package of your choice, and Font Effects (to create your own special effects, not just outline and shadow).

The package also includes an infinitely useful program called Spin Font, which takes any Bitstream font and lets you set it in paths, such as arcs and circles, and at angles. The program creates a .TIF file containing the finished text. You can also set headlines that exceed the normal 30-point limit of the LaserJet Plus and standard Series II.

To accomplish this, you have Spin Font create a .TIF file of the headline (with no angle, so that the text is straight), and insert it into your document as a graphic. If you distort the graphic, you can compress or expand the type as well.

❖ *Scaleable fonts for nonscaleable printers*

◆ Glyphix

➺ Swfte International, Ltd., P.O. Box 219, Rockland, DE 19732.
800-237-9383. Installation kit $79.95; Body Typefaces $49.95
for four weights; Display faces $24.95 each.

If you're lusting after a scaleable font printer, but would really rather spend the money on new living room furniture, a Hawaiian vacation, or even braces for the kids, lust no more. Get Glyphix. Glyphix is software which scales fonts "on-the-fly" like scaleable font printers do. But unlike those printers, where all the magic goes

FOUNDRY SERIES

Glyphix for WordPerfect

Scaleable fonts and special effects for the ink-jet & laser printers

on in the printer (or in the case of the LaserMaster—in the card), Glyphix is all software; you don't need any new hardware.

When you print, Glyphix determines what fonts WordPerfect needs, and then it generates them. It doesn't save them to disk, it just creates them as it sends them to the printer. You can choose any size type you want, from 1-point to 120-point—just like on a scaleable font printer.

Glyphix works seamlessly with WordPerfect. You load Glyphix, and it then loads WordPerfect automatically. You select fonts just as you do on scaleable font printers: you choose a typeface, then specify the size you want. You never have to make fonts in advance and there's nothing new to learn. Swfte, the creators of Glyphix, have done a great job making the software easy to install and transparent to use. You don't even know its there.

Glyphix was the first software of this type, and when it originally was released it was novel, but the fonts weren't great. Now *some* of the fonts *are* great. Some of their Foundry series of typefaces, such as Garamond Condensed, are virtually indistinguishable from Bitstream Fontware.

Glyphix even uses WordPerfect's special effects, such as outlines and shadows, and throws in 31 additional effects, including stripes, diagonals, squares, gray type, striped shadows, and reverses (white type on a black background). Reverses are normally impossible with a LaserJet, but Glyphix handles them.

Glyphix even conserves printer memory. When you are using large headline typefaces, Glyphix automatically downloads only the characters you've used.

Glyphix uses two types of fonts: their regular Business series (each package has one weight of each of four typefaces), and their higher-quality Foundry series. For real DTP you need four real weights of type, so I recommend the Foundry fonts.

The Business fonts are good, and some, such as Gibraltar (their version of Gill Sans), are very good, but each font only comes in the medium weight, so bolding is accomplished electronically and doesn't look good. Italics are also created electronically by "obliquing" or slanting the typefaces. This is OK, but not a true italic. I've seen italics. Italics are friends of mine. Obliqued typefaces are no italics.

As well as the special effects and the freedom to access any size font at any time, the other advantage of Glyphix is the amount of disk space you can save. The basic

Fontware starter set of fonts takes almost 600K of disk space. Glyphix's Foundry fonts take about 800K for four weights which you can print in 117 different sizes. Overall, Glyphix is the most economical way I know to have the convenience of scaleable fonts. And if you buy their Foundry series, they're excellent fonts as well.

◆ Publisher's PowerPak

- Atech Software, 5962 La Place Ct. #245, Carlsbad, CA 92008. (619) 438-6883, 800-748-5657. PowerPak software with three typefaces $139.95; Add-on typefaces $29.95 for two faces; Monotype Professional faces $79.95 for four weights of one face

If Glyphix is the Cadillac of on-the-fly font programs, Publisher's PowerPak is the Jeep. While Glyphix requires a LaserJet or compatible, PPP works on wide printer terrain. It supports over 300 printers, and you can even create files to send to a PostScript typesetter for high-res results. The font quality is not quite as good as Glyphix, but still surprisingly good. Equally surprising is the print speed. On a LaserJet, a full page took only about 35 seconds, including the font scaling. The next page took only 10 seconds.

PowerPak gives you all the advantages of scaleable font printers, such as the ability to print any point size you want at any time, and a gigantic saving in hard disk space. PowerPak can print type in sizes from 6 to 1000-point, and certain typefaces also include compressed, expanded, and outline versions.

Like Glyphix, PowerPak offers two types of fonts: their normal "add-on" typefaces, with each package containing one weight of two typefaces, or their "Professional" typefaces from Monotype.

I personally test hundreds of software packages a year, and I have to say that PowerPak surprised me with its simplicity and speed. There's nothing complicated or fancy about it. It works, right off the bat. And while that doesn't sound glamorous, it's high praise. While I don't recommend PowerPak for the truly picky among you, I do recommend it highly to laser users who want convenience and speed, and wholeheartedly to DeskJet and dot-matrix users who want good-looking output. It's difficult to tell that the DeskJet results aren't from a LaserJet, and even the dot-matrix results are good.

While you may want some of their add-on faces for their quirky styles, the normal faces (at $29.95 for two faces) don't have real italic and bold versions. Bolding and italicizing (actually oblique) are produced electronically.

The program works for both 5.0 and 5.1, and the same package includes versions for PlanPerfect and Microsoft Word. If you have a LaserJet, PowerPak signifies added convenience. But if you have a dot-matrix or DeskJet, PowerPak will change your life.

◆ Bitstream FaceLift for WordPerfect (See Bitstream listing on page 571)

Bitstream has recently introduced a $99 program called "FaceLift for WordPerfect." This new program works like Glyphix and PowerPak by scaling fonts in your computer and sending them to any LaserJet compatible printer. Unlike these others, only FL4WP uses Bitstream fonts. It's the best way to make Bitstream fonts easier and more convenient for users of LaserJet compatible printers.

FaceLift does several important things: it enables you to print type in any size from 2 to 500 point; it makes it easier to use type because you don't have to make fonts in advance in all the sizes you want; it can save you a lot of hard disk space because you don't need all those disk-based bitmap fonts; and you can use the same fonts for both FL4WP and FaceLift for Microsoft Windows.

FaceLift is very easy to install and use. Once installed, you select typesizes just as you would with a PostScript or LaserJet III printer, in fractional point increments. It supports all of Bitstream's 360 characters, as well as WordPerfect's character sets (some in graphics mode). Adding new fonts is *very* simple as well.

FL4WP uses Bitstream's new "Speedo" font format, but the fonts themselves are the same high-quality as their Fontware line. Because their "metrics" (widths) are the same, you should get the same line- and page-endings as you would with any Fontware typeface. This means you shouldn't have to reformat any older documents which used Bitstream fonts. While you cannot use Fontware fonts directly, it is possible to upgrade from Fontware to Speedo (call Bitstream for exact details).

FL4WP gives you control over which fonts are downloaded to the printer (for speed) and which are sent as graphics (to save memory) so you can tweak it to your specifications. Because Speedo fonts are designed to appear smoother than Fontware, they tend to print a bit heavier. With this in mind it's a good idea to adjust your printer to a lighter setting.

FL4WP comes with 13 typefaces: Swiss and Dutch in four weights (roman, bold, italic, and bold-italic) and four decorative faces including Park Avenue (not one of my favorites), Bitstream Cooper Black, Brush Script, and the exotic "Formal Script." A "Companion Pack" is also available. This is an excellent value and offers 24 additional faces for $199. These include four weights of: Bitstream Amerigo; Bitstream Charter; Century Schoolbook; and Futura Light (Italic, Condensed and Extra Black). Display faces include Swiss Compressed; Swiss Extra Compressed; Exotic (Peignot) Demi and Bold; Coronet Bold; ITC Zapf Chancery Medium Italic; and Clarendon roman and bold. If you're a Bitstream aficionado using a LaserJet II (or compatible), then interface with FaceLift.

A note for LaserJet III users of Bitstream type: Bitstream has released a conversion program available to transform Fontware scalable outlines into LaserJet III format. Contact Bitstream at 800-522-FONT.

◆ MoreFonts

→ MicroLogic Software, 6400 Hollis Street, Suite 9, Emeryville, CA 94608. MoreFonts $99.95; additional types $69.95 for four weights of one face

The name of this product reminds me of the jingle for Raisin Bran cereal: "More raisins than you have ever seen before; if you like raisins, plump, juicy raisins, you'll like Post Raisin Bran more . . ." In this case, it would go, "If you like fonts, flashy special effect fonts, you'll like MoreFonts More."

Unlike Glyphix or PowerPak, MoreFonts does not work inside of WordPerfect to scale fonts. MoreFonts is similar to Fontware or Type Director in that it creates fonts on-disk to be downloaded by WordPerfect. You also have the disk-space-saving option of just creating the fonts as you download them from within MoreFonts.

And while MoreFonts fonts are good, what makes them *really* special are the special effects. While a program such as Font Effects is designed to take your existing fonts and jazz them up, MoreFonts uses its own typefaces to create some of the most striking special effects I've ever seen. I mean it. Kaleidoscopic explosions of pattern, wood grain, airbrushed "fog," normal fountain fills, sunrise/sunset fountain fills created from lines (these are gorgeous), outlines, contours (outlines within outlines), drop shadows, 3-D drop shadows, gray patterns, normal reverses, and pattern reverses where the special effects create a box surrounded by black or white text.

You don't have to guess about what you're going to get either. If you have CGA, EGA, VGA, or Hercules, MoreFonts will show you the fonts, on-screen exactly as they will print. This allows you to fine-tune the special effects without endless trial-and-error printouts.

A type connoisseur friend of mine calls this type of stuff "jazz-bo," which is a pretty good description. While you can easily overdo these dramatic effects, when you want drama, effects from MoreFonts are extraordinary.

MoreFonts automatically installs these fonts into either 5.0 or 5.1. MoreFont's normal font generation is quite fast, so it's practical to generate the fonts as you download them. But the special effects require plenty of processor power and can take five minutes or so in larger sizes, so it's a good idea to create downloadable fonts on-disk for them.

The standard package includes four weights each of Times and Helvetica-like fonts, and one weight each of fonts which look like Broadway, Cooper Black, Coronet, University Roman, and Bodoni.

Additional packages include fonts which look like Helvetica Narrow, Avant Garde, Lubalin Graph, Bookman, Century Schoolbook, Palatino, Baskerville, Bodoni, and Tiffany. Each package of four weights costs $69.95. The font quality is quite good, but is best at 12-point and above. While not as good as Bitstream Fontware, I'd have to say that MoreFonts typefaces are as good, if not better than, HP/Compugraphic Intellifonts.

A single MoreFonts package will work with WordPerfect, Microsoft Word, Ventura, and Windows. For WordPerfect, the program creates fonts for LaserJet-compatible and DeskJet printers (DeskJets must have RAM cartridges).

MoreFonts is a great way to add incredibly flashy display typefaces for a modest cost.

◆ A Times Roman by any other name

In the review of Glyphix, I said it used "versions" of major typefaces. Swfte can't call their typefaces by those well-known names, however, and the reason might interest you. Then again it might not, so don't feel compelled to read any further. One of the strange points about typefaces is that they can't be copyrighted. The only part of them which is protected is their name. That's why many foundries have almost the same typefaces, but with different names. Swiss and Dutch can't be called Helvetica and Times Roman because while they look almost exactly like the originals, the names are copyrighted.

While foundries *do* license typefaces from each other (many of Bitstream's typefaces are licensed), sometimes they redesign the face slightly and give it a new name. Some foundries feel their redesigned face is an improvement over the original, and some of them are. Other times foundries do this because the original owner won't license it, and there's always the economy involved with not having to pay someone else.

A licensed typeface is almost always a guarantee of authenticity because the original foundry usually has the option to check the final product to make sure it meets their standards. Sometimes it's also a guarantee of quality, but not always. I've seen some licensed typefaces which were awful and some homegrown versions which were excellent, as some of Glyphix's are.

➜ What to look for in a font

That's why you've got to start looking at type for yourself. Look closely. I don't mean look under a magnifying glass, because few people read while looking through a loupe. I mean look closely, look at the quality. Does it look lumpy? Are all the characters the same weight, or are certain letters darker than others? Are they smooth or are they jagged? Is the baseline straight, or do certain letters print higher on the line than others, like on a bad typewriter. Is the typeface too heavy, so that even the normal weight looks bold? Or is it too light, so that parts of the characters disappear, giving the character a broken-up look?

Compare the typeface with other typefaces of the same resolution. Most laser printers print 300 dots per inch. Don't compare something from your laser printer to *Time* magazine and expect the two be the same quality. Laser printers now cost under $1,000, while traditional typesetting machines print up to 2450 dots per inch and cost at least $25,000. So there are going differences.

Look at real type from a real printer. Most type samples, including Bitstream's and Adobe's, are not laser-printed, they are typeset. Examples from some other companies are laser-printed, but then they are photographically reduced so they appear sharper. Your mileage may vary, which means that you *must* look at what actually comes out of the printer, not what's on the box. The companies aren't being dishonest; the samples are of their type, they just aren't shown at the same 300 dpi you will probably be using.

◆ Font Effects

➡ SoftCraft, 16 N. Carroll St. Suite 500, Madison, WI 53703
(608) 257-3300. Font Effects $95

LaserJet owners often feel like supporters of Jimmy Carter. There are lots of them out there, but for a long time they were soundly ignored. There are many more LaserJets around than there are PostScript printers, but PostScript printers garner all the attention. This might be because it takes a little more effort to get LaserJets to do some of the flamboyant things PostScript printers do.

One spectacular alternative is a program called Font Effects. Talk about value for money—it can take any LaserJet-compatible font and add shadows, create outlines, and stripe or fill them with gray or checkered patterns. This program creates some of the finest special effects I've seen for LaserJet fonts. You can create unlimited special effects on fonts, and they all appear razor sharp.

Let's say you need a font with narrow characters—a "condensed" font. You don't have to buy a new typeface package. You simply modify an existing one with Font Effects to make it half as wide. Or perhaps you need a short, wide font. With Font Effects, you can create a new font which is just as wide but only half as tall, or the same width and taller, or whatever you want. These variations allow you to use more words in a headline, and give you a greater degree of flexibility with the fonts you already own. The jagged edges often associated with resizing bitmapped fonts are not a problem thanks to a remarkable "fillet" function which fills in rough edges.

EFFECTS

But we're not through yet. Font Effects gives you inverted or reverse fonts which print white on black. White type on a black background may be more difficult to read than black on white, but it can also attract attention and add visual interest to a page. Font Effects will reverse most type up to 24-point. (Actually, Font Effects will reverse any size type, but because the LaserJet Plus limits the size of any single font, it won't print an inverted 30-point font.) The LJ Series II with added memory does not have this limitation, but with the standard 512K, large reverse fonts may not fit in memory. (Hint: Turn kerning off if you're going to use any of these reverse fonts.)

Font Effects does another trick I like: it creates "gray" letters, with the gray ranging from a smooth medium tone to a very coarse checkerboard light gray. You can even combine these special effects, creating narrow, outline, shadow, slanted, 22-point fonts. You can change a font as often as you like. The process itself takes anywhere from about one minute for smaller fonts, to as long as 10 minutes for resizing and filleting large fonts.

Font Effects provides 15 different features with which to modify type, and they can all be utilized in endless variations. These effects include outlines, pattern fills, contours (also called "inline," in which a white line is formed just inside the outside edge of characters), stripes, checkerboard, shades of gray, shadow, drop shadow, reverse, box, widen, narrow, embolden, slant, and fillet.

Font Effects is a great way to enhance the typefaces you already own, and can create distinctive fonts for logos, banners, advertisements, stationery, report covers—any circumstance in which big, flashy type is appropriate. For sensational-looking LaserJet fonts, Font Effects can't be beat. For information on installing Effected fonts with WordPerfect, see the review of the LaserFonts Manager earlier in this chapter.

➾ At long last keytops

If you produce computer documentation of any type, keystrokes are a must. You also know how hard it is to find something that looks like a keytop and looks good. I've known people who've gone to the extreme of designing key shapes, having them reproduced in rub-on sheets, and rubbing them on the finished pages. But now there's hope (at least about this). At my urging, SoftCraft, pioneers in computer

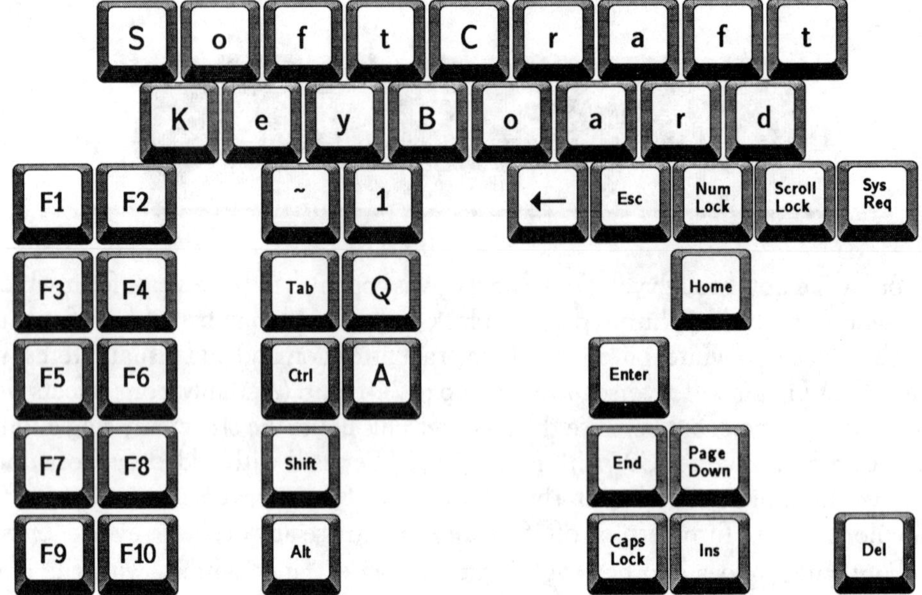

typesetting, developed a new font for LaserJets and compatibles called "Keyboard," or "Keytops," or something like that. Anyway, all you have to do is look at them to know they're going to be useful.

You'll also need SoftCraft's LaserFonts to install the font for WordPerfect, but this font will vastly improve the look of documentation. If you produce documentation, you are going to want to get your hands on a set of these babies.

When complete, the set will include all the keys on the keyboard, including the entire upper and lowercase alphabet, and all numbers and symbols. Hooray!

- Owners of the original LaserJet, see Chapter 21 for a new and unusual selection of fonts on cartridge from UDP.

◆ Additional soft font vendors

- DigiFonts, Inc., 528 Commons Dr., Golden, CO 80401. 800-242-5665, (303) 526-9435. DigiDuit Installation program and 8 typefaces $89.95; Additional typefaces, $29.95 per disk (of about 8); Complete library of 271 typefaces, $369.95; Installation programs for WordPerfect, Ventura, Windows/PageMaker, and Microsoft Word, $20 (each).

If you want the biggest type library at the smallest price, DigiFonts is your choice—around $460 buys a whopping 279 typefaces. DigiFonts uses their own proprietary font format, but the fonts are quite good. While not all DigiFonts' faces are as good as Bitstream's, the quantity and selection is overwhelming, containing scores of decorative display faces not available elsewhere.

Generating DigiFonts is very fast, even faster than the latest version of Fontware, and installation into WordPerfect is automatic. What's more, DigiFonts can automatically create outline and shadow fonts of any typeface, and other special effects such as pattern fills are also included. As an added bonus, all DigiFonts typefaces are compatible with Corel Draw.

If you want big type but have little printer memory, DigiFonts allows you to create fonts which contain only the characters you're going to use. This can save so much memory that you can actually print huge type, even with 512K.

Here's an example: a 72-point font in a normal US character set can take as much as 400K of printer memory. Obviously, that's not going to fit into the 380K available on the LaserJet II. But if all you want is a headline which reads "WAR DECLARED!" you really only need eight characters. A font with only those eight characters takes 43K and easily fits into memory.

If you use other programs that need downloadable fonts, such as Ventura or PageMaker, DigiFonts will install the same fonts into all these programs. This means you only need one copy of the fonts on your hard disk, which can save you megabytes of disk space. DigiFonts even maps characters correctly into the complex WordPerfect character set (and the character sets of the other programs as well).

➻ Mephistopheles Systems Design, 3629 Lankershim Blvd., Hollywood, CA 90068-1217. (818) 762-8150. $99 per typeface package

Mephistopheles bills their fonts as "Devilishly Good." I'd agree with them. They make the most carefully hand-tuned LaserJet bitmap fonts on the market. And don't worry—despite their name, they're anything but sinister.

While systems such as Fontware and Type Director use mathematical "hints" to create their bitmaps, the typographers at Mephistopheles use their eyes. Sometimes moving a single dot here or there can make the difference between a rough edge and a smooth one, or a font which is true to its original design and one that appears to be a little off. With careful "tuning," the finished fonts are sharp and, most important to those who care about type, true to their original designs.

All Mephistopheles fonts are licensed from Linotype, Monotype, Compugraphic, ITC, and other established type foundries. This means none of their fonts are "like-Optima" or "like-anything else." They *are* Optima, or the genuine article.

The plus side of hand-tuned bitmap fonts is that they are the highest quality. The downside is that they are more expensive, and, unlike font generation systems such as Fontware, they come in a limited number of sizes.

Mephistopheles has a very large library to choose from. While many of these faces are available from other vendors, Mephistopheles has many typefaces simply not available for the LaserJet from anyone else. These include New Caledonia; Caslon 3, 540, and Black (Caslon is a classic); Cochin (very popular and distinctive); Corona; David (Hebrew); Frutiger 45, 65, 75; many weights of Helvetica; Janson; Kabel (a distinctive deco sans serif), Kunstler Script (one of the most elegant traditional script fonts); Times (including Cyrillic layouts); Gill Sans (the *real* Gill Sans); Bembo; and Arial. If you're really into type, you'll appreciate Mephistopheles's fonts.

- Weaver Graphics, Fox Pavilion, Box 1132, Jenkintown, PA 19046. (408) 728-4000. LJ Fonts $29.95

Weaver makes great dingbats for LaserJet users. The complete set costs $60 and is a good way to add visual interest to documents. They sell all their fonts by individual weight (such as Times Roman Italic), so you can buy exactly what you want. Each weight includes sizes from 6 to 30-point, and costs $29.95. All Weaver's fonts are inexpensive and good. You will need a program such as SoftCraft's Font Installation in order to use these fonts with WordPerfect.

❖ *To clip art or not to clip art*

By this time you should know that WordPerfect combines text and graphics. If this revelation is a big surprise, you need professional help. Find a parade and join it. Most people have little trouble producing text (everyone thinks they're a writer), but fewer people consider themselves artists. Even with the array of graphics programs available, the old adage "Garbage in, garbage out" still applies. I find it much easier to "draw" in a draw program than a paint program because I can combine basic geometric shapes and come up with something vaguely recognizable.

If you've got a scanner, the world is your clip art. But remember that graphic images are covered by the same copyright laws that words are. Dover Publications sells a huge line of reasonably-priced books filled with copyright-free illustrations of everything from Renaissance and Victorian artwork to Art Nouveau and Art Deco designs and alphabets (pictured at right). Write or call for a catalog: Dover Publications, 31 East 2nd St., Mineola, NY 11501; (516) 294-7000. You can scan these images to your heart's content. However, don't scan material from a book (particularly THIS book) or magazine and expect to dis-

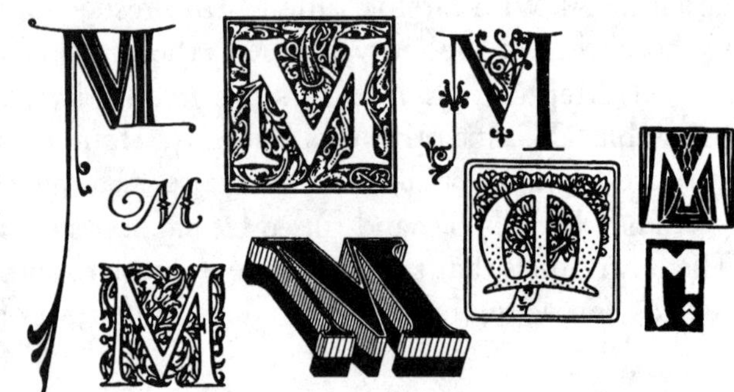

tribute it without infringing on someone's copyright. If you don't have a graphics program or a scanner, but still want to include art on your pages, electronic clip art is your best bet. I've used and can recommend the following clip art packages. Since taste and style are always subjective, I suggest you obtain catalogs from the following companies and choose the ones that match your style.

◆ Object-oriented clip art

These packages use draw-program-type line art format, and will always print a sharp image, no matter what the size. In addition, they always print at the highest resolution possible.

◆ PicturePak

➺ Marketing Graphics Inc., 4401 Dominion Blvd. Suite 210, Glen Allen, VA 23060-3379. (804) 747-6991. $145 per set (includes both .CGM and .PCX) or 3 for $350

When people ask me which clip art packages I recommend, I suggest Metro ImageBase for bitmapped art and PicturePak for object-oriented art. PicturePak's graphics are not only good-looking, but they are *useful*.

I have several packages of clip art, but many of them just don't have *useful* images. I mean, if you don't own a pet store, just exactly how often do you need a picture of a parrot? Not very often. But PicturePak covers the subjects which you'll use all the time: money, time, communications, the workplace, travel—real subjects, not just pretty pictures.

Each collection has a different business theme: Executive & Management, Finance & Administration, Sales & Marketing, Federal Governments, State & Local Governments, and US Maps and Landmarks. They may sound dull, but they aren't. Don't be thrown off by the government packages either. You don't have to be a politician to use them. Anyone in business can benefit from the excellent illustrations in these packages.

Each package contains both .CGM and .PCX versions of the same images. I recommend using the .CGM files with WordPerfect because you can make them any size from tiny to gigantic without loss in quality. If you want to customize the images, both Corel Draw and DrawPerfect accept CGM files. (Pictured: Sundial, money, letters.)

◆ PagePak

➜ Marketing Graphics Inc. 4401 Dominion Blvd. Suite 210, Glen Allen, VA 23060-3379. (804) 747-6991. $99

MGI has another little graphic trick up its sleeve and it's called PagePak. MGI's normal PicturePaks contain clip art images you place in graphics boxes but PagePak is a whole new genre of clip art. It should be called "page art," because that's what it is: full-page graphics which form the backgrounds for pages.

The package starts out simply enough with border graphics for applications such as coupons and classified ads. Then it blurs the line between clip art and page art with its full-page backgrounds for covers and title pages. These also include matching full-page designs for the insides as well.

Next, PagePak gives you full-page border artwork including a skyline newspaper, dart board, money, and a laptop computer screen, and a choice among three letterhead graphics: a fleur-de-lis, a globe, or a rose, along with matching envelopes, business cards, and labels.

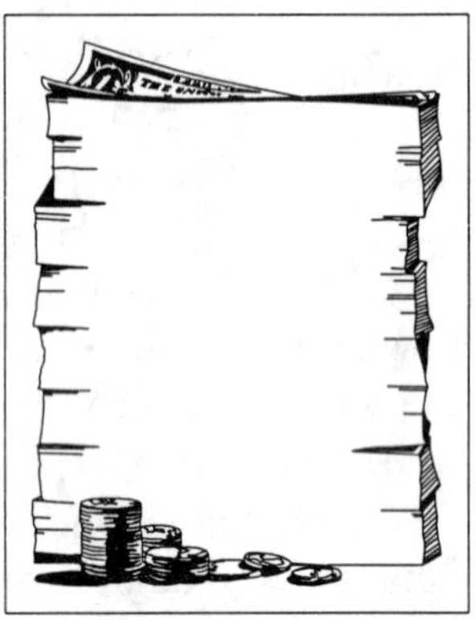

I don't recommend pinning your corporate identity to these graphics because so many other people will have them. But they are a professional-looking way to begin.

Then all hell breaks loose, and PagePak gives you memo backgrounds, fax sheets, "from the disk of," and maps of the world, USA, Canada, and Europe. Then two- and three-column newsletter backgrounds, invitations, presentations, and certificate designs.

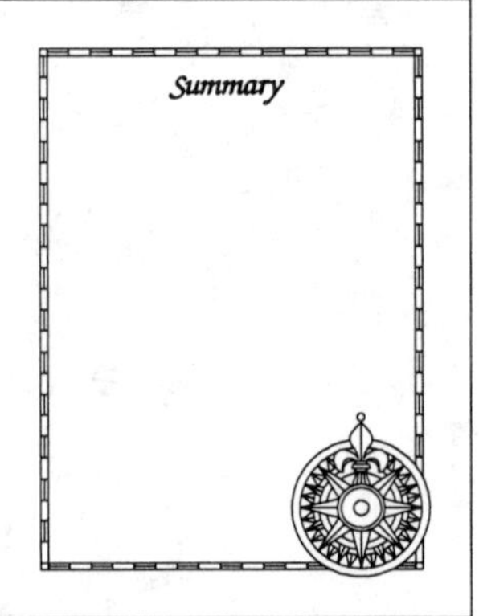

The designs include margin and advance codes for WordPerfect, but do not contain styles or font changes and are not optimized for any particular printer. PagePak is a revolutionary product which helps you add graphic impact on a full-page basis, and I recommend it highly.

(Pictured: a newspaper frame, money border, and presentation page.)

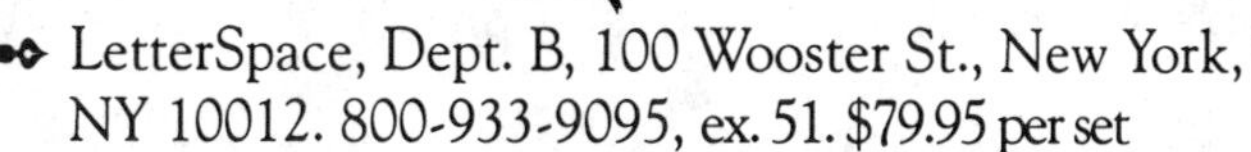

◆ DesignClips

➻ LetterSpace, Dept. B, 100 Wooster St., New York, NY 10012. 800-933-9095, ex. 51. $79.95 per set

This company's *Habitat Collection* offers sharp, striking libraries of graphic symbols I find especially suitable for logo design. These cleanly rendered images are not a bit fussy or old fashioned. A convenient way to enhance your pages with very modern, exciting graphics, these images are available in either draw or paint formats. Each disk of their Natural Environment Series is categorized by subject matter, and contains 50 images. Each image is in its own EPS file, which means you either need a PostScript printer or you must first convert them into WPG via Corel Draw to use them in WP. This is also true of all the EPS packages profiled here. LetterSpace does custom graphics too, so if you like these samples, you might want to give them a call. (Pictured above: graphics from Trees, Reptiles, & Mammals packages.)

◆ Images With Impact!

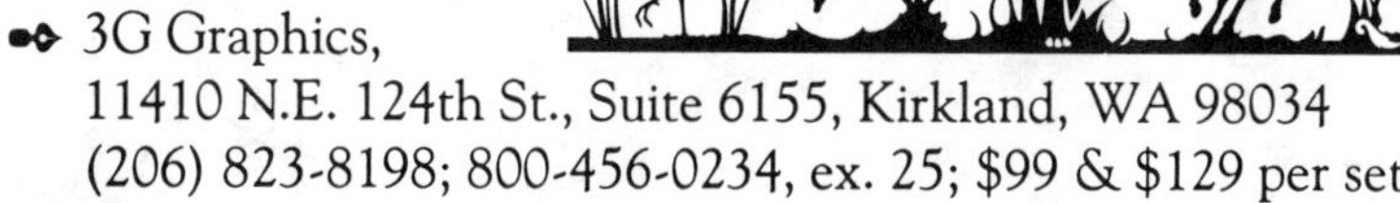

➻ 3G Graphics, 11410 N.E. 124th St., Suite 6155, Kirkland, WA 98034 (206) 823-8198; 800-456-0234, ex. 25; $99 & $129 per set

Packages of high quality clip art covering Business, Graphics & Symbols, and Accents & Borders are currently offered in EPS format only. The usual images (computers, money, travel, and food) are all here, but the Accents & Borders package rises above the norm. Over 260 images of historic, geometric, seasonal, sporting, and nature elements are offered in a variety of borders, frames, and ornaments. These are delightful designs that can be employed in a wide variety of ways to provide just the right note for that important page. A free color bonus disk is offered as an enticement for registered users. (Pictured: Animal border)

◆ Artbeats

➻ Artbeats, Inc., Dept. D, P.O. Box 20083, San Bernardino, CA 92406, (714) 881-1200, $99.95 per set

Artbeats offers four unique packages of background images, including high-tech geometric abstracts and nature-inspired images. Their newest package, Potpourri, includes confetti, paint splatters (pictured at right), fibers, lattice, and other patterns. These fun, attractive background graphics can provide a lot of interest for a page, and aren't to be missed. The files are available in .EPS and .CDR format (Corel Draw).

- **ClickArt**

  T/Maker, 1973 Landings Drive, Mountain View, CA 94043. (415) 962-0195. $129.95 per set

T/Maker's ClickArt EPS files take good advantage of PostScript's special effects. Each set includes 180 images which tend to be emphatically modern. ClickArt also offers some lively but low resolution (only 75 dpi) packages in bitmapped format at $69.95 per set. (Pictured: Phone & sissors.)

Bitmapped clip art

The next three packages all sell their wares in bitmapped, or "paint" format. These clip art packages allow you to use a program such as *PC Paintbrush* to manipulate the clip art (change its size, add text, invert it, stretch it, etc.). Remember, most bitmapped graphics can't be enlarged much or they get jagged.

- **Desktop Art**

  Dynamic Graphics, 6000 N. Forest Park Dr., Peoria, IL 61656. 800-255-8800. $75.95 per set, multiples are discounted

Desktop Art is the electronic wing of Dynamic Graphics, a large paper-based clip art company. Packages include Business, Four Seasons, Graphics & Symbols, Sports, Education, Artfolio, Health Care, and Borders and Mortices. The style of these graphics range from ultra-modern to traditional. They include realistic line illustrations, cartoon-type drawings, and decorative elements.

While the art itself is excellent, the packaging leaves something to be desired for WordPerfect users. A paint program such as PC Paintbrush is a virtual necessity for using Desktop Art, because so many images are contained in a single file. You need to separate the image you want and save it to a separate file. Unfortunately, you cannot crop these images adequately from within WordPerfect. The collections are discounted if you order more than one, and EPS packages are also available. Call for a catalog.

◆ Metro ImageBase

➻ Metro ImageBase, Inc., 18623 Ventura Blvd. #210, Tarzana, CA 91356. 800-843-3438. $145 per package

A late entry into the electronic clip art fray, Metro obviously has learned from the mistakes of its predecessors. To begin with, each file has a single image, so you don't need a paint program to edit them before you can use them. Next, each file is very large, often over 100K; even though the files are bitmapped, they offer high resolution and print a sharp image, even on Linotronic typesetters, because they were scanned at 800 dpi rather than at the 300 dpi capability of current laser printers.

The packages each consist of five high-density disks. Since these disks hold 1.2 megabytes, you'd be right to assume that you were getting 3.6 megabytes of art. But the art on these disks is compressed, which means that *each disk* really contains about 4 megabytes of art.

I'm not one to buy anything artistic by the pound (or megabyte) but the sheer size of the art tells you how sharp it's going to be on the printed page.

Most importantly, the art is wonderful. This is the most modern, attractive clip art I've seen for computers. The best thing you can say about clip art is that it doesn't look like clip art, and Metro ImageBase art doesn't.

Each package contains 100 images. Fourteen packages are now available, including Newsletters, Business Graphics, Art Deco, Four Seasons, Reports, Borders and Boxes, Exercise and Fitness, Nine to Five, Food, Weekend Sports, Team Sports, Computers, People, and Travel. This clip art is extremely varied and of excellent quality. I recommend it highly.

❖ *Graphics programs*

Here are a few graphics programs not covered in Chapter 18, *1-2-3 Publishing.*

◆ Corel Draw

➺ Corel Systems Corp., 1600 Carling Ave., Ottawa, Ontario, Canada K1Z 8R7. (613) 728-8200. $495

Corel Draw is a great graphics program. It's easy to use, relatively fast (because it runs under Microsoft Windows, you need a 286 at least), it comes with over 100 typefaces, and it gives you extraordinary control over type and graphics. If you want fancy type effects, whether or not you have a PostScript or scaleable font printer, this program is hard to beat, whether you use a PC or a Mac.

Even if you never use the drawing features, Corel is an exceptional tool for creating special type effects. This is because type is not only displayed on-screen exactly as it will print, but it can be manipulated in countless ways. It can be compressed, expanded, outlined, filled, rotated, or set to paths such as circles, arcs, boxes, or wavy lines. It can even be broken into its basic curves and manipulated as pure graphics, allowing for the creation of custom characters, which are the mainstay of logo design.

One of the elements which makes Corel's text control so special is that you can still edit text after it has been compressed, expanded, or automatically set to paths. Everything about the text can be changed: the typeface, size, kerning, word spacing, and vertical alignment. Corel's kerning feature is especially impressive because it allows for the infinitesimal control over characters which typographers need. The only time you lose the ability to edit text is when it's converted to curves for manipulation of character shapes.

Corel includes a program which converts fonts from *all* major typeface foundries, PC or Mac, including Adobe's Type 1 encrypted fonts. They call this program WFNBOSS, but I've dubbed it "Esperfonto" because it's a universal language for typefaces.

Corel Draw has also automated an important task which is manual in some other programs. Corel's "text to path" feature sets text along any path you draw. Setting text around circles or arcs is difficult and tedious to do manually, but Corel Draw does it accurately in seconds. The letters remain perfectly kerned. Text can fit inside or outside the circle or shape, and can be straightened and re-pathed at any time.

Corel Draw is an artist's dream, but it's also good for non-artists. I don't consider myself an artist because I can't draw. But I can make decent-looking pictures with Corel. Also, because Corel can import so many graphics formats, including EPS. It's the only PC-based graphics program, other than Adobe's own utterly impractical Illustrator for Windows program, which can import EPS files. While EPS files normally can print on PostScript printers only, you can bring them into Corel and then export them to WPG format for use in WordPerfect with any graphics printer. That's a pretty mean feat all by itself.

Corel also comes with a separate "autotrace" utility, called Corel Trace. While Corel has an autotrace feature built-in, this stand-alone program takes any PCX or TIF file and "traces" it, turning it into high-quality line art which can be scaled to any size without loss of quality.

If you have any artistic pretensions whatsoever, or just wish you had them, get Corel Draw. It's the most wonderful software, the kind that helps you produce on paper what you've seen in your mind, even if you never could before.

◆ Artline

Digital Research Inc., 60 Garden Court, Box DRI, Monterey, CA 93942. (408) 649-3896, 800-443-4200. $595

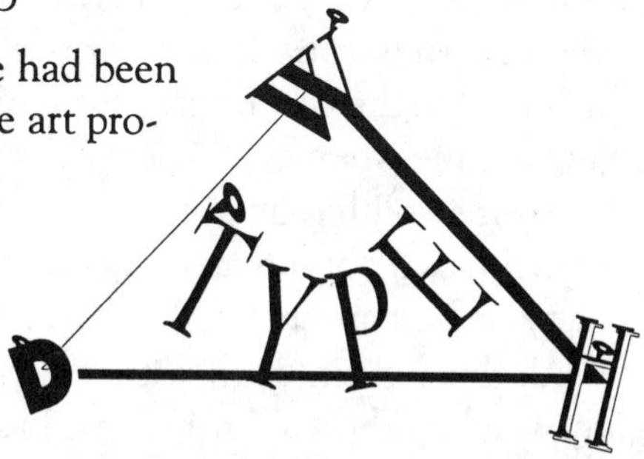

Until the new Version 2 arrived, Artline had been known primarily as a fast, XT-compatible line art program, and the first line art program to use real typefoundry fonts.

Artline 2.0 now can take its place with the big boys. It includes features like autotrace, fountains, 16 million colors, masking, blending, layers, undo, and text-to-path. Artline also forges new ground with its highly customizable user-interface, which allows you to design your own icons and designate their functions. The toolbox can be resized and it can contain as few or as many tools as you want. The tools can even be macro-like, automatically performing several functions. In a few years you're going to be seeing interfaces this innovative from everyone else, but this is just plain great today.

On the type front, this new version of Artline matches Corel Draw in that you can still edit text even after you stretch, rotate, or set it to a path. It's only when you convert the type to graphic curves that you can no longer edit it. DRI, the distributors of Artline, also promise that Adobe Type 1 font conversion will join the current Bitstream conversion. Artline has the best built-in autotrace feature yet. Of course, it can just plain autotrace like everyone else. It can also autotrace interactively, allowing you to change the level of precision based on the graphic itself. If one part of the graphic needs few points and long curves, you set the trace to a low number. If you reach a part of the graphic where you want super precision and many points, you stop, change the precision setting, then let it go. Artline has taken a feature which other programs let run wild and turned it into a very precise, interactive tool. This interaction means less need for editing later. It even has a unique halftone trace mode. This mode allows it to trace images from other programs, which even Streamline would choke on. This is superb software design.

This started out as Bitstream Goudy, but Artline allows you to customize fonts beyond recognition.

Another indication of Artline's good design is the way that it keeps track of complex paths and prevents you from creating one which is too complex to be printed by a PostScript printer. PostScript has serious limits, and while other programs blithely allow you to create paths which can't be printed, Artline won't.

Artline 2 includes: sophisticated layers which help you work on extremely complex drawings; "view bookmarks" which help you jump to commonly used views in a drawing; step in back or front one level at a time (rather than other programs which send to the very back or front in one jump); and the ability to show the actual object outline when moving or rotating, rather than just a bounding box.

Artline still has its excellent Illustrator-inspired Bezier drawing quill tool, and now includes a pop-up menu for editing Beziers, a la Corel. The only thing it can't do is place bitmaps in with line art, a limitation of GEM.

All this runs in 640K with no EMS required. CCP, the German software company which authored Artline, has brought it from an efficient but limited program to the Mercedes of draw programs.

◆ SLed

➻ VS Software, P.O. Box 6158, Little Rock, AR 72216. (501) 376-2083. $295.95

SLed is a fascinating hybrid of a paint program—a graphics power tool. The name stands for "Signature/Logo Editor" but that's a misnomer, because SLed is capable of far more than that. Not only can you perform the normal paint-type functions, but you can insert 300 dpi bitmapped fonts into your graphic, edit fonts as if they were graphics, and read and write images in .PCX and .IMG formats, and save them as downloadable fonts for use with word processing programs. SLed's most useful and unique feature is the manner in which it allows you to manipulate bitmapped type. You can enlarge it, reduce it, bolden or lighten it. You can write the font back to its original file, create a new file, or apply the new type as part of a graphic. I don't know of any other program for the PC that allows you to use high res fonts directly in a graphic, or manipulate them in such immediate, graphic ways.

If you have a LaserJet and desperately want reversed type, SLed can either create an entirely new reversed font from your downloadable fonts (which will print correctly on a LaserJet), or it can create just a headline or character in reversed type. SLed also lets you incorporate any LaserJet bitmapped fonts into a PostScript-printed page by saving them as paint files.

But unless you have CGA, EGA, or Hercules graphics, you're out of luck. Overall, SLed is a very handy program, especially when you want to play with bitmapped type.

◆ HotShot Graphics

⊸ SymSoft, P.O. Box 4477, Mountain View, CA 94040. (415) 941-1552. $245

Anyone who's ever written or even glanced at a software manual, recognizes the importance of screen dumps. I like to imagine that Bette Davis was really talking about software when she uttered the immortal line: "What a dump!" HotShot, an overnight sensation because of its ability to convert any text screen into a screen dump, is worthy of accolades, real or imagined.

While HotShot was confined to text screens, HotShot Graphics can create a screen dump of text or graphics. HSG includes all of HotShot's text screen editing features, including a paint program. While other programs can perform screen dumps (namely PC Paintbrush's Frieze utility and Halo's Grab), HSG is an entire system specifically designed to capture, edit, convert, and catalog screen dumps.

HSG's own format is compact: a 7K CGA screen dump converts into a 16K .PCX file. Conversion requires approximately 30 seconds per dump, and you can convert to .PCX, gray scale .PCX, TIFF, Encapsulated PostScript, or "printer-ready" format. You can scale as you convert, so normally tiny and distorted CGA screen dumps wind up looking great.

HSG includes all the original HotShot's annotation features for text screens, and a paint-type program for editing graphics screen dumps. The graphic editor doesn't function in CGA mode (although it will display graphics in CGA). HSG edits both its own files and .PCX formatted files. The paint program includes a fine selection of tools for curves, lines, circles, and squares, but will only fill in black, white, or one of 16 colors. If you use lots of screen dumps, HotShot Graphics will introduce you to a new artform.

❖ *Magellan—Finder of lost info*

➼ Lotus Development Corp.
55 Cambridge Parkway, Cambridge,
MA 02142. (617) 577-8500. $195

I can remember when a 5 megabyte hard disk was considered *big.* Of course, I'm the same person who can remember when gas was 25¢ a gallon, and even though this may make me sound like a grandfather, it wasn't all that long ago that these things were the reality. Now, 20 megabyte hard disks are considered small, 40 megabytes are the norm, and it's not even unusual to have 80 or 120 megabyte hard disks. All that's a blessing when you've got a mass of fonts, graphics, or text files, but it's a nightmare when you *misplace* something among 40,000,000 bytes. It's not unlike searching for a needle in a haystack.

While WordPerfect can search for words in a single directory of files, each time you search it has to all read the files. This can get old fast. More importantly, you can't have WordPerfect automatically search more than a single directory. I don't know about you, but I've got 52 directories on Drive C alone, and it's not practical to search through them one by one.

Magellan can help you to explore the deepest sub-directory of your hard disk and find whatever you need *in less than 15 seconds.* Honest. It's not one of those claims which was based on 1 megabyte of data on a '386—the time is based on a 60 megabyte, 28 millisecond hard disk running on an 8 mz '286. *Using Magellan is like turning your whole hard disk into a giant database.*

Magellan is the utility program someone should have come up with the very first moment hard disks hit the market, and it will quickly become an *indispensable* part of your life at the computer. Here's how it works. The magic is in the index. While the idea of an index isn't new, the way Magellan implements it is. In the past, indexes took hours to create and could take up a quarter or half of your hard disk. Magellan indexed my 60 megabyte hard disk in about 40 minutes, and the index took just over 1 megabyte of disk space. Each day it takes approximately 5 minutes to update the index to include all new files and changes, and that's it. There's none of this "keyword" nonsense which other programs force on you, as if you know in advance what you'll need to look for later on. Magellan indexes every single word (except for common words such as "and," "or," and "I," and you can even customize this list).

When you want to find something, you simply type in what you want to find. You can use "and," "or," and "not" to make the search more specific. Magellan searches its index, then comes up with a list of all the files which contain the words, numbers, or phrases you asked for. Magellan prioritizes them by the number of times the word or phrase is in the file, and what percentage of the file the matching words take. For example, in a search for "sheep," a file which mentioned "sheep" 65 times would be at the top of the list, while a very short file with only 5 "sheep" in it might be fourth. This indexing is so good on a hard disk that I can hardly wait to see how it can manage the mega-megabytes of CD ROM or WORM drives.

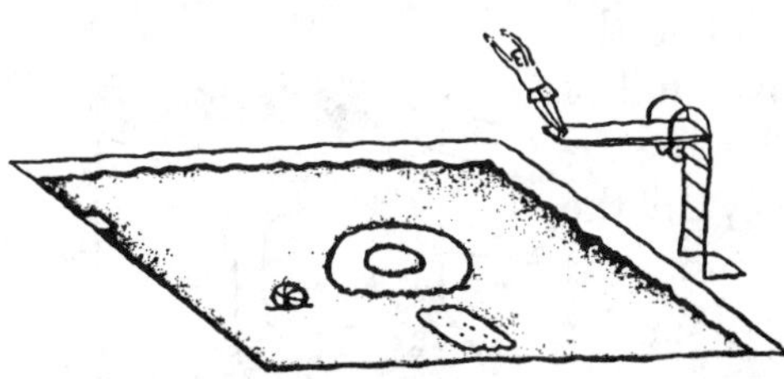

The next Magellan marvel is the inclusion of file "viewers" which display files from almost any program, including many graphics files. Magellan uses a split screen to show the file name on the left and the actual file on the right. Unlike other file management programs, Magellan shows the file just as it would appear if you were using the software which created it. 1-2-3 files look like 1-2-3 files, with the border and everything. WordPerfect files display perfectly.

Viewers are provided for the most popular software. Once you're found the file (or files) you're looking for, Magellan can "launch" the program that created the files. It loads the program and the file at once and takes only about 5K of memory in the background. When you leave the other software, Magellan returns on-screen.

Magellan has another interesting trick called "gather." This allows you to mark text on-screen and save it to a new ASCII file no matter what program was used to create the file. This permits you to selectively integrate information from many different files (and many different programs) and turn them into a single file.

The latest version of Magellan adds an undelete feature which even allows you to view the deleted file before you undelete it, the ability to ZIP, UNZIP, and index ZIPped files, backup and restore files by date, compare two files and create a new file listing the specific differences (this is faster than WordPerfect's compare, and the new file *only* includes the changes, but the file is in ASCII and doesn't use Strikeout or Redline codes), and verify (which helps you to verify if any of your files have changed, a good way to search for viruses). Magellan also includes more traditional file management tools such as copy, delete, rename, move.

I especially like the way Magellan can create groups of files. You can choose certain directories, or extensions, or just all files beginning with the letter "Z." Once you've created a group, you can display and find text only within those files. If you're like me, once a day I delete all my backup files. I created a group called "Delete Me" in Magellan and it instantly finds all files which end in .BAK (Corel), .BK! (WordPerfect), .$?? (Ventura).

Magellan includes a sophisticated macro system which allows you to automate repetitive tasks. Magellan "records" macros as you type. This means that macros aren't just for power users. If you are a power user, you can program macros as well. In fact, virtually everything in Magellan is well thought-out and easy to use. Even the on-screen help is as complete and detailed as the help in any other Lotus programs, such as 1-2-3.

The interface allows you to select commands either with function keys or by using the traditional Lotus / commands. While the documentation is beautiful and informative (full of useful tips), I wish that Lotus would assemble the excellent documentation for you. Actually, they call the manual the *Explorer's Guide,* and it's a lot of fun.

Overall, Magellan is a magnificent program. It's fast, it's easy, and it can save you a considerable amount of time each and every day. It's one of those programs you wonder how you ever lived without. *(The graphics on these pages are by artist Lonnie Sue Johnson from the Magellan manual.)*

❖ Punctuation & style checking— Good grammar are important

- Grammatik IV, Reference Software, 330 Townsend St. #135, San Francisco, CA 94107. 800-872-9933, (415) 541-0222. $99
- RightWriter, Rightsoft Inc., 2033 Wood St., Suite 218, Sarasota, FL 33577. (813) 952-9211. $99
- Correct Grammar, Lifetree software, 411 Pacific St., Monterey, CA 93940. 800-LIFETREE. $99

You need help. We all do. Good editors are few and far between. Unless my copy editor, Steve Paymer, happens to be available (unlikely, now that he's on-staff at *Roseanne*), what are you going to do? Even with Steve's eagle eye, it's easy to make mistakes while making his expert (not to mention comical) corrections.

I can recommend three different grammar checking programs. Each has different strengths, and which one you choose depends on what you need.

- **Correct Grammar**—finding genuine errors

Correct Grammar is the newest entry into this field, and its approach is unique. Rather than trying to search and destroy every single possible error, or to force users to adopt a more formal, less personal style, Correct Grammar focuses on what most people would consider *genuine* errors. Correct Grammar concentrates on grammar, not style, and this makes the program more convenient and less annoying than programs which call your attention to every single solitary little detail.

While the other programs will flag overused words, passive voice, long sentences, negatives, slang, sexisms, and euphemisms, Correct Grammar aims for the most obvious, common problems. The advantage of this approach is that it takes far less time to use than the others and, consequently, might be used more often. This is more important than it might seem. On a five-page file, a user could easily spend a half-hour with the other programs. With Correct Grammar, it would probably only take five to ten minutes. This is not because the program runs faster, or that it misses important problems, but because it is more selective in what it flags. It doesn't waste the user's time nit-picking.

Correct Grammar also seems tailor-made for use with WordPerfect. It runs from inside the WP and has the same look as WordPerfect, complete with menus along the bottom and similar function keys (F7 and F10 for Save, F2 for Grammar Search). Interactive mode allows the user to make changes as they are found, and Correct Grammar almost seems like an extension of WordPerfect rather than an entirely different program. The program also runs inside of Microsoft Word, Microsoft Works, WordStar, and SideKick.

In addition to interactive mode, Correct Grammar offers a "comment" mode. Unlike the other programs, which create straight ASCII comments, when used with WordPerfect 5, Correct Grammar creates real WordPerfect comments which display but don't print. The program also includes macros so the user can advance to the next comment or delete them all.

Correct Grammar is the right choice for users who don't need instruction in the basics, just a watchful eye for common but crucial errors.

RightWriter — when you need the all the help you can get

RightWriter goes to the opposite extreme. It tells you everything which might be wrong with your text. It provides the help needed by people who are extremely unsure of their writing ability.

RightWriter delves into every aspect of writing, including style issues. The program is especially aggressive about long, complex sentences, and this is exceptionally important if you want to avoid long, rambling sentences, like this one that you're reading right now. RightWriter also stresses the importance of the active voice in writing and calls attention to passive-voice sentences. You can also customize the program by adding terms specific to your industry, and add rules specific to your own writing style. RightWriter allows you to set it for various levels of writing, from Business to Informal. The program also provides an overall writing critique and two readability indexes.

In the following passage, Correct Grammar questioned only two items, the spelling of "dilling" and the unmatched parenthesis and quote mark. RightWriter called attention to nine items.

There is a problem of a severe nature in pickle division. It is clear that our current dilling system will not cut the mustard. We may possibly need to move on this reasonably quickly. To start, it would be advantageous to see if a new formula is do-able. (This should be looked into at once."

Unlike Correct Grammar and Grammatik, RightWriter does not work interactively, but marks up a file like this:

There is a problem of a severe nature in pickle division.
<* U12. WORDY. REPLACE BY severe problem *>
It is clear that our current dilling system will not cut the mustard.
^ <* S14. CONSIDER OMITTING: It is clear that *>
^ <* S16. CLICHE: cut the mustard *>
We may possibly need to move on this reasonably quickly. To
<* U13. REDUNDANT. REPLACE may possibly BY may *>
<* S17. WEAK: reasonably quickly *> ^
start, it would be advantageous to see if a new formula is do-able.
<* S13. REPLACE advantageous BY SIMPLER helpful or good? *>
<* U16. NOT A WORD. REPLACE do-able BY can be done *> ^
(This should be looked into at once.
^ <* P11. IS THIS PARENTHESIS CLOSED? *>
^ <* S1. PASSIVE VOICE: be looked *>

RightWriter can be launched directly from inside WordPerfect. Once it marks up a copy of your file, it reloads WordPerfect and the marked file. When you're finished making changes, RightWriter removes the marks.

➾ **Grammatik IV** – Best of both worlds?

If you can't decide between Correct Grammar and RightWriter, Grammatik IV might be your best choice. It's a cross between the two, with Correct Grammar's interactive mode and RightWriter's pickiness.

Grammatik IV can be run from inside WordPerfect. It's especially good at pinpointing incorrectly used homonyms like its/it's, and transpositions such as form/from. It's so-called "artificial intelligence" is surprisingly smart and can even finds sentences that are missing a word.

Grammatik is most effective in digging up cliches, improper punctuation, and, especially, improper use of the passive voice. The greatest advantage of Grammatik is that it's interactive. When Grammatik encounters something it considers a problem, it stops and presents you with several options. You can ignore the problem entirely (I've always been a firm believer in ignoring problems entirely), ignore a particular word or phrase, or disregard a specific type of problem entirely. Or, if you are able to accept criticism from a machine, have the program mark the problem in your file, or edit the problem yourself right then and there. Grammatik IV also includes an automatic correction feature which speeds changes but always keeps you in charge.

Grammatik offers extensive on-line help. If you don't understand a comment by the program, press F1 and a detailed explanation of that type problem appears. Some explanations run for four screens, so whatever you need to know is right there in front of you. Grammatik allows you to turn off any features you don't need (or like).

Version IV adds levels of style, including business, general, technical, informal, fiction, and custom. You can add your own rules for the program to catch, and the program now has a feature which removes all marks from the file when you're finished. Like RightWriter, Grammatik provides readability indexes so you can see the education level that is required to read your writing.

Reference Software, the publishers of Grammatik, also offer specialized dictionaries for WordPerfect's spell checker. These include Black's Law, Stedman's Medical Dictionary, and Oil Spell for the petroleum industry. (Can you spell Vaseline? I knew you could.) Grammatik is also available for the Mac. As good as these programs are, you shouldn't throw away your proofreader just yet.

◆ VCACHE - VOPT - VKETTE - VTOOLS

Golden Bow Systems, 2870 Fifth Ave. Suite 201, San Diego, CA 92103.
(619) 298-9349. VCACHE & VKETTE together $59.95; VOPT $59.95;
VTOOLS $49.95

Just a quick mention of a couple of programs which I find indispensable. VCACHE is an excellent disk cache program that utilizes conventional, extended, or expanded memory. It's the best disk cache I've used. VOPT is a disk cache specifically for floppies. Since I never have enough hard disk space, I store and download my fonts on floppies. VKETTE doubles the speed of this process and quickens the pace of all floppy-related functions.

VOPT is a remarkable program that prevents your files from being scattered about your disk. Both the *Mace* and *Norton* utilities can do this, but only VOPT can do it in 30 seconds a day. VOPT only moves the files that are not contiguous (not the entire disk, as Mace and Norton do). I put VOPT in my "autoexec.bat" file, and whenever I turn on the computer, it toils away, keeping my hard disk efficient. This results in a tremendous performance increase.

VTOOLS is a collection of handy little utility programs that make dealing with files easier. It allows you to find files anywhere on your hard disk, move files, change the date on files, compare two files, and perform many other bothersome tasks.

These little programs can make a big difference in how your system works. I, for one, couldn't live without them. (Okay, I could probably live, but I'd do a lot more whining and complaining and everyone around me would probably wish I were dead.)

◆ Less is more - PrintCache

➾ LaserTools Corp., 5900 Hollis St. Suite F, Emeryville, CA 94608. (415) 420-8777. $149

If you use a LaserJet Plus or Series II with 512K, you may have tried to print a full page of graphics at 300 dpi and found you couldn't. One solution is a program called PrintCache. Actually a "print spooler," it receives data as quickly as a laser printer, and then doles it out to the printer in the background while you continue to work.

PrintCache's "Optimization" feature can compress graphics so that they take up to 60% less space in the printer's memory. In my test, a graphics file which overflowed the LaserJet's memory and printed on two pages, printed perfectly on one page when optimized. Optimization does not affect downloadable fonts, and the difference will only be apparent on desktop published pages if many graphics are involved.

If this is all it did, PrintCache would be a worthwhile program, but PrintCache also does the work of a traditional print buffer. Instead of waiting for your slow printer, it stores the information that is sent to the printer and doles it out as the printer can take it. This means you don't have to wait around for the printer.

WordPerfect has background printing built in, but while this is working, editing is slower. Since PrintCache uses very little processing time, as opposed to WordPerfect's spool which takes a lot, PrintCache allows WordPerfect to get its processor-intensive work out of the way, so you don't have to suffer through sluggish performance.

Unlike other spoolers, which increase print time, printing with PrintCache takes no longer than printing directly to the printer. PostScript printers do not require (and cannot use) optimization; but they can use the spooler part of the program. I've found that WordPerfect can be finicky when printing to PostScript printers. If you try to continue editing while it is printing, it can freeze. PrintCache allows you to get back to work, rather than having to wait for WordPerfect's spool to finish.

21

No desktop is an island

Hardware options

While you may have used previous versions of WordPerfect on floppies, the desktop publishing features in version 5.0 and higher require a hard disk. For some of you, this may mean purchasing a new computer.

While WordPerfect runs fine on an XT-class machine, if you're serious about desktop publishing, you might want to consider an AT or compatible. These run at least four times as fast as an XT, and the performance improvement is dramatic, saving loads of time in View Document and in printing.

You can use at least 640K of memory, Hercules, EGA, or VGA-compatible graphics and monitor, and the largest hard disk you can afford—at least 20 megabytes (downloadable fonts take up an enormous amount of disk space).

Here are some AT compatibles I've tried and can recommend: the Zeos 386, the Victor 286, and WYSE 286 (all used for the production of this book), and the computers made by AST, Compaq, Dell, Epson, MultiTech, and even IBM. I especially love the keyboard on the Victor, with its big Return key and function keys on the side. It also works perfectly with everything I've tried: graphics cards, big-screen monitors, scanners, and printers.

The faster computers (386s and especially 386 SXs) are getting less expensive by the minute. We used a Zeos 386 for the desktop publishing of this book, and what a difference the speed makes. If you have the budget for a 386, get one; the time it saves you will be worth it.

Don't permit anyone to sell you more computer than you need, though. Don't be pressured into buying a PS/2 or any other computer unless you are sure it will perform better than a regular AT for your normal computer work.

The most important point to remember when purchasing a computer is to get one with a good warranty. Also, you need to determine that the company you buy from (the dealer or mail-order operation) will still be in business for the length of the warranty. Be careful about buying low-cost clones with unrecognizable brand names—you get what you pay for. Also get as much memory as you can afford (at least 640K DOS RAM, and some EMS if possible).

❖ Screen tests

If you are happy with your current computer, you still may want to purchase a larger monitor, or one with higher resolution. A big-screen monitor can save you time when formatting by giving you a much better idea of what your finished pages will look like when they are printed.

"What-you-see-is-what-you-get" really hits home to anyone who has spent long hours working with graphics for desktop publishing (DTP) while staring at a computer screen. Without a high-quality, high-resolution monitor, what you often see is fuzzy, and what you often get is dizzy. As graphics play an ever-increasing role in WordPerfect computing, high-res and full-page monitors are also becoming increasingly important.

Neither EGA nor Hercules (the current PC graphics standards) deliver very high resolution or display more than about a third of a page at a time. Even the Mac, known as a graphics computer, has a monitor with resolution only a little higher than the PC standards, and one which is often inconveniently small.

By comparison, the WYSE 700, the smallest and least expensive of the high-resolution displays, shows a full page in View Document with four times the resolution of Hercules graphics—in other words, it's four times as sharp.

Larger monitors, like televisions, aren't necessarily superior. Because the resolution of a monitor is independent of its size, a bigger monitor isn't always easier on the eyes. Here's why: 350 lines on a 12-inch monitor will be closer together and sharper than 350 lines on a 14- or 19-inch monitor. Characters and images on the smaller monitor appear sharper. All the monitors mentioned here come with their own high-res graphics cards. I'll cover two of the most popular monitors, each representative of its type. The first is a true full-page portrait monitor—it shows 66 lines of text and a life-size full-page in View Document (life-sized).

◆ MDS Genius

- Micro Display Systems, 1310 Vermilion St., Hastings, MN 55033. (612) 437-2233, 800-328-9524. Resolution: 736 x 1008 pixels; pixels per inch: 100 x 100; screen size: 8" x 11"; image area: 7.5" x 10.5"; One year warranty. $999

One of the first, and possibly best-known, full-page monitors for the PC was the MDS Genius. This monitor offers complete compatibility with all text-based programs. The Genius display is the only full-page monitor supported by WordPerfect, and the one I used while writing this book.

You can view up to 66 lines of text on the Genius, and that's more than a full page of type. While 66 lines is standard, utility programs that come with the monitor allow you to display up to 82 lines per screen. Remember that even 66 lines is more than a normal page of text, making the Genius an excellent monitor for writers, editors, and users with large spreadsheets.

Surprisingly, the display fills all 66 lines with more speed than many regular 24-line monitors. Text can be displayed black on white, or white on black, and even double height.

The Genius also offers the widest software support of any of the large screen monitors, so you can use it with a wide variety of graphics software; PC Paintbrush, HALO, and AutoCAD all list the Genius display on their install menus. This simplifies installation because no additional software drivers are necessary. The Genius is so popular that it is often the first large monitor new programs support.

The Genius has a resolution of 100 dots per inch. Because it displays 100 dots both horizontally and vertically, the pixels are considered "square," delivering a very accurate display of the printed page.

The Genius screen is so sharp that you can easily read the text page using View Document (except in facing pages mode). In full-page mode, details which are invisible on EGA or Hercules appear. In 200% mode, every detail, no matter how small, is clearly visible. The Genius is tall and narrow, however, and in facing pages mode, the pages are not much larger than on a standard screen.

The Genius full-page display emulates IBM monochrome and CGA—at the same time. The top half of the screen is monochrome, and the bottom simulates CGA, so the monitor is compatible with a great deal of graphics software which doesn't support its full-page, high-resolution mode. Programs such as 1-2-3 and Symphony can display a worksheet on the top half of the screen and a graph on the bottom. The CGA mode does not work with all programs, however.

Overall, the Genius is a versatile, doubly-useful monitor that enhances both graphics- and text-based software. If you do much writing or word processing, the full-page Genius can be an effective timesaver. Despite the $1795 price tag, this is no longer a luxury, but a means of reducing the number of test prints and improving your overall word processing and desktop publishing capabilities. Once you get used to 66 lines of text and a full-page View Document that you actually can read, it's difficult to imagine writing or editing with anything else.

◆ WYSE 700

➺ WYSE Technology, 3571 N. First St., San Jose, CA 95134. 800-GET-WYSE. Res: 1,280 x 800 pixels; pixels per inch: 125 x 105; screen size: 12" x 9"; image area: 10.1" x 7.6". One year warranty. $999

The WYSE 700 is not a true "full-page" monitor. It's a large, 15" high-res monitor that displays 25 lines of text, just like any other monitor, but with extremely high resolution in View Document mode. The Wyse's strength is its relatively low price and its relatively high resolution.

As well as functioning in high-res View Document mode, the Wyse functions in high resolution mode with GEM, Ventura Publisher, Windows, PageMaker, PC Paintbrush, HALO, AutoCAD, 1-2-3, Symphony, and most other graphics and CAD packages. If software doesn't specifically support the Wyse's high-res mode, the monitor is compatible with CGA. While CGA still has low resolution, it *looks* better on the Wyse than on regular CGA monitors.

Any text-based program (including word processing programs) can be used and the characters are exceptionally large and sharp characters. Text programs are displayed only as white characters on a black background, not black characters on a white background.

The Wyse has a wide screen that displays facing pages in a larger size than any other monitor I know of. You can actually read the type, and you just can't do that on most monitors (except in 200% mode). This may be the best value among high-resolution monitors for anyone who wants higher resolution and a medium-size display area. Wyse makes many other fine products, so give them a call.

❖ *Laser printers*

◆ LaserJets and compatibles

While there are many brands of laser printers, they are all based on engines from a few companies. Canon produces the engines for their own printers, as well as those from HP, QMS, and Apple. Canon engines can print up to eight pages per minute. Ricoh produces two different engines for their printers as well as those from TI, Acer,

Okidata, AST, Destiny, Epson, Quadram, and others. Ricoh's large engine (which I don't recommend) prints as many as eight pages per minute. Their small engine prints as many as six pages per minute. Kyocera produces their own engine, which is also used by Mannesmann Tally. It prints as many as ten pages per minute. NEC makes their own engines which can print as many as eight pages per minute. I say "as many as" because this rating is based on repeat printings of the same page. The printers are quickest when you send a file once, then tell the printer to print several copies of it.

Personally, I prefer Canon engines, because they are easy to set up and maintain, and they are economical. In my experience, you can actually print 4,000 pages on a single drum/toner unit that costs about $99. Other printers I've tried ran out of toner after only a few hundred desktop-published pages, and the toner cost $30.

Canon engines produce the best print quality and are also the quietest. If you think all laser printers are quiet, you should take a listen to some like the AST TurboLaser. When I turned on this Ricoh-engine printer my wife Toni ran into the room, ecstatic. She thought I'd finally bought a washing machine. (We finally *did* buy a washing machine and she's *really* happy now. Can you believe we've been married 14 years and never had our own washer? Several laser printers, but no washer.)

I used a LaserJet II and a QMS PS 810 to prepare all the material in this book because I admire their capabilities more than the others I've tried. I also used a LaserMaster LM 1000 for the final output. You, however, will have to decide for yourself.

There are several points to bear in mind. Don't buy a laser printer just because it's inexpensive. I've been witness to some really unpleasant machines that were loud, had terrible print quality, used excessive amounts of toner, and jammed often. I won't say the brand name, but the initials are "C. Itoh JetSetter" (my wife spells this "AST Turbolaser").

To achieve WordPerfect perfection, you need a laser printer that is either LaserJet- or PostScript-compatible. Some LaserJet emulations are excellent, such as that of the Mannesmann Tally. Others are close, but no cigar. "Close" often isn't close enough, so I'd recommend that you test the printer of your choice with WordPerfect and whatever fonts you intend to use. Cart all your disks down to the dealer and check it all out very carefully. Choosing the wrong laser printer can be an expensive mistake.

If you need a printer with two paper bins, look into the LaserJet IID, QMS PS 820 Plus, or Mannesmann Tally 910.

❖ Some items to consider when choosing a printer

- What does it emulate? How good is the emulation?
- If it has fonts built-in, are they identical in width to those available for LaserJets or PostScript printers? WordPerfect supports many laser printers, but Bitstream fonts will only work with LaserJet compatibles and PostScript printers.
- How much memory does it contain? The LaserJet has 512K standard and is expandable to 4 megabytes. Some models of Okidata only have 640K and there's no way to expand it. This limits the amount of graphics you can use.
- Can you expand the printer's memory? How much does more memory cost? Can you add PostScript?
- Can you use cartridge fonts, and if so, are they identical to the LaserJet fonts?
- Can it print on envelopes? This is a more important consideration than you might think. Not all printers can. You really can print envelopes efficiently in WordPerfect, so don't overlook this. Canon engines can print on envelopes. The small Ricoh engines can, the large Ricoh engines can't. Kyocera and NEC printers can.
- How much are consumables (toner, drum, etc), and how long do they **really** last?
- How loud is the fan?
- How long is the warranty?
- How fast does it **really** print? When a printer claims to print eight pages per minute, that refers to eight copies of the same page a minute, not eight different pages. Some printers are faster than others, even though they have identical ratings.
- Does the printer have a parallel port? If not, it's going to require a lot more time to print with WordPerfect.
- Print out a solid black page. How solid is the black? Is it even? Is it dark? Is it blotchy?
- Print out a gray screen that fills the page. Is it even or does it become lighter or darker around the edges?

◆ Hewlett-Packard LaserJet III

➡ Peripherals Group, 16399 West Bernadino Dr., San Diego, CA 92127. 800-752-0900. $2,395

If you're going to purchase any new laser printer, the very first one you should look at is the LaserJet III. Heck, this is the last printer you should look at, as well. The HP LaserJet is the standard by which all non-PostScript printers are measured. It's quick, quiet, and (amazingly) competitively priced (you can often purchase them for around $1,700). As with all Canon engines, the print quality is unsurpassed. The blacks are black, and text is sharp and crisp. You can use two font cartridges at a time, and envelopes print just fine.

Not only is this printer less expensive than the LaserJet II (which has now been discontinued), but it has built-in scaleable fonts, more memory, and a feature called *resolution enhancement.*

While the LaserJet III uses the same 300 dpi engine as the Series II, it includes a special chip which makes the resolution appear much higher. This chip can change the size of the laser beam and move it in 1/600th-of-an-inch increments so that it can fill in "jaggies." The results, while not as sharp as LaserMaster's 800 and 1000 dpi controller cards, is head and shoulders above other 300 dpi (and even 400 dpi) printers.

➡ PostScript-like features, LaserJet affordability

Like PostScript printers, the LaserJet III can rotate fonts to any angle, print white type on black backgrounds, and fill type with shades of gray. The III provides the freedom and ease of use of PostScript printers without the high price. No longer must you buy or generate fonts in every size you need, and your hard disk isn't choked with fonts. Font scaling is what most people have always wanted from PostScript. The LJ III makes it real and affordable.

The LaserJet III also is expandable enough to keep up with the times and nice enough not to turn its back on the past. You can add more memory easily, and a PostScript cartridge is also available. Unlike earlier PS cartridges, such as the Pacific Page, this one doesn't take forever to print. The printer includes a "video" port so that expansion boards, such as those from LaserMaster and Intel, can be used with the printer. The printer is also 100% compatible with all LaserJet II software and fonts.

Not everything is perfect. As with previous LaserJets, you should consider adding at least a megabyte of memory to get the most out of the printer.

The built-in Compugraphic fonts are just acceptable and not nearly as good as those from Bitstream and Adobe. CG-Times at 10-point is squashed, uneven, and downright ugly. CG's other downloadable fonts, while only $99 per set, also are not the highest quality. Not to worry—Bitstream offers a program which converts any Fontware typeface into LaserJet III format, and other major typeface foundries also will be offering fonts in this new format.

It's reasonably priced. It's high quality. It's reliable. It's expandable. With this combination of features, and HP's well-deserved reputation for quality and reliability, I don't see how you can go wrong with this printer.

◆ Hewlett-Packard LaserJet IIP

➻ Peripherals Group, 16399 West Bernadino Dr., San Diego, CA 92127. 800-752-0900. $1,495

The IIP (petite) is the III's baby sister. It's smaller, slower, doesn't have resolution enhancement or scaleable fonts, and you should be able to buy it for under $1,000. While the printer is cute and inexpensive, if you're going to be doing much DTP, the III is a better choice.

While the III prints eight pages per minute, the IIP prints four. That's not the problem it might seem because unless you're printing absolutely straight text with no graphics, or multiple copes of the same page, few laser printers actually print at their rated speed.

The IIP uses the same bitmapped fonts the Series II does, the same font cartridges as either the II or the III, and the same memory boards as the III. If the III isn't in your budget, the IIP is the next best thing.

◆ PDP 1-2-4

➻ Pacific Data Products, 6404 Nancy Ridge Dr., San Diego, CA 92121. (619) 552-0880. 1-2-4 Memory board from $295 to $1795

The only problem with HP's LaserJet II memory upgrades is that they aren't upgradable (the ones for the LaserJet IIP and III are). If you buy the one-megabyte board and later need more memory, you have to toss it and buy the two-megabyte board. This can get expensive. Pacific Data Products, the makers of the low-cost font cartridge, *25 in 1*, developed a memory upgrade system that makes sense. You can purchase their *1-2-4 board* with no memory, then add up to 4 megabytes. If you buy it with memory installed, you only save about $50 off HP's price, but because you can keep adding memory, you really save money when you need to upgrade. One of the reasons you'll need this extra memory is if you decide to use PacificPage, PDP's PS interpreter which requires 2 megs of memory. (A note about the PacificPage—it's good, but it's slow and doesn't use Adobe fonts.)

◆ Big fonts in little cartridges

➺ UDP Data Products, 1309 Laurel Ave., Manhattan Beach, CA 90266. (213) 545-5767. Desktop Publishing Font Cartridges, $379 each

An excellent new line of font cartridges from UDP offers fonts in sizes larger than previously available on cartridge. A Times Roman-like font in sizes from 8 to 30-point is on one cartridge, and the same sizes in a Helvetica-like font are on another. These cartridges contain 512K worth of fonts, and are a boon for anyone who uses WordPerfect on a network, doesn't want to spend time downloading fonts, or wants to save the memory that fonts normally take so they can print more graphics. These fonts are remarkably sharp and come with printer drivers so you can use them with WordPerfect. UDP is run by some very smart people—check 'em out.

◆ LaserMaster Series III Professional controllers

➺ LaserMaster Corp., 7156 Shady Oak Rd., Eden Prairie, MI 55344. (612) 944-6069. LX6 (with 4 megabytes of memory) $2,995; LX6 (6 megabytes memory) $3,995; LM 1000 $7,495

What's the fastest way to get WordPerfect to print two-and-a-half times sharper than the standard 300 dpi? The LaserMaster LX6 Professional printer controller board. The LX6 prints 800 x 800 dots per inch on a standard LaserJet II—that's seven times the resolution of a standard LaserJet. Everything from type to gray scale images looks four times as good, with a print quality which rivals typesetting machines costing $10,000 more.

The LX6 is capable of almost all of PostScript's type tricks, including scaling a single outline font from 3-point to 1200-point, rotating type, and printing white on black (although not with WordPerfect), or outline fonts. The only thing the LX6 doesn't do with type is make you wait around for it. The LX6 consists of a board which fits in any XT, AT, or 386-compatible computer. Connected to the optional I/O port of the LaserJet II (or IID) via a modular "telephone-like" cable, installing the board and software takes about 30 minutes, with the software installation being almost completely automatic.

If it isn't fast,
it isn't LaserMaster

An example of LaserMaster's special effects.

LM: A desktop publisher's dream

Another example of LaserMaster's special effects.

The LX6 is also extremely fast, usually printing a full eight pages a minute, which is as fast as the LaserJet's engine will allow. It also supports the LaserJet IID's duplex printing. The LX6 uses standard Bitstream Fontware typefaces, as well as all typefaces from Adobe and other "Type-1" fonts, (although currently only the Bitstream typefaces work with WordPerfect), so there's a huge library of high quality fonts from which to choose. The system uses all Bitstream font hints to create fonts on-the-fly that are just as sharp as bitmaps.

While it can take several minutes to download fonts to a PostScript printer, a LaserMaster can download a font in about a second. That means is that you never have to sit around thinking, "Do I have 20 minutes to spend on experimenting?" You can try as many different fonts, layouts and designs as you want because you don't have to wait for the results.

The LX6 comes with 135 fonts. You heard right. 100 more than standard PostScript printers. It includes the standard 35 fonts found in PostScript "Plus" printers. They are all "PostScript width-compatible," so it's possible to "proof" pages on the LX6 and then send them to a Linotronic for final printing while retaining correct character and line spacing.

While the LX6 is versatile, it is not PostScript-compatible, so you cannot print EPS files directly (but they're working on it). But unlike PostScript printers, LaserMaster products *never* run out of memory. You can use as many fonts as you want and graphics in any size — it doesn't matter, the page *will* print. That's not something you can say for PostScript.

For anyone who wants to use a laser printer as a final output device, the LX6 produces the sharpest pages I've seen output from a desktop laser printer. The LX6 and a LaserJet II (or III) cost around $4,800, about the price of a quality 300 dpi PostScript printer, and more than $15,000 less than the price of a Varityper 600. A six-megabyte version of the LX6 costs $3,995 (the additional memory is important for duplex printing). A network option is available for $995.

The LX6 is a realistic and reliable way to produce high-quality type and graphics. If you use WordPerfect and need the best quality output at the lowest cost, there is currently no competition for the LX6. If you can't cough up three big bills for the LX6 with 4 megabytes of memory, LaserMaster offers other less expensive options. For $1495 you can get a 2-megabyte version which provides 400 dpi and 35 fonts, or for $2495 you get the same 400 dpi and all 135 fonts.

For the high end, LM also offers the LM 1000, a printer controller board and 400 dpi printer. At print time you have the option of choosing either 400 dpi (for drafts) or 1000 dpi for exceptional quality. This duo provides resolution so high that it rivals the resolution of Linotronic typesetting machines and yet still provides high performance. If you want the highest print quality, choose the LM 1000 instead of the LX6. LaserMaster is always developing something new. Call and see what else they have up their sleeves (and tell them I sent you).

❖ *PostScript printers*

◆ QMS-PS 810

➻ Quality Micro Systems, P.O. Box 81250, Mobile, AL 36689. (205) 633-4500. $5,495

When comparing laser printers, it seems natural to compare them with cars. To begin with, they cost as much as cars did just a few years ago, and they inspire the same kind of loyalty, frustration, and joy in their owners.

With that in mind, meet the QMS PS-810, the Rolls Royce of PostScript printers. Its parallel port and fast 68000 processor make it the fastest PostScript printer for PC users. The LaserWriter NTX, even with its faster 68020 processor, is far slower because it lacks a parallel port, and printing through serial connections is slow. The QMS has parallel, serial, and AppleTalk ports, 2 megabytes of memory, and perfect Diablo and LaserJet emulations.

The 810 uses the excellent Canon SX engine that is small, quiet, and truly easy and inexpensive to maintain. Most important, it provides the best print quality of any 300 dpi laser printer (especially when the darkness control is set to 7 or 9). Solid blacks and crisp type are consistent throughout the long life of the toner/drum cartridge.

The QMS has a LaserJet emulation mode for your software that doesn't know from PostScript (or for pages with paint-type files that take forever to print with PostScript). The QMS, like all printers with Canon engines, is almost silent when not printing—there is virtually no noise, not even from the fan. This may seem trivial, but a quiet work space is always desirable and appreciated by others.

The paper path is perfectly straight, so the machine almost never jams. When it does, the top opens so far that it's a simple task to clear the jam. Thick envelopes run through the machine smoothly, and the "face-up" tray in the back stacks them neatly. The drum even covers itself (it's shy and modest) when you open the printer top, so you won't accidentally scratch it when clearing infrequent paper jams.

In general, the QMS PS-810 is the premier PostScript printer for PC users in every aspect: type quality, speed, reliability, convenience, and cost of operation. But then, you get what you pay for, and you pay a premium for the QMS.

◆ NEC LC 890

- NEC Information Systems, 1414 Massachusetts Ave., Boxborough, MA 01719. (617) 635-4400. $4,795

If the QMS is a Rolls Royce, the NEC is more like a Pinto. It gets you where you're going, and offers lots of little convenience features, but just doesn't have as much style, speed, or reliability.

It comes standard with 3 megabytes of memory, a full megabyte more than many other PS printers. The blacks are solid, and it has PostScript, as well as excellent LaserJet and Diablo emulations. It can be equipped with two paper trays, so it is efficient for office use. It has serial, parallel, and AppleTalk ports, and a convenient LCD control panel mounted on the front, with no knobs or dip switches in the back.

However, even though this printer has more memory than the QMS, it's not nearly as fast. The print quality is acceptable, and the blacks are solid, but the output is not as impressive as that produced on Canon SX engines, such as the LaserJet or QMS PS-810. Type from the NEC appears noticeably heavier, even on the lightest setting; it also seems more jagged and not as sharp as type from the QMS. "Toner fuzz" is often apparent around the edges of characters, and pages lack the crispness you get from the QMS.

I have three other complaints. The fan is loud, and this is an important consideration when the machine runs all day. This NEC is louder than a floor fan I have in my office. This can be irritating when turning the printer off and on, and reinitializing the printer several times a day is impractical.

Paper jams are another annoyance that occur with more regularity than with Canon printers because the paper path is not as straight, and the paper's position in the hoppers encourages paper curl and dust. The cover of the printer does not open very wide, which makes removing a jam or getting inside the printer at all difficult.

Appendix

Design Glossary
Recommended Reading
Product Directory
Index
About the book
About the author
Keystroke/code chart

Design Glossary

Alley. The space between columns of type on a page. See **Gutter**.

Alignment. Designation regarding the ends of lines of type, such as flush right, flush left, justified, or centered.

Ampersand. Name of the type character "&," used in place of "and."

Artwork. Images, including charts and photos, prepared for printing. It can refer to whatever is meant to be reproduced, whether it be a drawing, photograph, or text, and is treated as an artistic element on the page.

Ascender. The part of a lowercase letter that rises above the body of the letter, as in b, d, f, h, k, l, and t.

Baselines. Invisible lines where the bottom of each character rests.

BF. Copyreader's abbreviation indicating that the copy should be set in boldface type.

Bleed. Printing that extends off the edge of a sheet or page after trimming.

Block. A standard paragraph in which the first character of the first line is not indented. Block paragraphs also contain a blank line between paragraphs.

Blurb. A short summary of a book's contents to be used on the jacket copy. May also refer to a longish caption or a short block of text treated as a **readout**.

Boards. In traditional printing, the typeset copy is pasted up on a board. In desktop publishing, if you are not going to use a laser printer for your final output, you may still need to employ paste up boards for the printer to use in preparation for duplicating.

Body copy. The bulk of text in a publication. The stories and articles are the body of your publication. Headlines are not body copy, as they are set in *display type.*

Boldface. A heavier, darker version of a regular typeface.

Boxed. Matter enclosed by rules or borders.

Bullet. A large dot used as a graphic element in body copy.

Byline. A line telling the reader who wrote the article. Usually follows the headline and comes before the body copy, but can also appear at the end of an article. The byline is usually set in boldface type.

Camera Ready Copy. Finished pages prepared for the printer's camera. The camera is a *copy* camera, which photographs pages so that they can be used with the printing press. The whole idea behind desktop publishing is the ability to produce these completely ready-to-go-to-the-printer pages.

Capitals. The large letters of the alphabet. Also know as "caps" or "uppercase letters."

Captions (or Cut-lines). Sentences or paragraphs of descriptive text accompanying illustrations. They are usually set in a different style of type (often italics or boldface) to distinguish them from body copy.

Characters. Individual letters, figures, punctuation marks, etc., of the alphabet.

Clay-coated paper. A paper with an especially smooth surface, recommended for use in laser printers because the ink doesn't smudge on it. It is heavier than regular copy paper, and so can easily be sprayed with adhesive or glued with rubber cement for manual pasteup.

Clip art. Illustrations, usually black and white, which can be used without securing permission from the artist or paying royalties.

Columns. Vertical rows of text. The purpose of a column is to make reading easier by keeping lines of text shorter, while still allowing you to use a lot of text on a page.

Comp. The abbreviation for *comprehensive,* an accurate layout displaying type and illustrations in position on a page. Mainly used in advertising agencies to show clients various different layouts.

Condensed type. Narrow version of a regular typeface.

Copy. All the text on your page. Available in various flavors, the most plentiful of which is body copy.

Deckhead or deckline. The lines following the headline and preceding the byline, usually imparting more information about the article. See **Headline and Subhead.**

Descenders. The part of a lowercase letter that falls below the body of the letter, as in g, j, p, q, and y.

Display type. Type set larger than body copy (which is usually about 10 or 12 point), for headlines, readouts, etc. Attention-grabbing display typefaces are employed for effect in advertisements, promotional materials, etc.

Drop cap. Display letter that is inset into the text. May also be raised.

Dummy. A type of blueprint for page layouts. You mark off sections of a page where stories or artwork will be placed later. Dummies are a quick and efficient way to decide what will go on each page.

Editing. The process of checking copy for fact, consistency of style, spelling, grammar, and punctuation prior to typesetting.

EM. A printer's unit of measurement, refers to the width of the letter "m," used for inserting white space in a line of type.

EN. Another printer's unit of measurement, also refers to the width of the letter "n," used for inserting white space in a line of type. Sometimes called a "thin space."

Family of type. All the typestyles of available typefaces (roman, italic, bold, condensed, expanded, etc.).

Flop. *Howard the Duck* (sorry, Steve); To turn an image over so it faces the opposite way. This is usually done with portraits so that they will face the correct way on the page. A mirror-image.

Folio. Page numbers.

Font. Complete assembly of all the characters (upper and lowercase letters, numerals, punctuation marks, etc.) of one size and one typeface. Special characters (those not in a font), are called "pi" characters (bullets, arrows, stars, etc.).

Footer. Text appearing at the bottom of a page, such as a page number or chapter title, etc.

Formatting. The process of designing pages on the computer.

Galley. A long sheet of typeset text not yet in page format, often used to proof text.

Graphics. Art and other elements (including type) used on a page as a visual statement.

Grid. An arbitrary geometrical pattern that divides the area of the page into horizontal and vertical shapes (columns).

Gutter. The blank space where two pages meet at the publication's binding, or the blank space between columns of type.

Hairline. A fine line or rule, the finest that can be reproduced in printing. The next largest size in many systems is a half-point line, followed by a one-point line.

Halftone. The process of reproducing photographs so they can be printed on a large press. Photos have a "continuous-tone" that are converted into a "halftone" by photographing the original through a fine cross-line screen. This is necessary for quality reproduction of the photos, and is performed at the printers' before plates are produced for printing.

Hanging Indent (Outdent). A style in which the first line of copy is set full measure, and all the lines that follow are indented.

Hard copy. Type which is printed on a piece of paper, as opposed to type on the screen of a computer. It is useful to print out a hard copy of a page as a rough draft for proofing before you print out a final version.

Header. A line of text (such as the title of a publication, name of article or chapter), appearing at the top of a page.

Headlines. Lines of type (set in a display type, a larger size than body copy), telling readers what the story or article is about. They are often accompanied by subheads (or deckheads), which are smaller headlines. Also abbreviated as "hed."

Hung initial. Display letter set in the left-hand margin.

Indent. An indented paragraph is the most common style. The first line of each paragraph is indented, usually 3 or 5 spaces, with no blank lines left between paragraphs. The indent can be longer or shorter, depending on the effect you want.

Initial cap. The first letter of a body of copy, set in a display type for decoration or emphasis. Often used to begin each chapter of a book, it may be either dropped into a paragraph or raised above it.

Insert. A separately prepared and printed piece which is inserted into another printed piece or a publication.

Italic. Letterform that slants to the right: *Italics appear like this.*

Jumphead. The headline appearing above an article continued from another page. The jumphead may only contain one or two words of the original headline.

Jumpline. The line which is to be continued from the end of a column of text, stating the page the article jumps to. Also at the top of the column, under the *jumphead,* stating where the article was continued from.

Justified type. Lines of type that align on both the left and the right of a column's full measure.

Kerning. Adjusting the space between letters so that part of one letter extends over the body of the next. Kerned type is more pleasing to the eye.

Kicker. The words positioned just above the headline. Usually in a smaller typesize, flush left, sometimes underlined. Also called a "teaser."

Landscape. A horizontal page, printed so that the width of the page is greater than its height. A vertical page is called *portrait.*

Layout (or Make-up). The placement of all elements, including text and graphics, on a page. Layout is the design process, and **make-up** involves the physical paste-up of the elements. In desktop publishing, layout is also referred to as *page composition* or *page processing.* A layout specifies the sizes and styles of type, the positions of illustrations, spacing, and general style.

Leading (pronounced ledding.) The term originates from a time when thin strips of lead were inserted between lines of type to achieve proper spacing. Leading determines the amount of white space between lines of type, and can be expressed as "10/11," or "10 on 11,"(10-point type with 11-point leading).

Letterspacing. Adding space between individual letters in order to fill out a line of type and improve appearance.

Ligatures. A ligature refers to two connected characters, like "ff" is when typeset, or the "ae" in *Encyclopædia Britannica.* Kerned pairs of letters, such as the "ff" and "fi," may fit closely together enough so as to resemble ligatures, but most software doesn't support them (since they are not included in many fonts).

Line drawing. Any artwork created by solid black lines, usually with pen and ink.

Linotron. Trade name for phototypesetting machines and systems manufactured by Mergenthaler Linotype.

Logotype. "Logo" for short. Two or more type characters joined together for use as a trademark or company signature. Can also refer to any type and artwork combined to represent a single graphic element or distinctive symbol.

Lowercase. The small letters, as opposed to the capitals.

Measure. The length of a line of type, normally expressed in picas, or in picas and points.

Mechanical. The camera-ready pasted up assembly of all type and design elements located in exact position on artboard or illustration boards; instructions for the platemaker are contained either in the outside margins or on an overlay.

Modem. Short for modulator/demodulator, this is a device used to transmit data from one computer to another, via telephone lines. Utilized in desktop publishing to send files to a typesetter for higher quality.

Non-repro blue. A type of light blue pencil used especially for marking camera-ready copy or paste-up boards because the marks will not reproduce when photographed.

Oblique. Roman characters that slant to the right. Not true italics, but similar.

Offset printing. A system which uses special printing plates created directly from photographs of the original pages. Your camera-ready copy is used as the original page.

Outdent. Text on the first line of a paragraph which prints to the left of the paragraph margin.

Orphan. The last word or line of a paragraph stranded at the top of a column of text. Or the first line of a paragraph stranded at the very bottom of a column of text. This is undesirable and should be adjusted whenever possible. See also **Widow**.

Page composition. Identical to layout. The design and placement of all the elements on a page. Also called *page processing.*

Pagination. The process of putting pages into consecutive order. In page composition programs, **batch pagination** is a process in which text is automatically flowed onto pages in consecutive order. Some programs require you to **paginate manually** by using a mouse to place the text on each page individually.

Pasteboard. Laminated chipboard utilized for paste up.

Paste-up. The process of placing the type and graphic elements on the pasteboard in preparation for camera-ready copy. When the paste-up is completed it is called a *mechanical.*

Photomechanical. The complete assembly of type, line art, and halftone art in the form of film positives. Used for checking proofs and monitoring the production of printing plates.

Pica. A typographic unit of measurement equal to one-sixth of an inch. Column width is measured in picas.

Pi characters. Special characters of a font, such as arrows, bullets, stars, copyright symbols, etc. as: ® © ™ ⇐ ⇒.

Point. Smallest typographical unit of measurement, approximately 1/72 of an inch. Type is measured in terms of points, the standard sizes being 6, 8, 10, 12, 14, 18, 24, 30, 36, 42, 48, 60, and 72 point.

Portrait. A vertical page, printed so that the width of the page is less than its height. A horizontal page is called *landscape.*

Press run. The length of the printing run, or the number of sheets to be printed.

Printing plate. A surface, usually composed of metal, that has been treated to carry an image. The plate is inked, and the ink is transferred to the paper by a printing press.

Production artist. A person who performs paste up.

Proofreader. A person who checks for accuracy by reading type that has been set against original copy. Proofreaders may also read for consistency, fact, and style.

Proofs. A trial print or sheet of printed material that is checked against the original manuscript, and then subsequently used for corrections.

Raised cap. Display letter that is set above the text. The "R" at the beginning of this entry is a raised cap. May also be dropped into the text.

Readouts (or callouts or pull quotes). A readout is a section of text which is set apart from the body copy for use as a graphic element. It pulls out an important quote or statement from the text, and is set in a larger typesize than the body copy. Readouts are not headlines or sub-heads, but are most often duplicates of sentences or paragraphs of body copy used for emphasis. However, readouts can also contain sentences or paragraphs that are *not repeated* in the body copy.

Ream. A unit of measure for paper of any size: 500 sheets of paper.

Reverse type. Type that drops out of the background and assumes the color of the paper. Normally white type on a black background.

Rules. Black lines, used for a variety of effects, including borders and boxes. They come in a range of thicknesses *weights* that are measured in point sizes, the thinnest of which is called "hairline." Rules may be dotted, dashed, or contain a number of lines of various weights.

Rulers. Measuring devices which help you place *rules* (lines). On the computer screen, rulers are used as electronic measuring devices.

Running head or foot. Title or other information at the top or bottom of every page of a publication.

Sans serif. Without serifs. A clean, modern typeface, such as Helvetica (Swiss).

Scanner. A device, connected to a computer, which can convert a typewritten page or artwork (such as a photograph or line drawing), from the printed page into data which is compatible with the computer.

Serifs. The curves and flourishes at the ends of letters. Times Roman (Dutch) is a serif typestyle.

Sidebar. A shorter story than the primary one it supports, containing specific information relating to one aspect of the main article. Used to highlight a particular point, or present related or background information.

Signature. A printer's term referring to a single sheet of paper with several pages printed on each side. The sheet is then folded into "booklets" from which books and magazines are assembled. One fold creates a four-page signature, two folds, an eight-page item.

Subheads. Can be placed directly after a headline or above certain paragraphs, highlighting a specific area of body copy. Subheads stand out, and help the reader find specific topics.

Text. The body copy on a page or in a book, as opposed to the headings.

Thumbnails. Small, rough sketches used to explore designs for page layout.

Typeface. Used interchangeably with *typestyle.* A typeface is a font, such as Times Roman. Typeface can also refer to a type family designation, such as bold or italic.

Type family. A range of typeface designs that are all variations on one basic style of font. A family is usually made up of roman, italic, and bold faces.

Typestyle. Used interchangeably with *typeface.* A typestyle indicates a particular font, such as Optima.

Typography. The art and process of working with and printing from type.

X-height. A typesetting term used to represent the height of the main body of the lower case letters of a typeface, excluding the ascenders and descenders.

White space. Refers to the blank space that frames or sets off text and graphics. Also called *negative space.*

Widow. A relative of the orphan: a single word on a line by itself at the end of a paragraph. It's unattractive and makes the text harder to read.

Wordspacing. Adding space between words to fill out a line of type and improve appearance.

WYSIWYG. What You See Is What You Get (printed.) Pronounced "wissywig" or "wizzywig," depending on how you pronounce *Caribbean.* Refers to the ability to display a close representation of the printed page on the computer screen.

Read more about it

There are several books that deal specifically with desktop publishing, and a few of them that address both design and electronic publishing techniques. Here are a few of the best.

◆ Desktop Publishing

Desktop Publishing With Style 2nd Edition, *a complete guide to design techniques and new technology for the IBM PC,* Daniel Will-Harris, 1989. This practical and amusing overview offers sound advice on all MS-DOS software, hardware, and graphic design. Includes in-depth coverage of fonts, printers, paint and draw programs, scanners, utilities, graphics cards, and monitors. Replete with design tips, it graphically shows how to achieve professional results with Ventura, PageMaker, and the big three word processors, and includes over 45 full-page examples of newsletters, reports, flyers, etc. $24.95.

LaserJet Unlimited, Second Edition: *How to get the most from your Hewlett-Packard LaserJets,* Ted Nace and Michael Gardner (Peachpit Press), 1989. Packed with up-to-the-minute information, this book covers everything you ever wanted to know about LaserJets — utilities, compatibility, typesetting techniques, and tons of tips and tricks. An indispensable tool for all LaserJet and Series II owners. $24.95.

◆ Graphic Design

Mastering Graphics, Jan White (R. R. Bowker), 1983. An excellent book for serious students of design; it details the principles of design and layout in clear, concise terms. Those who produce newsletters, brochures, and many other publications will appreciate the many examples and understandable way in which the material in this book is displayed. $29.95.

Editing by Design, Jan White (R. R. Bowker), 1982. A useful book for the editor who wants to learn more about communicating effectively in print. Also helpful for the art director who wants an improved understanding of how to effectively present written material. Covers all the basics, including type specifications, cropping photos, and numerous design alternatives. The author spent 22 years as an art director for major magazines and what he doesn't know about graphic design isn't worth knowing. $34.95.

Graphic Design for the Electronic Age, Jan V. White (Watson-Guptill), 1988. The subtitle for this book is "the manual for traditional and desktop publishing," but the emphasis is on graphic design rather than desktop publishing specifics. No particular software or hardware is referred to, although electronic typographic considerations are dealt with extensively. This book draws on material from several of White's other informative and useful books, and is well worth the price. If you can only afford one of White's books, this is the one. $34.95.

Graphic Idea Notebook: *Inventive techniques for designing printed pages,* Jan V. White (Watson-Guptill), 1980. Another work by the master of the genre, Jan White. With this book, transforming ordinary material into provocative publications looks easy. A book to stimulate your imagination and open your eyes to the many possibilities by which you can enhance your publications with special handling of graphics. $22.50.

Graphics Handbook, Howard Munce (North Light), 1982. A book about design not written by Jan White? How did this wind up in here? Well, this is a good book, too. Not as detailed as White's, but excellent for the beginner. This book attempts to take the fright and mystery out of the design and preparation of simple printed pieces, and it really does simplify some of the mechanics. Generously illustrated with hundreds of graphic examples of the most popular applications. $14.95.

◆ Typography

Rookledge's International Typefinder, *the essential handbook of typeface recognition and selection,* Christopher Perfect & Gordon Rookledge (PCB International), 1983. An absolute classic. Although essential is an appropriate word, the subtitle could easily have been "the *perfect* handbook of typeface recognition," because that's what it is. The volume is well-structured, dividing 700 typefaces into a logical progression and highlighting the special identifying characteristics of each font. For anyone interested in type, this book is an Aladdin's cave, full of wondrous treasures. $24.95.

Photo Typography, Allan Haley (Scribner's Sons), 1982. The author is a vice president at ITC (International Typeface Corporation), and his book offers valuable guidelines and insight into effective typesetting and design standards. If you need more in-depth information about specific fonts, including their history, distinct characteristics, and usage, read this book. $18.95.

The Art of Typography: *Understanding contemporary type design through classic typography,* Martin Solomon (Watson-Guptill), 1988. This book explores aesthetic elements and contains numerous examples to illustrate attractive composition and design. Includes a variety of problem-solving ideas and a comprehensive directory of typefaces. $29.95.

Designing With Type, *a basic course in typography,* James Craig (Watson-Guptill). Often used as a textbook for design students, this manual thoroughly examines five popular typefaces and demonstrates how they can be applied to a multitude of publications. Also includes a type gallery of over 120 faces. The author has written several other books about design and typography, and is well-equipped to share his vast knowledge with readers. $24.95.

Decorative Letters, *Copyright-free designs,* Carol Belanger Grafton (Dover Publications), 1986. Over 800 decorative letters of the alphabet to add spice to a variety of publications. For standard LaserJet users, these ornamental letters are especially effective when used as large dropped or raised capitals. $3.50.

◆ Producing Newsletters

Slinging Ink, Jan Sutter (William Kaufman), 1982. All about newsletters, from start to finish. $12.95.

Editing Your Newsletter, Mark Beach (Van Nostrand Reinhold), 1983. Practical information on the writing, editing, design, and layout of newsletters. $18.50.

◆ Offset Printing

Getting It Printed, Mark Beach (Coast to Coast), 1986. A how-to book on working with print shops and graphic artists, with an emphasis on the basics of getting the job done. $29.50.

Printing It, Clifford Burke (Wingbow Press), 1972. Written by a printer, this books offers sound advice on how to get a print shop to produce a publication to your satisfaction. $12.95.

◆ Periodicals

Desktop Communications, an IDC publication. This magazine is very useful for anyone who wants to improve their business by using computers. Full of detailed, practical articles and the latest trends in this ever-growing field. Subscriptions are $24 a year. IDC, PO Box 941745, Atlanta, GA 30431.

Step-By-Step Graphics, published by Dynamic Graphics. This magazine is jam-packed with informative articles about specific design techniques, with special focus on how to improve the visual communication process. High quality and comprehensive. Subscriptions are $42 a year for six bimonthly issues. Step-By-Step Graphics, 6000 N. Forest Park Dr., Peoria, IL 61614-3592, 800-255-8800.

The WordPerfectionist, monthly newsletter of the WordPerfect Support Group. The aim of this publication is to provide help and guidance to users of WordPerfect. In that it is not affiliated with WordPerfect Corp. and is extremely user-friendly, a healthy mix of information is achieved. This newsletter will help you keep up with WordPerfect's metamorphosis and idiosyncrasies. Subscriptions are $36 a year from The WordPerfectionist, P. O. Box 1577 Dept. DTP, Baltimore, MD 21203 or call (800) USA-GROUP.

WordPerfect, the Magazine, published by WordPerfect Publishing. This monthly magazine features articles about business, professional, and industrial applications for WordPerfect, as well as covering third-party products and services. Subscriptions are $15 a year. WordPerfect Publishing, 288 W. Center St., Orem, UT 84057.

◆ WordPerfect

Instant Access Guide to WordPerfect 5.0, Michael Seif and Karen Rockow (Price/Stern/Sloan), 1988. If you need additional information on WordPerfect's basic commands and functions, I can recommend no better step-by-step guide. We served as editors for this book and worked closely with the authors to insure that this would be a quick and efficient reference. The book takes a visual approach by using screen graphics, key symbols, and cross-referencing of minimal text to show people how to learn to use the program. With its bright blue cover and spiral binding, the book is very helpful for the new user, as well as the infrequent user who needs a quick refresher. ISBN 0-89586-725-7, $14.95

— Toni Will-Harris

Product Directory

Arts & Letters
Computer Support Corporation
15926 Midway Road
Dallas, TX 75244 (214) 661-8960

Cambridge Computer Z88
Sinclair Systems
424 Cumberland Ave.
Portland, ME 04101
(207) 761-3700

ClickArt
T/Maker, 1973 Landings Drive
Mountain View, CA 94043
(415) 962-0195

Corel Draw & Tabin
Corel Systems Corporation,
1600 Carling Ave., Ottawa, ON
Canada K1Z 7M4 (613) 728-8200

Desktop Art
Dynamic Graphics
6000 N. Forest Park Dr.
Peoria, IL 61656 800-255-8800

DigiFonts
528 Commons Dr.
Golden, CO 80401
800-242-5665, (303) 526-9435

Font Effects
SoftCraft, 16 N. Carroll St.
Suite 500, Madison, WI 53703
(608) 257-3300

Fontware
Bitstream, Athenaeum House
215 First Street
Cambridge, MA 02142
800-522-3668

Genius Full Page Display
Micro Display Systems
1310 Vermilion St.
Hastings, MN 55033
612-437-2233, 800-328-9524

Glyphix Fonts
Swfte International, Ltd.
P.O. Box 5773
Wilmington, DE 19808
800-237-9383

Grammatik III
Reference Software, 330 Townsend
#135, San Francisco, CA 94107
800-872-9933, (415) 541-0222

HALO DPE
Media Cybernetics Inc., 8484
Georgia Ave., Silver Springs,
MD 20910 800-446-HALO

Harvard Graphics
Software Publishing Corporation
P.O. Box 7210, 1901 Landings Drive
Mountain View, CA 94039-7210
(415) 962-8910

Hewlett-Packard LaserJet Printers
H-P Peripherals Group, 16399 West
Bernadino Dr., San Diego, CA 92127
(619) 592-8182

HiJaak
InSet Systems, Inc.
71 Commerce Dr.
Brookfield, CT 06810
800-828-8088, (203) 775-5866

Hot Shot Graphics
SymSoft, P.O. Box 4477
Mountain View, CA 94040
(415) 941-1552

LaserFonts
SoftCraft, 16 N. Carroll St. #500
Madison, WI 53703 (608) 257-3300
Also LF Manager, Font Effects,
LaserFonts & LaserGraphics, Word
Processor Pack, Spin Font

LaserMaster LM 1000, LX6, Glass Page
LaserMaster Corp.
7156 Shady Oak Rd.
Eden Prairie, MN 55344
800-LMC-PLOT

LaserTorq
LaserTools Corp.
3025 Buena Vista Way
Berkeley, CA 94708
800-346-1353

LJ Fonts
Weaver Graphics
Fox Pavillion Box 1132
Jenkintown, PA 19046
(215) 884-9286

Lotus 1-2-3, Freelance
Lotus Development Corporation
55 Cambridge Parkway
Cambridge, MA 02142
800-345-1043

Metro Image Base Clip Art
Metro ImageBase, Inc.
18623 Ventura Blvd., #210
Tarzana, CA 91356 800-843-3438

NEC LQ 890 PostScript Printer
NEC Information Systems
1414 Massachusetts Ave.
Boxborough, MA 01719

Nekoosa Laser 1000 Paper
Nekoosa Paper Inc.
100 Wisconsin River Dr.
Port Edwards, WI 54469
(715) 887-5271

PC Paintbrush Plus
Zsoft, 450 Franklin Road, #100
Marietta, GA 30067
(404) 428-0008

PDP 1-2-4 Memory Board
Pacific Data Products
6404 Nancy Ridge Dr.
San Diego, CA 92121
(619) 552-552-0880

Perspective Jr. (formerly Boeing Graph)
Three/D/Graphics
860 Via de la Paz
Pacific Palisades, CA 90272
(213) 459-8525

Publisher's PicturePak & PagePak
Marketing Graphics Incorporated,
4401 Dominion Blvd. Suite 210
Glen Allen, VA 23060-3379
(804) 747-6991

QMS-PS 810
Quality Micro Systems
P.O. Box 81250, Mobile, AL 36689
(205) 633-4500

Ricoh PC Laser 6000
Ricoh Corporation
155 Passaic Ave., Fairfield, NJ 07006
(201) 882-2000

RightWriter, Rightsoft Inc.
2033 Wood St., Suite 218
Sarasota, FL 33577
(813) 952-9211

Toshiba T-3100
Toshiba America, Inc.
Information Services Div.
2441 Michelle Drive
Tustin, CA 92680
800-457-7777, (714) 730-5000

ScreenExtender
Stairway Software
700 Harris St., #204
Charlottesville, VA 22901
(804) 977-7770

SLed
VS Software, P.O. Box 6158
Little Rock, AR 72216
(501) 376-2083

VCACHE - VOPT - VKETTE - VTOOLS
Golden Bow Systems
2870 Fifth Avenue, Suite 201
San Diego, CA 92103
(619) 298-9349

Victor 286
Victor Computers, 380 El Pueblo Road, Scotts Valley, CA 95066
(408) 438-6680

VP PLanner & VPP Plus
Paperback Software International,
2830 Ninth Street
Berkeley, CA 94710

Will-Harris Designer Disk 5
Designer Disks, Dept. B
PO Box 1235
Point Reyes, CA 94956
Available by mail order only—not sold in stores

Windows Graph
MicroGrafx Inc.
1820 North Greenville Ave.
Richardson, TX 75081
(212) 234-1769

WordPerfect
WordPerfect Corp.
288 West Center, Orem, UT 84057
800-321-5906

Words & Figures
Lifetree, 411 Pacific St.
Monterey, CA 93940
(408) 373-4718

Writer Series Font Cartridges
GNU, 100 Hilltop Road, Box 414, Ramsey, NJ 07446 (201) 825-1222

WYSE 700 Monitor
WYSE Technology
3571 N. First St.
San Jose, CA 95134 800-GET-WYSE

ZEOS 386
Zeos International Ltd.
530 5th Avenue NW, #1000
St. Paul, MN 55112
800-423-5891

❖ *Further communications*

- If you would like to send me examples of what you are producing with WordPerfect, I would be happy to take a look at them and offer suggestions for improvement or answer questions—I like hearing from readers.

  If you want a reply, be sure and enclose a self-addressed stamped envelope, though. Write to me at:
  DWH - Dept. Q, Box 1235, Point Reyes, CA 94956

Notes

Index

!

A

F

H

Q

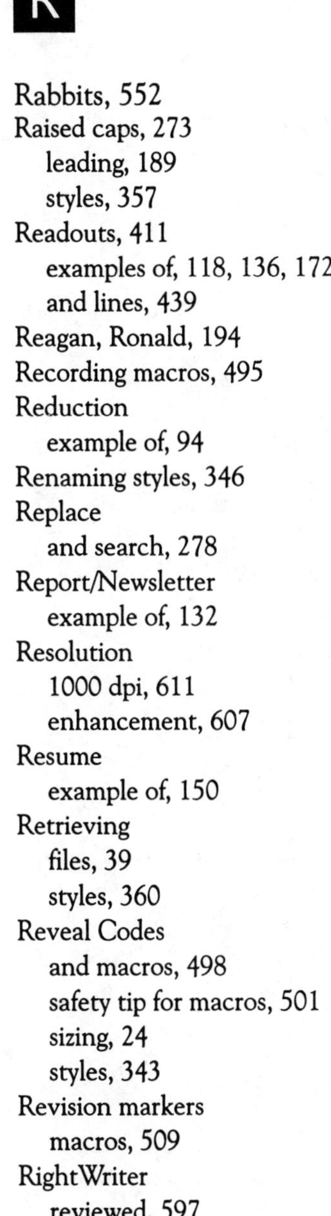

R

S

About the book

This entire book was written and edited in WordPerfect 5.1. I started with a beta version and worked my way through many upgrades. The body text is set in Bitstream Fontware Goudy Old Style. The headings, subheads, and keystrokes are Hammersmith, Bitstream's Fontware version of Gill Sans. The diamond subheadings are Zapf Dingbats. All pages were printed 8 1/2 x 11", and reduced by 18% (to 82% of their original size). This improved the quality of the type and graphics. For speed and quality, the final printing of the book was accomplished with a LaserMaster LM1000 at 1000 dpi on Nekoosa Laser 1000 paper.

A LaserMaster LX6 was also used with a LaserJet II and III (code name: *Galaxy*) for 800 dpi output. A QMS-PS 810 was used for proofing everything in the early stages of the book, when it was one of the few printers WordPerfect 5.0 supported. Later it was used for the PostScript example pages in Chapter 4, *Show & Tell*. All of those examples are documented as to what specific fonts, graphics programs, and printers were used to produce them.

The computers used for writing and producing the book were a ZEOS 386 (screaming machine), Victor 286 (AT compatible), WYSE 286 (AT compatible), and Toshiba T3100 (portable AT compatible). The monitors were the full-page MDS Genius, WYSE 700, and Toshiba plasma display, all of which are supported in high-resolution graphics modes by WordPerfect. We also used a LaserMaster GlassPage 1280.

Screen shots were created with Hot Shot Graphics (SymSoft) on the WYSE, and InSet/HiJaak on the Genius. I also used HiJaak for graphic file format conversions. I used a Cambridge Computer Z88 (a-one-and a-half-pound portable computer with 512K memory) for taking notes on those rare occasions when I was allowed to leave the house. Since moving to the woods of Northern California, I no longer had the need for appliances to prevent overheating, but I could have used some uninteruptible power supplies for those raging electrical storms. Maybe for the next edition.

We ate altogether too many Entenmann's chocolate chip cookies, and let our Canon combination answering machine/fax machine insulate us from the rest of the world during the preparation of the book. I sat on a genuine Balans chair (you know, the backless pretzel-shaped things where your knees rest on little pads), and I was inspired by the sounds of nature and a Japanese-style stone fountain from the Cherry Brook Potters of Canton, Connecticut.

Both Toni and I had frogs covered in fabric from Liberty's of London perched on top of our monitors to provide amusement during those 18-hour sessions with WordPerfect.

One last note: You would not be reading this book if it were not for the special people at Peachpit Press. They make hard work worthwhile.

—DWH

What's a nice comedy writer like Daniel Will-Harris doing in a field like this—computer books—the ultimate techno-snooze? Well, his first computer book, *Desktop Publishing With Style*, received much popular and critical acclaim, and if you can make a computer book entertaining and informative, the future is yours.

Daniel has always been interested in any form of communication, from finger painting to being editor-in-chief of his college paper. It was on that paper that he met his first (and hopefully only) wife, Toni, who is responsible for the art direction of his books and that last parenthetical. Since escaping Los Angeles, they now live in the Northern California woods with their pet sheep, Selsdon.

For many years Daniel worked as a writer for television and the musical theater. When he discovered what computers offered a writer, he was hooked and has been a slave to technology ever since. He has written for many magazines, which led to his current predicament: he writes a monthly column for *Desktop* magazine, among others (on a deadline that pops up with frightening regularity).

Daniel paid his dues for many years as contributing editor for a best-selling line of computer books by Peter A. McWilliams. Daniel and Toni also desktop published the camera-ready pages of Peter's most recent book, *The Personal Electronics Guide*, for Prentice Hall, and they recently edited a series of computer books for yet another publisher.

As a past writer of technical manuals and user guides, Daniel enjoyed the many free trips to Japan (from where he's schlepped home a lot of those little pastel plastic geegaws). He's also in great demand as a lecturer, and to conduct seminars about desktop publishing and writing with a computer—yes, he knows it's tough work being the leader in the desktop publishing/graphic design field,

but someone's got to do it. After so much experience with computers, it was a natural step to start his own consulting firm and become a parasite of the rich and famous. As a consultant, Daniel deals primarily with people in the entertainment industry and the media, such as William F. Buckley, Gene Roddenberry, Disney Studios, Hanna-Barbera, KUSC, the *LA Weekly*, and Time/Design, headquartered in Denmark (more free trips). Just so you know, he feels that name dropping, if used judiciously, is a virtue.

You don't do all that schmoozing with celebs for nothing, so it should come as no surprise that he's served as a consultant on many feature films, most recently for *Half Moon Street* director Bob Swaim. Living proof of the "it's all who you know school," he's also appeared in several motion pictures, including *Love Letters*, with Jamie Lee Curtis, *The Mae West Story*, with Ann Jillian, and *Saturday the 14th* with Ray Walston.

In his spare time, Daniel likes to collect anything art deco, or stuffed, and to get away for dinner at his favorite restaurant in Belgium. His greatest ambition is to have some spare time before the turn of the century.

CODE	KEYSTROKE	COMMAND
[ ]	[HOME] [SPACE]	Hard Space
[-]	-	Hyphen
-	CONTROL-	Soft Hyphen
[/]	F1 or [HOME] /	Cancel Hyphenation
[AdvToLn]	SHIFT-F8 O A I	Advance to Line
[AdvUp]	SHIFT-F8 O A U	Advance Up
[AdvDn]	SHIFT-F8 O A D	Advance Down
[AdvRgt]	SHIFT-F8 O A R	Advance Right
[AdvLft]	SHIFT-F8 O A L	Advance Left
[AdvToPos]	SHIFT-F8 O A P	Advance to Position
[Brdr Opt]	SHIFT-F8 O B	Border Options
[Block Pro]	ALT-F4 SHIFT-F8	Block Protection
[BOLD]	F6	Bold
[C/A/FlRt]	(Automatic after Center, Align or Flush Right)	End of Tab Align or Flush (5.0 only)
[Center Pg]	SHIFT-F8 P C	Center Page Top to Bottom
[Cndl EOP]	SHIFT-F8 O C	Conditional End of Page
[Center] or [Cntr]	SHIFT-F6	Center
[Col Def]	ALT-F7 D	Column Definition
[Col Off]	ALT-F7 C	End of Text Columns
[Col On]	ALT-F7 C	Beginning of Text Columns
[Comment]	CONTROL-F5 C C	Document Comment
[Color]	CONTROL-F8 C	Print Color for Font
[Date]	SHIFT-F5 C	Automatic Date/Time Function
[DEC TAB]	F6 (or [TAB] with decimal or right tabs)	Decimal Tab
[Dorm HRt]	Automatic	Dormant Hard Return (5.1 only)
[Decml Char]	SHIFT-F8 O D	Decimal/Thousands Separator-character
[EXT LARGE]	CONTROL-F8 S E	Extra Large Print
[Fig Opt]	ALT-F9 F O	Figure Box Options
[Figure] or [Fig Box:]	ALT-F9 F C	Figure Box
[FINE]	CONTROL-F8 S F	Fine Print
[Flsh Rt]	ALT-F6	Flush Right
[Font]	CONTROL-F8 F	Base Font
[Footer]	SHIFT-F8 P F	Footer
[Force]	SHIFT-F8 P O	Force Odd/Even Page
[Form]	SHIFT-F7 P S	Form (Printer Selection)
[Header]	SHIFT-F8 P H	Header
[HLine:]	ALT-F9 L H	Horizontal Line
[HPg]	CONTROL-ENTER	Hard Page Break
[HRt]	[ENTER]	Hard Return
[Hyph On]	SHIFT-F8 L Y O	Hyphenation
[HZone]	SHIFT-F8 L Z	Hyphenation zone
[->Indent]	F4	Indent
[->Indent<-]	SHIFT-F4	Left/Right Indent
[Index]	ALT-F5 I	Index Entry
[ITALC]	CONTROL-F8 A I	Italics
[Just:]	SHIFT-F8 L J (F L R C)	Justification (Full, Left, Right, Center)
[Just Off] (5.0)	SHIFT-F8 L J N	Right Justification Off
[Just Lim]	SHIFT-F8 O P J	Word/Letter Justification Limits

CODE	KEYSTROKE	COMMAND
[Kern]	SHIFT-F8 O P K	Kerning
[L/R Mar]	SHIFT-F8 L M	Left and Right Margins
[LARGE]	CONTROL-F8 S L	Large Print
[Ln Height: Auto]	SHIFT-F8 L H A	Leading/Line height auto
[Line Height: #"]	SHIFT-F8 L H F	Leading/Line height Fixed
[Link:]	CONTROL-F5 S C	Spreadsheet Link
[<-Mar Rel]	SHIFT-[TAB]	Left Margin Release
[Open Style]	ALT-F8	Open Style
[Ovrstk]	SHIFT-F8 O O C	Overstrike Preceding Character
[OUTLN]	CONTROL-F8 A O	Outline Font
[Outline On]	SHIFT-F5 O O	Outline On
[Outline Lvl #]	ALT-F8 & SHIFT-F5 P	Outline Style
[Par Num]	SHIFT-F5 P	Paragraph Number
[Par Num Def:]	SHIFT-F5 D	Paragraph Numbering Definition
[Pg Num]	SHIFT-F8 P N	New Page Number
[Pg Numbering:]	SHIFT-F8 P P	Page Number Position
[Pg Num Style:]	SHIFT-F8 P N S	Page Number Style
[REDLN]	CONTROL-F8 A R	Redline
[Set Fig Num]	ALT-F9 F N	Set New Figure Box Number
[Set Tab Num]	ALT-F9 T N	Set New Table Box Number
[Set Txt Num]	ALT-F9 B N	Set New Text Box Number
[Set Usr Num]	ALT-F9 U N	Set New User-Defined Box
[SHADW]	CONTROL-F8 A A	Shadow Font
[SM CAP]	CONTROL-F8 A C	Small Caps
[SMALL]	CONTROL-F8 S S	Small Print
[SPg]	(Created automatically)	Soft Page Break
[SRt]	(Created automatically)	Soft Return
[StkOut]	CONTROL-F8 A S	Strikeout
[Style On]	ALT-F8	Styles/Paired
[Subdoc]	ALT-F5 S	Subdocument (Master Documents)
[SubScpt]	CONTROL-F8 S B	Subscript
[Suppress:]	SHIFT-F8 P U	Suppress Page Format
[SuprScpt]	CONTROL-F8 S P	Superscript
[T/B Mar]	SHIFT-F8 P M	Top and Bottom Margins
[Tab]	[TAB]	Tab
[Tab Opt]	ALT-F9 B O	Table Box Options
[Tbl Def:]	Table Definition	ALT-F7 T C
[Tab Set]	SHIFT-F8 L T	Tab Set
[Tbl Box] or [Table]	ALT-F9 T C	Table Box
[Text Box]	ALT-F9 B C	Text Box
[Txt Opt]	ALT-F9 B O	Text Box Options
[UND]	F8	Underlining
[Undrln]	SHIFT-F8 O U	Underline Spaces/Tabs
[Usr Box]	ALT-F9 U C	User Box
[UsrOpt]	ALT-F9 U O	User Box Options
[VLine:]	ALT-F9 L V	Vertical Line
[Vry Large]	CONTROL-F8 S V	Very Large Print
[Wrd/Ltr Spacing]	SHIFT-F8 O P W	Word and Letter Spacing
[W/O On]	SHIFT-F8 L W Y	Widow/Orphan Protect On
[W/O Off]	SHIFT-F8 L W N	Widow/Orphan Protect Off

More from Peachpit Press. . .

101 Windows Tips and Tricks
Jesse Berst and Scott Dunn
This power-packed, user-friendly survival guide gives you tips and tricks to make Windows faster, easier, and more fun. Icons and illustrations lead your eye to the key points, and friendly explanations get you up to speed in a hurry. *(216 pages)*

Corel Draw 2.0: Visual QuickStart Guide
Webster & Associates
This is a highly visual tour of Corel Draw, including an interactive "Walkabout" tutorial disk. *(160 pages)*

Desktop Publishing Secrets
Robert Eckhardt, Bob Weibel, and Ted Nace
This is a compilation of hundreds of the best desktop publishing tips from five years of *Publish* magazine. The tips cover all the major desktop publishing software and hardware products, including Ventura Publisher, PageMaker, WordPerfect, CorelDRAW, Windows, PostScript, fonts, laser printers, clip art, and more. *(550 pages)*

The LaserJet Font Book
Katherine Pfeiffer
A guide to LaserJet fonts and to using type effectively. Hundreds of LaserJet fonts from over a dozen vendors are displayed, accompanied by complete information on price, character sets, and design. *(320 pages)*

LaserJet IIP Essentials
Steve Cummings, Mike Handa, and Jerold Whitmore
Covers configuration and use of the IIP with word processing, database, spreadsheet, and desktop publishing programs. *(340 pages)*

The Little DOS 5 Book
Kay Yarborough Nelson
A quick and accessible guide to DOS 5. This book is packed with plenty of tips as well as an easy-to-use section on DOS commands. It also covers DOS basics, working with files and directories, disk management, and more. *(160 pages)*

The Little Laptop Book
Steve Cummings
Now you can get on the fast track to notebook and laptop computing. This book covers choosing a laptop, protecting it from theft and damage, hot tips on applications and utilities, printing on the road, and telecommunication. *(192 pages)*

The Little Windows Book, 3.1 Edition
Kay Yarborough Nelson
This second edition of Peachpit's popular book explains the subtle and not-so-subtle changes in version 3.1. *(144 pages)*

The Little WordPerfect Book
Skye Lininger
Teach yourself the basics of WordPerfect 5.1 in less than an hour. This book gives you just what you need to start creating simple letters, memos, and short reports—fast. Gives step-by-step instructions for setting page margins, typing text, navigating with the cursor keys, and more. *(160 pages)*

The Little WordPerfect for Windows Book

Kay Yarborough Nelson

This book gives you the basic skills you need to create simple documents and get familiar with WordPerfect's new Windows interface. It also covers more advanced topics, such as formatting pages, working with blocks of text, using different fonts, and special features including WordPerfect's new mail merge, tables, equations, indexes, and footnotes. *(200 pages)*

PageMaker 4: An Easy Desk Reference

Robin Williams

At last—this highly acclaimed reference book is available for PC users. This essential book for PageMaker users lets you look up how to do specific tasks using a unique three-column format. *(768 pages)*

PageMaker 4: Visual QuickStart Guide

Webster and Associates

Provides a fast, highly visual introduction to desktop publishing in PageMaker 4.0 for the PC. Packed with 300 illustrations, you learn by seeing. Section One leads you on a brief guided tour of the entire program; Section Two presents information by task; Section Three provides a reference of menu commands. *(176 pages)*

The PC is not a typewriter

Robin Williams

PC users can now learn Robin Williams' secrets for creating beautiful type. Here are the principles behind the techniques for professional typesetting, including punctuation, leading, special characters, kerning, fonts, justification, and more. *(96 pages)*

Ventura Tips and Tricks, 3rd Edition

Ted Nace and Daniel Will-Harris

This book was described by Ventura President John Meyer as "the most complete reference for anyone serious enough about using Ventura." Packed with inside information, speed-up tips, special tricks for reviving a crashed chapter, ways to overcome memory limitations, etc. Features a directory of over 700 products and resources that enhance Ventura's performance. *(790 pages)*

Winning! The Awesome & Amazing Book of Windows Game Tips, Traps, & Sneaky Tricks

John Hedtke

This book provides rules and explanations for setting up, running, and mastering each game in the Microsoft Entertainment Packs. In addition to giving the complete rules and instructions for the games it explains their hidden features. Finally, it shows some sneaky tricks learned directly from the games' programmers that let you rack up huge scores in record time. Whether you're an occasional dabbler or a hopelessly irredeemable addict, this book will show you how to have even more fun with Windows. *(232 pages)*

WordPerfect: Desktop Publishing in Style, 2nd Edition
Daniel Will-Harris
Peachpit's popular guide to producing documents with WordPerfect 5.1 or 5.0. *(650 pages)*

WordPerfect for Windows, Visual QuickStart Guide
Webster & Associates
A visual tour of WordPerfect for Windows, including an interactive "Walkabout" tutorial disk. *(280 pages)*

WordPerfect for Windows with Style
Daniel Will-Harris
This generously illustrated handbook gives step-by-step instructions for creating good-looking business documents using WordPerfect for Windows. The book shows a variety of documents and provides the exact commands, codes, and keystrokes used to create each one. Includes valuable insights into styles, graphics, fonts, tables, macros, clip art, printers, and utilities. Daniel Will-Harris combines technical accuracy, detailed and easy-to-understand explanations, and just plain fun. *(350 pages)*

Order Form

(800) 283-9444 or (510) 548-4393
(510) 548-5991 fax

#	Title	Price	Total
	101 Windows Tips & Tricks	12.95	
	Corel Draw 2.0: Visual QuickStart Guide (with disk)	24.95	
	Desktop Publishing Secrets	27.95	
	The LaserJet Font Book	24.95	
	LaserJet IIP Essentials	21.95	
	The Little DOS 5 Book	12.95	
	The Little Windows Book, 3.1 Edition	12.95	
	The Little WordPerfect Book	12.95	
	The Little WordPerfect for Windows Book	12.95	
	PageMaker 4: An Easy Desk Reference (PC Edition)	29.95	
	PageMaker 4: Visual QuickStart Guide (PC Edition)	12.95	
	The PC is not a typewriter	9.95	
	Ventura Tips and Tricks, 3rd Edition	27.95	
	Winning!	14.95	
	WordPerfect: Desktop Publishing in Style, 2nd Edition	23.95	
	WordPerfect for Windows: Visual QuickStart Guide (w/disk)	27.95	
	WordPerfect for Windows with Style	23.95	

Tax of 8.25% applies to California residents only.	Subtotal		
UPS ground shipping: $4 for first item, $1 each additional.	8.25% Tax (CA only)		
UPS 2nd day air: $7 for first item, $2 each additional. Air mail to Canada: $6 for first item, $4 each additional.	Shipping		
Air mail overseas: $14 each item.	**TOTAL**		

Name		
Company		
Address		
City	State	Zip
Phone	Fax	
❑ Check enclosed	❑ Visa	❑ MasterCard
Company purchase order #		
Credit card #	Expiration Date	

Peachpit Press, Inc. • 2414 Sixth Street • Berkeley, CA • 94710
Your satisfaction is guaranteed or your money will be cheerfully refunded!